AN AESTHETIC
EDUCATION IN
THE ERA OF
GLOBALIZATION

AN AESTHETIC EDUCATION IN THE ERA OF GLOBALIZATION

GAYATRI CHAKRAVORTY SPIVAK

Harvard University Press
Cambridge, Massachusetts
London, England
2012

Library of Congress Cataloging-in-Publication Data

Spivak, Gayatri Chakravorty.
An aesthetic education in the era of globalization / Gayatri Chakravorty Spivak.
p. cm.
Includes bibliographical references and index.
ISBN 978-0-674-05183-6 (alk. paper)
1. Aesthetics—Study and teaching—Philosophy.
2. Literature—Study and teaching—Philosophy.
3. Culture and globalization—Philosophy.   I. Title.
BH61.S67   2011
111'.85—dc22   2011013286

MAITREYI CHANDRA
and
the memory of
LORE METZGER

Sisters

Contents

Preface

THIS IS A COLLECTION spanning at least twenty-three years. Looking back, I discover in them what Derrida called a *théorie distraite* in the introduction to *Psyché*, when he discovered shared theoretical motifs in the essays collected in his book.[1] In this book, after writing the Preface, I have actively looked for a distracted theory (poor but accurate translation) of the double bind. Following the rule of "In literary criticism, when you look for something, you find it," I've found it. The point is, of course, that now I feel that a double bind is rather more than the suggestion that having found it, you can play it. (That, incidentally, was the problem with "strategic use of essentialism.")

As I say in the Introduction, there is often the suggestion in them that the humanities can somehow learn to resolve double binds by playing them. I have often suggested that "Three Women's Texts and a Critique of Imperialism" (springing up out of teaching an undergraduate class in 1978 at the University of Texas–Austin), "French Feminism in an International Frame," and the translation of "Draupadi" with a critical introduction (both written in reaction against recognition of my "French" expertise), and, finally, "Can the Subaltern Speak?," represented the start of a new direction in my thinking.[2] The first essay here, "The Burden of English," represents the responsibility of such a turn, looking homeward, my first professional presentation at an institute of tertiary education in India. The double bind here is between caste and class, necessarily also understood as race and class. The hope at the end of the piece refuses to acknowledge that certain contradictions between the preserved performatives of indigeneity and civilizationism cannot even enter the security of a double bind. Doubt rather than hope, or, archaic rather than residual. Couldn't see it or say it then. But the Introduction brings us there.

This first foray into Indian tertiary education was immediately followed by the second essay in this book, "Who Claims Alterity?," written in 1987 by invitation for *The Statesman*, the oldest daily newspaper in my hometown of Calcutta, celebrating the fortieth anniversary of Indian Independence. For some vague reason, I think this is not quite what the paper wanted. I expanded the piece for presentation in the series called "Remaking History" for the Dia Art Foundation. Many people had bought tickets. I used to live in Pittsburgh then. The American writer, filmmaker, and visual artist Gary Indiana was in the audience, I remember. That with-it crowd in Chelsea, when it still retained its attractively lugubrious streetfrontage, was puzzled by the auto-critique of a member of the model minority, before the term was invented. Did these two rather disparate hosts mind the double bind: between metropolitan minority and postcolonial majority perspectives in a tug of war in the same subject?

"How to Read a 'Culturally Different' Book," the next piece in the book, was written in response to an individual request. Badrel Young, Pakistani-British, who taught at the time at a Council school in Hackney, was assigned R. K. Narayan's *Guide* as a text for the multicultural classroom. She asked me to give some "Hindu mythology" as background. This essay emerged in response. Harish Trivedi, Professor of English at Delhi University, who remains critical of my postcolonial stance, complained that I don't treat *Guide* as an "Indian" novel. I don't know how to. Is that a double bind? In the fifth essay, "Culture: Situating Feminism," chronologically askew upon the Table of Contents, I spell it out: "Culture is its own irreducible counter-example."

Ruedi Kuenzli asked me to keynote at the Midwestern Modern Language Association in 1991. Ruedi is a tremendously conscientious person. In response to his call, all I felt was a desperate honesty, thinking to inhabit the double bind between being a Calcuttan and being a New Yorker. I had just come to Columbia then but I already felt the seduction of New York. By March 2011, I have lived longer in New York than in Calcutta. I remember my Columbia colleague Leonard Gordon in the audience. I knew he was in touch with the Bengali academic community in the United States. Quite unreasonably, I wanted him to see that, in my prepared remarks, there was no trace of Bengali identitarianism.

In the lineaments of globalization, to recognize this cultural predicament as a performative double bind rather than the "double bind" represented so that it can cover over the contemporaneity of capital is to refuse to acknowledge damage control.

I think "Acting Bits/Identity Talk," the seventh essay, was written for a conference arranged by the National University in Singapore. That visit is forever marked for me by the death of my friend Bimal Krishna Matilal. I was coming to Singapore from Bangladesh (my "activist" life began in 1986). I had spoken to Bimal before leaving the United States. It was not possible to phone from Bangladesh, since I was in rural areas. I called as soon as I got to Singapore. He was already dead.

There is a bit about flatulence in the essay. This is of course embarrassing. I remember a South Asian professor commenting after my talk that it had resembled a series of farts. I am used to the hostility of men (sometimes women) of my own cultural inscription. I did not say then what I feel I can write now.

Bimal Matilal died of multiple myeloma. Toward the end his rib cage had collapsed and was pressing on his lungs. We would work together as long as he could but then his mind would cloud and he would ask me to sing. All through this time, I think because of the pressure on his lungs, he was constantly flatulent and this embarrassed him considerably. To ease him I had brought up the passage in *Glas*—"Ontology cannot lay hold of a fart"—commenting on Genet, who writes on farts, and Bimal had brought up the discussion of bodily winds in the *prāṇāyāma*. This is the double bind between body and mind, the place of an impossible ethics for the mature Lévinas, the baby marked for death as it is born.[3]

The semester I gave "Teaching for the Times," the sixth essay, I was a visiting professor at the University of California at Riverside. The air there was full of Derrida. The eighth essay, "Supplementing Marxism," was written there. It was a very special audience. I hope to write a book on Derrida after I put the slim book on Du Bois in press. "Touched by Deconstruction" (2000) and "Notes toward a Tribute to Jacques Derrida," written with this audience in mind (my "school-mates"), will find their place there.[4] Here the double bind is self and other. I've put "What's Left of Theory?" next to it because it gives the tremendous double bind between the counter-intuitive and the intuitive in the learning of a theory made for changing the world.

It was written in response to Judith Butler's invitation to present a paper at the English Institute, at rather short notice. It was a busy semester. But my tremendous loyalty to Butler, which has led to, and will lead to, much work together, made me respond to this first call. I should, however, also mention that I have an overblown respect for the Institute. I continue to believe that it is the scholarly apex of the profession. I have carried around a burden of intellectual insecurity since my undergraduate days as a consequence of everyday sexism, especially applied to seemingly charismatic females. An invitation to the Institute I could not refuse.

Yet I had little time to prepare. I took therefore the lesson that I was teaching at the time in my Marx seminar and let it carry me where it would. It led me outside the classroom, not surprisingly. This repeated gesturing toward the outside of the teaching machine from the inside is my rise and fall.

I have been teaching this course on Marx since the late 1970s, when I started teaching at the University of Texas at Austin. We read about a thousand pages of selections from various texts, German and English side by side. The brief is to think "Marx" as a textual figure in the writing and not to read the text because one will need it for some project of cultural theory. Although I have written bits and pieces of my class experience here and there, I cannot imagine writing the book that I always say will rise from there: Can there be a socialist ethics? I cannot, yet, "imagine that which I know."[5]

In 1981, ravaged by the departure of a beloved partner, I gave a talk at the Whitney Humanities Center at Yale on the gender injustice of Christopher Lasch's *The Culture of Narcissism*.[6] A couple of years later, in response to Ralph Cohen's invitation, I gave a more extended version of it ("Echo," the tenth essay) at the University of Virginia. I knew Jacqueline Rose would be in the audience. I read my Freud as carefully as I could. I had established my profound friendship with Bimal Krishna Matilal in 1985. My intellectual exchange with Professor Matilal, who believed that Indic rational critique was an instrument for philosophizing rather than merely a cultural artifact, allowed me to understand (or imagine) Freud in the context of Ovid in a more generous way. I could begin to read Freud as a body-mind philosopher.

In 1992, another friendship began. Assia Djebar and I acknowledged a resonance with each other. It was this writer of Mediterranean Algeria, a feminist Muslim who has been fascinated by the history of the Berber language, who gave me a sense of "echo at the origin." We have encountered her already in "Acting Bits."

Muslim Europe, but only by way of France. Can I call this theory? I feel that my use of psychoanalysis in this essay is different from its use as a descriptive taxonomy. The double bind here is more obvious, having to do with the imperative to ab-use, of which I speak in the Introduction.

One consequence of this one I've already introduced as looking homeward. The next essay, "Translation as Culture," thematizes this double bind, in its very structuring suggesting that it can be played both ways. On the one hand a "diasporic" teacher of English at a university and on the other hand an upper-class, caste-Hindu, radical-minded Indian citizen, both a dime a dozen, so to speak. It is, of course, up to readers to catch the

unexpected asymmetries of this deliberate shift in voice, merely cited. The
first part was given as a keynote at the Annual Convention of the International Association of Commonwealth Literature (IACL) in Oviedo, Spain.
The provenance of the second is explained within the text.

I have placed "Translating into English" next, where the double bind is
how to inhabit the readerly position when one is the published implied
reader and, of course, the scary double bind of betraying the mother
tongue into the global idiom. I have put "Nationalism and the Imagination" next to that, because that brought these asymmetries home; for that
meeting of the IACL was upon homeground, in Hyderabad, India. (A version revised for delivery in Bulgaria, *Nationalism and the Imagination*, was
published by Seagull Books in 2010, and translated into French and published by Payot in 2011.) The double bind there described is between the
underived private and the tremendous public function of nationalism. The
problem here is that we do inhabit that unacknowledged double bind; to
acknowledge it would destroy that habitation. One of the reasons why this
must be used to supplement globality. Hope against hope.

In my first seminar with Paul de Man in 1961, I gave a paper on Rabindranath Tagore. He is an invariable resource for Bengalis abroad and at
home. In my first lecture in India, you will have noticed, I spoke of Tagore.
Given all the double binds I have been describing, it is not surprising that
of all Tagore's prose fiction, I am most moved by *Gora*. It seemed to me impossible, of course, not to attempt the *Kim/Gora* couple. It always irritates
me when *Gora* is taught in indifferent English, simply as a narrative of nationalism, exemplary outside of Tagore's varied itinerary in prose and verse. Yet,
without a tradition of Bengali teaching, can it be otherwise?

Valiantly trying, I taught *Gora/Kim* in an undergraduate narrative class
at Columbia. I have no doubt that I was not able to convey very much
beyond the usual clichés of colonial discourse.

The Society of Fellows at Columbia is a fairly traditional organization
and, as such, has, quite correctly, not sought to involve me in its workings.
Ann Waters, a student of Nicholas Dirks at Michigan, was a member of
the Society one year. At her invitation, I presented a paper at the Society for
the first and the last time. The paper was an account of the class on *Gora/
Kim*.

When Sugata Bose at Tufts asked me to give a paper at a valedictory
conference for Amartya Sen (he was leaving Harvard to be the only Master of color at Trinity College, Cambridge, for a bit), "Resident Alien,"
the fourteenth essay, was the only appropriate thing to hand. I suppose it
must have crossed my mind that Sen and I were both resident aliens in
the United States. In that crowd of South Asianist historians and social

scientists, the paper seemed embarrassing. I have brought forward "Ethics and Politics" here, for it situates both Sen and Tagore. The double bind of history is lodged in the future anterior, the unexpected results of activist education; but also in the swing between coercion and consent in teaching. This is the biggest double bind, the biggest proof against the possibility of a just society, and it holds my life as an unanswered question: Can vanguardism be supplemented?

In *Gora*, Tagore thematizes the supplementation of vanguardism by removing *Gora* from the Hindu vanguard; but *Gora* remains the representation of a resident alien from above. In the next essay, "Imperative to Reimagine the Planet," I attempt to imagine those from below, who would be citizens. This is a different imagining from "Teaching for the Times," in response to a different kind of call.

In December 1997 my dear friend Willi Goetschel paid me the extraordinary compliment of asking me to give the lecture inaugurating the turn of a foundation named Stiftung Dialogik from Holocaust asylum to migrant multiculturalism, in his native Zurich. Goetschel is now the President of the Stiftung, but at that time the founding President Hermann Levin Goldschmidt, whose wife, Mary, had been the initial founder of this particular asylum route, was still alive. There too, I did not say quite what the group wanted. But, as I recount in the piece, Goldschmidt's genius allowed me to respond to that gap.

I repeat that I find it tedious to go on endlessly about my particular diasporicity. Come what may, I cannot think of what used to be called "the brain drain" as either exile or diaspora. I feel that as a literary intellectual, I am here to use my imagination, not only to imagine the predicament of diaspora, exile, refuge, but also to deny resolutely that the manifest destiny of the United States is (to appear) to give asylum to the world. As such, I often have to confront the question of "speaking for" groups that are not my own.

I have responded to this question so many times that a particular reference would be silly. Yet I seem never to be heard. Let me repeat, then. Why has this Enlightenment model of parliamentary democracy (representing a constituency, "speaking for" them) become the master-model for rejection of diasporic academic work? Why has the imperative to imagine the other responsibly been lifted? Ponder the answer, please, as you read this section. This plea was already there in the decade-old first version of this book. Today I locate the double bind as between the uselessness of human life (planetarity) and the push to be useful (worldliness).

In the spring of 1998, I taught a senior seminar on reading. The class was exceptionally focused, very smart, small. The reading of *Lucy* that follows is an account of how the class read that novel. If "How to Read a 'Culturally Different' Book" reads in the imagination-retrieval mode "for the multicultural classroom," "Thinking Cultural Questions" reads in the formalist mode for the student of English. It was written in the British Library in London, in the nine planned days that I had to wait for the floodwaters to recede from Dhaka so that I could fly to Bangladesh. In its present form, "Reading with Stuart Hall in 'Pure' Literary Terms," it is related to the work of Hall because it was subsequently published in a Hall Festschrift. It was in 1996 that I began reclaiming the undergraduate teaching of English literary criticism. It was what my teachers at the University of Calcutta trained me for. You will judge if it was a good move. The double bind here is between "truth" and rhetoric.

"The Double Bind Starts to Kick In," earlier called "Moral Dilemma," frames this more teacherly turn. It should interest the general reader that I have been able to read bits of it to my History of Literary Criticism undergraduate class in order to explain to them why I cannot teach a regular survey. I should also like to thank Emily Donaldson, a student of this class in 1998, who inspired me by saying "Professor Spivak, you are not even a hard A, you are a hard B." Students have explained to me subsequently that, when my more famous colleagues teach undergraduate surveys, they teach them as "easy courses with few requirements," so that students with "harder" majors, or pre-law and pre-medical students, can skate through them and earn credits. This gave me a clue to how close to home are those operations of the trivialization of the humanities and the privatization of the imagination. I would also like to thank Christopher Brady, the only science major (Biology), who lasted the class, although he was obliged to drop to a pass-fail grade, because the class was too demanding. That you cannot inhabit this double bind, change it into the single bind of course descriptions, should be obvious.

The essays that follow have crept into the kind of doubt that finally emerges in the Introduction. I can tabulate more easily here. "Terror: A Speech after 9/11": between existing models of secular law and the need for accommodating the intuition of the transcendental. "Harlem": between development and impulse to resistance (this will find a fuller statement in my Du Bois lectures, delivered at Harvard in November 2009). "Scattered Speculations on the Subaltern and the Popular": between subalternity as a position without identity and the massive identitarian affect of an epistemological engagement with specific cases of subalternity. "World Systems and the Creole" and "Rethinking Comparativism" spell out the double bind at the heart of comparativism; I think of the death of the discipline, precisely because of that more extreme sense of a double bind. In

"The Stakes of a World Literature" it is a subaltern song that spells out the double bind and will repeat it as all the other double binds in the book.

"Sign and Trace" and "Tracing the Skin of Day" are catalog essays, both of which spell out the double bind in wanting to sign the trace—which finds a way out in renouncing verbality altogether, but never with complete success.

Gender is the last word. Figure out the double binds there, simple and forbidding.

Introduction

GLOBALIZATION TAKES PLACE only in capital and data. Everything else is damage control. Information command has ruined knowing and reading. Therefore we don't really know what to do with information.[1] Unanalyzed projects come into existence simply because the information is there. Crowd sourcing takes the place of democracy. Universities become adjuncts to what is called international civil society; the humanities and imaginative social sciences bite the dust. At this point, some of us remind ourselves that the legacy of the European Enlightenment is Doubt. Hope (or lack of hope) and sentimental nationalism (or sentimental postnational globalism) are where much of our world stands now. This book is about productively undoing another legacy of the European Enlightenment—the aesthetic. Productive undoing is a difficult task. It must look carefully at the fault lines of the doing, without accusation, without excuse, with a view to use. That is never far from my thoughts, but I must confess, in this era of the mantra of hope, undoing the Aesthetic that was the cousin of Doubt has made this Introduction less upbeat than the chapters in this book, where, in dark times—hope still seemed a valuable alternative.

The chapters themselves are in praise of learning the double bind—not just learning about it. Given the humanities' need to be supported in the academic world, this consistent praise often led to the conviction that the humanities could somehow learn to resolve double binds by playing them. But the fact that such convictions are shared, on different registers, not only by the humanities, and that the other ways of knowledge management can be made more consistent with the axiomatics of electronic capitalism has shifted the grounds of this conviction.

The most pernicious presupposition today is that globalization has happily happened in every aspect of our lives. Globalization can never happen to the sensory equipment of the experiencing being except insofar as it always was implicit in its vanishing outlines. Only an aesthetic education can continue to prepare us for this, thinking an uneven and only apparently accessible contemporaneity that can no longer be interpreted by such nice polarities as modernity/tradition, colonial/postcolonial.[2] Everything else begins there, in that space that allows us to survive in the singular and the unverifiable, surrounded by the lethal and lugubrious consolations of rational choice. Other kinds of institutional knowledge assume this base implicitly. What is the nature of this aesthetic education? There can be no global formula for it. I, most at home in institutions of tertiary education, give an idea in this book that can be described as sabotaging Schiller.[3]

When knowledge management tries to undo the double bind on these shifting grounds and calls it the practice of sustainability: doing the minimum of something in order to do the maximum of something else, it is a displacement of Schiller's transformation of Kant's critical philosophy, about which more later. Such top-down, balancing-out calculations may also be why Kant calls "mere reason" morally lazy. The world needs an epistemological change that will rearrange desires.[4] Global contemporaneity requires it. This too will be part of our concern in this book.

The humanities version of sustainability, in the early days, was to maximize imaginative training and minimize the mind-numbing uniformization of globalization. (Clues can be found for this in the British Romantic Movement.) As we were trying to achieve this, the increasingly corporatized and ambitious globalist university in the United States supervised the minimalization of the humanities and the social sciences—in order to achieve the maximum of some version of globalization.[5] When these essays were crafted, that tendency had not found its full flowering. Some of us were at the beginning of institution building at two ends of the spectrum, with hope and cautious confidence. Although the Gulf War (1991) and then the war in Iraq (2003–) were happening, the peculiar "end" of the Cold War, a conclusion perhaps too quickly drawn from the implosion of the Soviet Union, seemed something still to work with. Today the conjuncture has moved along—global social movements have fully internationalized into an alliance with feudality in the North. The humanities and social sciences are peripheral at the top. The only hope for me lies at the subaltern end; and that cannot inform a university press book! The only link here may be work with a certain Gramsci, but that work postdates these essays. I will refer to it here. It will be the readers' task to scan it between the lines of the book.

In the body of the book, there is also, occasionally, an unexamined conviction in the history-defying originality of the aboriginal. I have since come to realize that it might have come from a "feudal" protection and preservation that were no more than a ruse of primitivist benevolence.

The reconsiderations and realizations that I have here outlined are reflected in this Introduction, and not always in the body of the book. I ask, as usual, for an interactive reader. The Introduction opens with the double bind: learning to live with contradictory instructions. It traces a Kant–Schiller–Marx–de Man trajectory, where the European proper names are metonyms for epochal changes. Toward the end, the Introduction moves on to a place that contradicts the virtue of acquiring the skill of playing the double bind: schizophrenia as figure, reterritorialized and recoded. The Introduction ends with Gramsci's exhortation: instrumentalize the intellectual, in the interest of producing epistemological change, rather than only attending upon the ethical, in subaltern and intellectual alike.[6] I have invoked the world, as an unexamined empirical given, in the interstices of the Introduction.

The most pervasive double bind undoes the individual-collective dichotomy by way of a thinking, of death, that would undo the human-animal dichotomy as well. "The general future of mankind has nothing to offer to individual life, whose only certain future is death."[7] If I had the book to write over again, I would include readings of Tillie Olsen's *Tell Me a Riddle* and Christine Brooke-Rose's *Subscript* and *Life, End of.*[8] These are novels that dare to stage the ethico-political in general, together with aging and dying, relating without a relationship to textual practice. Is it because of the Baubo-factor—that women past reproduction can cast a cold eye upon reproductive normativity—that these are old women's texts? A post-normative queeredness? Is this why J. M. Coetzee chooses old woman protagonists as trace of the author in *The Age of Iron,* and the Elizabeth Costello texts?[9] Maybe on this register, the literary can still do something. Maybe not.

Please work at this double bind between Introduction and book as you read. I have provided a Preface that charts an intellectual trajectory: Should we credit the pessimism of the intellect of the Pre-Post-face weighted by the conjuncture, or the optimism of the will of the essays? No sustainability here; given the times, who wins loses.

In 1992, asked to give the first T. B. Davie Memorial lecture at the University of Cape Town after the lifting of apartheid, I suggested that we learn to use the European Enlightenment from below.[10] I used the expression "ab-use" because the Latin prefix "ab" says much more than "below." Indicating both "motion away" and "agency, point of origin," "supporting," as well as "the duties of slaves," it nicely captures the double bind of the postcolonial and the metropolitan migrant regarding the Enlightenment. We want the public sphere gains and private sphere constraints of the Enlightenment; yet we must also find something relating to "our own history" to counteract the fact that the Enlightenment came, to colonizer and colonized alike, through colonialism, to support a destructive "free trade," and that top-down policy breaches of Enlightenment principles are more rule than exception.[11] This distinguishes our efforts from the best in the modern European attempts to use the European Enlightenment critically, with which we are in sympathy, enough to subvert![12] But "ab-use" can be a misleading neographism, and come to mean simply "abuse." That should be so far from our intentions that I thought to sacrifice precision and range and simply say "from below." This too rankles, for it assumes that "we," whoever we are, are below the level of the Enlightenment. A double bind, again.[13]

The phrase "double bind" comes from Gregory Bateson's *Steps to an Ecology of Mind,* first published in 1972.[14] To begin with, the double bind was a way for him to understand childhood schizophrenia qualitatively. Bateson was, however, aware that "both those whose life is enriched by trans-contextual gifts and those who are impoverished by trans-contextual confusion are alike in one respect: for them there is always or often a 'double take.'" In other words, inhabiting thus the two ends of the spectrum, the double bind could be generalized. At one end, the need for cure; at the other, to recognize the healer. He was also aware of the need for the catachrestic concept-metaphors for which there can be no literal referent. In his essay on "A Theory of Play and Fantasy" he defines "the play of two individuals on a certain occasion"—play and therapy—never distant from what we are calling an aesthetic education—by way of "a set-theoretical diagram." It is when "the mathematical analogy breaks down" that he systematically outlines how the therapist must work at the limits of the double bind of the "abstract" and the "concrete" (EM, pp. 186–187). In the contemporary context, we can call this the double bind of the universalizability of the singular, the double bind at the heart of democracy, for which an aesthetic education can be an epistemological preparation, as we, the teachers of the aesthetic, use material that is historically marked by the region, cohabiting with, resisting, and accommodating what comes from the Enlightenment. Even this requires immense institution-changing initiatives, thwarted by the bureaucratic spirit accepted above and below. And yet, there is "the good teacher," "the good student," on the way to collectivity. Doubt and hope . . . [15]

In his essay Bateson spelled out the training of the imagination in terms of a *mise-en-abyme,* an indefinite series of mutual reflections:

speaking of "dilemma[s] . . . not confined to the contexts of schizophrenia" (EM, p. 258), he distinguishes between "people and . . . robots in
the fact of learning . . . from passing on from solution to solution, always
selecting another solution which is preferable to that which preceded it"
(EM, p. 240). He "enlarge[s] the scope of what is to be included within
the concept of learning" by way of "hierarchic series [that] will then
consist of message, metamessage, meta-meta message and so on" (EM,
pp. 247–248). This "training," the bulwark of an aesthetic education,
habitually fails with religion and nationalism: "Up in the dim region
where art, magic, and religion meet and overlap, human beings have
evolved the 'metaphor that is meant,' the flag which men will die to save,
and the sacrament that is felt to be more than 'an outward and visible
sign, given unto us'" (EM, p. 183); it is interesting that Freud mentions
the same two items—"Throne and Altar"—in "Fetishism," as the moni-
tors of fetishistic illogic.[16]

Play training, an aesthetic education, habitually fails with flag and sacrament, throne and altar. Bateson described habit altogether unsentimentally. A practitioner's line connects him here to the Wordsworth of the
Lyrical Ballads, interested in undoing the bad epistemo/affective consequences of nascent capitalism, and to Gramsci looking to produce the
subaltern intellectual out of "the man [sic] of the masses" in a place and
time where clan politics were not unknown.[17] Here is Bateson:

> In the field of mental process, we are very familiar with this sort of econom-
> ics [of trial and error adaptability], and in fact a major and necessary saving
> is achieved by the familiar process of habit formation. We may, in the first
> instance, solve a given problem by taking them out of the range of stochas-
> tic operation and handing over the solutions to a deeper and less flexible
> mechanism, which we call "habit." (EM, p. 257)

The passage above was written in 1959. Ten years later, at a symposium on the double bind, Bateson generalizes habit. Here the practitio-
ner/philosopher's connection is with the Freud who attempted to go beyond
the pleasure principle to a more general "organic compulsion to repeat
[that] lie[s] in the phenomena of heredity and the facts of embryology"
(SE 18, p. 37). Here, again, is Bateson:

> By superposing and interconnecting many feedback loops, we (and all other
> biological systems) not only solve particular problems but also form habits
> which we apply to the solution of classes of problems. We act as though a
> whole class of problems could be solved in terms of assumptions or prem-
> ises, fewer in number than the members of the class of problems. In other
> words, we (organisms) learn to learn. . . . [The] rigidity [of habits] follows
> as a necessary corollary of their status in the hierarchy of adaptation. The
> very economy of trial and error which is achieved by habit formation is only

possible because habits are comparatively "hard programmed." ... The economy consists precisely in not re-examining or rediscovering the premises of habit every time the habit is used. We may say that these premises are partly "unconscious", or—if you please—a habit of not examining them is developed. (EM, p. 274)

The aesthetic short-circuits the task of shaking up this habit of not examining them, perhaps. I said to begin with that in the earlier stages we could find in British Romanticism our models. But as long as we take the literary as substantive source of good thinking alone, we will fail in the task of the aesthetic education we are proposing: at all cost to enter another's text. Otherwise, we will notice that William Wordsworth's project is deeply class-marked, and that he does not judge habit. He is clear about being superior to others in being a poet, unusually gifted with a too-strong imagination, capable of organizing other people's habits. I will quote at length to show his lack of interest in working with the subaltern, although he certainly acknowledges the power of their "real" language. His chief interest is in changing the taste of the readers of poetry; his confidence in "the poet's" (the trace of the author?) gifts is elaborately expressed in these passages, again even as the (unself-conscious?) power of the "real" language of "men" is recognized:

> For our continued influxes of feeling are modified and directed by our thoughts, which are indeed the representatives of all our past feelings; and, as by contemplating the relation of these general representatives to each other, we discover what is really important to men, so, by the repetition and continuance of this act, our feelings will be connected with important subjects, till at length, if we be originally possessed of much sensibility, such habits of mind will be produced, that, by obeying blindly and mechanically the impulses of those habits, we shall describe objects, and utter sentiments, of such a nature, and in such connexion with each other, that the understanding of the Reader must necessarily be in some degree enlightened, and his affections strengthened and purified. (LB, p. 126)
>
> [The poet] is a man speaking to men: a man, it is true, endued with more lively sensibility, more enthusiasm and tenderness, who has a greater knowledge of human nature, and a more comprehensive soul, than are supposed to be common among mankind; a man pleased with his own passions and volitions, and who rejoices more than other men in the spirit of life that is in him; delighting to contemplate similar volitions and passions as manifested in the goings-on of the Universe, and habitually impelled to create them where he does not find them. To these qualities he has added a disposition to be affected more than other men by absent things as if they were present; an ability of conjuring up in himself passions, which are indeed far from being the same as those produced by real events, yet (especially in those parts of the general sympathy which are pleasing and delightful) do more nearly

resemble the passions produced by real events, than any thing which, from the motions of their own minds merely, other men are accustomed to feel in themselves; whence, and from practice, he has acquired a greater readiness and power in expressing what he thinks and feels, and especially those thoughts and feelings which, by his own choice, or from the structure of his own mind, arise in him without immediate external excitement. . . . (LB, p. 138)

But, whatever portion of this faculty we may suppose even the greatest Poet to possess, there cannot be a doubt but that the language which it will suggest to him, must, in liveliness and truth, fall far short of that which is uttered by men in real life, under the actual pressure of those passions, certain shadows of which the Poet thus produces, or feels to be produced, in himself. However exalted a notion we would wish to cherish of the character of a Poet, it is obvious, that, while he describes and imitates passions, his situation is altogether slavish and mechanical, compared with the freedom and power of real and substantial action and suffering. So that it will be the wish of the Poet to bring his feelings near to those of the persons whose feelings he describes, nay, for short spaces of time perhaps, to let himself slip into an entire delusion, and even confound and identify his own feelings with theirs; modifying only the language which is thus suggested to him, by a consideration that he describes for a particular purpose, that of giving pleasure. . . . (LB, pp. 138–139)

But it may be said by those who do not object to the general spirit of these remarks, that, as it is impossible for the Poet to produce upon all occasions language as exquisitely fitted for the passion as that which the real passion itself suggests, it is proper that he should consider himself as in the situation of a translator, who deems himself justified when he substitutes excellences of another kind for those which are unattainable by him; and endeavours occasionally to surpass his original, in order to make some amends for the general inferiority to which he feels that he must submit. (LB, p. 139)

Thus he may be a "man speaking to men." For him, however, Marx's third thesis on Feuerbach would have held no appeal: that since the knowledge gap between teacher and taught cannot be circumvented, not to let this develop into a power gap is a constant task that will keep society always in the state of upheaval that is necessary for liberation. (The English translation of upheaval—*Umwälzung*—is usually "revolution" rather than "upheaval," thus destroying Marx's important warning: the educators must be educated.)[18] The deeply individualistic theory of the Romantic creative imagination in Wordsworth must remain anti-systemic.[19] By contrast, Gramsci's entire energies are devoted to producing the subaltern intellectual, by instrumentalizing the "new intellectual":

The history of industrialization has always been a continuing struggle (which today takes on an even more marked and rigorous [*rigorosa*] form)

against the characteristic of "animality" in man. It has been an uninter-
rupted, often painful and bloody process of subjugating natural (i.e. animal
and primitive) instincts to ever [sempre] new, more complex and rigid habits
of order, exactitude and precision, making possible the increasingly complex
forms of collective life which are the necessary consequence of industrial
development. This struggle imposed from outside, and the results to date,
though they may have great immediate value, are to a large extent mechanical: the new habits have not yet become "second nature." . . . Up to now all
changes in modes of existence and modes of life have taken place through
brute coercion. . . . The selection or "education" of men adapted to the new
forms of civilization and to the new forms of production and work has
taken place by means of incredible acts of brutality which have driven the
weak and the non-conformists into the limbo of outcasts or eliminated them
altogether.[20]

(It should be mentioned here that Gramsci manifests what all projects
of "education" do, a need to establish a distinction from a homogeneous
"animality." Derrida has analyzed this at great length in *The Animal
That Therefore I Am*.[21] It is a compromise that we cannot escape. We see
this in the rhetorical staging of Derrida's essay "University without Conditions."[22]) Gramsci and Bateson, interested in education and therapy,
could not be satisfied with habit alone as more than the ground of epistemic change. Indeed, Bateson came to think of therapy itself as a species
of double bind: "The difference between the therapeutic bind and the
original double bind situation is in part the fact that the therapist is not
involved in a life and death struggle himself. He can therefore set up relatively benevolent binds and gradually aid the patient in his emancipation
from them" (EM, pp. 226–227). And, since his task is psychological rather
than epistemological, he stops at making it very clear that habit does not
question. It is Gramsci who insists, at least by implication, that the premises of an argument must indeed be "rediscoverable," "re-examinable," by
the man of the masses as he is educated to be a citizen. I take the liberty
of quoting myself:

> If we want to "change the world," alter-globalism must think of the educa-
> tion of the disenfranchised into disinterest in a double bind with the interest
> of class struggle: "democracy . . . cannot mean merely that an unskilled
> worker can become skilled," writes Gramsci. "It must mean that every 'citi-
> zen' can 'govern' and that society places him, even if only abstractly, in a
> general condition to achieve this."[23]

In an important comment on Marx, Gramsci distinguishes between the
psychological, the moral (our word would perhaps be "ethical"), and the
epistemological. Our task is to "ab-use" this, not to excuse its seeming

systemic confidence (belied by much of the hesitation of what Gramsci wrote in prison), nor to accuse it of that very thing, but to see in the addition of the epistemological a way of reading Gramsci with "history in the reading":[24]

> The proposition contained in the Preface to *A Contribution to the Critique of Political Economy* to the effect that men acquire consciousness of structural conflicts on the level of ideologies should be considered as an affirmation of epistemological and not simply psychological and moral value. From this, it follows that the theoretical-practical principle of hegemony has also epistemological significance, and it is here that Ilyich [Lenin]'s greatest theoretical contribution to the philosophy of praxis [i.e., Marxism] should be sought. In these terms one could say that Ilyich advanced philosophy as philosophy in so far as he advanced political doctrine and practice. The realization of a hegemonic apparatus, in so far as it creates a new ideological terrain, determines a reform of consciousness and of methods of knowledge: it is a fact of knowledge, a philosophical fact. In Crocean terms: when one succeeds in introducing a new morality in conformity with a new conception of the world, one finishes by introducing the conception as well; in other words, one determines a reform of the whole of philosophy.[25]

The relationship between education and the habit of the ethical is as the relationship without relationship between responsibility and the gift that we must imagine in order to account for responsibility—an unrestricted transcendental deduction, if you like.[26] Training for the habit of the ethical can only be worked at through attending to the systemic task of epistemological engagement. We "learn to learn" (Bateson's more general phrase) how to teach from the historico-cultural text within which a certain group of students might be placed. Thus Gramsci invokes

> the active relationship which exists between [the intellectual] and the cultural environment he is proposing to modify. The environment reacts back on the philosopher and imposes on him a continual process of self-criticism. It is his "teacher." . . . For the relationship between master and disciple in the general sense referred to above is only realised, where this political condition exists, and only then do we get the "historical" realisation of a new type of philosopher, whom we could call a "democratic philosopher" in the sense that he is a philosopher convinced that his personality is not limited to himself as a physical individual but is an active social relationship of modification of the cultural environment.[27]

An aesthetic education teaches the humanities in such a way that all subjects are "contaminated." I have repeated that I have not much hope for this in the current context. Let me at least quote Gramsci's hope:

The mode of being of the new intellectual can no longer consist in eloquence, . . . but in active participation in practical life, . . . superior to the
abstract mathematical spirit; from technique-as-work one proceeds to
technique-as-science and to the humanistic conception of history, without
which one remains "specialised" and does not become "directive" (specialised and political).[28]

I will come later to Gramsci's "techno-scientific" lesson, "superior to the
abstract mathematical spirit." For now, let us remember that the prison
notebooks, being notes to oneself for future work, are necessarily in an
open form that requires careful acquaintance with the protocols of the
text. I would like to propose that the training of the imagination that can
teach the subject to play—an aesthetic education—can also teach it to discover (theoretically or practically) the premises of the habit that obliges
us to transcendentalize religion and nation (as Bateson and Freud both
point out). If, however, this is only a "rearrangement of desire" or the
substitution of one habit for another through pedagogical sleight-of-
hand, there will be no ability to recover that discovery for a continuity
of epistemological effort. We must learn to do violence to the epistemo-
epistemological difference and remember that this is what education "is,"
and thus keep up the work of displacing belief onto the terrain of the
imagination, attempt to access the epistemic. The displacement of belief
onto the terrain of the imagination can be a description of reading in its
most robust sense. It is also the irreducible element of an aesthetic education. In the context of the beginning of the twenty-first century, to learn
to de-transcendentalize religion and (the birth of a) nation into the imaginative sphere is an invaluable gift. But this particular function of reading
is important in a general and continuing way as well. Elsewhere I have
argued that this type of education, with careful consideration of social
context, can be part of education from the elementary level, where it is
even more formal rather than substantive. In this book, that argument
flashes up here and there, but the general terrain of the book is tertiary
and postgraduate education, the reproduction of citizens and teachers.
This is where we use the legacy of the Enlightenment, relocate the transcendental from belief, with a view to its double bind, producing a sim-
pler solution: privatize belief, rationalize the transcendent. This particular solution, offered as liberal education as such, suits capitalism better.

We saw briefly how Bateson takes the double bind out of the limited
context or narrow sense of a mental "disease." Indeed, it may have become, for him, a general description of all doing, all thinking as doing, all
self-conscious living, upstream from capitalism, a question of degrees.
Contradictory instructions come to us at all times. We learn to listen to

them and remain in the game. When and as we decide, we know therefore that we have broken the double bind into a single bind, as it were, and we also know that change will have to be undertaken soon, or, things will change: task or event. Knowing this, the typical emotion that accompanies decisions—ethical, political, legal, intellectual, aesthetic, and indeed decisions of the daily grind—is a spectrum of regret and remorse to at least unease, otherwise self-congratulation followed by denial or bewilderment. This is different from the unexamined hope which animates much globalist and alter-globalist enterprise today, in the United States as in the global elite.

I will think of our relationship to the European Enlightenment and to "ab-use"/"use from below" by the Gramsci-Bateson model as I unfold my argument, always keeping in mind the uneven diachrony of global contemporaneity. This revises the unquestioning emphasis on the legacy of British and German Romanticism or the feudal benevolent primitivism of the global South. Indeed, it also revises the philosophical error of confidence in accessing the ethical reflex directly, rather than insist on an epistemological preparation into the possibility of a relationship without relation: the reflexive re-arrangement of desires, a recruiting of English teachers reaching hearts and minds, against the interests of a maximal capitalism and unmediated cyber literacy as the greatest good. My re-territorialization of Schiller may be an example of this. Remember also that a gendered access to the Enlightenment, which was often a way out of indigenous gendering, is doubled over a double bind, if possible.

Of course, the Enlightenment also had a strong element of control and, epistemologically, it harbored an encyclopedist impulse, which matched the classifying impulse that seems the strongest virtue of classical science. The study of literature can also make uncritical use of this. It is not necessarily a bad thing to do but this is not what globalization needs from an aesthetic education as supplement.

It is well known that literary studies became disciplinarized concurrently with colonialism. In broad strokes, it may be argued that their construction as an object of discipline and study was also the inauguration of their exhaustion. As they became less and less useful to the self-determination of capital, they began to legitimize themselves by varieties of scientism. Hard-core structuralism and discourse analysis were part of this from the 1940s on down. The present tendency toward quantitative analysis of literature belongs to the same impulse. Literature can, of course, be studied in as many ways as one likes. The purpose of an aesthetic education is not, however, served by protective scientism. All double binds are well settled there under a seemingly scientific control.

Sometimes these scientists of the literary critical scene say that the close readers are emphasizing the "author function." On the contrary, readers who are reading literature closely to exercise the imagination to play the double bind are, like Bateson, interested in form rather than the author. The death of the (authority of the) author (in establishing contextual correctness as literary criticism) is the birth of the reader (concentrating on the practice of reading)—a good formula from the 1960s that remains useful today, in sparer times. We would use the formula as a double bind, rather than understand it as turf battle.

For the sake of convenience, let us assume that the European Enlightenment can be philosophically metonymized by the Peace of Westphalia and Kant—the integrity of nation-states and the public use of a self-constrained reason. Here is another limit to this study. Other imaginations of the Enlightenment will generate other narratives. I believe my argument can, mutatis mutandis, work with them.[29]

The Peace of Westphalia announces the distant possibility of a Euro-partial, nation-state-specific globality which we have learned to acknowledge as European imperialism, as a social formation. Whatever we might call "history" is not a continuous narrative, except by the most sweeping metonymic generalizations. In that mode, we can read the self-conscious gesture of Westphalia also as announcing the symbolic end of an old world, just around the corner, itself metonymizable as a change in the meaning of the word "empire." Whatever the Holy Roman Empire might have meant had to come to an end in 1795, chronologically over a hundred years later, but the semiotic change is supposed to have been launched with Westphalia, birthplace of Voltaire's Candide. The Ottoman and Russian imperial formations, "inclusive" in different ways, became increasingly out of joint from this narrative, this mole-like semiotic recoding which accompanied what can be computed as the self-determination of capitalism, equally reductively, of course.[30] In the post-Soviet conjuncture, they become, in their diachrony, today, our warning signals when we generalize. With this expanded self-presentation of the norm, epistemic formations outside were exceptionalized, and anthropologized when "known." This is coming undone in global contemporaneity, but the dominant presuppositions, including ours, remain the same. (Proposing alternative non-European epistemes is a variant of the old anthropologism.) "Local subjectivities within imperial space [remain] secondary."[31] In global contemporaneity, thus, one way to "democratize" is to make space for rogue capitalism, taking advantage of the simultaneity of capital/data movement, even if it means military or party/clan violence, carrying with it the aura of the civilizing mission accompanying transformative projects from imperialism to development. This aura carries over to the question of minority rights within developed civil societies, where it engages postcolonial radicalism of a more political sort, whereas "majority" and "minority" are Euro-U.S. constructs relating to democracy as body count. As Marx pointed out, capital is reduction. The change in the meaning of "empire" is the opening of the possibility of accessing an "other side of the world," nation by European nation, and paradoxically, the beginning of the dream of cosmopolitanism by a particular class.

When Goethe and Marx wrote about world literature, they presupposed this specifically European access to a world rather than the entire empirical world taken as a source of the literary. Goethe might have caught its aporetic nature by insisting on a "striving" toward it. Scientific socialism saw it as accomplished fact.[32] Kant, when he wrote as public intellectual rather than philosopher, also spoke of a world this way. That is the world that inhabits his thought of a cosmopolitheia, a constitution for world governance. We must remember that in these contexts state-formation preceded democratization, one of the crucial factors in overcoming clan through capital.[33]

In order to understand the "world"'s double bind toward the European Enlightenment, let us look again at that prescient document, Kant's bid for cosmopolitheia, "Toward a Perpetual Peace," as it emerges as a considered reaction to what may be considered a follow-through from the Peace of Westphalia: the Treaty of Basel (1795).[34] We are looking at a source-narrative of "European" access to a "world." Kant's understanding of this in terms of colonialism seems at first exemplary. Yet the rest of the argument also seems exemplary, for us in a less interesting way. Admittedly with irony, Kant sees capital (he calls it "money," but his argument is unmistakable) as the great equalizer, and proposes an implicitly master countries' world governance—since no other method of establishing equality is proposed—predicated upon a containment as well as a permission to warfare. Kant's prohibition of something like the U.S. intervention in Iraq, which commenced in the late twentieth century and continued into the twenty-first ("No state shall forcibly interfere in the constitution and government of another state") is uncanny; yet the following is also allowed:

> The spirit of commerce [*Handelsgeist*] sooner or later takes hold of every people, and it cannot exist side by side with war. And of all the powers (or means) at the disposal of the power of the states, financial power [*Geldmacht*] can probably be relied on most. Thus states find themselves compelled to promote the noble cause of peace, though not exactly from the mainspring [*Triebfeder*] of morality. . . . In this way, nature guarantees perpetual peace by the actual mechanism of human inclinations. (PP, p. 114)

An early statement of MacDonaldist globalization as human nature as nature's cooperation with mercantile capitalism; the connection is mechanical—the talk is of an inappropriate mainspring.

This detail, easily missed, the irony of the opening passage of the work, and the philosophical sharpness of a closing injunction point toward the urgency of our task of ab-use (not abuse). The text signals its undoing and re-location, if we attend.

The opening passage, a "literary" invocation of a pub-sign, suggests that the only perpetual peace—"eternal peace" *(der ewige Friede)* would be more idiomatic—is that of death. In the closing invocation the sentence that I have in mind is "The deceit [*Hinterlist*] of a shady [*lichtscheu*]"— Kant's wording is stronger than most English translations—"politics [*Politik*] could however easily be thwarted [*vereitelt*] through the publicization of philosophy's maxims [*von der Philosophie durch die Publicität jener ihrer Maximen*], would it but dare to allow the philosopher to publicize his own maxims" (PP, p. 130).

Let us focus for a moment on the word "maxim":

> I call all subjective grounding propositions [*Grundsätze*] that are found [*hergenommen*] not from the nature [*Beschaffenheit*] of the object [Latin spelling] but from the interest of reason in regard to a specific [*gewiss*] possible perfection of the cognition of the object [Latin spelling], maxims of reason. Thus there are maxims of speculative reason, which rest unsupported [*lediglich*] on reason's speculative interest, even though it may seem as if they were objective principles [*Principien*].

Before I continue with the quotation, I would like to comment on the translation modifications that I have made in it. Normally, this would be part of a "Translator's Note." I bring it up in the text because the difficulty of translating the nuances of Kant's sustained practice allows a common reader, like me, or the reader of a literary-critical book, like this one, to miss the sustained private grammar of values. And, of course, a general assumption of continuous translatability is waylaid by the diachronic heterogeneity of our globe that I persistently invoke. For example, Kant has a sustained practice of distinguishing between *Grundsätze* and *Principien*. The former belongs within the outline of philosophizing as truth within what I call an "intended mistake." They are the propositions that ground philosophizing. The latter is part of the objective world of pure reason as it is transcendentally deduced by the philosopher, without the ability to produce evidence. Indeed, whenever Kant uses Latin spelling—as in the case of the two uses of the word "Object" as *Objekt* rather than *Gegenstand* in our passage—Kant makes this distinction. In most English translations *Grundsätze* and *Principien* are both translated "principles." This effaces the distinction between the philosopher philosophizing by programmed "intended mistake" and the philosopher bringing philosophy to crisis by transcendentally deducing the characteristics of the ideas of pure reason, the crucial difference that a reader like Schiller must ignore as he changes aporias to reversible chiasmuses. I have also changed "taken" to "found," because the notion of something already laid down or programmed for the philosophizing subject, available in the German deep background in *hergenommen,* is made more active if "taken" is kept. I want to insist that none of the English words in the excellent Cambridge translation is "wrong." It is just that they seem here, surprisingly, not to have practiced the literalism that sympathy with Kant's private grammar would have produced. I have written about this in "Translating into English" (Chapter 12 in this book). To continue with my comments on translation modification, let me point at "unsupported" for the *lediglich.* "Solely" is more idiomatic. But the idea of uncoupled as in a single person that *lediglich* carries is I think lost if we read nothing but "solely." This way we can see that maxims like *Grundsätze* are subjective and principles as *Principien* are objective and the former cannot be taken objectively, although, and this is important, they might seem objective. Are we beginning to get a sense of what advice Kant is giving to the politicians? To understand that what they work with is interested rather than rational? In the protocol of Kant's philosophical texts, some words relate to the programmed exigencies of the philosophizing reason and, mutatis mutandis, mere reason; others to the description of the functioning of pure reason. The former group is more often than not German and more colloquial; the latter Latin and more formal. Thus it is with *Grundsatz* and *Princip.* To translate both "principle" is to lose an important and continuing nuance.

Let us continue reading Kant:

> If merely [this carries with it the place of "mere" reason within Kantian architectonics] regulative grounding propositions [*Grundsätze*] are considered as constitutive, then as objective principles [*Principien*] they can be in conflict, but if one considers them *merely* [emphasis added] as maxims, then it is not a true conflict, but it is merely a different interest of reason that gives rise to [*verursacht*] a divorce [the metaphor of a marriage programmed to come undone is already available in *lediglich*] between ways of thinking. Reason has only a single united [*einig*] interest, and the conflict between its maxims is only a variation and a reciprocal limitation of the methods attempting to be sufficient to this interest [*ein Genüge zu tun*].[35]

Without a theory of Reason as such, Kant's assertion of a single united interest of Reason can itself be (or not be) read as within the programmed "intended mistake." An unavoidable double bind, which Schiller must avoid, or turn into a series of balances ending in play.

A "maxim," then, is something the philosopher devises in order to come to terms with the transcendental gap at the origin of philosophy. The conduct of the politician, at best "rational" in an altogether narrow sense, cannot be aware of this self-framing cautionary and pre-cautionary gap.

I should like to think that this framing of "Toward a Perpetual Peace" is the space in Kant where we can turn the text around into a permission not to excuse or accuse, but to use (ab-use), take the anaesthetized Enlightenment as self-deluded, a ruse for dupes, a place for excuses. The aesthetic might enlighten to crisis. One can hope that an education through the aesthetic can protect the rational choice of the political by understanding it as produced by the philosophers' methodological need for maxims rather than the unquestioned conviction of the supremacy of reason. Hope. Wish. No guarantees. A responsible buttressing of the possibility of the political in view of the tremendous uncertainties of the ethical.

This was Kant's effort to bring Plato's book on constitutions up to date. After all, Plato only knew a city-state. Kant had the world. Greek and Enlightenment colonialisms self-represented differently—an epistemic difference. Derrida points at the contradiction between a "borderless" world and Kant's demand for an unconditioned policing of the truth.[36]

This formulation of cosmopolitheia troubles us because it seems allied to imperialism contemplating the world in its grasp. On the other hand, we want to rewrite it to suit us, from the toughest definition of politics to the most mysterious confines of literary theory. And not all of us can perform the translation into a thinking of a just world. Can class and gender struggle, so exploited by the benevolent harbingers of capital and clan, be sustained, can vanguardism be persistently supplemented by a (preparation for) mature aesthetic education in the tertiary and post-tertiary, so that it informs the general culture of the citizen?

It is with such questions in mind that we always remind ourselves of Kant writing specifically as a philosopher. And, in the management of the transcendental from belief to philosophizing reason (a faculty never named by Kant, but one of the driving subjects of *The Critique of Pure Reason* that can be accommodated within my broad and vulgar "definition" of the imagination, "thinking absent things," hardly distinguishable from thinking—not to be confused with Kant's tightly housed *Einbildungskraft*)—by way of the transcendental deduction, Kant is our master.[37] In "Terror" (Chapter 18 in this book) I have commented on how he turns grace itself, metaleptically, into an "effect," which, when successfully incorporated into thought (imagined?) can allow us to overcome the moral laziness of mere reason. I have welcomed this last (non)faculty within my vulgar definition of the imagination. In the same spirit of vulgarization, let me point out that Kant calls the filling of the dialectic that results from the transcendental deduction "an illusion." We could think that the Hegelian Eurocentric teleology, filling philosophy with history, is pre-empted here. The content is irreducibly absent in Kant's thinking of the transcendental dialectic, and hence my feeling, that "the ability to think absent things" is not too far away.

As a philosopher, Kant wrote in a fractured voice, unacknowledged by him, of course, but that is another story. Writing about the "world" in the context of the practical function of pure reason, for example, he wrote as follows:

> Its execution is always bounded and defective, but within bounds that cannot be determined, hence always under the influence of the concept of an absolute [absolut] completeness. . . . In it [the practical idea] pure reason even has the causality actually to bring forth . . . the idea of a necessary unity of all possible ends, it must serve as the entire original and limiting condition for everything practical. (PR, pp. 402–403)[38]

But when we use practical reason as such we should proceed in the following way:

> But where reason itself is considered as the determining cause (in freedom [in der Freiheit]), hence in the case of practical principles, we should proceed as if we did not have before us an object of sense but one of pure understanding, . . . and the series of states can be regarded as if it began absolutely [schlechthin] (through an intelligible cause). (PR, p. 613)[39]

Writing about pure reason, the "as ifs," not just "world" but "self" as well, are clearly shown to be things needed so both experience and philosophizing can be possible. This is the best of the European Enlightenment, which recognizes the limits of its powers without either theologizing or pathologizing them. Ulysses among the sirens, who tempt with absolute knowledge.[40] When Nietzsche writes: "Truth is the kind of error without which a certain kind of living being could not live. The value for life ultimately decides," the rhetorical power of the word "error" and the clear designation of the decision to something other than the conscious philosophizing mind makes us miss the family resemblance between his statement and Kant's notion that a "world" and a "self" must be assumed in order for the human being to think that he (for Kant) has experience. An "as if" is as much error as truth. Your interest makes you decide which word you will use. And Kant's use of Anlage, a word that comes close to programming, carries the idea of an agency outside of the mind as consciousness. If we can use this "from below" (ab-use, rather), we can have an enlightened practice that is not merely opposition.

Again, a double bind.

Academic and mechanical Marxists are as superstitious about the words "ethical" and "aesthetic" as academic and mechanical feminists used to be of something vaguely understood as "biology."

I have often spoken of Melanie Klein, establishing biology as the terrain of ethical semiosis. Here let me point out the obvious failure of any Marxism to produce the impulse to redistribute without state control and enforcement. The breakdown of the first wave of Marxist experimentation through the seduction of capitalism for leaders and people alike may have something to do with the absence of the ethical aspects of communism in the epistemological project of popular education. If ethics and aesthetics are defined as devoid of and even as opposed to the political, which is confined to a certain state-formation and structure and a certain management of the economic, we can hope for a short or enforced life for the communist system. The fact that the relationship between a globalized socialist system, an unconditional ethics, and an open aesthetics is at best a double bind does not remove the problem. A quantified literary criticism is little more than a parlor game compared to the seriousness of the situation. These considerations lead to the epistemological projects that we call "education." Otherwise, we would be obliged to give a wider scope to what George Caffentzis notes in the context of the Peak Oil Complex: "At first glance, [it] . . . could transform the modality of the [anticapitalist] movement's slogan, 'Another World is Possible,' to 'Another World is Necessary for there to be a World,'" but he is finally obliged to say: "For the most part, it is a politics of alternative energy without an alternative society."[41]

Current cosmopolitical double binds come clearer if we put Kant's philosophical writings in relation with his political writings. As mentioned above, Kant never defined the subject of philosophy, philosophizing reason, merely brilliantly tabulating the not incontrovertible facts that establish experience as necessary. This is the most spectacular scene of the double bind. Our own more quotidian general tendency is to deny the double bind, even if we are adroitly managing it in practice by short-term single-binding, persistently hedged. The denial can take the form of emphasizing a single pole of the swing of the double bind as the correct solution. Eurocentric visions of rational choice or state—from Rawls to Kavka—are simply too many to mention—with Human Rights and alterglobalization on the way. Or it can suggest balance as a possible solution. (Our most persuasive current balancing act, as I mentioned in the beginning, is "sustainability.")

In *On the Aesthetic Education of Man,* Friedrich Schiller tried to undo the double bind of mind and body by suggesting the *Spieltrieb*—the "play drive," art as a balancing act that will save society.[42] It is commonly understood that he is influenced by Kant. I am a bit obsessed with Schiller because he, a non-philosopher, made the kind of mistake which a general reader of philosophy must necessarily make, turn the desire inscribed in philosophy into its fulfillment. He has been chided by Paul de Man for making this mistake about Kant, and also for the equally pervasive one of psychologizing Kant. (One might add that this last is so pervasive a misreading of Kant that an early deconstructive formula can be applied to it: there must be something in the text that allows for such psychologizing; no excuses, although one must mark the places in the texts where the possibility for such "mis"readings arises. Mark also how Kant himself deals with them. This is where Kant's ultimately mechanical intuition of the functioning subject comes into play. Our task is also "psychologizing" to an extent—repeating Schiller's mistake and transforming balance to an open series of double binds.)[43]

For our present purposes, we need only note how Kant manages the crisis of the double bind. I have noticed one case in chapter 1 of *A Critique of Postcolonial Reason.*[44] In this Introduction, I have been suggesting that the other big one—I must philosophize, man cannot philosophize (understanding cannot access the ideas of pure reason)—is managed by the transcendental deduction. I recite the important passage: "I therefore call the explanation of the way in which concepts can relate to objects a priori their transcendental deduction, and distinguish this from the empirical [evidentiary] deduction" (PR, p. 220). As I have already pointed out, Kant forbids us to fill this gap with content, and calls such moves a "transcendental illusion, which influences ground rules [*Grundsätze*] whose use is not ever meant for experience" (PR, p. 385).

Schiller is unequivocal about resolving the double bind:

> All the disputes about the concept of beauty which have ever prevailed in the world of philosophy, and to some extent still prevail today, have no other source than this: either the investigation did not start with a sufficiently strict distinction, or it was not carried through to a pure and complete synthesis. (AE, p. 125)

The drive toward form and the drive toward matter "cancel each other out, and the will maintains perfect freedom between them" (AE, p. 135). "As soon as two opposing fundamental drives are active within him, both lose their compulsion and, in the opposition of two necessities gives rise to *Freedom*" (AE, p. 137). And nowhere is his domestication of Kant more apparent than in the celebrated definition of the aesthetic: "If we are to call the condition of sensuous determination the physical, and the condition of rational determination with us logical or moral, then we must call this condition of real and active determinability the aesthetic" (AE, p. 141). From here it is no more than a step to an idealized account of education, to which the tough effortfulness of the Gramsci-Bateson model can bear no resemblance:

> He must learn to desire more nobly, so that he may not need to will sub-limely. This is brought about by means of aesthetic education, which subjects to laws of beauty all those spheres of human behavior in which neither natural laws, nor yet rational laws, are binding upon human caprice, and which, in the form it gives to outer life, already opens up the inner. (AE, p. 169)

Yet here and there, the aporetic intuition of the German nineteenth century does emerge, when, for example, Schiller talks about the effort to make the aesthetic emerge as something "which . . . might . . . serve as a pledge in the sensible world of a morality as yet unseen" (AE, p. 15). But, as the famous 11th Letter shows, he thinks of the Self as undivided, as something which can "annul time," or "subjugate the manifold variety of the World to [its own] unity" (AE, p. 77). The philosophical rigor of the unacknowledged, fractured Kantian subject is not to be found here. This kind of confidence seems altogether sympathetic in the season of unexamined hope that we are attempting to undo. Our social problem seems to be summed up so accurately by Schiller! "The moral possibility is lacking, and a moment so prodigal of opportunity finds a generation unprepared to receive it" (AE, p. 25).

It may be adduced that Kant and Schiller show us two different ways of living in the double bind. If so, ab-using this enlightenment is to expand the scope of this by an "intended mistake": to bequeath a geography to it. I can claim that the chapters in this book are instances of such mistakes. Schiller did not intend his mistake; he was a Kantian. We are not invested in the value of intention. And yet, as I have insisted for a long time, in the field of agency, the fragile instrument of intention drives us. And therefore, it is on the ground of intended versus unintended mistakes that we can differentiate ourselves from Schiller.

Indeed, Kant's own text can also be described as an intended mistake, where the intention is the program of reason and the "mistake" is the only correct procedure open to the philosopher. In Kant's world this phrase would not apply. Kant takes care of it through the transcendental deduction. As we have seen, the guarantee chosen against the possibility of "mistake" is not amenable to evidentiality: "no clear legal ground for an entitlement to their use either from experience or from reason" (PR,

p. 220). "Mistake" can only be used as a catachresis here, and the intent is programmed as the mark of reason. As I write, I begin to suggest more and more that the relationship of this style of reading with the Enlightenment is a taxonomy of "mistakes." Kant's intended, but managed; Schiller's unintended; ours intended and acknowledged; and all subject to the general taxonomic rule of future anteriority. By contrast, the style of the Enlightenment is generally recognized to be access to the self-identical, reasonable norm. Can this be historically our role? To make the Enlightenment open to a(n) (ab)-use that makes room for justice, because it takes away the absoluteness of guarantees and secures it from the mordant satire of a *Candide?*

Prabhat Patnaik, the Indian economist, would find a paragraph such as the above incomprehensibly "postmodern," and would be indignant if he were called "mistaken." Yet, when in the field of general education, he invokes Gramsci and writes as follows, he is with us:

> What is meant by the "nation building" task of higher education however (I have elsewhere called it, following Antonio Gramsci, the task of creating "organic intellectuals" of the people) is something very different from these suggestions. It is indeed a striving for knowledge, for excellence, but unrestricted by the hegemony of the existing ideas which typically emanate from the advanced countries. These ideas must of course be engaged with, but higher education in developing societies cannot remain a mere clone of what exists in the advanced countries. Developing societies must go beyond the mere imitation of research agendas set by the established centres of learning in the advanced countries in order to take account of the people's needs.[45]

In our own ways, sufficiently different, we are both asking for a displacement of the Europe/non-Europe economy of correctness. I call it a "mistake"; he can call it the right way. It may even be the disciplinary difference between the humanities and the social sciences. It may be the secret of an aesthetic education today.

I will move to de Man by way of Derrida's globalizing last move toward "a New Enlightenment," a deconstruction of the first moves (though he never gave up on what I have called the constraints of the Enlightenment, a polytroping Mediterranean Ulysses calling up the siren song of deconstruction without giving fully in) that curb universalization (no "globalization" as academic buzz word in 1968!) by means of the trace. I think there is a difference between Derrida's New Enlightenment and the ab-use I am proposing. Yet I feel that in order for the reader to judge, I must draw her attention to those pages in *Rogues.*[46] Those pages continue the insistence on the Enlightenment throughout Derrida's writings, now, perhaps from a "different" intention contained within the program of deconstruction.

Early in his career, Derrida seemed to have felt that the thinking of the trace would halt the unintended "transcendentalizing" of Kant's transcendental deduction—the structuralist transformation of language into a cause without a cause, displaced from an effect without a cause (which already literalizes the figure of metalepsis)—and thus the securing of the definitive predication of "man." In line with this thinking, I have suggested that an important example of Kant's account of philosophy within the bounds of reason (there may be no other kind) may retain the marks of the operation of the trace, without any necessary psychological figuration.[47]

Kant put a line through fourteen paragraphs in his own copy of the first edition of *The Critique of Pure Reason* (PR, pp. 305–311). In the second edition he added two opening paragraphs, but kept the fourteen deleted paragraphs as they were. In my fancy, they are forever "under erasure," making visible the mechanical (eighteenth-century?) undergirdings of a method to which Kant's language usually gives a more philosophizing (though not psychologizing) cast.[48] And it is here that Kant seems to admit to the idea that his task as a philosopher is to bring under control something as indecisive as a trace:

> Since there is still something that follows, I must necessarily relate it to something else in general that precedes, and on which it follows in accordance with a rule, i.e. necessarily, so that the occurrence, as the conditioned, yields a secure indication of some condition, but it is the latter [the condition] that determines the occurrence. (PR, p. 307)

(We should note that "occurrence" here is *Begebenheit*, with the connotation of a given, rather than *was da geschieht* in the passage quoted in note 48, with the connotation of something taking place, which is also translated "occurrence.")

Kant is talking about the apprehension of sequence as causality. The philosopher must have the apprehension of an objective sequence, because otherwise the subjective apprehension of sequence would be "entirely undermined" (PR, p. 307). And what is the object that will yield objectivity? By the dry logic of these fourteen paragraphs, Kant gives an altogether impersonal answer: "That in the appearance which contains the condition of th[e] necessary rule of apprehension [that distinguishes it from every other apprehension] is the object" (Ibid.). We are looking at the management of the undermining risk of the trace. Later Kant will tell us that the object that will give us real objectivity "cannot be given through any experience" and we must "regard all the concatenation [*Verknüpfung*] of things in the world of sense as if they had their ground in [an entity created by reason functioning rationally]" (PR, p. 611).

If we want to follow this line of thought, this trace, so to speak, we can even suggest that Derrida puts the trace in the place of transcendental deduction. Here is Kant:

> To seek an empirical deduction of [space, time, and the concepts of understanding] would be entirely futile work, for what is distinctive in their nature is precisely that they are related to their objects without having borrowed anything from experience for their thinking [*Vorstellung*]. Thus if a deduction of them is necessary, it must always be transcendental. . . . A tracing [*Nachspüren*] of the first strivings [*Bestrebungen*] of our power of cognition to ascend from individual perceptions to general concepts is without doubt of great utility. . . . Yet a deduction of the pure a priori concepts can never be achieved in this way; it does not lie down this path at all, for in regard to their future use, which should be entirely independent of experience, an entirely different birth certificate than that of an engendering [*Abstammung*] from experiences must be produced. (PR, pp. 220–221)

We cannot not notice that the question of securing a better birth certificate (transcendental deduction) than a mere tracing of experiential birth is all too clear. A fatherly origin, not a motherly engendering.

When in 1968 Derrida wrote "I have attempted to indicate a way out of the closure of this framework via the 'trace,'" he was ostensibly speaking of Saussure's espousing of language as causeless effect. "In and of itself, outside its text [*hors texte*], it is not sufficient to operate the necessary transgression," the paragraph closes.[49] I suggest that "transcendental deduction" can be put in the place of "transgression" and it would make sense. For Kant closes off ("the closure of a framework") the trace by transcendental deduction.

I therefore think that it is the connection of the "as if" with the suppression of the trace-structure in the interest of the more secure birth certificate of the transcendental deduction, establishing the performative conventions of philosophy, as it were, that makes Derrida write, nearly forty years later, in a section subtitled "The Neutralization of the Event," that the idea of a "world," as in "worlding" or "globalization," is itself one of those architectonic, trace-stopping, event-neutralizing "as ifs" in Kant's thought.[50]

I am suggesting, then, that the working of the trace resists figuration. I will also suggest that the impulse of the "human" is to turn the trace into sign—upstream from the debate about the figure and its literalization. Derrida mimes his "human all-too-human"-ness by making the final move toward a New Enlightenment, to expand the scope of reason, to "save the honor of reason," even as, in the posthumously published *The Animal That Therefore I Am*, he frames the human itself in the "animot."[51]

De Man's own reading of Schiller in *Aesthetic Ideology* specifically mentions that Schiller turns the stalling of philosophy at the transcendental deduction into a chiastic reversibility. This is because Schiller takes Kant's catachrestic use of psychology into a reference to psychological development. With these unintended "mistakes" (Schiller thought he was reading Kant right and even making a practical advance upon him), what emerged was a philosophy of balance.

De Man reads Kant as a philosopher for whom philosophizing was recognized as menaced by philosophizing to the last instance. He reads Schiller as domesticating Kant's critical incisiveness in order to re-valorize what he thought of as the "aesthetic." (Kant's own use of "aesthetic" is altogether more complex, as a sort of ambivalent refuge, beautifully captured in the phrase "truth" [a charming name] which he uses to name the island within which this lake is situated to which the philosopher travels altogether like Ulysses among the sirens [PR, p. 354]. We recall Derrida's revision of the Ulysses position. No handy sailors to wax his ears. Ab-use of the Enlightenment.) I will suggest that in the end de Man finds a way to point at persistent domestication as a way to handle the aporetic. I do of course go even so far as to suggest that for Kant philosophizing is precarious precisely because it too may be a species of domestication programmed by the very nature of the rational being.[52] De Man describes this as Kant's system breaking down under its own critical weight (AE, p. 134). Although de Man acknowledges that the *Spieltrieb* or "play drive" complicates the idea of balance in the interest of education, he faults Schiller for always assuming continuity between language and "man," which Kant's entire system, implicitly, could not presuppose. If Kant's system is always about to break down under its own critical weight, Schiller smoothly moves from polarity to polarity. Today's praise of the humanities must not make this niche-marketing mistake. Kant works with laws, Schiller with drives. (Our earlier comment on words like *Grundsatz* or maxim points at Kant's carefully shoring up philosophy—as "intended mistake" by an understanding grabbing at the intent of the law?—against the evidentiary impregnability of transcendentally deduced laws.) Kant's dynamic sublime stages the limits of the imagination. Schiller rewrites the difference between the mathematical and the dynamic sublime as the theoretical and practical sublime and valorizes his rewriting over what he perceives as Kant's difficulties. As usual, where imagination is a name in Kant for a structural moment with programmed functions in an architectonic of faculties, in Schiller it is a phenomenal human capacity. Therefore their expectations from the imagination are different. Schiller misses the hierarchy where, in Kant, the intellect trumps the imagination, and has an altogether un-Kantian conception of freedom. (For Kant the invocation of freedom is imbricated in the programmed machinality of practical reason. De Man sums it up by saying: "Schiller appears as the ideology of Kant's critical philosophy."[53]

In spite of Andrej Warminsky's careful attempt at teasing out de Man's notion of ideology as it was going to be contained in the theoretical conclusion ["Rhetoric/Ideology"] of his projected book *Aesthetics, Rhetoric, Ideology,* I will not here ponder the meaning of this sentence beyond a comment, a question, a displacement, as follows:

The comment: "Ideology" has something to do with idealism here. De Man repeatedly faults Schiller for undoing Kant's critical philosophy by resorting to idealism.

The question: Leaving it to the appropriately delicate and learned critical intelligence to tease out and develop a possible de Manian theory of ideology, can we draw out a rule of thumb here from what already exists—that attention to rhetoric will alert us to the staging of idealism subverting the critical? This attention is ideology critique, and, if we combine this with the post-Althusserian conclusion that ideology allows us to live, it may lead us toward the responsibility of the "intended mistake."[54]

The displacement into such an intended mistake will come at the end of this chapter. We will attempt to shake the Schillerian balance into a double bind, by way of Bateson's treatment of "Play," and we will come to the ab-use of the Enlightenment.)

Here now is the last move of my Introduction. I will move to the contradictory swing of the double bind—and say that this best lesson of European philosophy, not just by chance concurrent with the use of the difference (between needing and making) at the heart of the human by capital, cannot be remembered today: that smart work, saving work, comes, when you know its limits, with an auto-immune knowledge, alas. The Internet remains parasitic upon the human imagination which then sees in it a Faustian promise. It seems wonderful from our left perch when ecologists today can summon the whole world in the interest of biodiversity, fighting monocultures. Capitalism appropriates the organic world, but it's a fair fight, perhaps? When the metaphor of the monocultures of the mind is given its full potential upon the terrain of linguistic diversity, we see the situation break down. There is no adequate analogical fit between the mind and the sense-perceptible world. The natural or sense-perceptible world needs the help of capital-use—its uniformity—to access minds. Minds, in order to become amenable to the appropriately social use of capital, and therefore the ethical use of the earth, need to grow away from the universalization of capital—and court singularity, of texture—so that the structures can keep working efficiently.

Linguistic diversity can only curb the global. *Death of a Discipline* was too hopeful a book.[55] In the ferocious thrust to be "global," the humanities and the qualitative social sciences, "comparative" at their best, are no longer a moving epistemological force. They will increasingly be like the opera, serving a peripheral function in society. As to whether they will draw as much corporate funding as opera—whose glamour the curricular humanities and social sciences cannot hope to match—remains to be seen. Already it is the relatively glamorous think tanks and monolingual "interdisciplinarity" (read shrinking diversity and Americanized monoculture) that are gaining funding. U.S. "core curricula"—minimally "politically correct" by including "multicultural" classics—again in English translation—are traveling internationally. (It is ironic that China—with its bi-millennial tradition of imperial civil service core curricula—is a top candidate on this list.)

In this climate a plea for aesthetic education can hope for no more than a coterie audience—opera goers masquerading as "popular culturalists," hoping for an impossible just world with the desperate outreach through the rhetoric of "to come"—a recognition of the aporetic, of the double bind. Muscular Marxists are giving way to the corporate-funded feudality of the digitally confident alterglobalists. Deep language learning and unconditional ethics are so out of joint with this immensely powerful brave new world-machine that people of our sort make this plea because we cannot do otherwise, because our shared obsession declares that some hope of bringing about the epistemological revolution needed to turn capital around to gendered social justice must still be kept alive against all hope. The essays in this book were mostly written before these latest developments, the contradictory swing of the double bind. Treating this Introduction as a postface as well, then, let me, in conclusion, schematize:

Kant gave us headwork as limit-knowing "intended mistake." Strong enough to undermine the unquestioning and impersonal, seemingly rational confidence of the social productivity of capital but irrelevant to the irreducible personal self-interest that accompanies the rational confidence in productivity. It is therefore not surprising that, as we pointed out above, Kant himself has confidence in commerce as bringing peace—without commenting on the inadequacy of the absence of violence in the interest of commerce as the ethical marker of a just society. Marx's mistake was to think that the workers' self-interest would decline if the secret of social productivity were revealed. Some had thought that the solution lay in ethical instruction. It was Gramsci's genius to understand that the point

was to deconstruct Marx by inserting the lever in Thesis 3 and epistemologizing the project: instrumentalizing the new intellectual to produce
a "revolutionary" subject as proletario-subaltern intellectual, so far invariably lost in the vanguardism of the immediate aftermath of revolutions. A disinterested episteme can allow and withstand the interruption of
the ethical. Study humanism, said Gramsci, in somewhat the same spirit as
some of us say deep language learning and literary textuality train the
ethical reflex.

Meanwhile, back at the ranch, Schiller had neutralized Kant's courage
by changing grounding error to reversibility. All "in-between" solutions
make this move. Paul de Man notices that the *Spieltrieb,* being part of
human programming, is, however remotely, related to Kant's "can't help
philosophizing" scenario. This is where the lever can be inserted to deconstruct Schiller from reversibility into double bind. Indeed, Kant's
philosophizing as "intended mistake," where intention is a drive, can also
be read as the scenario of a double bind—between philosophy as truth
and lie, psychology as figure or letter. ("Nothing but a figure," says de
Man. "Nothing but," legitimation by reversal—a double bind.)

All this adds little to the opening of this Introduction. Let us push the
argument forward by pulling up another item from that opening: that
Schiller's *Spieltrieb* has something in common with Bateson's "play." It
protects the subject from double bind as schizophrenia. The conclusion of
this Introduction has taken us from the upbeat postcolonial task of ab-
using the European Enlightenment to the bleak landscape of the contemporary Euro-U.S. academy, turning out "the scholar," the *Gelehrt,* the felicitous subject of the Enlightenment, as an epistemologically challenged
market analyst. The Enlightenment is sick at home. It is time to recode
and reterritorialize a message from the 1970s, a time when globalization
in its contemporary form was starting to get moving. The Euro-U.S. subject must court schizophrenia as figure.[56] In our dwindling isolation cells,
we must plumb the forgotten and mandatorily ignored bi-polarity of the
social productivity and the social destructiveness of capital and capitalism by affecting the world's subalterns, in places where s/he speaks, unheard, by way of deep language learning, qualitative social sciences, philosophizing into unconditional ethics. Behind every "ethical" use of the
Internet is "good" education—familial, cultural, institutional—in our sense
"aesthetic." Without this pre-set good education—immigrant literatures
and movements as the end, Sino-Arabo-Indic civilizational golden-ageism
as alternative, dreams of digital democracy, the feudality without feudalism of world social fora—are all self-serving dead ends. The fear of this
bi-polarity produces two apparently opposed current tendencies: the praise

of Empire and alter-globalization, sharing some common sympathies.[57] If, instead of each identitarian group remaining in its own enclave, some of us engage in ab-using the enabling violation of our colonial past to converse with each other, we may be able not only to turn globalization around, but also to supplement the necessary uniformization of globalization with linguistic diversity. But such hope is out of joint; better doubt.

With teaching: an aesthetic education; hope against hope, the idiom of the classroom. Scholars such as Lynn Hunt and Martha Nussbaum are certain that the humanities will bring enlightenment. "You could make the argument—well, I could anyway —" Charles Isherwood writes,

> that some of the havoc caused by the subprime mortgage crisis [of 2008] can be traced to a collective amnesia on the part of the powers that be about the essence of human nature. At one point Alan Greenspan argued that it was not the lack of regulation that caused the firestorm; it was an excess of greed on Wall Street. He didn't see that coming? This apparent ignorance of our baser nature among top-tier economists should be quickly cured, lest more problems be caused. I hereby recommend for them a crash course in what men and women are, and what they will do to survive and prosper when the restraints of civilization fall away. I prescribe an evening in the hair-raising company of "Blasted."[58]

You have to be taught to (want to/how to) read "Blasted" so that you feel what Charles Isherwood, or Martha Nussbaum, or yet Lynn Hunt feels. Or else you may simply want to invest in the piece: a variety of greed. Schiller was indeed wrong in his understanding of Kant. But who is exactly right? Schiller's problem was not that he was wrong, but that he did not run with his version of his wrong, as did Kant, as did Nietzsche, as did Derrida, in different ways. All communicated action, including self-communicated action, is destined for errancy. This is so commonsensical a point that it is almost not worth making. Yet it is so hard to make this enter into theory. In order to conserve felicitous cases, we seem to be obliged to ignore destinerrancy.

I would rather suggest that we must know what mistake to make with a specific text and must also know how to defend our mistake as the one that will allow us to live. I assume that the passing of a text into my grasp is a mis-take, of course. As we move toward the subaltern, we can only learn through mistakes, if that remote contingency arrives.

Let us now turn to Gramsci's "techno-scientific" knowledge, "superior to mathematical abstraction." That knowledge and that abstraction may be read as the secret of Marx's message to the worker, required lesson for every leader involved with factory organization, as was Gramsci, and often missed by readers of Marx involved with party organization alone, or with academic textual debates. It is the "jumping-off point" *(Sprengpunkt)* for the understanding of political economy, the homeopathy or medicine/poison character *(pharmakon)* of labor quantification ("abstract average" in Marx).[59] The point is simple. If the surplus generated by the definitive human difference, between making capacity and need, is used by the workers willing to quantify their work for use in social welfare, we will have scientific socialism. The model of the will and consent is simple here, sharing a simplicity with the agential concept of the vote. "How many votes for the unconscious," asks Derrida, thus revising both Reich and Nancy into a double bind.[60] The point is that Marx did not situate this agent into a developed theory of the subject. The French Freudo-Marxists of the 1970s told us that Freud was like Marx, and complicated Marx in the process.[61] Perry Anderson complained that because Marx did not theorize the revolutionary subject, post-structuralism could arise.[62] On the other side, the entire alienation-reification camp implicitly supposed that Marx did in fact theorize at least the possibility of a free subject and launched their critique of capitalism as a critique of quantification (abstract average) roughly as dead labor over living.[63] In fact, what Marx did not theorize was the (post/para)revolutionary subject. Why should the agent of the "social" as quantification used for agential freedom of intention from capitalism devote their freed intention to the building of a welfare society, where the "social" is understood, by Marx and Marxists, in a general humanistic sense? (The "socius" of Deleuze and Guattari has psychiatry as its allegory of reading, and sees itself as a different sort of corrective, which, although important, is not relevant here.)[64] Here the play of the word "social"—on the one hand the ferociously original adjectives *gesellschaftlich* or *vergesellschaftet* in the sense of an association based on labor quantified as *pharmakon* and on the other hand the fuzzy noun, at best theorized through a deep background in theories of anthropologists such as Lewis Morgan.[65] The proletarian needs to be taught only the lesson of the first. This is where Gramsci steps in. He realizes that just the abstract mathematical techno-scientific lesson is not enough. The new instrumentalized intellectual must do more. Through his intelligence, experience, and enforced leisure, he comes to realize that Marx was able to think the social as *pharmakon* because he himself understood the social as consensual welfare of the class-diversified collective through his own humanistic education. Hence Gramsci's insistence that the proletarian (plus the subaltern) needs to be the subject of a humanist education.[66] It is in the interest of this that all implicit support of the "progressive bourgeoisie" (Lenin's celebrated phrase for the historical ally of the revolutionary vanguard)—in short the Venn diagrams of hege-mony and the state—must be understood as *pharmaka*.[67]

In "Supplementing Marxism" (Chapter 8 in this book), the under-standing of the problem of the paleonymy of the social leads to a pre-scription for the ethical. This related to my confidence in the accessible originality of the aboriginal that I have mentioned in passing. The expan-sion of my work to a subaltern group of modern India—rather than a feudally "preserved" aboriginal community—has made me realize that my idea that the ethical could be called up simply because it was thought of as "cultural conformism ready for modernization" depended on the fact that my first batch of schools was in a district that is even more "backward," and the subalterns there had been kept in a cruel "cultural isolation" as if in a museum by the benevolent landlord, who only under-stood duty toward the subaltern as fighting the party and the feudalist culturalist writer whose work I have translated. In other words, the seem-ingly untarnished presence of a salvageable ethical sediment was the re-sult of systematic subordination under benevolent despotism which I had not understood until those particular schools were closed because some boys were beginning to question authority in however unsystematic a way even as the girls were robotized. Gramsci was right in thinking the project epistemological. One must attend upon the interruption of the ethical. It cannot be part of a plan directly.

I said above that on the register of the Baubo, perhaps the literary can still do something. Or perhaps not. Let me end with gender, then, since reproductive heteronormativity is the world thing with which we secure the space between making and need, long before the emergence of capital from that fault. It is a space of neither reason nor unreason, altogether irreducible. Recall Oedipus's lament: "O marriages, marriages, you put us in nature, and putting us back again, reversed the seed, and indexed fathers, brothers, children, kin-blood mingled, brides, women, mothers, a shameful thing to know among the works of man."[68] If only we had been animals, without the abstraction of kinship inscription as a secondary revision, there would have been no sin.

Gender is our first instrument of abstraction.

If I give you a tiny working definition of culture—which "Culture: Situating Feminism" (Chapter 5 in this book) spells out—you will get a sense of this. Let us think culture as a package of largely unacknowl-edged assumptions, loosely held by a loosely outlined group of people, mapping negotiations between the sacred and the profane, and the rela-tionship between the sexes. To theorize in the abstract, we need a differ-ence. However we philosophize sensible and intelligible, abstract and concrete, etc., the first difference we perceive materially is sexual difference. It becomes our tool for abstraction, in many forms and shapes. On the level of the loosely held assumptions and presuppositions that English-speaking peoples have been calling "culture" for two hundred years, change is incessant. But, as they change, these unwitting *pre*-suppositions become belief systems, organized suppositions. Rituals coalesce to match, support, and advance beliefs and suppositions. But these presuppositions also give us the wherewithal to change our world, to innovate and create. Most people believe, even (or perhaps particularly) when they are being cultural relativists, that creation and innovation are their own cultural secret, whereas "others" are only determined by their cultures. This habit is unavoidable and computed with the help of sexual difference sustained into something feminists who are speakers of English started calling "gender" in the last forty years. But if we aspire to be citizens of the world, we must not only fight the habit of thinking creation and innovation are our own cultural secret, we must also shake the habit of thinking that our version of computing gender is the world's and simply ignore it unless we are specifically speaking of women and queers.

Thought of as an instrument of abstraction, gender is in fact a position without identity (an insight coming to us via Queer Studies from David Halperin), sexualized in cultural practice.[69] We can therefore never think the abstracting instrumentality of gender fully. With this brief introduction I will go to the conclusion of de Man's "Kant and Schiller" and myself conclude this Introduction.

This is the displacement announced on page 25.

De Man did not meddle with gender. Yet he singles out a passage in Schiller that en-genders the aesthetic and leaves it deadpan. Allow me a longish quotation:

> Hypotyposis for Kant is . . . a very difficult problem that again threatens philosophical discourse; whereas here [in "On the Necessary Borderlines in the Use of Beautiful Forms"] it is offered by Schiller as a solution. . . . The sensory . . . becomes a metaphor for reason. This extends to humanity, which, it turns out, is not entirely a principle of closure, because humanity is not single—but it has a polarity, it has the polarity of male and female that inhabits it, and this is how Schiller copes with that problem. "The other sex," he says, the female sex, "can and should not share scientific knowledge with man, but by ways of its figural representation, it can share the truth with him. Men tend to sacrifice form to content. But woman cannot tolerate a neglected form, not even in the presence of the richest content. And the entire internal configuration of her being entitles her to make this stern demand. It is true, however, that in this function, she can only acquire the material of truth, and not truth itself. Therefore, the task which Nature

disallows women, the other sex, this task must be doubly undertaken by
man if he wishes to be the equal of woman in this important aspect, in this
important aspect of his existence. He will therefore transpose as much as
possible out of the realm of the abstract, in which he governs and is master,
into the realm of the imagination and of sensibility. Taste includes or hides
the natural intellectual difference between the two sexes. It nourishes and
embellishes the feminine mind with the products of the masculine mind, and
allows the beautiful sex to feel what it has not thought, and to enjoy what it
has not produced by its labor" (*Werke,* 21: 16–17). That much for women.
Schiller's humanism is showing some of its limits here. At any rate, the theoretical conclusion of this passage would be that just as the sensory becomes
without tension a metaphor for reason, in Schiller, women become without
oppression a metaphor for man. Because the relation of woman to man is
that of the metaphor to what it indicates, or that of the sensory representation to reason.

In the same way, Schiller's considerations on education lead to a concept
of art as the metaphor, as the popularization of philosophy. Philosophy, as
you saw, is the domain of men; art is—basically, the beautiful is—the domain of women. The relationship is that of metaphor.[70]

I have no interest in rescuing either Schiller or de Man into good gender politics, whatever that might be. It is not a secret that "feminization"
is a putdown. Yet, by itself "feminization" cannot necessarily be a putdown.
And the aesthetic, for Schiller, is a powerful thing, fit for princes, which
can save the world from itself. It cannot be denied that these peculiar
deployments of woman are the moment of transgression which calls for
displacement, and my task is to undertake such a displacement.

Suppose we attempt to reverse and displace the ancient binary until
"woman" is a position without identity. I say "attempt" because the force
of the effort is the force of reading and thinking, since interest determined
by sexual difference cannot disappear. Keeping this in mind, I recall our
efforts in the early days of academic feminism: to distinguish between
male tasks and domestic (female and servant) tasks, as one-time only and
repeated because forever necessary, respectively. Something you can footnote as opposed to cooking and cleaning, let us say. Schiller's woman is
upper class at first glance. If, however, you look closely at the passage de
Man quotes, you will see that the distinction between access to truth and
access to figuration is a displacement of the distinction between one-time
and repetition that we discussed as historically assigned to male and classed
male/female. It is in this sense that one can add the concept-metaphor of
female to Baubo to think the place of the aesthetic as useful to shore up a
world gone awry by rational choice and the extreme abstract rationality
of the electronic, where imagination itself is empiricized into reasonable

programming, even as the imagination as event inevitably escapes. This is how Gramsci's shorthand phrase "humanist history" can be expanded in today's context, and this is how we must instrumentalize ourselves as new intellectuals in the hope of a good world in the aporetic mode of "to come." In a previous book I announced a death, and here I announce a hopelessness, because life and hope are too easily claimed by the camp of mere reason. Perhaps it would be more appropriate to end this Introduction with an impossible "female" task—in Schiller's sense and mine.

Let me end with the invocation of such a task in the conclusion of Jacques Derrida's *Rogues*. It is not a thankless task, but a gendered task, a necessary repetition of difference rather than the one-time-only securing of good theory, where gender is a position without identity, Schiller's injunction to feminize the aesthetic, the last best gift to me, a woman, his first Ph.D., bequeathed against the grain by my disgraced teacher, Paul de Man.

Here is the double bind. "To be responsible . . . would be to invent maxims of transaction for deciding between two just as rational and universal but contradictory exigencies of reason as well as enlightenment." Note the word "maxims."

And here is the task: "It remains to be known, so as to save the honor of reason, how to translate. For example, the word reasonable. And how to pay one's respects to, how to . . . greet . . . beyond its latinity, and in more than one language, the fragile difference between the rational and the reasonable."[71]

In the preface to *Allegories of Reading,* de Man describes a "shift," not an "end"—"a shift from historical definition to the problematics of reading . . . typical of my generation, . . . of more interest in its results than in its causes"—careful words, camouflaging the "causes" as "uninteresting."[72] Yet, the "pugnacious literalism" that this teacher taught makes this student sniff at those very causes: shifting a generation born in Europe in the 1920s away from historical definition to a problematics of reading which, for them, remained contained within the canonical principles of literary history.

Critics have noted these words, of course, and fitted them in with other instances of contrast between history and language. No one, however, seems to have noticed that de Man is speaking not just of himself but of his generation. My generation was born when de Man's generation was flirting with fascism, the uninteresting cause of a subsequent shift from history to reading. We came of age outside of Europe, when their war, where we fought for our masters, inaugurated the end of territorial imperialism. I am now a good bit older than de Man was when he died. "Typical

of my generation" is this concern for preserving the dreams of postcoloniality in the face of globalization. It is the story of that parabasis that
was for me the most sustained lesson of Paul de Man: displacing the lesson of Paul de Man to another theater.

De Man goes on to say that the shift from history to reading typical of
his generation "could, in principle, lead to a rhetoric of reading reaching
beyond the canonical principles of literary history which still serve, in
this book, as the starting point of their own displacement."[73] "Reaching
beyond." Displaced to another place. How far beyond? As far as I pull,
in these times? Altogether elsewhere? At least into an understanding, as
the best universities counsel students to cut their dissertations to market
demands, that an aesthetic education inevitably has a meta-vocational
function?

Instrumentalize the essays that follow, then. Comfortably condemned
as they are to use material from and in the dominant, they must be undone on the way to subalternity, remembering that in subalternity also
reasonable and rational hang out as a difference. That any reader will waste
the time to learn to parse the desires (not the needs) of collective examples
of subalternity is my false hope.

CHAPTER ONE

The Burden of English

For Maitreyi Chandra

SPOKE for the first time professionally in India at Miranda House, an elite women's college in Delhi. Its then principal, Dr. Lola Chatterjee, had transformed it into an institution also of radical learning. I was indeed honored that my colleagues at Miranda House had invited me to deliver the first V. S. Krishna Memorial Lecture. By all accounts, Professor Krishna had been an exemplary teacher and scholar. I did not know her. I did, however, feel enough of her presence from conversation with her friends to have a sense of her and to want to greet her prematurely absent shadow. This was my greeting, on a theme that bound our lives together: the burden of English studies in the colonies. She and I were both students of English literature in a colonial and postcolonial situation. She had the added experience of teaching in that context, an experience I never really acquired. At that time, just beginning to inaugurate the cultural double bind for myself, I felt that her past and my future held something in common—a burden. I used the word "burden" in at least its two chief senses. First, the content of a song or account. In this case, expanding the metaphor, the import of the task of teaching and studying English in the colonies. And, second, a singular load to carry, in a special way.

I am not speaking of English language policy but of the teaching, specifically, of English literature. Let me start with a passage from Ngũgĩ wa Thiong'o's *Decolonising the Mind* to show how much, in spite of obvious differences, the predicament of the teaching of English literature in postcolonial India has in common with the situation, say, in postcolonial Kenya:

A lot of good work on Kenyan and African languages has been done at the Department of Linguistics and African languages at the University of Nairobi. . . . They . . . acknowledge the reality of there being three languages for each child in Kenya, a reality which many patriotic and democratic Kenyans would now argue should be translated into social and official policy. Kiswahili would be the all-Kenya national and official language; the other nationality languages would have their rightful places in the schools and English would remain Kenya people's language of international communication. But I am not dealing so much with the language policies as with the language practice of African writers.[1]

I, too, am dealing with practice, not policies, but not the language practice of Indian writers. I am dealing, rather, with the language practice of teachers: the situation of the Indian teachers of English.

What is the basic difference between teaching a second language as an instrument of communication and teaching the same language so that the student can appreciate literature? It is certainly possible to argue that in the most successful cases the difference is not easy to discern. But there is a certain difference in orientation between the language classroom and the literature classroom. In the former, the goal is an active and reflexive use of the mechanics of the language. In the latter, the goal is at least to shape the mind of the student so that it can resemble the mind of the so-called implied reader of the literary text, even when that is a historically distanced cultural fiction. The figure of an implied reader is constructed within a consolidated system of cultural representation. The appropriate culture in this context is the one supposedly indigenous to the literature under consideration. In our case, the culture of a vague space called Britain, even England, in its transaction with Europeanness (meaning, of course, Western Europe), Hellenism and Hebraism, the advent of Euramericanism, the trendiness of Commonwealth literature, and the like.

"Global English" was not yet a player. Our ideal student of British literature was expected so to internalize this play of cultural self-representation that she would be able to, to use the terms of the most naive kind of literary pedagogy, "relate to the text," "identify" with it. However naive these terms, they describe the subtlest kind of cultural and epistemic transformation, a kind of upward race-mobility, an entry, however remote, into a geo-political rather than merely national "Indian"-ness. It is from this base that R. K. Narayan can speak of "English in India" as if it were a jolly safari arranged by some better-bred version of the India Tourist Board and, conversely, it is also upon this base that a critical study of colonial discourse can be built.[2]

It is with this in mind that many decolonized intellectuals feel that the straightforward ideal of teaching English literature in the theater of decolonization continues the process of producing an out-of-date, British Council–style colonial bourgeoisie in a changed global context.

I am not suggesting for a moment that, given the type of student who chooses English as a field of study in the general Indian context of social opportunity (whatever that might be), this kind of ideological production is successfully achieved. The demand for a "general cultural participant" in the colonies has at any rate changed with the dismantling of actual territorial imperialism. Today, the student of English literature who is there because no other more potentially lucrative course of study is open to him is alienated from his work in a particular way. To make him/her the subject of an "aesthetic education" is a peculiar problem.

It cannot be ignored that there is a class-argument lurking here, although it is considerably changed from my student days in the mid- to late 1950s. The reasons why a person who obviously takes no pleasure in English texts chooses English honors are too complex to explore here. At any rate, the class-value of the choice of English honors is gendered, and is different according to the hierarchy of institutions—in the metropolitan, urban, suburban, and rural centers. The same taxonomy as it operates among students of English literature as a Pass (general subject rounding out the study of the Honors subject, or part of a non-honors general bachelor's degree) and the teacher's accommodation within it as Brit Lit become less and less normative, are much more demographically and politically interesting. I have not the skills to study it, and so will turn to a more literary-critical topic and return to the "implied reader." As the years have passed, it is on the subaltern elementary level that I have confronted the immense problem of the preparation for an aesthetic education. But I was not to know it then.

The implied reader is imagined, even in the most simple reading, according to rudimentary or sophisticated hypotheses about persons, places, and times. You cannot make sense of anything written or spoken without at least implicitly assuming that it was destined for you, that you are its implied reader. When this sense of the latent destiny of the texts of a literary tradition is developed along disciplinary lines, even the students (mostly women) who come to English studies in a self-consciously purposive way—all students at Miranda House would have to be included here—might still be open, under the best circumstances, to an alienating cultural indoctrination that is out of step with the historical moment. This becomes all the more dubious when the best of them become purveyors of native culture abroad.

I should like to look first at a few literary figurations of this alienation. I want next to plot some ways of negotiating with this phenomenon. As I have already suggested, this alienation is a poison and a medicine, a base upon which both elitism and critique can be built. The institutional curriculum can attempt to regulate its use and abuse.

I will discuss a few literary figurations of the gradual cultural alienation that might become a persistent accompaniment to the successful teaching of English literature in India. I employ the word "figure" here from the word "figurative" as opposed to "literal." When a piece of prose reasonably argues a point, we understand this as its literal message. When it advances this point through its form, through images, metaphors, and indeed its general rhetoricity we call it figuration or figuring-forth. Rhetoric in this view is not mere *alaṃkāra* (ornamentation). The literal and the figurative depend upon each other even as they interrupt each other. They can be defined apart but they make each other operate.

Indeed, literature might be the best complement to ideological transformation. (Today the force of the "might" wavers.) The successful reader learns to identify implicitly with the value system figured forth by literature through learning to manipulate the figures, rather than through (or in addition to) working out the argument explicitly and literally, with a view to reasonable consent. Literature buys your assent in an almost clandestine way and therefore it is an excellent instrument for a slow transformation of the mind. For good or for ill. As medicine or as poison, perhaps always a bit of both. The teacher must negotiate and make visible what is merely clandestine.

To emphasize my point that the assent the implied reader gives to literature is more than merely reasonable, indeed perhaps clandestine, my first example is a text where I am perhaps myself the type-case. To make of "myself," written into a cultural text, the example of alienating assent, is a direct challenge to the hegemonic notion of the "willing suspension of disbelief," still an active orthodoxy coming via such influential figures as the Anglo-American T. S. Eliot, the English I. A. Richards, and the Euramerican Herbert Marcuse.

It is not a text written in English, although some of you may have read it in indifferent English translation. It is the short story "Didi" (1895) or "The Elder Sister" by Rabindranath Tagore.[3] My point here is to illustrate how the implied reader is drawn into patterns of cultural value as she assents to a text, says "yes" to its judgments, in other words, reads it with pleasure. When we teach our students to read with pleasure texts where the implied reader is culturally alien and hegemonic, the assent might bring a degree of alienation.[4]

It is a simple story. Shoshi was the only daughter of an elderly couple. Her husband Joygopal was hoping to inherit their property. Her parents had a son in late middle age. After their death, Shoshi takes her orphaned infant brother to her bosom almost in preference to her own sons. Joygopal, enraged by the loss of his inheritance, does everything to take it away from the orphan boy, and indeed tries to precipitate his death by neglecting a serious illness. At this point, the English magistrate for the area comes on tour. Shoshi delivers her brother over to the magistrate. She soon dies mysteriously and is cremated overnight.

I have read this story many times. I am not only its implied reader, but its successful implied reader. Even after all these readings, my throat catches at the superb sentimental ending: "Shoshi had given her word to her brother at parting, we will meet again. I don't know where that word was kept" (p. 290). This assent is so strong, in other words, that the analysis of it that I will now begin and that I have performed before cannot seriously interfere with it. This is why literature is such an excellent vehicle of ideological transformation. For good or for ill. As medicine or as poison.

It is, for women of my class and inclination *(pravritti),* a major ingredient in the centering of the subject that says "yes," first to reading, and then to reading something, so that more of that subject can be consolidated and sedimented; so that it can go on saying "yes," indefinitely. (There are different systems of representation that operate centering for different classes or *varna*s, different inclinations. And the weave is interrupted with the patchwork of intervention and contingency. To give an example of a different class, a different history, a different set of inclinations: it is "religion" thrown into the potential sign-system of "citizenship" as concept and metaphor that wins the assent of the young woman whose class-family-*pravritti* insert her into the Rashtriya Sevika Samiti.)[5]

How then is my assent given to this story? To what do I assent? How am I, or indeed how was I, historically constructed as its implied reader so that I was able to read it with pleasure within my cultural self-representation?

Many of Tagore's short stories are about emancipated women. This story is about a village woman whom love for her brother emancipates to the extent that she can see that the impartial white colonial administrator will be a better *ma-baap* (parent) than her self-interested Indian kin. Yet, as a woman, she cannot choose to give herself over to him. Does she choose to remain behind? Or is she, for herself, a prisoner of the patriarchal system from which she delivers her brother by assigning the

Englishman as her father? (This is, of course, a central patriarchal theme, this giving of the name of the father to the Englishman, for the issue is inheritance and the passage of property.) At any rate, the implied reader, whose position I occupy for the moment as the daughter of upper-middle-class female emancipation in urban Bengal, cannot be sure if Shoshi chooses to remain with or is a prisoner of patriarchy, and, indeed, still cannot be sure where she stands within this situation. This must remain what Meenakshi Mukherjee has called an "interesting but elusive and unverifiable statement" for the moment. I will speak of the thrill of ambivalence later. Here all I need to say is that, in order to assent to the story, to derive pleasure from a proper reading, one must somehow see the entire colonial system as a way out of indigenous patriarchy.[6] In "Can the Subaltern Speak?" I have written about the cultural politics of this conviction in the matter of the abolition of the self-immolation of widows in 1829. In most of his prose writings Rabindranath was also not simply telling a story or making a point but also fashioning a new Bengali prose.[7] You will therefore accept the suggestion that the texture of the levels of prose plays a strong part in the fabrication of the implied reader's assent.

Tagore endows only Shoshi with full-fledged subjectivity. It is in the service of building that subject that Tagore deploys that stunning mixture of Sanskritized and colloquial Bengali that marks his writing of this period. There is some cultural discrepancy in creating Shoshi as the subject-agent of a romantic love or *prem* that is still not the legitimate model of the cementing emotion of the institution of the Indian marriage. Rabindranath brings this about through an expert manipulation of the model of *biraho* or love-in-absence abundantly available in classical Sanskrit. Any careful reader will see the marks of this in the construction of Shoshi's subjectivity.

The discrepancy involved in the Sanskritization of Shoshi's subjectivity as the agent of *prem* is never treated ironically by Tagore. It is in the interest of constructing her as the subject or agent of *sneho* or affection that a benevolent irony makes its appearance, but always only at the expense of her brother Nilmoni. There are many instances of this. I will quote a tiny fragment simply to remind myself of the pleasure of the text: "*krishokaay brihatmastak gombheermukh shyambarno chheleti.*"

This fantastic collection of epithets, reading which it is almost impossible to depart from pure Sanskrit phonetics, is a measure of the registers of irony and seriousness with which Tagore can play the instrument of his prose. The available English translation, "the heavy-pated, grave-faced, dusky child," is, of course, hopeless at catching these mechanics.

Why read a high-culture vernacular text as we think of the burden of teaching English? Let us backtrack. The goal of teaching such a thing as literature is epistemological but also epistemic: transforming the way in which objects of knowledge are constructed; perhaps also shifting desires in the subject. One object of knowledge, perhaps the chief object, is the human being, inevitably gendered. It is always through such epistemico-epistemological transformations that we begin to approximate the implied reader. In our case, the approximation is mediated by the new vernacular literatures secreted by the encounter described, for this writer with a profound imperialist irony, as "the Bengal Renaissance." That particular mediation has been commented on ad nauseam and is indeed a cliché of Indian cultural history. Like most clichés, this one has become part of the "truth," of Indian cultural self-representation. And in the fabrication of this truth, Tagore's role is crucial.

Some of Tagore's most significant epistemic meddling is with women. Women constituted by, and constituting such "minds" become the culturally representative "implied reader." Therefore the problem of the teaching of English literature is not separated from the development of the colonial subject. And women being notoriously the unfixed part of cultural subjectivity as it is represented by men, the construction of the feminine subject in colonial vernacular literature can give us a sense of the classroom molding of minds preserved in literary form. To read vernacular colonial literature in this way, as preparing the ground for, as it is prepared by, British literature in the colonies, is to challenge the contrast often made, in "Western" colonial discourse studies, between "Western" literature as "central," and third world literature—in this case "Indian" (!)—as "marginal" or "emergent." Expanding Ashis Nandy's idea of the "intimate enemy," or my own notion of "violating enablement," it seems more productive to consider the heterogeneity on both sides. In order to make systemic changes, we need systemic taxonomies. In that conviction, we must repeat that two discontinuous ways in which the opposition center/ margin or dominant/emergent is undone are gender and class. Thus it seems important to look at Tagore's participation in the project of epistemic transformation by way of a rural woman. This is more interesting in the business of the construction of the implied reader precisely because Shoshi, the central character, does not belong to the class of women who will read the story felicitously, "in its own time." This class-separation allows for a feeling of identity-in-difference which seems a much more flexible instrument of epistemic transformation as a site of negotiations. What happens when an exceptional underclass woman is herself a creative reader of British literature will be considered in the next section.

Shoshi is developed as an agent of romantic love in elegant Sanskritic prose in descriptive third person with no hint of indirect free style.[8] In other words, rhetorically in the text, she is given no access to a Sanskritized subjectivity. In her case, what will be shown is the subordination of love or *prem* for her husband to affection or *sneho* for her orphan brother. The entire network of Indian patriarchy, including colonial functionaries as well as Shoshi's own untransformed conjugal epistemology, would like to keep Shoshi in the gendered private sphere, as her husband's adjunct. Shoshi enters the public sphere by establishing direct contact with the British colonial authority and chooses to re-enter the patriarchal enclosure. She is destroyed by this choice.

Keeping within the allegory of the production of the colonial subject, with something like a relationship with the implied reader of British literature, we see the orphaned brother as the full-fledged future colonial subject, mourning his sister—his personal past—but encircled by the sahib's left arm, the right implicitly pointing to a historical future. It is Shoshi, however, who supplements the picture, choosing to remain in the static culture, while sending the young unformed male into the dynamic colonial future. A gendered model, this, of the colonial reader, not quite identical with the "real" reader and therefore, in a patriarchal system of reckoning, more like a "woman."

How, then, can we construct a model of the woman or man of the urban middle class, themselves woven and patched as well by the same strands, of the same stuff, reading in the exciting identity-in-difference frame of mind, the subject laid out in the pages of the story? A richly constructed, richly praised female subject who chooses to remain within the indigenous patriarchal structure; with confidence in the Magistrate as foster-father, another mark of her heroism. This is the complex of attitudes that is the condition and effect of any appropriate reading of the story. The structure survives; Madhu Kishwar will not call herself a "feminist" because the word is too much marked by the West, but will work for (other) women's rights.[9]

The Magistrate is constructed as a subject who might be privy to the thrill of this ambivalence. The possibility is lodged in this exchange: "The saheb asked, 'Where will you go.' Shoshi said, 'I will return to my husband's house, I have nothing to worry about.' The saheb smiled a little and, seeing no way out . . ."

By contrast, the neighbor Tara, who opposes husbands if they are scoundrels at the beginning of the story, and roars out her rage at the end, is displeased when Shoshi leaves her husband's house to look after her sick brother: "If you have to fight your husband why not sit at home

and do it; what's the point in leaving home? A husband, after all"
(p. 288).

The Magistrate (Brit Lit) (perhaps) understands best of all that Shoshi
must sacrifice herself to her own culture, but takes charge of Nilmoni (the
indefinite future). A crude but recognizable model of what the "best"
students manage—saying "yes" and "no" to the Shoshi-function, as it
were—in our Brit Lit classes.

I want now to show how this necessarily limited and divided assent to
implied readership is parodied in Kipling's *Kim,* within five years of the
publication of "Didi." It is for reasons such as this that it is particularly
necessary not to differentiate British and Indian literatures as "central"
and "marginal," in a benevolent spirit; a legitimation by reversal of the
colonial cliché whose real displacement is seen in the turbulent mockery
of migrant literature—Desani or Rushdie. Here is Kipling's:

> Hurree Chunder Mookerjee, . . . an M.A. of Calcutta University, [who]
> would explain the advantages of education. There were marks to be gained
> by due attention to Latin and Wordsworth's Excursion . . . also a man might
> go far, as he himself had done, by strict attention to plays called Lear and
> Julius Caesar; the book cost four annas, but could be bought second-hand
> in Bow Bazar for two. Still more important than Wordsworth, or the emi-
> nent authors Burke and Hare, was the art and science of mensuration. . . .
> "How am I to fear the absolutely non-existent?" said Hurree Babu, talking
> English to reassure himself. It is an awful thing still to dread the magic that
> you contemptuously investigate—to collect folklore for the Royal Society
> with a lively belief in all the Powers of Darkness.[10]

By contrast, Tagore is performing in the narrative, through the representation of an apparent epistemic transformation of the central female
character, as a productive and chosen contradiction: self-sacrifice to culture while bequeathing the future to the colonist in loco parentis; Kipling
describes in this minor male character as an unproductive contradiction:
bondage to a superstitious and mercenary indigenous culture while mouth-
ing sublime doctrine, the distinctive failure of the colonial subject. (We
know that Kipling understood the good Indian in an earlier, feudal, semiotic; and was incapable of bringing to life an Indian woman as subject or
agent of profound inner change.)

At least two kinds of point can be made here. By contrast to Kipling—of
course Kipling is an interested choice on my part—Tagore's complicated
and complicit structure remains preferable as a mode of assent in the
colonies. In the frame of indigenous class-alliances and gendering it becomes dubious. The activist teacher of English can negotiate this only if
she works to undo the divide between English and vernacular literatures

laid down in our institutions. (Here in the earlier dispensation I am recommending playing the double bind through the teaching of literature—mirabile dictu!) The teacher can use her own native language skills and draw on the multilingual skills of the students in class. More important, Departments of Modern Indian Literatures, the Departments of Literature in the State Vernacular, and Departments of Comparative Literature must work together so that the artificial divide between British and Native is undone.

I should like to make clear that I am not conflating British and colonial/Commonwealth literatures. Nor am I suggesting a collapsing of boundaries. I am proposing that the complexity of their relationship, collaborative/parasitical/contrary/resistant, be allowed to surface in literary pedagogy. They are different but complicit. I will recite this refrain again, for it is a common misunderstanding.[11]

As contrast to Tagore's class-divisive gendering I will draw on Binodini Dasi's *My Story*.[12] To contrast Kipling's dismissal of the agency of a productive contradiction to the colonial subject, I will point at Tagore's *Gora* as a counter-*Kim*.[13] (*Gora* will be discussed further in Chapter 14.)

Gora ("Whitey"—the word applied to the British tommy is here a perfectly acceptable diminutive from Gaurmohan) appeared five years after the publication of *Kim*. The heroes of both novels are Irish orphans of the Indian Mutiny, turned Indian. But there the resemblance ends. Gora becomes both a nationalist Indian and a tremendously orthodox Brahman. At the end of the novel he finds out that he is not only not a Brahman, but not even a Hindu or an Indian by birth. It is then that he realizes that he is most truly Indian, because he chooses to be so. His realization is embedded in a discourse of woman. First his identification of India with his (foster) mother who, unlike his (foster) father, did not observe caste difference: "Ma, you have no caste rules, no loathing, no contempt. You are my India." Then the summons to the hitherto spurned untouchable servant: "Now call your Lachchmia. Ask her to bring me a glass of water." And finally the mother's request to him to acknowledge the love of the emancipated Brahmo heroine, expressed obliquely as a request to summon a male friend: "Gora, now send for Benoy" (p. 572).[14] Rather different in historical "feel" from Kim O'Hara with the Lama on a hilltop, the end of *Kim*.

If I were commenting on the thematics of the half-caste as "true" Indian, I should contrast this figure with Mahasweta Devi's Mary Oraon, and again the registers of class and gender (and of course coloniality and postcoloniality) would come into play.[15] But contrasting half-caste Mary to Kipling's Irish-as-Indian hero, one would have to notice there the feudal, and here the nationalist axiomatic; the codified past as opposed to a possible dynamic future. Kim's return is acted out again by E. M. Forster's Fielding; their futures are not seriously marked by the colonies. For Gora agency is bestowed by the colony as nation. The theme of choice is important here as well.

But Gora is not a divided subject in the same way as Shoshi. If he chooses a return to culture, he is also the inheritor of the future. The theme of sacrifice is less ambivalent and therefore less interesting in Gora. The colonial reader is as race- and gender-divided from Gora as she would be class-divided from Shoshi. And from that race- and gender-distanced position, the system of representations she assents to is again not quite accessible to the staging of her own identity, but this time "from below," not, as in the case of the indigenous woman, "from above."[16] The cultural choice and bequest of the future can inhere in the same fantasmatic character: the white man turned Indian by choice.[17] The development of readership thrives in the difference and deferment staged between hero and reader, whether from above or below. In a former colony, the institutional teacher of imperialist and colonial literature can open this space of difference (never an identity) only by way of persistently undoing the institutional difference between that literature and the literature(s) in the mother tongue(s). It is then that the active vectors of these differences, negotiating gender, class, and race, would begin to appear.[18]

Let us now consider a performance of this undoing, in the very house of performance, during the colonial era. I am referring to the Calcutta professional theater at the end of the nineteenth century. To give an example of the undoing of institutional difference I will quote from Binodini's *My Life* at length:

Girish-babu [the eminent actor Girishchandra Ghosh (1844–1912)] taught me with great care the performance of parts. His teaching method was wonderful. First he explained the essence [bhab—bhava] of the part. Then he would ask us to memorize it. Then when he had time he would sit in our house, with Amrit Mitra, Amrit-babu (Bhuni-babu) and others, and tell us the writings of many different British actresses, of eminent British poets such as Shakespeare, Milton, Byron, Pope, as if they were stories. Sometimes he would read the books aloud and explain. He taught various moves and gestures [hab-bhab] one by one. Because of this care I started learning acting-work with knowledge and intelligence. What I had learnt before was like the cleverness of parrots, I had experienced little. I had not been able to say or understand anything with argument or reasoning. From now on I could understand my own performance-selected part. When big British actors or actresses came I would be eager to see their acting. And the directors of the theatre would take pains to accompany me to see English theatre. When we returned home Girishbabu would ask, "Well now, let's hear something about what you've seen." (pp. 78–79; translation modified)

Here indeed is teaching to perform. Men teaching women the trick of the "inside" of their captors, as the captors themselves code that "inside," with instruments supposedly generated in a deeper "inside," for general decipherment in an "outside," the British audience, who supposedly possess "insides" that are resolutely considered quite different from those held by these men and women. But the devout colonial subject, decent dupe of universalism, thinks to learn the trick perfectly. The performance of the teaching and of the learning is not mere mimicry. Deliberate, canny, wholesale (representation of) epistemic transformation—producing something in the future anterior—is what we are witnessing here. This is not the *Nātya Sāstra* warmed over.[19] The idea that apprenticeship with the West introduces analytic learning in place of rote learning is a sentiment that thoroughly informed the debates on education in the nineteenth century and continues to this day: it was heard in February 1991 from an Indian woman dancer who learned her stuff from an old-fashioned Indian male master but went on to collaborate with a European male director whose method was not unlike Girishbabu's.[20]

A later passage allows us to sense how completely the principle of reasonable learning affected the epistemological project representing the epistemic:

I had no taste for other topics of conversation. I liked only the accounts of the great British actors and actresses that respected Girish-babu gave me, the books he read to me. When Mrs. Sidnis [Siddons] left theatre work, spent ten years in the married state and then returned to the stage, where in her acting the critics noticed what fault, where she was excellent, where lacking, all this he read and explained to me from books. He would also tell me which British actress practised her voice by mingling it with birdsong in the woods, this too he would tell me. How Ellen Terry dressed, how Bandman made himself up as Hamlet, how Ophelia dressed in flowers, what book Bankimchandra's *Durgeshnandini* imitated, in what English book *Rajani* found its idea [*bhab*=thoughts], so many things of this nature, I do not know where to begin. Thanks to the loving care of respected Girish-babu and other affectionate friends, I cannot recount how many tales by what great English, Greek, French, and German authors I have heard. I did not only listen, I collected ideas [*bhab*=mood] from them and reflected upon them ceaselessly. As a result of this my nature [*shabhāb*—*swabhāva*] became such that, when I went to visit a garden, I did not like the buildings there, I would search out the secluded spots resplendent with wild flowers. I would feel that perhaps I lived in those woods, ever-nurtured by them! My heart would throw itself down as it witnessed beauty so intimately mingled with every plant and bud. It was as if my soul would start to dance with joy! When I sometimes went to a riverbank it would seem as if my heart would fill with waves, I would feel as if I had played in the waves of this river forever. Now these waves have left my heart and are throwing themselves about. The sand on the banks of the river at Kuchbihar is full of mica, most lovely, I would often go alone to the riverbank, which was quite far from my living quarters, lie down on the sand and watch the waves. I would feel as if they spoke to me. (pp. 80–81; translation modified)

The rhetoric of this extended passage lays out the construction of the colonial subject as contradictory implied reader of the imperial text. Binodini was indeed receiving an education in English and European literature in a way that no university student does. To be sure, to learn to read well is to say "yes, yes" to the text, if only in order to say "no," in other words to perform it, if only against the grain. But between that general sense of performance and the narrow sense of performing in order to simulate there is an immense difference in degree. Binodini was not obliged to get her information right; the proper names are often askew. (Ellen Terry comes out "Ellentarry" in Bengali, a single word, and "Ophelia" inhabits the same register of reality as Mr. Bandman and Mrs. Sidnis.) Yet here we see the difference between knowing and learning. She identifies with Bankim, the master-creator recognized as the successful colonial subject by the very babu-culture of Bengal that Kipling mocks. If Bankim had taken the *bhab* of British Literature, so would she; he to write, she to interpret through performance. Reading-in-performance is a species of writing, as Bankim himself recognized:

> One day Bankim-babu came to see the performance of his *Mrinalini,* and I was playing the part of "Manorama" at that time. Having seen the part of Manorama being played Bankim-babu said: "I only wrote the character of Manorama in a book, I had never thought to see it with my own eyes, seeing Manorama today I thought I was seeing my Manorama in front of me." (p. 81; translation modified)[21]

The public sphere of professional theater and the private sphere of the self interpenetrate in the longer passage in a clearer and more intense model of what can happen in the classroom. In the consummate rhetoric of this gifted craftswoman, the epistemic simulacrum is obstinately sustained. The translator has taken care to preserve every "as if," every "perhaps." (It would have been possible to construct the Bengali sentences without them.) It is not a "real" nature that Binodini imagines as the place of eternal nurture. It is rather the planted woods in a garden-house. In the passage about the waves, the location of the waves is made nicely indeterminate; but in fact the waves, ostensibly the vehicle of union, preserve separation between river and heart, displacing it from figure to figure. This rhetorical effusion does not break step with the ritual language celebrating her dead protector within which the autobiography is framed. It seems appropriate that we, in search of a model for the colonial subject as implied reader, should be implicated in the reader function of this thoroughly benevolent and utterly dominant male.

Binodini was no rural subaltern. In her own words: "I was born in this great city of Calcutta, in a family without resource and property. But not to be called poverty-stricken, for, however painfully, we scratched together a living. . . . My grandmother, my mother, and the two of us, brother and sister" (p. 61; translation modified).

A family of women, quite within the other discursive formation that can look upon marriage as a socio-economic institution of exchange for consumption: "But with our sentience our sufferings from poverty increased, and then our grandmother perpetrated a marriage between my infant brother of five years and a girl of two and a half [the play between infant—*shishu*—and girl—*balika*—is her own] and brought home her mother's negligible quantity of ornaments. Then our livelihood was earned through the sale of ornaments" (p. 61; translation modified).

It is not only the play between *shishu* and *balika* that signals that Binodini, writing at the age of 47, after her brilliant and thwarted attempt at staging herself, in every sense, as female individualist, is still unemphatically at ease with the pragmatic patriarchal culture that thwarted her; although her expressed sentiments will not draw from it. The next few sentences quietly emphasize this; for it is the love *(sneho)* of the older women rather than the unconsummated child marriage that remains in memory: "My grandmother and respected Mother were most affectionate [*snehomoyee*]. They would sell the ornaments one by one at the goldsmith's shop and give us all kinds of food stuff. They never regretted the ornaments."

The brother died soon after the marriage. What happened to the child bride deprived of her ornaments for the subsistence of the other women? We cannot know. But there can be no doubt that the tragedy of feminism is played out not only in the obvious and visible masculist suppression of Binodini's ambitions, but also in the widening gap between the obscurity of the unremembered child widow and the subtle and layered memoir of the autobiographer.[22] The male suppression of the competitive female is a poignant story, where the politically correct judgment is trivially obvious, but it is not the only story in coloniality. The feminist has the dubious task of marking the division in womanspace. Tagore may have found it difficult to stage the estranged wife Shoshi as the full-fledged colonial subject, insert her fully into the contradiction of implied readership, make her the agent of both *sneho* and *prem,* but the prostitute-performer Binodini straddles the gap with ease. In prostitution, sublated through performance upon the colonially fractured stage, the old lesson in *lāsya* is destroyed and preserved on another register as *prem.*[23] Although Binodini is bitter and contemptuous about the men's refusal to let her own a part of her beloved Star Theatre, and indeed to keep their promise of preserving her proper name by naming it "B-Theatre"—curious synecdoche, known only to the knowing—her extraordinary language of exalted devotion to her dead protector, her companion in the long years after her departure from the stage, rings with greater affect, as does the explicit (auto)eroticism of her singular love poems, where the agency of the male lover is only present to the extent that it is necessary for the topos of male inconstancy. Marriage may be an institution that crumples when the woman is epistemically fractured, but residential (rather than itinerant) prostitution can be re-coded as a peculiar liberty. How far do we want to take this as an allegory of colonial reading?

In the Brit Lit classroom today, an answer might be concocted in terms of Hanif Kureishi's *The Buddha of Suburbia.*[24] The shifts are: a century in time, coloniality through postcoloniality to migrancy, a literary representation by a male author who "read philosophy at King's College, London" (jacket blurb). Here too an uncomfortable opposition between native and migrant can be undone or put under erasure (crossed out while leaving visible).[25] Again, not conflation; perhaps the very shock of the reconstellation lets "truths" flash forth. No such confidence in playing the double bind today, readers.

The central character Karim will not be allowed to be English, even as Binodini was not allowed to be an entrepreneurial professional individualist, although she carried bricks on her head for the building of the theater, and he is "Englishman born and bred, almost. . . . Englishman I am (though not proud of it), from the South London suburbs and going somewhere. Perhaps it is the odd mixture of continents and blood, of here and there, of belonging and not, that makes me restless and easily bored" (p. 3).

This is the flip side of Binodini's restless self-separation on the glittering sand of the Kuchbihar River; the style difference may be between

Romanticism and existentialist modernism (small *e*, small *m*: *The Catcher in the Rye, Under the Net*), rather than only that between India and Britain.[26] Let the student notice that Karim, as he learns performance from British and American directors, is being asked to be "Indian," or portray migrants favorably. He must dye his skin browner (his mother is working-class English) as he is given Mowgli's part in Kipling's *The Jungle Book,* and produce "an Indian accent," which he finally, during performance, begins to "send up" with occasional lapses into Cockney.[27] Yet outside the theater, he lives in the incredible violence of racism in contemporary London, which is also vividly described in the novel.

Karim's father, a Muslim, becomes a Buddhist from do-it-yourself books and finds fulfillment with an "artist" woman. Yet there is real good sense in him, real unworldliness, and there is love between them, however sweetly sexist.

Dominant British society shuttles between racist violence and approval of the "real" Indian. Once again, it is the productive epistemic fracture of the colonial, postcolonial, hybrid subject that is denied. The expectations are Kipling's Mowgli, or the Buddha of Suburbia. The transformation of the father is given in the third person. Let us consider what the son says, in the first person, about learning to act.

"India" is an imagined ingredient with material vestiges here, important in the survival technique of the fabrication of a hybrid identity. With a different political impulse from the malevolent racist British underclass, or the benevolent racist British artist, we too would like to keep alive the divide between "real" Indian and migrant "Indian." Without collapsing the difference, what if we attended to the fact that Binodini's imagined "England" and the representation of Karim's imagined "India" are both "created" under duress? We would begin, then, to plot an alternative literary historiography. Binodini thought of the duress as imaginative freedom. We are not surprised that Karim is represented as creatively happy when he puts together his stage Indian. The intimate enemy, a violation that enables. The teacher of British literature in the former colonies must look at this phenomenon carefully, to let the differences appear in their entanglements.

Here, then, are the passages from *The Buddha of Suburbia*. Karim is re-thinking the Indian character, having been criticized for his initial negative representation of an Indian immigrant:[28] "At night, at home, I was working on Changez's shambolic walk and crippled hand, and on the accent, which I knew would sound, to white ears, bizarre, funny and characteristic of India" (p. 188).

He is at his father's best friend Anwar's funeral (the two had come to Britain from Bombay many years ago):

> There was a minor row when one of the Indians pulled out a handy com-
> pass and announced that the hole hadn't been dug facing in the right direc-
> tion, towards Mecca. . . . But I did feel, looking at these strange creatures
> now—the Indians—that in some way these were my people, and that I'd
> spent my life denying or avoiding that fact. I felt ashamed and incomplete at
> the same time, as if half of me were missing, and as if I'd been colluding
> with my enemies, those whites who wanted Indians to be like them. Partly
> I blamed Dad for this. After all, like Anwar, for most of his life he'd never
> shown any interest in going back to India. He was always honest about this:
> he preferred England in every way. Things worked; it wasn't hot; you didn't
> see terrible things on the street that you could do nothing about [this is con-
> tradicted by the graphic descriptions of racist violence in London]. He
> wasn't proud of his past, but he wasn't unproud of it either; it just existed,
> and there wasn't any point in fetishizing it, as some liberals and Asian radi-
> cals liked to do. So if I wanted the additional personality bonus of an Indian
> past, I would have to create it. (pp. 212–213)

How very different from the "uncreative" sacrificial choice thrust upon the rural woman or the unfetishized choice of a culture without the bonus of a past accessible to the "white migrant" imagined in the colonial context! Again, leisurely classroom consideration of the difference will make appear how the representations of "race," of "gendering," of "religion/ culture," construct the chain of displacements upon which these examples may be plotted. "Nation" and "class" relate to these links on other levels of abstraction.

For Binodini, the professional theater had promised an access to feminist individualism which residential prostitution denied. Down along a chain of displacements, casual prostitution and the stage have become confused for Kureishi's character Karim, although in the "real" world, professional prostitution still has a confining relationship to the media. At any rate, the identity forged in the theater had come to organize Binodini's own staging of her identity in honorable residential prostitution recalled in later life. "The acting bit of her lost its moorings and drifted out into real life."[29] There is no such bleeding over in the representation of Karim. The character who plays the sexual field is the Paki. When he "wants the additional personality bonus of an Indian past," he reverses the demands of his protector, and "creates":

> There were few jobs I relished as much as the invention of Changez/
> Tariq. . . . I uncovered notions, connections, initiatives I didn't even know
> were present in my mind. . . . I worked regularly and kept a journal [My

Story]; . . . I felt more solid myself, and not as if my mind were just a kind of cinema for myriad impressions and emotions to flicker through. This was worth doing, this had meaning, this added up the elements of my life. And it was this that Pyke [the director] had taught me: what a creative life could be. . . . I was prepared to pay the price for his being a romantic, an experimenter. He had to pursue what he wanted to know and follow his feelings wherever they went, even as far as my arse and my girlfriend's cunt. (p. 217)

Karim is a character in a book. The fact that this passage about creativity and the discovery of a coherent identity is much less gripping than Binodini's passage about divided self-creation cannot be taken as representative of the difference between the colonial reader's longing for the metropolis and the migrant's fancy for his roots. It is simply that our students might be encouraged to place it on that chain of displacements that will include *Gora, Kim,* and *The Jungle Book*. Through attention to the rhetorical conduct of each link on the chain, the student might be encouraged, to belabor the by now obvious, neither to conflate nor oppose, but to figure out gender and class difference in complicity. In the next essay, we will draw attention to the moment when the half-caste tribal woman in "The Hunt" fabricates identity for the object (rather than the individualist subject) by intoning a word that would allow the indigenous exploiter to be constructed within the script of Oraon performance. Mahasweta offers a link in the chain away from migrancy into subalternity.

What I am suggesting, then, is that, in the postcolonial context, the teaching of English literature can become critical only if it is intimately yoked to the teaching of the literary or cultural production in the mother tongue(s). In that persistently asymmetrical intimacy, the topos of language learning, in its various forms, can become a particularly productive site. I am not speaking here of becoming an "expert" of the mother tongue, for the benefit of those who are thoroughly ignorant of it in the metropolis, a temptation to which many of us have given in. I am speaking of a much less practical thing: becoming "inter-literary," not "comparative," in the presence of long-established institutional divides and examination requirements. It is a kind of homoeopathic gesture: scratching at the epistemic fracture by awkwardly assuming a language to be an "epistemic system" and staging a collision between Kipling and Tagore, Didi and Binodini, "Mary Oraon" and "Karim." The authority of cultivating the felicitous implied readership is questioned in such teaching and learning. Any number of "correct" readings can be scrupulously taught here, with some degree of assurance that the reader's space of the mother tongue will secure the quotation marks by way of repeated colonial and postcolonial encounters, among them the one in the classroom.

Great clumps of topics are pulled up with this style of teaching; access to subjectivity and access to the other's language are among them. Such topics allow us to float into Commonwealth literature, even without access to the various native traditions or emergences. The peculiar authority in this floating reading is of the contingent reader who might have that access. An interruptive authority, for the text is in English. Again, speaking in full globalization, the globality of English, this scenario seems out of joint.

Let us consider an example: The last scene of Nadine Gordimer's *July's People*.[30] Successful black insurgency in South Africa. A family being protectively steered into the village of their former servant, July. Barriers falling, people learning about being human, the nature of power, being gendered, the master-servant dialectic. The emergence of July's proper name—Mwawate—in itself the kind of topic that rocks the centralized place of the "implied reader." As if man Friday should have a history. When people have been pared down a good bit, we encounter an event impossible to conceive earlier in the book. Mwawate speaks to his former mistress, the central character in the book, in his own language, with authority, dignity, and irritation. I will first quote the preparatory moments: "She knew those widened nostrils. Go, he willed, go up the hill to the hut; as he would to his wife. . . . The only way to get away from her was . . . to give up to her this place that was his own" (p. 152).

Then a furious exchange in English about why had he stolen little things; why had she given him only rubbish; why had he accepted rubbish; almost farcically resembling what Jan Nederveen Pieterse has called "the dialectics of terror": "not discussed is the initial . . . terror, which includes the institutional violence of the denial of . . . human rights and [of imperialist] occupation."[31]

It is in response to this frustrating exchange that Mwawate speaks:

You—he spread his knees and put an open hand on each. Suddenly he began to talk at her in his own language, his face flickering powerfully. The heavy cadences surrounded her; the earth was fading and a thin, far radiance from the moon was faintly pinkening parachute-silk hazes stretched over the sky. She understood although she knew no word. Understood everything: what he had had to be, how she had covered up to herself for him, in order for him to be her idea of him. But for himself—to be intelligent, honest, dignified for her was nothing; his measure as a man was taken elsewhere and by others. She was not his mother, his wife, his sister, his friend, his people. He spoke in English what belonged in English:—Daniel he's go with those ones like in town. He's join.—The verb, unqualified, did for every kind of commitment: to a burial society, a hire purchase agreement, their thumbprints put to a labour contract for the mines or sugar plantations. (p. 152)

Gordimer is playing a whole set of variations on the topos of languages as epistemes. To begin with, the imperious gesture, of the pronominal address as imperative: "you," but even before that, and surreptitiously, the sudden incursion of Mwawate's "inside" into the novel: "Go, he *willed*" (emphasis added). It remains paratactic—cannot be staged as becoming syntactic in the hands of this white author woman writing about a female white protagonist, precisely because both are painfully politically correct. The sentences can start only after that enabling shifter, "you," (staged by the writer as) pronounced by the imperfect speaker of English. Put this on a spectrum of contemporary artists using this topos in many different ways: Toni Morrison, J. M. Coetzee, Guillermo Gómez-Peña, Jamelie Hassan.[32]

In the hands of a radical creole writer like Gordimer, the implied black reader of a white text cannot be in a subject-position, not even a compromised one like Shoshi's. The text belongs to the native speaker. But the rhetorical conduct of the text undermines and complicates this a lot. The desire of the radical native speaker is in that sentence: "She understood although she knew no word." How fragile the logic of that sentence is; there are no guarantees. It is as if the white magistrate in "the elder sister" should enunciate the desire for understanding Shoshi's ambivalence, which the writer as classed male colonial subject articulates by way of the representation of his slight smile. And in Gordimer's text there is the strong suggestion that rather than understand the "burden" of Mwawate's words, the peculiar situation of being addressed by him in his tongue produces in her an understanding of a narrative of, precisely, the infelicity of their communication. His measure was elsewhere. "He spoke in English what belonged in English."

Just as Mwawate's subject-space is syntactically inaccessible in the rhetoric of the novel, so is the dubious assertion of "understanding" unmoored from the passage that tells you what she understood. And, in addition, the man speaking his mother tongue—the other tongue from English—is deliberately distanced by a metonym with nature: Mwawate flickering, adjacent to the moon and the parachute silk clouds. Put this on a spectrum with the neat divisive locatives of nature and mind in Binodini's self-staging!

What is it that Mwawate says in English? It is the matter of public organizations: "he's join." This is not a "mistake," just as Dopdi Mejhen's
"counter" is not.[33] In its profound ungrammaticality, it undoes the dominant language and pushes its frontiers as only pidgin can. Put this calm
approach on a spectrum with Kipling's mockery, Rushdie's teratology,
and Tagore's colonial prose.

It is not possible for an "expatriate English professor," as Madhu
Jain described me in a December 1990 issue of *India Today,* to produce
a thick analysis of the burden of English teaching in India. Let
me remind my readers that I have not attempted to comment on the
importance of English as an international medium of exchange. (For
the record, the proportion of honors to pass students in English at
Delhi University is 602/13,900, 580/15,700, 660/17,300, 748/18,800,
and 845/19,800—for 1986–1990, respectively.)[34] All I seem to have
done is offered impractical suggestions: to undo the imported distinction between center and periphery as well as some indigenous institutional divisions by looking at literature as the staged battle-ground of
epistemes.

It may not be altogether as impractical as it seems, at first glance, to
the embattled local teacher. I am speaking, after all, of disturbing the
arrangement of classroom material as well as our approach to them. Predictably, this would be against the interest of the student, who would
have to sit for an examination that expects ferocious loyalty to a colonial
curricular arrangement. (This is an argument we daily face, mutatis mutandis, in terms of bilingualism in the United States; in the 1960s and
1970s it was Black English.) Can one share the dilemma with the students while preparing them for the regular exam papers? A time-honored
strategy of politicization through pedagogy. The counter-argument here
is the cynicism of students in a demoralized society, where English learning at institutes of tertiary education has given way to call centers, in a
way unimaginable by Ngũgĩ in the 1970s. Paradoxically, the language
remains most difficult to learn precisely for those students who would be
most susceptible to such politicization. (In the United States, this translates, as imperfectly as all translations, to the justified cynicism of the
urban underclass student toward the smorgasbord of cultural studies.)
Alas, the answers to that one are lost or found, lost and found, in the
transactions in the classroom. It is to the most practical aspect of our
trade that I dedicate these ruminations.

Would such a technique of teaching work outside of modern literature? And if so, with *adivasi* (formal name for the alleged aboriginal)
creation-myths and the reclaiming of "African" mythic traditions by

writers and filmmakers of contemporary Africa? Or only with *Beowulf* and the *Mahabharata?* One looks forward to an alternative literary historiography of postcoloniality critical of the hierarchical imprint of "the Commonwealth," or, as today, a thinking that situates the postcolonial as a moment in the history of cultural politics.

CHAPTER TWO

Who Claims Alterity?

S A POSTCOLONIAL, I am concerned with the appropriation of "alternative history" or "histories." I am not a historian by training. I cannot claim disciplinary expertise in remaking history in the sense of rewriting it. But I can be used as an example of how historical narratives are negotiated.[1] The parents of my parents' grandparents' grandparents were made over, not always without their consent, by the political, fiscal, and educational intervention of British imperialism, and now I am independent. Thus I am, in the strictest sense, a postcolonial. As a caste Hindu, I had access to the culture of imperialism, although not the best or most privileged access. Let me, then, speak to you as a citizen of independent India, and raise the necessary critical and cautionary voice about false claims to alternate histories. False claims and false promises are not euphoric topics. I am also a feminist who is an old-fashioned Marxist and some of that will enter into this discussion of the cultural politics of alternative historiographies.

How are historical narratives put together? In order to get to something like an answer to that question, I will make use of the notions of writing and reading in the most general sense. We produce historical narratives and historical explanations by transforming the socius, upon which our production is written into more or less continuous and controllable bits that are readable.[2] How these readings emerge and which ones get sanctioned have political implications on every possible level.

The masterwords implicated in Indian decolonization offered four great legitimizing codes consolidated by the national bourgeoisie by way of the culture of imperialism: nationalism, internationalism, secularism, culturalism. If the privileged subject operated by these codes masquerades as the subject of an alternative history, we must mediate upon how they (we) are written, rather than simply read their masque as historical exposition.

Writing and reading in such general senses mark two different positions in relation to the uneven many-strandedness of "being." Writing is a position where the absence of the weaver from the web is structurally necessary. Reading is a position where I (or a group of us with whom I share an identificatory label) make this anonymous web my own, even as I find in it a guarantee of my existence as me, one of us. Between the two positions, there are displacements and consolidations, a disjunction in order to conjugate a representative self. (Even solitude is framed in a representation of absent others.) In the arena of cultural politics, whose disciplinary condition and effect are history, anthropology, and cultural studies, this disjunction/conjunction is often ignored. The socius, it is claimed, is not woven in the predication of writing, not text-ile. It is further claimed that, when we push ourselves, or the objects of our study, forward as agents of an alternative history, our own emergence into the court of claims is not dependent upon the transformation and displacement of writing into something readable. By that reasoning, we simply discover or uncover the socius and secure the basis of cultural or ethnic power through the claim to knowledge. By that reasoning, power is collective, institutional, political validation. I do not advise giving up this practical notion of power. If, however, we "remake history" only through this limited notion of power as collective validation, we might allow ourselves to become instruments of the crisis-management of the old institutions, the old politics. We forget at our peril that we get out of joint with the pre-text, the writing of our desire for validation, which one can only grasp by being "nominalistic, no doubt: power is not an institution, and not a structure; neither is it a certain strength some are endowed with; it is the name that one lends to a complex strategical situation in a particular society," so that one can read that writing.[3]

I will soon go on to discuss Indian postcoloniality from this perspective. But first I will make a brief detour via Marx.

Of all the tools for developing alternative histories—gender, race, ethnicity, class—class is surely the most abstract. It is only when we forget this that we can set aside class-analysis as essentialist. In the volumes of *Capital*, Marx asks the German worker to grasp, as a preliminary to the planned change involved in remaking history, the abstract determinations of what is otherwise merely suffered as concrete misery.[4] In the language that I have been using, one might summarize Marx as saying that the logic of capitalism weaves the socius like the textile of a particular set of relationships. Power and validation within this socius are secured by denying that web and transforming/displacing it into "natural" readability. I think it is not excessive to see these general senses of reading and writing at work, for example, when Marx asks the worker to understand (read?) the coat s/he produces as having more signification than it does as itself. Capital is a writing, which we must not read merely in terms of producing objects for use, a few for ourselves and many more for others, and not being given enough money to get more for ourselves. Reading the archives of capitalism, Marx produces a critique, not of cultural, but of economic politics—hence a critique of political economy, political economism.[5] In the current global postcolonial context, our model must be a critique of political culture, political culturalism, whose vehicle is the writing of readable histories, mainstream or alternative. I think it might be useful to write power in Marx this way: "power is the name that one attributes to a complex strategical situation"—the social relations of production—forming a particular society, where 'society' is shorthand for the dominance of (a) particular mode(s) of production of value."

The most useful way to think value is as something "contentless and simple" that must be presupposed as the name of the possibility of measuring what is produced by the human body/mind machine—a thing that is not pure form, cannot appear by itself, and is immediately coded.[6] As Gayle Rubin on the one hand and Gillles Deleuze and Felix Guattari on the other have suggested, in their very different ways, this coding operation is not merely economic; it can be understood in the fields of gendering and colonialism.[7] This does not involve allegiance to the narrative of the evolution of the modes of production as the only lexicon of readability, or the presupposition that class-analysis is the only instrument of readability. (As for the strategy for dealing with the sexism of Marxists, it seems to me not very different from that for dealing with the sexism of non—or anti—Marxists.)

Yet this counterintuitive thought of value should not make us imagine that we can ourselves escape the codes inscribing the real. We are obliged to deal in narratives of history, even believe them. In fact, it is easier to believe in Marx's historical passions than in his methodological delicacy, and many of us feel that to label one ideology and the other science is only provisionally justified in situations of political calculation. In the celebrated postface to the second edition of *Capital,* Marx offers us a historical narrative: he argues that Germany was unable to develop the discipline of political economy more or less because in the late eighteenth and early nineteenth centuries it had not participated in the first stages of the development of industrial capitalism. Hence Germany had no bona fide political economists, who were the ideologues of industrial capitalism. When German savants talked political economy, they produced a bizarre *Mischmasch der Kenntnisse*—a jumble of knowledges.

> The peculiar historical development of German society (that the capitalist mode of production came to maturity there after its antagonistic character had already been revealed), therefore excluded any original development of "bourgeois" economics there, *but did not exclude its critique*. In so far as such a critique represents a class, it can only represent [*vertreten*] the class whose historical task is the overthrow of the capitalist mode of production and the final abolition of all classes—the proletariat. (C 1, pp. 95, 98; emphasis added)

The position implicit in the work of the "Subaltern Studies" group of historians is that, since the colonies were not the theater of the development of industrial-capitalist class differentiation, if postcolonial intellectuals keep themselves strictly to the discourse of class-analysis and class-struggle, they might produce a *Mischmasch der Kenntnisse*. The peculiar historical development of colonial society, however, does not exclude the critique of class-analysis as a normative imposition of the instrument of reading. Insofar as such a critique represents a group with a name, it is the subaltern.[8]

It seems obvious to some of us that the disenfranchised female in decolonized space, being doubly displaced by it, is the proper carrier of a critique of pure class-analysis. Separated from the mainstream of feminism, this figure, the figure of the gendered subaltern, is singular and alone.[9] Insofar as such a figure can be represented among us, in the room where this piece was first given as a talk, it is, first, as an object of knowledge, further, as a native-informant style subject of oral histories who is patronizingly considered incapable of strategy toward us, and finally, as imagined subject/object, in the real field of literature. There is, however, a rather insidious fourth way. It is to obliterate the differences between this figure and the indigenous elite woman abroad, and claim the subjectship of an as-yet-unreadable alternative history that is only written in the general sense I invoke above. (This has now become altogether more material in globalization and alter-globalization.)

This fourth person is a "diasporic postcolonial," or a cosmopolitan postcolonial who is the typical participant in international civil society. Who or what is she? (The central character of Mahasweta Devi's "The Hunt," altogether different from the two figures described above, my chief literary example of remaking history in this piece, negotiates a space that can, not only historically but philosophically, be accessible to her.)

We all know that the world was divided into three on the model of the three estates in the mid-1940s when neocolonialism began.[10] We also know that, during the immediately preceding period of monopoly capitalist territorial conquest and settlement, a class of functionary-intelligentsia was often produced who acted as buffers between the foreign rulers and the ruled.[11] These are the "colonial subjects," formed with varying degrees of success, generally, though not invariably, out of the indigenous elite. At decolonization, this is the "class" (as I indicate above, class-formation in colonies is not exactly like class-formation in the metropolis) that becomes the "national bourgeoisie," with a hand in the carving out of "national identities" by methods that cannot break formally with the system of representation that offered them an episteme in the previous dispensation: a "national" buffer between the ruler and the ruled.

A good deal of this repetition of the colonial episteme in the presumed rupture of postcoloniality will come into play in Mahasweta's story. For the moment let us hold onto the fact that de-colonization does quite seriously represent a rupture for the colonized. It is counterintuitive to point at its repetitive negotiations. But it is precisely these counterintuitive imaginings that must be grasped when history is said to be remade, and a rupture is too easily declared because of the intuition of freedom that a merely political independence brings for a certain class. Such graspings will allow us to perceive that neocolonialism is a displaced repetition of many of the old lines laid down by colonialism. They will also allow us to realize that the stories (or histories) of the postcolonial world are not necessarily the same as the stories coming from "internal colonization," the way the metropolitan countries discriminate against disenfranchised groups in their midst.[12] And the contemporaneity of globalization has dated these instruments of analysis. The diasporic postcolonial can take advantage (most often unknowingly, I hasten to add) of the tendency to conflate the three in the metropolis. Thus this frequently (though not invariably) innocent informant, identified and welcomed as the agent of an alternative history, may indeed be the site of a chiasmus, the crossing of a double contradiction: the system of production of the national bourgeoisie at home, and, abroad, the tendency to represent neocolonialism by the semiotic of "internal colonization."

Throw into this chiastic field a phenomenon I invoke often: the shift into transnationalism in the early 1970s through the computerization of the big stock exchanges (this was my way of presaging "globalization" in the early 1980s).[13] Of course, changes in the mode of production of value do not bring about matching changes in the constitution of the subject. But one is often surprised to notice how neatly the ruses change in the arena that engages in coding subject-production: cultural politics. And the universities, the journals, the institutes, the exhibitions, the publishers' series are rather overtly involved here. Keeping the banal predictability of the cultural apparatus in transnational society firmly in mind, it can be said that the shift into transnationalism brought a softer and more benevolent third worldism into the Euramerican academy. This was indeed a *ricorso* from the basically conservative social scientific approach that matched the initial dismantling of the old empires. It is in this newer context that the postcolonial diasporic can have the role of an ideologue. This "person" (although we are only naming a subject-position here), belonging to a basically collaborative elite, can be uneasy for different kinds of reasons with being made the object of unquestioning benevolence as an inhabitant of the new third world. (S)he is more at home in producing and simulating the effect of an older world constituted by the legitimizing narratives of cultural and ethnic specificity and continuity, all feeding an almost seamless national identity—a species of "retrospective hallucination."[14]

This produces a comfortable "other" for transnational postmodernity, "ground-level activity," "emergent discourses." The radical critic can turn her attention on this hyperreal third world to find, in the name of an alternative history, an arrested space that reproaches postmodernity. In fact, most postcolonial areas have a class-specific access to the society of information-command telematics inscribed by microelectronic transnationalism. And indeed, the discourse of cultural specificity and difference, packaged for transnational consumption along the lines sketched above, is often deployed by this specific class. What is dissimulated by this broad-stroke picture is the tremendous complexity of postcolonial space, especially womanspace.[15]

As I must keep repeating, remaking history is a tall order, and we must not take collective enthusiasm or conviction as its sole guarantee. In order to emphasize this point, I will fall into the confessional mode, give you an insider's view of what it "feels like" to taste the freedom offered by political independence in its specific historical moment.

My academic generation in India, approaching seventy now, were children at the time of the Indian Independence, unlike the "midnight's children" who were born with the Independence, and served Salman Rushdie to symbolize the confusion of a new nation seeing itself only as rupture, a monstrous birth.[16] These children of the middle class have become college and university teachers, cultural workers, government servants, political activists, the women household managers with a foot in the women's movement, the professions, the arts. I know surprisingly few executives or scientists as old friends. Our childhood and adolescence were marked by a dying fall that had to be rearranged as an upbeat march. We were not old enough to analyze, indeed sometimes to know, the details of the scenario until later. Those years marked the collapse of the heritage of nineteenth-century liberalism out of which the nationalist alibi for decolonization had been painstakingly fabricated. We could not know then, although it was being bred into our bones, that the people were not behaving like a nation, that the dubious euphoria of 1947, division and violence barely managed, was now turning into a species of *Jawaharlalvisādayoga*—the Sorrow of Jawaharlal—out of which a chauffeur of a different kind would drive the national automobile into a new and changed space called the Indian Union.[17] It was beyond our grasp to understand that the grandeur of an internationalist "national" commitment within a necessarily furtive left under imperialism—the undivided Communist Party of India—was just as necessarily breaking up into a split-level insertion into electoral politics. Yet our academic humanist generation would bear the political melancholy of this change. We wrote essays in our school magazines at Gandhi's murder. Yet we had already, in the curious logic of children, settled that the "partition riots" (between Hindus and Muslims at Independence), like the "famine of '43" (artificially produced by the British government in order to feed the military during World War II), marked a past that our present had pushed firmly back. In other words, as middle-class children and adolescents, my academic generation was thrust in the space of remaking history, negotiating a new history. This is the subject-position of the children of the national bourgeoisie in decolonization. The adolescent imagination could be persuaded that the disturbing reminders of the past were no more than the ashes that the phoenix leaves behind as s/he leaps into the air reborn. We were already marked by this excusing structure (productive of unexamined allegories of nationalism) when, like everyone else, we perceived that, in terms of religious fundamentalism as a social formation, every declared rupture with the past is always also a repetition. Today's monumentalizing of the "partition" as unspeakable, and the dismissal of the partition of East India because unmanageably cultural-negotiatory, seems a displacement of that structure.

The potential executives, scientists, and professionals from that generation were the first big brain drain to the United States. If, as children and adolescents, they suffered the same contradictions that I mention above, they understood them, I think, more in terms of broken promises.

These people, mostly men, did well in the United States. By and large, they did not trouble themselves about the struggles of the 1960s and 1970s in this country. Hard-working, ambitious, and smart, they were upwardly class mobile to begin with. They received some of the benefits of the struggles they did not join. As the only colored community (although, like the colonial subject of the previous dispensation, they basically identified with the whites) in the United States that did not have a history of oppression on the soil, they were often used in affirmative action employment and admission where blacks, Hispanics, and "Asian-Americans" (meaning U.S. citizens of Chinese and Japanese extraction) were bypassed. The constitution of the Indian community is changing rapidly, and beginning to assume some of the more working-class and small bourgeois dimensions of the Indian diaspora in the Afro-Caribbean and Great Britain. It can nonetheless be said, I think, that the first generation of Indian-Americans, just entering university, often innocently searching for their "roots" and their "heritage" (following a route laid down by internal colonization), are the children of the people I have been describing. Some of these young women and men will no doubt lend a certain confessional authenticity to third worldist alternative histories in the coming years. (It might be more interesting for them to intervene in internal colonizing in India, but that suggestion, at that time beside the point, is now happening, with "India rising," and is still beside the point of this chapter, though in rather a different way.)

The sources of the tremendous vitality of underclass British subcontinental culture—rigorously to be distinguished from the Indian academic community in Britain—are to be found in the sort of sectarian "household" religion that has been the strength of subaltern consciousness on the subcontinent.[18] The children of this community (the underclass British subcontinentals) are now producing the "indy-pop" or "panjabi new wave" music that can already be compared in the politics of its provenance to jazz or soul in the United States. These groups are now written up in funky magazines and Sunday supplements of national dailies, listed in city lights, featured in political theater and cinema.[19]

A large percentage of the Hindu contingent of Indian-Americans is, in an odd sort of way, fundamentalist. The so-called upanishadic religion of which they promote the fundament is a version of the sanitized Hinduism woven in the nineteenth century, whose most stunning achievement was its co-existence with a polytheism read as personal allegory. It is idle to deny the emancipatory energy of this innovation in its own time. In contemporary America this emancipatory force is channeled into recoding the entry into the great rational abstraction of the constitutional we the people.[20] Thus it is that the average cultured "secularist" Hindu Indian-American is often engaged in propagating a fantasmatic Hindu cultural heritage as the flip side of participation in the fantasy of the land of opportunity, a free society ruled by law and the popular mandate. The postcolonial diasporic as native informant finds a nurturing and corroborative space in this group, privileged in India as the non-resident Indian (NRI; and now PIO—"person of Indian origin," carrying a passport that bestows everything but citizenship), who gets investment breaks as well as invitations to opine on the Indian spiritual heritage. This provides a continuous multicultural insertion point into laundered Judaeo-Christianity as secularism in the dominant.[21]

This system of cultural representation and self-representation is the U.S. semiotic field of citizenship and ethnicity. The cultural fantasies of origin of the prominent "ethnic groups" in the United States (including the English and the French) and their imprint on the countries of their origin are well known. (Israel, Ireland, Poland, and Cuba are four other examples.)[22] All of these groups (excluding the English) had a history of varieties of oppression on the soil that lent an urgency to the fantasies. In the Indian case, export-import has been speeded up for reasons that I have tried to sketch.

Now, if one returns to the melancholy story of the years of Independence, whose shadow fell on my childhood, then one begins to see that the cultural, communal (religious), and class heterogeneity native to the subcontinent has been asserting itself in spite of the unifying hopes on assorted sides, based on those assorted concept-metaphors: nationalism, secularism, internationalism, culturalism.

Any extended discussion of remaking history in decolonization must take into account the dangerous fragility and tenacity of these concept-metaphors. Briefly, it seems possible to say that an alternative and perhaps equally fragile mode of resistance to them can only come through a strategic acceptance of the centrifugal potential of the plurality and heterogeneity native to the subcontinent. Yet heterogeneity is an elusive and ambivalent resource (except in metropolitan "parliamentary" or academic space), as the recent past in India, and indeed on the globe, have shown. Its direct manipulation for electoral or diplomatic results constitutes devastation. (Manipulation in commercial interest can lead to a dynamic "public culture.")

It is only in situations like this that institutionally placed cultural workers have the obligation to speak predictively. These scrupulous interventions are in fact our only contribution to the project of remaking history or sustaining ever-shifting voices with an alternative edge. In a sense our task is to make people ready to listen, and that is not determined by argument. Indirect and maddeningly slow, forever running the risk of demagogy and coercion mingled with the credulous vanity and class interests of teacher and student, it is still only institutionalized education in the human sciences that is a long-term and collective method for making people want to listen. As far as I can see, remaking (the discipline of) history has its only chance on this unglamorous and often tedious register.[23]

Therefore I propose the persistent establishment and re-establishment, the repeated consolidating in undoing, of a strategy of education and classroom pedagogy attending to provisional resolutions of oppositions as between secular and nonsecular, national and subaltern, national and international, cultural and socio-political by teasing out their complicity.[24] Such a strategy of strategies must speak "from within" the emancipatory master narratives even while taking a distance from them. It must resolutely hold back from offering phantasmic, hegemonic, nativist counternarratives that implicitly honor the historical withholding of the "permission to narrate." The new culturalist alibi, working within a basically elitist culture industry, insisting on the continuity of a native tradition untouched by a Westernization whose failures it can help to cover, legitimizes the very thing it claims to combat.

In a longer piece of which this is a part, I go on now to deal with the emphasis on technical education in contemporary India, and suggest some alternatives. That discussion would be pertinent to comments on "remaking history" with India as its space of agency. That it is not pertinent here should remind us that our perfectly appropriate collection is still within a "parochial decanonization debate."[25] Remaining then within the system(s) of representation negotiated by internal colonization, let me simply remark that the kind of predictive pedagogy that I engage in the longer piece is, however hardheaded, always to come.

That peculiar space, of a future that is not a future present, can be inhabited by paralogical figures.[26] In chapter 3 of *A Critique of Postcolonial Reason* I have attended to two such paralogical figures. I have indicated in this essay why the subaltern female seems particularly meaningful within postcolonial themes. I will now look, therefore, at such a paralogical literary case that rewrites ethnicity and reads race appropriatively—in the strong senses of reading and writing that I brought up earlier.

I will look again at Mahasweta Devi's "The Hunt."[27]

In the previous pages, I have suggested that the disavowal of postcoloniality in the name of nativist ethnicist culturalism is a species of collaboration with neocolonialism, especially in its benevolent instance. Not to be able to see error on the other side is to feed the arrogance of the benevolent neocolonialist conscience. By contrast, Mahasweta's story makes visible the suggestion that the postcolonial negotiates with the structures of violence and violation that have produced her.

History cannot be reversed or erased out of nostalgia. The remaking of history involves a renegotiation with the structures that have produced the individual as agent of history. In "The Hunt," the figure for this negotiation is the rewriting of ethnicity and the reappropriation of rape. And the name of the agent of this remaking is Mary Oraon.

A word on "figure." I do not mean to read Mary as the representative of the postcolonial, or as an example of directly imitable correct practice. I am looking rather at the logic of her figuration, at the mechanics of the fabrication of the figure called Mary. I will read the fabrication of the narrative in this way as well. Our usual way of reading involves character and plot. Often we call our reading "political" if we read these two items as allegorical in the narrow sense. My reading of the figuration of Mary and her story is not unrelated to these practices, but tries to take into account that the line between aesthetics and politics is neither firm nor straight.[28]

Mary Oraon. Oraon is the name of one of the largest of the three-hundred-odd tribes of India. In Hindi, the national language, the tribes are called *adivasi*s (original inhabitants; see my comment on p. 568, note 9). In English, they are referred to collectively as the "scheduled" tribes, because of the special sanctions (honored altogether in the breach) written for them in the Indian constitution. With the "scheduled" castes, the lowest Hindu castes (the outcastes), these original inhabitants are the official subalterns of the Republic of India. In the language of the government as well as that of political activists they are the SCSTs (Scheduled Castes/Scheduled Tribes, where "schedule" stands for "quota"). They are outside of the seven religions listed in the Indian national anthem: Hinduism, Buddhism, Sikhism, Jainism, Zoroastrianism, Islam, and Christianity. This then is Mary, simply Oraon, simply identified with her tribe. But she was christened Mary. Her father was a white planter who raped her mother before leaving India for Australia. If we think of the postcolonial, figuratively, as the living child of a rape, the making of Mary is, rather literally, its figuration. She is not a "true" tribal.

Mary, servant in the house of a caste Hindu, is and is not a Christian. All the appropriate categories are blurred in postcoloniality.[29] Her mother stopped being a Christian when a Hindu in independent secular rural India would not hire her for fear of caste contamination. Mary will marry a Muslim. This negotiability of "religions" is rather different from the official post-Enlightenment secularist agenda, devastated, as I have mentioned earlier, by the violent communalism on the soil.

It is not only secularism as defined through the culture of imperialism that is put into question in Mahasweta's story. The reinscription of post-coloniality as the product of an enabling violation puts the militant "tribal" in the place of the bourgeois intellectual as its representative figuration. (Today secularism is a double bind for me: the need to keep in place a secularist law that took for granted that educated Judaeo-Christian, educated Muslim-Buddhist-Hindu, etc. protected the intuition of the transcendental through an inherited humanism, seemingly privatizing it in favor of the rule of law.)

Every detail in that figuration shuttles between "literal" and "metaphorical." Admiration for the courage of the White, for example, is part of the subaltern repertoire. Thus Jalim, Mary's boyfriend, comments on her insistence upon the commitment of marriage rather than mere cohabitation. "Yes, there is something true in Mary, the power of Australian blood" (IM, p. 3). She herself puts it with an impersonal rage against her mother that can provide a text for decoding: "When you see a white daughter you kill her right away. Then there are no problems." "What about you if she'd killed," one of the tribal boys asks. "I wouldn't have been" (IM, p. 5).

Describing her mind-set authorially, Mahasweta writes: "She would have rebelled if they had imposed the harsh injunctions of their own society upon her. She is unhappy that they don't. In her in-most heart there is somewhere a longing to be part of the Oraons. She would have been very glad if, when she was thirteen or fourteen, some brave Oraon lad had pulled her into marriage" (IM, p. 6).

Mahasweta is careful not to privilege this mind-set into the self-marginalizing or self-anthropologizing ethnic's project of dining out as an exile or an expression of her semi-tribal voice-consciousness. The provenance of this scenario and these sentiments is the one or two Hindi films Mary has seen. The overcoming of caste and creed barriers for the sake of love is one of the basic themes of the immensely productive Hindi film industry, now somewhat misleadingly called Bollywood.[30]

The description of Mary's everyday life as a bridge between the "outside world" (represented by the obscure rural township of Tohri) and the arrested space of Kuruda (the little community on the borders of which the tribals live) is orchestrated to provide empirical sanction for Mary

Oraon as the name of woman, worker, postcolonial. I will pass over that rich text and focus on the moment when, "suddenly one day, stopping the train, Collector Singh descends with Prasadji's son, and Mary's life is troubled, a storm gathers in Kuruda's quiet and impoverished existence" (IM, p. 6).

The train no longer stops at Kuruda, as it did in British India, when the white planters lived there. The train is a widely current metonym for the unifying project of territorial imperialism, the "colonialism" of which Mary is the postcolonial.[31]

"Collector"—a petty revenue collector under the British raj—could be a proper name or a descriptive honorific. The man acts with what Lukacs would have called "typicality." He violates the land by selling the sal forests of the area, cheating the small landowners of a fair price. He violates the tribe by employing them as wage labor at a murderous rate of exploitation and entertains them with quantities of liquor and a travesty of the commodified so-called mass-culture of the West. In fact, the story of the silent sal forests is also a carefully articulated historical metonym. As follows:

The ecology of the sal tree is thoroughly intertwined with the precapitalist communal economy and social relations of the tribes. Its transformation into colonial constant capital was performed through the imposition and production of the elaborate social relations of white planter and tribal servant. The transformation of the culture of imperialism in postcoloniality is figured forth by the incompetent but good-natured Indians living in the nooks and crannies of the great plantation houses. The real legatee of the imperialist economic text, the necessary trajectory from high bourgeois to petty bourgeois social manipulation under decolonization, is the despicable Collector Singh, who remobilizes the sal forest into constant capital and the tribals into variable capital without inserting them into generalized commodity exchange.[32] Marx described this a hundred years ago as "capital's mode of exploitation without its mode of production."[33] Mary Oraon, the not-quite-not-tribal, not-quite-not-Indian, is the not-quite-not-self-conscious, not-quite-not-self-identical agent who would defeat this continuous narrative of exploitation.

I will not focus on this aspect of the story either. For our present purposes, I must concentrate on Mary's appropriation of the structure of rape as not-quite-not-man. And here, the aspect of Collector Singh that becomes important is his attempt to violate Mary sexually and his various related exchanges with Mary. The narrative resolution of this sequence happens on the day and night of the spring festival of the Oraons.

Mary, as the vigilant and alert critic of what is violating the land and the people, rewrites the festival, turns it from the hunt game to the hunt. She brings the festival to crisis—literalizes the metaphor—to be able to act. The "authentic" version of the tribals monumentalizes the past. There the sexual division of agency is intact. The men know. The women masquerade: "they [the women] don't know why they hunt. The men know. They have been playing the hunt for a thousand million moons on this day. Once there were animals in the forest, life was wild, the hunt game had meaning. Now the forest is empty, life wasted and drained, the hunt game meaningless. Only the day's joy is real" (IM, p. 12).

If for the men the ritual of the hunt seems a functioning metaphor, for the women, allowed every twelve years to perform the hunt, the ritual is staged as a catachresis, an analogy without an accessible historical or literal pole, in classical rhetoric a metaphor in abuse. Mary undoes this gendered opposition. She dynamically literalizes the literal catachresis of the hunt by negotiating with the structure of rape—violation as such—and appropriates it as a weapon. For her the forest does come to hold an animal, and the reality of the day's joy is both "real" and "full of meaning." How does she operate this? It is the festival that rewrites the collector as animal, for her, and legitimizes him as prey.

Some years ago, writing on *Jane Eyre*, I had described the scene where Jane first encounters Bertha Mason as a situation that made indeterminate the difference between human and animal so that the narrative could move Jane from the letter to the spirit of the law (CPR, p. 121). This is not such a "making indeterminate," but rather its opposite. Let us consider the text. Mary is returning from work, the monotone of the festival music is in the air, Collector accosts her on the lonely path:

> At first Mary was scared. . . . After a good deal of struggling, Mary was able to spring out of his grasp . . . long sideburns, long hair, polyester trousers, pointed shoes, a dark red shirt on his back. Against the background of the spring songs Mary thought he was an animal. An-i-mal. The syllables beat on her mind. Suddenly Mary smiled. (IM, p. 13)

Mary makes the rendezvous with him, intending to kill him. But she cannot kill him without help from the inscribing power or from the ritual. There is, once again, a negotiation and a transformation. The tribal women at their post-hunt picnic are at that very moment getting drunk on liquor donated by Collector. For Mary he brings "imported liquor" to the tryst. This substitutes for the festival music and Mary begins to drink. "Yes the face is beginning to look like the hunted animal's." Indeed Mary transforms that face. She "caresses it . . . gives him love bites on the lips.

There's fire in Collector's eyes, his mouth is open, his lips wet with spittle, his teeth glistening. Mary is watching, watching, the face changes and changes into? Yes, becomes an animal" (IM, p. 16).

One is not sure who speaks the next question: "Now take me?" In this moment of indeterminacy, Mary appropriates rape. She holds him, lays him down. The machete becomes the phallus of violation. The killing of the ritual beast is also a punishment for the violation of the people, of the land, as also a historically displaced return for the violation of her birth: "Mary lifts the machete, lowers it, lifts, lowers."

Every detail seems to bristle with "meaning." Violating, Mary feels sexually replete. This is a negotiation with the phallus, not merely masquerading as a man. Before the kill, dancing, "she had clasped Budhni [an old tribal woman], and said, 'I'll marry you after I play the hunt. Then I am the husband, you the wife.'" After she returns from the kill, "she kisse[s] Budhni with her unwashed mouth."

A great deal more can be said about Mahasweta's articulation of the negotiative, strategic postcolonial in the figure of the gendered subaltern. I will do no more than comment on her use of the word *bonno*, which I have translated as "wild" in the following passage: "A great thirst dances in her blood. Collector, Collector, I'm almost there. Collector wants her a lot. . . . With how much violence can Collector want her? How many degrees Fahrenheit? Is his blood as wild as Mary's? As daring?"

What blood is named "wild" here? The blood of the forest-dwelling tribals? (The word *bonno* literally means "of the forest.") Or the blood of the violating Australian? (In its signifying scope, *bonno* also means "brute.") A group of bourgeois feminist English professors, intellectuals, and organizational activists, strongly charged with ethnicist pride in its own place, thought that the word could only mean Mary's return to tribal authenticity.[34] Mahasweta's peculiar burden might well be that the wildness of the blood is both Mary and Oraon and purely neither.

I hope it is clear by now that, in the space that I occupied in front of the New York audience at the Dia Art Foundation that evening, the demand that only the Indian tribal can speak as the Indian tribal for the Indian tribal at their tribunal tries mightily to make invisible the mechanics of production of that space, this book. By those demands, Gayatri Spivak attitudinizing on the occasion of Mahasweta Devi writing about the tribal can be at best cathartic. Attend rather to this: my contractual situation as a postcolonial is in a place where I see claims to the subjectship of alternative histories coming, and becoming called for, in an often unexamined way. A literary pedagogy, choosing texts carefully, can at least prepare another space that makes visible the fault lines in slogans of the European Enlightenment—nationalism, internationalism, secularism, culturalism—the bulwark of nativism, without participating in their destruction. This, strictly speaking, is de(con)structive pedagogy. Like all good teaching in the humanities, it is hopeful and interminable. It presupposes and looks forward to a future anterior of achieved solidarity and thus nurses "the present." In the strictest sense, then, (para)logical: morpho-genetic (giving rise to new ways of reading, writing, teaching in the strongest sense), without terminal teleological innovation. Its "present" is a field of value coding, in a sense of "value" that is not logically (but not necessarily chronologically) prior to the economic; the political, the economic, the affective are entangled there.

In the contractual site that held speaker and audience that evening, or in this book, the remaking of history is a persistent critique, unglamorously chipping away at the binary oppositions and continuities that emerge continuously in the supposed account of the real. The cultural politics of repetition are in play with the strategically necessary gesture politics of rupture attendant upon the political independence that is the minimal requirement for "decolonization." As it happens, generations like "my own" (I could just hear the purist murmur of "essentialism" from theoretically correct friends), straddling the transition, and groups like my own (again!), diasporics circulating within patterns of "internal colonization," can put one item on the agenda when they speak to a group like "that audience" (again and again!), serious metropolitan radicals, when the speakers belong to the trade of cultural work: I repeat, a persistent unlearning of the privilege of the postcolonial elite in a neocolonial globe.

A false hope, as I now repeat.

CHAPTER THREE

How to Read a "Culturally Different" Book

ONE OF THE PAINFULLY slow results of the demand for a multi-cultural canon is the inclusion of Global English on the college curriculum. The results of this uncertain victory are often dubious, because neither teacher nor student is usually prepared to take the texts historically and/or politically. This chapter is an attempt to walk a conscientious teacher through a limpid novel, R. K. Narayan's *The Guide*.[1]

In the late 1950s, the term "Indo-Anglian" was coined by the Writers' Workshop collective in Calcutta, under the editorship of P. Lal, to describe Indian writing in English. Although the term has not gained international currency, it is useful as a self-description.

The first question to be asked of a piece of Indo-Anglian fiction is the author's relationship to the creative use of his or her native language. This question is not identical with that asked by Ngũgĩ wa Thiong'o, referenced in Chapter 1 of this book.

The complexity of Ngũgĩ's staging of the relationship between English and Gikuyu also involves the relationship between dominant literature and subordinate orature. To draw that parallel in an admittedly asymmetrical way, we should have to consider the millennially suppressed oral cultures of the aboriginals of India. We have not yet seen an Indo-Anglian fiction writer of tribal origin; we are far from seeing one who has gone back to his or her own oral heritage. Indeed, anyone aware of the ruthless history of the expunging of tribal culture from the so-called Indic heritage and the erasure of the tribal paraph—the authenticating flourish above or below the signature—from Indian identity will know that the case is difficult to imagine.

By contrast, literary activity is usually prolific in the mother tongue of the writer of Indo-Anglian prose or poetry. The writer of Indo-Anglian literature might represent this dynamic base of regional public culture as if it were no more than a medium of private exchange or a rather quaint simulacrum of the genuine public sphere. This artificial separation of public and private is, strictly speaking, a cultural class-separation. The relationship between the writer of "vernacular" and Indo-Anglian literatures is a site of class-cultural struggle. This struggle is not reflected in personal confrontations. Indeed, the spheres of Indo-Anglian writing and vernacular writing are usually not in serious contact. By "class-cultural struggle" is meant a struggle in the production of cultural or cultural-political identity. If literature is a vehicle of cultural self-representation, the "Indian cultural identity" projected by Indo-Anglian fiction and, more obliquely, poetry can give little more than a hint of the seriousness and contemporaneity of the many "Indias" fragmentarily represented in the many Indian literatures.

In fact, since the late 1960s, as metropolitan (multi)cultural studies began to establish itself through the good works of the Birmingham School, inaugurated by Richard Hoggart's *The Uses of Literacy* and continued under the able direction of Stuart Hall, the Indo-Anglian writer began to acquire and transmit an increasingly "postcolonial" aura of cultural self-representation.[2] How does international cultural exchange of this sort operate? This question should be kept alive, not answered too quickly. A too quick answer, taking the novels as direct expressions of cultural consciousness, with no sense of the neocolonial traffic in cultural identity and the slow and agonizing triumph of the migrant voice, would simply see them as repositories of postcolonial selves, postcolonialism, even postcolonial resistance.

However difficult it is to fix and name the phenomenon, one might consider it carefully because its tempo is so different from the boomerang-effect of the cultural shuttle in fully telematic (computerized and videographic) circuits of popular culture. Consider merengue in New York: the artists are in Santo Domingo, the market is supported by the Dominicans in New York, and the trend changes from the original "pure" strain as fast as you can count. Consider Rap in South Africa, where the singers themselves acknowledge American influence, and remark on how African the U.S. groups sound; the South African newscaster considers this a cultural re-appropriation of what originated in Africa; and the U.S. group compliments the South African group on being so comprehensible in English, of having so little "African accent." Consider the Chicaricano "border art" of the Mexican artist Guillermo Gomez Peña that we discuss in "Teaching for the Times," Chapter 6 in this book.

The only Indo-Anglian postcolonialist novel in this telematic tempo is Shashi Tharoor's *The Great Indian Novel,* inspired by Peter Brook's *Mahabharata,* which prompted the author to read the *Mahabharata* for the first time, in its condensed English version as the play-script for Brook's production of the epic.[3] The novel is an amusing verbal comic-strip series superimposing the struggle among the great nationalists of the Indian Independence Movement upon the family feud at the heart of the ancient epic. Translation is immediate here. *Maha* is literally "great" and *Bharata,* all complexities of history and geography forgotten, can be taken as identical with the contemporary (Hindi) name for India. *Maha-Bharata* = Great India; the postcolonial politicians' fantasy to make the present identical with the hallowed past, and thus win votes for a politics of identity at degree zero of history.

This example remains an anomaly. The spoof is inaccessible to the international readership of Commonwealth literature. And the Indo-Anglian novel is simply not a part of "popular" culture on the subcontinent, whether global "kitsch" or indigenous "folk." To think of the Indo-Anglian novel, even in its aggressively postcolonial manifestations as "popular," is to think of *Sons and Lovers* as a novel of the international working class. The tragedy (or the bitter farce?) of *The Satanic Verses* is that, precisely through electoral manipulation in India, it became available to, though not read by, the "people" of whom it spoke.

By contrast, the general tempo of two-way traffic in the course of change in the Indo-Anglian novel in India and in its readership, institutional or otherwise, is less tractable. The change that we begin to notice in the early 1970s is an exuberantly mocking representation of the native language. In the wake of swiftly changing global cosmopolitan identities riding like foam on waves of diversified diasporas, what was an upper class, upwardly mobile, or upwardly aspiring private relationship to a vernacular in national peripheral space is literally "re-territorialized" as the public declaration of ethnic identity in the metropolitan space of the newish migrant writer, borrowing his or her discursive strategy from the field prepared for the new immigrant by the only slightly less new.[4] Although *The Satanic Verses* might be the classic case of this, the landmark text, before the preparation of its readership, is Desani's *All about H. Hatterr,* a virtuoso novel where "English" attempts to claim its status as one of the Indian languages (belonging to a national underclass) through the technique of sustained literal translation of the vernacular rather than islands of direct monstrous speech in a sea of authorial Standard English.[5]

Writers like R. K. Narayan (Nayantara Sehgal, Kamala Markandeya, Ruth Prawer Jhabwala, Mulk Raj Anand, Raja Rao, et al.) pre-date this hyperreal scramble for identity on the move.[6] The "internal evidence" for this is the stilted English of the dialogue in their novels, whenever it happens between the rural or underclass folk they often choose to represent, and of the representation of the subjectivity of such characters in so-called indirect free style.[7] The situation of the underclass, or rural characters, or yet of the language of indirect free style, is dealt with quite differently in the vernaculars. With this earlier group of reportorial realist writers, then, one must be especially aware of the relationship with the vernacular.

The group started publishing fiction in English well before Indian Independence in 1947. Narayan's first book, *Swami and Friends,* was published in 1935. The emergence of a mode of production of identity recognizably "postcolonial" by a younger group meant a setting wild of the private space of the mother tongue. Negotiated political independence set this earlier group adrift, away from the current from which the postcolonial monstrous would emerge. They became novelists of the nation as local color, the nostalgic rather than the hyperreal.

The representation of the temple dancer in *The Guide* stands out in this miniaturized world of a nostalgia remote from the turbulence of postcolonial identity. The story, given in flashbacks, in between an autobiography, in the book's present, of the male lead released from prison and sheltering in an imageless temple, to a devotee who authenticates his felicity as a saint, can be summarized as follows:

With the coming of the railway station, Raju's father's shop moves up in class. With his father's death, Raju is able to respond to this upward move. He becomes not only a railway store owner but also a flashy and resourceful guide of conducted taxi tours of local beauty spots. On such a tour he meets Rosie/Nalini, daughter of a temple dancer (henceforth *devadāsi*— female servants of the Lord), the dancing in her blood strictly suppressed, first by a personal ambition that prompts her to take a master's degree in Political Science, and second by an archaeologist/art historian husband. Raju the Guide seduces her, she comes to live with him, his mother leaves home with his scandalized uncle, he makes immense amounts of money by setting her up as a dancer and being her agent, and he goes to jail for forging her signature in order to prevent re-establishment of contact between herself and her husband. She disappears from the scene. After a brief stint in prison, he emerges and takes shelter in the temple. He attracts one follower and then, as a result, an entire village full of devotees. When he is urged to fast and stand knee-deep in water for twelve days to end a regional drought, he starts telling his story to Velan, his follower.

The novel is not arranged in this straightforward way. It begins with Raju talking to Velan in the temple. We are not aware that the account is a confession, for two contradictory motives bleed into each other: avoidance of the hardship of fast and penance, and avoidance of "enforced sainthood."[8] We only know these motives toward the end of the book. In the meantime, some of the chapters begin to move out of the frame narrative as regular flashbacks. To put it in code, the reader begins to say "yes" to Raju's past by inhabiting the roguish personality of a past character so unlike the present. That is the historically established power of the indirect free style of storytelling. The reader does not have to exercise his mind to get used to experiment. When the story makes no difference to Velan, the reader can say "yes" to that indifference as well.

(Given primitive distinctions such as first world–third world, self-other, and the like, I tend to classify readers by slightly less crude stereotypes. In that spirit, and in the strict interest of decolonizing the imagination, let it be proposed that, for the metropolitan reader or teacher reading or teaching Commonwealth literature, the limpid local color prose of this style is quite satisfactory. For the rather special Indian readership of Indo-Anglian fiction, this class-distanced hyperreal is also satisfying, perhaps because it conveys a cozy sense of identification at a distance, thus identity-in-difference. The person who reads "popular" vernacular literature for fun will not read *The Guide*. The reader of "high" vernacular literature will, if she reads English literature with her antennae up, be dissatisfied with the "subjectivity" opened up by the free indirect style, precisely because the limpid prose would seem a bit "unreal," a tourist's convenience directed toward a casual unmoored international audience.)

Narayan tells us that the novel was written in a hotel room in Berkeley, California. There is a sizable literature of displaced writers writing from abroad in the various vernacular literatures. *The Guide* has no need to make use of that convention. To classify readers in this way is a denial of contingency, which seems a particular loss when talking about literature. Deconstruction has taught us that taking contingency into account entails the immense labor of forging a style that seems only to bewilder.[9] If literary study is to work with established metropolitan colonial history, it seems best that one stay with the outlines of rational agency and give a hint of postcolonial heterogeneity according to the impoverished conventions of mere reasonableness.

This fake saint then becomes a sacrifice. To what? Faith is not, after all, reasonable. And the line between virtue and the sustained simulation (making something happen by insisting it is so) of virtue is hard, perhaps finally impossible, to fix. So the book can suggest, in the end, that perhaps Raju is a miracle-worker, after all: "Raju opened his eyes, looked about, and said, 'Velan, it's raining in the hills. I can feel it coming up under my feet, up my legs—' He sagged down" (p. 220). A nice bit of controlled indeterminacy there, resting upon one of the most firmly established European cultural conventions: transition from Christian psychobiography to Romantic Imagination.[10]

(In a broader field it is seen as the transformation of Christianity into "secular" ethics, theology into philosophy. Michel de Certeau and Michel Foucault have, among others, speculated about the relationship between these changes and the turn to capitalism.[11] The dominant Hindu "colonial subject" in India came to terms with his Hinduism with the help of the epistemic trick allowed (often clandestinely) by this shift. At the colonial limit, sacred geography thus became an interior landscape. The problem of irrational faith was interiorized into allegory in the narrowest possible sense. Religion as cultural allegory allowed the Indo-Anglian writer of the first phase to produce an immediately accessible "other" without tangling with the problem of racism or exploitation. Raja Rao is perhaps the most striking example of this.)

In the literary history of Britain, one reads this transition or transformation by way of the nineteenth-century project of re-writing Milton: by Blake, Wordsworth, Shelley. In Wordsworth's "Hail to thee, Urania!," Imagination is supposed at last to be triumphant.

Alas, this high register, where literary production is in the same cultural inscription as is the implied reader, cannot be employed for the epistemic ruses of the colonial subject. No Indo-Anglian writer of Narayan's generation can speak of his education in English literature without self-irony, however gentle. Narayan offers a vividly ironic account of his own education in English literature in chapters four, five, and six of his *My Days: A Memoir*. It would be difficult to imagine from this book that his conversations with his grandmother and the street-people might have taken place in his native Tamil. "Thus ended one phase of my life as a man of Madras; I became a Mysorean thenceforth."[12] This meant a bilingual move—from Tamil to Kannada—for an adolescent. Can one surmise that the bilingualness of the move was not significant for largely English-speaking Narayan? Of course, from this memoir or indeed, from the self-contained small-town world of *The Guide*, one would not be able to guess either that Tamil has one of the longest continuous literatures in India, and that both Tamil and Kannada were active in literary production and experimentation at the time of the writing of *The Guide*.[13] For example, the literary and cultural-political universe inhabited by Anantha Murthy, the Kannadese novelist, is at many removes of "concreteness" in terms of the weaving together of the fabric of national identity, torn from end to end in the current conjuncture. Native readers of Tamil and Kannada literature suggest that there might have been a surreptitious and unacknowledged one-way traffic between Indo-Anglian writing produced by Tamilian and Kannadese writers and the vernacular literatures in this case. This writer, whose mother tongue is neither, cannot vouch for this judgment without extensive research, although she is au courante in her own.

In Narayan's own estimation at least, the novel's core is the predicament of the male lead.[14] Rosie/Nalini is therefore merely instrumental for the progress of the narrative.

My method of considering this instrumentality will be "allegorical" in the most ordinary sense (one-to-one correspondence, as we used to say), or semiotic in the most formulaic way (this "means" that). This may be the only way in which the literary critic can be helpful for the study of culture and, for the historical study of the aftermath of colonialism and the postcolonial present. It is an enabling limitation, a découpage for the sake of the disciplines.[15]

Rosie/Nalini is, then, the remote instrument of Raju's enforced sanctity. How does Narayan represent her so that the narrative of Raju's transformation may be revealed? Let us notice, first of all, that she is absent at the actual transformation, the present of the frame-narrative. She is only instrumental in getting him to jail. Release from that chain of events, release from imprisonment, is release into the road to sanctity.

The story is not just a boy-girl story, however. It is also a decently muted tale of access to folk-ethnicity (protected by that nice indeterminacy already mentioned). Here the main burden of the frame narrative is that Raju transforms Rosie into Nalini or lotus. But that is represented as an inauthentic entry into folk-ethnicity. The author makes clear that that attempt was the vulgarization of culture in the interest of class-mobility. Raju transforms Rosie into Miss Nalini, and, as her impresario, becomes besotted by his access to money and the attendant social power. Within the miniature field of Indo-Anglian fiction this authorial judgment is the celebration of tradition over modernity that its readership can devoutly endorse, at a tasteful distance. And, since Raju's obsession interferes with his obsessive love for Rosie, it resonates on the boy-girl register as well. It is by a neat and accessible irony that his forgery, prompted by "love" (he wants to keep Rosie from further contact with her husband), is mistaken for "love of money."

Rosie has tried to lift herself from the patriarchal ethnos by going the route of institutional Western education. But dancing is in her blood. If the railway train as a harbinger of progress and class-mobility is a cliche of the literature of imperialism, the *nautch* (dance) girl is a cliché of the imagining of British India. Raju is first taken by her in a passage indicating the rhythm in her blood:

> He [a derelict cobra man] pulled out his gourd flute and played on it shrilly, and the cobra raised itself and darted hither and thither and swayed. . . . She watched it swaying with the raptest attention. She stretched out her arm slightly and swayed it in imitation of the movement; she swayed her whole body to the rhythm—for just a second, but that was sufficient to tell me what she was, the greatest dancer of the century. (p. 58)

But Raju the entrepreneur cannot bring Nalini to life. It is her husband the gentleman-archaeologist who wins her back, at least in spirit. There is a bond between them in their passion for their cultural labor. Narayan has the modernist literary tact not to conclude her story, and Raju's last word on it shows his inability to grasp the mysterious bond. Reporting to him in prison, his secretary Mani explained that

> the only article that she carried out of the house was the book [her husband's book about the caves—a counter-Guide that we never get to read]. . . . Mani said, "After the case, she got into the car and went home, and he got into his and went to the railway station—they didn't meet." "I'm happy at least about this one thing," I said. "She had the self-respect not to try and fall at his feet again." (p. 205)

She is not needed in the last phase of the book: the phase of ethnicity over culture. India is folk-kitsch. E. M. Forster had written the "Temple" section, in this conviction.[16]

Although (or perhaps precisely because) the dancer is not central to the novel, a feminist reader or teacher in the United States might wish to know a little more about the temple dancer in order to grasp the representation of Rosie/Nalini.

The source book most readily available to her is Frédérique Marglin's *Wives of the God-King*.[17] Although for most metropolitan teachers of Commonwealth literature the terrain of *The Guide* exists as "India," the reader might have specified it to herself as Southern India from internal and external signals.[18] The state where Marglin did her fieldwork is not Narayan's South, but Orissa, where the Southeast meets the Northeast. How does the Orissan *devadāsi* (or *dei*), imprisoned in her own temple-community of women in a gender-hierarchy that mixes "tradition" and "modernity" in its unique blend, communicate with her counterpart in the South, in Mysore or Bangalore? Certainly not in their mother tongue. In fact, it is unrealistic to think that there can be actual situations of communication between them. These are subaltern women, unorganized pre-capitalist labor, and it is not yet possible to think of them as Indian collectivities of resistance, although the Indian Constitution appropriately thinks of them collectively as victims and thus offers a redress that has never been fully implemented in the individual states. Indeed, current feminist activism around this issue, dependent upon the direction and organization of the women's movement in various regions, is much more forceful and visible in the states of Maharashtra, Karnataka, and Tamil Nadu (roughly Narayan's area) than in Orissa, Marglin's field of work. The language-barriers that allow the Indo-Anglian writer precisely to represent one of them as our implausible Rosie keep her locked in isolated communities. The patriarchal system that informs *The Guide* so that Raju can finally occupy the temple as saint makes the temple her prison.

(There are a very few rags-to-riches stories of the daughters of temple dancers becoming great artistes, but Narayan's focus on Rosie is too slight for us to feel that this is the point of her representation. To emphasize that point, Rosie's entry into secondary and post-secondary education would have had to be dramatized.) Is literature obliged here to be historically or politically correct? Because it is not, this sort of literary criticism is a category mistake, derided as "politically correct." But it should be considered that literature is not obliged to be formally excellent to entertain, either. Critical evaluation is dismissed as "pedantic" by the real consumers of popular culture. Here again is class-negotiation. This way of reading, pointing at its cultural political provenance, can be useful in the specific situation where the heterogeneous agency of the colonized in postcoloniality cannot be imagined, although the details of colonial history are known professionally.

As the feminist reader moves into *Wives of the God-King,* she notices a peculiar blandness in the reporting of the *devadāsi*'s prostitution. This curious apologetic finessing of judgment, invariably called cultural relativism, has become an unavoidable mark of the field-investigator who has become sensitive to the risks of neocolonial knowledge but will compromise with it. This is perhaps exacerbated by the investigator who learns the social practice as artistic performance (in this case Odissi dance), now the property of the middle and upper middle classes.[19]

The transmogrification of female dance from male-dependent prostitution to emancipated performance helps the indigenous colonial elite engage in a species of "historical (hysterical) retrospection" which produces a golden age.[20] Raju in *The Guide* is represented as entering the hallucination without any particular historical thickening.

Dr. Marglin's traffic with a great many Indian men, acknowledged in her book, is coded as exchange with a student of the *devadāsi* system or a student of Odissi, eager cultural self-representation in response to altogether laudable white interest in our heritage; rather different from the traffic between men and women described in her chilling prose. It would be impossible to suspect from this account that feminists have internationally battled and are today battling (not the least in India) against this view of the role of the woman in reproduction:

> The chastity of the wives of the temple brahmins is crucial not because it is they who transmit the characteristics of the caste and the kula to their children, but to ensure that only the produce of that species of seed that has been sown in it is the one that will be reaped and not the produce of some other species of seed. A woman, like a field, must be well guarded, for one wants to reap what one has sown and not what another has sown, since the produce of a field belongs to its owner. Such an idea was expressed long ago by Manu: . . . . This theory by the ancient law-giver certainly corresponds well to what is the case today in Puri. . . . Women are like the earth, and the earth is one, although it is owned by many different types of men. . . . The woman palace servant (dei) told me that her mother answered her query [about menstruation rituals] . . . in the following way: . . . "God has taken shelter" (in you). . . . "You have married and you'll do the work of the god . . .". The "work of god" and "the shelter of the god" she said referred to the fact that from that time on she would start her rituals in the palace and would become the concubine of the king.[21]

Wives of the God-King is a thoroughly vetted and rather well-known book. It is hard to imagine that it was published in 1985! The author takes at face-value the invocation of the golden age by orientalist and bourgeois alike. The usual anti-Muslim explanation of the decay of Indian (read Hindu Aryan) culture under the Muslim rule, and hence the deterioration of the *devadāsi*s into prostitutes draws this from the author:

> This view is representative of many if not most English-educated Indians today. The historical research necessary to confirm or refute the above statement was beyond my abilities, even if the records were available, which is highly doubtful. My training has prepared me to do ethnography, which happily the particular historical circumstances of Puri made possible.[22]

"Ancient sources" are so regularly proclaimed, that our inquisitive feminist literary critic will probably be daunted away; especially since there are repetitions of post-colonial piety and the claim that if Dr. Marglin had been born a hundred years ago, her views would have coincided with those of Annie Besant, the noted Theosophist. Would the feminist investigator check this claim by consulting Mrs. Besant's biography? Amrita Srinivasan has given a fine analysis of the relationship between the Theosophist interest in saving the dance rather than the dancer and the establishment of Western-style residential schools for dance, like Kalākshetra (lit. the artistic field) in Chennai (then Madras) by the indigenous elite.[23]

There seems nothing to link the women in Marglin with the world of *The Guide* except to imagine that the daughters of one of these hapless women had been able to enter the educational system with nothing but her mother's good wishes as her resource.

And if the Indian colleague or friend who is the U.S. feminist's "native informant" happens to be a not untypical woman from the emancipated bourgeoisie, the work of her own uneven emancipation will have been undertaken by the slow acculturation of imperialism, that is, in its neocolonial displacement, the topic of our discussion. If this imaginary informant happens to be a careful student of the dance-form, she has learned the entire social ritual as ritual reverently museumized in an otherwise "modern" existence. She might see the dance as directly expressive of female resistance in its very choreography. The result of this innocent ethnic validation is Cultural Studies as alibi.

Vigilance, then, about class as we read the novel and look for background. Impatient non-major students of required English courses often mutter, Can we not just read for pleasure? Their teachers were taught to offer a consolation from U.S. New Criticism, Knowing the rules of the game does not detract from pleasure. But reading in the style of Cultural Studies, looking into the class-provenance of form and information, may not enhance pleasure. The most it can do is to give a clue to the roadblocks to a too-quick enthusiasm for the other, feeding "the missionary impulse" surreptitiously, in the aftermath of colonialism, even as it attempts to offer untrained resistance to the arrogance of the discipline.

One of the most tedious aspects of racism as the science of the everyday is the need to refer every contemporary act of life or mind performed by the cultural other to her cultural origin, as if that origin were a sovereign presence uncontaminated by history. In order to stem that tide vis-à-vis Narayan's novel, some brief and inexpert comments on the so-called ancient texts are offered below. My gratitude to Dr. Mandakranta Basu, who has helped locate the texts.

There are no known direct references to dancing in the temple in the oldest books of dance theory and trade talk on dance practice, *Nātya Sāstra* and *Abhinaya Darpaṇa*. (The current debate seems to be between where the limits of dance and drama are fixed.) There is a passage in the

Nātya Sāstra (second or third century CE) on how to transform the body into a space of writing and turning. The yoking of dance to the body is in order proficiently to lead toward what is signified by the body as a collection of *akṣara* or letters. "Leading toward"—*abhinaya*—is crudely translated "drama" by English translators, so that even without the *devadāsi* we fall into the Aristotelianized problematics of mimesis. There is no mention of temple-dancing in this early text, though an interesting distinction between the improper and proper use of the signification-representing body, in consecrated lust and in the consolidation of attraction respectively, is made.[24]

A millennium later, the *Nātya Sāstra* is being legitimized as holy knowledge or *Veda* in the *Sangitaratnākara*.[25] *Lāsya* or carnal affection is being recuperated into theogony. The word relates to the root *las,* which, at its most rarefied, means "to appear in shining." "Phenomenality" itself, captured in German *Erscheinung,* meaning, in classical Greek, roughly, "coming to appear."

It is not surprising that the *Sangitaratnākara* also gives a list of social rather than interpersonal occasions where dance is appropriate: coronations, great feasts, voyages, valedictions to divine images after periodic festivals, marriages, meetings with the beloved, entries into the city, the birth of a son. Dance enhances the auspiciousness of all these activities. No temple dancers yet. *Lāsya* can still mean only dance, which belongs to the ceremonial life of kings and well-placed householders.

The first mention of temple dancing is located in the mediaeval collection of stories called *Kathāsaritsāgara* or the *Sea of Stories*.[26] Aparna Chattopadhyay offers a theory of West and Central Asian provenance and offers connections with Corinth and Phoenicia. Legitimation by "Vedic" origin becomes all the more interesting.

Of particular interest is the twelfth-century *Kuttinimatam* (The Art of the Temptress) by Damodargupta. Here the stylization of seduction through body movements is taught as a practice by an older prostitute to a younger.[27]

Who knows exactly how *lāsya* changes into the art of lust? Muslim conquest is about as useful as the International Jewish Conspiracy. Words change meaning bit by bit, here-excess, there-lack. We find fossils of "earliest use" and strain this intimate mystery of linguistic change at ease from the incomprehensible social field of manifestation and concealment and sublate it into one line of a dictionary.[28] Any history that tries to imagine a narrative of the subaltern woman's oppression must imagine that familiar lexicographical space, that line in the dictionary, into the uncanny, the strange in the familiar. That space is the mute signature of the process by which the woman becomes a ventriloquist, beginning to act as an "agent" for *lāsya*. If this painful invitation to the imagination does not produce the disciplinary writing of history, then, as an apologetic outsider, I would submit that it might strengthen the discipline to recognize it as a limit.[29]

As part of preliminary on-site research, I viewed documentary footage shot by Dr. Veena Sethi when she traveled with the Indian National Commission on Self Employed Women in 1987. I discovered the existence of this footage on a research trip to India in December 1990. In that material, there is a discussion, in the presence of the temple pimps, between the *devadāsi*s and the activists. Some resistance to rehabilitation can be sensed in that conversation. This may be due to the presence of the pimps, to the class-separation between activist and subaltern, to the bitter awareness of the absence of follow-up to keep "the new way of life in place," and/or to patriarchal ventriloquism.[30]

If the *devadāsi* cannot speak to an unreconstructed subalternist history, and in the entrepreneurial fantasy of Indo-Anglian fiction, she also cannot speak by way of capital logic.

(*Shramshakti* [labor-power], the impressively heavy report of the Commission, published in 1988, mentions the encounter with the *devadāsi*s in a few paragraphs in the prefatory material and moves on to "regular" prostitutes:

> Another group of women represented at this Pune meeting were the Devadasis, of whom there are many here. Most of them are girls of poor, landless, low caste families who dedicate their girls to the service of God. Their "services" are taken for granted by upper class men. Although this practice is sanctioned by tradition and religion, these women usually end up in prostitution or begging. There is no one to look after them when they grow old, and no source of income. Some of them develop diseases which remain untreated. In this meeting, they requested education for their daughters, old age homes, and some income generation programme. A blind woman asked for reservation for the blind in jobs, and special training in telephone exchanges, chalk making, or cane making. At the Kolhapur Devadasi Vikas Centre, there were 50 devadasis present. Shantibai said that she was dedicated to the Devi because her father had promised (God) to do so if he got a son. Now her father is old and blind, and that son is in jail. The Commission heard numerous similar cases: they had been dedicated to God in exchange for a son. Chhayabai and Ratnabai said they were made devadasis purely because of poverty. "There was not enough at home to feed everyone." So they lived in the temple and got fed there. At the age of 13 they started serving the devi with men, and started bearing children. In all cases,

the men do not stay with the devadasi or the children. Then the devadasis have to resort to begging. On Tuesday and Friday near temples they have some income out of begging alms. But generally they have lost their capacity to earn by hard honest labour. Their priority is education for their children, which is problematical. Because the father's name is not given, the children are often not admitted.)[31]

This report was published three years after Marglin's book. The tenor of the conversations seems somewhat different. The reader is convinced of the contrast between the U.S. anthropologist and the Indian activist. (Although a single example does not prove a case, a single counter-example makes human generalizations imperfect.) I am nonetheless arguing that even an effort as thoughtfully organized as SEWA's cannot allow the agency of the *devadāsi* to emerge, because she is not written in the idiom of organized or unorganized labor, self-employment or other-employment (autocentrism vs. extraversion in broader registers), namely, capital logic.[32]

In the body of the report, the "occupation" *devadāsi* does not emerge in the many tables. The master-list, included in the chapter headed "Demographic and Economic Profile," includes thirty "types of skill." The last two are "others" and "no skill." The percentage distribution is Rural: 0.97 and 89.69 and Urban: 3.26 and 69.48. How would the *devadāsi* be docketed? Is *lāsya*—the convincing representation of lust—still her skill?

There is no reason at this point not to credit the tiny but significant report of their agency (out of which comes demand): "Their priority is education." There can be no doubt that education is perceived by them as a way out of the vicious impasse of female proletarianization (reduced to nothing but your body) outside of capital logic. It is not difficult for R. K. Narayan to put his finger on this pulse. But we are concerned with another story: that at the utterly remote other end of the trajectory denoted by "education" (international conferences), one must still engage in the question of "decolonizing the imagination." I should be able to say right away that one of the important tasks of the local women's movements in the *devadāsi* areas is to fight in an organized way against the lethal requirement of "the father's name." The novel can ignore this hurdle and present the query as coming from Raju's mother, and immediately deflected by Raju himself—a proof of his masculine ingenuity. But we, decolonizing our imagination, must admit that, even if this first barrier is crossed, and justifiably, in the imagination of these hapless infirm *devadāsis*, education is an instrument of upward class-mobility. These women are correct in perceiving that it is class-jumping that gives the woman "freedom" in patriarchy (and access to feminism as a matter of choice).[33]

If their daughters and granddaughters emerge for the "New Europe" as objects of domination and exploitation only when they emerge in the "New Europe" as migrant labor, this obscure moment of the agency of the infirm *devadāsi*s ("their priority is education for their children") remains a negligible part of a minor agenda, rather than the most serious necessity for educational reform "originating" out of a subaltern or subproletarian priority. This is the question not of militant centers of localized "pedagogy of the oppressed," but of overhauling the presuppositions in general national education. If the subaltern—and the contemporary *devadāsi* is an example—is listened to as agent and not simply as victim, we might not be obliged to rehearse decolonization interminably from above, as agendas for new schools of postcolonial criticism. But the subaltern is not heard. And one of the most interesting philosophical questions about decolonizing remains: who decolonizes, and how?

Let us get back on the track of our feminist teacher. She will encounter a debate about the "real" *devadāsi*: Was the "real" *devadāsi* a "free woman, an artist?" Is her present condition a result of the collusion between colonial and nationalist reformists, supported by men of her own community who stood to gain by her fall?

Amrita Srinivasan advances an affirmative answer to this question. She offers a challenge to the critical imagination when she "anthropologizes" colonial reform and asks us to consider the ways in which it rewrote its object: "If sacrificial infanticide and sati had been banned earlier as 'murder,' then by the late nineteenth century temple-dancers were being presented as 'prostitutes,' and early marriage for women as 'rape' and 'child-molestation'" (AS, pp. 178–179). She situates the Theosophist impulse mentioned by Marglin: "The British government officials and missionaries were not slow to play up non-Brahmin suspicion of Indian nationalism, coming as it did from the largely Brahmin-dominated Theosophical circles and Congress alike" (AS, p. 197). Marglin treats Orissa; Srinivasan treats Tamil Nadu (R. K. Narayan's Madras). And she is on target about the appropriation of the dance form by the elite:

> By 1947, the programme for the revival of sadir [the name of the dance-form of the Tamil *devadāsi*s] as Bharatanatyam, India's ancient classical dance, was already well underway with the patronage and support of Brahmin dominated Congress lobbies of elite Indians drawn from all parts of the country. (AS, p. 197)

Her analysis of the precolonial *devadāsi*'s controlling position within "the efficacy of the temple as a living centre of religious and social life, in all its political, commercial and cultural aspects" (AS, p. 184) is indeed an attempt at decolonizing the imagination, however difficult it might be to agree that "the conscious theological rejection [on the part of the *devadāsi?*] of the harsh, puritanical ascetic ideal for women in the bhakti sects, softened for the *devadāsi* the rigours of domestic asceticism in the shape of the widow, and the religious asceticism in the shape of the Jain and Buddhist nun" (AS, p. 191).

If one must see conscious agency here, one might think of Marx's suggestion that the capitalist carries the subject of capital. For although it is no doubt true that in Tamil Nadu the *devadāsi* was free of marriage and domestic duties, Srinivasan herself shows us that there can be no doubt that the *devadāsi's* exceptional sexual status was tightly and gender-divisively controlled in the interest of economic production:

> In the *nāgeswaram* tradition the women of the group were scrupulously kept out of public, professional life. . . . Married girls were not permitted to specialise in the classical temple dance and its allied music. . . . The *devadā-sis* represented a badge of fortune, a form of honour managed for civil society by the temple. . . . The *devadāsi* acted as a conduit for honour, divine acceptance and competitive reward at the same time that she invited *"investment,"* economic, political and emotional, in the deity. (AS, pp. 186, 183; emphasis added)

In this context, to claim that "the *devadāsi* stood at the root of a rather unique and specialised temple artisan community, which displayed in its internal organisation the operation of pragmatic, competitive and economic considerations encouraging sophisticated, professional and artistic activity" (AS, p. 192) might be to emphasize social productivity isolated from forces and relations of production. Perhaps in reaction against the colonial-nationalist elite collaboration, Srinivasan has created a bit of a static utopian past as well. She is surely right in noticing the interest of the men of the group in pushing through colonial reforms so that the *devadāsis'* economic "power" could be broken. But to perceive these forces as supervening upon a freely functioning structure seems unconvincing. In fact the *devadāsi* structure was subsumed in a general patriarchal structure. As Gail Omvedt puts it: "Can any special section of women be free of patriarchy in a patriarchal society?"[34]

Srinivasan's utopian solidarity for these competitive, robustly celibate prostitutes (her Indo-centric re-definition of "celibacy" is her boldest attempt at unsettling our imagination) is combined with contempt for contemporary popular culture which must also be examined:

> In the midst of new forms of vulgarity surrounding the dance profession today, such as the commercial cinema, it is the *devadāsi* tradition alone

which is propagated by the elite schools as representative of the ancient and pure *Bharatanatyam.* . . . If the *devadāsi*'s dance was a sacred tradition worth preserving and the legislation (justified though it was on the grounds of anti-prostitution) came down with a punitive hand not on prostitutes in general but on the *devadāsi* alone—why did the *devadāsi* need to go? (AS, p. 198)

This question cannot be asked alone but must be put in the context of broader questions: Why did precapitalist institutions disappear under imperialism? Why can the *devadāsi* not be fully captured in capital logic today? Srinivasan's own economic argument would suggest that this pre-colonial economic institution was "supplemented" by capital-formation. The *devadāsi* had to go not only because she was the member of a non-Christian female artist's community who challenged notions of female chastity (Srinivasan's argument) but because the structure of competition and production in the community was precapitalist (also her argument). Because of her functionalist utopianism, she cannot see that the commodification of woman's body in art in the commercial cinema is not different in kind from its imperfect commodification in the commercial temple. They are two links on the chain of displacement of capitalist/colonial production.

Let us attempt to project this sequential displacement onto a cross-section of class-stratification:

a) As Gail Omvedt suggests, the contemporary predicament of the *devadāsi* is a social tradition pressed into the service of capitalism ("pimps from the Bombay prostitution industry pay for the dedication ceremony, and often pay something to the girl's parents, in order to directly recruit the girl for a commercial brothel in Bombay").

b) The *devadāsi* dance forms of Odissi and Bhāatanātyam have, as their felicitous goals, the commodification of superstars in "high" cultural performances. (On the authority of a male dancer, reputedly the son of a *devadāsi,* now a regular teacher of classical dance in Puri, the actual performance of the *devadāsi*s was much more improvisatory; the various stages of the dance were not as fixed.)

c) The *devadāsi* dance forms in the convention of the musical film commodify women's bodies in "popular" cultural performance. With this projection, the debate about the *devadāsi* would be as fully inscribed in women's class-stratification as the sources of metropolitan information about the cultural other.

Do *devadāsi*s visit the commercial cinema? What have they thought of the film version of *The Guide?* It seemed impertinent, indeed absurd, to put the question to the oldest living *devadāsi* in Puri, a woman ravaged by poverty and disease, one of Marglin's informants.

The film is an indigenous translation of Narayan's novel. It is part of the immensely popular internationally distributed and prolific Bombay Film industry. Here *The Guide* is lifted onto an altogether broader canvas. Almost every detail of the film recorded below is absent in the novel and in contradiction with its spirit.

Folabo Ajayi, a renowned dancer from Nigeria, said recently to Sanjukta Panigrahi, an internationally renowned cultural performer of Odissi, that she had been partially prepared for Ms. Panigrahi's live performance by the many filmic representations of Indian dance that she had seen.[35] Thus the "popular," scorned by the Indo-Anglian novelist, and treated with amused contempt by his or her Indian readership, can mediate the relationship between practicing artists.

The film thus speaks for India, as does Indo-Anglian fiction. The translation of the absent Tamil-Kannadese specificity into Hindi makes nonsense of the material situation of the *devadāsi*. The terrain of the film is now Rajasthan, an area that allows the regulation long-skirt costume popular in Hindi film.

Narayan is apart from "the people," a ruefully apologetic but affectionate commentator. "He never misses an eccentricity of Indian English," offers *The Times* of London as a jacket blurb. *The Guide* in the Hindi film version is the condition and effect of the vox populi. As such, the film brings into bold relief the multiculturalism of (the now-precarious) official Indian self-representation, the religious tolerance of the Hindu majority that was still ideologically operative in the Nehruvian atmosphere of the 1960s, and the protected subject/object status of the woman in love and performance ("Your caste is the same as Uday Shankar's and Shantha Rao's," says the film's Raju, mentioning two famous Indian dancers, the histories of whose production are about as different as can be). These cultural generalizations catch a moment in postcolonial history that still hung on to the shreds of the dream of decolonization immediately after Independence, especially in the first two areas. The violence of the translation of the English novel into the national language (not the appropriate vernacular) forces into the open the relay between Empire and Nation, English and Hindi, and the rivalry between.

At this stage, the American girl-reporter is still the boorish outsider. The sequence of the reporter questioning the dying and saintly Raju is repeated in *Gandhi*, but of course one dare not say that Attenborough cites *The Guide*.

The novel is in English, the film fights with it (in both senses), and neither scenario captures the different beat of Indian literatures. The film mocks the ugly American and gives shelter to vernacular heterogeneity in certain brief moments, under the paternalist arm of the multicultural nation. It is possible to suggest, although such suggestions are always debatable, that, since the Emergency of 1975, the de-emphasizing of the federal structure, the manipulation of electoral politics, the attempt at centralizing power, and the emergence of the new politics of fragmentary consolidation(s) of opposition, as well as the rise of Hindu fundamentalism; the presentation of multiculturality and Hindi as protector of the vernaculars is not part of the current "task of the translator" in India. The first item, re-programmed within dominant global capital, has now moved to the space of migrant postcoloniality. *The Satanic Verses* opens with the citation of a song from a 1960s film *Shri 420,* where the invocation of unity in diversity is even broader in scope.[36]

At the beginning of the film of *The Guide,* we have a scene where a betel-leaf vendor rattles off a list of the places from where the ingredients of the little betel-leaf pack of spices *(pān)* have come: the nuts from Mysore, the leaves from Calcutta, the limewash from Bikaner, the caoutchou from Bombay. And Raju answers back: You seem to be fostering national unity from your *pān*-stall alone. In the very next sequence, Raju the guide is shown managing at least two Indian languages and English with some degree of flair.

These two invocations of national unity stand at the beginning of the film, to "set the mood," as it were. The fight with English, however, plays an integral part in making the heavily moralized story come across to the reader. When Raju is first established as a holy man, two village priests challenge him with a Sanskrit *sloka* or couplet. Raju is of course clueless in Sanskrit. After an electric pause, he comes back at them in English: "For generations you've been fooling these innocent people. It's about time you put a stop to this!" The priests are bested, for they do not know English. The villagers rejoice. Raju is legitimized.

Of course Raju is himself a fraud as well. He has to be if the story is to remain a transformation story. But the seriousness of the message in English cuts across the mere story-line and indicates a major theme: the new nation will get rid of religious bigotry through the light of Western reason. The West is now to be used as an equal rather than a subordinate. This is the promise of decolonization; immediately broken by that other relay race: between colonialism and neocolonialism, and the rise of isolationist fundamentalism which stages the West only as violator.

A metropolitan focus on popular history sometimes denies this first confident hope of decolonization. It can also be argued that it is the denial of this hope by global capital and racism in postcoloniality and migrancy, and its popular dissemination, that has brought us to the general scene of super-state powers versus guerilla counter-warfare and particular scenes of domestic confusion and violence.

Let us review the situation schematically. (a) The gendered subaltern woman, the contemporary *devadāsi,* can yield "real" information as agent with the greatest difficulty, not the least because methods of describing her sympathetically are already in place. There is a gulf fixed between the anthropologist's object of investigation and the activists' interlocutor. She slips through both cultural relativism and capital logic. (b) The "popular" film forces the issues of the immediate post-decolonization nation up into view because it speaks to and from the "people" as it constitutes itself for representation and self-representation as the Constitutional subject; it also transforms itself into its asymmetrical opposite through the circuit of distribution—as commodity it performs the function of representing the nation to an international (though not inter-national) audience. (c) The Indo-Anglian novel in the colonial mode puts the lid on (a) and (b) by its apparent accessibility.

And an "Indian" commentator is not necessarily helpful. That is to fetishize national origin and deny the historical production of the colonial subject. Indo-Anglian fiction and Commonwealth literature have now been disciplinarized in Indian English departments. The history and management of the university in the colonies are by and large conservative. Here for example is a Reader in English at a reputable Indian university, sounding like the usual unproblematic *Reader's Guide:*

> The next important novel of our study should be *The Guide* (1958), which is perhaps the most widely discussed of Narayan's works. The book, which has all the ingredients of a commercial film (indeed it was made into one), both on the maturity of the comic vision and in the novelist's artistic sophistication shown in the treatment of his theme (a sophistication which was lacking in the earlier novels), transcends the limits of a seemingly bizarre story. The authenticity in the treatment of Raju, an ordinary tourist guide with no extraordinary qualities except a certain cunning with which he plays on the gullibility of the village folk and Rosie the dancer, shows Narayan's artistic restraint in projecting Raju as a saint. It is this restraint which makes Raju's character and Narayan's art look credible.[37]

Upon being questioned, the author of this passage dismissed the film as not faithful to the novel.[38] True and false, of course. In this passage the making of the film is parenthetical, and perhaps what one is discussing in the present essay is the relationship between the text and that parenthesis.

At the end of the film, English is withheld by the saintly and triumphant Raju. He is fasting, waxy, bearded and swathed—in some shots deliberately made up to look like a standing photograph of the nineteenth-century popular visionary Sri Ramakrishna, one of the most recognizable icons of liberated Hinduism. The reconciled Rosie—here the film diverges wildly from the novel—holds him up and an immense crowd is gathered. An American reporter appears. She is in safari clothes. She asks a few inane questions, "Do you believe in science," "Have you been in love," et cetera. The moribund saint answers in Hindi through an interpreter, and surprises her with an English-language answer in the end. The American answers with a delight that is, alas, still typical: "You speak English!" The journalist too denies history by conveniently mistaking the progressive bourgeoisie for the primitive.

Another important theme de-subtilized by the film is: Woman with a capital W. Rosie is a failed enterprise in the modernization of culture in the novel. In the film she appears in the house of an unreally opulent good-whore *devadāsi* mother who inserts her into the mainstream through marriage.

In response to the stylistic requirements of the morality play of decolonization, the greatest identity-change is undergone by Rosie's husband, who becomes the lascivious instrument of the *devadāsi*'s daughter's social liberation. In the novel he is rather an odd obsessive archaeologist who is troubled by his wife's dubious profession. He is privately christened "Marco" by Raju because his obsession puts Raju in mind of "Marco Polo," a cliché figure for the small-town guide. In the film he becomes that anomalous and detested thing, a Eurasian Indian (a reminder that we were not always "equal to the West"), whose last name becomes "Marco." Rosie is Rosie Marco before she becomes Miss Nalini.

Both Raju and Nalini become more and more like fashionable Delhi and Bombay undergraduates and young executives as their love progresses. Indeed, although the end of the film is ideologically most satisfying in terms of the new nationalism, this love-story is the part that, in context, is trend-setting.

This is also where "form" and "content" split apart to put into the field of vision the fault lines in the self-representation of the nation, precisely in terms of the woman as object seen. For this genre of musical film, especially in the 1960s, is always an elaborately staged frame for song and dance. These are Bombay musicals actively transforming the filmic conventions of the Hollywood musical and re-coding the myth of India in the process. What is remembered across classes, genders, nations—years afterward, in other countries—are the songs by famous artistes lip-synched by famous actors and actresses and, in *The Guide*, the spectacular solo and group dance numbers. Here the cultural good is most visibly de-authenticated and re-territorialized. In the strictest sense of commodity (a product produced for exchange) the three classical dance traditions of India, and multiple folk forms are put into a hopper, swirled around with free-form musical structuring to produce a global "India."

One of the most cliché items routinely noticed in Indian classical dance is the mudra—or the range of expressive hand-head-eye gestures. The Sanskrit word *mudrā* is also coin—a common concept-metaphor straddling the money-form and the simple semiotics of stylized gesture, capable of considerable elaboration, but incapable of incorporating contingency. It is also, characteristically, the word for engraving, imprint. It is not by chance, then, that it is through this already in-place value-form that the expressive repertoire of the Hollywood musical rushes in, culture-marked with the proper name "India," ready for exchange.

The film is plotted in easy doubles. If Raju is purified through jail and drought, Nalini is purified through her search for and discovery of Raju. In usual patriarchal fashion, that process is not shown but implied. Let us consider it through a few moments of the "real" time of our film, rather than the flashback temporality of the narrative.

At the jail gate, six months after Raju's good-conduct release, Raju's mother and Nalini arrive polarized, the former on foot from the village, the latter by car, just back from London. Their reconciliation starts the flashback in response to the mother's question: "If you were going to step out, why did you marry?"

In the flashback, her dance-impulse is opened up at her own request. One of the film stills, framed by the bare legs of the rural snake-dancer, shows us the couple caught in the gaze of the dancer, whose graphic symbol is shaped like the female sex. The focus of the riveted gaze of the couple is indeterminate.

But dancing as such is not important to the film's Rosie. It is revealed through a conversation between Rosie and Mr. Marco (where the juxtaposition of sculptured dancers and Rosie makes the point that he is not in touch with life) that Rosie needs to dance because Marco cannot give her a child. Thus the cultural politics of the film do not allow the commodity-value of the dance-woman to be anything more than a splendid distraction which gives national information outside the nation, unaffected by the forces fabricating "national identity" out of progressivism and nostalgia. The function of the novel (giving information without attention to its historical production) has more in common with the dynamic kitsch of the film's frame than one would suspect; it is just that the target-audiences are different. The transformation of the classical mudra (money-form of expressive equivalence) into the vocabulary of the musical comes to a climax in the final dance, ending this central part of the film, where Waheeda Rahman's eyes, arms, and hands combine an expressive (or free) understanding of gesture with vestiges of the (bound) traditional lexicon of the mudra, visible through the crescendo of music and tempo as she brings the refrain to its repeated conclusion: *"Hai, hai re hai, sainya be-iman"* (Alas, alas, [my] lover [is a] traitor). Whatever the eyes do, the mouth is fixed in a rictus that signals the separation of the dance from the direct expression of anguish or anger. From a complex set of perspectives, this is the *devadāsi* as living doll, stunningly expert in her art. Here the representation of *lāsya* is indeed again a skill, distanced by the work of the screen.

The first version of this essay was written in Princeton, New Jersey. The circulating library of videotapes in a Princeton shopping mall where I obtained a videotape of the film is one of thousands spread across the United States and indeed all countries where there is a sizable Indian immigrant presence. The value of the film in class-heterogeneous migrant subcultures has globalized the film differently from its earlier popular international presence, which continues on its own course. It has already been suggested that the current situation of the fabrication of "national" identity in India makes of the film an anachronism. This new globalization brings it clear out of the nation-theater, into the space of cosmopolitan diasporic culture, at the other end from the radical cacophony of *The Satanic Verses*. At the end of the opening sequence of the central movement of the film (Miss Nalini's dancing career), where she is shown as receiving a prize, the film cuts to Raju's gloating face. In the place of the original fadeout, we read the following message:

World Distribution
Esquire Electronics Ltd.
Hong Kong

There seems to be an appropriate if obscure typographic felicity that "Esquire" is in the copyright typeface of the U.S.-based men's magazine.

If the gendered subaltern, the young Maharashtrian *devadāsi* encountered by the SEWA group, is at one end of the spectrum, this message on the screen, inside as well as outside the film, points at the immense network at the other end. The space in between is not a continuity. It offers a cross-section where the travestied premodern marks the failure of modernization into the circuit of postmodernity. In the meantime, the muted modernism of the novel is in the classroom that molds the traditional disciplinary dominant in the pluralist academy.

The film accommodates two minor and completely outdated gestures toward Hindu-Muslim secularism quite absent in the novel. As Raju lies in the arms of his mother and Nalini, Gaffur (the Muslim taxi-driver from his days as a guide) arrives, drawn by rumor. The villagers will not let him enter. Raju insists. They embrace. And, on a more atmospheric level, a popular folksong, praying for rain, from what was then East Pakistan (now Bangladesh), is played in the film's otherwise Hindi songtrack. Since Bangladesh is a Muslim-majority area of the subcontinent, the prayer is addressed to Allah, and the Bengali is Urdu-ized enough for one line of the song to pass as Hindustani. Only one word needed to be altered and in the syllabic space released is inserted the name of Rama, the Hindu god-king who was Gandhi's totem, and in whose name India is being "ethnically cleansed" of its Muslim population in the 1990s, and lately, after the sobriety of electoral victories, claimed into a Hindu-ness (hindutva) deliberately mistranslated "Indianness." If in the embrace of Gaffur, the nineteenth-century Ramakrishna is glimpsed, the coupling of Allah and Rama in song brings the Mahatma himself to mind. In the contemporary context of religious strife, these overdetermined moments would have to be either suppressed or elaborated.

CHAPTER FOUR

The Double Bind Starts to Kick In

THIS IS AN EARLY articulation of the double bind, when I was still training teachers among the tribals in aspic, just about when I was beginning to put together the first version of this manuscript. I had not yet elaborated the thought of the double bind and it is now of some interest to see how it makes its appearance to define as a dilemma what has become a curious enablement, even in my professional solitude. I have inserted my current position as a running parenthetical commentary.

How is it possible to reconcile what I learn in the field with what I teach for a living? This chapter shows how an answer seems to have formulated itself in practice. (The answer was wrong because the cultural generalizations about the aboriginals were wrong. A grounding error, however.) The reconciliation is fractured. The problem could have been more easily solved if I had decided to "teach" (transcode for academic use) what I learned in the field. I hope you will work out from what follows why this is not an option for my stereotype of myself, why that solution would have been more a part of the problem, for me, than this incoherence. I give you the dilemma, as its reconciliation. The first section is about what I learn in the field: other women. (Now I would say I try to learn to learn from below: to engage with subalternity, not too different from the metaphor of the "suture" I used in "Righting Wrongs."[1]) The second section is about how that has changed what I teach for a living: literary criticism. (Now the meaning of "living" has expanded into a scary literality.)

To begin with, some presuppositions. Radical alterity—the wholly other—must be thought and must be thought through imaging. To be born human is to be born angled toward an other and others. To account for this the human being presupposes the quite-other. This is the bottom line of being-human as being-in-the-ethical-relation. By definition, we cannot—no self can—reach the quite-other. Thus the ethical situation can only be figured in the ethical experience of the impossible. This is the founding gap in all act or talk, most especially in acts or talk that we understand to be closest to the ethical—the historical and the political. We will not leave the historical and the political behind. We must somehow attempt to supplement the gap. To try to supplement the gap that founds the historical-political is a persistent critique. I believe it is in that spirit that Susan Bazilli, editor of *Putting Women on the Agenda,* writes: "In the present South African climate we are faced with the task of determining the future of law and its relationship to women. To do so we must always be cognizant of narrowing the gap between law and justice."[2]

I. What I Learn in the Field: Other Women

(I now find "other people's children" to be a concept-metaphor that works with urgency as shorthand for the democratic impulse that travels across the class-gender and city-country, North-South divide. Negotiating with the grounding presence of the sheer selfishness of reproductive heteronormativity, releasing it toward the other, as it were.)

Narrowing the gap between law and justice, as I understood it then, has something like a relationship with supplementing the founding gap between the historico-political and the ethical in a persistent critique. Let me get at this by way of a historico-political scenario. Let us consider a specific imaging of the other—not the general impossible figuration of the quite-other. Let us think rather of interested modern constructions of the other woman. "Modern" in this formulation would mean the period of "modernization," opened up by the end of World War II. It began with the establishment of the Bretton Woods Organizations, of the United Nations, of the General Agreement on Tariffs and Trade—between 1945 and 1948. It was the beginning of the end of European colonialism. The middle of our century is the initiation of neocolonialism. Colonialism had a civilizing mission of settlement. Neocolonialism had a modernizing mission of development. In the 1970s, the circuits of dominant capital became electronified. We entered the phase of "postmodernization." Robert B. Reich, the former U.S. Secretary of Labor, has called this "electronic capitalism."[3] (These are the beginnings of what we now call globalization.)

Territorial colonialism is not at an end, of course. But national liberation struggles and their image-making are no longer the dominant mode.
As Raymond Williams would suggest, in a formulation that I repeatedly
use, whether these residual discourses, the discourses of national liberation in the era of "modernization," emerge as alternative or oppositional is case-specific. This has become particularly true since the inauguration of the new economic world order, a new phase—the phase
of postmodernization—since 1989. The Report on the World Conference
on Women in Mexico City which led to the Declaration of Mexico issued
by the United Nations in the name of women in 1975 declares, "True
peace cannot be achieved unless women share with men the responsibility for establishing a new international economic order."[4] A decade later,
the Nairobi Forward-looking Strategies for the Advancement of Women
consolidated a plan which I have heard Bella Abzug describe as "the
beginning of global feminism." (The canny reader will take us forward
to Beijing, Beijing + 15, and its classification of "women's reality" by the
headings of the "Platform for Action." Although eminently efficient and
benevolent, these headings are in a double bind with the far less bold and
confident but far wiser premises of an aesthetic education.)

I believe the intent of the Declaration and the Strategies, as indeed of
the Platform for Action, to have been generally equitable toward women.
But the task of *establishing* a new world economic order could only de-
volve upon women in a dominant position. And, if it is correct to insist
that "because a form of production that does not correspond to the capitalist mode of production can be subsumed under its forms of revenue
(and up to a certain point this is not incorrect), the illusion that capitalist
relationships are the natural condition of any mode of production is further reinforced," then it cannot be denied that, without sufficient understanding of this, these international efforts have not necessarily created
an ethical relationship between the feminists of the dominant and the
object of their goodwill.[5] (I was just obliged, in 2010, to give this reminder to a tremendously benevolent young female sociologist in Estonia, commenting on eco-villages! The entry of the old communist bloc
onto the capitalist scene has changed nothing.)

In 1985, we had not yet fully acknowledged our access to a postmodern electronic capitalism in the field of gender ideology. International
feminist politics was still in the condition of modernizing. The condition
and effect of constructing other women was "women *in* development."
In the globalizing postmodern, she is embedded in the more abstract frame
of "Gender *and* development," which is the current slogan of the agencies
inaugurating our "modernity" that I mention above.

Modernization was international. Postmodernization is global. The boundaries of nation-states are now increasingly inconvenient, yet must be reckoned with, because the limits and openings of a particular civil society are state-fixed. The globalization of capital requires a post-state system. The use of women in its establishment is the universalization of feminism of which the United Nations is increasingly becoming the instrument. In this re-territorialization the collaborative international non-governmental organizations (NGOs) are increasingly being called an international civil society, precisely to efface the role of the state as agent of social redistribution. Saskia Sassen has located a new "economic citizenship" of power and legitimation in the finance capital markets.[6] Thus, elite, upwardly mobile, generally academic women of the new diasporas join hands with similar women in the so-called developing world to celebrate a new global public or private "culture" often in the name of the underclass or the rural poor as "other." (I now call this phenomenon, going far beyond feminism, "feudality without feudalism.")

This is one location of "the problem of thinking ethics for the other woman." How can we invite the operators of "Gender and Development" to experience ethics as the impossible figure of a founding gap, of the quite-other?

The hero of the colonial adventure was Europe, understood as Britain, Holland, Belgium, Spain, France, Portugal, Germany, and Italy (roughly in that order). At the moment of neocolonialism, the relay passed to the United States. In postmodern electronic capitalism, even the United States, conceived homogeneously, cannot be specified as the place of the self that causes the other. The self that runs the other machine has become so diversified that you can hardly give it the name of a continent or country. In Robert Reich's words: "Electronic capitalism enables the most successful to secede from the rest of society. It is now possible for top level managers, professionals and technicians to communicate directly with their counter-parts around the world." North and South, Self and Other are made indeterminate in this conjuncture. (Again, and in the bottom strata of society, the problem is bigger than women, although the usefulness of women as alibis for feudal radicalism remains intact.)

Although Eurocentric economic migration continues to rise, as the new North-South divide is exacerbated by the forces of economic restructuring, instituted to consolidate a uniform system of exchange the world over, ostensibly to establish a "level playing field," the assumption of a narrative continuity between colonialism and postcoloniality is not what belongs to globalization proper, which is more finance than trade. (Today, the ideological shift toward contemporaneity underscores the irrelevance of postcolonialism strictly defined. The organic intellectuals of globalization are alter-globalists.) It was the detritus of the old colonialisms that were pushed out by the ravages of neocolonialism into global labor export. Those tendencies made "multiculturalism" an issue in northwestern Europe as never before. Each nation-state in the European Union confronted the issue in its way, referring to either its old colonial experience or its position on the refugee circuit. Austria has its Albania; Holland its Suriname; Sweden its Estonia. The "cultural short fall" of this is showing itself in the inauguration of "postcolonialism" in these areas, academically.

If we want to track this slightly earlier field in the United States, we note that the inception of postcolonialism in this country was initially in response to the coming of age of so-called new immigration after Lyndon Johnson relaxed the quota system in 1965. It has mingled, of course, with the regular waves of economic migration and asylum-seeking that follow basically the same trends as in the case of northwestern Europe. The results of U.S. postcolonialism (more academic), and multiculturalism (more sociopolitical), have, however, been perceived to be in conflict with the demands of older minorities, especially African-Americans and Hispanics. Thus, the value coding of postcolonialism and multiculturalism cannot be the same in the European Community and the United States, although both are restricted phenomena where dominant images of the subordinate can still be color-coded, which is not the case, of course, in the global South. It is by way of a critique of this that I mention the postmodern global frame where Europe, the United States, and their others are no longer a clear-cut issue. Contemporaneity on the World Wide Web.

In Eurocentric economic migration rather than in electronic globality, as we travel down in class, the denial of the *cultural* subjectship of the abstract *rational* structures of "democracy" to the felicitous Euro-U.S. agent becomes active rather than reactive; patriarchal rather than analytic; and becomes transvalued and displaced into demands for preserving the inscription and superscription of the woman's body as an image of a cultural "self"—as the other in the self. These abyssal shadow games also involve woman, but they are not necessarily European images, or Euro-U.S. images. (This has now changed, haphazardly, in France and in Holland.) It takes place within indigenous patriarchy, and, however intimately they might be related to modernity, they are consolidated in the name of tradition. (This is now more discursively convenient as the modernity/tradition polarization is becoming less so.) And although the women themselves are ambivalent about these moves, they are often seen as mute victims and/or as Enlightenment subjects speaking up for diversity. As such, they provide an alibi for cultural absolutists who want to save them from their "culture" as well as cultural relativists who must see this as anticolonialism. An (unacknowledged) double bind.

In quite another way, the representation of "Europe" or the United States in the place of the self in such situations becomes suspect. For though the women and men demanding the inscription and superscription of the woman's body as cultural icon are themselves the recently hyphenated, they are also the new Europe or the new United States. In the United States this is even more problematic since the so-called Euro-Americans are themselves hyphenated and the natives have been "othered." Even this is not the whole story. For the hyphenated European or American is, of course, gender and class divided. Since it is the woman who is most citational, put within quotation marks in order to sanction all kinds of social actions—from automobile commercials to war to globalization itself—the upwardly mobile, hybrid female European or American can negotiate the class divide, and even the race divide, in the name of the gendered cultural subject acting for a fantasmatic Europe or, as the case may be, the United States. Whereas in the underclass, disappointed in the expectation of justice under capitalism, the migrant falls back upon "culture" as the originary figuration of that founding gap between the quite-other and the other, in patriarchy, this cultural figuration is a gendering internalized by both male and female, differently. This too is part of "the problem of thinking ethics for the other woman." How can we, in the face of discrimination from above, and alas, from minorities with a longer history of U.S. nationalization, however unjust, persuade the migrant or refugee that a systemic figuration of the violence of the founding gap closes the (im)possibility of ethics, especially given the history of patriarchal figurations, the (im)possibility of an ethics of sexual difference?[7] How can we, their academic champions, remind ourselves that the depredations of globalization—indiscriminate dam-building, patenting indigenous knowledge, pharmaceutical dumping, trade-related intellectual property measures, biopiracy, culture-fishery and the replacement of the welfare state by the managerial state—touch those who stayed in one place? That today, as Roberta Cohen of the Brookings Institution Project on Internal Displacement tells us: "The most realistic count of internally displaced persons is . . . 20 to 25 million: nine to ten million in Africa, five million in Asia, five million in Europe, and two million in the Americas. Their number now exceeds that of refugees"?[8] How can we say to Joan Tronto, when she writes: "I start from the assumptions about the need for a liberal, democratic, pluralistic society in order for all humans to flourish," that such societies can flourish in one part of the world at the expense of another and within one globalized state at the expense of the disenfranchised and that capitalist globalization has exacerbated this?[9] I therefore fear that the more "late twentieth century American society . . . take[s] seriously . . . the values of caring . . . traditionally associated with woman," the less it will want to learn, under all the garbage of domination and exploitation, these virtues shining in societies where the welfare state is now not allowed to emerge as the barriers between national and international economy are removed; and where, in the name of "gender training," precisely these virtues must be impatiently undermined rather than nurtured even as the millennial gender-compromise that they have brought about is shattered.

There is a difference, almost a fracture, between globality and development on the one hand, and immigration and multiculturalism on the other. The located gendered subaltern, often less viciously gendered than the underclass migrant, but facing the global directly, falls through the fracture. The upper-class, hybrid female is, first, "woman" for the international civil society serving today's "economic citizen"—the finance capital market in the business of development. Secondly, she is "woman" as subject of postcolonial, multiculturalist theory. And finally, she is "woman" as trainer of other women to become "woman," eligible for benevolence, for "development" coded loosely as ethical-political action.

It is in the interest of the coalition between these women and metropolitan feminism that we are obliged today to forget the economic narrative. These women originally from the global South, the hybrid postmodern North, are indistinguishable from the indigenous elite women of the South upon whom, by a crude and classless theory of national identity and the universalist politics of feminist solidarity that is hand-in-glove with biased cultural relativism, the donor agencies are relying more and more. Twenty-five years ago, Samir Amin, writing about what he called "Levantine merchant princes," mentioned the difficulty of assigning a country to them. These women are their modern ideological counterparts. Their economic counterparts, female and male, with the glass ceiling and the feudalism of heterosexist "love" worked in, are the secessionist community described by Robert Reich.

If it were my plan today simply to recount the economic narrative, I would draw a sharp contrast between the triumphalism of the sixth volume of the United Nations Blue Book series, a 689-page document titled *The Advancement of Women, 1945–1995* (from which I have already cited), and parenthesis-ridden, unedited versions of the Platform for Action by which women's oppression had to be codified by the World Women's Conference in 1995. I would comment on the parentheses which marked all of the things said by all of the "consensus-breaking" women who came from all over the world, ironed out in the final version. I would comment on the procedures by which governmental and non-governmental delegations and spokespersons have been and are organized. I would analyze the efficacy of women's credit-baiting without infrastructure in the name of micro-enterprise. But our task is supplementation. I will backtrack to the road not taken with a request to you to keep this narrative framing in mind.

Radical alterity, if one can say it, appears to require an imaging that is the figuration of the ethical as the impossible. If ethics are grasped as a problem of relation rather than a problem of knowledge, it is not enough to build efficient databases, converting the "gift," if there is any, to the "given" (datum), upon which calculating "aid" can be based. It is necessary to imagine this woman as an other as well as a self. This is, strictly speaking, impossible. Imagination is structurally unverifiable. Thus, the image of the other as self produced by imagination supplementing knowledge or its absence is a figure that marks the impossibility of fully realizing the ethical. It is in view of this experience of the figure (of that which is not logically possible) that we launch our calculations of the political and the legal. The gift of time grasped as our unanticipatable present, as a moment of living as well as dying, of being hailed by the other as well as the distancing of that call, is launched then as reparation, as responsibility, as accountability.

This is an account of the double bind of the ethical as spelled out in the thinking of Melanie Klein, Emmanuel Lévinas, Jacques Derrida, and Luce Irigaray.[10] When one decides to speak of double binds and aporias, one is haunted by the ghost of the undecidable in every decision.[11] One cannot be mindful of a haunting, even if it fills the mind. Let me then describe a narrower sense in which I am using the word. When we find ourselves in the subject position of two determinate decisions, both right (or both wrong), one of which cancels the other, we are in an aporia which by definition cannot be crossed, or a double bind. Yet, it is not possible to remain in an aporia or a double bind. It is not a logical or philosophical problem like a contradiction, a dilemma, a paradox, an antinomy. It can only be described as an experience. It discloses itself in being crossed. For, as we know every day, even by supposedly not deciding, one of those two right or wrong decisions gets taken, and the aporia or double bind remains. Again, it must be insisted that this *is* the condition of possibility of deciding. In the aporia or the double bind, to decide is the burden of responsibility. The typecase of the ethical sentiment is regret, not self-congratulation.

I have given an account of the general aporia of the ethical. Let me now describe an only seemingly more restricted aporia, thoroughly fore-grounded in the postmodern global, between capital and culture. Globalization is the implications, as I have said, of the financialization of the globe, the establishment of a uniform system of exchange. This is a computation of the globe into the abstract as such. Marx already knew this when he placed capital in the place of the idea in the Hegelian system. But in postmodern electronic capitalism, globalizing capital, finance capital, is also virtual. You cannot be against globalization; you can only work collectively and persistently to turn it into strategy-driven rather than crisis-driven globalization.

In this particular situation, then, globalization is also the site for a potentially right decision. In order to operate this critique one must tangle with the abstract, with the virtuality of "virtual money."[12] The benevolence of the global feminism that I describe above is usually satisfied with the coding of this abstraction as "development," and does not learn to decode.

In this rarefied and Marxist understanding, globalization, capital financializing the globe, is the abstract as such, the abstract as virtual, pure structure. By contrast, culture is the irreducibly text-ile where the edge of the cloth where we are woven always unfurls ahead, in a future forever anterior. Culture alive is always on the run, as I will say again and again. For the sake of a continuous contrast we can call it the concrete as such. But, in fact, it is discontinuous with capital as the electronic virtual. It is caught always abreactively, after the fact, in a hybrid tangle of idiom, less organized than language. It always serves to code the economic, which is always lent its structure. How is it foregrounded in the postmodern global and how does it connect to imagining the other woman?

Let us take a step back and narrativize ruthlessly. The construction of the colonial subject, to code colonialism as administration and civilization, was predominantly the forging of a class alliance with the colonized, the kind of alliance that produced Edward Said and Gayatri Spivak. The tragedies of gender and nationalism allow us to conclude that questions of gender were subsumed there. I discuss Family Law and "custom" briefly below.

The construction of the postcolonial subject was to code the failure of decolonization as multiculturalism, in metropolitan space, to race, itself rewritten as a fantasmatic national identity as its subject. So if the first was class, the second is race as multiculture—cultural rights. Identitarian politics succeeds insofar as class and gender remain subsumed to this notion of a national and postnational identity.

The construction, on the other hand, of the *globalized* subject is through the manufacturing of a gender alliance. The female subject/agent of globalization often collectively legitimatizes itself in the name of a generalized ethical agenda. This is where she crosses the capital/culture aporia on the side of capital. Yet to work for global justice as a principle is as right a decision as to work for strategy-driven globalization. But the interests of globalization from above and from below cancel each other. This too contributes to the problem of thinking ethics for the other woman.

In 1998, *National Geographic* showed pictures of women saluting the male fieldworkers of the Grameen Bank as they vow not to have too many children.[13] Will mainstream feminism ever think critically of this model of cultural indoctrination, even as Grameen gets more savvy?

Different officers of Women's World Banking repeatedly invoke Chandra Behn, a member of the celebrated Self Employed Women's Association or SEWA, as their legitimation. At the same time, they speak of opening "the huge untapped market of poor Southern women to the international commercial sector." When SEWA was founded in the early 1960s, Ela Bhatt, the founder, had no such ambition. "The World Bank's [Consultative Group to Assist the Poorest] . . . appears to be narrowly focused on microlending as an end in itself. And the means to that end, critics charge, may do more damage to 'empowerment leaders' like SEWA than good."[14]

This was the placing of the poorest women of the South upon the spectral grid of finance capital. "Pay up every week or else" is once again the instrumentalization of body and the money-form in the interest of the abstract. SEWA had made the subaltern women co-operative owners of their own bank, precisely to bypass the predations of commercial capital as they started life changes: driving by strategy, not driven by crisis-management. Under the initiator Ela Bhatt's fierce left-labor Gandhianism, the free-choice cultural-identity slot was anti-Fordist, bi-religious (Muslim/Hindu) worker's pride, which lasts to this day, although one senses a certain unease now, among the working-class Hindu women, in pronouncing the "*la ilaha* . . ."—there is no God but God—the Muslim credo.

Grameen Bank had initially started lending to women allegedly because the repayment rate was higher. I have as research here fifty-odd rural women's testimony, spontaneously offered because I had agreed with their skepticism.

Bangladesh, established in 1971–1972, fell into the beginnings of electronic capitalism and became a little-noticed U.S. military and political "colony of expediency." It is in this arena, in 1976, that Grameen, indigenous enterprise, made its pitch. Ela Bhatt was a women's activist labor lawyer. Muhammad Yunus, the initiator of Grameen, was a Professor of Economics at the University of Chittagong. In the Grameen Bank loan camps the coding of women was into "discipline": up-and-down exercises (even for women in advanced pregnancy, according to my rural informants), salutes, the bank's fieldworkers always two Bangladeshi men in Western clothes. There was no freedom-of-choice coding here; the curious training into "discipline" did not catch; even as, somewhat later, the hygienic habits imposed inside Export Processing Zones were not carried over into daily habit—a real contrast to rural primary health care practiced by rural female para-medical fieldworkers. This is what the *National Geographic* is re-coding as reproductive right.

SEWA was about the conscientization of women as self-employed workers—recoding work-situations they already inhabited—somewhat like Marx's recoding of the factory worker as the *agent* of production. Grameen was a bank that initially established itself upon women's good repayment record. Like the nimble-fingered lacemakers moved into electronic worker-positions without identity, entailing cultural coding as "women in development"—women's feudal loyalty was here moved into loyalty as bank-borrower (and now as free choosers of reproductive freedom). The connection between credit and micro-enterprise was not necessarily perceived unless directed externally from governmental and nongovernmental sources. It was in the wake of the possibility of full globalization that women's micro-credit came into its own, an "untapped market for the commercial sector." The World Bank has factored gender into all its projects now. Women's micro-credit organizations are springing up all over. The "cultural" recoding of that positioning is a culture of woman-ness. As I have mentioned above, the key phrase now is therefore "Gender *and* Development," for the word "woman" is being "culturally" negotiated as these very poor women blink on and off with their "200,000 loans averaging $300 each" and their "over 95% repayment rate," upon the grid of the spectral network, with the extra fast turnover of finance capital, emptying money again and again of its money-being.[15] The fieldworkers of women's World Banking preach women's liberation as a quick fix—more accessible as "free choice of free femininity" than the mysterious rituals of "discipline" could be, although they too are now being brought into line. Now Professor Yunus too can speak in terms of women's liberation.

(After the Nobel, he is global. Before, only the circuit of capital into which his beneficiaries were inserted was so. His intentions are unexceptionable. He preaches private-sector socialism, a near-absurdity.)

It is hard for feminist cultural studies to access this circuit without falling into global-local binarities or banalities, a substitute for the older modernity-tradition patter. I am suggesting their constant displacement by paying attention to women's positioning on the axis of abstract capital, needing "cultural" coding.

This much at least is clear: to imagine or figure the other as another self, you need to engage the moving edge of culture as it leaves its traces in idiom. To reduce it to language—to semiotic systems that are organized as language—was a structuralist dream. But at least, whatever the subject-position of the structuralist investigator, there was rigor in the enterprise. Its tempo was different from the impatience of a universalist feminism re-coding global capital. From existing evidence, it is clear that individual-rights or universalist feminists infiltrate the gendering of the rural South to recast it hastily into the individual rights model. They simply take for granted that colonized cultures are inevitably patriarchal. I will not enter into historical speculation. I will take shelter in a figure—the figure or topos, that in postcoloniality the past as the unburied dead calls us. This past has not been appropriately mourned, not been given the rites of the dead, as the other system brought in by colonialism imposed itself. There was no continuous shedding of a past into an unmarked modernity.

I am not necessarily suggesting that there can be such continuity. It is just that when a sense of that continuity is absent, in different ways, in an entire culture, there are immense problems in the practice of freedom in a modernity not marked by a locational adjective. In later chapters, I will speak of Khaled Ziadeh and Farhad Mazhar to speak of these predicaments of infelicitous or unmourned modernities.

In the field of political culture, to engage in a strategy-driven globalization, to step into a modernity not forever marked by the West and contrasted to a tradition necessarily defined as static, it is to the past as the call of the unburied dead that the postcolonial must strain to gain access.

(In the intervening years, I have realized, as I have plunged more and more into the specific task of the uncoercive rearrangement of desires at two ends of the spectrum—represented here as a double bind—that strategy-driven globalization is the old goal of international socialism recoded into the global; and that it still needs supplementation by a persistently repeated, diversified, aesthetic education for all. But I get ahead of myself.)

Men and women are both in this situation of attending to the past so that it can be understood as another access to contemporaneity, but not equally. For, first, across the classes, it is women who are generally asked to hold the marks of a necessarily stagnating traditional culture. And second, unable to confront the real source of domination, it is upon the domesticated woman, in the private sphere, that the underclass man, frustrated by globality, vents his frustration. And, finally, family law, a strictly codified—rather than dynamically flexible—version of precolonial laws, allowed to flourish by colonizing powers to keep indigenous patriarchy satisfied, still functions across the immigrant-feminized labor export divide. Thus it is possible to argue that unequal gendering is exacerbated under colonialism, subsequently in underclass migrancy, and thrust into a bewildering simulacrum of freedom in the underbelly of globalization. To undo this is not a matter of a quick-fix gender training, bringing the international feminist into the fragility of the family.

Assia Djebar complicates the metaphor with the double difficulty of regaining an active perspective for women in the unperformed burial rites for the dead, old culture, when the colonial culture seemingly gave access to the new. In anguish, Djebar's fictive persona raises a cry in turn. "If only," she writes, "I could occupy with desire one of those singular women."[16] Here is a figure as an experience of the impossibility of recapturing a cultural past in order to mourn it so that new life can begin.

Yet, I have also argued that the figure of the experience of the impossible *is* the condition of possibility of deciding. In the aporia or double bind, to decide is the burden of responsibility. What can the mourning work of postcoloniality look like when it slips from figure to accountability? Let us reopen Susan Bazilli's book: "We must always be cognizant of narrowing the gap between law and justice." With this in mind we turn to Mary Maboreke's essay "Women and Law in Post-Independent Zimbabwe: Experiences and Lessons."[17] At the time, Mary Maboreke taught in the faculty of law at the University of Zimbabwe in Harare and was involved in gender-sensitive constitutional law. (She is currently the head of the Women, Gender and Development Directorate of the Organization of African States, headquartered in Addis Ababa.) She, like other feminist constitutionalists in Southern Africa, is engaged in re-inventing customary law so that the constituent subject of the new nation can insert the subaltern into the circuit of hegemony. Her project is the opposite of the hasty gender-training undertaken by today's globalizing feminists. It is with respect to this that I insist on working with the cultural idiom, as in invisible mending. Reinventing gendered "custom" is rather different from coercing into rights-claims. This is particularly apposite for Central and Southern Africa, since "custom" there was a largely colonial construct meant not only to regulate women but to keep power frozen in the hands of tribal chiefs.[18]

The way in which customary law had constructed the woman as a separate subject created a wedge through which the failure of decolonization could begin to fester. (And now some smart PR person reconstructs her as the success of international civil society by inscribing "I am powerful" above her face.) The examples can be multiplied all across formerly colonized countries. To heal this wound, the violence of the founding gap mentioned in my opening words must be a reminder of the importance of the quite-other in being-human. There is no trace of the ethical in from-above do-gooding to sustain the commercial sector.

The figure produced by the cultural topos of an unfinished mourning, an unburied dead, inhabits a fractured modernity in an altogether quotidian way:

> Most African people have neither completely moved away from the customary way of life ["customary" = customary law] nor have they remained squarely rooted within it. In most cases, they have a foot in each world. Very often the modern executive, moving sleekly along the streets of the capital city is "transfigured" into an ancestor-worshiping traditionalist overnight when he or she goes "home" to the rural area to appease some disgruntled ancestor or avenging spirit believed to be manifest in some misfortune.[19]

You cannot engage one without engaging the other. This has become urgent in the ideology of the contemporary.

II. What I Teach for a Living: Literary Criticism

What is to be done here, now, with what we are as agents? I use a working definition of agency: institutionally validated action. At the limit the distinction between subject and agent breaks down, for the coming-into-being of a subject across that founding gap—the programming of the synthesis with the quite-other (which my ancestors, incidentally, located in the synchronicity of the pulmonary system using the air of alterity or *ātman*)—may well be an instituting that keeps us in subjectship. Short of that marginal general moment, present in each thought of agency, we can say, in the narrowest possible sense, that we are validated by the academic institution, in the United States, as teachers of English literature, to act upon the sensibilities of our students, uncoercively, by their consent. As such, what is to be done? If I do not look at the problem of thinking ethics for the other woman in this practical way, I contribute to both its ghettoization and its development into an instrument of intellectual black-mail, a travesty of the ethical angle.

What I am interested in here is promoting the habit of mind that can be open to experience ethics as the impossible figure of a founding gap, of the quite-other. The companion task, of reading material by and on other women, can lead to self-aggrandization unless the habit of mind is produced at the same time. Two formidable problems are faced by people like me who have a foot in both worlds. First, that serious students in the Brit Lit classes are generally not the serious students in the other women classes. And, second, that the relevant material by other women in their counter-globalizing, other-womanly role is in activist field reports in the idiomaticity of the many languages of the world, rather than in the inter-views of well-vetted oral history.

(Today, the effort to promote habits of mind straddles both sectors. The gap between the two sectors is ever-widening in the subalternization-machine of capitalist globalization; yet the connections are ever stronger. Not quite not a double bind.)

I proceed in the faith that it is not only the past of the colonized that has to be laid to rest and mourned. I have already suggested that the situation of the person in metropolitan space, of the politically correct woman in metropolitan space, is also endangered. It is not possible to be good anymore because it is preferable to be ignorant, especially in a place like New York. There is so much seemingly benign encouragement to think that New York *is* the world. The entire global situation can be turned into the situation of the migrant in New York. (Other capital cities can be substituted.) New York is not even a mega-city if one considers the ratio between the heights of buildings and the way in which the subdivisions are localized at ground level. Confronted by this benign yet unjust triumphalism, I begin to teach by choice the se-quence courses in literary criticism in the English major: teaching the canon, otherwise; using the beginnings of modern British criticism as an instrument.

These are undergraduates. I start with the *Preface* to *Lyrical Ballads,* chapters 13 and 14 of the *Biographia Literaria,* and "A Defence of Poetry."[20]

We try to understand these three texts (and there were others) as wanting to say, at the inception of the ravages of the economic system attendant upon the Industrial Revolution, that the imagination, which is our inbuilt capacity to other ourselves, can lead perhaps to under-standing other people from the inside, so that the project would not be a complete devastation of the polity and of society through a mania for self-enrichment. (Via Bateson and Gramsci, I can now situate their passion in their historical moment, as I hope the Introduction to this volume makes clear.)

Coleridge allows us to plot the literary-critical agent's access to the esemplastic Imagination as a barred rupture or founding gap;[21] Wordsworth to broach the topic of the importance of connective passion with little stimulus—imagination as real virtuality. We can go on then to Shelley's analysis of the information explosion—"we cannot imagine what we know"—and contrast the real virtuality of the Imagination with the existential impoverishment of virtual reality as it is devised today, until we learn to "'upload' ourselves into a suitable computing machine as a way of extending our lives and acquiring a more robust physical constitution. . . . You will pass from sentient being to insentient robot."[22]

Even as we touch upon the colonial connections of these figures to establish parity with our own connections with globalization, I spend time demonstrating how the textual figure "Wordsworth"'s genuine admiration for the imaginative proficiency of rustic culture is, however distanced, not a species of primitivism; and now I would give some of this time to pointing out his lack of engaging with them. Shelley's expansion of the "poetic" function (which we later contrast with Jakobson's), seeing the metaphor, establishing connections between dissimilars, as the instrument of the Imagination and the very name of the "love" that is the secret of morals, allows the class to see how far metropolitan literary criticism had gone to think that othering, another name for the ethical angle, might save their world from the moral impoverishment otherwise signaled by economic growth. I keep alive the connection with the students' own desire to do good in the world. When turned off by Shelley's ecstatic tone, a student is asked to describe something s/he really enjoyed recently. I mimic the student's ecstatic tone as exactly as I can (no diss-ing) and then read the offending Shelley passage. And so on. Any trick to train them into a mental habit of othering rather than merely provide them with tools to describe.

And yet, the great experiment didn't work. The poets had no real involvement with infrastructure. Our situation is even worse because we don't even have as much enthusiasm. We are in a conjuncture which is rather like theirs: at the inception of globalization, as they were at the inception of industrial capitalism. If you think that Coleridge, Wordsworth, and Shelley are just dead white men, remember that you are becoming chromatists—using skin color only as color. There are anglo-clones in this classroom who are not the pinky-brown that we normally call white. And you are being genitalists and reducing feminism to the kind of genitals that we are sitting on. If you look at what they are doing, you should learn from them today. Poetry has become a sort of narcissism. But in terms of visual arts, we still think this. I am constantly asked to help curators launch shows in museums where they invite the street in and make the barrio (or Brick Lane) into a show. It is exactly like the earlier attempt—except somewhat less well-theorized than Wordsworth's and Shelley's belief that you could with poetry exercise the imagination, train in ethics ("public taste")—in the othering of the self and coming as close as possible to accessing the other as the self.

Then we read Arnold and Pater. What has happened between the first three and these two is the institutionalization of English literature as a subject that can be taught at a university. The first teaching of English literature, as a subject, as a faculty (as it were), was in India, not in Britain. And not only was it in India, it was at my college. I tell them I am their native informant. The first group of poet-critics was figuring the impossible. People like Arnold yoke the power of the imagination to the indigenous upper class in the colonies. Under the impetus of a pedagogic incentive much stronger than merely academic, my ancestors othered themselves and became colonial subjects. When Wordsworth wants to become transparent so that he can enter the minds of persons who have been uncontaminated by the Industrial Revolution and become a conduit and actively enter the passions of the reader so that by exercising this othering through the imagination, the person who can no longer be excited without external stimulation because of the horrible factory life in cities, will get training in ethics by robustly imagining the other, and Shelley says Roman law is "poetic" in his enlarged sense, they are still figuring an experience of the impossible if we read the way I am reading.

(In the intervening years, as the two kinds of work got entangled in shared double binds, I realized that although the British Romantics seemed useful to nuance the confidence in the individual will carried by the New York end students wanting to help the whole world, they themselves had not cared about the subaltern. Wordsworth had merely used them. There was a lesson for me there, which has led to where I am now, still learning. Poetry coming out of the eighteenth or nineteenth century will not help the epistemico-epistemological crisis of globalization. And Marx takes humane postrevolutionary impulses for granted. I came upon Bateson, Du Bois, and Gramsci—still no gender-interest among subalternists. African lawyers rewriting customary law no longer translate into training the imagination into the "modern" classroom in New York and/or Belera. But I've learned ab-use, sabotage. Hong Kong seems to take Meaghan Morris out of the radical ghetto where "a self-serving Western critique . . . maps a *univocally* global status for English and a (presumed) new world order."[23] But the subaltern floor of the globalist can use the European Enlightenment rather better, twisted into unrecognizable rules of thumb. Reading practice, not just content. We knew this but dismissed it as "formalism." And now it looks to be too late. It is a pity I will not write about the contortions in the villages: the poetry of the decimal system. But I will not entertain the solidarity tourists. I get ahead of myself. Read what follows with this parenthesis in your mind.)

Back to the old story. By the time Arnold and Pater write, that figure of the experience of the impossible has been transformed into the institutional practice of producing the colonial subject. We have moved from figure to calculus. When Wordsworth or Shelley uses poetry as the subject of a proposition, or Coleridge uses imagination thus, they are describing faculties of the mind or mental phenomena. They are making a critique of individual will. They talk about the poetic sensibility as something which can in fact be unlike the individual will because it is given over to a principle and faculty of the subject which is larger than the outlines of the will.

On the other hand, when Arnold uses the word "culture" as a subject of propositions, he does not have a theory of the mental theater at all. The study of perfection does not involve tapping a different *faculty* of the mind but a change in the reading list. When Arnold uses the word "culture" as a subject, in fact it occludes the requirement that there be custodians of culture. The verbs are all verbs of coercion; there is no verb of othering and indeed, the non-individual subjects are not names of super- and supra-individual, even sub-individual faculties of the mind, like all psychological phenomena, like poetry being emotion recollected in tranquility and so on. Here is Arnold; notice the verbs of coercion and notice the use of culture as a subject which clearly occludes (not very much, but nonetheless does) the collectivity of the custodians of culture. Perfection managing a restricted democracy.

> Perfection as culture conceives it, is not possible while the individual remains isolated. The individual is required under pain of being stunted and feebled in his own development if he disobeys to carry others along with him in his march towards perfection. To be continually doing all he can to enlarge and increase the volume of the human stream sweeping thitherward.[24]

Now this notion of the individual coerced by perfection as conceived by culture to draw people along in a stream is quite different from the poetic sensibility as an othering mediator between those subjects that are still uncontaminated by the Industrial Revolution or the past and our world which cannot imagine what it knows, which then can learn this way. (At the other end it was still women reconstructed by informal world governance agents, not even subalterns kept "subaltern" in the interest of feudal benevolence. I didn't know then that nothing is uncontaminated by history. The subaltern just has no access to redress—this I knew but could not use when the double bind between the two ends of the spectrum—sorry, mixed metaphor—seemed simply a high-flown "moral dilemma," the earlier title of this piece, unrevised.) I tell the students that if you want to see how much this has come full circle, you'll notice that it is not as if people don't believe this anymore except today it is done by patenting the DNA of so-called primitive tribes that are quite uncontaminated by the narrative of the Industrial Revolution that leads finally to globalization so that our bodies can in fact recover from the environmental ravages of this history. Whereas these folks are in fact trying to deal with it in terms of the mind and that's why they fail because they did it only in terms of the mind; nonetheless they figured the impossible whereas after institutionalization it comes into Arnold. Arnold's project of providing better reading material resembles our attempts to do no more than expand the canon. Arnold's success in producing the colonial subject is like the conviction shared by the global feminist dominant that feminist aid is to make the rest of the world like us.

I love Pater. I certainly teach him with gusto and affection. But I do point out that he was supported by his fellowship at Brasenose College. He was not a rich man, he was not even a very important man; he was a little mouse of a man, he was not like old Matthew Arnold. He was just a very smart man. It was possible to burn like a hard gem-like flame while drinking from the college cellars and eating at High Table, as we save the world from Columbia U.

"To maintain this ecstasy is success in life. In a sense it might even be said that our failure is to form habits, for after all, habit is relative to a stereotyped world and meantime it is only the roughness of the eye that makes any two persons, things, situations, seem alike."[25]

Now this passage—that our failure is to form habits—is quite reminiscent of Shelley's chat about de-familiarization, that poetry takes the veil of familiarity away from reality. Shelley's final point, however, is to show us how, by metaphorizing our humanity, we can perceive others as similar, when they are not in fact similar, not in reason similar, not by database similar. This is the flip side of de-familiarizing the familiar—because our very well-known self and environment are othered. This is Shelley's argument: by restoring the metaphoric nature of common language, taking the veil of familiarity away, you are able to metaphorize the connection between all human beings. Whereas Pater's argument has become that by de-familiarizing you will see that no two persons are alike.

It has gone full circle. And the circle did not include the problem we are facing. "Metaphorizing" humanity is sabotageable, as we will see in "Rethinking Comparativism," Chapter 23 in this book.

Now when these students ask me why I am teaching the canon, I say to them it is not to excuse them, but not to accuse them either. We must see our complicity; we are in the same kind of situation in the bosom of the super-power, wanting to be good. We are where Arnold is: we want to be the custodians of culture; we want to expand the canon. We know unless this multicultural material, this feminist material, is introduced into the canon, culture will not be perfect. Thus our usual radical project is not all that different. Therefore we should learn from this. We must at least try not to get involved, like Arnold, in the repeated construction of the colonial subject, the construction of, the consolidation of, or the expanding, and changing the composition of the upper classes in Britain. Rather than do that, learn from the difference between the figuring of the impossible in imagination in Shelley, Wordsworth, and Coleridge, and then the institutional experiment, the production of the colonial subject in this case, the postcolonial subject, the benevolent and trivial humanist subject in the super-power. For us the multicultural feminist counter-canon is Arnold's "sweetness and light." Tell me next time how it is that you can lay your past to rest so that your project, your institutional project can look a little bit different.

Of course I teach them Derrida and Barthes, Lacan and Irigaray, Hortense Spillers and Jacqueline Rose, Saussure and Jakobson, etc. But in order to channel them into thinking the other through idiomaticity, I have to involve them in revising for gender and race what was best in British literary criticism. For the only language that I share with them, in which they are "responsible," is English. My students cannot help believing that history happened in order to produce them. I invite them into the history of this noble failed experiment to think of themselves as not the best, not the worst, but somewhere in between. The literary imagination is programmed to fail but it can figure the impossible.

(I should mention here that a lot—not all—of what one learns from eating deconstruction travels and survives in understanding and working at the village schools.)

For gender-sensitivity *within this tradition* I open Virginia Woolf. I re-cite a move from Virginia Woolf here to show that the opening of this "perhaps" for readers to come is not confined to some essentialized or naturalized hybrid. "'I' is only a convenient term for somebody who has no real being," Woolf writes in one of her most persuasive texts. "Lies will flow from my lips, but there may *perhaps* be some truth mixed up with them; it is for you to seek out this truth and to decide whether any part of it is worth keeping."[26]

Woolf places us in the classic paradox—"I will lie"—and writes the reader in the "perhaps." It is in this mode that she gives a random name to that "I" that is merely a convention: Mary Beton or Mary Seton. And it is also within this mode that she acknowledges the compromised foundations of metropolitan agency. Mary Beton owes her £500 to imperialism, her eponymous aunt "died by a fall from her horse when she was riding out to take the air in Bombay," and she herself sees money as a better alternative to democracy (RO, p. 37). In the final movement, Woolf takes us into the impossible possible of the "perhaps," only as fiction can. She puts Mary Beton to rest (RO, pp. 104–105) and speaks "in my own person" (RO, p. 105). She inaugurates a ghost dance, asking all aspiring woman writers to be haunted by the ghost of Shakespeare's sister, and quite gives up the "room of one's own and £500 a year" in her closing words: "I maintain that she would come if we worked for her, and that so to work, *even in poverty and obscurity,* is worth while" (RO, p. 114; emphasis added).

For race-sensitivity I open, first, for Cultural Studies, the W. E. B. Du Bois who wrote, as African-American metaphorizing the other, "I sit with Shakespeare and he winces not," and went on to describe the colonial (rather than the enslaved) subject in "The Negro Mind Reaches Out."[27] Next, from within the framework of reverse-othering described by Du Bois, I read what I consider to be the first significant essay of postcolonial criticism, Chinua Achebe's "An Image of Africa."[28] It is the othered subject asking for the redress which we are trying to teach as a mental reflex.

(It's a different Du Bois that I sit with now, as note 57 in the Introduction will attest.)[29] And so I go, asking the students to enter the 200-year-old idiomaticity of their national language in order to learn the change of mind that is involved in really making the canon change. I follow the conviction that I have always had, that we must displace our masters, rather than pretend to ignore them. Teaching English, I must use its history to undo its problems, one of the greatest at that time being the one mentioned in my original title: a moral dilemma. In displacement I was making the first move toward ab-use; and the dilemma morphed into a double bind, at first enabling, now not so.

A word in conclusion, a reminder of the fracture or incoherence in this essay in another way. What I describe in the second section is an obstinate attempt at a formal training of the imagination in the classroom. Filling it with substance would take us back to the first section. The obvious gap between the two cannot be filled by only academic labor, not to mention an academic lecture. Right on, I say to my earlier self.

Culture: Situating Feminism

HAVE BROUGHT forth this essay here, embedding a 2001 presentation, because it will, almost brutally, allow the reader to instrumentalize what has gone before. The project of parsing cultural difference has given way to attending upon subalternity; the question of woman has transformed itself. The immediately preceding essay gives a sense of where things (in me and in the world) have changed, and where they have not.

Let me first offer the short description of "Culture," written for a British think tank just before 9/11. I will then pull at a definition sentence, and go into feminist contemporaneity by way of stereotyped, seemingly autobiographical testimonies that further advance the Preface of this book. When we fall into "Teaching for the Times," the next chapter, the limits of the U.S. university will come clearer.

Here, then, is "Culture":

Every definition or description of culture comes from the cultural assumptions of the investigator. Euro-U.S. academic culture, shared, with appropriate differences, by elite academic culture everywhere, is so widespread and powerful that it is thought of as transparent and capable of reporting on all cultures. It is, however, also a multiform cultural system, marking the descriptions and definitions it produces. Cultural information should be received proactively, as always open-ended, always susceptible to a changed understanding. The specialist speaks from the ever-moving, ever-shifting ground of her or his cultural base, knowingly pushed back or unacknowledged as transparent.

Culture is a package of largely unacknowledged assumptions, loosely held by a loosely outlined group of people, mapping negotiations between the sacred and the profane, and the relationship between the sexes. On the level of these loosely held assumptions and presuppositions, change is incessant. But, as they change, these unwitting presuppositions become belief systems, organized suppositions. Rituals coalesce to match, support, and advance beliefs and suppositions. But these presuppositions also give us the wherewithal to change our world, to innovate and create. Most people believe, even (or perhaps particularly) when they are being cultural relativists, that creation and innovation are their own cultural secret, whereas others are only determined by their cultures. This habit is unavoidable. But if we aspire to be citizens of the world, we must fight this habit.

When the tendency to think of our own culture as dynamic and other cultures as static is expressed by a powerful group toward less powerful groups, a political problem arises. This problem surfaced in the 1960s, when the volume of migration from the old colonies increased greatly. A new subdiscipline called "Cultural Studies" emerged, first in Britain, then in the United States, and now available in universities worldwide. This is a happening within academic culture. The Cultural Studies position can be roughly summarized this way: colonizers founded Anthropology in order to know their subjects; Cultural Studies was founded by the colonized in order to question and correct their masters. Both disciplines study culture, the first the culture of others as static and determining, the second the culture of one's own group—as dynamic and evolving. As a result of this polarization, anthropology has launched a comprehensive auto-critique.

In spite of its auto-critique, anthropology can only study the self-conscious part of cultural systems, drawing from it more academic conclusions than the practitioners of the culture, even when it slips into Cultural Studies and focuses, in the style of Pierre Bourdieu, upon aspects of the culture of the metropolis. Cultural Studies studies that self-conscious part as if it worked for real cultural change, at least for the investigator within the culture studied. But the part that works for change escapes the study of cultural dynamics. Culture alive is always on the run, itself the irreducible counter-example. For the Cultural Studies investigator, that incommensurable part is lodged in either the academic culture s/he shares with the anthropologist or the moving wedge of the metropolitan culture into which s/he has entered as a participant.

Before the advent of modernity, the country-to-town movement, the field-to-court movement, the movement along the great trade routes, operated to create the kind of internal split of cultural difference within the same culture that may be the real motor of cultural change. Across the spectrum of change, it is the negotiation of sexual difference and the relationship between the sacred and the profane that spell out the rhythms of culture, always a step ahead of its definitions and descriptions.

The word "culture" belongs to the histories of Western European languages. If we want to move into the elusive phenomenon in other places, below the shifting internal line of cultural difference, we will not look for translations and approximations of the word. Such synonyms carry on their back the impulse to translate from the European, which is a characteristic of the colonized intelligentsia under imperialism, and thus is the condition as well as the effect of that differentiating internal line. They will not let us go below it. We must rather learn a non-European language well enough to be able to enter it without ready reference to a European one. We may encounter creole versions of the word "culture" which will complicate our argument. But they are neither the same word nor its translation.

Anthropologists and comparative historians learn field languages but customarily do not enter them so that they become languages of reference. Cultural Studies investigators typically do not relate to their native languages or the languages of their immediate or remote places of origin as languages of reference. The only route for learning languages in this way is through instruction in reading verbal art in these languages and instruction in philosophizing through ethical systems in them. This would require educational reform.

Such efforts might make us realize that all cultural process, even in the belief-system and ritual sector, moves because human beings imagine and create fictions of all kinds, including the rational fictions that extend philosophy; and that it is not possible for one of us to have access to an exhaustive sense of all the cultures of the world. Study of diversity in metropolitan space should make us aware of the limits to the production of cultural information outside the metropolis.

Let me qualify everything I have said by suggesting that in the field of culture alive there are no mistakes. Cultural continuity, made possible by cultural change, is assured by cultural explanations, coming from all sides, insiders and outsiders, rulers and ruled. The study of cultures is part of culture—the anthropologist's picture of elders initiating young men and women, as well as these very words you read. Culture is a place where different explanations always collide, not just by races and classes, but by genders and generations. Culture is its own explanations. It is possible that the assumption of a collectivity sharing a culture is not an essential truth, but a millennial increment of the need to explain.

Zoom now to 2010, a lecture on "Situating Feminism." That task is easily done. Just recount the triumph of the Euro-specific (even Anglo-specific) model—Mary Wollstonecraft—embedded in the history of both capitalism and Marxism, traveling through coloniality and globalization, with a missionary impulse at work.

However, as is clear from the outset of this book, I am in the Du Bois–Gramsci tradition. (In fact, the Du Bois connection will come clear in my next book.) I believe in an aesthetic education for everyone. All that I have said in the Introduction to this book can be summarized as follows: by aesthetic education I mean training the imagination for epistemological performance.

As I have insisted in "Culture," every definition or description of culture comes from the cultural assumptions of the investigator. The question of feminism particularly involves this generalization. Let me then situate my stereotype of myself as a middle-class Calcutta girl in the 1950s:

Feminism was in the air among the smart literary set when I was coming into my own in the 1950s in Calcutta. I belong to the school that thinks that "text" is a web or a weaving, including the web of what one calls a life. Thus, this phenomenon, marking "feminism" in the stereotype of my life, is, to me, "textual." One could put it in a more (and less) understandable way by saying that "feminism," probably the English word, was not for me a bookish affair, although one was constantly naming books, especially *The Second Sex*.[1]

I now realize that something not specifically called feminism was woven into that web by my parents, who were proto-feminists, insofar as, bearing some opprobrium from the larger family, they brought the girls up exactly like the boy, emphasizing intellectual achievements rather than preparation for marriage. Our greatest source of pride was that our mother, unlike the women of her class and generation, had earned a master's degree in Bengali literature in 1937, when she was 24.

Father died when I was 13. He had been insistent in recognizing me and my sisters and mother, and perhaps women in general, as agents. I was in practice a thoroughgoing woman-for-woman person by age 15, when mother released me from the possibility of an arranged marriage. She showed me by her example how to be such a thing: through her indefatigable work to establish a working women's hostel in the Calcutta of the 1950s and 1960s, as well as her hard work with other women's organizations, for travel and moral uplift, for the employment of destitute widows, and what can only be called undercover work toward the establishment of the first institutional Ramakrishna Mission nunnery, finding interim habitations for intellectual women who wanted to leave patriarchal life, for whatever reason.

Once again, I wasn't reading a book, but I was intertextually involved in the making of a life: feminist intuitions implicit in the direct family, and "feminist" positioning explicit in the peer group.

The first influential text was probably Engels, *Origin of the Family*.[2] A close second was Betty Friedan, *The Feminine Mystique*, but that was simply because, as an assistant professor in my twenties, I was asked to introduce her to a crowd of thousands at the University of Iowa, in the mid-1960s.[3] After that, it's hard to say what influenced me. I was doing feminism, producing feminist texts, before I could recognize an influence.

Cixous's "Laugh of the Medusa" was moving, though, from the start, I was not a single-issue feminist.[4] Gayle Rubin's "sex-gender system" remains useful to this day, for permutations and combinations.[5]

One of the good things for me about feminism is that it doesn't, like Marxism, have a named book at the origin.

A very general definition of work for feminism is to research how humankind is not nice to women and queers in different ways, and to see how this operates a structure of approved violence at one end and alibis for the interventionist missionary impulse at the other. It also allows feminism to mix with patriotism as the world is undoing the rule of law by way of the mantra of leadership-role model—and indeed enforcement.

Let us now go back to "Culture" and borrow another bit. Let us assume that culture is a set of largely unacknowledged assumptions, held by a loosely outlined group of people, mapping negotiations between the sacred and the profane and the relationship between the sexes, with sexual difference unevenly abstracted into gender/gendering as the chief semiotic instrument of negotiation. Nationalism and religion come into play here. We have already seen Gregory Bateson's and Sigmund Freud's agreement in this regard (see the Introduction, page 5).

These are among coding ingredients (permissible narratives) at our disposal. Sexual difference and reproductive heteronormativity (RHN) are the irreducible. Briefly, this is upstream from straight/queer/trans. "Hetero" here is the antonym of "auto." For example, the queer use of childbearing is the extra-moral use of difference. I got an e-mail from one of my Italian translators today: "the notion of 'reproductive heteronormativity' which, as far as it seems, has never been translated into Italian yet, and which would sound, translated as it is as '*eteronormatività riproduttiva*,'

which is not particularly clear [*sic*]. I think it would be better [as] '*ripro-
duzione etero-normata*' which would be closer to the idea of 'reproduction' thru 'traditional' heterosexual intercourse." My response: "Sorry
'reproductive heteronormativity' does not mean 'reproduction thru 'traditional' heterosexual intercourse. The phrase is clumsy in English too. I
hope you will preserve its awkwardness in Italian." We are in a double
bind with the RHN through the variety of our sexualities. This normativity extends to reproduction, with all its psychic uses, so that "human" can
be established and distinguished from experiencing beings. Hence
"norms." And as for the analogy with difference as producing semiosis, it
is a formal, not a substantive argument. "Norm" for me is not an endorsement, but a description that frames my struggle against sexisms.

Let me now move to the other end, consolidated gender culture, where
one coding of the difference is taken as cultural fact.

Responding to Helen Thomas's repeated question, "Why do they [Al
Qaeda] hate us?," I wrote:

> In 1916, assuming they would win the war, France, Russia, and Britain di-
> vided up the remains of the 600-year old Ottoman Empire, drawing fron-
> tiers, creating the Middle East. Lebanon and Iraq were directly controlled;
> others kept in spheres of influence. Haifa, Gaza, and Jerusalem were an
> Allied "condominium." Arms control was strictly European. The Arab powers
> learned of this in 1917, at the end of the war. Previous agreements, assuring
> Arab independence, seemed to have disappeared. The makings of a cultural
> memory.
>
> The Ottoman Empire was corrupt but, except for focused examples such
> as the Armenian genocide, generally the carrier of an attitude of conflictual
> coexistence towards religious difference.[6] Now a master race that clearly
> thinks itself justified in controlling and systematizing the locals, without
> any social contract, often by remote control, steps in. An inchoate resent-
> ment starts in people who cannot combat this palpable transformation at
> the ground level. Women feel this strongly, especially in traditional societ-
> ies, where they think of men as holding their dignity. The cultural memory
> thickens.

Quick-fix gender politics, to which I will come in a moment, simply
attempts to abolish this and transform this into feminine self-interest,
although in the Middle Eastern theater, especially Palestine, there is not
much room for such interference. If one understands, however, that RHN
offers us a complicated semiotic system of organizing sexual/gendered
differential, we might be able to see that this placing of specifically one's
dignity in one's partner, so that it is her/his public indignity that cannot
be borne, is not necessarily male-identified, and not necessarily a direct
reflection of social oppression. Indeed, this desire can be rearranged. I

remind the reader of my description of an aesthetic education: the training of the imagination in epistemological performance through a rearrangement of desires.

But of course the spectrum of requirement through passion to place one's dignity in one's partner can also accommodate violence. But what isn't medicine and poison if you are teaching use rather than doing good, epistemological involvement rather than material succor? The problem here is one of indeterminacy, because violence is part of desire, pleasure, education, but acknowledgment of violence distorts the mechanism unless framed—and in the matter of feminism this is where the intuition of the transcendental comes in.[7]

I use this phrase to mean the arguer's sense that s/he cannot provide adequate evidence for a conviction. As we noticed in the Introduction, Kant theorizes this as transcendental deduction. Most of us are convinced of the evidentiarity of our convictions, but still have inchoate feelings (generally disavowed, hence intuition) that there is something other than the evidentiary.[8] Without this we can neither mourn nor judge.

Abstract structures, such as democracy and the state, and indeed capital, cannot accommodate this as such. The state is thoroughly compromised into managing global capital. Multicultural democracy (a contradiction in terms) and international civil society both applaud only the social productivity of capital and all structural constraints are lifted as obstacles and the needy are seen as individual occasions. I mentioned at the start that human behavior toward women and the queer ranged from violence to alibi. It is the asymmetries between these alternatives that constitute the socius.

Today, with the abstractions of capital commanding social movement, violence and alibi coexist in a chiasmus rather than as a critical pair which would be an asymmetrical riddle that must leave space for an intuition of the transcendental. Whether Foucault is right or wrong, they seem to organize themselves into an *irréductible vis-à-vis*.[9]

As example of this achieved chiasmus I will cite a tiny slice of an academic feminists' electronic everyday. (Here the world has changed little in its presuppositions, although the instruments of capitalism have sharpened since the earlier essay.) I will end with the autobiographical, coming to the point that below the radar you cannot choose only to "empower" women—violence will not be undone this way.

I remind the reader of my discussion of placing one's dignity in the other. (It is of course only an example, but I chose it to point at the different ways in which we would treat it as part of an aesthetic education as contrasted to feminist intervention from within the international civil society.) As I produce my short list, do notice two things: (1) that the interventions listed would simply develop self-interest in the woman below, and (2) that those interventions would solve problems from above—thus producing a sort of clueless global subject in place of the more consolidated colonial subject of yore—by impatiently locating need (alone) rather than speculating on desire.

Here, then, is a selection from a random and typical list of notices that came my way last week. We take such notices for granted, as proofs of the feminist activism of the international civil society, and do not usually notice that they cannot imagine the necessity for what I am defining as "aesthetic education."

1. The first one announces the appointment of a new special representative of the Secretary General (SRSG) on sexual violence in conflict, Margot Wallström from Sweden, Minister, CEO, most popular woman in Sweden, and Chair of the Council of Women World Leaders. "Violence against women is the most common but least punished crime in the world," she has quite correctly said, adding that she would lobby for the recognition of sexual violence in war as a war crime. She added that increasing the role of women in decision-making processes will be a priority for her. "For gender justice advocates," the e-mail continued, "this SRSG appointment opens a vital channel of communication to the UN Secretary General as SRSGs often conduct widespread consultations with various stakeholders' commitment to the challenges faced by women around the world."

Now defining violence against women as a crime and punishing the perpetrators is an excellent thing. But already in "Can the Subaltern Speak?" I was suggesting that a good law was without effect because women's subjectivity was not engaged. This is even more important today, when it is a world we attempt to govern. This is the way in which I discussed law as enforcement in the long note to the Introduction. This may be the moment to quote a story told by David Livingstone that tells of a powerful African chieftain assuring him that Christianity would be incontrovertibly established in his domain if he were allowed to enforce it with his whip:

> Seeing me anxious that his people should believe the words of Christ, he [Sechele, chief of the Bakuena] once said, "do you imagine these people will ever believe by your merely talking to them? I can make them do nothing except by thrashing them; and if you like, I shall call my head men, and with our Litupa (whips of rhinoceros hide) we will soon make them all believe together."[10]

The "stakeholders" are there because the women "cannot represent themselves, they must be represented."[11]

2. The second e-mail announces that the NGO Working Group on Women, Peace and Security launches a new monthly policy note: "The February MAP [Monthly Action Policy] includes an appeal to France, which currently holds the Security Council Presidency, to honor its stated commitments to ensure that women's rights are upheld." An Algerian-French activist just complained bitterly to me about women at Columbia University daring to speak of French postcoloniality. What then about the international civil society? "Point to ways," the e-mail says, "in which these reports should include important considerations relevant to the protection of women's rights, articulate a comprehensive strategy regarding sexual violence," abstract words that can be filled with the force of meaning only if the imagination is trained for epistemological performance through language learning. This can be said even more forcefully about their next "recommend[ation:] the development of the Team of Experts, as well as the proposals to strengthen the UN response to sexual violence in conflict." These experts probably know the local languages. But here class and, yes, cultural difference kick in—feudality without feudalism operates as impatient stakeholding benevolence. Let us refer to another passage in the description of "Culture" I mention on page 119.

This is not to say that the people from that culture who have remained in the nation of origin in social strata separated from the general academic culture are more authentic representatives of the culture in question. It is to say that there is an internal line of cultural difference within "the same culture." This holds not only for the nation of origin but also for the state to which the cultural minority has immigrated. The academy is a place of upward class-mobility, and this internal cultural difference is related to the dynamics of class difference. It is related to the formation of the new global culture of management and finance and the families attached to it. It marks access to the Internet. It also marks the new culture of international non-governmental organizations, involved in development and human rights, as they work upon the lowest social strata in the developing world.

3. The third e-mail announces a meeting of the European Union and NATO on women, peace, and security:

> The EU's efforts will include a stepping-up of the co-operation on women, peace and security with the African Union. The EU will also intensify bilateral efforts towards governments and actors that bear responsibility for the most serious violations of women's rights, and support capacity building of partner countries. March 3—Join us for lunch at the UN at our annual meeting.

Now, "capacity building" is a good goal. But when the European Union and NATO do this for African countries, we have to crack the code to put in the taxonomy of gender as alibi, with the notoriously politicized U.S. Department of Justice tier system of states (the United States excepted) as our guide.[12] We are also helped when we notice the credentials of the chief guest:

> Our special guest speaker is Ellen Iskenderian, President and CEO of Women's World Banking (WWB), the world's largest network of microfinance institutions and banks. Women's World Banking was established following the First World Conference on Women held in Mexico City, 1975. Since that time they have been the leader in microcredit loans to women in developing countries.
>
> Ms. Iskenderian, who joined WWB in 2006, has more than 20 years of experience in building global financial systems throughout the developing world. Ms. Iskenderian is a leading voice for women's leadership and participation in microfinance, and a strong advocate for the role of capital markets in the sector.

I have written at length about credit-baiting elsewhere.[13] Here let me repeat what I have cautioned in the Introduction: to remember the necessarily forgotten and mandatorily ignored bi-polarity of the social productivity and the social destructiveness of capital and capitalism.

4. The fourth e-mail shows us the alibi at work. It is an announcement from the National Council for Research on Women ("If it matters to women it matters to everyone" [no race-class-gender here!]).

First an announcement of the Council Mission: "The National Council for Research on Women is a network of more than 100 leading U.S. research, advocacy, and policy centers with a growing global reach. The Council harnesses the resources of its network to ensure fully informed debate, policies, and practices to build a more inclusive and equitable world for women and girls." Its modest goal is information retrieval.

Next come title and time: "'From Turbulence to Transformation,' Wednesday, March 3, 2010 3:00–5:00 pm." And then the place: "At Goldman Sachs: 32 Old Slip at Front Street, 2nd Floor Auditorium New York City, Sponsored by Deloitte." At a time when the country and the world are outraged against investment bankers in the United States, they take gender as alibi. I spoke of PLATO this way in the 1980s.[14] Nothing changes. This is the production of the alibi. The following promise can only be read with deep alarm and irony:

> At this critical yet promising moment in history, join our panel of visionary leaders for an in-depth exploration of the most pressing issues of our time. What are the challenges and opportunities for advancing real and substan-

tive social change that creates a better world for women and girls? Panelists will share their vision, strategies, and the action steps needed to promote more equitable and inclusive societies locally, nationally and globally.

We then have the names of three corporate women and gendered organizations committed to civil society enterprise. Capitalist feminism as body count, light years away from an aesthetic education for the gendered subaltern:

Edith Cooper, Managing Director and Global Head of Human Capital
    Management, Goldman Sachs
Letty Chiwara, Manager, UNIFEM Cross Regional Programmes
    (invited)
Jacki Zehner, Founding Partner, Circle Financial Group (moderator)
Co-sponsors: Americans for UNFPA; Center for Women in Government & Civil Society at SUNY Albany; John Jay College of
    Criminal Justice Gender Studies Program; New York Women's
    Social Entrepreneurs; The White House Project; Women's Forum,
    Inc.; US National Committee for UNIFEM

What does it "mean," with full connotative weight, that "This event is free and open to the public"? A common Marxian statement comes to mind: Capitalism offers no extra-economic coercion; domination versus exploitation. It is of a piece with a world where there is rage against investment bankers that "RSVP is required for security purposes." "Free and open" means you do not have to pay for it (seemingly, of course), and you do not have to be invited.

This casual look at a random list, the e-mail harvest of a feminist's everyday, shows us how deeply we have moved away from anything this book might suggest. If you wish to move away toward the other end of this restricted spectrum, to women who have moved away from corporate life, the *New York Times* magazine for February 21, 2010 has a silly article praising "femivores"—an ignorant neologism—women who have literalized Voltaire's *Candide*'s hilarious advice: "but we must cultivate our garden."[15] They have not moved from the corporate world. They are subsumed in it.[16]

Because we, as feminists, live in this peculiar capitalist soup, my testimony as my stereotype to Frigga Haug concentrated on this matrix:

How feminist am I in my salaried work, how engaged, how intellectual? It seems to me that our first instance of engagement is in how we have chosen to support ourselves, even if unwillingly, because with that support we think we can be engaged feminist intellectuals outside. I often think that feminism is in my bones, but what feminism is it that is in my bones? If I ponder about it in your pages, I will not be speaking about social engagement as a feminist. When it comes to social engagement, I repeat, you must think of how you have chosen to support yourself—because, in spite of yourself, that is how you have—depending on what you have chosen—inserted yourself in the abstract circuit of capital and the repercussions of your action determine your "engaged" work.

If capital is the strongest agency of validation into modernity, and has been since the seventeenth century, when previous imperial formations and mercantile formations change into the capitalist mode of production—in this place I am held by a much older agency of validation, reproductive heteronormativity. Let us say that it is between these two—capitalism as modernity and reproductive heteronormativity as the chief recoding instrument of capital, thoroughly internalized—that the engagement of the feminist shuttles.

The job is everybody's choice of a mode of living. Like many "engaged" persons, I also have another job that is outside of this choice. This is my engagement with maximal teacher training in backward areas of West Bengal, now for over twenty years. In the opening I said that the instrumentalization of the salaried job for the propagation of the "real" job is not perhaps very intelligent—and we are speaking of the feminist intellectual. We must think through engagement in terms of the relationship or non-relationship between the two "jobs." If the relationship is to instrumentalize, then I think there is a "reaction formation" which wants to deny the often-larger social role of the one unwillingly chosen. This applies to a salaried job as much as it does to a feudal job such as marriage. Let us carefully think through the meaning of "freedom of choice."

"Freedom of choice" is something that is denied to race-class-gender-compromised people. Therefore, in our activism, we cannot ignore "freedom of choice" as a desirable opportunity for which we must strive to build the best possible social and political infrastructures. But the freedom from oppression that spells out "freedom of choice" cannot be an end in itself. We must keep in mind that the end is the freedom to be able to understand that an achieved juridico-legal, socio-political "freedom of choice" should allow the individual to realize that this concept-metaphor has been, in the narrative of modernity, deeply imbricated with capitalism disguised as a pursuit of happiness. Alas, it is in the area of the unwillingly chosen and kept "job" that we in fact, and in our lives, act out the limits of freedom of choice—and this is where the truth of our engagement lies. This irreducible compromise should tell us more about our engagement than the sustainable activism—the maximum of compromise in order to achieve the minimum of activism.

In order for what we recognize as feminism to operate as an engagement, we must presume socialist norms, which are written within capitalism, because mere socialism means turning the use of capital from capitalist to socialist uses. Where there is no agency of turning and the development of capitalism not noticeable except inchoately, by the remotely victimized, the task has been picked up today by the international civil society, which I have described as "self-selected moral entrepreneurs" on many occasions. These people are confident that gender redress can be computed in terms of making the phenomena of gendering accessible by general terms provided by world governance style documents, every unit fought over in prep com meetings, everything most simply understood, as in a PowerPoint presentation, as in knowledge management plans, decisions made by logic rather than subject-engagement. A certain kind of anti-capitalism, not invariably present in this sector, which is often dependent, and happily so, upon corporate funding, substitutes for a proactive socialism here. The slow and deep language learning that must accompany accessing cultural infrastructures so that real, long-term change might be envisaged is largely absent. The distinction between problem solving and the uncoercive rearrangement of desires—between Doctors Without Borders and primary health care, let us say—is almost universally ignored in this sphere. This kind of "feminist engagement" is not noticeably "intellectual," if the intellectual is a person who analyzes the existing situation before choosing the most convenient instrument for solving a problem that has been constructed as a "case" by looking at the grid established by people on a completely different level of capitalist society.

In this sort of below-the-radar rural situation, in eastern India, at least (that is another problem: we tend to generalize too soon, because of the alliances of the international civil society with the benevolent feudal feminism of the global South), the problem-solving approach can apply to clearly visible cases of domestic violence. Given the entire infrastructure in place hierarchically in local and district-level administration, nothing achieved here will last when the engaged persons leave, as they necessarily must, unless there is maximal follow up and, more important, an engagement supported by deep language learning, and a renunciation of the conviction of having all the answers. Such work cannot recognize the millennially established structures of feeling and desires to be as tenacious as those shared by the activists. This is why for health and education, in these areas we must engage children rather than adults if we are to destabilize internalized accepted gender patterns of behavior, and they must be destabilized at the same time as desires are rearranged to develop intuitions of a democratic state. Real change must be epistemic rather than merely epistemological, home as well as school. Therefore we are obliged to remember that all these efforts, however carefully undertaken by the engaged intellectual, might be able to bring to bear is offset by the development of ethical and epistemic semiosis in the subaltern household, cradled in an often traumatic childrearing which is so deeply involved in the lessons of millennial class apartheid and gender division that it continuously creates the problem that one is trying to solve. Class apartheid here is more crippling than gender divisions. As from subaltern space you enter the rural middle class, engendering shows its uglier face.

Therefore, autobiographically and confessionally, rather than in an instructive mode, let me say that, in the metropolis, encountering a sort of feminism that must itself fight with on-the-ground phallogocentrism, recently internalized postfeminism, mainstream gay movements reproducing the morphology of reproductive heteronormativity, continuing juridico-legal fights, and confronting the underlying unexamined gender-benevolence of the international civil society allied with the feudality of the global South, I encounter upon subaltern ground a situation where involvement with women is pleasant—but their delighted reaction cannot be taken as evidence of the success of engagement—and therefore, giving time, skill, undermined by repeated mistakes because human equality as human sameness is too easily assumed, my feminist engagement goes into a pre-active moment, so that male and female children can learn simply to be the same and different, starting from nothing but having been born by phallus and vagina, with phallus and vagina, nourished by breast, by guile, protected and destroyed by physical violence and subservience.

I must end now. If I don't get packed, I miss my train. These regular ten-day trips of intense labor remain bookended by the salaried work and the lecture circuits that provide the travel. I take pleasure in being validated by the absence of financial recognition from the other end—nothing but harassment from the U.S. Internal Revenue Service periodically. Let me end with what I had to produce so that I could at least deduct travel and expense from my income and the detailed account of my everyday that was demanded in order for this not to be questioned year after year:[17]

Village Research Project [Written for the U.S. Internal Revenue Service]

No grant proposals written to preserve intellectual freedom. Professor Spivak's project relates to the fact that national liberation does not always lead to a good and democratic society. Current research in the area (Fareed Zakaria, Jack Snyder etc.) states that no society below a certain per capita level is "ready for democracy."[18] Zakaria, Snyder and others in the field are social scientists. Professor Spivak's research, relating to the work of such rare thinkers as John Shikwati in Kenya, investigates the reason for their opinion. Typically, a newly liberated country, in the absence of established democratic infrastructure, is obliged to put planning and development in the hands of a vanguard. In the absence of a people educated in the habits of democracy, there are no constraints upon the vanguard. It is for this reason, perhaps, that social scientists declare the place "unready for democracy." The generosity of Human Rights NGOs does not confront this problem but perceives education as a "human right." Typically, such work ends in fundraising, building schools, providing textbooks, and making this part of peacekeeping enforcement. Spivak insists that focus must be placed on the quality of the education. There are three points here. (a) Without deep language learning and long-term effort no cultural infrastructure can be accessed. Here Spivak's salaried work (she has been teaching full time at U.S. universities for forty-five years) as member of the Institute of Comparative Literature & Society, with its insistence on deep language learning ignored in today's speed-oriented globalized world, joins her rural research. (b) The current quantified tests for educational success are unable to assess results here. (c) Because these largest sectors of the electorate have been oppressed sometimes for millennia (as in the case of India or China), their cognitive mechanism has been damaged and educational generalizations such as Dewey's or Montessori's do not apply. Work such as Paulo Freire's early attempts relates to making populations aware of oppression. (Freire's word is "conscientization.")[19] Spivak believes that democratic habits and the intuitions of citizenship are developed in children under such difficult circumstances by changing their intellectual habits rather than developing political movements. In order to bring this about, Spivak is also interested in developing "green" habits in extreme poverty and interacting with state leaders and the rural gentry to see how such educational efforts can be stabilized. Under Spivak's research guidance, such efforts are being initiated in China and Africa.

Currently, Spivak's research base is seven hamlets. On each research visit Spivak participates in two training sessions per hamlet and meets with educators collectively on the final day to assess progress. Some time is spent in social interaction and monitoring "green" habits. This immense project is not yet well developed enough to result in direct publication, but incidental publication is all over the place.

As I mentioned above, apart from insisting whenever possible that the girls and the boys receive equal attention, and some other interventions of which I cannot speak, I can do little at the level of the children. I have three wonderful woman teachers, from poor rural gentry, uneasily cooperating against the deeply ingrained prejudices of their origins; I commend them in this—I may even go so far as to say I love them.

On the level of the rural adult female population, there are the two, wives of the adult males most active in these circles, who had come forward in the beginning—to befriend me by serving me hand and foot. They were women of good faith from the lowest stratum of village life, I let them sleep in my own bed under the same mosquito net—a most unusual one-of-a-kind piece of behavior to which they acceded—but I felt increasingly that I had to incur a lot of unnecessary expense so that they could come to the various schools really as a way to visit other villages that they could not otherwise visit easily, and that apart from these jaunts, their presence was merely a convenience because they cooked for all of us. With great ambivalence, at a certain point I asked them not to come to the committee house any more, and of course they were hurt. Yet my friendship with them continued because one of my schools was in their residential hamlet. I have now instituted the practice of "inviting" them at the final day's general training meeting for all the teachers, followed by lunch. They enjoy the fact that they sit in chairs with me, chatting, while the men cook—and we point this out repeatedly, laughing. Is this anything?

The government has programs for "quota women" about which there is research and experience, showing that although the practice should continue, it is at the moment so much in the hands of powerful men that it is only the kind of supplementing that we are practicing and recommending, training the imagination for epistemological performance, that will change the situation, in the remote to distant future.[20] Examples of exceptional women can be brought forward. I congratulate them, and befriend them when I can. But, following Adrienne Rich's commencement address to Smith College in 1979, I repeat the valuable lesson that exceptional women do not prove the rule.[21] Otherwise, there are projects for so-called self-help groups toward opening individual bank accounts. Opening bank accounts as an end in itself and then engaging in fantasmatic tasks of cottage industry or general rural activities does not seem to me to be bringing in the sort of feminist systemic change that we are thinking about. Remember I have experience here.

In the meantime, the more energetic of the two women I am speaking of, deeply cradled in the ideological shelter of reproductive heteronormativity, is often angry with me because I sacked both of her sons from the position of teacher after they had harmed the children through many many months of inefficient and uncaring teaching. I have just been obliged to discuss bad teaching with her second son, who has been made extremely ambitious to escape his group in some other way—through country-town-level "spoken English" "computer training," etc. That is a pitiful employment preparation, but who can blame him? He pays no attention to the children at all, teaches them with dismissal and impatience—keeping the job only because it brings in some money before he can get a better job. The woman is once again tremendously angry with me because she can perceive this only as a blow to her self-esteem, drawing her identity from her husband, a low-level factotum at the Party office, and from her sons. If I were doing gender training, as I have indicated above, this is where desires would need to be shifted, with great gentleness, rather than oppositional sentiments produced. I must, however, remain focused upon the children, the only possible guarantee of an epistemic future. For now, I consider the fact of her being able to express her anger a step forward in establishing equality. With this absurd story of the limits to single-issue feminism, I close these hesitant remarks, drawn from my last instance.

I insist, then, upon my repeated frustration, also the condition of possibility for all my work now: I cannot generalize in the subaltern theater.

Let me return to the comforts of generalization, to what holds the entire gender mechanism as it is held by it—other people's children. My ideas about disciplinary change, in a double bind with reproductive heteronormativity, are based on "other people's children." As you will see in Chapter 23, I make this connection also about rethinking comparativism in elite post-tertiary education.

I want to understand something (understanding everything is impossible) about bypassing the necessity of "good" rich people solving the world's problems. "Good" rich people are dependent on bad people for the money they use to do this. And the "good" rich people's money mostly goes to bad rich people. Beggars receive material goods to some degree and remain beggars.

My desire is to produce problem solvers rather than solve problems, epistemico-epistemological change, in other words.[22] In order to do this, I must continue to teach teachers, current and future, with devotion and concentration, at the schools that produce the "good" rich people (Columbia University) and the beggars. (The latter are seven unnamed elementary schools in rural Birbhum, a district in West Bengal; this work cannot be done with an interpreter and India is multilingual. I am therefore confined to West Bengal, which speaks my mother tongue.)

I must understand their desires (not their needs) and, with understanding and love, try to shift them. That is education in the Humanities.

I have only recently been invited to participate in the elite tertiary and post-tertiary institutions in India, where English (which I believe is also an Indian language) can be understood. Although I feel most at home there, because of the presence of critical intelligence, I cannot linger.

If before I die there is even one student who develops something like democratic judgment, quite different from justified self-interest against oppression from all sides, there is perhaps hope. There was such a boy in another area, in an even more "backward" district, where I started these efforts. The local ex-feudal chief closed the four schools there, in my absence, destroying twenty years' work because nothing threatened this "good" rich local more than judgment among those whose problems he solved. The boy had not advanced far enough to retain what had only just begun. He has fallen back into the ranks of the rural destitute. The life of my exemplary local assistant has been destroyed.

This is the area—among these children—where I fall into the most unacceptable kind of identitarianism.[23] I am a woman, therefore women. You work it out.[24]

CHAPTER SIX

Teaching for the Times

T HE PREVIOUS chapter situates these "times" as belonging to tertiary and post-tertiary education in the United States. This is especially true of the perception of feminism. Instrumentalize what follows situationally, then, and remember, nationalism is a tough perennial. The more it claims to have rhizomatically ruptured, the more it covers repetition. *Plus ça change* . . .

Since its inception, the United States has been a nation of immigrants. The winner among the first set of European immigrants claimed, often with violence, that the land belonged to them, because the Industrial Revolution was in their pocket. And the story of its origin has been re-presented as an escape from old feudalism, in a general Tocquevillian way.[1] It is well known that in the Founders Constitution, African slaves and the Original Nations were inscribed as property in order to get around the problem of the representation of slaves as wealth: "The key slogan in the struggle against the British had been 'no taxation without representation.' . . . The acceptance that slaves as wealth should entitle Southern voters to extra representation built an acknowledgement of slavery into the heart of the Constitution."[2]

Here we have extreme cases of marginalization where the term itself gives way: de-humanization, transportation, genocide. I will not begin in that scene of violence, but rather with the phenomenon that has now kicked us from opposition to the perceived dominant: the "model minority" sector of documented "new" immigration.[3]

Let us rewrite "cultural identity" as "national origin validation." (Global contemporaneity manages itself by constructing fantasmatic

"nationalisms" unmoored from the state!) Let us not use "cultural identity" as permission to difference and an instrument for disavowing that
Eurocentric economic migration (and eventually even political exile) is in
the hope of justice under capitalism. That unacknowledged and scandal-
ous secret is the basis of our unity. Let us reinvent this basis as a spring-
board for a teaching that counterpoints these times, this place. This is all
the more important because "we"—that vague, menaced, and growing
body of the teachers of culture and literature who question the canon—
are not only oppositional any more. We are being actively opposed because what used to be the dominant literary-cultural voice—the male-
dominated white Eurocentric voice—obviously feels its shaping and
molding authority slipping away. We seem to be perceived as the emerging dominant. What are the role and task of the emerging dominant
teacher? Since one of the major functions of tertiary and post-tertiary
education is to facilitate employment, let us also consider the problems of
educating the educators of the emerging dominant field; in other words,
let us consider both the undergraduate and the graduate curricula. I will
inevitably touch upon our possible (false hope!) meta-vocational usefulness, mentioned in the Introduction.

Access to the Universal/National Origin Validation on the Undergraduate Curriculum

In a powerful paper on "The Campaign against Political Correctness:
What's Really at Stake?," delivered at the Institute for Advanced Study at
Princeton, Joan Wallach Scott lays bare the shoddy techniques of the opposition to the emerging dominant as it constituted itself at the end of the
last century:

> Serious intellectuals have only to read the self-assured, hopelessly ill-
> informed and simply wrong descriptions of deconstruction, psychoanalysis,
> feminism or any other serious theory by the likes of D'Souza, Richard Bern-
> stein, David Lehman, Roger Kimball, Hilton Kramer, George Will—and
> even Camille Paglia—to understand the scam. . . . Their anger at the very
> scholars they long to emulate . . . seems to have worked in some quarters.
> That is partly because the publicists have assumed another persona beside
> that of the intellectual: they pretend to represent the common man—whom,
> as elitists, they also loathe.[4]

This brilliant and shrewd paper focuses on the American scene a decade ago. Today, opposition has emerged within the humanities. Let us
remain upon the scene as it was, when Joan Wallach Scott could correctly
demonstrate that the opposition was desperately claiming a "universal-

ity" that, in my view, has already slipped out of their grasp. She quotes S. P. Mohanty, who "calls for an alternative to pluralism that would make difference and conflict the center of a history 'we' all share," and Christopher Fynsk as offering "the French word *partage* [meaning] . . . both to divide and to share," as an informing metaphor of community.[5] I will keep these suggestions in mind, even as I necessarily note that these good voices are not among the strongest today. Emergence into an at best precarious dominant does not for a moment mean that our battle for national-origin validation in the United States is over. It simply means that we as a collective of marginals are fighting from a different position now and we face the need to consolidate ourselves in new ways, which I have tried to indicate in my opening words. Being reactive to the dominant is no longer the only issue. I agree with Scott's and Mohanty's and Fynsk's general point: conflict, relationality, divide and share. In the U.S. context these remain good marching orders. But difference and conflict are hard imperatives. Difference becomes competition, for we live and participate—even as dissidents—within institutions anchored in a transnational capitalist economy. Our "limited physical supply of what is at stake makes it easy to overlook the fact that the functioning of the economic game itself presupposes adherence to the game and belief in the value of its stakes."[6]

My point is that the stakes in question are not just institutional but generally social. Eurocentric economic migration as a critical mass is based on hope for justice under capitalism. The task of the teacher is as crucial as it is chancy, for there is no guarantee that to know it is to be able to act on it. To continue with the quotation from Bourdieu above:

> How is it possible to produce that minimal investment which is the condition of economic production without resorting to competition and without reproducing individuation? [In other words, is pure socialism possible?] As long as the logic of social games is not explicitly recognized (and even if it is . . .), even the apparently freest and most creative of actions is never more than an encounter between reified and embodied history . . . a necessity which the agent constitutes as such and for which [s]he provides the scene of action without actually being its subject.

"Reified history" is in this case our monumentalized national-cultural history of origin combined with ideas of a miraculated resistant hybridity; "embodied history" our disavowed articulation within the history of the present of our chosen new nation-state. This "encounter" does not translate to the scene of violence at the origin that I laid aside at the opening of this chapter.

In the classroom I spend some time on Bourdieu's caution: "and even if it is [recognized] . . ." I draw it out into the difference between knowing and learning. Without falling into too strict an adherence to the iron distinction between performative and constative, two ways of saying/doing, I still have to hang on to a working difference between knowing about something and learning to do something.[7] The relationship between knowing and learning is crucial as we move from the space of opposition to the menaced space of the emerging dominant.

A chapter in a book will not allow the meditative tempo of the classroom. Let me therefore ignore Bourdieu's parenthesis and emphasize the point Bourdieu makes, keeping myself, for the moment, confined to the institution. I will return to the more general point of new-immigration-in capitalism later.

As long as we are interested, and we must be interested, in hiring and firing, in grants, in allocations, in budgets, in funding new job descriptions, in publishing radical texts, in fighting for tenure and recommending for jobs, we are in capitalism and we cannot avoid competition and individuation. (The meta-vocational use relates to the possibility of "pure" socialism—always "to come.") Under these circumstances, essentializing difference, however sophisticated we might be at it, may lead to unproductive conflict among ourselves. (As I will argue in Chapter 20, "Scattered Speculations on the Subaltern and the Popular," it is different in the underclass.) If we are not merely the opposition any more, we must not lose the possibility of our swing into power by crumbling into interest groups in the name of difference. We must find some basis for unity. It is a travesty of philosophy, a turning of philosophy into a direct blueprint for policy making, to suggest that the search for a situational unity goes against the lesson of deconstruction. If we perceive our emergence into the dominant as a situation, we see the importance of inventing a unity that depends upon that situation. I am not a situational relativist. No situation is saturated. But imperatives arise out of situations and, however unthinkingly, we act by imagining imperatives. We must therefore scrupulously imagine a situation in order to act. Pure difference cannot appear. Difference cannot provide an adequate theory of practice. "Left to itself, the incalculable and giving idea of justice [here as justice to difference] is always very close to the bad, even to the worst, for it can always be reappropriated by the most perverse calculation."[8]

In the interest of brevity I am collapsing a good few philosophical moves needed to make this argument acceptable.[9] I can only ask you to take it on trust that those moves can be made. What is important for me, in order, later, to pass into the second part of this chapter, is simply the conviction that we, the so-called oppositional discourses in the United States, must find a practical basis for unity in global contemporaneity, even if to nurture false hopes.

Consider this good passage from Jonathan Culler, also quoted by Joan Wallach Scott:

> A particular virtue of literature, of history, of anthropology is instruction in otherness: vivid, compelling evidence of differences in cultures, mores, assumptions, values. At their best, these subjects make otherness palpable and make it comprehensible without reducing it to an inferior version of the same, as a universalizing humanism threatens to do.

I repeat, good words, words with which we should certainly claim alliance. Yet, today in particular, we must also ask: Who speaks here? Who is the implied reader of this literature, the researcher of this history, the investigator of this anthropology? For whose benefit is this knowledge being produced, so that he or she can have our otherness made palpable and comprehensive, without reducing it into an inferior version of their same, through the choice of studying literature, history, and anthropology "at their best"? Shall we, today, be satisfied with the promise of liberal multiculturalism that these disciplines will remain "at their best," with a now-contrite universal humanism in the place of the same, and us being studied as examples of otherness? Or should we remind ourselves of Herbert Marcuse's wise words in the 1960s? I will speak of our difference from the 1960s in a while, but Marcuse's words are still resonant over against the promises of liberal multiculturalism: "Equality of tolerance becomes abstract, spurious. . . . The opposition is insulated in small and frequently insulated groups who, even when tolerated within the narrow limits set by the hierarchical structure of society, are powerless while they keep within these limits."[10]

It is certainly important that we have opened up third world literature job descriptions on the MLA job list, yet I am insisting that we will remain powerless collaborators in repressive tolerance if, in higher education in the humanities, we do not re-think our agency. Predictably, my agenda in the end will be the persistent and shifting pursuit of the global history of the present.

Other voices are asking questions similar to mine. I would cite here Aihwa Ong's piece "Colonialism and Modernity: Feminist Re-Presentations of Women in Non-Western Societies," which ends with these important words: "We begin a dialogue when we recognize other forms of gender- and culture-based subjectivities, and accept that others often choose to conduct their lives separate from our particular vision of the future."[11] To claim agency in the emerging dominant is to recognize agency in others, not simply to comprehend otherness, or even to recognize as other.

A distorted version of this recognition is produced in liberal multiculturalism. Yet we have to claim some alliance with it, for on the other side are the white supremacist critics of political correctness. It is no secret that liberal multiculturalism is determined by the demands of contemporary transnational capitalisms, our place within which we are obliged to disavow. Procter and Gamble sends business majors abroad to learn language and culture. In 1991, the year before this paper was first presented, the National Governor's Association Report queried, "How are we to sell our product in a global economy when we are yet to learn the language of the customers?" If we are to question this distorting question while utilizing its material support, we have to recognize also that the virulent backlash from the current racist dominant in this country is behind the conservative geo-politics of the times as well. We are caught in a larger struggle where one side soldiers to exploit transnationality through a distorting culturalism and the other knows rather little what script drives, writes, and operates it. It is within this ignorant clash that we have to find and locate our agency, and attempt, again and again, to throw the clashing machinery out of joint, even as UNESCO and the Preservation lobby fix and preserve "cultural heritages," one by one. What actually happens in a typical liberal, multicultural classroom "at its best"? On a given day we are reading a text from one national origin. The group in the classroom from that particular national origin in the general polity can identify with the richness of the texture of the "culture" in question. (I am not even bringing up the question of the definition of culture.) People from other national origins in the classroom (other, that is, than Anglo) relate sympathetically but superficially, in an aura of same difference. The Anglo relates benevolently to everything, "knowing about other cultures" in a relativist glow.

What is the basis of the sympathy and the feeling of same difference among the various national origins in such a best-case scenario? Here the general social case writes our script. The basis for that feeling is that we have all come with the hope of finding justice or welfare within a capitalist society. (The place of women within this desire merits a separate discussion.) We have come to avoid wars, to avoid political oppression, to escape from poverty, to find opportunity for ourselves and, more important, for our children, with the hope of finding justice within a capitalist society. Only to discover that the anglo-clone supremacist/culturalist class wants to claim the entire agency of capitalism—re-coded as the rule of law within a democratic heritage—only for itself; to find that the only entry is through a forgetfulness or museumization of national origin in the interest of class-mobility. And in the liberal multicultural classroom we go for this, sometimes seemingly as resistance, but at best as competition, necessarily in the long-term interest of our often disavowed common faith in democratic capitalism: "a necessity [as Bourdieu reminded us] which the agent constitutes as such and for which [s]he provides the scene of action without actually being its subject." This necessity is what unites us and unless we acknowledge it ("and even if we do") we cannot hope to undertake the responsibility of the emerging dominant. Let me digress for a moment on a lesson such an acknowledgment can draw from history. If by teaching ourselves and our students to acknowledge our part and hope in capitalism we can bring that hope to a persistent and principled crisis, we can set ourselves on the way to intervening in an unfinished chapter of history which was mired in Eurocentric national disputes. False hope.

"The Law is the element of calculation, and it is just that there be Law, but justice is incalculable, it requires us to calculate with the incalculable."[12] Now that the Bolshevik experiment has imploded, and China is doing "sustainable communism," we cannot afford to forget that the incalculable dreams of the vestiges of Second International Communism (rather than the overt history of its demise in national competition), placed within the calculus of the Welfare State, were quietly eroded by the forces of what is politely called "liberalization" in the third world and by privatization in the first. The calculations with the incalculable are concealed in many passages of the later Marx, the most memorable being the long paragraph at the end of the chapter entitled "The Illusion Created by Competition" in *Capital,* volume 3, where, in a series of five massive "ifs" (the rhetorical bulwark of the element of calculation), Marx comes to the conclusion: "then nothing of these [capitalist] forms remains, but simply those foundations of the forms that are common to all social modes of production."[13] If, if, if, if, if; I will quote this passage again. The line between democratic capitalism and democratic socialism is here being undone, with a certain set of impossible conditions. Persistent critique is being replaced by blueprint. The new immigrant ideologue today acts out the impossibility of that blueprint. In the face of that impossibility she must persistently investigate the possibility of the push from democratic capitalism into democratic socialism, the only struggle that fits the scene. That was Gramsci's dream. It is no secret that, in the developing countries, it is the forces of feminist activism and the non-Eurocentric Ecology movement that did attempt to regenerate the critical element into that dream of displacement from capitalism to socialism. Ethnicity, striking at the very heart of identity, was the incalculable and mystical principle that is open for the "most perverse calculation" in that larger field. The role and agency of the U.S.-based marginal movement and its claims to ethnicity were therefore up for re-invention. That was indeed my theme in the 1990s. Today both these sectors have been claimed by (alter)globalization. My earlier emphasis on educating the educators has become contaminated. Let us return to the undergraduate classroom.

In spite of our common-sense estimation of the best-case scenario, national-origin validation in the general multicultural classroom remains crucially important, for the various national origins, in order to undermine the symbolic importance, all out of proportion to its content and duration, of the test in American History and Civilization taken for the Immigration and Naturalization Service (INS), which establishes that, from now on, the history of the racial dominant in the United States is the migrant's own.

I have already suggested that the place of women within the desire for justice under capitalism may be different. Amy Tan's controversial *The Joy Luck Club* animates this difference in every possible way.[14] The competitive difference among marginal groups, the difference between economic migration (to the United States) and political exile (in China), the necessity and impossibility of the representation of the "culture of origin," culture as negotiable systems of representation between mothers and daughters, the role of university and corporatism in "moving West to reach the East" (T, p. 205), the extreme ungroundedness of identity in the obsessive pursuit of perspectives, can all be used for political pedagogy in the invention of unity.

Let me indicate the inaugural staging of the economic argument, rehearsed many times in the novel:

> After everybody votes unanimously for the Canada gold stock, I go into the kitchen to ask Auntie An-mei why the Joy Luck Club started investing in stocks. . . . "We got smart. Now we can all win and lose equally. We can have stock market luck. And we can play mah jong for fun, just for a few dollars, winner take all. Losers take home left-overs! So everyone can have some joy. Smart-hanh?" (T, p. 18)

Contrast this egalitarian Joy Luck by way of investment to the original Joy Luck Club, four women attempting to contain political exile by force of spirit. This is the frame narrator remembering the reminiscence of her recently dead mother. They are refugees from the Japanese, in Kweilin:

I knew which women I wanted to ask. They were all young like me, with wishful faces. . . . Each week we could forget past wrongs done to us. We weren't allowed to think a bad thought. We feasted, we laughed, we played games, lost and won, we told the best stories. And each week, we could hope to be lucky. That hope was our only joy. . . . I won tens of thousands of yuan. But I wasn't rich. No. By then paper money had become worthless. Even toilet paper was worth more. And that made us laugh harder, to think a thousand-yuan note wasn't even good enough to rub on our bottoms. (T, pp. 10, 12)

In this perspectivized field of identity, only the Polaroid produces the final ID. Here is the last scene of the novel, where the Chinese-American frame narrator meets her long-lost Chinese half-sisters. No attempt is made to provide interior representations of their memories:

I look at their faces again and I see no trace of my mother in them. Yet they still look familiar. . . . The flash of the Polaroid goes off and my father hands me the snapshot. . . . The gray-green surface changes to the bright colors of our three images, sharpening and deepening all at once. And although we don't speak, I know we all see it: Together we look like our mother. Her same eyes, her same mouth, open in surprise to see, at last, her long-cherished wish. (T, pp. 331, 332)

It is at her peril that the reader forgets the authoritative cherished wish that is given in the opening epigraphic tale:

The old woman remembered a swan she had bought many years ago in Shanghai for a foolish sum. This bird, boasted the market vendor, was once a duck that stretched its neck in hopes of becoming a goose. . . . When she arrived in the new country, the immigration officials pulled her swan away from her, leaving the woman . . . with only one swanfeather for a memory. . . . For a long time now the woman had wanted to give her daughter the single swan feather and tell her, "This feather may look worthless, but it comes from afar and carries with it all my good intentions." And she waited, year after year, for the day she could tell her daughter this in perfect American English. (T, pp. 3–4)

Tan's risk-taking book offers us a timely concept-metaphor: the dead mother's voice achieves perfect American English in the regularizing graph of the Polaroid. It is left to us to decode the scandal with sympathy and responsibility, the feather becomes pen.

The Earlier Scene

Since Reconstruction, the first major change in the Constitution after the Civil War, the various waves of immigrants have mingled with one of the supportive, original agents of the production of American origins: the African-American (not the First Nations).[15] But even here, the emphasis on assimilation given in the melting pot theory followed the pattern of Anglocentrism first, and a graduated Eurocentrism next, with the lines of dominance radiating out of that presumptive center. Indeed, this is why the older immigrant elements in the multicultural classroom may or may not strengthen the undermining of the INS test, if the issue is the invention of unity rather than difference. This is the pedagogic imperative, to change the "may not" to "may," in the interest of a different unity. We are not disuniting America. If we are not aware of this as participating agents, the tremendous force of American ethnicity can be used in the service of consolidating the new world order out of the ashes of the socialist experiment, simply by re-coding capitalism as democracy.

I have so far put aside the uprooting of the African and the redefining of the First Nations in the interest of the new and old immigrants. Also to be placed here is the itinerary of the Chicano/a/Latino/a, unevenly straddling the history of two empires, the Spanish and the U.S., one on the cusp of the transition to capitalism, the other active today. We remembered this especially in 1992, when I revised the speech; the time for remembering extends.

For me, an outsider who came to the United States in 1961, the voice that still echoes from the Civil Rights/Black Power movement is from the Ocean Hill–Brownsville School District Struggle of 1968.[16] I had received my Ph.D. the previous year. My experience in India, as it attempted to decolonize its school-system, was not far behind. This is why it is not the more famous struggles that I monumentalize but rather words retained by force of memory. I am not even sure who it was that said them. It may have been the Reverend Galamaison: "This is a struggle against educational colonization." The other day I caught a voice on television, of a little African-American girl who was then a student in that school district, now a mature woman who spoke of her experience and remarked: "We became third world. We became international."

In this perspective, in the area of the struggle against internal colonization, it is the African-American voice in the United States that has become postcolonial. Paradoxically, the rising racist backlash (now surrounding an African-American president) is an acknowledgment of this. Emergence into postcoloniality from internal colonization is not measured in statistics. It is a general and often unperceived change in the positioning on the socius. Once again, so that I am not misunderstood, I want to emphasize that this is not a signal for an end to struggle. It is that, thanks to unceasing effort, the struggle moves to another register. A second wave of backlash rage was on the rise. With an awareness of that register Joan Wallach Scott asked her astute question and made her judgments in terms of class. In 2010, because of color at the helm, race and capital have joined against health care:

> The special treatment that came with high social status never seems to have been seen as a compromise of university standards. (One has to wonder why it was that, for example, the test scores of blacks are stolen from the admissions office at Georgetown Law School and published by disgruntled conservatives, while those of alumni children of influential politicians were not. One can only conclude that the call for a return to a meritocracy that never was is a thinly veiled manifestation of racism.)

In terms of internal colonization, the original groups have not equally emerged into postcoloniality. If I read the signs right (and I may not), the Latino/a/Chicano/a segment has, on one side, been moving for some time toward a recognition, in literary-cultural studies, of "our America" in the entire (North-Central-South) American continental context, not contained within internal U.S. colonization, as the African-American must be. A move toward globality. On the other, specifically the Chicano element is engaged in the restoration of the major voices within internal colonization, reflected, for example, in Ramón and José Saldívar's work on Amerigo Paredes, as well as speaking up for "border culture."[17]

The thought of sublating internal colonization is articulated differently in the context of the First Nations.

At a conference on the Literature of Ethnicity, John Mohawk anguished that Native American writing was not stylistically competitive with the kind of sexy postmodernism that some of our best-known colleagues celebrate in the name of postcoloniality. The embattled phrase "stylistically competitive" was not his. But I will use that phrase again before I end.

Since the Native American voice has been most rigorously marginalized even within marginality, I want to spend some time on the work of a Native American scholar, Jack D. Forbes, who is claiming a new unity with African-Americans. As I have indicated, this unity cannot be based on a choice for justice under capitalism, but rather in the investigation of the institution of the so-called origins of the United States: a sublation of internal colonization.[18] Before making the claim to this divided unity, Forbes lays bare the mechanics of constructing another unity, in another political interest. He gets behind dictionaries to capture the elusive lexical space in-between meaning shifts, by sheer empirical obstinacy. He teases out usage to show the emergence of juridico-legal practice and

rational classification. This is an invaluable quarry, on the level of aggre-
gative apparatuses (power) and of propositions (knowledge), for a future
Foucauldian who will dare to try to take these further below, into the
utterables *(énoncés)* that form the archival ground-level (not ground) of
knowledge and the non-symbolizable force-field that shapes the shifting
ground-levels of power.[19] I cannot readily imagine such a person, for the
pouvoir-savoir (ability-to-make-sense) in question involves

> 300 to 400 years of intermixture of a very complex sort, [and] varying
> amounts of African and American ancestry derived at different intervals and
> from extremely diverse sources—as from American nations as different as
> Naragansett or Pequot and the Carib or Arawak, or from African nations as
> diverse as the Mandinka, Yoruba, and Malagasy. (F, pp. 270–271)

For the perceptive reader, then, Forbes's book at once opens the horizons of Foucault's work, shows the immense, indeed perhaps insuperable
complexity of the task once we let go of "pure" European outlines, and
encourages a new generation of scholars to acquire the daunting skills for
robust cultural history. This work is rather different from the primitivist
patronage of orality. It is in the context of this complexity that a new
"unity" is claimed:

> In an article published in the *Journal of Negro History* [James Hugo] John-
> ston remarked: "Where the Negro was brought into contact with the Ameri-
> can Indian the blood of the two races intermingled, the Indian has not dis-
> appeared from the land, but is now part of the Negro population of the
> United States." The latter statement might offend many Indians today, who
> still survive, of course, in great numbers as Native Americans, but none-
> theless the significance of Johnston's thesis as regards the extent of Native
> American–African intermixture remains before us. (F, p. 191)

This point of view is to be contrasted with the persuasive and representative usual view of the substitution of one collective identity by another: that the Indian population dwindled, was exported, and was replaced by Africans and imported slaves from the West Indies.[20] It is in the
pores of such identity-based arguments that Forbes discovers the survival
of the Native American, in the male and female line. By focusing on the
vast heterogeneity and textuality of the description of mixed groups,
Forbes shows that the emergence of the "other," as the other of the white,
may be, at best, an unwitting legitimation by reversal of the very dominant positions it is supposed to contest. My argument thus is a corollary
of Forbes's. Forbes points out what we caricature by defining ourselves
as the "other (of the white dominant in metropolitan space)": "It would
appear that both Americans and Africans began to appear in exotic pag-

eants and entertainments staged in London during the seventeenth century. It is not always possible to clearly ascertain the ethnicity of the performers, since Africans were sometimes dressed up as Americans, or perhaps vice versa" (F, p. 56).

In the discontinuous narrative of the development of racism, how are we to compute the relationship between that usage and the 1854 California State Supreme Court statement that "expresses a strong tendency in the history of the United States, a tendency to identify two broad classes of people: white and non-white, citizen and non-citizen (or semi-citizen)" (F, p. 65)? Are we, once again, to become complicitous with this tendency by identifying ourselves, single ethnic group by group, or as migrant collectivity, only as the "other" of the white dominant? Shall we, "like so many Europeans, [remain] utterly transfixed by the black-white nexus either as 'opposites' or as real people" (F, p. 172)? Given that, in the literally postcolonial areas like Algeria or India, white racism is no longer the chief problem, Forbes's historical reasoning is yet another way of bringing together the intuitions of global resistance.[21]

Yet even in this work, where isolationist concerns broaden out into global decolonization of scholarship, one must note the absence of a feminist impulse. The Native American woman, being legally free, was often the enslaved man's access to "freedom" in the United States. And slavery itself is "matrilineal." These two facts provide the motor for a great deal of Forbes's narrative of interaction. Yet black Africans and Native Americans, so resourceful and imaginative in probing the pores of the hide of history, never question the gender secrets hidden in them. It is correctly mentioned that Native American practices included the thought of "individual freedom and utopian socialism" (F, p. 266). But it is not noticed that there is feminism in those practices as well. What is it to define as "free," after enslavement, genocide, colonization, theft of land, tax-imposition, women who had, before these acts (masquerading today as social cohesion), been culturally inscribed as "freer"? What is it to become, then, a passageway to freedom after the fact? What is the "meaning" of matrilineage-in-slavery, mentioned in parentheses—"(generally slavery was inherited in the female line)" (F, p. 240)—where lineage itself is devastated?

The Global Field/Transnational Literacy on the Graduate Curriculum

With the name of woman I pass from "Access to the Universal" into "The Global Field," of uneven decolonization, and make an appeal to decolonize feminism as it studies feminism in decolonization. With plenty of help from feminist historians and social scientists, I taught myself to teach a course on "Feminism in Decolonization." From personal experience, then, I know how much education an educator (namely, myself) needs in this venture. "Feminism in Decolonization" is a political rewriting of the title "Women in Development." I am encouraged to see that a critique of the feminist focus on women in development is one of the main premises of the piece by Aihwa Ong that I have already cited. This gives me an opportunity to recite once again that, in this effort, we have to learn interdisciplinary teaching by supplementing our work with the social sciences and supplementing theirs with ours.

It is through the literature of ethnicity that we customarily approach the question of globality within literary-cultural studies defined along humanist disciplinary lines. The word *ethnos* in Greek meant "one's own kind of people" and therefore we take it to mean, by extension, "nation." Side by side with the Greek word *ethnos* was the word *ethnikos*—other people, often taken to mean "heathen, pagan." It is not hard to see how the New Testament would use these already available words. Like many ideas belonging to Christianity, these words were pressed into pejorative service in English, to mean "other (lesser) peoples," in the Age of Conquest. In the nineteenth century, as conquest consolidated itself into imperialism, the word becomes "scientific," especially in the forms "ethnography" and "ethnology." We are aware of the debates between the British ethnologist-ethnographers on the one hand, and anthropologists on the other, as to whether their study should be based on language or on physical characteristics. The discipline concerned itself, of course, with ideas of race, culture, and religion. The connections between "national origin" and "ethnicity" are now politically in place without question.

I think the literature of ethnicity writes itself between *ethnos*—a writer writing for her own people (whatever that means) without deliberated self-identification as such—and *ethnikos,* the pejoratively defined other reversing the charge, (de)anthropologizing herself by separating herself into a staged identity. The literature of ethnicity in this second sense thus carries, paradoxically, the writer's signature as divided against itself. For the staging of the displacing of the dominant must somehow be indexed there. A woman's relationship to a patriarchal or patriarchalized ethnicity makes her access to this signature even more complex.

There is a dominant generalized or world-systems approach to the ethnicity of the *ethnikoi* that has some affinity with Freud's suggestion, nearly eighty years ago, that the search for cultural identity is a species of narcissism:

We have learnt that libidinal instinctual impulses undergo the vicissitude of pathogenic repression if they come into conflict with the subject's cultural and ethical ideas. . . . What he projects before him as his ideal is the ersatz of the lost narcissism of his childhood in which he was his own ideal. . . . The ego ideal . . . has a social side; it is also the common ideal of a family, a class, or a nation.[22]

The standard world-systems estimation of ethnicity, not unrelated to the failures of systemic communism, is something like the following: "Seen in long historical time and broad world space, [nations and ethnic groups] fade into one another, becoming only 'groups.' Seen in short historical time and narrow world space, they become clearly defined and so form distinctive structures."[23] Although I am in general sympathy with the resistance to "the intellectual pressure to reify groups," I cannot work with this world-systems view of ethnicities in globality. The long view and the broad space are so perspectivized that to learn to acquire them in order to produce correct descriptions may be useful only if supplemented unceasingly.

Sublimation and the symbolic circuit stand over against what Freud represents as cultural-ethical pathogenic repressions that may be represented as movements against the individual or social psychic system. On the literary-critical side, Fredric Jameson represents such representations. And therefore he has been reading third world literature for some time now as allegories of transnational capitalism. It is because I agree with Jameson that I would like to insist here upon a different definition of allegory, not just a symbolic order of semiosis. Otherwise, caught between accusations of political correctness and liberal multiculturalism, we are denied the right to say, "Heresy by itself is no token of truth."[24]

I take as my motto the opening words of *Abarodh-bashini* or Lady-Prisoner, a critique of veiled female life published by Rokeya Sakhawat Hossain, an Indian Muslim woman, between 1915 and 1917. She shows that not only the signature of the writer of ethnicity but also the signature of the patriarchally imprisoned woman is self separated: "We have become habituated after living for so long in prison; therefore, against the prison we, especially I myself, have nothing to say. If the fishwife is asked, 'Is the stink of rotten fish good or bad?' What will she respond? Here I will make a gift of a few of our personal experiences to our reader-sisters, and I hope they will be pleased."[25]

Rokeya Hossain allows me to produce a more responsible sense of allegory: the fishwife-as-feminist who, like Hossain, admits to being unable to distance herself from her own imprisonment, "admits," in other words, "to the impossibility of reading [her] own text" as she herself says, can only produce fragmentary instances "against the inherent logic which animate[s] the development of the narrative, [of imprisonment], and dis-articulates it in a way that seems perverse."[26] On that model, since we are imprisoned in and habituated to capitalism, we might try to look at the allegory of capitalism not in terms of capitalism as the source of authori-tative reference but as the constant small failures in and interruptions to its logic, which help to recode it and produce our unity. "Allegory" here "speaks out with the referential efficacy of a praxis."

Learning this praxis, that may produce interruptions to capitalism from within, requires us to make future educators in the humanities transna-tionally literate, so that they can distinguish between the varieties of de-colonization on the agenda, rather than collapse them as "postcoloniality." I am speaking of transnational literacy. We must remember that to achieve literacy in a language is not to become an expert in it. I am therefore not making an impossible demand upon the graduate curriculum. Literacy produces the skill to differentiate between letters, so that an articulated script can be read, re-read, written, re-written. Literacy is poison as well as medicine. It allows us to sense that the other is not just a voice, but that others produce articulated texts, even as they, like us, are written in and by a text not of our own making. It is through transnational literacy that we can invent grounds for an interruptive praxis from within our hope in justice under capitalism.

If we were transnationally literate, we might read sectors that are stylis-tically non-competitive with the spectacular experimental fiction of cer-tain sections of hybridity or postcoloniality with a disarticulating rather than a comparative point of view. Native American fiction would then allegorically intervene in reminding us of the economic peripheralization of the originary communist, pre-capitalist ethnicities of the fourth world. We can link it to the fact that, even as we admire the sophistication of Indian writing in English, we have not yet seen a non-Christian, tribal, Indo-Anglian fiction writer in English. And we will also discover that all stylistically non-competitive literature cannot be relegated to the same transnational allegory in the crude sense.

Take, for example, the case of Bangladesh. You will hardly ever find an entry from Bangladesh on a course on postcolonial or third world litera-ture. Stylistically non-competitive on the international market. The United Nations writes it as the lowest on its list of developing countries, its women at the lowest rung of development. Our students will not know that, as a result of decolonization from the British in 1947, and liberation from West Pakistan in 1971, Bangladesh had to go through a double de-colonization; that as a result of the appropriation of its language by the primarily Hindu Bengali nationalists in the nineteenth century, and the adherence of upper-class Bangladeshis to Arabic and Urdu, the Bangladeshis have to win back their language inch by inch. (I speak of this at greater length in Chapter 12, "Translating into English.") Some of this may be gleaned from Naila Kabeer's essay on Bangladesh in Deniz Kandiyoti, *Women, Islam, and the State*.[27] But apart from a rather mysterious paragraph on "progressive non-government organizations," there is no mention in it of the fact that, because of the timing and manner of Bangladesh's liberation, the country fell into the clutches of the transnational global economy in a way significantly different from both the situation of the Asia-Pacific and the older postcolonial countries. Also, that the worst victim of the play of the multinational pharmaceuticals in the name of population control is the woman's body; that in the name of development, international monetary organizations are substituting the impersonal and incomprehensible State for the older, more recognizable enemies-cum-protectors: the patriarchal family. In this situation, the most dynamic minds are engaged in alternative development work, not literary production. And class-fixed literary production as such in Bangladesh is not concerned with the text of the nation in transnationality, but rather a nation-fixed view which does not produce the energy of translation.[28]

About thirty years ago, in an essay that was allegedly refused entry into the Norton Critical Edition of *Jane Eyre* because it was too oppositional, I wrote these words:

> A full literary reinscription cannot easily flourish in the imperialist fracture or discontinuity, covered over by an alien legal system masquerading as Law as such, an alien ideology established as only Truth, and a set of human sciences busy establishing the "native" as self-consolidating Other. . . . To reopen the fracture without succumbing to nostalgia for lost origins, the literary critic must turn to the archives of imperial governance. (CPR, pp. 131, 132)

Over the last decade, I have painfully learned that literary re-inscription cannot easily flourish, not only in the inauguration of imperialism, but also in the discontinuity of re-colonization. The literary critic and educator must acquire and transmit transnational literacy in a system that must be allegorized by its failures. This intimation of double bind has now changed completely from a balancing act. There is a mad scramble on among highly placed intellectuals to establish their "colonial origins" these days. Such efforts belong with the impatience of world systems literary theory, with portmanteau theories of postcoloniality, with the isolationism of both multiculturalism and anti-racism, and cannot keep the fracture or wound open. This is the infinite responsibility of the emergent dominant engaged in graduate education in the humanities. Otherwise we side with the sanctimonious pronouncement of a Lynne Cheney: "Of course I support multi-cultural education. I want each child to know that he can succeed."[29] Woodrow Wilson had, I believe, suggested at some point that he wanted each American to be a captain of industry! Faith in capitalism gone mad in the name of individualism and competition.

Over against this super-individualist faith, let me quote the Declaration of Comilla (1989), drawn up in Bangladesh, by the Feminist International Network of Resistance to Reproductive and Genetic Engineering, under the auspices of UBINIG, a Bangladesh Development Alternative collective, proposing once again an interruptive literate practice within development:

> We live in a limited world. In the effort to realise [the] illusion [of unlimited progress leading to unlimited growth] within a limited world, it is necessary that some people [be] exploited so that others can grow; Woman is exploited so that Man can grow; South is exploited so that North can grow; Animals are exploited so that people can grow! The Good Life of some is always at the expense of others. Health of some is based on the disease of others. Fertility of some is based on the infertility of others. . . . What is good for the ruling class should be good for everybody?[30]

I can just hear world-systems theorists murmuring, "moralism." But then the moralism of liberal multiculturalism allows us to forget these women's admonition. Like the fishwife, we cannot tell if the stink of rotten fish is good or bad when we disavow our own part or hope in U.S. capitalism.

I heard a colleague say recently, only half in jest, that the newest criticism no longer considered the "literary" part of literature to be that important. On the contrary. We expand the definition of literature to include social inscription. Farida Akhter intervening angrily against "the agenda of developing countries enforcing population policies on others" at the Third Plenary of the World Women's Congress for a Healthy Planet on November 11, 1991 has something like a relationship with the absence of classy postcolonial women's literary texts from Bangladesh on the U.S. curriculum. If those of us who direct dissertations and teach future teachers still peddle something called "culture" on the model of national-origin validation (crucial to the general undergraduate curriculum), we have failed to grasp the moment of the emerging dominant, to rend time with the urgency of justice. Indeed it is the new immigrant intellectual's negotiable nationality that might act as a lever to undo the nation-based conflict that killed the Second International.

Conclusion

I close with two passages from Assia Djebar's novel *Fantasia*.[31] Algeria, like India, is an older postcolonial state. The old modes of decolonization at the time of national liberation are crumbling in both, although India is now altogether more active on the globalizing circuit. Transnational literacy allows us to recognize that we hear a different kind of voice from these countries, especially from singular women, from Mahasweta, from Assia Djebar.

In the case of Djebar, that crumbling could be staged as a profound critique of Fanon's false hopes for unveiling in *A Dying Colonialism*. Here are Fanon's famous words:

> There is the much discussed status of the Algerian woman . . . today . . . receiving the only valid challenge: the experience of revolution. Algerian woman's ardent love of the home is not a limit imposed by the universe. . . . Algerian society reveals itself not to be the woman-less society that had been so convincingly described.[32]

And here is Djebar, in *Fantasia:* Staging herself as an Algerian Muslim woman denied access to classical Arabic, she gives a fragmented version of the graph-ing of her bio in French, of which I quote the following fragments:

> The overlay of my oral culture wearing dangerously thin. . . . Writing of the most anodyne of childhood memories leads back to a body bereft of voice. To attempt an autobiography in French words alone is to show more than its skin under the slow scalpel of a live autopsy. Its flesh peels off and with it, seemingly, the speaking of childhood which can no longer be written is torn to shreds. Wounds are reopened, veins weep, the blood of the self flows and that of others, a blood which has never dried. (D, pp. 156, 178)

Identity is here exposed, by the historically hegemonic imperial languages, as a wound, for those who have learned the double-binding "practice of [their] writing" (D, p. 181). This double bind, felt by feminists in decolonizing countries as well as, though differently, in Eurocentric economic migration, is not ours. The wound of our split identity is not this specific wound, for this wound is not necessarily, indeed rarely, opened by a hope in Anglo-U.S.-EU-based capitalism.

One of the major motifs of *Fantasia* is a meditation upon the possibility that to achieve autobiography in the double bind of the practice of the conqueror's writing is to learn to be taken seriously by the gendered sub-altern who has not mastered that practice. And therefore, hidden in the many-sectioned third part of the book, there is the single episode where the protagonist speaks in the ethical singularity of the *tu-toi* to Zohra, an 80-year-old rural mujahida (female freedom fighter) who has been devastated both by her participation in the Nationalist struggle and by the neglect of woman's claims in decolonized Algeria. The achievement of the autobiographer-in-fiction is to be fully fledged as a story-teller to this inti-mate interlocutor. Telling one's own story is not the continuist imperative of identity upon the privileged feminist in decolonization.

Rokeya Sakhawat Hossain, an upper-class Indian woman, had not kept a journal, but spoken as the fishwife. Djebar's French-educated her-oine attempts to animate the story of two nineteenth-century Algerian prostitutes, Fatma and Meriem, allegorically interrupting Eugène Fro-mentin's *Un été au Sahara,* a masterpiece of Orientalism. She succeeds, for Zohra's curiosity flares up: "'And Fatma? And Meriem?' Lla Zohra inter-rupted, catching herself following the story as if it were a legend re-counted by a bard. 'Where did you hear this story?' she went on, impa-tiently." The "I" (now at last articulated because related and responsible to "you") replies simply: "'I read it!' I retorted. 'An eye-witness told it to a friend who wrote it down'" (D, p. 166).

This unemphatic short section ends simply: "I, your cousin, translate this account into the mother tongue, and report it to you. So I try my self out, as ephemeral teller, close to you little mother, in front of your vege-table patch" (D, p. 167). She shares her mother tongue as instrument of translation with the other woman.

In the rift of this divided field of identity, the tale shared in the mother tongue forever interrupts (in every act of reading) and is forever absent, for it is in the mother tongue. The authority of the "now" inaugurates this absent autobiography in every "here" of the book: The fleeting framed moment undoes the "blank [*blanc*] in the memory" of the narrator's per-sonal childhood, which only yields the image of an old crone whose mut-tered Quranic curses could not be understood (D, p. 10).

The final movement of *Fantasia* is in three short bits, what remains of an autobiography when it has been unraveled strand by strand. First a tribute to Pauline Rolland, the French revolutionary of 1848, exiled in Algeria, as the true ancestress of the mujahidat.[33] Revolutionary discourse for women cannot rely upon indigenous cultural production. If the tale told to Zohra is a divided moment of access to autobiography as the tell-ing of an absent story, here autobiography is the possibility of writing or giving writing to the other identifiable only as a mutilated metonym of vio-

TEACHING FOR THE TIMES 157

lence, as part object. The interrupted continuous source is, once again, Eugène Fromentin. There is one unexplained Arabic word in the following passage, a word that means, in fact, pen:

> Eugène Fromentin offers me an unexpected hand—the hand of an unknown woman he was never able to draw. He describes in sinister detail: as he is leaving the oasis which six months after the massacre is still filled with its stench, Fromentin picks up out of the dust the severed hand of an anonymous Algerian woman. He throws it down again in his path. Later, I seize on this living hand, hand of mutilation and of memory, and I attempt to bring it the qalam. (D, p. 226)

Everything I have written in this chapter has been a meditation upon the possibility that, at this divided moment, we should not only work mightily to take up the pen in our own hands, but that we should also attempt to pick up the *qalam* offered us in uneven globalization, and, with the help of our Polaroid, attempt to figure forth the world's broken and shifting alphabet. No balance, women's work, a persistent double bind.

CHAPTER SEVEN

Acting Bits/Identity Talk

T HIS CHAPTER is a collection of fragments, hence "bits" in its title. If there is a guiding thread, it is the conviction that, if you fix on identity, it gives way. (The curious example from Derrida on page 178, resolutely literal-minded, takes this notion to the seeming absurdity, which is always philosophy's counterexample.) The two fields where this lesson is often forgotten are middle-class metropolitan migrancy (an exchange of civil society which must give itself an alibi: I was elsewhere), the subject of the previous chapter; and middle-class cultural self-marginalization in the third world (this is elsewhere).

At the close of the last chapter, it was clear that in *Fantasia: An Algerian Cavalcade,* Assia Djebar places herself on a chain of great autobiographers: Augustine, the Berber who wrote not only his theology but his *Confessions* in the language of Rome; and Ibn Khaldûn, son of a family that fled Southern Arabia, who wrote not only his history but his Ta'arif (identity) in Arabic.[1] Situating herself thus, she acts out a definition of identity as a wound, exposed by the historically hegemonic languages (D, pp. 156, 178, 181). I proceed from there to present a series of citations of "myself" engaged in identity talk.

The relationship between the texts of the conqueror and the autobiographer is part of the spectacular "arabesques" of *Fantasia.* This is the divided field of identity, that a "feminist-in-decolonization"—as the sign of a(n) (l)earned perspective, not an autobiographical identity—can uncover between Books IX and X of the *Confessions,* in Ibn Khaldûn's "sudden . . . yearning to turn back on himself . . . [to] become . . . the subject and object of a dispassionate autopsy" (D, p. 216).

The language and education policies of the French in Algeria and those of the British in India are rather different.[2] The articulation of patriarchy with Hinduism and with Islam is also significantly different. Yet there is a strong structural bond between the delicacy of Djebar's staging of temporary storytelling and my position, some nine months before I read *Fantasia,* lecturing in my mother tongue, in Kolkata, on the subject of "Deconstruction-Translation," in front of a university audience, many of the senior members of which were my former fellow students. It was a situation of the public acknowledgment of the responsibility of Bengali identity among Bengalis in their felicitous habitat. Kolkata is the capital of West Bengal, the center of Indian Bengali high culture. It was also a situation of the testing of the expatriate by the locals—a presentation of an identity card as it were, just the opposite of the group identity easily claimed in "Teaching for the Times," Chapter 6 in this book. The locals were ferociously well-prepared in deconstructive matters as well as their humanist critique. Any suspected patronizing (I was terrified) would have been not only an error of judgment but a betrayal precisely of the con-tamination of my identity by prolonged contact with the United States. (In the event the patronage came from the other side. In the Sunday Supple-ment of *Ananda Bazar Patrika,* the Bengali-language daily with the largest circulation, my identity was validated. I was hailed as a "daughter of Bengal," but also embarrassingly complimented on my control over my native language.)

For me the most interesting thing, in retrospect, about my careful exer-cise on "Deconstruction-Translation" was that I could get into it only by staging an error in a dictionary definition of "identity," the English word. I will again turn to Assia Djebar before I advance my argument.

In the previous chapter, I commented on the final movement of *Fanta-sia,* with one unexplained Arabic word meaning, in fact, pen: "I seize on this living hand, hand of mutilation and of memory, and I attempt to bring it the *qalam,*" writes Djebar (D, p. 226).

This fragmentary finale begins with two French dictionary entries about a term signifying an item in the rhetoric of the Algerian woman's body. The entries read the figure in two opposed ways. One says that *tzarl-rit* means "to utter cries of joy while smacking the lips (of women)." The other says that the same word means "shout, vociferate (of women when some misfortune befalls them)" (D, p. 221).

Structurally, although not in expressed affective character, I can find something like a relationship, between this inauguration, of the bestowal of writing through a European's mutilation/memory, by way of an example of the limits of European lexicography; and my own opening, of the translation of Derrida's writing (on) translation, by way of an example of the limits of the lexicography of English. There, women's corporeal rhetoric: *tzarl-rit;* here men's transcendental logic: "identity" itself.

(I am, of course, somewhat absurdly straining to share the field of identity with Assia Djebar, rather than some identically produced, rooted Indian sister. Who, she? Is there some pertinence to the fact that what I self-cite below is an example of the very first time that I have translated my own Bengali prose into my own English? But am I not always doing that, in a way that I cannot fathom? There, then, women's corporeal rhetoric; here below men's transcendental logic; mistakes in dictionaries.) I quote:

> In the field of rational analysis, a feeling of recognized kinship is more desirable than nationalism, which conjures with history to invoke motives lying beyond individual reasonableness. Therefore I have started with the family resemblances between deconstruction and Bhartrhari-Nāgārjuna, so that I can tangle deconstruction with our own idamvada.[3] Idamvada is a weird translation of the word identity. Usually we translate identity as vyaktisatva, svarupa, ekarupatā and the like. The other day in the United States I saw in a students' English dictionary that the source of the word "identity" was given as Latin idem or Sanskrit idam and both were cited as meaning "same." Now the meaning of the Latin word idem is not exactly "same" in the sense of one, but rather "same" in the sense of multitudes or repetitions. That which is primordial [*anādi*] and unique [*ekamevādvitiam*] is not idem, it is rather that which can be cited through many re-citations. To make these two meanings one is a clandestine patching up of a loose part of the text-ile fabric of conceptuality. At least from the outside it seems that in our solemn recitation of Hindutva [Hindu-ness, a key word of Hindu nationalism] this clan-destiny or ruse is at work. The little Sanskrit that I learnt under the able guidance of Miss Nilima Pyne at the Diocesan School in Calcutta [I beg the U.S. reader not to lose sight of the social textile here] allowed me to suspect that the Sanskrit idam is also not the undiminishing singly manifest [*akshaya ekarūpa*]. Then I looked at the dictionary. Idam is not only not the undiminishing selfsame, as a pronoun it does not have the dignity of a noun, is always enclitic or inclined towards the noun, always dependent upon the proximity of a particular self, and must always therefore remain monstrative, indexed. All over the world today "identity politics" (that is to say a separation in the name of the undifferentiated identity of religion, nation, or subnation) is big news and almost everywhere bad news.[4] The unremarkable and unremarked ruse in the United States students' dictionary [Merriam-Webster's college edition, I think] makes visible the fraud at the heart of identity politics. As a memorial to that publication I submit this outlandish deconstructed translation of "identity," only for this occasion—not ahamvada

[ego-ism as ipse-ism] but idamvāda. Deconstruction-work shakes the stakes of the spirit's ahamvāda to show idamvāda, and therefore we protect ourselves in the name of a specific national identity, we do not want to know it, we dis-pose of it rather than pro-pose it.[5]

Here then am I, Gayatri Chakravorty (the newspaper dropped the Spivak), speaking on identity as a Bengali ("daughter of Bengal") to Bengalis. As I have remarked in note 3, all the terminology is general Indic (although the matrix language, here English, is Bengali) rather than specifically Bengali. I am Indian, and there is another Bengal, the Eastern part of the landmass, another nation-state, Bangladesh. The next fragment of identity comes from Gayatri Chakravorty Spivak, an Indian in Bangladesh. The language is the same. The fragment is, in a sense, doubly cited, for it is an account of something that happened in Bangladesh that I presented, at a conference on Institutions of Culture at the National University of Singapore, again as an academic among academics, speaking of another place, an Asian among, largely, Asians; another identity bit acted out. (A U.S. colleague teaching at the time in Australia was reported as complaining, after what follows, "This sort of theory can't lead to practice." If he should read these pages, and he well might, I would gently respond that even if the relationship between theory and practice were vectored—which I cannot for a moment credit—the vector is the other way here—theory desperately attempting to digest practice.) I quote:

(Preamble—I start from the assumption that men and women occupy different positions in the making of culture. Any discussion of culture that does not take this into consideration is symptom more than explanation. Women are either silenced or ventriloquial not-quite subjects who hold up the culture or, if conscientized, resist.

For the last few days we have been talking about the cognitive mapping of unisex cultures. But institutions in culture must precomprehend an institution or instituting of culture, not simply as a chronologically prior event but as a philosophically subtending layer. In fact at this level, continuous with the possibility of being in the world, "culture" is one of the many names that one bestows upon the trace of being othered from nature, and by so naming, efface the trace. This intimate proximate level is already sexed and ready for the supplement of gender, like that other most intimately distanced text of culture, the so-called experience of the inside of the body. However we narrativize the difference-deferment of cultural identity or the subjectship of culture, in this place "culture" is a word like "value" in Marx, simple and contentless, immediately codable as ground of difference. What I have liked about Derrida over the years is the obstinate naïveté that makes him repeat the necessary but impossible questions beginning with "What is. . . ." The one that has engaged me most for the last couple of years is: "What is it to learn?" Particularly because the subjectship of ethics and the subjectship of culture, past the threshold of naming, in and out of claims to alterity, is in the hands of only those who can enter or counter globality. I am frustrated that I cannot hear the subaltern, if that is a name of culturing apart. "What is it to learn, these lessons, otherwise?" I am not interested, in other words, in legitimizing the global by reversing it into the local. I am interested in tracking the exorbitant as it institutes its culture.

This is a question I can neither answer nor stop asking. And as an effect of this predicament, or an adjunct to it, perhaps even a companion to it, or perhaps to shut it out, I find myself turning fragments of the institution of culture, conventionally primary or secondary, into cases. Cases of exorbitant normality rather than diseases; cases of confounding the instituted laws. I want to be able to offer four of these cases in the following pages. I think of these slippery things as cases because I do not want them to prove a theory by becoming post-dictions and making the theory—metaleptically—pre-dictive; but perhaps they do? I do not want them to be illustrations of our arguments. But perhaps they are? At any rate these case reports inevitably produce a series of working analyses and descriptions, failures for me, for they seem to lead somewhere when they would rather not conclude.

How do I know a case is a case, Simon During had asked during the conference. The best I can offer is to say that I see a shaped outline in a fragment, it begins to make sense, and it fits into a case. And then, what is it a case of? This has not yet been a thing I have worried about in my project of unlearning learning in order to ask: What is it to learn? But, for the moment, since a question generates an answer, let me say cases of subject-ing, cases of agent-ing, thus cases of identi-fying, cases of the staging of culture as the originary synthesis with the absolute other; everything that we leap over when we start with the object of cultural studies or the politics of culture. But the real answer is you tell me, when you have read these pages.

The first case is just an account of a conversation, a fragile exchange that I have no business setting down here.)

I was at the top of this bit of coast before I came to Singapore, in the edge of the armpit of the Bay of Bengal, the waterlogged islands of Kutubdia and Maheshkhali and the town of Cox's Bazar, the places hit by the cyclone and tidal wave of April 29, 1991. Every act of life there is a major effort. I did not think of these efforts and encounters while I was there except to reflect repeatedly and bitterly upon the contrast between the cheerful relief and rehabilitation efforts of grassroots workers, mostly women, in the area, and the hyperreal videographic image of the absolutely abject and dependent victim that was the only item in international circulation.[6] These places are not outside of globality; in another context I could tell the story of the presence there of the U.S. task force and its tremendous popular critique as one episode in a serial narrative.[7]

When I returned to the capital city of Dhaka, Farhad Mazhar, a male activist, a pharmacist-poet who knows his Marx and Hegel, asked me:

"What did you see?" I had not thought of this yet. But, since a question generates an answer, I scrambled to legitimize myself with this man of work. Beside me were sitting a high school graduate woman from a country town who is a teacher at a barefoot school, not a player in the culture of the coastal islands; and a woman law graduate, considerably more articulate but less of a worker, just beginning to worry about the problems of Bangladeshi rape law. I knew what I was saying was too cumbersome, but the case got made nonetheless.

I had seen, I said, that life and death are in the rhythm of water and land for these people and not only for the very poor among them. They build in the expectation of obliteration, planned obsolescence at the other end. Everyone, including the health and relief workers from other parts of Bangladesh, half a notch above the lowest of them in class, remarks on the fact that loss of land and kin seems to leave a noticeably impermanent mark on the inhabitants of this area. Yet they are not "fatalists"; they grieve and want relief, to rebuild in the face of certain loss, yet again. This is an eco-logical sense of being-in-the-world. The way I found myself putting the case was in terms of the young Marx's perception of species-life rather than species-being, where human life and death are no more than Nature breathing in and out.[8] Marx was obliged to narrativize the case in both a logical and a historical way: for him, both logically and historically, this space was a determination where revolution or planning would not "take." And in the understanding of history as sequence, knowing how to help presumed knowing what should be wanted, easier within a "scientific" vision of the formation of class; but not on this coastline. Here the cultural rather than the class subject was repeatedly being instituted, or instituting itself in an eco-logy, a logic of a greater household or *oikos,* where the subject of the logic is not necessarily worlded as human in the common individualist sense. For my interlocutor, Mazhar, this was proof that, after the critique of consciousness as appropriation, Marx had not theorized property adequately; and that the task of alternative strategies of development that respected subaltern agencies of the institution of culture must learn to rethink property. I had no such confidence; I was stalled at "what is it to learn" and offered a contradiction that I had also seen. Today Hardt and Negri's too easy claim to a digital access to common wealth gives the lie to the difficult rhythm of the pre-digital and endangered subaltern commonwealth.

If this was an eco-logic where the unlikely material subject was the pulse of the tide and the rhythm of the waterlogging of wind, I was in no way ready, daily encountering these very people's savvy discussion of the U.S. task force—that had taken its helicopters back home, that had dropped supplies already available and moving in much larger quantities in the slow-moving trawlers, that had created more trouble in their medical facilities because they could not communicate, that had been contemptuous to the locals, all comments heard from these very people—simply to narrativize them as an earlier pre-scientific stage where the proper help was to "control" nature so that these people could be redefined as passive and graduate to a more or less remote commitment to, or critique of, capitalism. What would it be to learn otherwise, here? Better offer the contradiction: they will not move except as unwilling refugees.

It is commonplace now to say that the expansion of colonialism transformed habitation or land, from its status as reference for the dominant subject, so that space could become a signifier for the colonizer: nation into empire. It is becoming a commonplace that, for the migrant or nomad or yet hybrid the dynamics of the transformation of land or space is now a script or graph rather than a containing system of signs. Smadar Lavie has written on Israeli holding action here, energetically defining an "identity" for the Bedouin, that master-nomad, since the late 1960s.[9] But the tenacious clinging to land in this coastal area seemed something else: a postponement of the eco-logic that otherwise instituted the cultural moment for these people. What was it to learn to help, here? I could respect the relief-workers' bemused on-the-spot decision that this other kind of resistance to rehabilitation must not be allowed to develop into an aporia. The work of rehab must continue. But the vestiges of intellectual sophistication I possessed saw through with distaste the long-distance theorist's dismissal of the aporia as anachrony or his embracing of it as the saving grace of a-chrony. I was adrift. I knew the ways of cutting the drift or *dérive,* of course. Silence the subaltern by talking too much. Describe, account, print.

I cannot close this case. I will go back, asking again: "What is it to learn?" In a minute I will make an enormous leap into the much more comfortable and recognizably political arena of the institution of culture in hyphenated art in the first world: Lebanese-Canadian. But I cannot leave this case without reminding myself that even in this liminal culture, by religious naming Muslim-Hindu and Buddhist, women have an ironic relationship to both eco-logic and the positing of land as the postponement of that logic. In exogamy, these women shift their loyalty from father's land to husband's, quite as many of our non-U.S.-origin female colleagues do. In reproductive culture, these girls' knees scissor in at adolescence and slowly open wider and wider as the rhythm of childbearing in the rhythm of tide and wind is seen as the definitive predication of gendering. Perhaps deconstruction rewrites Marxism for me by the fearful sense that even species-life, *Stoffwechesel* or material alteration of nature, cannot be without gendering if disclosed in the institution of culture. The move into globality here is either the utter dehumanizing of reproductive engineering or the processing zones of international subcontracting, or yet the extension of domestic labor in post-Fordist exploitation.

If the previous part was written in the wake of the U.S. task force, the following bit was written in the shadow of war as intercultural performance, where an old politics of identity successfully managed an absolute politics of culture.

In February 1991 I was in a pretty villa on Lake Como, owned by the Rockefeller Foundation. We were conferring on intercultural performance. I flew back to Toronto, to read a paper, on my birthday. I was musing on identity, thinking that my entry into identity had been "experienced" by my mother, as pain, relief, attachment; that the famous birth-trauma, opening the ontic, remained inaccessible to "experience," to onto-logy as auto-bio-graphy. I was considering how powerfully this is used for an ethics of sexual difference by Luce Irigaray in her "Fecundity of the Caress."[10] The man behind me started up a conversation. He told me with considerable relish that we had started the ground war in Iraq.

I felt the force of that shared "we" so strongly that I knew that I would start with talk of war that evening in Toronto. This identity-bit, in the most colloquial sense, can only be described through the political affect of the Green (no longer phenomenally so) or Alien Registration (Identity) Card. An unnameable identity, named only as "alien," yet strong enough, again, for public self-identification with the protesters in the nation. I quote:

> I have been struck by the extent of a certain kind of judeo-christian religiosity and patriotism on both sides of the War in the United States: Because we are good Jews and good Christians, and because we are Americans, we must punish Saddam for misbehaving and kill the people of Iraq; or, because we are good Jews and good Christians, and because we are Americans, the people of Iraq are our brothers and sisters, however devilish or clownish Saddam might be.

To put it in code: "legitimation by reversal," of a war, of the new imperialism. Millennially, whenever there has been a certain kind of classic victory, the imperialist powers have reshuffled what remains in order to create a new empire. The apparent winning of the Cold War and the dissolution of the Warsaw Pact had to be organized by the United States so that the positions could be reshuffled, so that we could have a new world order before the European Economic Community could become the United States of Europe.

In the context of the Eighteenth Brumaire of the Bolshevik Revolution, these words relating to cultural politics are already out of date. Economic abstractions have a slower tempo, and hence the following passage still retains a certain pertinence:

> The Western powers will be kind enough to destroy their lands, and those whose lands are destroyed will be made to pay the cost of destruction. But the Western powers will be equally kind enough to engage in the reconstruction of the prostrate, devastated lands, for which the victims of devastation will have to fork out money a second time around. . . . The opportunities, as currently assembled, are so tempting that a scramble is on among contractors and engineers hailing from different Western countries. They have not the least doubt that whatever the temporary difficulties, that beast, Saddam, is bound to receive his just desert, and Kuwait and its oil will be regained for the West.[11]

The most frightening thing about imperialism, its long-term toxic effect, what secures it, what cements it, is the benevolent self-representation of the imperialist as savior.

Therefore, listening to the U.S. protest movement as well as the voice of the new patriotism, some noticed how difficult, even impossible, it would be to transform that cement into an international voice that acknowledges global cultural diversity with respect rather than mere benevolence. Some were reminded over and over again of the lessons that we learned in our lives, about the sense of mission that secures and cements imperialist victories in the economic and the political fields by persuading the victim to produce assent. Here is a double bind with the ab-use of the Enlightenment.

What we call "experience" is a staging of experience, sometimes on the small screen. In this sense, an earlier experience is being staged on this new, displaced imperialist scene: the horror of an absolute act of intercultural performance. One of the many tasks of the activist intellectual is to offer scrupulous and plausible accounts of the mechanics of staging. A most tenacious name, as well as the strongest account of the agency or mechanics of the staging of experience-in-identity is "origin": "I perform my life this way because my origin stages me so." National origin, ethnic origin. And, more pernicious: "You cannot help acting this way because your origin stages you so."

The notion of origin is as broad and robust and full of affect as it is imprecise. "History lurks in it somewhere," I had written, but now I think that sentence would have to be revised: History slouches in it, ready to comfort and kill. Yet to feel one is from an origin is not a pathology. It belongs to that group of grounding mistakes that enable us to make sense of our lives. But the only way to argue for origins is to look for institutions, inscriptions; and then to surmise the mechanics by which such institutions and inscriptions can stage such a particular style of performance. This preserves and secures the minority voice in Anglo cultures and also reveals the manipulation of the very same minorities into superpower identification in the violent management of global cultural politics.

In a crisis the intellectual as activist does not always stop to divide a fully mobilized unity. Stands get taken on both sides because, at ground level, democracy is body count—the more the better. That is how changes in agency are inaugurated; higher lawmaking is pushed by bodies mobilized into "the same voice." At a moment of crisis one does not speak up against the absolute intercultural translation that may be cementing both protest and blind patriotism. Even if one knows from the staging of the experience of history that this absolute inter-culturalism is also that which cements imperialist malevolence, one does not speak up, one joins. In a crisis, no hand is clean. Analysis is action there, performance is art. One does not speak of art there as a specific terrain, and does not mention the possibility that rights as written by law are not "experienced" as such by an individual-in-identity but rather animate an abstract agent-in-experience.

When I speak of art specifically my take is a schoolteacher's take: art and literature and music for me are audio-visual teaching aids in the construction of cases. Naïve but useful if one is groping to state the question: what is it to learn? In this view, art also performs the short haul/long haul two-step I have just described in terms of the performance of protest. The videographic performance of war and its aftermath pretends to be analytic as well as performative. It tries to fluff the important difference and relationship between the short haul joining together for body count and the long haul speaking up to displace the legitimation by reversal.

I refer the reader to an earlier piece where I discuss a treatment of Salman Rushdie's novel *Midnight's Children*, part of a mixed-media show called "Inscription" by the Lebanese-Canadian artist Jamelie Hassan.[12] In it Hassan wrenches the title of Rushdie's novel from its context. She is working to confuse the possibility of absolute translations, in the field of identity as well as performance.

Like Rushdie, I am from the Indo-Pakistani subcontinent. We are, then, talking about my own context, productive of my own identity as decolonized subcontinental; another identity-bit. By relocating it, Hassan puts my own identity in parentheses, shows that "my" context is also unsaturated and open, like all contexts. The effort at fracturing my identity is precisely not to sanctify the memory that I was awake, as a child, upon that midnight, between the 14th and 15th of August 1947, when an India divided into India and Pakistan became independent. Hassan makes me learn the ropes. She has unmoored the date, away from Rushdie's India and Pakistan, and given it over to the children of Egypt—who seem, to most sympathetic spectators in North America, and they are in a minority, to be the children of Palestine. And I say, it's all right.

This is the kind of stripping that must be undertaken together if ethnic identities in the so-called first world are to become culturally and politically productive.

A year later, having had my first lesson, I was adrift in Djebar.

Thus adrift, "my" generation (on the cusp of postcoloniality and migrancy, the contemporary prophets of postcoloniality in hybridity) can hail the new American and place her with the Africans and the American nations that built today's America in unacknowledged blood. To confect the new American out of the pipe-dream of "We the People," or out of the bogus concept of the world's Policeman, or yet to give "democratic ideals" a kind of moral luck, is to forget the violence at the origin. When we engage in identity turf battles, we forget this unacknowledged heritage, accept the staging of the United States as enlightened white and behave as if the ethnic scene in the United States represents the globe. This representation is a version of the dream of white America. Here the connection between teaching for the times and being in history come clear.

Think of it this way: what we call culture, in ways that I have attempted to frame in Chapter 5 and at many removes from the vestigial originary space I grappled with in the case of coastal Bangladesh, may be shorthand for an unacknowledged system of representations that allows you a self-representation that you believe is true.[13] Then the culture of the United States, even before the establishment of the United States as such (the kind of place that, say, Goethe looks forward to at the end of *Wilhelm Meister's Apprenticeship,* the dream of old Europe come true) is, in that understanding, the dream of interculturalism: benevolent, hierarchized, malevolent, in principle homogenizing, but culturally heterogeneous. And that particular hegemonic U.S. cultural system of self-representation, abundantly available in and for the socius, begins to usurp, for the United States, the entire globe. And the fact that every national origin is written with a hyphen before the word "American" tends to get forgotten. The next step is Arthur Schlesinger and Lynne Cheney, armed with *The Dis-uniting of America,* moving on toward "the liberal revolution."[14] But not every artist performs that way.

The other kind of emphasis on being a new American is not at all so benign. It is what is called, these days, "border culture." This stops the easy traffic in ethnicity where the sign system in use, English, belongs to the master. Here are some words from "Border Notebook" by Guillermo Gomez Peña, the Chicarrican artist from Tijuana–San Diego:

> dreamt the U.S. had become a totalitarian state controlled by satellites and computers. I dreamt that in this strange society poets and artists had no public voice whatsoever. Thank God it was just a dream. In English. English only. Just a dream. Not a memory. Repeat with me: Vivir en estado del sitio is a translatable statement; to live in a state of siege es suseptibile de traduccion. In Mexican in San Diego, in Puerto Rican in New York City, in Moroccan in Paris, in Pakistani in London. Definitely, a translatable statement. Vivir en estado de alerta is also translatable, my dear. To live in a state of alert, with your wings ready to flap and your eyes ready to question. Why? Why? A child of the Mexican crisis, a new foreigner in the art world, out to exhibit his wounds in immaculate neon coffins. Why? Why? Why? Why? Why? Why? San Diego Channel 10. Super Mojado loses his cool in the middle of an interview. The producers are crapping their pants. Yeah.[15]

I wrench together this anguish with a short passage from Toni Morrison's *Beloved,* the most extreme example of the withholding of translation.[16] Let us look at the scene of the mother tongue changing from mother to daughter, identity transfer, the institution of a culture that will yield Toni Morrison. (We have to remember that chattel slavery is matrilineal.) The scene in the novel is not of a change, but a loss. For the narrative is not of immigration but of slavery. Sethe, the central character of the novel, remembers "what Nan"—her mother's fellow-slave and friend—"told her she had forgotten, along with the language she told it in. The same language her Mam spoke"—the African language—"and which would never come back. But the message, that was. That was, and had been all along" (B, p. 62).

Yet the representation of this message, as it passes through the forgetfulness of death, to Sethe's ghostly daughter Beloved, is of a withholding. Morrison writes, "This is not a story to pass on" (B, p. 275). Even between mother and daughter, a certain historical withholding intervenes. If the situation between the new immigrant mother and daughter—when the mother talks protecting honor and the daughter talks reproductive rights—provokes the question as to whether it is the birth or death of translation, here the author represents, with violence, a certain birth in death.

A death in the birth of a story that is not to translate or pass on. Strictly speaking, therefore, an aporia or unbridgeable gulf. And yet it is passed on, with the mark of untranslatability on it, in the bound book *Beloved* that we hold in our hands. The most extreme case.

Contrast this to the confidence in accessibility in the house of power, ministry of culture or official feminism, where history is waiting to be restored. The scene of violence between mother and daughter reported and passed on by the daughter Sethe, a former slave, to her daughter Denver, who carries the name of a "white-trash girl"—Morrison's Sethe's words—in partial acknowledgment of women's solidarity in birthing, is the condition of impossibility of the book *Beloved*. It celebrates its own impossibility in this tragic way. Here is Sethe telling the story of that impossibility to her daughter: "She picked me up and carried me behind the smokehouse"—her slave mother whose language she could no longer speak—

> Back there she opened up her dress front and lifted her breast and pointed under it. Right on her rib was a circle and a cross burnt right in the skin. She said, "This is your ma'am. This," and she pointed. . . . "Yes Ma'am," I said. "But how will you know me? . . . Mark me too," I said. . . .
>   "Did she?" asked Denver.
>   "She slapped my face."
>   "What for?" [the daughter now asks this mother]
>   "I didn't understand it then. Not till I had a mark of my own." (B, p. 61)

Which is of course a different mark, because the owner is different. This scene, of claiming the brand of the owner as my own, is an example in extremis of what we are talking about; claim the Enlightenment as a double bind. On the other side is a resistance that cannot speak itself as resistance. An example, if the reader's attention span is long enough, of radical monstration, *idamvāda* undoing *ahamvāda*.

This scene, of claiming the brand of the owner as my own, to create in this broken chain of marks owned by separate white male agents of property an unbroken chain of re-memory in enslaved daughters as agents of a history not to be passed on, is of necessity more poignant than, let us say, the wonderful creole writer Coetzee's novel *Foe*, where Friday, the slave whose tongue has been cut off, actually writes something on his slate, "on his own," when the metropolitan anticolonial white woman wants to teach him writing. And when she, very anxious, wants to see it, he withholds it by rubbing it off, *idamvāda* as erasure.[17] And yet even Morrison's powerful staging, in a U.S. text in the tradition of the novel, is productive in a mode that the washed-up coastline of the southeastern edge of Bangladesh, the northern edge of the landmass off the coast of which the Singaporeans, my immediate audience, so successfully inscribe themselves, cannot share. Yet, I can hope, like Djebar's autobiographer-heroine Isma, to earn the right to be an ephemeral storyteller of this episode and arouse curiosity about the remote ancestors of the U.S. task force.

The scene in *Beloved* passes between mother and daughter and then the mother withholds the passing of it—because of course she cannot mark her child. In slavery and less extremely in migrancy, the dominant mark is to be made by the master, in order to be claimed as "my mark." The speaking in English in Jamelie Hassan's "Meeting Nasser," the child turning forward and speaking in English, is not given by the mother who speaks Arabic. This precarious moment in the scene of cultural translation, when suppressed or ignored, produces at the other end the performance of today's war, or the uncaring gift of the task force. This precarious scene of claiming the brand of the owner as my own, to create in this broken chain of marks owned by separate white male agents of property an unbroken chain of rememory in enslaved daughters, teaches us the lesson that we must, as agents, claim that mark as Elizabeth Hassan, the new immigrant child in Jamelie's installation, is doing, as in a much more violent moment the slave mother is doing, as Guillermo Gomez Peña is doing. It is not a gift to be given. It is not a gift that you give at the end of a gun, or off a helicopter, a gift that the other accepts with victory signs or an abject letter.

The lesson of the impossibility of translation in the general sense, as Toni Morrison shows it, readily points at absolute contingency. Not the sequentiality of time, not even the cycle of seasons, but only weather. Listen to this incredible passage and quietly relate this to the tedium of my first case: "By and by, all traces gone. And what is forgotten is not only the footprints but the water and what it is down there. The rest is weather. Not the breath of the disremembered and unaccounted-for; but wind in the eaves, or spring ice thawing too quickly. Just weather" (B, p. 275).

That too is time. Geological time, however slow, is also time. One must not make history in a deliberate way. One must respect the earth's tone. One might be obliged to claim history from the violent perpetrator of it, in order to turn violation into the enablement of *idamvāda,* but that is another story. After the effacement of the trace, no project for restoring the origin.[18] That is "just weather," here today as yesterday. With this invocation of contingency, where nature may be the great body without organs of woman (that passage of Marx again) we can begin to see that the project of translating culture within the politics of identity is not a quick fix.

When I talk about the postponement of eco-logic by positing land as the *da* of *da-sein,* or of the border art where Gomez Peña goes back and forth from Tijuana to San Diego, where Jamelie Hassan goes back and forth from the Islamic world to the world of eastern Canada, where Toni Morrison crosses through slavery from Africa into the United States— for this, the word Derrida would offer us is *navette,* a shuttle, perhaps between the heterosexist homoerotic world and the Queer. Identity giving way.

Glas is a kind of typographic miming. It is written in bits and pieces. On the left-hand side is the homoerotic traditional tale of Western philosophy, on the right-hand side the criminal male homosexual Jean Genet. As we read, we are obliged to be a *navette* between the two sides in order to find out what every extraordinary page might "mean."

> Navette is the word. . . . The word—la navette—is absolutely necessary. It will have had to be there. . . . It is a small metal vessel in the form of a boat. . . . And then the weaver's navette coming and going, woven in a chain. The weave is in the navette. . . . Isn't elaboration [Derrida is using it in the expanded sense—*elaborare,* to work out] a weaver's movement?[19]

In the early Derrida the text is one of the master metaphors that persistently question mastery. The text is textile, from the Latin *texere,* to weave. But here he seems to give up the concept-metaphor of the text. The weaver's shuttle, the *navette,* smoothly going back and forth between the two sides is not going to serve here.

The question/statement (half a quote from Genet) with which the book begins, in the right hand column, is: "'What remained of a Rembrandt torn into small, very regular squares and rammed down the shithole' is divided in two" (G, p. 1b). What remains, what is the irreducible remains of art, or, for us, of identity, when it is torn up into a million ID cards and stuffed into English divides (at least) into two. You cannot say that the result is a smoothly woven text: "Yet we have mistrusted the textile metaphor. This is because it still keeps . . . a kind of . . . naturality, primordiality, cleanliness. At least the textile metaphor is still more natural, primordial, proper than the metaphor of sewing of the seam [*couture*]" (G, p. 208b).

Couture carries the echo of the *coupure* or cut—the cut from the place or origin.

Derrida is learning this lesson by looking at the gay man's text. We are in the house of identity: what is the name of (the straight white) man? It is in the left-hand column that the homoerotic commedia of the authoritative answers to that question (disguised, of course, as the question of Man) is played out. Hegel is accusing Kant of being a fetishist because he does not introduce love into religion, and Freud is launching the fetish into indeterminacy by speculating with it.

But what is this fetish without which the white mythology of the identity of man cannot act out? Again and again Derrida puts in *Glas* texts on the so-called African fetish found in Hegel, to show that these mythographers have not earned the right to speak of the fetish. The withheld translation of Africa has been suppressed (G, pp. 207a–211a).

For Hegel the fetish is an animal substitute for the Eucharist: this notion is implicit when Hegel, Marx, and Freud use the fetish as a counterconcept in their text, even though Freud does unmoor it. For the notion of the fetish, it is not interesting to weave with a *navette* between Marx, Hegel, Freud, Kant. Derrida is going to have to cut holes and put their fantasy of the African fetish that one cannot restore, in a text written in English, in French. He is going to have to patch it on the text to see what difference it makes.

Meanwhile, on the right-hand side Genet is in the harem of transvestites and criminal gay men, on another orbit from the text of the identity of "man." They are putting on all kinds of *fétiches,* dildos, grape clusters on the crotch, et cetera, as that text unfolds. Who is the authority for whom, and how is the *navette,* shuttling from Hegel and Company to Genet and his accomplices weaving anything at all? Derrida suggests that we will have to think now, rather than of textile, a weave, as in the old dispensation, of the kind of sewing and patching that betrays, exposes what it should hide, dis-simulates what it signals, makes the TV screen crap its pants.

Therefore he can do nothing other than cite:

> Cit[ing], as perhaps you have just seen, only to displace the syntactic arrangement around a real or sham physical wound [the Freudian fetish, covering the phallic mother's (absent) phallus, is never far away] that draws attention to and makes the Other be forgotten. . . . All the examples stand out, are cut out [*se découpent*] in this way. Regard the holes, if you can. (G, pp. 215b, 210b)

This is not the confident postmodernist citation where what is cited is emptied of its own historical texting or weaving. This is a citing that invokes the wound of the cutting from the staged origin. I harmonize with Djebar here: autobiography is a wound where the blood of history does not dry. Postmodernist practice manages the crisis of postmodernity— the displacement of the dream of mere modernization as the text of imperialist wish-fulfillment at its best.

By the graphic of the Queer fetish Derrida is led to the absurdity where ontology itself gives way. Genet writes of roses shooting whiff after whiff at our faces (the rose is a character in this gay brothel as well as one among many fetishes)—and Derrida, in the middle of one of these passages, comments, "The essence of the rose is its non-essence: its odor insofar as it evaporates. Whence its effluvial affinity with the fart or the belch: these excrements do not stay, do not even take form" (G, pp. 58b, 59b). "Fart" in French is *pet,* so to repeat identically, absolute translatability becomes *re-péter,* each fart different because of what the body must take in to live. A familiar case of the daily failure of ontology. Rather than the idea infinitely repeatable and therefore always identical, the repetition becomes something that cannot be caught. "How could ontology lay hold of a fart?" (G, p. 58a). He rewrites the ontico-ontological difference by reminding us of the body's being: the ontic, which in Heidegger is the intimacy of being, to which the being is so proximate or close that no ontology can lay hold of it, in the late Heidegger becomes, perhaps, a certain kind of fetish, the spirit covering over the uncertain periodicity and peculiar incorporation (identity?) of the present-in-absence ghost. His politics change; he invokes an originary or primordial *Zusage.*[20]

The digestive system is deeply culturally marked. What are the limits to ontology here? *Glas* on the right-hand side starts with the shithole. The outside limits to Kant's sublime were long ago located in vomit.[21] Derrida's work in the 1980s, once again around the Eucharist and that assimilated creole Augustine, obstinately asks: "What is it to eat?" In this unemphatic moment in *Glas,* Derrida asks a question that causes embarrassment.

The text, that too "primordial" metaphor, is a *navette* between *Geist* and *Gäschen,* between spirit and a fart, between the transcendent breeze and the wind that makes us embarrassed, marked by the body's materiality. What Derrida is looking at is the way we are when we are close to ourselves. This lecture—in Singapore—would have been an exercise in the discomfort of controlling flatulence if it had been an after-dinner lecture. And when one is alone and proximate to oneself, one finally gives way to the totally unembarrassing comfort of the signature of the body being itself (as it were)—nobody there to be embarrassed or repelled. It is simply the end of the public sphere, for the moment. It is difficult to hear this question: How can ontology—the philosophy of being—lay hold of a fart? There is none of the glamor of sexuality here, or of the so-called spectrum of sexual practices. How can ontology lay hold of a fart? An ontology can always put its hand on whatever remains in the john—the shit—but never on the whiffs let out by roses. The text is a gas, the mark of the spirit in one's body. The text is an imperfect *navette* between *Geist* and fermentation, *Gäschen,* the little gas. The ontic as fart or belch, the signature of the subject at ease with itself decentered from the mind to the body that writes its inscription. This is also the embarrassment offered by the subaltern victim in the flesh, scratching herself and picking her nose.[22]

But if you cannot catch it, how can ontology lay hold of it? This is not as glamorous as either mind or body, either high-toned mind-talk or highly attitudinizing body-talk. There is crisis, there is the long-haul politics of culture, but this rag and bone shop remains the counter-case of cultural institution. As indeed of the philosophy of Being, highest talk of identity in another guise. This singularity blows gas in the face of political mobilization and fundamental ontology alike.

Let's get out of here. Zoom now to the other end of the spectrum. We have considered varieties of creole and migrant art and theory, writing by a woman who takes the history of slavery seriously, responsibly, art and theory which try to cope with the problem of the politics of translation, the politics of culture, the politics of identity.

Now let us touch the responsibility of the "national" artist seeking an international audience. Not the artist who is an immigrant, but the artist who has remained in decolonized space, to represent that culture to the persons in metropolitan space eager for other cultures. This is a great narrative indeed; and upon this register I think that the national artist has a very strong responsibility not to take advantage of the sanctioned ignorance of the West.

Recently in Italy I saw a performance by a woman, an Indian artist, a dancer, which was broken up by an Italian director. What he was actually doing onstage (I was reminded of the Olympia in Hoffman's story, Freud's treatment of "The Sand-man") was actually making her do her classical dance and then asking her to break up her sequences, taking away her music, and then slowing the sequences down as much as possible, making her do 5 percent of the sequence and then putting other women—whom he no doubt treats the same way—together so they could do a peculiar kind of a dance together under his control. And in the representation of this happening—which filled me with terror, because that is how we were produced by assenting to imperialism—at a certain point, he makes her say that she had resisted him for a long time until she realized that he was not going to take away her style. When questioned by Trinh T. Minh-ha, as to how she believed that he would not take away her style, she said confidently, "He promised me nothing. I believed him."

We are afraid of this kind of seductive winning of the assent of the colonized, so that the result is a kind of ventriloquism which then stands in for free will. Our own complicity in our production is another kind of translation of cultures, access to a museumized identity, roots in aspic. The national artist in the third world has a responsibility not to speak for the nation in response to a demand made by this craving for intercultural exchange. Everything is susceptible to exchange, but commodity is something made for exchange. Identity as commodity.

And so I would like to turn to the film *The Voyage Beyond,* by the Bengali filmmaker Gautam Ghosh. This is not a film about contemporary India, but of India in the last century. It is the story of a very young girl being married off to a dying old man. They are in a burning ghat on the borders of the Ganges or Ganga. At a certain point the outcast, the untouchable, wins her to sexuality. She is there because she's going to be sati, a widow who self-immolates. At the end, she is washed away in the waves of the Ganga as is her dying husband.

This is basically the story. Actually the film engages in a peculiar species of auteurism by borrowing the proper name of a magisterial text of Bengali fiction, Kamal Majumdar's *Antarjaliyatra* (1961). The metropolitan viewer cannot know this. The result, in this particular case, is a sort of violation of the transcoding or translation between two media. (I know that films are not supposed to be "faithful" to novels; that is not my point.) I believe that it is this possibility of violating the particularity of this novel as historical icon that kept Satyajit Ray and Mrinal Sen from attempting its filming.

If in the context of the other cases I have said that sometimes it is necessary to withhold translation, as in the extreme case staged by Toni Morrison, here, going 180 degrees, I am suggesting that in certain macro-contexts there is also room for a gesture of "faithfulness to the original." Faithfulness to the original considered as one case among many, not a case that should be idealized. In a certain historical conjuncture, when the West is avid for third world culture, it sometimes becomes the appropriate case. Given the experimental verbal authority of this novel, no film using the title *Antarjaliyatra* can avoid auteurism. A new Macbeth is a new Macbeth. I will not attempt to comment on the verbal experimentation of *Antarjaliyatra.* Let me, however, say a word or two about the general project of the book. It does have something to do with the question of identity. The idea of identity is often marked by the names of continents, huge chunks of the world: Asian identity, third world identity. The author of this book attempts the nearly impossible task of grasping identity in the extremely proximate or close-up place—the place where, in philosophical rather than cultural discourse, Derrida/Genet locates the wind that is not spirit—where it has not yet reached the level of adjectival description. In the layer of its incessant and inchoate emergence, close to the body, if the body too is understood as a kind of patchwork, between bone and blood, nerve and twitching muscle. Kamal Majumdar chooses the liminal space of the burning of the body and three human beings relating differently to that event-to-come: an event that hangs over the text, but never happens. The dying brahmin, the woman in imminent death-in-life, and the untouchable, who is the facilitator of the flame that consumes the body. The filmmaker shatters this project by staging the burning ghat as a realistic referent carrying a realistic amount of local color, a stage for a broadly conceived psychodrama played out by easily grasped stock characters: the good and earthy untouchable, the good, colonially touched doctor who is not quite good enough, the patriarchally oppressed woman awakening into struggling self-consciousness through sexual liberation. Hinduism as precolonial superstition, heterosexuality as woman's liberation: a screen easy to work out from a base of minimal knowledge.

What the author of the novel is trying to do takes as understood a fully formed ideological subject, to whom the reader is invited to be ex-centric. In other words, Majumdar expects the reader to have enough internalized perception of a certain kind of Hinduism, as a heteropraxic cultural system, to have earned the right to be asked to consider the following question: how do the affects work when such extreme dispensations as sati and the caste system operate as a felt cultural norm? This kind of a question is extremely important today in my nation-state of origin where Hindu fundamentalism is violent, where even children and young girls are sometimes being convinced that to be a good citizen of India one has to internalize an absolute version of the majority religion, which cannot admit that it is a negotiated mistranslation. Again an attempt at the cultural or political translation of origins.

In this context, to redo the book for a national audience would have been quite different from doing it for an international audience. This is not the place to develop those suggestions.

Let us go back to the novel's project. His question: how do the affects work when such extreme dispensations as widow-burning and the caste system operate as a felt cultural norm? How could our mothers and grandmothers have assented to this, and remained human? There is no possibility here for the viewer to interpret the film from a position of cultural superiority. This is a question that can only be asked by us as Hindus, to ourselves. This text is exactly not for the outsider who wants to enter with nothing but general knowledge, to have her ignorance sanctioned.

Majumdar wants to avoid critical distance as far as possible, because he knows it is not fully possible. He articulates the most extreme system of belief, not because he wants to give himself distance, but because he wants to acknowledge proximity, because he wants to get at that most difficult thing, perspectival normativity. In other words, he is not distancing himself by portraying these three people as "normal." He is trying to perspectivize the idea of normality as such by choosing the hardest possible case. He is perspectivizing all normality, yours and mine as well, not just "Asian" or "historical." And—this is a difficult point but I want to continue to emphasize it—the base of normality out of which normality in general is thus unmoored is a rather specific Bengali cultural base, a general "identity," if you like. From out of this base, presupposed only to be put under erasure, Kamal Majumdar seems to ask a question that I can, since I write in English, put to you almost exactly in the words of John P. Leavey Jr. and Richard Rand as they have translated the French of Jacques Derrida: "How does one give the *seing* [a thumbprint as well as one's breast] to an affect?" (G, p. 425).

It is easy to get information about the identity of an entire continent, or to put one's signature on a concept, support it or oppose it. But how does one claim the normality of an affect in extremis as one's own, in the place of the *seing* rather than the signature? One way is to unmoor affect from the natural person and place it in ideology—can this be done except from above?

Again, this is a question that I can neither not ask nor answer. Turning away from this limit, let us notice cruder ways of fabricating identity. Let us look at the way in which Ghosh changes the introductory verbal material from novel to film.

At the beginning of the film, Ghosh's subtitle writer takes a feeble whack at giving the viewer a bit of potted history. In 1829 Lord William Bentinck abolished the self-immolation of widows, echoed by names like Ram Mohun Roy in the dialogue. In the Bengali film, there is nothing but the title and the opening credits. Let us now turn to some of the sentences in the preface of the book, dealing precisely with the identity or rather the subject-position of the assigned reader or viewer: "The affective-icon of this book is Ramakrishna's, the poetic icon Ramprasad's. . . . I am certain our country still thinks of the Ganga as its life, our country still touches immortality, everyone will understand our story. My profound respect to the reader."[23]

Who are these two named figures? Ramprasad Sen, an eighteenth-century clerk patronized by Raja Krishna Chandra Sen, is not exactly a figure unknown to the West. Some of his exquisitely and deceptively simple poetry in praise of Kali was translated into French fifty years ago. He is a constituent figure of Bengali culture. He is part of that great movement of re-inscribing Kali into an affective goddess, both mother and daughter, violent only out of radical innocence, not malevolent but a punisher, in sheer childlike impatience with evil.[24] This Kali is the book's icon, not the peculiarly monstrous figure behind the untouchable in a sequence toward the end of the film, where he is talking to the young bride, reminiscent of nothing so much as Coppola's insensitive imaging of the Bodhisatva icon in *Apocalypse Now*.

Ramakrishna, a mystical visionary of the second half of the nineteenth century, is another constituent figure of contemporary Bengali culture who is not unknown to the West. Centers of the Ramakrishna Mission began to be established in the West from the very beginning of the twentieth century. His conversations have been translated into English. Christopher Isherwood wrote a sympathetic biography about ten years ago. Ramakrishna is one of the most moving affective reformers of Hinduism, attaching himself to a Kali who closely resembles Ramprasad's beloved goddess. He is a perspectivist, attempting affectively to enter the subjectivity of a Muslim, a Christian, a woman. He is absolutely opposed to the caste-system. This is not the place to comment on what has happened to Ramakrishna's vision as it has become socially institutionalized. What is important for the question of the identity of the reader/viewer is that this figure is the affective icon of the book.

Majumdar writes: "The new Bengal has been created by remembering him, by keeping him in mind. He took away a bit of fear in the natural human being in the raw, from his own wakeful state by saying: 'Is a human being a small thing, eh!' "

The book's "icons" are a certain Ramprasad's and a certain Ramakrishna's, longing for an absence of violence, of cruelty, of caste, and of addiction to flesh. Whatever one feels about desire and its (un)fulfillment, one is free to suppose a Gautam Ghosh trying to transcode this complex finespun textile of desires into filmic idiom. Instead he appropriated, abdicated, and banalized, putting the name of William Bentinck on the screen of Ramprasad Sen and Ramakrishna Paramahansa.

The Voyage Beyond is actually what is called a "topical" film. It is made in the atmosphere of great interest in Sati following Rup Kanwar's self-immolation a few years ago. Feminist mobilization and resistance to Sati on that occasion was certainly widespread and important. In that legalized context, it was understandably not possible to approach gendered subjectivity with any subtlety. The movement had to remain on the level of female agency. A filmic representation of woman-in-Sati is not confined to such restrictions. What does Gautam Ghosh do with the relative autonomy of this art-form? There are at least five looks at different points of the film that consolidate the representation of the young bride Jashobati in the film:

a) An unconsummated look before the exchange of garlands that seals the marriage.
b) A look at the temple of the grotesque goddess asking for a repetition of the sexual encounter.
c) A rounded gaze at the stone printed with the palm-mark of the burnt widow.
d) A look at the end with Jashobati pinned on the woodframe evocative of the seasonal status of goddesses regularly deposited in the river.
e) The visually exciting representation of the unfocused look of the eye painted on the boat.

The least convincing bit of "liberated" script, "Am I your plaything?" is not accompanied by any orchestration of the gaze.

Considerations of the first three should accompany a viewing of the film. I would like to point out here that Jashobati looking out of the disposable goddess-frame and the lovely boat with the pair of eyes that cannot gaze carry a heavy cultural message without cultural logic. The suspension of two particular deaths—the natural death of the old man and the forced unnatural death of the young wife—deaths that do not happen, is here re-coded as a return to a cultural base without any cultural justification. To play thus with textual subtlety seems to me to be an abdication of the responsibility of the national artist, trafficking in national identity (in the name of woman) for international consumption.

For it is against the grain of this responsibility of the national in the international that we feminist internationalists strain. I am thinking now of the worldwide group called Women Living under Islamic Law, going all the way from North Africa to Indonesia with members from immigrant communities in the first world.[25] These feminist internationalists must keep up their precarious position within a divided loyalty, to being a woman and to being in the nation, without allowing the West to "save" them. Their project, menaced yet alive, takes me back to my beginning. It is in their example that I look at myself as a woman; at my history of womaning, revised in advance in "Culture: Situating Feminism," Chapter 5 in this book. Women can be ventriloquists but they have an immense historical potential of not being (allowed to remain) nationalists; of knowing, in their gendering, that nation and identity are commodities in the strictest sense: something made for exchange. And that they are the medium of that exchange. Bride by bride, the first diasporics.[26]

When we mobilize that secret ontic intimate knowledge, we lose it, but I see no other way. We have never, to quote *Glas,* been virgin enough to be the Other. Claudine Hermann, a lawyer who has practiced both in Afghanistan and in France, gives me my closing words: "We have always known how [in 'culture'] to see women through the eyes of men. And in something called life, to see men through the eyes of women. We have always known how wide the gap is."[27] We have always been schizoid and, I might add, hermaphrodite. Not androgynous, but a bit of a hermaphrodite who is secure in the conviction that sex and gender are structurally not identical. Cultures are built violently on the enforced coercion that they are. War is its most extreme signature; and, like all signatures, patriarchal.[28] Our lesson is to act in the fractures of identities in struggle. The lesson in this chapter is, once again, the double bind of identity itself.

CHAPTER EIGHT

Supplementing Marxism

AN THE DOUBLE BIND of identity be escaped by thinking collectivity? Received wisdom might say so. Yet in Marx, the source
of our most analytical theory of collective practice, a double
bind comes to inhabit the "social." In 1992, it had seemed that attending
to the ethical would be the necessary supplementation. As indicated in
the Introduction to this book, it is in systematic and systemic interventions in the epistemological that the task for the times lies. In 1992, Derrida
was laying out communism in the mode of messianicity without messianism.
I thought I would supplement Marxism as socialism, as follows:

I will make six points telegraphically. First: Early and late, Marx painstakingly established a definition for the term "social," which involved a
rationalization of the merely individual. To grasp this rationalization is
class-consciousness. In the context of industrial wage-labor, this rationalization can be called, in contemporary language, the quantification of
labor into socialized labor-power. Although in the passage I have quoted
on page 198 Marx imagines the socialized welfare state, in the mainstream of his thought he is interested in the worker participating in the
quantification of his or her socialized labor-power as the owner of the
means of production, in order to produce surplus for the maintenance of
society. Two uses of the idea of the social are at work here. The first use
is the Enlightenment project of the public use of reason, but with a proletarian rather than a bourgeois subject—legitimizing by reversal and
opening the door to totalitarianism when practiced by the vanguard
upon an epistemically unprepared population. This is where an ab-use
through an aesthetic education—a persistent and impossible supplement-

ing of vanguardism—that acknowledges the unacknowledgeable fracturing of reason in Kant's critical method rather than transform it by substituting balance through play is proposed. The play might be cousin to Hardt and Negri's digital idealism. When, however, Marx uses the word "social" or "society" to project or describe the goal of the public use of reason he seems to be relying on an unresearched, incoherent, humanist notion.[1]

Karl Marx was aware of educational problems, of course. His move away from the academy is proof of that perhaps. I have also cited the third thesis on Feuerbach in the Introduction. It cannot, however, be denied that the major problem for him was the rational struggle, against capitalism, to appropriate capital for social productivity, and that he had a privileged education. In the event, in the gap between these two uses of the "social," systemic Marxisms bloom, fester, and fail. Any reformist critique of Marxism that further rationalizes the social ignores and runs the same risk.[2]

Second: by contrast, the strongest humanist support of Marxism is the critique of the reification of labor. This implicit critique, sometimes unrecognizable as such, and sometimes surrounded by more spectacular arguments, runs like a red thread from great national liberation movements all the way to romantic anti-capitalism. In its vaguest yet most robust articulation it asserts that labor itself must not be commodified and is grounded in a binary opposition between labor and commodity.[3] Marx's notion of the use of reason as class-consciousness in a socialized society, however, was the recognition that labor as a particularization of labor power was a commodity, although of a special kind. (I have argued this at greater length in Chapter 9 in this book, "What's Left of Theory?"). In Marx's view, it is only with this understanding that the agents of production, the workers, can move to become agents of the social. Indeed, Marx describes the common double nature of commodity and work as "the pivot [der Springpunkt] around which the understanding of political economy revolves [dreht um]."[4] It is because of this pivotal concept that he recommends the explanation of the circuit of capitals spelled out in terms of the commodity as the most serviceable for class-conscious worker bent upon change, upon appropriating the surplus for redistribution. Without work on the second use of "social," which I believe is insufficiently thought through in Marx, neither the possibility nor the impossibility of such moves can be grasped (see note 2).

Third: If the Marxian project of class-consciousness were not anchored in a full saturated, rationalized class subject and secured by the assurance of a certain end, it could serve to give shape to a persistent critique of capitalism; to combat the humanist critique of reification which can be and is co-opted and modernized to recode unreconstructed global capitalism as democracy. A brief presentation permits telegraphic sketches; therefore let me say that this persistence may juggle to an uneven three-step where communism is a figuration of the impossible in view of which capitalism and socialism can be perceived with some effort as each other's double bind.

This is the next step from the heterotautological double bind between "social" and "social": the "social" is (appropriates) (not) "social."[5] In 1992, I was busy transforming the double bind into the chiasmus of the Nietzschean (rather than Derridean) notion of difference, by quoting Derrida's passage on Nietzsche as if it were a self-description:

> The same, precisely, is *différance* . . . as the displaced and equivocal passage of one different thing to another, from one term of an opposition [here capitalism and socialism] to the other. Thus one could reconsider all the pairs of opposites . . . on which our discourse lives, not in order to see opposition [between capitalism and socialism] be erased but to see what indicates that each of the terms must appear as the *différance* of the other, as the different and deferred within the systematic ordering of the same.[6]

No wonder I was calling the swing between capitalism and socialism "effortless" in those days after the fall of the Wall. Such is the seduction of hope that I was ignoring the Gulf War of 1991. Today we know that what was consolidated in the failure of state as well as revolution, namely, the international civil society, also consolidated the reduction of double bind into sustainability, for the convenience of a capitalism seemingly only for social productivity, the epistemic problem reduced to calculation. There is no supplementation of Marxism there.

Derrida has shown appropriate irritation with the harnessing of deconstruction by "a community of well-meaning deconstructionists reassured and reconciled with the world in ethical certainty, good conscience, satisfaction of service rendered and the consciousness of duty accomplished, or more heroically still, yet to be accomplished."[7] I was troubled in 1992 that he might be dismayed if I say that in this sketching of the three-step where communism is a figuration of the impossible in view of which capitalism can be effortlessly perceived as socialism's *différance* (as I had in 1992), I had brutally reduced his work to formulas. I was on target with the figuration of the impossible; I quote, "the law is the element of calculation and it is just that there be law. But justice is incalculable. It requires us to calculate with the incalculable."[8] But now I have graduated (I hope) from a difference misperceived as pushing away in time and space to the more active notion of double bind. (*Différance* is simply the common-sense fact that to begin with anything is to differentiate it from everything it is not and therefore there never can be a clean beginning. Common sense is hard.) No guaranteed formulas any more. Only loss of hope.

It will not do to reduce our task of supplementing Marxism to a push and pull between communism and socialism either: Socialism is in the element of calculation and it is just that there be socialism, but communism is incalculable. It requires us to calculate with the incalculable, precisely what Marx left dangerously uncalculated. What Marx left uncalculated was the epistemological burden of training the socialist subject. I owe another formula to my friend Teodor Shanin: socialism is about justice, not primarily about development. For the second part of my sketched three-step is where capitalism and socialism must, through training in epistemological performance, be understood and felt as one another's double bind (the 1992 wording had been "can be effortlessly perceived as each other's *différance*"). And, even if (riffing now on Foucault and breaking up the *pouvoir/savoir* or can/know description of a successful episteme) the *savoir* may be there through imaginative training, the *pouvoir* is elsewhere. Unless the impossible project of aesthetic education is everywhere, this will not succeed. The very first waves of capitalist colonialism show unwitting signs of this, soon corrected. The proof is in the varieties of what in the case of the British became the Bloomsbury Fraction at home and the colonial subject abroad. Today all we have is a tremendous bad faith in the dismissal of secularism as colonial/orientalist and, in another neck of the woods, not entered by the secularism debaters, the bad faith of a corporatism that teaches self-interest to the untheorized subject of Human Rights.[9] A conference can only ask a question, whither Marxism, remembering that a blueprint of this *différance* is teleologically given in the final pages of the third volume of *Capital*.[10]

Fourth: What role can my group play? Again, a telegraphic definition. "My group." The middle-class professional migrants who entered the United States after Lyndon Johnson relaxed quotas in 1965, leading to a 500 percent increase in Asian immigration, otherwise called the brain-drain, disguising the poaching it sometimes was. (I have spoken of them in Chapter 2 of this book, "Who Claims Alterity?") More important, I am speaking of their children, Americans psychologically held together or centered in the expectation of civil agency in the United States—strictly to be distinguished from "cultural" assimilation.[11] I am speaking of, and indeed for, this group because when we talk about Marxism at academic conferences in the United States, we so often lay out grand plans whose agents, if they exist, never come to these conferences. Or we lay plans which presuppose incredible systemic changes. What I am going to suggest will no doubt make no more than a minute contribution to the great collective persistent critique that I sketched in point three, but it is something we can do tomorrow, or in fact, today.

Of the earlier generation of these migrants I speak only of those not directly involved in the financialization of the globe, rentiers of the new world order, so to speak. Indirectly, the entire group, having migrated, has a stake in dominant global capital; leaving postcolonial problems, leaving the failure of decolonization, coming with the hope of justice under capitalism. This fact, which recodes itself as the often unacknowledged ease of having left, appears as various sorts of psychic phenomena which, in another code, may perhaps be called "reaction-formations." (Please remember, I am not speaking of refugees and exiles, or of the underclass, but rather of relatively well-placed economic migrants after 1965, the new immigrants who became model minorities. We have to take into account that, even within this group, women are most often exilic, since they seldom have a "real choice" in the decision, and are often obliged to act out a custodianship of "culture"—in food habits, dress habits, sexual codes, and the like—in migrancy. Indeed, this is a knot in the red thread of this entire book and leads to the re-territorialization of the veil from Assia Djebar to Leila Ahmed.[12])

The most noticeable of these "reaction-formations" in the current conjuncture is an unexamined culturalism, which in turn allows the recoding of capitalism as democracy.[13] Of course matters are rather more indeterminate if one pauses to ponder, but my register allows the abstract, telegraphic, rational-expectations language with which we make sense of our lives.

Unexamined culturalism has now developed into a culturalism that is part of policy, often gendered, for good or ill. One cannot diagnose it away as group "reaction-formation," although some elements of the socius can perhaps still be mobilized along those lines, if we accept its dictionary definition: "Psychological attitude or habitus diametrically opposed to a repressed wish, and constituted as a reaction against it. . . . In [psychic] economic terms, reaction-formation is the counter-cathexis of a conscious element: equal in its strength to the unconscious cathexis, it works in the contrary direction." This precarious pathology—the American dream cooked in a hallucinatory culturalism—makes the place of nationality or nationalism willy-nilly negotiable, in many different ways. The energy of that negotiation can be more productively channeled into the area where responsibility has an unavoidable bond with freedom of subjective consciousness or purity of intentionality. If we as a group are in the grip of a dream of reparation by our culturalism, our negotiable nationality can, through teaching and learning of rational transnational awareness, come to realize that in the current post-Soviet conjuncture, to work at the *différance* of capitalism and socialism in the heart of dominant capitalism may be more reparatory toward the places we left behind than the culturalism that feeds, financially and otherwise, the various fanaticisms that lodge in the fault line between nation and state opened up by that very conjuncture. This last sentence is not only telegraphic but telescopic. Believe me, I unpack every phrase and clause of it daily in areas and arenas where I have more time and greater responsibility. Here I must acknowledge again that I have, without offense, I hope, made use of a bit of Derrida in my reductive way, a passage previously cited in this book: "One can doubtless decenter the subject, as is easily said, without challenging anew the bond between, on the one hand, responsibility, and, on the other, freedom of subjective consciousness or purity of intentionality."[14] Giving shape without end to what I have telescoped into a sentence is, I hope, one small way of accepting that challenge. This last bit relates to the epistemological production of the subaltern intellectual, as citizen, "Maoist," or ethnic (see Chapter 9, note 35).

Fifth: A word now about another way of working with the rational kernel of Marx's rational thought in the context of a more diversified struggle in which some of us also take part. To tabulate: feminism, anti-racism, anti-colonialism. Here I will repeat a conviction that has been growing over the last few years. In this context the nascent crisis theory implicit in much of Marx, especially in some sections of the third volume of *Capital,* has to be added to that kernel forever broken and restored on the track of the double bind. What I have continued to say is that these movements, the three that I have mentioned, should swallow and digest these dynamic materials rather than seek to fit correctly the authoritative label "Marxist." If I may once again analogize, somewhat fancifully, from individual pathology to the history of the present, I would say that today it is a necessarily incomplete incorporation. Incorporation seems a particularly productive act of semi-mourning for the perpetually deferred death of an insufficiently rationalized systemic vision.

Sixth: If we think transnationally, rather than only in the Group of Seven theater, we cannot emphasize the role of the state centrally. In order for the machinery of the state to participate in persistent socialism as the difference and deferment of capitalism, we need the regionalist movements of resistance to Development, capital *D,* keeping their distance from the specifically international civil society. Let us set out the improbability of setting the socialist calculus in motion by way of a telegraphic account of what it looks like from the perspective of the global other side, including those ex-communist countries attempting to be satisfied with the promises of an underdeveloped capitalism. For it is impossible to escape the orthodox constraints of a neoliberal world economic system which in the name of Development (capital D) and now sustainable development removes all barriers between itself and fragile national economies, so that any possibility of social redistribution is severely damaged. Further, the people who have politico-economic power or consumerist ambitions in much of the old third world share a common interest in and therefore often welcome subordination (invariably represented as aid or collaboration) by dominant global capital. In this situation of increasingly lost hope, confusion, and the failure of decolonization, the always dubious hyphen between nation and state is violently renegotiated by dystopic fanatics in the old third world as well as in the newly defined second in the name of a once glorious and pure nation. Enthusiastic movements have always known that the best chance for action or a feeling of agency is to guarantee a cure that will bring about the return of the glorious repressed of history—"we were powerful once"—as its cathartic end. The script is violence in the name of action. Caught between the specters of development and nation, the state is not the prime mover of the socius. The located movements of resistance to development have a critical relationship to the state. Much of the strength of that critical relationship comes from that culture's active and interminable digestion of the pulverized and augmented rational kernel of Marx's thought. These movements are obviously better networked in the old third world, and the supportive networks in the first world however little they now attempt to decolonize their sense of resistance. These specific networking lines are hard to lay down in the newly defined second world, and it is still hard to swallow a culture as medicine that has so lately been a poison.

These two movements I speak of are the two I know best: the non-Eurocentric ecological movement and the non-Eurocentric movement against reproductive and genetic engineering, the latter relating to so-called population control imposed upon the North by the South. They are regional rather than international (a) because of their critical relationship to the many so-called nation-states they encompass, and (b) because at their best they still try to learn from rather than impatiently transform subalternity and womanspace, areas that have not been considered as central resources for the conceptualization of the modern state.

(Subalternity is the name I borrow for the space out of access to the welfare mechanisms, however minimal, of the state—both located, and undocumented migrant. The subaltern is not necessarily to be confused with unorganized labor, women as such, the proletarian, the colonized, the object of ethnography, political refugees, et cetera. Nothing useful comes out of this confusion. The word becomes useless then, not that a useless word is necessarily a bad thing when we pause to ponder.)

The traffic with the incalculable in the non-Eurocentric ecological movement is sometimes driven not by the logic of the consumption of resources alone, but by the conviction that change is hardly ever possible on grounds of reason alone. In order to mobilize for nonviolence, for example, one relies, however remotely, on incanting the sacredness of human life. "Sacred" here need not have a religious sanction but simply a sanction that cannot be contained within the principle of reason alone—a non-philosophical kin to the transcendental deduction. In this sense, nature is no longer sacred for civilizations based on the control of nature. The result is global devastation due to a failure of ecology. It is noticeable that less advanced groups in the fourth world still retain this sense as a matter of their cultural conformity. I am not exoticizing or romanticizing the aboriginal; they are not all "radicals." It is a matter of their cultural conformity, if only because they are still subaltern. What we are dreaming of here is not how to keep the aboriginal in a state of excluded cultural conformity, but how to learn and construct a sense of sacred nature by attending to them—which can help mobilize and drive a globe-girdling ecological mind-set beyond the reasonable and self-interested terms of long-term global survival. We want to open our minds to being haunted by the aboriginal. We want the spectral to haunt the calculus.

As has been suggested in the Introduction, the idea that this cultural conformity was robust enough to be recoded came from a museumization practiced by benevolent despots in the area of my initial educational struggle. Indeed, the convictions of the leaders of the struggle seem now to be caught in that feudality that I have learned since then to recognize. The World Bank is more matter-of-fact:

> The world's remaining indigenous peoples—estimated to number more than 250 million in seventy countries—possess knowledge fundamental to the sustainable management of resources in these regions. In cooperation with the Center for Indigenous Knowledge, the Environmental Department prepared a bank discussion paper entitled "Using Indigenous Knowledge in Agricultural Development" (Warren 1991). Region-specific technical papers are being prepared to support the implementation of the directive.[15]

World Bank assistance comes at the request of states. I have spoken of the state in globalization, as it continues the process started with the neo-colonialism in the middle of the last century. I need not belabor the point. The fight over patents is news to no one.

In the tug-of-war between capitalism and socialism, the World Bank manages the ecological movement. The movement is now nestled within the more inclusive climate change lobby, in its incessant pursuit of the sustainability of capital accumulation. The movement against reproductive and genetic engineering confronts the multinational pharmaceuticals and their conglomerative associates. (In the lower reaches, these are movements that have eaten and daily chew—actively ruminate upon, as Nietzsche would say—the hard nut of Marxist economic theory; and they daily half-mourn the tug of capitalism, even in their own resistance. But half-mourning is also half-jubilation. This is where, in the upper reaches, emphasis on capital's visible social productivity alone, and the concealment of incessant subalternization win.)

All initiatives of population control or genetic engineering are cruelly unmindful of the dignity of reproductive responsibility. The imperative collective calculus for winning the right to sexual preference and pleasure, the right to equitable work outside and in the home, and the right to equality in education must be supplemented by the memory that to be human is always and already inserted into a structure of responsibility. To distinguish this strictly from heterosexual communitarianism, we must connect with the subaltern presupposition where heterosexual reproduction is a moment in the general normativity of a homosexuality for which the sexual encounter itself is a case of the caress.[16] This originary queerness contains and is contained by reproductive heteronormativity (RHN), invaginated by the law of genre.[17] As I have suggested in "Culture: Situating Feminism," Chapter 5 in this book, today's metropolitan, governmentalized queer couple uses the difference of heteronormativity in an extra-moral sense. There is no continuous logic between this and the logic of capital. The double bind between capital/social and that between the two Marxist uses of the "social," however, are determined by this problematic as well, for everything within the pleasure principle and a little bit beyond is held by RHN.

"Supplementing Marxism" is the title of this chapter. Supplementing here does not only mean stuffing the holes in Marxism as Marxism stuffs our holes. As my intractable ending shows, I have not forgotten Derrida re-citing Rousseau: the supplement is dangerous because it opens us to the incalculable.[18]

CHAPTER NINE

What's Left of Theory?

Marx

It is perhaps no surprise that, in the absence of a practical left in the United States, a dwindling enclave in the academic and journalistic world continues to debate the theory-practice binary opposition with a vigor matched only by its lack of consequence outside the academy. But the U.S. academy is our home, and insofar as the consequences of this debate affect our hiring and firing practices, it is worth commenting on it in a strictly academic way. I should add here that our handful of elite universities, with larger and more managerial global spheres of influence, protect their conservatism with a viciousness not necessarily imaginable outside that charmed circle, ideologically controlling the constitution of their student body when the formal law of the land will not allow more visible lines of separation. In this sorry field, then, I begin, as usual, in the classroom.

Every couple of years for the last two decades, I confront the task of explaining to a new group of graduate students that, although the difference between use and exchange seems immediately available to intuition, use-value and exchange-value are in the same form: the value form. To put something in the value form means to abstract it, so that it can be measured. This is as true of use-value as it is of exchange-value. When we use something up, we do not in fact measure it. (Today an exception might be made of foods with their nutritional value tabulated on the label.) But that does not in fact mean that the thing cannot be put in the value-form. It is only in this sense that use-value is a fiction.

Marx was trying to explain the value-form as the possibility of abstraction across the board because it was going to come in handy to explain the special character of capital, but the insight was altogether counter-intuitive. By this insight, use-value, generally a fiction, is not a fiction for capital. Capital consumes by measure. This is labor-power, not labor. It is the use of the use-value of labor, not the use of labor. Counter-intuitive lesson.[1]

And then comes the other lesson, better known but commonly left unconnected with the first one: that the capitalist pays back less value (in the money-form) than s/he borrowed (in the labor-power form). This is because when labor-power is used, it produces more value than its concrete pre-measurable personal base requires to reproduce itself potentially as measurable into use-value for capital: labor-power. Socialism will voluntarily keep the use of labor-power undisturbed in form but equitable in fact, and save the difference for redistribution.

It is essential to understand the abstraction involved in the value-form, whether in use or exchange, in order to understand this argument. Commodification of labor into labor-power is a potentially good thing in this argument, for it alone can provide the wherewithal for socialism. Use (concrete) over exchange (abstract), more goods for the working class to use, and fewer for the capitalist to exchange, is far too Luddite a binary opposition to account for the theoretico-practical breadth of Marx's work. Ownership of the means of production, dictatorship of the proletariat, critique of reification, when anchored in this binary, cannot confront the self-determination of capital (I use the nineteenth-century expression advisedly) as globalization: global finance capital necessarily interrupted by world trade. On the other hand, if the counter-intuitive Marxian lesson—in the value-form both use and exchange are abstract, and the capital-labor (power) relationship is that capital uses the abstract(ed labor)—is learned, the socialist grabbing and saving the difference (surplus and/or interest) for redistribution can mean the difference between crisis-driven and strategy-driven globalization.

It is difficult to grasp this because Marx was ahead of his time. It is also difficult because working-class culture clung to a robust empiricism which was the muscular side of the querulous academic empiricism that commanded the authoritative translations (in the narrow as well as the general sense) into English.

From all accounts, Frederick Engels was not a querulous man. But he can be counted as Marx's first English translator, a metonym for the empiricist havoc that constructed a practical Marx who repeated good common sense, namely, use/concrete, exchange/abstract, alienation of labor a crime against the working class. No. Marx's tone is different: Labor for him is use of labor-power by capital. And, "it is an extraordinarily cheap kind of sentimentality which declares that this method of determining the value of labour-power, a method prescribed by the very nature of the case, is brutal. . . . When we speak of capacity for labour, we do not speak of labour, any more than we speak of digestion when we speak of capacity for digestion" (C 1, p. 277).

Let us read one critical page of *Capital* to see the process at work (see Figure 1). Marx is theorizing and Engels is running interference, with the intention of making things clearer for the implied working-class reader. In the two previous paragraphs, Marx has been telling us that we must leave behind the intuition that value first appears in the exchange-relation, in quantitative abstraction. Marx urges the reader to make the difficult counter-intuitive move, to grasp abstraction in use-value. "Of course when we exchange, the common factor in the exchange relation . . . is its value. We must now consider value *independently of this* [*the exchange*] *form of appearance*. A use-value or good [*Gut*] therefore, has value only because abstract human labour is objectified in it" (C 1, pp. 128–129; emphasis added).

In the use form of appearance, value does not become intuitively manifest to us because we do not engage in exchange. But, as I suggest above, Marx's clear implication is that, unless we are able to think it, we will not be able to understand the relationship between capital and worker and the commodity will remain a fetish. Thus it is the role of the abstract—the spectral, if you will—that we must grasp rather than reject. Here we can see that he is clearly undoing the use(-value)/exchange(-value) binary opposition or semantic nexus that still haunts our common sense. Yet, as he approaches the end of the clinching paragraph, Engels undermines the theoretical effort, crucial to the establishment of the point around which the lever of social justice will turn (C 1, p. 132). The heterology of the social is downstream from this.

In the value-form, use as well as exchange suffers abstraction. When labor is abstracted into labor-power, it is used for capital accumulation by the capitalist; only if it is still abstracted into labor-power can it be thus used by associated workers, for socialism. (The ownership of the means of production must not be understood on the model of collective private property here.) Instead of reading this, we get a bit of formula-talk, that generations of leftists have learned by rote, leaving out the crucial words "use-value" and "labor-power": "Now we know the substance of value," Engels writes. "It is labour." Yet Marx was attempting to emphasize the value-form: not labor, but labor as labor-power. "We know the measure of its magnitude," Engels continues. "It is labour-time." For the their value might fall below that of bricks. In general, the greater the productivity of labour, the less the labour-time required to produce an article, the less the mass of labour crystallized in that article, and the less its value. Inversely, the less the productivity of labour, the greater the labour-time necessary to produce an article, and the greater its value. The value of a commodity, therefore, varies directly as the quantity, and inversely as the productivity, of the labour which finds its realization within the commodity. (Now we know the *substance* of value. It is *labour*. We know the *measure of its magnitude*. It is *labour-time*. The *form*, which stamps *value* as *exchange-value*, remains to be analysed. But before this we need to develop the characteristics we have already found somewhat more fully.)*

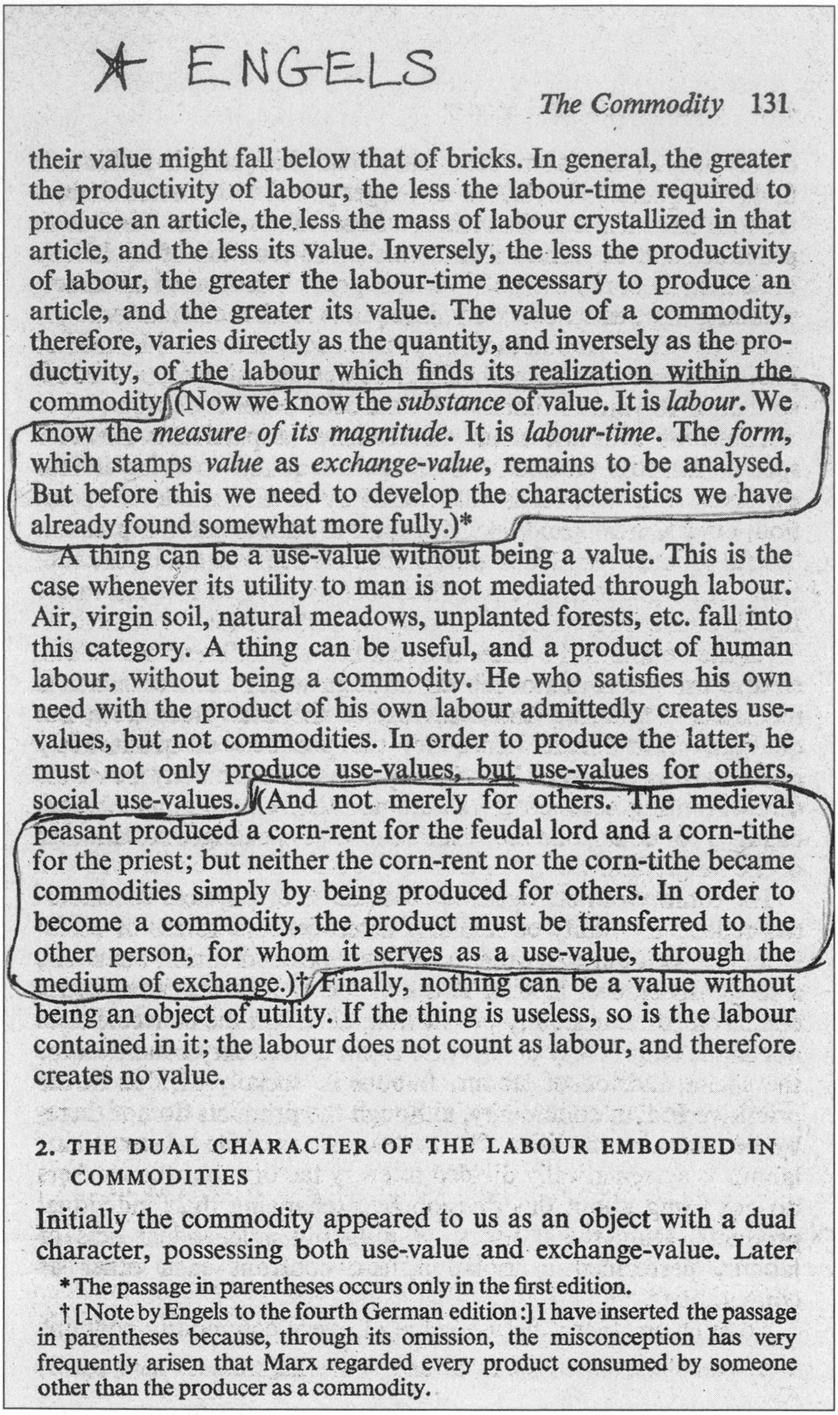

A thing can be a use-value without being a value. This is the case whenever its utility to man is not mediated through labour. Air, virgin soil, natural meadows, unplanted forests, etc. fall into this category. A thing can be useful, and a product of human labour, without being a commodity. He who satisfies his own need with the product of his own labour admittedly creates use-values, but not commodities. In order to produce the latter, he must not only produce use-values, but use-values for others, social use-values. (And not merely for others. The medieval peasant produced a corn-rent for the feudal lord and a corn-tithe for the priest; but neither the corn-rent nor the corn-tithe became commodities simply by being produced for others. In order to become a commodity, the product must be transferred to the other person, for whom it serves as a use-value, through the medium of exchange.)† Finally, nothing can be a value without being an object of utility. If the thing is useless, so is the labour contained in it; the labour does not count as labour, and therefore creates no value.

2. THE DUAL CHARACTER OF THE LABOUR EMBODIED IN COMMODITIES

Initially the commodity appeared to us as an object with a dual character, possessing both use-value and exchange-value. Later

* The passage in parentheses occurs only in the first edition.

† [Note by Engels to the fourth German edition:] I have inserted the passage in parentheses because, through its omission, the misconception has very frequently arisen that Marx regarded every product consumed by someone other than the producer as a commodity.

Figure 1: Page from Karl Marx, *Capital: A Critique of Political Economy.*

Marxian argument this is irrelevant without the transformation of labor into labor-power. And Engels's next sentence, "The form, which stamps value as exchange-value, remains to be analyzed," reinforces the very use-exchange semantic nexus that Marx was attempting to dislodge in the value form.

Between 1867 and 1873, Marx re-read *Capital*. From the second edition, to which he wrote a magisterial postface, he removed the Engelsian passage. Engels preserved it in a note. English translations restore it to the text. Rather a lot of the received pieties of Left conservatism in the metropolis are this sort of failure of translation, an inability or refusal to surrender to the counter-intuitive original.

By chance I was reading both Plotinus on Beauty and Marx on the Commodity, for my undergraduate and graduate classes last semester. I was struck by the tenacity of Marx's classical training. Marx unpeels value in a style of argumentation remarkably similar to the Plotinian unpeeling of beauty. Marx was keen on Aristotle. His theoretical object choice is in step with Aristotle. Theory takes as its object things that are birthless and cannot be verbally articulated.[2] Marx is looking at the circuits of capital, the birth of whose originary accumulation cannot be philosophically grasped, only narrativized.[3] Marx shifts gears from philosophy to history, so to speak, a favorite move of classical German philosophy.[4]

In keeping with this methodological proviso, and still undoing the use-value/exchange-value split, Marx offers a few counter-examples. Keeping just value for the découpage of his labor theory, he consigns value-at-the-origin to Nature, where the possibility of measure exists as the incommensurable. Thus the very first counter-example—earth and air—has incommensurable use-value because human labor has not gone into its making. This, one may say, remembering the Aristotelian notion of theory, is the birthless, unphrasable end of the forms of appearance of value. The other three counter-examples are: (1) Use-value produced with labor but producing no commodity (the thinking of abstraction must be possible here). (2) Use-value for others—social *(gesellschaftlich)* use-values—where abstraction must surely be thought, although the value is not deployed within general commodity exchange. And, finally, (3) arguing from the other side, Marx indicates the need to assume *Nutz*—sheer usefulness—in use as well as exchange, so that it cannot be kept separate for use-value alone. This hint of the complicity (folded togetherness) of usefulness and the abstract mensurability of value is unfortunately not clear in English translations.

After Marx's death, Engels explains away the counter-intuitive politics of theory by predicating the commodity only in exchange.

It was Engels who provided the decisive cuts. The history of the left rose and fell in them.

In the classroom, we give accounts of the world beyond. Only in that spirit can one connect our problem of reading with the predicament of what Perry Anderson magisterially called Western Marxism more than twenty years ago.[5] We remember that our failure in reading, anchored in so frail a thing as the disappearance of real language requirements in this era of the triumph of English, as the instrument of a globalization that would be for Marx both medicine and poison, is part of the picture. We are implicated in what we study. What we are recounting is what we now call a cultural difference. British (U.S.) empiricism (pragmatism) over against continental rationalism, leading to a failure of reading (translation). It is with this intimate connection, not-quite-not-a-consequence, in mind that we turn to one possible temporizing of the predicament of Western Marxism.

After 1919, Western Marxism moved through cultural critique, varieties of the New Left, structuralist Marxism, and now Marxism on the deconstructive model. After 1989, capitalism triumphant has led through to globalization—nearly complete abstraction, finance capital; and the attendant damage control, of which Schiller is the specific, hopeless, final, and persistent remedy. Deleuze and Guattari's fantastic insight, that capital was—let us say almost—the abstract as such and capitalism codes it is no longer sufficient. Finance capital is let us say almost the abstract as such and world trade codes it.[6] Now I begin to think also of reproductive heteronormativity, with gender as the first instrument of abstraction, conjuring with sexual difference as its originary differential. What I had earlier seen as a "structural homology" has now stepped forward into the argument.

In "Can the Subaltern Speak?," the point was that the British and the caste-Hindu reformers only concentrated on the visible violence of Sati, passed a widow remarriage law without any infrastructural involvement, and left the miserable rule-governed life of the ordinary Hindu widow unchanged.[7]

A structural homology may be advanced here. As long as we remain only focused on the visible violence of world trade, endorse the credit-baiting of the poorest rural women of the Southern hemisphere in the name of micro-enterprise without any infrastructural involvement, the subaltern remains in subalternity.[8] And we legitimate the world trade coding of the finance capital market by reversal.

In this situation, the untrammeled power of the abstract financialization of the globe economically and ideologically managed from within capital—world trade—cannot be managed (supplemented) by opposing perspectives from within. Today Marx's ghost needs stronger offerings than Human Rights with economics worked in, or the open-ended messianicity of the future anterior, or even responsibility (choice or being-called) in the Western tradition. The need is to turn toward ethical practices—care of others as care of the self—that were defective for capitalism.[9] Marx must be turned around to those who lost in the capitalist competition, again and again; in order to turn this ferociously powerful form of capital around to the social.

By now the reader knows the error of placing a specifically archaic hope in the aboriginal staged in aboriginality, without epistemological care, or indeed planning for the ethical. I pull again on the red thread: aesthetic education as training the imagination for epistemological performance.

Caught in our cultural difference, English-dominance and pragmatism, we cannot think of abstraction as useful—for capital and therefore for socialism. Caught in his cultural difference, Europe-dominance and rationalism, Marx could not think this need. First, as an organic intellectual of industrial capitalism he could only advise a public use of reason (understanding and turning around the spectralization of labor-power) from below. It must of course be admitted that, in his unrelenting analysis of what it was that the workers must free themselves from, namely, the workings of capitalism, he did not devote as much time to the how, beyond this faith in Reason. If only the worker grasps this twofold nature of the labor contained in commodities (as labor and its spectralization, labor-power), s/he will grasp the blasting point (*Springpunkt*, modern German *Sprengpunkt*) of political economy, and revolution is almost sure to follow.[10] This is clearest in *Capital*, volume 2, where Marx recommends the commodity-circuit explanation of capitalism to workers because commodity capital, as the direct product of the capitalist production process, recalls its origin and is therefore more rational in its form, less lacking in conceptual differentiation, than money capital, in which every trace of this process has been effaced, just as all the particular useform *(Gebrauchsform)* of commodities are generally effaced in money.[11] Here are the rational bones within the flesh of the marketplace that will guarantee freedom from capitalism. (The money-circuit, the favorite mode of explanation of vulgar economists, is constantly described as irrational.) Here we develop insights from Chapter 8.

It is still only the story of freedom from. When it came to the presumably postrevolutionary moment of freedom to establish socialism, no provision for something like an epistemic guarantee could be or was thought.

Toward the end of his life, Marx gave a picture of a socialist community, which we recall in "Imperative to Re-imagine the Planet" (Chapter 16 in this book):

> If however wages are reduced to their general basis, i.e. that portion of the product of his labour which goes into the worker's own individual consumption; if this share is freed from its capitalist limit and expanded to the scale of consumption that is both permitted by the existing social productivity . . . and required for the full development of individuality; if surplus labour and surplus product are also reduced, to the degree needed under the given conditions of production, on the one hand to form an insurance and reserve fund, on the other hand for the constant expansion of reproduction in the degree determined by social need; if, finally both (1) the necessary labour and (2) the surplus labour are taken to include the amount of labour that those capable of work must always perform for those members of society not yet capable, or no longer capable of working— . . . then nothing of these forms remains, but simply those bases [*Grundlagen*] of the forms that are communal [*gemeinschaftlich*] to all social modes of production.[12]

What is not given here is why people as a whole would want to exercise the freedom to arrange for the upkeep of other people. The establishment of governments that enforce this are, first, again that reliance on abstract structures that we are questioning here. The Introduction speaks of an augmentation of enforcement in world governance today. Secondly, the machinations of electoral politics do not usually support a cause because of a desire to help others. This calls for a persistent struggle for epistemic transformation in the future anterior.

Although Marx left the question of the will to socialism begged, we cannot afford to do so. The post-Soviet rhetoric of the indispensability of the United States is often couched in the language of a moral mandate (although the politicians know that it is no more than lip service). A thousand people are not much of a specimen, of course. But if the behavior of managerial passengers on international flights over the last ten years gives a clue, the guess can be ventured that, in full-swing globalization, the supposed inheritors of the Enlightenment legacy as the torch passed from Europe do not insist on the freedom to arrange for the upkeep of the species-being of others. They get better and better at making money (manipulating the now electronic spectral, as Marx had hoped the workers would the rational spectral), but, when left to their own devices, their talk—and, rather infrequently, their reading—would lead to the following rational expectations: that they understand power as it is inscribed in a simple semiotic.[13] They understand simple sentimentality about family as well as gender-struggle as the latter relates to the semiotic of power. This sentimentality can accommodate charity, stretching sometimes to structured community work; all accompanied by the mira-culating power of American superiority, as it makes them superior as in-dividuals.[14] Is this what Marx was shooting for? I think not, since his assumption was an implicit entailment of the ethical in the agential grasping of the spectral.

At the other end of the spectrum, thinkers who can think collectivity cannot think responsibility and vice versa. In his latest book, Mahmood Mamdani charts the extent to which British colonial policy constituted a monolithic tradition or custom in equatorial Africa in order to assign power to chieftaincy.[15] For him the antonym of tradition remains rights. Commenting that "a departure from the accent on individual rights in received liberal notions . . . [entailed that] circumstances of birth prevail . . . over choice of association in shaping one's life possibilities." Mamdani relates this to other historically specific details but his attempt at under-standing its particular significance (p. 202) misfires. If birth is given its full philosophical expansion as the unanticipatable fall into time, it can form the shifting bedrock—Foucault's *socle mouvant*—upon which to base one's quest for remnants of responsibility in what is precisely not liberal, but precapitalist notions of radical alterity.

One cannot for a moment deny that the problems here are great. At least three types can be tracked here, the first peculiar to equatorial Africa, the other two common to other oppressed systems containing a certain degree of internal coherence. First, the establishment by colonial authori-ties of group-specific traditions gave ethnic rights to group members be-longing to a region but only race rights (comparable but of course not equal to those of whites) to the out-of-state black traveler. Can lines of generality, outside of rights-talk, and involving responsibility-talk as birth-right, be inscribed here? I ask in ignorance. It seems at least as mas-sive and intractable a problem as Marx's idea of entailing the ethical in the spectral. Secondly, these systems, if and when institutionalized, give rise to relatively inflexible hierarchies. We must compare them— discontinuous as the terms of comparison must be—to the contemporary power semiotics mentioned above; avoiding cultural conservatism, on both sides. But how does one weigh cultural systems? Another massive and intractable task. But so was the promise of full socialism. Thirdly, these systems, reactive to colonial domination of the males, often turn increas-ingly gender-compromised. At least for Southern Africa (this indicates the limits of my knowledge, not of the field), there is activist feminist work engaged in the framing of gender-sensitive constitutional law.[16] Hence the lineaments of responsibility in African tradition are, in Mamdani's reading, particularly difficult to track. In his reading, there may be nothing (authentic) left with which to associate labor in the interest of the social.

Speaking of tradition in a vaguer non-European form, Michel de Certeau comments with rare understanding on "collective fragments of memory [which] constitute, whether consciously or unconsciously, the roots or the 'fixed points by which a collective irreducibility is engraved in individual members.'"[17] Yet he too cannot get beyond the language of "collective rights as capable of balancing the economy that, in the name of individual rights, exposes the entire social reality to the great universal light of the market and of the administration" (p. 157). On the other side, Lévinas's *autrui* is a non-phenomenological abstraction. His *visage*—too quickly translated as visage or face—is mostly a nominal construction from *viser*, to be directed toward, the verb of intentionality. The singular/universal remains a perennial moral dilemma, an ethical conundrum. Granted that this may be the outline of an irreducible experience of the impossible. But how can we loosen the bracket, how contaminate this austere landscape with the unevenness of grouped persons without falling into the abstraction of collective rights?

As I have argued elsewhere, the place of the subject of rights is empty because, even in statutory law, it must be written in the normative and privative language of abstract equality. To fill it with an impossible ethical singularity without jettisoning the usefulness of the abstract calculus is what was contemplated in earlier work. Now the task is seen in its practicality and its impracticability becomes visible. Systems where responsibility inheres as birth-right—thus programming an indeterminacy that frees it from the deliberations of conscience—can support a sense of rights alone when we have moved from freedom from to freedom to. (This is responsibility in an extra-moral sense, if you like, counter-intuitive to Enlightenment moralisms.) Rights, being altogether self- and selves-directed, is too weak a concept to make the move.

To go any further here would be to anticipate the argument.

Metropolis

Let us acknowledge the protocol of Marx's initial movement, from speculations about the subject of labor in the Economic and Philosophical manuscripts to the definition of the agent of production in the *Capital*s. This agent, only a part-subject, since its labor is part of an abstract flow, will turn the lever, as commodified labor, of political economy, to veer capital into *pharmakon*, a medicine always ready to turn poisonous if the socialist dose falls short. This is where Gramsci supplements Marx's implicit "moral and psychological" charge with an "epistemological" urgency (see pages 8–9). Detractors and sympathizers of diverse persuasions will grant alike that the epistemes or mind-sets foreclosed by the capitalist/socialist teleology, defective for capitalism, survive in more or less habitable ruins in un-Enlightened sectors and enclaves of the planet, as more or less recognizable remain(s). Perhaps these are not ruins. The question to ask may be of the order of "what remain[s] of a Rembrandt torn into small, very regular squares and rammed down the shithole. . . . As the remain(s)."[18] The memorable opening lines of the counterhegemonic right-hand column of Derrida's *Glas* provides working orders. One can make a tight analogy here. The structural outlines of responsibility-based cultural practices begin to atrophy into residual scaffolding as industrial capitalist imperialisms impose the dominant structures, whose motor is rights-based. (It needs of course to be said that as soon as a culture systematizes responsibility, the contingency of responsibility begins to atrophy even without the intervention of an alien dominant.) Working para-sitically upon and under the dominant, they may at worst be no more than meaning-less connective behavior—bits and pieces of syncategorematic social idiom—small, very regular squares. Rammed down the shithole of an ethnic practice determined by elite and/or colonial policy, what remain(s) . . . as the remain(s)?

This question, if read as the question of cultural identity, for which reading there is, of course, no guarantee, shows that we are looking at an effortful project of developing something de-formed and de-constituted, fragmented into disjointed joinings, through a species of prayer to be haunted, which will both support and critique the institutional supports that guarantee agency. It must be remembered that the success of the prayer to be haunted is unanticipatable. And you cannot just call any attempt at multiculturalism a successful ghost dance. To repeat:

> At certain points the dominant culture cannot allow too much residual experience and practice outside itself, at least without risk. It is in the incorporation of the actively residual—by reinterpretation, dilution, projection, discriminating inclusion and exclusion—that the work of the selective tradition is especially evident.[19]

Another habit-formula for cognitive tuning.

At the end of that chapter, Raymond Williams counsels observing the pre-emergent. It is a measure of his strength that he does not counsel its plotting in some calculus. And it is in the space of this observation that we install the prayer to be haunted, the strengthening of the imagination to learn broadly.

No mystical exercise this, but an effortful suspension of/from the calculus. Since the English Institute, where this chapter was first presented,
has its being in the literary, let us consider a literary example before pro-
ceeding further. I do not have the political taste to offer an example via
cultural identities outside of Europe. All I need here is an instance of the
prayer to be haunted. I choose a text that moves you and can move most
in my classroom.

As we have seen, Virginia Woolf offers us an opinion upon one minor
point—a woman must have money and a room of her own if she is to
write fiction—in a fictive space that she introduces in the robust mode of
paradox: "Lies will flow from my lips, but there may perhaps be some
truth mixed up with them; it is for you to seek out this truth."[20]

She closes this nested or framed space of paradox with a line not written: "The very first sentence *that I would write here*, I said, crossing over
to the writing-table and taking up the page headed Women and Fiction, is
that it is fatal for any one who writes to think of their sex" (RO, p. 104;
emphasis added). The lovely unwritten passage is put to rest with the long
mesmeric vowels of high modernism taking a page out of impressionist
painting: "The taxi took the man and the woman, seeing them come together across the street, and the current swept them away, I thought,
hearing far off the roar of London's traffic, into that tremendous stream"
(RO, pp. 104–105).

When Woolf starts to speak, "in my own person" (RO, p. 105), she urges
what I have described as the prayer to be haunted by the spirit of Shakespeare's sister, buried "where the omnibuses now stop" (RO, p. 113), the
singular spirit of all women (each woman) of talent who could not enter
writing because they were not written in the *socius* as such. She urges her
reader not to be confined in the mere calculus of rational expectations:
"A thousand pens are ready to suggest what you should do and what effect you will have. My own suggestion is a little fantastic, I admit; I pre-
fer, therefore, to put it in the form of fiction" (RO, p. 113). And, in another striking paradoxical move, she concludes by unspeaking a room of
one's own and £500 a year in the very last words of her book: "The dead
poet who was Shakespeare's sister will put on the body which she has so
often laid down. . . . She would come if we worked for her, and . . . so to
work, *even in poverty and obscurity*, is worthwhile" (RO, p. 114; emphasis added).

There is something like a relationship between this chiastic structure of a
double paradox as a figure of what and how to do and the hesitant suggestions recently advanced by me to *Stiftung-Dialogik,* a Swiss foundation,
included in "Imperative to Re-imagine the Planet," Chapter 16 in this book.

In that essay I try to reconstruct a bit of the traces of an organized episteme defective to capitalism. As I have suggested above, few people know better than Mahmood Mamdani how very nearly erased such traces are. He has meticulously documented the construction of custom by colonial governmentality, in order to constitute itself thereby. Yet, if we are not committed to recovering an authentic origin, the lineaments of this hybrid ethos can perhaps yield, in the chanciness of the future anterior, and by way of effortful prayer (a performative rather than a belief-marked namable "religious" practice), some restraining dynamic upon the abstract structure of civility into which they must be grafted. Otherwise, the Enlightenment leads to exploitation, and stagnant custom leads to genocide; and the promises of cyberpolitics do not produce an epistemic or ethical alternative.[21] One resource here can be the new virtualized demographic frontiers—connecting migrant groups to mother country—that establish Internet and other electronic shadow lines within the boundaries of the modern state. Is it merely to be communitarian to insist that, if not dismissed as reactionary, these shifting frontiers can offer a foothold for what's left of theory? Put in utterly practical terms, it involves a certain kind of left-work that is to be distinguished from both union organizing (old-style empiricization of spectrality) and human rights-ism (new-style bourgeois moralist political, economic, and military blackmail).

Respect for, and systemic (rather than merely museal) integration of the para-capitalist mind-set of the migrant underclass into the efficient abstractions of civil society as an indefinitely continuing effort: such is the last-ditch model offered here for a metropolitan practice to supplement Marxism. Living in a society where the only ethical model is a triumphalist corporate philanthropy matched by a trade-related human rights paradigm and global military policing, such offers can reflect no more than Gramsci's famous pessimism of the intellect and optimism of the will, expressed in a classroom that is increasingly committed to vocational professionalism. The next section will take a step backward to move toward a history of the vanishing present outside the metropolis. The object is to reconsider the metropolis, indeed, the urban, everywhere: as telos.

Rural/Indigenous

At the very beginning of *The Economic and Philosophical Manuscripts,* Marx writes a couple of sentences where the story of land-related agency still waits to be told.

Briefly, agency here (as invariably in my work) is the name of institutionally validated action. Writing at the beginning of the consolidation of industrial capitalism, Marx's entire energy is and must correctly be devoted to showing the worker that s/he is the agent of production, and this agency is validated by the institution of capital accumulation. This chapter attempts to demonstrate, above, how Marx argues the turning (troping?) of this agency into social-ism rather than capital-ism. Such an argument requires an urbanist teleology, for its workshop is the factory:

> Let us therefore, in company with the owner of money and the owner of labour-power, leave this noisy sphere [the marketplace], where everything takes place on the surface and in full view of everyone, and follow them into the hidden abode of production, on whose threshold there hangs the notice No admittance except on business. Here we shall see, not only how capital produces, but how capital is itself produced. . . . When we leave the sphere of simple circulation or the exchange of commodities, which provides the free-trader vulgaris [still offering the mythic level playing field of the global free market] with his views, his concepts and the standards by which he judges the society of capital and wage-labour, a certain change takes place, or so it appears, in the physiognomy of our dramatis personae. He who was previously the money-owner now strides out in front as a capitalist; the possessor of labour-power follows as his worker. (C 1, pp. 279–280)

In spite of tremendous changes in the factory mode of production, its stagnancy and near-disappearance in post-Fordism, and the slow increase in importance of commercial and now finance capital, metropolitan theorists (Southern and Northern) are still caught within the urbanist teleology that Marx required. Thus it is quite unrealistic to expect Marx himself to have been prescient to a miraculous degree. Therefore Marx—in spite of all his homeopathic pharmacology of capital and labor (that the poison of commodification, when applied to labor, may lead to the medicine of socialism) and his lifelong sensitivity to originary indeterminacy (an opening we saw shut by Engels)—could only think land and labor teleologically.[22] Indeed, it is a tribute to Marx's philosophical intuition that a trace of the road not taken remains in those notes scribbled by the young man of twenty-six trying to think wage through.

Sentence one: It is therefore only for the worker that the separation of capital, landed property and labor is a necessary, essential and pernicious separation. Sentence two is separated and italicized in the manuscript. Marx must derive the agent of production through factory work. He buries the trace of an aporia lurking in that necessary, essential, and pernicious thing with an invocation of the finality of a merely human death: "So for the worker the separation of capital, ground rent and labour is fatal." Aporia here is the nonpassage that Derrida ruminates upon in *Aporias*.[23]

If agency is validated action, for Marx this validation will come only from industrial capitalism. The rest is history. As the automobile commercial says, You trade a commodity, you don't drive it. Marx had tried to self-drive labor-power, as commodity, without considering the episteme. Only agency here, for the history of the subject (that within which agency—a part larger than the whole, therefore "invaginated") is European and can be taken as given: if not Hegel, then the *Communist Manifesto*.[24] If a history determines consciousness, the ideology is German. We still live in the aftermath.

We are faced here with a world ravaged by the sheer rationalist convictions of capitalo-socialism, a predicament no less daunting than the confrontation with Western metaphysics. Seeking to encounter the other of those convictions where the Enlightenment has reached unrecognizably, as I have done for over a quarter of a century, with respect, humility, and a desire to learn, I cite Derrida's words for my metropolitan readers, hoping, in the iteration, in the alter-ing attendant upon all citation, to displace those words, however slightly, from the metropolis:

I [gave] in to the word *aporias,* in the plural, without really knowing where I was going and if something would come to pass, allowing me to pass with it, except that I recalled that, for many years now, the old, worn-out Greek term *aporia,* this tired word of philosophy and of logic, has imposed itself upon me, and recently it has done so with greater insistence [*de façon plus insistante*].

The cited thought of non-passage is a passage.

Let us step back into the manuscripts again.

It is not often noticed that Marx's premature dismissal of the nation form of appearance, a tendency shared by most Western Marxists today, is concatenated or linked with the teleologization of the separation of land and labor that we noticed a moment ago. As Marx starts reading *The Wealth of Nations* and taking the notes that form the first part of these manuscripts, the object of his analysis is named *Nationalökonomie* or national economy. The lineaments of political economy do emerge as Marx takes notes, but the antagonist is still the *Nationalökonom,* sometimes almost a de-propriated (generalized) pseudonym for Smith. In some famous pages of the Notebook on Capital as assembled in the Dietz edition of the *Grundrisse,* Marx considers the genealogy of the nation-form in a secondhand way, via contemporary anthropology, looking forward to the separation of the subject from land, to the development of appropriate agency and its institution—industrial and postindustrial capitalism, toward urbanization.[25] By 1867, as the much-revised text of *Capital* is published, the critique is of political economy, the nation has disappeared, and Adam Smith is altogether de-propriated and de-authorized. The very first words of Marx's book are "the wealth of societies" (C 1, p. 125). The *Grundrisse* had established the national as an atavistic residual: blood-tie to land. The social is the rational emergent, the result of the strategy-driven manipulation of the abstract average. The argument is that we must progress from national wealth to social wealth, treating the problem of nation-thinking as a mere inconvenience, rashly brushed aside.

Now the *Umdrehung* or turning around of political economy is the embattled *(zwieschlächtig)* commodity-character of socialized labor. Unlike the automobile commercial, in Marx's hands this commodity is driven, traded, spectralized as futures. Labor's agency is in its commodity-character as labor-power. Labor can blossom or dance where body is soul as Reason holding the dancer in the dance as *zwieschlächtig.* This thinking is not immediately practicable. But no thinking has such closure. I have tried to show here how, perhaps unavoidably, even its thinking was not permitted. Engels's benevolent interpolations are emblematic of the impatience that insists that theory leave no residue, no remains. As we used to hear from the knee-jerk Marxists: theory and practice are united in the concept. From Western liberals of the left, with nothing left to lose, periodically: what's left of theory? And from the lone self-appointed heir of Marx: messianicity and the ghost dance. I continue to tease out the possibilities of the Marxian text.

The previous chapter has argued that it was in the untheorized space of the social that Marxism foundered, unable to acknowledge the practical demands of the double bind. This chapter tries to outline the precipitate and derivative covering over of land and nation that allowed the word "social" to emerge. Yet, in the paragraph, precisely near the end of the chapter entitled "The *Schein* of Competition"—illusion, yes, but also glow, lure, and even, in the echo of *Erscheinung,* carrying the normativity of "appearance," which is a necessary form, illusion only if mistaken for the contentless (Marx cannot quite say form, or idea)—one can read, in the language of hope, the trace of an avowal that the social cannot be merely the spectral as rational. Here are the concluding words of that paragraph, quoted above: "then [after all the socializing moves have been made] nothing of these forms remains, but simply those bases [*Grundlagen*] of the forms that are communal [*gemeinschaftlich*] to all social [*gesellschaftlich*] modes of production"(C 3, pp. 1015–1016; translation modified).

Here is the trace of the community in the rational spectral: the urban telos carrying the previous formation of the *Gemeinschaft* in its subjunctive future, a trace of the "humanist" meaning of "social" in the rational homeopathy of socialism. The translation loses the tiny nuance, massive in its implications, by rendering *gemeinschaftlich* as common.

A nonpassage, then, as a residual invoked in so progressivist a system as Marx's must be! And the thought of non-passage forces a passage. Let us approach Marx's Eurocentric internationalism.

The question, Why did capitalism not develop equally everywhere? (implicitly asked and answered today by the waves of economic migration) had to be answered by some logic of difference by Marx. One of the notions that developed in response to this question was species-being *(Gattungswesen)*. At age 26, Marx turned his back on both academic radicalism and street activism and began to read again. The copious notes, with large chunks of the read material handcopied, obligatory before the days of the Xerox machine, are the explosive first part of the *Economic and Philosophical Manuscripts*. In the latter parts, the young Marx writes from what he already knows, loosely affected by the reading whose tracks constitute the earlier sections. It is in these later sections that he writes of species-being, the assumption that every human being is capable of, and must, take himself or herself as an example of being-human in general. No doubt this is a classical German philosophical cliché. But nonetheless, his conviction at that early stage was that socialism would make it possible for this to be empirically true in the case of each human being. It was therefore, at least in those early days, his practical motive force.

He was to lose this idea soon. But the idea that there was a difference that one had to account for and obliterate accompanies him into the new project of agent-formation. He comes of course to the idea of *Mehrwert*, literally more-value rather than the grander surplus-value. The commonly narrative account of this formulation has been given at the opening of this essay. The more philosophical account would be to say that Marx sees that one can define the human being as being more than himself or herself, because s/he is worth more than him/herself with the production of *Mehrwert*. This would be a naming of the human on a self-difference. But Marx wants a narrative or chronological account as, once again, he moves from a version of autonomy to a version of heteronomy—conclusions determined by facts rather than reflection. In this case, the facts are an imaginative making of the probable *(poiesis)*, rather than an *istoria*.[26] Upon this path, Marx and Engels lead themselves into the story of the Asiatic mode of production.[27] It is not enough simply to give it a decent burial. That allows us to forget that, although its factual correctness—that there was a mode of production in Asia where state tax and ground rent were the same—has long been disproved, *poiesis* did prove *philosophoteron* (better equipped to feed the love of knowledge) than *istoria*. That the main reason for lack of historical movement in the developing world was that the latter never produced real cities but only military encampments still carries a certain weight (its only serious competitor being an equally poetic cultural conservatism). It became the thing with which to adjudicate as to whether a country could be the locus of communism as well.[28] The old Russian topos of the flight from Asia—Peter the Great and the initiation of the Great Game—was displaced in the great Lenin-Plekhanov debates. The notion accounted for either being different or being the same. And it was clinched around the impossibility of producing cities. In the new postcoloniality of the post-Soviet epoch, we should be aware that capitalist colonialism also urbanized. (The writer's birthplace Calcutta is one such urban formation.) Indeed, the Bolshevik Revolution, mutatis mutandis, can be read as Marx understood 1848 in "Eighteenth Brumaire." A tremendous opening that, step by sequential step, served to consolidate the executive power of finance capital over a seventy-year span, and then dissolved itself. And through it all, the ideologeme of the City remained thoroughly embedded in the self-representation of Europe as the custodian of the *Polis* or *Civitas*.

This exercise on the edge of aporias has been to pass through to the history of the present. Here is the storying needed to keep the argument moving. It is in fact the story of a storying of the rewriting of the logical model of social justice into a narrative of population movements. The big international so-called non-governmental organizations (NGOs) that are in fact working for the Bretton Woods organizations call themselves an international civil society (briefly, everything that is not the state) today. This exacerbates the weakening of the nation-states, which are increasingly powerless in the developing world, as the barriers between their fragile economies and international capital are gradually removed. And even in the so-called developed world, the international circuits of electronic capitalism (finance and trade) increasingly bypass the redistributive demands of the state. The particular phenomenon of the *non*-governmental organizations (hardly a substantive description) is a reaction to this. In this predicament Western Marxism has not been able to give up the narrative of movement from the rural to the urban. The most unfortunate consequence of this has been to describe transnationality—the characteristic of a certain capital-formation—as not much more than the movement of people. This leads Etienne Balibar to write off class-consciousness or agency-consciousness (quite distinct from theories of fully self-present subject-consciousness) and suggest that the best way to understand mass movements would be in terms of population movements.[29] And Derrida in effect transforms Marx—although in theory protected by the alterity of the absolute arrivant—into an arrivant, a species of migrant. The exilic hybrid as marrano becomes the name of the human condition, where the secret keeps the Marrano even before the Marrano keeps it (A, p. 81). In his brilliant work *On Hospitality*, cited earlier, the figure remains the foreigner at the door. As in the case of Balibar, this is the one moment in an otherwise incandescent work that remains opaque and insistent. Any supplementation of this thinking will see that, for the subaltern in the narrow sense, the foreigner at the door is the World Bank, the IMF, and the World Trade Organization, sustained by the United Nations, fine-tuned by the international civil society, often empirically represented by the hapless local field representative, not physically recognizable as foreign at all. Such a realization is no discredit to Derrida, who has always acknowledged the consequences that the thought of a divided origin is the nonethical opening of ethics.[30] And this reminder of the narrow senses of arrivant, hospitality, foreigner will also be acceptable to the philosopher who has been ever mindful of paleonymy. Indeed, the asymmetry of interest that tips the balance for the migrant and the messiah is linked to the double bind of deconstruction. But his followers are not always alive to these checks and balances.[31]

Bound no doubt by my own double bind, I add, then, to the undocumented immigrant the subaltern in the South, the rural landless, the aboriginal. Here also, literary examples will guide me into my argument. Let us remind ourselves that, in the initial redefinition of the Gramscian word "subaltern," as recorded by Ranajit Guha, it is the name of the space of difference inhabited by those who have no access to the lines of mobility within a society.[32] Let us also remember that there are no test cases, that singularities overflow definitive determinations, the event escapes performative conventions, a caution Marx was obliged to deny. This is where, today in an institutionally hopeless place of underfunded difference misunderstood by its own inhabitants, the vocational usefulness of an aesthetic education still lingers. A literary example, then:

Mahasweta Devi's novella *Pterodactyl, Puran Sahay, and Pirtha* takes place in the shadow of the so-called green revolution and at the time of publication upon the much-debated terrain of so-called subaltern Maoism.[33] Abujhmar, one of the few "real" places named in the text, is in today's Chattisgarh state (PT, p. 109). Puran Sahay the settler Indian journalist (albeit the "settlement" was 3,000 years ago) travels to report the famine in Pirtha, an aboriginal area:[34]

> The survey map of Pirtha Block is like some extinct animal of Gondwana-land. The beast has fallen on its face. The new era in the history of the world began when, at the end of the Mesozoic era, India broke off from the main mass of Gondwanaland. It is as if some prehistoric creature had fallen on its face then. Such are the survey lines of Pirtha Block. (PT, p. 99)

The figuring of geological time puts the (post)colonial figuring instrument of the survey under erasure. The lineaments of the other of the human cover the self-and-other established by this old settler colony in antiquity. Since the remotely precapitalist colonizers (today's Hindu Indians) have inscribed themselves as postcolonials in the wake of the most recent Independence, this is an untold story.

The Mesozoic is invoked again in a passage where the pterodactyl has taken up the peculiar corporeality of a specter. This time, the ghost's otherness to the humans—however they themselves may be separated by ancient colonial history—is clear. Mahasweta is chasing planetarity here, as did Toni Morrison (see page 171): "just weather." The pterodactyl refuses the food laid out by the aboriginal. And, as for the ancient settler, today's "real" Indian, today the so-called intellectuals who code the subaltern as "Maoist," rather than note that the word *Maobadi* (not "Maoist") has been recoded to signify a violent refusal? "Who can place his hand on the axial moment of the end of the third phase of the Mesozoic and the beginnings of the Cenozoic geological ages? . . . The dusky lidless eyes remain unresponsive" (PT, pp. 155–156). I can read this text as an unwitting reinscription of the Freudian uncanny.[35] With this second instance we have entered a doubly inscribed cave, an inner shrine room inside Bikhia's cave-dwelling. Pterodactyl's cave is the home of the wholly other.

After the representation of the ghost's death, Mahasweta moves us through to yet another cave with all the accouterments of a womb-archetype; the way down lies through an underground passage with dripping walls. The last cave, the place where the pre-human past is buried, is once again a place of the obliteration of historiography, just as, in the first figuration of the extinct animal of Gondwanaland, the geography of survey maps has been overwritten. In the final cave, Puran cannot tell if the wall-paintings are archaic or contemporary.

I can read this erasure of colonial, postcolonial, and indeed human timing in order to take a step backward to move toward what I will call the spectralization of the rural, calling into question the urbanist teleology of the European tradition. For Devi's novella is framed in the green revolution, the first inkling, in the rise of neocolonialism, after the dismantling of territorial imperialism, that land would be a major player in the gradual transnationalization of the pharmaceutical industry, the source of chemical fertilizers as well as chemical instruments of coercive contraception. The efficient cause for Puran's trip to Pirtha is a famine that cannot be constituted as evidence according to the statistical manipulation of the postcolonial state. And the counter-intuitive absurdity of family planning in a place that cannot be acknowledged as starving provides the contempt that is the pervasive tone of the text toward national policy.

After the European recession of the 1870s, Lenin already knew that the major theater of spectralization had shifted to commercial capital.[36] Already spectralized labor-power, use-value in capital accumulation, had lost its unique power to socialize capital as agent of production. One of the longest chapters in Lenin's book *Imperialism* is entitled "Banks." He could not envisage a World Bank yet.

The development of the spectralized capital dependent upon commerce through the circulating mediation of the banking system, with industry (theorized by Marx as labor-power) apparently invisible in a supportive infrastructural role, surplus-value invisible as anything other than interest, allows the explanation of capital that Marx had laughed at in *Capital*, volume 2, to establish itself as the dominant explanation:

> The production process appears simply as an unavoidable middle term, a necessary evil for the purpose of money-making. . . . Enrichment as such appears as the inherent purpose of money-making. . . . [Money capital] is expressed as money breeding money. The creation by value of surplus-value is not only expressed as the alpha and omega of the process, but explicitly presented as the glittering money form. (C 2, pp. 137–138)

The apparent disappearance of labor-power (industry), and its concomitant use-exchange binary opposition, and the critique of reification, also still attached to considerations of industry, made it possible for academic post-Marxism to emerge. The criticism from the Left, in other words, seemed to have nothing to do with the conjuncture, to metropolitan cultural radicals of various convictions. Time and space will not allow a discussion here of the various ways in which these intellectuals resolved their problems. It goes without saying that world economic behavior was largely untroubled by these controversies. Yet we must speak of the world in the classroom. And the same forces that substituted information command for knowing or learning (whatever that may be) in the classroom wrought a change in the nature of commercial capital: electronification.

Commercial capital works through banks. For finance capital, the bank is a matheme on the screen. If this is the morphological change in the determination of capital, the narrative support came from the fall of the Soviet Union. Globalization can now be seen as the establishment of the same system of exchange globally—made possible by electronification. Since this is also the method by which information can be stored and disseminated, it also causes (and is caused by) infoglut. At certain levels, this detailed proliferation of information helps globalization as such. Hence, TRIPS (trade-related intellectual property) on such things as bio-diversity, human genome patenting, et cetera. On the more strictly educational levels, it creates a seductive simulacrum of learning. Global telecommunication is the industry that is linked to, but not identical with, globalization—in form; given that it must, unlike the circuits of finance capital, which are abstract—have a narrative (or at least decipherable) content, it can be used for political manipulation, crisis management, and damage control.

For those of us still mesmerized by the urbanist teleology of the right and the left, the changes seen upon urban built space are the most visible. It is possible, however, that the real terrain of globalization is the spectralization of the so-called rural. Again, the evolutionist narrative explanation and argument is that the former colonies must be modernized. The development of bank-based commercial capital in neocolonialisms showed up a fault-line in Marx's teleology. The urban had been an alternative. In postcoloniality, the rural was engaged directly.

Today's global front is in what can be called the country, not the city at all. To learn that is to move from postcoloniality to globalism, from below. The space that is not the global—global being roughly synonymous with the old social minus the centralized pivot of socialism—is now thought from the centrality of the global: as the rural, the local, the ecological, the aboriginal. In the age of biopiracy, databasing both indigenous knowledge and body, the *Encyclopedia of Life Support Systems* launched by UNESCO, must define the aboriginal period as associated with inactive approaches in which there is no concern for environmental degradation and sustainability.[37] It was of course as impossible for the aboriginal to think sustainability as it was for "Aristotle to decipher . . . the secret of the expression of value, because of the historical limitation inherent in the society in which [they] lived" (C 1, p. 152). Yet the practical philosophy of living in the rhythm of the ecobiome must now be dismissed as of no concern.

[As I repeatedly insist, this untroubled view of the aboriginal is now contaminated. I have indicated that "Pterodactyl" mentions an actual place, Abujhmar. The piece was written in 1987, for the fortieth anniversary of the independence of the Indian nation-state, perhaps the first big indicator of the passing of territorial imperialism. If one looks at the geological descriptions of this terribly isolated place, the lineaments of the story can be appreciated, although the hero Shankar is implausible in the real. By 2000, the tribal state of Chattisgarh is established and Abujhmar becomes the site of the events mentioned on page 214. Even as global capital marches toward the financialization of the globe, the repressive postcolonial state is opposed haphazardly by violence coded in the language of the legacy of Marxism by left intellectuals. I cannot enter into the details of the resistance to aesthetic education by these same intellectuals in this space.]

The task, it seems to me, is not to cultivate this supremacist benevolence, but to revise—*re-viser*, re-turn—to rethink the separation of land and subject, the project that Marx was unable or unwilling to entertain fully because of the historical limitation inherent in the society in which he lived. The story of industrial capitalist imperialism may be a contained episode in an epic temporization that is not necessarily unilateral.

From commercial to finance capital, transnationalization to globalization, it is the spectralization of the rural that is now the dominant. The silicon chip puts the rural into a general equivalent form, not money but data. Capital uses the spectrality of the rural. The Global Environment Fund is controlled by the World Bank and the United Nations Development Program. Finance capital, the abstract as such, cannot operate without interruption by the empirical. The haphazard list below, involving the spectralization of the rural, is coded by world trade:

Biodiversity (the enormous variety of plant species in Nature), electronified for biopiracy (patenting them illegally with Northern patents though legally by unilaterally established latter-day laws by the North, as in the famous Neem case); monocultures (mutant hybrid high-yield seeds suppressing variety, in the process depleting and literally killing the soil) produced by way of chemical fertilizers, themselves blips on the screen of capital. As the commercial says: You see coffee, Sprint sees data. Indigenous knowledge transformed into database, murdering the world's oldest cultures by invoking a common heritage. Trade-Related Intellectual Property Rights and Trade-Related Investment Measures abreactively punish the collectivities millennially working at the premeasurable rural for not establishing property rights over its value coding.[38]

Deforestation-reforestation and the management of waters (for example, cutting down forests that are important to indigenous life- and knowledge-systems, and replanting with eucalyptus, which can produce 75 percent pulp-wood but depletes the moisture in the soil and disturbs the balance of living organisms in regions drastically; destroying mangrove and salinating arable land to establish foreign direct export shrimp culture and devastating long-established human and other life-systems; and the like) belong to the earlier (more commercial) phase but augment the latter. And the credit-baiting of rural women for phantom micro-enterprise is the latest twist: small-scale, commercial-in-the-finance-capital market, where the perennial need of the rural poor is exploited for the commercial sector with no locally operated infra-structural change. This is an important and complex issue that is beyond the scope of this book. Suffice it to say that this invariable power choice of monocultures has something like a relationship with the dismissal of literary production in languages without capitalist power as parochial.[39] It is with this connection in mind that I ask you to read the following remarks.

No conurbation is structurally necessary for the spectralization of the rural. As we have been insisting, pure finance capital—the abstract as such—is impossible. In its coding through world trade (discourse of level playing field) and the commercial sector (discourse of money begets money or better than the moneylender) it invokes land and the embodied female subject. And it is here that the always partially spectralized rural confront the forces of the global encounter face-to-face (discourse of common heritage in patenting). Resistance networks long in place run interference for the operation of the globalizing agencies, which shift, twist, turn, and manage these crises as interruptions of their spectralizing global sweep. This unending series of interruptions, which I, as a literary critic reading the social text in the broadest and most active sense, have learned to recognize by hanging out in the text of this new activism, can be rhetorically named the irony of the main text of global regularization if we understand irony as "the permanent parabasis of an allegory (of globalization) . . . the systematic undoing, in other words, of the abstract."[40]

Parabasis—a step beside yet upon a ground—is when the Chorus stepped out to tell the public how to respond to the main text of the Old Comedy, the freer form of Greek drama of which Aristotle postpones discussion. No Marxist can be unmindful of the grandeur of the spectral motor of globalization as such. The Moor (Marx's nickname), as the dark double of the Enlightenment, wanted the agent of production to drive that motor by understanding its own spectralization as use-value of the capital that could become useful for global socialism. For this too-philosophical revolution he needed the narrative of the urban. We who criticize both the pure spectrality of a revolutionary program without epistemic support and the urban as telos advanced metaleptically (substituting effect for cause) find in the negotiating-interruptive model of the constant turning around of globalization against the vicious greed of the super-power an interminable and therefore more practical figure: a permanent parabasis. The model is eating (again and again) rather than book writing (once and for all, repetition unavoidable but unwelcome), "women's work," "slaves' work," as we said in the Introduction.

In the theater of metropolitan immigration—in "Imperative to Re-imagine the Planet" (Chapter 16 in this book)—we have proposed a model of give and take between responsibility-based cultural systems and abstract civil society and the rule of law. There politics and civil society are sustained by the European story of urbanization. In this new spectral-ization, the paradoxical new complicity (folded togetherness) of the global, we must supplement the classic socialist method, even when un-moored from a telos- or job-security orientation; even when mindful of the feminization of labor and the disappearance of the factory in elec-tronic post-Fordism. For unlike labor-power, the earth and the *bios* are not renewable. The incommensurable counter-examples cited in *Capital*, volume 1 are here in the value-form and not use-values at all: A thing can be a value without being a use-value. You see coffee, Sprint sees data. The alternative line of land-related agency left behind in the *Economic and Philosophical Manuscripts* snakes forward in bursts, in ways that Marx could not have foretold. Subalternization must be recognized as the persistent menace to the agent of production.

This spectral rural is not the empiricity of green fields and vials of blood; it has, in the manner of catachreses, no literal referent. Unlike what Paul Virilio thinks, it is not the metropolitan or transnational traveler whose experience of "com[ing] back to Paris from Los Angeles or New York at certain times of the year [when] you can see, through the window, pass-ing over the pole, the setting sun and the rising sun that offers us the new global time; showing the beyond of the geographical city and the advent of human concentration in travel time."[41] The new global time is virtual, somewhere in our heads—*Gedankenschnelle*. The contempt in the fol-lowing sentence is no more than an expression of the sanctioned igno-rance of the European:

> The global metropolitics of the future electronic information highways in itself implies the coming of a society no longer divided so much into North and South, but into two distinct temporalities, two speeds: one absolute, the other relative. The cut [*coupure*] between developed and underdeveloped

countries being reinforced throughout the five continents and leading to an even more radical rupture [*rupture*] between those who will live under the empire of real time essential to their economic activities at the heart of the virtual community of the world city, and those, more destitute than ever, who will survive in the real space of local towns.[42]

The time of seed and DNAs is not real or local time; it is irrelevant to subject-speak, open only to an open place of agency. The definition of the subaltern is now being rewritten. It is the group that, although or perhaps because, cut off from ordinary lines of mobility, is being touched directly by global telecommunication: the spectrality of indigenous knowledge, the databasing of DNA-patenting of the most remote groups, the credit baiting of the poorest rural women.

Arrived here, the writer of this essay no doubt reveals her double bind. But it seems that the epistemic undertaking here is not only messianicity, not only the responsibility of being human, but the mind-set that names the *bios* with the name of an alterity that harbors good and bad, the sacred, if there is any. The infinite patience of learning so unproductive a mind-set, from compromised sources rather than declaring a futurity of new solitude-loving philosopher companions (theoretical), or protecting the intellectual property rights of the indigenous (practical)—has no place in an essay prepared for the impatience of publishers' deadlines in the international book trade. Its place is outside my classroom here.

Coda

1. Marx the rationalist wanted to build socialism with the bones beneath the flesh. He required an urbanist telos.
2. Actually existing socialism managed to strengthen the bones of capitalism in the long run.
3. Triumphant global finance capital/world trade can only be resisted with irony.
4. The model is actually existing Southern hemisphere–based network movements.
5. To strengthen this, metropolitan multicultural policy might strengthen the scaffolding of civil rights abstractions with the cement of cultural systems defective for monstrous self-enrichment; with an aesthetic education for all.
6. Otherwise strong economic systems in the Northern hemisphere can offer a society with low unemployment, few social services, and tremendous gaps between the rich and the rest as the good society.

7. Globalization studies might reconsider their urbanist telos and take account of the new system's engagement with the bones of the rural/indigenous.
8. The impossible solution is the infinite unguaranteed patience to learn to learn from below how to teach the subaltern.
9. Otherwise corporate philanthropy and/or international protectionism see millions as only bodies or human capital.
10. This coda cannot be acted on from a U.S. classroom.

CHAPTER TEN

Echo

STARTED to think specifically about Narcissus when I came across Christopher Lasch's *The Culture of Narcissism*.[1] At that point the epistemological and the agential seemed separate, or only accessed together through thoughts of postcoloniality and the doubly bound relationship between women and the colonial Enlightenment. Now things have shifted, and the reader will step on new terrain.

The book was an attack on the few social gains made by feminism. Yet Narcissus was a boy! What seemed particularly unjust was the description of the young executive as "the happy hooker," when we are still fighting the equal wages debate at all levels.[2] (The word "Yuppie" had not yet come into the common language.) Prostitutes, however, were already organizing precisely because their class-position was rather different from that of young executives.[3]

I turned to Freud and found that he too had located the richest examples of narcissism among women, especially women unfulfilled by the secondary narcissism of motherhood. Where was Echo, the woman in Narcissus's story? This chapter is an attempt to "give woman" to Echo, to carve her out of traditional and deconstructive representation and (non)representation, however imperfectly, and remember that "women's work" is the model aesthetic education—to borrow and anticipate the speech of the other.

There is a curious moment, peculiarly susceptible to racist misuse, in Freud's "On Narcissism: An Introduction":

> We have learned that libidinal instinctual inferences undergo the vicissitudes of pathogenic repression if they come into conflict with the subject's

cultural and ethical ideas. . . . What he projects before him as his ideal is the Ersatz of the lost narcissism of his childhood, in which he was his own ideal. . . . The ego ideal . . . has a social side; it is also the common ideal of a family, a class or a nation.[4]

It is certainly at least implied here that the felicitous emergence of the superego (for Freud no doubt the subject of the Enlightenment) happens because there is something other than mere conflict between cultural and ethical ideas and the libidinal instinctual inferences. The full-blown version of this particular theme—of non-European cultures being stuck in varieties of narcissism and its vicissitudes—is not uncommon. Asia and Africa are always supposed to have had trouble with Oedipus.[5] (Very broadly and irreverently speaking, if as a man you can't get to Oedipus, you are stuck with Narcissus. Women can't pass through Oedipus, and therefore the secondary narcissism of attachment to the (boy-)child saves them from themselves, from penis-envy and so forth.) Their growth is arrested on the civilizational scale. Hegel trumped Freud in this in his plotting of the itinerary of the Spirit in Art.[6]

In the case of India, which in a certain way I "know" best, Sudhir Kakar, the eminent psychoanalyst, has diagnosed the Indian male type as arrested in the moment of Narcissus.[7] V. S. Naipaul, visiting India for the first time in 1962, fell on this diagnosis with a vengeance. Although he has put down his earlier overreaction against India to his own ancestral Indo-Caribbean past in a later book, this particular definitive view seems unchanged; "underdeveloped ego" in the first book, infantile golden-ageism in the second.[8] These are the two moments: Narcissus and the ego ideal (see OTM, pp. 207–209). Thus you might say that I am interested in the psychoanalytic Narcissus because, in a kind of "colonial" reconstellation of the matter of "Greece," he is made to stand at the door of the free discourse of Oedipus. I now suggest that listening to Sophocles otherwise we might access the baseline sense that where we are animals, claims to Enlightenment are chancy (see the Introduction, note 68). This is not the other-enabled ethics of the early Lévinas. It is the possibility of ethics sketched out in *Otherwise than Being*, not an ethics of alterity implying the family romance, but based on the fact that we all start aging and dying when we are born, before identity.[9]

I have always felt uneasy about the use of psychoanalysis in cultural critique since it is so culture-specific in its provenance. Like many others, I too have felt that Marxism, focusing on something on a much higher level of abstraction than the machinery, production, and performance of the mental theater, and as obviously global as capitalism, is not open to this particular charge. (To say capitalism is all over the place is not as universalist as to say everyone has the same-pattern psyche.) Although I feel the weight of Derrida's critique of institutional psychoanalysis in the world, especially in such deeply ambivalent questions as psychiatric care for the Union Carbide victims in Bhopal, since I am not qualified to speak of psychoanalysis as clinical practice, I must leave it largely alone.[10] For the use of feminist psychoanalysis in understanding sexual difference and gendering I feel some sympathy because it is so actively contestatory. But general cultural critique has always seemed to me to be quite another matter. Without the risks or responsibilities of transference, at least implicitly diagnostic and taxonomic, ignoring geopolitical and historical detail in the interest of making group behavior intelligible, and not accountable to any method of verification, the brilliance of psychoanalytic cultural criticism has always left me a bit suspicious.

Yet Freud has remained one of my flawed heroes, an intimate enemy. To his race, class, and gender-specificity I would apply the words I wrote about Charlotte Brontë almost thirty years ago, now to be found in *A Critique of Postcolonial Reason:* "If even minimally successful, my reading should incite a degree of rage against the gendered/imperialist narrativization of history, that it should produce so abject a script for him."[11]

Both Freud and Marx move me in their engagement with ethics. Freud thought he had revised Kant, the representative ethical philosopher of the Enlightenment.[12] In spite of all Freud's claims, it is his vulnerability as a moral philosopher that is for me a lesson of history.

It was finally my contact with the ethical philosopher Bimal Krishna Matilal that allowed me to make room for Freud in my intellectual world. Professor Matilal argued that nineteenth-century Indologists were basically correct in estimating that India had no tradition of moral philosophy in the Western European sense. But they had not been able to grasp either the Indic tradition of rational critique or the tradition of practical ethics in India. According to Matilal, the latter was based on the reading of narrative instantiations of ethical problems. We read some of the *Mahābhārata* together in this way. I realized that this way of doing rather than exclusively talking about doing (the other, of course, is also an ethical decision; this in fact is at the root of my unease with the use of psychoanalysis in cultural critique) ethics was a rather widespread, rather global, phenomenon, not confined to non-European cultures. It had been ranked as "popular" by most high-cultural, European-model, moral philosophical systems. (I am not speaking, of course, of diagnosing story lines as formal allegories, drawing morals from parables, or attention to the "moral dimension" of fiction.) Freud was not only "reading" his analysands, he was also reading Sophocles, and he missed on the passage that everyone misses. Jon Elster's *Ulysses and the Sirens,* which I was reading at the time, seemed an example of moral philosophizing on that "popular" model.[13] And psychoanalysis, as a challenge to systematic moral philosophy, had certainly read received narratives and the sequentially constructed narratives of analysands as instantiations of socioethical problems. As a cultural critic rather than a clinical practitioner, I was not obliged to take the conclusions as scientific system. As a being in ethics, I could share them as malleable situational lessons, even turn them, as in the reading of that crucial passage in Sophocles.

Professor Matilal also suggested that the moral dilemma was the most important terrain for the exercise of this type of practical ethics as encountered in the Indic tradition. The ethical double bind was the rule rather than the exception. Freud's recognition of the aporia between terminable and interminable analyses, and Derrida's thinking of ethics as the experience of the impossible, resonated with this suggestion.[14] Derrida's work is also a critique of traditional European systematic moral philosophy, after all. Further, this particular privileging of the aporia in the field of ethical decision seemed quite apposite to the tale of Narcissus. As I will attempt to show in my reading of Ovid, it is a tale of the aporia between self-knowledge and knowledge for others. In this matter of knowledge for others I also received an impetus of interest from my discussions with Bimal Matilal. He discussed an argument advanced by Gangesa, a twelfth-century linguist, that the production of truth was not necessarily dependent upon the speaker's intention. (This is *bhrāntapratārakavākya,* the case of the deluded deceiver, who speaks the truth while thinking to lie.)[15]

I felt that Ovid himself, against his probable intentions, had monumentalized in neglected Echo the random possibility of the emergence of an occasional truth of a kind, less striking than Oedipus's ill-translated complaint against kinship inscription, but clear in its rhetoricity.[16]

Freud's "On Narcissism," written on the threshold of *The Metapsychological Papers,* is philosophically bold. The desire of psychoanalysis is to tap the para- and pre-logic that produce the subject's logic, and also the logic of the subject's illogic. Thus at the opening of the essay, Freud quietly asserts that at the origin "of the hypothesis of separate ego- and sexual-drives" (SE 14, p. 79) there is no grounding unity but only a riddle, the grounding riddle or *Grundrätsel* of biology.

Unlike the Sphinx's riddling question to Oedipus, which for Hegel signifies the turn to Europe, "it is as idle to dispute" this absence of ground "as to affirm it" (SE 14, p. 79).[17] The theory of the separation of the ego and sexual drives, as necessary to psychoanalysis as is the separation of Mind and Knowledge to Hegel, arises simply out of the fact that "it is a necessary hypothesis that a unity comparable to the ego cannot be available [*vorhanden*] to the individual from the start" (SE 14, pp. 76–77). This acknowledgment of risk, the revelation of the ground of the cure as a necessary methodological presupposition, is the Freud of the dilemma who resonates with all my predilections for the dilemma as the type case of the ethical situation, the double bind that binds this book. For us it is perennially conjunctural; for Freud the conjuncture is the staging of the subject. (If there is an objection to seeing the analyst's behavior as a species of ethical behavior as colloquially understood—doing the right thing for the other person in light of the best knowledge available—then this resonance will fail.) How then does he interrupt the risk with the claim to science?

> I am of the opinion that that is just the difference between a speculative theory and a science built upon the interpretation of the empirical. The latter will not envy speculation its privilege of having a smooth, logically unassailable foundation [*Fundamentierung*]. . . . The fundament [*Fundament*] of science . . . is observation alone. (SE 14, p. 77)

It is a nice reversal of received ideas: speculation is logically firm; science is logically ungrounded but has an observational foundation. It will not surprise us that the science is anthropology and the observation field-work: speculation about "the mental life of primitive peoples," which then allows him to draw conclusions about "the mental life of children," although in the sentence describing the nature of these observations he conflates the two groups of people, as though primitive peoples were childless (SE 14, p. 75). In fact, if the analogy between primitive peoples and children were not scientific, the fundament of the science would be blown away. I am obliged to notice that the ground of the differentiation between the speculative and the scientific is becoming rather shaky here as well. We are told not to try to grapple with the grounding biological riddle of sexual difference as providing a basis for a theory arguing the ego's initial separation from sexual drives because it would be as ridiculous as attempting to prove inheritance by arguing from the kinship of all races. Does not the childlike behavior of primitive peoples belong to the same order of argument? In fact, is it not, in a certain way, exactly the opposite of arguments about the universal kinship of races? If the other term of the analogy brings the activities of the analyst practicing terminable analysis into the same workaday register as the settlement of legal disputes, then the entire justification of the scientificity of the diagnosis of narcissism is dubious.

What does Freud observe when he tells us that "this extension of the libido theory receives reinforcement from our observations and views [speculations?] on the mental life of children and primitive peoples" (SE 14, p. 75)? "In the latter," he continues, "we find characteristics which, if they occurred singly, might be put down to megalomania. In the children of today, whose development is much more opaque [*undurchsichtbar*] to us . . ." (SE 14, p. 75). Why are the characteristics of remote primitive peoples transparent to "us"? So that they can offer a basis for the firm foundation of science? And why do "we expect to find an exactly analogous attitude" (SE 14, p. 75) in the children of today? Is this not the same sort of desire for a methodological certainty that had been sternly put in its place earlier? Once the analogy is "found," or rather the declaration of its expectation is offered as its finding, the primitive peoples are not heard of again.

I am of course not complaining that Freud is not sufficiently scientific. I have already said that it is the Freud who acknowledges dilemmas with whom I am in sympathy. I am remarking that the scientific basis that Freud needs is deeply marked by a rather offensive sort of casual racism for which there is certainly no precedent in the authoritative staging of the Narcissus narrative in Ovid. Freud was a man of considerable classical education and a sensitive reader. One might even invent a curious connection between Ovid's stated project in the *Metamorphoses* and Freud's stated project in the narcissism essays. Freud: I am "replacing the special chemical substances [of the organic soil *(Boden)* of the psyche] by special psychical forces" (SE 14, p. 78). And Ovid's *Metamorphoses* begins: "My mind is bent to tell of bodies changed into new forms."[18]

Yet Freud leaves Ovid alone. In fact, Ovid's Narcissus, at first sight, seems to suffer from Freud's version of secondary narcissism. In one Freudian articulation at least, primary narcissism is an "absolute self-sufficien[cy] from which we step, toward noticing a changeful world outside and the beginnings of finding objects, by being born [*mit dem Geborenwerden*]."[19]

Here the mother is nothing but, in Luce Irigaray's word, an "envelope."[20] By contrast, in Ovid Liriope's womb has a history. It comes to envelop Narcissus by a primary rape by Cephisus, demidivine violence as sexual violence that does not offend the political economy of the gods. The entire pretext of Tiresias and Echo as major players is crosshatched by a story of punishment and reward. When Freud and Lacan use the narratives as psychoethical instantiations they ignore this framing. (It may be argued that Lacan dispenses with the story lines of Oedipus and Narcissus.)[21] But Lacan is not a monolithic proper name. I cannot now spend time on the various turns in Lacan's career, or on the connection between proper names and the psychoanalytic institution. Here suffice it to say that the idea of the Mirror Stage, Lacan's reinscription of Narcissus, was launched in 1936. And in the 1949 version Oedipus is present without qualification; and the end of psychoanalysis is a rewriting of Narcissus's *iste ego sum* (I am that) into an ec-static "Thou art that." For Lacan, it is in this that "is revealed to [the patient] the cipher of his mortal destiny."[22] (I will argue that it is Ovid's Narcissus who is an icon of mortiferous self-knowledge.)

Lacan's mirror-stage baby assumes his "specular image" jubilantly, thus "exhibit[ing] in an exemplary situation"—exactly as narratives instantiate active ethical structures—the "primordial form . . . [that] situates the agency of the ego, before its social determination, in a fictional direction, which will always remain irreducible for the individual alone."[23] Freud's secondary Narcissus is unenlightened.

How different this modern Narcissus—plotted (in both the early Lacan and Christopher Lasch) in terms of a rather banal contrast between group ("social") and individual ("fictional") or, in an admittedly subtler form in Freud, of an irreducible secondariness which alone gives a clue to the primary fiction, again a methodological underived fiction—from Ovid's Narcissus, emerging from a scene of responsibility and punishment.[24]

As Freud and Lacan use an approximation of the Narcissus narrative for ethical instantiation, they ignore its framing. Indeed, as I look into the mass of learned literature on both the Narcissus tradition and narcissism, not only do I notice a singular absence of independent attention to the narrativization of Echo (the Renaissance practice of Echolalia has rather little to do with the rhetorical philosopheme called Echo), but also an ignoring of the frame.[25] In the first draft of this chapter, I myself, although attentive to the frame, had not noticed Echo's part in it, and wrote as follows:

> The Narcissus story in Ovid is introduced by other accounts of sexual difference and divine violence. It unfolds while on earth a child torn from its mother's womb—because the mortal Semele could not withstand her lover Jove's heavenly glory, a sight she craved by Juno's vengeful temptation—gestates in the Father's thigh, God appropriating woman's power. In the preamble of the Narcissus story as such stands Tiresias. He too names a site where sexual difference is suspended. To become woman was his initial punishment for disturbing the copulation of holy serpents. Retaining the memory of maleness he had realized that being-woman was a punishment. He had repeated his offense deliberately—an act of self-knowledge which will find its parallel in Narcissus—and won back maleness: a transformation-punishment that is thus also the fulfillment of his desire. Now he retains the memory of having-been-woman. He gives the opinion that women have greater sexual pleasure, an opinion contradicted by Narcissus' fulfillment

and Echo's perpetual lack that we encounter in the embedded story. Juno punishes him with blindness, Jupiter compensates with clairvoyance.

In the second draft, Echo's figuration became clear. She too had served Jupiter. As he played with nymphs, she would engage Juno in prudent chat. It is this beguiling prudence that Juno takes from her: you can no longer speak for yourself. Talkative girl, you can only give back; you are the respondent as such. Jupiter does not give her anything in return.

It is within this asymmetrical frame of transgression, punishment, and dubious reward that the Narcissus story is framed. The story of Narcissus is a tale of the construction of the self as object of knowledge. I will suggest below that the account of Echo is a story of a punishment that is finally a dubious reward quite outside of the borders of the self.

The story of Narcissus is framed, then, in the value-coding or gendering of affect in a spectacular dynamics of transgression and reward. For Narcissus himself, we remember Tiresias's famous line: He will live as long as he does not know himself. He can instantiate, in the kind of reading I am proposing, the construction of the self as an object of knowledge. (It is perhaps in the recognition of this mortiferous autoerotic model of self-knowledge that Rousseau made Narcisse the artist.)

There is a moment of exquisite anguish before the boy can describe his predicament: *et placet, et video; sed quod videoque placetque, non tamen invenio* (M, p. 154, lines 446–447) (It pleases, and I see it; but I cannot reach what I see and what pleases). In his description, it is clearly knowledge of the division in identity that kills and inscribes him in nature. He points and declares, *iste ego sum:* "I am that. . . . I now know my image. . . . I have what I desire. Strange prayer for a lover, I would that what I love were absent. . . . Death is not serious for me for in death I will leave my sorrow" (M, p. 156, lines 463–471).

It should be noticed that *sum* in Narcissus's declaration is grammatically precarious in this declaration, yet possible. When Freud topologizes the psyche, it is the impossibility of self-knowledge as such that is captured in *wo Es war soll Ich werden* (where it was, I shall become). Narcissus's formula might run: *Wo Es ist, bin Ich nicht* (where it is, I am [not]), the limit of the possibility of self-knowledge. In Freud's ethical reading of narratives, however, this relationship cannot be established. Freud's reading is no different from the magisterial Christian reading of *Paradise Lost*.[26]

And therefore we remain accustomed to interpreting the declaration of the Ovidian Narcissus as a psychic problem. Attending to the frame and the text, I am obliged to say: if this is pathogenic repression, what is on the other side is family romance. And Ovid's Narcissus, unlike Freud's, is not incapable of wishing for his own death.

Insofar as I am supposed culturally to be banished from Oedipus, I relate the narcissian proposition to another type of ethical instantiation in a narrative moment. Here is the utterance of Mary Oraon in "The Hunt." Mary is the girl-child of rape, of an Indian tribal by a colonial Englishman, as Narcissus is the boy-child of divine rape. Mary is the emblem of the subaltern postcolonial, as we have seen in Chapter 2.

"My mother should have killed me when I was born," says she.

"And then, what about you?" asks another. "I would not have been," she answers.

This is the moment of Narcissus: If I make disappear what I cannot not desire, I disappear too. But this is only one end of the shuttle. We move now to Echo.

Echo in Ovid is staged as the instrument of the possibility of a truth not dependent upon intention, a reward uncoupled from, indeed set free from, the recipient. Throughout the reported exchange between Narcissus and Echo, she behaves according to her punishment and gives back the end of each statement. Ovid "quotes" her, except when Narcissus asks, *quid . . . me fugis* (Why do you fly from me?) (M, p. 150, lines 383–384). Caught in the discrepancy between second person interrogative *(fugis)* and the imperative *(fugi)*, Ovid cannot allow her to be, even Echo, so that Narcissus, flying from her, could have made of the ethical structure of response a fulfilled antiphone. He reports her speech in the name of Narcissus: *quot dixit, verba recepit* (M, p. 150, line 384)—he receives back the words he says. The discrepancy is effaced in the discrepancy of translation. In English, Echo could have echoed "Fly from me" and remained echo.[27]

Narcissus is punished with the knowledge of the relationship between death and self-knowledge because he had not responded to the desire of others. But this punishment is not in the name of Echo. Here too Echo, by definition dependent, remains uncoupled from the effect of herself as cause. It is another youth of indeterminate sex who brings Nemesis down upon Narcissus. You scorn us, know yourself. Child of rape, know as your Mother knows—for Tiresias's answer about the consequences of Narcissus's self-knowledge had been given to Liriope—you disappear if you act on your knowledge. Echo is dead in the narrative before this happens. And in her brief exchange with Narcissus, she marks the withheld possibility of a truth outside intention.

Is there a radical counterfactual future anterior, where Echo, against her intention, a poor thing at best, will forever have exercised the negative transference ("fly from me" between question and order) that will have short-circuited the punishment of mortiferous self-knowledge? Is that the impossible experience of identity as wound? The *a-venir* of a history not written? But this can only be the radical interruption of ethical hope, which must be cut down to logical size so a calculus can be proposed. Let us look at Echo's death.

In an interruption of narrative time, Echo comes to echo farewell, to echo the rites of mourning. At the moment of Narcissus's death, his sisters come to mourn him and in the place of the body find the flower. The body seems to have been inscribed into nature by sheer force of the *agon* of self-knowledge. The flower nods at the water here on earth to be the *a-letheia* (truth as unforgetting) of the limits of self-knowledge as Narcissus still gazes upon the waters of Lethe—though, unlike the Loeb translation, Ovid does not mention the image: *in Stygia spectabat aqua* (M, p. 158, line 505, translated in the Loeb edition as "he kept on gazing on his image in the Stygian pool").[28]

By contrast, Echo's echoing farewell comes from a space already insufficiently inscribed—an insufficiency that is the name not of the limits of self-knowledge but of the possibility of deconstruction. The rest of this chapter will elaborate this theme.

At first there is nothing but voice and desiccated body. Finally there is nothing but voice, "for they say that her bones were turned to stone." Ovid uses a peculiar formulation: *vox manet* (M, p. 152, line 399). Received wisdom has it that it is *scripta* that *manent*. It is writing that remains. But in this singular space, voice remains, the body become stone. "The structural possibility of being severed from its referent or signified (and therefore from communication and its content) seems to me to make of every mark, even if oral, a grapheme in general, . . . the nonpresent remaining of a differential mark cut off from its alleged 'production' or origin."[29]

Let us now consider this figuring of Echo in two related but different ways. First, how does it give us the offer of a precarious foothold outside of the subject-position of the "wild" psychoanalyst cultural critic, producing an irresponsible simulacrum of the analyst in her consulting-room?

Just as Oedipus has to be male, Echo has to be female. (Narcissus as figured can go both ways and, as we have seen, in the banalized psychic-problematic interpretation, has been most often located in the female.) Echo is female-figured because the asymmetry of the reward-punishment compensation circuit between herself and Tiresias is equalized, still asymmetrically, from the moment of the impossibility of echoing as punishment between the Latin interrogative and imperative forms of "fly from me," the two subject-positions named Narcissus and Echo in the exchange, where someone called Ovid (the analysand? the cultural critic? the received storyteller as writer? us?) has to take a role and fill in with "what happened," which is never exactly "what happened" marked with a difference, here the difference between question and response, questioner and respondent. Guarding this difference is Echo's punishment turned into reward, a deconstructive lever for future users. We remember that even if Echo had been able to echo and act according to mere punishment with no difference of subject-position, the response would have been a refusal to answer or (we cannot be sure) a suggestion that this particular respondent is inappropriate. Thus: N. Why do you fly from me? E. Fly from me—I cannot answer you or I am not your proper respondent: a deferment independent of, indeed the opposite of, the sender's intention. A difference and a deferment together are, strictly speaking—but can one be strict about this?—the (non)law of differance not letting an originary identity be declared. Here is the figuration of Echo's "reward." Her punishment fails (in order) to mark differance. Ovid covers it over with telling; we open it to secure a peculiar foothold. It is this mode of utterance that is covered over in Ovid's report, that Echo says "fly from me[?]."[30] In the rest of the narrative, through the representation of a stable-yet-unstable, same-yet-different, non-originary voice that remains, an unintentional vehicle of a possible cure—figured though separated accompaniment of a successful mortiferous self-knowledge that cannot advance—is glimpsed, a cure that is one possible case among many.

For Echo is obliged to echo everyone who speaks. Her desire and performance are dispersed into absolute chance rather than an obstinate choice, as in the case of Narcissus. If the ever-renewed narcissus flower is a "natural monument" to the fulfillment of Narcissus's desire-as-punishment out of this world, the lithography of Echo's bony remains merely points to the risk of response. It has no identity proper to itself. It is obliged to be imperfectly and interceptively responsive to another's desire, if only for the self-separation of speech. It is the catachresis of response as such. Echo's mourning is outside the opposition of mourning and a melancholia only half of which is narcissism. She is inscribed as destinerrance as such. She gives the lie even to Derrida's absent interlocutrice, whom Derrida echoes and corrects (reaching for Narcissus and Ovid in one) in *The Post Card:*

> P.S. I forgot, you are quite right: one of the paradoxes of destination, is that
> if you wanted to demonstrate, expressly for someone, that something never

arrives at its destination, it's no use. The demonstration, once it has reached its end, will have proved what one should not demonstrate. But this is why, dear friend, I always say "a letter can always not arrive at its destination, etc."[31]

In my ethically instantiated reading of the Ovidian narrative, the traces of Echo occupy the position of something like an analyst. Under the broken rebus—legendary bones and paradoxically persistent absent voice, connected by nothing at all—that is her mark or guarantee that she will be around, the mastership of truth (Derrida's critique of the Lacanian analyst), is the experience of the impossible (Derrida's description of ethics).[32] Echo will not have been dragged into the circuit of political imitations.

And now the second question: What ethical instantiation does this figuration of Echo offer "us"—the worldwide collectivity of conscientized feminists of color from bourgeois origins or in passive capitalist social relations? We must catch the undoing moment of Echo as she attends, at a distance, every act of cultural narcissism. This feminist is culturally divided from the women at the bottom. I have already indicated in "Acting Bits/Identity Talk" (Chapter 7 in this book) that what she sees as her face she knows to be an "it" which she loves and of which she desires the disappearance, which is the precarious moment of the Ovidian Narcissus; in order not to speak for, speak to, listen to, but respond to the subaltern sister. In the current conjuncture, national identity debates in the South and "liberal" multiculturalism in the North want her to engage in restricted-definition narcissism as well. Simply put: love-your-own-face, love-your-own-culture, remain-fixated-in-cultural-difference, simulate what is really pathogenic repression in the form of questioning the European universalist superego. If this position can raise a "why do you fly from me?" toward the subaltern separated from the feminist, then the feminist might, just might, ventriloquize the "fly from me" toward that Narcissus-face, both the self-knowing Ovidian and the deluded Freudian. In fact, the subaltern herself is also sometimes caught in the desire for Narcissus and the "fly from me" gesture, on another level. Once there is an effort to engage in the politics of subalternity-on-the-move, who questions and who answers "fly from me" is not at all clear. The only thing we know is that "be like me, be my image" can never be on the agenda, from either side. I should also emphasize that this "imitation" cannot be the slow-motion thinking-through of a raised consciousness. In the field of decisions, it can only be the sort of much-practiced reflex that shows the steps in slow motion if anyone cares to analyze after the fact; and analysis, notoriously, is inadequate to its object. If, under such circumstances, the imitation of Echo takes us this far, we have to remember that Echo produces the possibility of a cure against the grain of her intention, and finally uncoupled from intention. Echo will not have been dragged into the circuit of adequate political imitation. The "practice of freedom," especially in the context of women divided into feminists and women, does not come simply because of the fact of gaining something called independence. In the context of the difference between Isma (colloquial Arabic for "she is called," with the proper name to be filled in, and thus, in this case, a blank), central character in *Fantasia,* a self-knowing woman (and therefore mortiferously aware of the limits of self-knowledge, caught in the moment of the Ovidian Narcissus) who has learned the practice of the writing of the hegemonic language and women in her so-called traditional culture, Assia Djebar has written something called "a-phonie," which I discuss below. At this date, I am still speaking of *Fantasia.*[33]

As an Algerian woman who has learned the practice of French writing, Assia Djebar is not-quite-not-Narcissus, with some doubt about claiming the historicophilosophical "I," for traditional women of her class will insist that she insert her "self" into a received orality—strictly speaking, a graph ("the stitched seam of arche-writing, condition of the [so-called oral] language, and of writing in the narrow sense")[34]—as the only appropriate mode of expression for her, her "law of genre":[35]

> Each gathering, weekly or monthly, carries over the web [*tissu*] of an impossible revolt. Each speaker [*parleuse*]—the one who clamors too high or the one who whispers too fast—is freed. The "I" of the first person will never be used: in stereotyped formulas the voice has deposited its burden of rancor and of rales rasping the throat. Each woman, flayed inside, is eased in the collective listening. And the same for gaiety, or happiness—which you must guess at; litotes, proverb, to the point of riddles or transmitted stories, all the verbal stagings are unrolled for unpicking fate, or exorcizing it, but never to strip it bare. (F, pp. 154–155)

Over and against this chain of mere whispered souvenir that survives in the acknowledgment of the exclusion from the writing of classical Arabic she moves to French for a narrative memoir. Yet she cannot be the Rousseauistic Narcisse of French tradition either. She must make the other acknowledgment as well: that the French dictionary cannot grasp the rhetoric of the Algerian woman's body. The fragmentary finale of *Fantasia* begins with two French dictionary entries that read a figure in that corporeal tropology in two opposed ways. I have written of this in "Acting Bits/Identity Talk" (Chapter 7 in this book), but here I elaborate further. One: *tzarl-rit* means "to utter cries of joy while smacking the lips (of women)."[36] The other: *tzarl-rit* means to "shout, vociferate (of women when some misfortune befalls them)."[37] Mourning or jubilation, Narcissus cannot know.

Caught in this middle space, all she can insert, ambiguously, is a sheltering a-phonie, a concept-metaphor for which I find no literal referent: "All words, too lit-up, become braggadoccio, and aphonie, untamed [*inentamé*—the history of the language will allow un-broached] resistance" (F, p. 178).

A-phonie, midway between women's oral culture and patriarchal scripture, is a willed imitation of Echo's warning-in-longing that must continue to fail, since one cannot Echo willingly. It is the impossibility in view of which the risk of legal battles like the fight for a uniform civil law must be undertaken. And if this is interpreted in terms of the mirror-stage narcissism of Enlightenment phallocracy, *vox manet*.[38] If I read the deconstructive embrace between Djebar's Isma and Ovid's Echo as an ethical instantiation, here is what emerges: something relating to the need of a uniform civil code for men and women, not personal codes that keep women minors; something that would make it impossible for patterns of transgression and reward to be asymmetrically gendered, in the calculus of the law. Negotiating without much choice with various structures inherited from colonialism, necessarily fighting to write the body in the normative, privative, rational abstractions of a uniform civil law, rather than a culturally inherited and imperially consolidated personal code, the body "bereft of voice," is a stone (F, p. 156). In this divided field, the recovery of a woman's voice is useless in autobiography and equally anthropologistic if it does not acknowledge that the woman-in-culture may be the site of internalized phallocracy. It is thus that, between writing in French and the culturally patriarchal woman's voice, Djebar gives to the supercolonized woman the task of a-phonie: not a writing, not a graph, but not the phonocentric, responsibility-rather-than-rights-based, patriarchal-functionalist, unmediated woman's voice either. This may claim "identity" with the impossible dimension of the rhetoricity of Ovid's Echo: *vox manet*.

In "Can the Subaltern Speak?" I wrote of Freud as a monitory model (CPR, p. 217). Here too, as I read narrative as guide to action and limits to action, Freud remains an ally, as class, race, and gender-bound, in his different ways, as no doubt am I. Assia Djebar's brilliant essay on the gaze in Delacroix can be included in this alliance.[39] The deconstructive embrace that holds the elite texts reporting on the nineteenth-century subaltern and the subalternist historians is another example. The elite allies can serve as monitory models for the decolonizing feminist, but they—Ovid, Freud, Delacroix, colonial elite—lose their lineaments in the process. They are ab-used. They cannot serve when we try to learn—outside of the closed circuit of the production of academic knowledge—

the impossible response to the gendered subaltern. In her own separate enclosure, the subaltern still cannot speak as the subject of a speech act. Dishing out our personal pain in academic bestsellers serves women on the make or catharsizing voyeurs. And Rigoberta Menchú, a spirited subaltern who has networked herself into the structure of hegemonic discourse, immediately becomes the object of right-wing critique.

What follows is an extended appendix. Readings such as the above are read, if at all, with a certain "political piety," as a "third-world intervention" and then laid aside when the serious mainstream work of deconstruction is undertaken. I have therefore included the following three examples:

I am in a deconstructive embrace with Claire Nouvet's "An Impossible Response," which I read after completing the preceding pages.[40] It is a brilliant and much more adroit example of the same genre of reading as mine. Our embrace is asymmetrical, as are all embraces. The asymmetry can be tabulated as a difference in stakes, which cannot not be reckoned (with) in ethical-instantiation readings. Her stake seems to be the figurality of the self. What my stake is the reader will decide. Within the warmth of an embrace, then, I reckon our asymmetry: in spite of her careful reading of Echo, Narcissus remains the hero of the predicament of the "self." He it is who, character or figure, with the help of Echo, figure or character, thematizes or figurates the impossibility signaled in Nouvet's title.

In place of the "self," the Ovidian text, seen as "deconstructing itself" (Nouvet) rather than rhetorically giving us a clue for turning it around to use Echo (Spivak), is invested by Nouvet with a certain sovereignty. Much of this sovereignty is established by allowing it to perform an undermining of "character" by "figure."[41] I see this as a contemporary fading-away of the "polytheist" habit of mind of thinking being and principle in an agile slippage.[42] One focus does not necessarily "undermine" or "correct" the other (although that power-claim is the substance of "polytheisms" as sites of conflict) in a "live polytheist" discourse. However Max Müller binarized it over against "Western exceptionalism" (Wikipedia!), for the *dvaitin* (see Chapter 21, note 14), henotheism is the god focused on is God then.[43] Who knows how a "Roman" thought a "Greek" story? I am not interested in a vulgar Heideggerian narrative of religion-in-ethics. But it does not seem necessary to censor the genealogical imagination either.

Perhaps it is this imperative to keep Narcissus center stage that does not allow Nouvet to notice Echo as also in an anterior and asymmetrical frame of punishment and reward with Tiresias. Therefore she must inscribe Ovid's inability to let Echo be Echo as Narcissus unechoed (IR,

p. 121). Indeed, if the failure of echo between interrogative and imperative is finessed by Ovid in reported speech, Nouvet's text, replete with
quotations, gives this "passage" (in every sense) as three pages of report.
This stake in the "drama and story" of the "self" seems to limit the question of the feminine. Since the unbalanced parallel of Tiresias and Echo
as male and female singularities is not seen, at a certain point in Nouvet's
essay, Echo is simply seen as "the feminine" rather than "bad girl," "talkative girl," "girl of deluding tongue," as in Ovid. In a few pages of her essay, the "self" becomes genderless, until the resounding first person plural
at the end of the essay operates simply in terms of being-human:

> Ovid's text opens a dangerous question: if a humanist self-assertion is
> "criminal" [I should have trouble here because of the failure of the polythe-
> ist imagination, the confusion of self-recognition and self-knowledge, and
> the meaning of "punishment"], can we ever hope to avoid this crime? . . . It
> is by definition "incomprehensible" since it revokes the very notion of a
> self. We therefore cannot pretend to comprehend it, but can only expose
> our "selves" to its questioning, a questioning which can only disturb the
> comfort of our "good conscience" by confronting us to the uncertain status
> of our "subjectivity," of our "selfhood," and even of our "humanity." (IR,
> pp. 133–134)

Ethics are not a problem of knowledge but a call of relationship (without relationship, as limit case). But the problem and the call are in a deconstructive embrace: Narcissus and Echo. If we see ourselves only as
subjects (or "selves") of a knowledge that cannot relate and see the "self"
as writing, our unavoidable ethical decisions will be caught in the more
empirical, less philosophical "night of non-knowledge," the necessarily
decisive single bind inevitably (mis)taken for a solution to the double bind,
a "decenter[ing] of the subject, as is easily said, without challenging anew
the bond between, on the one hand, responsibility, and, on the other, freedom of subjective consciousness or purity of intentionality . . . a parade
of irresponsibilizing destruction, whose surest effect would be to leave
everything as it is," and to flatten gender.[44]

If we move to Echo as the (un)intending subject of ethics, we are allowed to understand the mysterious responsibility of ethics, that its subject cannot not comprehend.[45] In fact, if in the curious protocol of a deconstructive embrace I transgress Nouvet's text by displacing the
antecedent of "it" from "Ovid's text" to "Echo," the move is made. Yet
this is not simply to make Echo say I am it now *(nunc sum ego iste),* for we
are levering her out where Ovid's text signals its loss of sovereignty, that it
cannot catch her as such, make her act Echo. Because she is obliged to give
to Ovid's text this self-deconstructive sovereignty, Nouvet describes the

Narcissus split as self-recognition rather than self-knowledge.[46] It is, of course, not a question of right or wrong readings. Between different ethical-instantiation fields, the difference may be no more than between seeing the glass half-full rather than half-empty. For Nouvet the self-recognition is inscribed in negatively charged language, as a "problem" and a "decomposition" (IR, pp. 124, 125). For us, Narcissus's self-knowledge is an accession to a clarity that is so clear that it will not lead to relation: to know that to know the self is to slip into visible silence: some call it writing. We may call it an ancient disclosure of the general U.S. epistemological training today. If Ovid and Freud are other readers/writers of a narrateme in a tradition of ethical performance, then "Ovid" (the reader function of the Narcissus story in *Metamorphoses*) is as much a text as his "text," and deconstruction is as much an experience of the impossible as it is a response to the impossible as an impossible response. Today a loss of hope, for the stakes are the world.

My stake in Echo will not allow me to ignore Freud's ignoring of Ovid's staging of (Narcissus and) Echo. Freud is part of the precomprehended scenario of "An Impossible Response," emerging via Blanchot's invocation of the primal scene as scene of writing.[47] An in-house reading, where the text is sovereign in its self-deconstruction, even as the "self" becomes (dis)figured. It is perhaps this that makes for the peculiar blind spot of the essay: the reading of Narcissus's death as a liquefaction (IR, pp. 125–128). It is indeed an "ambiguous" death, not because it is a liquefaction, but because it is a burning as well as a liquefaction. The two vehicles of the similes that describe Narcissus's demise are "yellow wax" and "hoar frost." How render both, as does Nouvet, to "water"? It is only if we remember the yellow flower and Narcissus in Styx that we can "understand" Echo as still "around." "Is there anyone around?" is not, strictly speaking, a question whose "response ... inhabits the question" (IR, p. 110). Its answer may inhabit the question, when Echo answers, by default. *Vox manet,* but only sometimes as resident answers.

Under the rebus of Echo then—since we are nowhere without a blind spot—I invite Nouvet to share mine. Rather than overlook the play of burning and melting, I "naturalize" *in-fans* (speech-less) into more than a pun with infancy, into a historically and specifically feminine infancy of speech (as ambiguous as liquefying through burning) that can no longer be written when self-knowledge inhabits the ambiguity of a "live autopsy," a contemporary rearticulation of Narcissus's desire for the death of the loved object: *un parler d'enfance qui ne s'écrit plus* (a speaking of infancy which can no longer be written), in an impossible response to which Djebar proposes a-phonie, not Narcissus's disaster but Echo's peculiar "reward": to "fail" to order flight from fixation with, in this case, a self that cannot accede to an "I," to an *ego sum,* to the *iste ego sum* of writing, which would itself have been unable to ask for that failed response except through the failure of self-knowledge, imagining that the shadow flees the shadower. I ask Claire Nouvet to attend to a-phonie, Echo's responsibility. This would allow her to escape the tedium of the Oedipal chain (here represented by Blanchot-Schlegel, one might have included Rousseau) reading Narcissus. Insert Echo as the unintending force field that teaches us "that the imperative quality of 'il faut' proceeds in fact from a relentless and demanding uncertainty" (IR, pp. 131–132). Echo the brothers in a self-knowledge that "kills."

One question remains: Can this narrative be read without the specific ethical burden of the feminist in decolonization? By definition, ethical-instantiation readings must have different stakes, different experiences of impossibility. I have already referred to Freud's mature reflection upon the impossibility of an adequately justified psychoanalysis. Keeping that aporia in view, I offer here the outlines of a reading from "a general psychoanalytic position," as if, beset by schools and subschools as the "science" is, such a thing were possible. I have chosen André Green's *Narcissisme de vie, narcissisme de mort* (Narcissism of Life, Narcissism of Death) simply because it is neither too conservative nor too current, innovative in one or two details without being aggressively original, and not yet in touch with feminism.[48]

Green remains within the invariable telos: Narcissus marks an arrest where there should be a passageway to others or the Other. Given his stake in the telos within the forgotten ethical impossibility of psychoanalysis, I will show how his text too asks for supplementation by Echo.

First, of course, Narcissus. Green has an intuition of the part of mortiferous self-knowledge, the part he calls "epistemophilia . . . implying the erotization of the process of thought" (NVM, p. 33).

Green's contribution in this text is the suggestion of a positive and a negative narcissism, and epistemophilia is the negative. But without Echo, the death generated by positive narcissism lacks the dignity of the Ovidian narrative:

> For shame, the only way open is that of negative narcissism. A neutralization of affects is at work, a mortiferous enterprise where the work of a Sisyphus operates. I love no one. I love only myself. I love myself. I do not love. I no. I O. Same series for hatred. I hate no one. I hate only myself. I hate myself. I no. I O. This series of propositions illustrates the evolution towards the affirmation of the megalomaniac I as the last step before disappearance. (NVM, p. 207)[49]

Yet Echo struggles to break through the argument. Here is the description of the psychic apparatus, admittedly the boldest Freudian breakthrough: "It is logical to admit that the effect of structuration [condition and effect of the apparatus] must come *from elsewhere* if the Self is thus engaged in the instantaneousness of the present" (NVM, p. 93; emphasis added). Narcissus immobile, Echo from elsewhere.

In an uncanny description of the project of psychoanalytic thought, Green writes, ostensibly about narcissism: "Narcissism is the effacement of the trace of the Other in the Desire of the One" (NVM, p. 127). We see the effacement at work when, considering negative narcissism in a woman, Green faithfully emphasizes her penultimate declaration, "My mind is blank and I can't think," but ignores her final remark: "Since I cannot work, I telephone someone" (NVM, p. 157). "Tele-phone," distant-voice, *vox manet,* an effort at domesticating Echo; but she will not yield to imitation, to the apparatus that would harness the distant voice to matching questions and answers.

"Echo" in lower case gives us a clue to her foreclosure. When Green proposes a complex of the dead mother, he says, in passing, "in fact, the complaint against X was really against a mother absorbed perhaps by something else, and unreachable without echo, but always sad" (NVM, p. 235). Echo's dispersal into the common language has not only foreclosed her narrative, but reversed and scrambled the narrative: an unreachable desired mother of the homosexual son.

Speaking of the treatment of moral narcissists, Green writes, "To the extent that it [transference] remains expressed by way of the words of the analyst in terms of objects, it has little echo on this material covered over by the narcissistic carapace" (NVM, p. 201). Again, a longing for Echo, lost in the history of the language, not facing the terrifying ethical possibility that Echo/Transference might be as "absurd" as Narcissus/Self-representation (NVM, p. 139).

Our reading proposes a shifting of the stakes. For us Narcissus is not necessarily a stalling of/in the self where there should be a passageway to others or the Other. There is access to the founding dilemma of ethics if we read the Narcissus-Echo pair as an icon (or, more accurately, a graph) of the passage, crossed easily and imperfectly in the exchange of everyday life, and authoritatively in the production of theory on all levels of civil and military enterprise. Then at "ground" level, where justification is sought and offered, we see the knowledge of the self as writing, stalled; and the symbolic circuit not as a relatively fixed Eurocentric scenario, but a contentless, enclitic, monstrative vector, its definitive responsive character unfilled with the subject's intention, though the intentional mo-

ment (Echo's speech toward Narcissus, Oedipus's complaint) is not absent. Incidentally, this would enrich and dislocate Lacan's geometry of
the gaze in interesting ways.

Who can deny that, in the construction of the subject's history, the
driving force of the symbolic is a desire for self-knowledge, although full
self-knowledge would mean an end to symbolicity? Why, in spite of so
many hard lessons to the contrary—not the least from the vicissitudes of
many cultural and gender-inscriptions—do we still cling to the rotarian
epistemology of advancing from the Imaginary to the Symbolic?[50]

The plausibility of this reading is marked by Echo's struggle for emergence in the text. She will be found in the text, even as she marked the
moment of textual transgression in Ovid. One re-forming entailed by this
intervention is to make the self "writing" and "male"—and to make the
Symbolic "feminine." Will this change a historical habit? I can hope.

I am in another sort of deconstructive embrace with my old graduate
school friend Samuel Weber, both of us students of the predeconstructive
Paul de Man, excited early by Derrida's work, untroubled by changes in
critical fashion, in our own different ways attempting to carve out political trajectories within what we know and learn. It is no surprise to me
that in his *Legend of Freud,* Weber does not give sovereignty to the self-
deconstructive "text" (here Freud) but produces a new reading from where
it transgresses itself in terms of its own protocols.[51] In doing so, Weber
produces a reading of psychoanalysis where narcissism is not a stage to
be superseded, but rather plays a constitutive and operative role. I give
below a summary of Weber's remarkable rewriting of the Freudian enterprise, and end, again, by rescuing Echo, struggling to break through.

Weber sees "speculation," reflection in the mirror or speculum, as itself
narcissistic, and sees the project of the adequation of the self and of
thought as an unwitting description of the narcissistic predicament. He
provides a brilliant summary of scholarship in support of his contention
that both French and Anglo-American Freudians "have shared the conviction that Freud articulated the death-drive as an alternative, or even
antidote, to the power exercised over his thought by the theory of narcissism" (LF, p. 124). Although he is, I believe, somewhat unjust to Lacan
here, he also suggests that in Freud, as opposed to what we find in Lacan,
the scene is not one of progression from the Imaginary to the Symbolic, but
"that there is an other scene of the Symbolic, of the Fort-Da game, and it is
precisely: the Imaginary, in all of its aggressive, narcissistic ambivalence"
(LF, p. 97).[52] It is unjust to Ovid too, of course. The acknowledgment of
the mortiferous quality of the self as writing is inscribed in Ovid's narrativization; and Narcissus longs for death. I resonate, nonetheless, with

Weber when he suggests that Freud's thought would develop according to the paradigm of a dynamic disunity of which narcissism is the organized, if ambiguous, part.

> What is at stake here is the possibility of elaborating and rethinking what Deleuze has called the "transcendental" nature of speculation in terms of a certain notion of narcissism, one that is never fully explicated in the writings of Freud, but which is all the more powerfully at work in his texts because it remains, in part at least, implicit. . . . The power of narcissism then, would entail not simply the symptom of an individual subject, "Freud": but rather the theoretical project of psychoanalysis itself, putting its limits into play. (LF, pp. 128, 125–126)

"The power of narcissism." Where does it come from? The last words Echo gives back to Narcissus, to his *emoriar, quam sit tibi copia nostri* (M, p. 150, line 391)—translated in the Loeb edition as "May I die before I give you power o'er me!"—are *sit tibi copia nostri!* (I give you power over me). *Copia nostri* is "our plenty, our plenitude," but also "the provisions that we have laid up for the future," even "our forces," as in military forces, the same metaphor as in *Besetzung*, lost both in "cathexis" and *investissement*. Following the powerful tricks of Ovid's text, Narcissus's ambivalence toward death here—"May I die," nothing more than a rhetorical exclamation—is turned into truth independent of intention (explicit-implicit in Weber's text, *bhrāntapratārakavākya* in Gangeṣa), even as Echo bequeathes her reserves to him by way of an "imperfect" repetition.

Let us step out of the psychoanalytic enclosure for a moment here and repeat that, in terms of a feminism as such (whatever that might be), *sit tibi copia nostri* is a variation on the old game of playing female power within the male establishment. The Narcissus-Echo relationship is more complex. The homeopathic double bind of feminism in decolonization, seeking in the new state to cure the poison of patriarchy with the poison of the legacy of colonialism, can read it as an instantiation of an ethical dilemma: choice in no choice, attendant upon particular articulations of narcissism, ready to await the sounds to which she may give back her own words.

Back in Weber's text, let us now trace Echo's struggle to step forth. I believe her lineaments in the following passage are clear enough for me not to have to retrace them at this stage. Indeed, the mortiferous Narcissus and Echo as devious voice are indistinguishably imbricated here:

> The very *Stummheit* (muteness) of the death drive precludes it from ever speaking for itself; it is inevitably dependent on another discourse to be seen

or heard. And that discourse, however much it may seek to efface itself before the "silence" it seeks to articulate, is anything but innocent or neutral. The death drive may be dumb, but its articulation in a theoretical and speculative [or risky activist, from the broad feminist perspective mentioned above] discourse is not. (LF, p. 129)

It is in the following passage that I find it disturbing that Echo still remains foreclosed. Weber is describing Freud's imprisonment within the discourse of the same, even as he gropes for radical difference:

> If Freud's initial stories deal with men, betrayal, and ingratitude, death enters the scene with—as?—the passive female. . . . The *Schicksalzug* (trait of destiny) that Freud asserts it represents, is . . . a recurrent fatality linked to the female: she either eliminates the male or is eliminated by him. But nothing is more difficult to do away with than this persistent female: you kill her once, and her soul returns, "imprisoned in a tree"; you "slash with (your) sword at (the) tall tree," and a voice comes to accuse you. The activity of the subject, in this final story, consists indeed of a repetition, but what he repeats, actively, is the narcissistic wound that never heals without leaving scars. (LF, p. 134)

Freud's story comes from Torquato Tasso's *Gerusalemme Liberata* (1576), a text that is itself among the European reinscriptions of Ovid. If he had paid as much attention to Ovid, the "persistent female" might have come to undo the Freudian Narcissus. In the event, I agree with Weber that "for Freud . . . the stories he has told are not versions of the narrative of narcissism, but evidence of something radically different. And yet, when he seeks to describe that difference, it emerges as more of the same" (LF, p. 135).

"The two sources of psychoanalytic concepts are psychoanalytic practice on the one hand, and the epistemological horizon on the other" (NVM, p. 32). Good words, with which psychoanalysts of any school would find it hard to disagree. I have spoken only of the latter. Psychoanalytic practice, being a species of performative ethics within the calculus of professional exchange, must suit its terms to every analytic situation. My chapter must remain scrupulously parasitic to that space, rather than claim it for an irresponsibilizing cultural diagnosis. Let's step off in closing, beyond "humanity" and short of it, where Ovid and Freud are flashes of species-being in the great ecosystem of species-life. Narcissus is fixed, but Echo can disseminate. Whales, those paleo-mammals that were once creatures of the earth, echo-locate objects and other inhabitants in the sea world, which is not their home but merely their makeshift dwelling place. The interior of the body, inside Narcissus's carapace, can give us back echoes that hi-tech can intercept to bypass the "Self."

Ava Gerber's stunning "body art" can be an example of an impossible imitation of Echo, attending to the failed narcissism of U.S. body culture. Wallace Stevens's "beauty is immortal in the flesh" celebrates every change in the flesh as beauty, down to its inscription in the economy *(Haushaltung)* of nature after what the Biblical Elders would decipher as decay and death.[53] James Joyce is another flash in the system, canniest of men on the track of women: "Hush! Caution! Echoland!"[54]

CHAPTER ELEVEN

Translation as Culture

I WROTE AN INTRODUCTION to the translation of *De la gramma-tologie* in 1973. A Parisian intellectual mocked me, thinking I would be Echo in the minimal sense to Derrida's Narcissus. He was wrong on both counts. I told him I would put my signature on it and, in that time of innocence, stumbled upon Echo-in-translation. Here are three moments on that path, between 1997 and 2009, the last one least hopeful. This first essay offers the simulacrum of a double bind: how one speaks abroad, and at home.

Oviedo

In every possible sense, translation is necessary but impossible. Melanie Klein, the Viennese psychoanalyst whom the Bloomsbury Group killed with kindness, suggested that the work of translation is an incessant shuttle that is a "life."[1] The human infant grabs on to some one thing and then things. This grabbing *(begreifen)* of an outside indistinguishable from an inside constitutes an inside, fit to negotiate with an outside, going back and forth and coding everything into a sign-system by the thing(s) grasped. One can call this crude coding a "translation." In this never-ending weaving, violence translates into conscience and vice versa. From birth to death this "natural" machine, programming the mind perhaps as genetic instructions program the body (where does body stop and mind begin?) is partly metapsychological and therefore outside the grasp of the mind. Here is originary bio-power, body translating into mind and vice versa, asymmetrically, critically. Thus "nature" passes and repasses into "culture," in a work or shuttling site of violence (deprivation—evil—shocks the infant system-in-the-making more than satisfaction; some say *Paradiso* is the dullest book of *The Divine Comedy*): the violent production of the precarious subject of reparation and responsibility. To plot this weave, the reader—in my estimation, Klein was more a reader than an analyst in the strict Freudian sense—translating the incessant translating shuttle into that which is read must have the most intimate knowledge of the rules of representation and permissible narratives which make up the substance of a culture, and must also become responsible and accountable to the writing/translating presupposed original.

The subject in the shuttling described by Klein is something that will have happened, not something that definitely happens; because, first, it is not under the control of the *I* that we think of as the subject and because, second, there is such a thing as a world out there, however discursive. In this understanding of "translation" in Melanie Klein, therefore, the word "translation" itself loses its literal sense, becomes a catachresis.

In a discussion with Dr. Aniruddha Das, a cell biologist who was working on how cells and parasites recognize what to attack in the body, I asked why he used the word "recognize," such a mindy word, even a word that has to do with intellect and consciousness. Why use that word to describe something that goes on in the body, not really at all in the arena of what we recognize as mind? Wouldn't the word "affinity" do for these parasites' "knowing" what to attack? He explained to me that no, indeed, the word "affinity" would not do, and why it is that precisely the word "recognize" had to be used. (I cannot reproduce the explanation but that does not matter for us at this moment.) He added that the words "recognition" and "recognize" lose their normal sense when used this way. There is no other word that can be used. Most people find this difficult to understand. And I started laughing. I said, yes, most people do find it difficult to understand; what you have just described is a catachrestic use of the word "recognition." In other words, no other word will do, and yet it does not really give you the literal meaning in the history of the language, upon which a correct rather than catachrestic use would be based.

In the sense that I am deriving from Klein "translation" does indeed lose its mooring in a literal meaning. Translation in this general sense is not under the control of the subject who is translating. Indeed the human subject is something that will have happened as this shuttling translation, echoing inside to outside, from violence to conscience: the production of the ethical subject. This originary translation thus wrenches the sense of the English word "translation" outside of its making. One look at the dictionary will tell you the word comes from a restricted ("supine") Latin past participle (of *transferrer*, "to transfer"). It is a done deal, a ceaseless future anterior, something that will have happened without our knowledge, particularly without our control, the subject coming into being.

When so-called ethnophilosophies describe the embedded ethico-cultural subject being formed prior to the terrain of rational decision making, they are dismissed as fatalistic. But the insight, that the constitution of the subject in responsibility is a certain kind of translation, of a genealogical scripting, which is not under the control of the deliberative consciousness, is there also in Melanie Klein, hardly a fatalist. What is interesting about Melanie Klein is that she does indeed want to touch responsibility-based ethical systems rather than just rights-based ethical systems and therefore she looks at the violent translation that constitutes the subject in responsibility. It is in this sense that the human infant, on the cusp of the natural and the cultural, is in translation, except the word "translation" loses its dictionary sense right there. Here, the body itself is a script—or perhaps one should say a ceaseless inscribing instrument.

When a translator translates from a constituted language, whose system of inscription and permissible narratives are "her own," this secondary act, translation in the narrow sense, as it were, is also a peculiar act of reparation—toward the language of the inside, a language in which we are "responsible," the guilt of seeing it as one language among many. Translation in the narrow sense is thus a reparation. I translate from my mother tongue. This originary *Schuldigsein*—being indebted in the Kleinian sense—the guilt in seeing that one can treat one's mother tongue as one language among many—gives rise to a certain obligation for reparation. As I will argue in "Rethinking Comparativism" (Chapter 23), this is the rough side of comparativism. I am a slow translator, and for me it is the shuttle between the exquisite guilt of finding the mother tongue or the substitute mother tongue when I translate from French—every "original" is a place-holder for the mother tongue—shuttle between that guilt, a displacement of some primordial *Schuldigsein,* and the reparation of reality-testing, where each of the languages becomes a guarantee of the other. Each is assumed to be or to possess the generality of a semiotic that can appropriate the singularity of the other's idiom by way of conscientious approximations.

Singularity and generality, idiom and semiosis, private and public grammars. It is as if the play of idiom in semioticity becomes a simulacrum, or case, of the ethical as such, as the unaccountable ethical structure of feeling is transcoded into the calculus of accountability. The idiom is singular to the tongue. It will not go over. The semiotic is the system which is generalizable. This element of transcoding is what locates the recognizable violence of the recognizably political within the general violence of culturing as incessant and shuttling translation, a point much harder to grasp without familiarity with the discourses of the gift.

I don't just mean discourses of the gift à la Heidegger, Lévinas, and Derrida as they underpin, let us say, Derrida's wonderful *Given Time*.[2] I also mean discourses of the gift as they are available in ethnophilosophies. In my own case, for example, it is the discourse of *matririn* or "mother debt"—an accountable translation of the gift of time. Unless one is familiar with the discourses of the gift it is harder to grasp the general violence of culturing as incessant and shuttling translation. Klein locates this in whatever single object first signifies pleasure/pain, good/bad, right/wrong and allows itself to be concatenated into signifying the unmotivated giver of the gift (of life). I grasp my responsibility to take from my mother tongue and give to the "target"-language through the ethical concept-metaphor of *matririn*, "mother-debt"—a debt *to* the mother as well as a debt (that) the (place of the) mother *is*. For the father debt I can give you chapter and verse; it is my chaptering and versing in a publishable genealogy. I cannot provide a citation for *matririn*. The aphorism: *matririn* is not to be repaid, or cannot be repaid, was part of my childhood every day, as it is of my intellectual life now. The mother-debt is the gift of birth, as it is imaged to be, but also the accountable task of childrearing (literally *manush kora*, "making human," in my mother tongue). One translates this gift-into-accountability as one attempts to repay what cannot be repaid, and should not be thought of as repayable.

For me, it is within this open-ended, nature-culture frame that all recognizable violence of the recognizably political within the general violence of culturing can be located—in an element, of transcoding as well as translating. I will stay with the element of transcoding in this first part, with the location of the recognizable violence of the recognizably political. I leave aside for the moment the other terrain of culture as translation, where recognition begins in differentiation.

Let us now speak of idioms and semiotic systems within this frame. I learned this lesson of the violence of transcoding as translation, from a group that has stayed in place for more than thirty thousand years, by way of secondary research.[3] That lesson was contained in the philosopheme—the smallest unit of philosophy: "lost our language," used by the Australian aboriginals of the East Kimberley region. The expression "lost our language" does not mean that the persons involved do not know their aboriginal mother tongue. It means, in the words of a social worker, that "they have lost touch with their cultural base," they no longer compute with it, it is not their software. In the Kleinian metaphorics, it is not the condition and effect of their nature-culture shuttling. Therefore, what these inheritors of settler-colonial oppression ask for is, quite appropriately, mainstream education, insertion into civil society, and the inclusion of some information about their culture in the curriculum. Under the circumstances this is the only practical request. The concept-metaphor "language" is here standing in for that word which names the main instrument for the performance of temporizing, of the shuttling outside-inside translation that is called life. What the aboriginals are asking for, having lost generalizing control of the semioticity of their system, is hegemonic access to chunks of narrative and descriptions of practice, so that the representation of that instrumentality, as a cultural idiom rather than a semiotic, becomes available for performance as what is called theater, or art, or literature, or indeed culture, even theory. Given the rupture between the many languages of aboriginality and the waves of migration and colonial adventure clustered around the Industrial Revolution narrative, demands for multilingual education here become risible. All we have is bilingualisms, bilateral arrangements between idioms understood as essentially or historically private, on the one side, and English on the other, understood as the semiotic as such. This is the political violence of translation as transcoding, the contemporary translation industry about which many of us write. It is not without significance that I cannot check the lexicality of this "loss of language" against any original.[4]

Recently I found corroboration in what Lee Cataldi and Peggy Rockman Napaljarri have written about the Warlpiri people of Central North Australia:

> For Warlpiri people, the coming of the Europeans was "the end of the Jukurrpa" . . . [—]simultaneously an account of the creation of the places in [their narrative], an account of the mythical but human behavior of the ancestral figures, and a mnemonic map of the country with its important, life-giving features for the purpose of instructing a younger listener. . . . Rosie Napurrurla and many others are very aware that the intrusion into their lives and land of the dominating, metropolitan culture of the West meant the end of the Jukurrpa as a world-view [I would call it a discursive practice], as a single, total explanation of the universe. It is apparent that many Warlpiri people are much more clearly aware of the nature of cultural conflict and the nature of the two cultures than Europeans are [and, I would add, than are some academic theorists]. Such awareness is the privilege of the loser in this kind of conflict.[5]

When we establish our reputations on transcoding such resistant located hybridity, distinct from the more commonly noticed migrant hybridity, we lose the privilege of the loser because we claim that privilege.
The translators in Cataldi and Napaljarri's book placed their effort within
resources for a cultural performance of the second degree. They were not
themselves constricted by the violence of this culture performing itself, as
originary and catachrestic translation—the coming into being of the responsible subject as divined by Klein.

After spending three or four days with a Canadian artist of Islamic origin, I asked her a question. We had gotten to know each other well. "I
want you to tell me," I said, "when you confront a situation where you
have to make a decision between right and wrong, do you turn to Islam
for the ethical answer? I quite understand that you and I must join in
undermining the demonizing and dehistoricizing of Islam that is current
in North America today, but this is a different kind of question. It is the
difference between a generalizable semiotics that writes our life, and a
cultural idiom that we must honorably establish so that we can 'perform'
it as art." And she said, after a long time, "I've never been asked this question, but the answer is no."

The translators of the Warlpiri texts place their effort as a resource
for a cultural performance, an idiom, rather than the violence of culture
turning over, in and as the human subject, as originary and catachrestic
translation. I quote again:

> Although it is true that Warlpiri people no longer live within the logic and
> constraints of the world-view known as the Jukurrpa, it is also the case that,
> like other traditional Aboriginal people, they have succeeded in creating for
> themselves a way of life which is unique and distinctive, nothing like the
> European culture with which they have to live. We hope that something of
> the spirit of this social creation is communicated by the translations and the
> narratives in this book.[6]

Alas, we cannot discover how that tradition worked as a violent catachrestic translation shuttle of the outside-inside when it was indeed the
semiosis of subject-making. The Industrial Revolution put paid to that
possible precolonial anti-essentialism, that placing of subject-making in
alterity. And therefore any mention of tradition is silenced with the remark that that is just essentialist golden-ageism, and sometimes it is indeed that. On the contrary, I am mourning the loss of aboriginal culture
as underived fictions that are the condition and effect of the subject's
history merely because it is the founding crime of the world we live in.
There is no question of unwriting or rewriting history here. The bad-

faith, hybridistic essentialism of discovering diasporic hybrids and offering that transcoding of the popular as in itself a radical gesture cannot bind that wound of history. I am certainly not interested in censoring work. What I am objecting to is the kind of silencing that is operated when the transcoding of diasporic cultures mingling becomes in itself a radical gesture. It's that claim to effortless resistance, short-circuiting efforts to translate where "languages have been lost," about which I feel dubious. Many regions thrown together in labor export is not "vernacular cosmopolitanism." Cosmopolitheia is world governance, far indeed from the scene of translation.

Cataldi and Napaljarri, our translators, inhabit an aporia, a catch-22. Some of their material "is derived from land-claim documents," already a site of transcoding a mnemonic geography into the semiosis of land as property. Their book appears in a series that believes in "the global interdependence of human hearts and minds," which can be double-talk for the financialization of the globe, "culturalization" of electronic capital, alibi for the contemporary new world order, post-Soviet exploitation.

Their book appears in such a series, "printed on acid-free paper that meets the American National Standards Institute Z.39.48 standard." What is the relationship between the scene of global ecology and the appropriation of traditional knowledge as trade-related intellectual property in the name of biopiracy coded as bioprospecting? What is the relationship between standardized environmentalism on the one hand and traditional knowledge systems on the other, compromised by unequal development and the "green revolution"? Mnemonic geography and satellite positioning technology (see the Introduction, note 5)? This is also a transcoding question. Just as we cannot content ourselves with collecting examples of diasporic hybridity, so also can we not just read books translating "other cultures," as I have done here. We must work at the screen if we are really interested in translation as a phenomenon rather than a mere convenience because we cannot learn every language in the world.

Precisely in the pages showing the most stunning Warlpiri paintings is an insert, advertising 52 percent student rate savings on *Time* magazine and a free stereo cassette player "for your spare time." The act of the insertion is the mechanical gesture of a subordinate employee or a machine, completely at odds with the apparent intent of the translators. The international book trade is a trade in keeping with the laws of world trade. It is the embedding network which moves books as objects on a circuit of destined errancy. At one end, the coming into being of the subject of reparation. At the other end, generalized commodity exchange. We translate somewhere in between. Even as the translators consign this text of Warlpiri dreaming (Jukurrpa) to this exchange, they cannot grasp, because of the depredations of history, the way in which the totalizing dreaming was an operative anti-essentialist semiosis, the infant shuttling between inside and outside and reality testing, the shuttling of violence and conscience making the subject in responsibility emerge. This book is interesting because it shows that the Warlpiri are themselves aware of this. They point at contemporary social creation. Some assume that subalterns (those cut off from cultural mobility) have nothing but idiom which the historian translates into systematicity. I have at least chosen a text where this view is laid aside and corrected.

In November 1996, I was in a gathering of about twelve hundred aboriginals in a settlement on the outskirts of Akarbaid village in western West Bengal. (These "aboriginals" are supposedly the descendants of the population of the Indian subcontinent before Indo-European-speaking peoples started trickling into that landmass.) Toward evening Mahasweta Devi asked Lochan Sabar, an eighty-four-year-old aboriginal, to "tell Gayatri about the time when you were involved in India's Independence Struggle."

The historians' collective named Subaltern Studies have been engaged since the early 1980s in questioning the nationalist historiography of Indian Independence, suggesting that it ignores the continuous tradition of insurgency among peasants and aboriginals. Here was I confronted by a man who was on the cusp of that binary opposition, between bourgeois nationalist historiography and the subaltern. This Lochan Sabar, himself an aboriginal who had not left that way of life, had taken part in the Independence Struggle and was getting the pension of a "freedom fighter."

He begins telling his story, a story that has been told many times before. I alone do not know it in that company. He is using the word "Gandhi" from time to time. He has translated his experiences in the freedom struggle into an oral formulaic mode, which I could at that point recognize because I had read A. B. Lord as an undergraduate.[7] Mahasweta turns aside and tells me, "By the way, he's not referring to Mahatma Gandhi." Any person in the position of a bourgeois leader staging himself as subaltern is being given the name Gandhi. Gandhi after all was no subaltern; he staged himself as one, took off his suit—so any time that some charismatic intellectual populist leader is described Lochu is using the word "Gandhi." In terms of the way in which they mythicize, "Gandhi" has become a type word. This shakes me up. Next, whenever there comes a moment in his epic recounting when what the academic subalternist historians describe as religion coming into crisis and becoming militancy comes to pass, Lochan Sabar marks it with the exclamation *Bande Mataram!* (Praise to the Mother!), without catching it in the web of his narrative.

Those of you who have seen Satyajit Ray's *Home and the World* will remember this as the slogan of the freedom fighters.[8] These are the opening words, in Sanskrit, of the nineteenth-century nationalist song written by Bankim Chandra Chatterjee.

Sanskrit is the classical language of the Hindus. The very word means "refined" (as opposed to "natural," "raw"). The refinement of the original Indo-European speech traditions into that form would be politically exactly opposed to the culture of the aboriginals. How shall one compute Lochan Sabar's negotiation with this?[9] Further, the Mother in the song is Bengal-cum-India. The Bharatiya Janata Party, the Hindu Nationalist Party in India, wants to claim it as the national anthem in place of the more secular one in actual use. Lochan is not aware of this; he is not Hindu, only an unlettered animist whose religious idiom is contaminated by Hindu folk practice. He is transforming the hegemonic nationalist account, Gandhi as well as Bankim, into the semiotic conventions of subaltern or Sabar telling. He is deflecting Bankim's own effort, related to the British ideology of restoring Bengal to its Hindu lineaments against the Muslim rule that the British had brought to an end. Bankim attempted to establish a Hindu Bengali nationalism which would gradually vanish into "Indian" nationalism. He negotiates the Islamic component of Bengali culture; the aboriginals are nothing but children to him. Bankim's brother, Sanjiv Chandra Chatterjee, had written the immortal sentence, memorized by every schoolchild in my day: "The savage has beauty in the forest, as does the child in its mother's arms." In the process, denying the lexicalized Arabic and Persian elements of Bengali, Bankim lexicalizes Sanskrit into Bengali as Lochan Sabar weaves his words into subaltern formula.

I can see both as generalizing, from idiom to semiosis, differently. Lochan's is not just an idiomatics, which the historian then transcodes and makes available in the more general semiotic of a recognizable historiography. My friends, fellow Subalternists, said, "But, Gayatri, you say you won't transcode it because you have this kind of primitivistic piety towards these tribals, but nonetheless you are saying it, aren't you?"

Indeed, this too is a moment of destined errancy. Just as *Yimikirli* enters the international book trade, so does my anecdote. I would like to place them on a taxonomy with the docketing of every hybrid popular phenomenon as a radical gesture as such, and yet mark the difference. This is not an example of "vernacular nationalism."

There was a moment when another man, who didn't know what was going on, cried from the opening of the enclosure, "Lochan, sing, sing for us," and Lochan Sabar said loudly and with great dignity, "No, this is not a moment for singing. I am saying History." He himself was making a distinction between entertainment and knowledge.

I too am a translator, into English. Some say I have not grasped either Derrida's French or Mahasweta's Indian spirit. I seem now engaged in an even more foolhardy enterprise, to catch the translations from the other side. It was in that spirit that I began my speech with a quotation from the Warlpiris. And thus I end, with a quotation from Lochan Sabar. I embed them both in translation in the general sense, translation as catachresis, the making of the subject in reparation.

The year after my speech at Oviedo, I received the Translation Award from the National Academy of Letters in India and delivered an acceptance speech in 1998. There is a certain continuity between the two events. In the former I question the metropolitan hybridist. In the latter I take the national identitarians to task. I take the liberty of appending my acceptance speech as the appropriate conclusion to this essay.

New Delhi

I am deeply honored that the Sahitya Akademi have decided to acknowledge my efforts to translate the fiction of Mahasweta Devi. I want to begin by thanking Mahasweta Devi for writing such spectacular prose. I want to thank my parents, Pares Chandra Chakravorty and Sivani Chakravorty, for bringing me up in a household that was acutely conscious of the riches of Bangla. My father was a doctor. But we children were always reminded that my father's Bangla essay for his matriculation examination had been praised by Tagore himself.

And my mother? I could not possibly say enough about her on this particular occasion. Married at 14 and with children coming at the ages of 15 and 23, this active and devoted wife and mother, delighted every instance with the sheer fact of being alive, studied in private and received her M.A. in Bengali literature from Calcutta University in 1937. She read everything I wrote and never complained of the obscurity of my style. Without her constant support and interest, and indeed without the freedom she gave me in the 1950s, herself a young widow then, to lead my life as my errant mind led me, I would not have been able to write these words for you today.

Samik Bandyopadhyaya introduced me to Mahasweta Devi in 1979. Initially, I was altogether overwhelmed by her and took her at her word. Now long familiarity has brought a more judicious approach.

In 1981, I found myself in the curious position of being asked to write on deconstruction and on French feminism by two famous U.S. journals, *Critical Inquiry* and *Yale French Studies,* respectively. I cannot now remember why that position had then seemed to me absurd. At any rate, I proposed a translation of Mahasweta's short story "Draupadi" for *Critical Inquiry,* with the required essay on deconstruction plotted through a reading of the story.

When I look back upon that essay now, I am struck by its innocence. I had been away from home for twenty years then. I had the courage to acknowledge that there was something predatory about the nonresident Indian's obsession with India. Much has changed in my life since then, but that initial observation retains its truth. I should perhaps put it more tactfully today or acknowledge the strong collaboration India-side.

Why did I think translating Mahasweta would free me from being an expert on France in the United States? I don't know. But this instrumentality disappeared in the doing. I discovered again, as I had when I had translated *De la grammatologie* ten years earlier, that translation was the most intimate act of reading, Echo in a double bind. Not only did Mahasweta Devi not remain Gayatri Spivak's way of freeing herself from France, but indeed the line between French and Bengali disappeared in the intimacy of translation. The verbal text is jealous of its linguistic signature but impatient of national identity. Translation flourishes by virtue of that paradox.

The line between French and Bengali disappeared for this translator in the intimacy of the act of translation. Mahasweta resonated, made a *dhvani,* with Derrida, and vice versa.[10] This has raised some ire, here and elsewhere. This is not the occasion for discussing unhappy things. But let me crave your indulgence for a moment and cite a couple of sentences, withholding theory, that I wrote in a letter to my editor Anjum Katyal of Seagull Books, when I submitted to her the manuscript of my translation of "Murti" and "Mohanpurer Rupkatha" by Mahasweta Devi:

> [In these two stories] the aporias between gendering on the one hand ("feudal"-transitional, and subaltern), and the ideology of national liberation (as tragedy and as farce) are also worth contemplating. But I am a little burnt by the resistance to theory of the new economically restructured reader who would prefer her NRI neat, not shaken up with the ice of global politics and local experience. And so I let it rest.

That hard sentence at the end reflects my hurt and chagrin at the throwaway remark about Gayatri Chakravorty Spivak's "sermonizing" offered by the reviewer, in *India Today,* of *Imaginary Maps,* the very book that you have chosen to honor.

I was hurt, of course. But I was chagrined because "sermonizing" was also the word used by Andrew Steer, then Deputy Director for the Environment at the World Bank, in 1992, when I had suggested, at the European Parliament, that the World Bank re-examine its constant self-justificatory and fetishized use of the word "people." At both Oviedo and New Delhi, my concern is for the constitution of the ethical subject—as life/translator (Klein), narrow-sense/translator, reader-as-translator.[11]

Why did I decide to gild Mahasweta's lily? Shri Namwar Singh, Professor of Hindi at Jawaharlal Nehru University, who presided over the occasion, will remember that instructors at the Department of Modern Indian Literatures at Delhi University had asked me in 1987 why, when Bangla had Bankim and Tagore, I had chosen to speak on "Shikar," one of the stories included in *Imaginary Maps*. I am most grateful to the Jnanpith committee for correcting such errors.[12] My devotion to Mahasweta did not need national public recognition. I was her first English translator.

To ignore the narrative of action or text as ethical instantiation is to forget the task of translation upon which being-human is predicated. Translation is to transfer from one to the other. In Bangla, as in most North Indian languages, it is *anu-vada*—speaking after, *translatio* as *imitatio*, Echo. This relating to the other as the source of one's utterance *is* the ethical as being-for. All great literature as all specifically good action— any definition would beg the question here—celebrates this. To acknowledge this is not to "sermonize," one hopes.

Translation is thus not only necessary but unavoidable. If the text speaks, there will be Echo. And yet, as the text guards its secret, it is impossible. The ethical task is never quite performed. "Pterodactyl, Puran Sahay, and Pirtha," one of the tales included in *Imaginary Maps,* is the story of such an unavoidable impossibility, where the unavoidable—the planetary—is only too easily—seemingly—avoided. Even by the general outlines of the historical narrative accepted by the state, the Indian aboriginal is kept apart or othered by the descendants of the old settlers, the ordinary "Indian." In the face of the radically other, the pre-historic pterodactyl, the planetary necessarily (mis)represented by a creature, the aboriginal and the settler are historially human together. The pterodactyl cannot be translated. But the aboriginal and the settler Indian translate one another in silence and in the ethical relation, interrupting the popularizing epistemology of the journalist.

This founding task of translation does not disappear by fetishizing the native language. Sometimes I read and hear that the subaltern can speak in their native languages. I wish I could be as self-assured as the intellectual, literary critic and historian, who assert this in English. No speech is speech if it is not heard. It is this act of hearing-to-respond that may be called the imperative to translate.

We often mistake this for helping people in trouble, or pressing people to pass good laws, even to insist on behalf of the other that the law be implemented. But the founding translation between people is a listening with care and patience, in the normality of the other, enough to notice that the other has already silently made that effort. This reveals the irreducible importance of idiom, which a standard language, however native, cannot annul.

And yet, in the interest of the primary education of the poorest, looking forward to the privative norms of democracy, a certain standard language must also be shared and practiced. Here we attempt to annul the impossibility of translation, to deny provisionally Saussure's warning that historical change in language is inherited. The toughest problem here is translation from idiom to standard, an unfashionable thing among the elite progressives, without which the abstract structures of democracy cannot be comprehended. Paradoxically, here idiomaticities must be attended to most carefully. I have recently discovered that there is no Bangla-to-Bangla dictionary for this level (the primary education of the poorest) and suitable to this task (translation from idiom to standard).[13] The speaker of some form of standard Bengali cannot hear the self-motivated subaltern Bengali unless organized by politically correct editing, which is equivalent to succor from above.

It is not possible for us to change the quality of rote learning in the lowest sectors of society. But with an easy-to-use same-language dictionary, a spirit of independence and verification in the service of rule-governed behavior—essential ingredients for the daily maintenance of a democratic polity—can still be fostered. The United Nations, and non-governmental organizations in general, often speak triumphantly of the establishment of numbers of schools. We hardly ever hear follow-up reports, and we do not, of course, know what happens in those classrooms every day. But a dictionary, translating from idiom to standard even as it resists the necessary impossibility of translation, travels everywhere. It is only thus that subalternity may painstakingly translate itself into a hegemony that can make use of and exceed all the succor and resistance that we can organize from above. I have no doubt about this at all.

I am sorry I will not be with you when these words are read. I am writing them by the light of a hurricane lantern in a tiny room in Jonara, a settlement of a certain denotified tribe. In the next room is a number of male tribal adults, one of whom came willingly and learned so much from me in four hours of concentrated work that another, older, came a bit later and learned some and later asked me to prepare the other one so he can teach the adults until I come again. (My teacher training work, which I do systematically in the morning, is with groups of children and their teachers.) Now a group of adult males are murmuring in the next room, poring over letters and words, one of them a student in the local high school who was, until now, separated from his elders because idiom cannot translate itself into standard.

In the afternoon, the only barely literate bride whom I had seen last year said to me in the presence of senior women, "I've forgotten everything." Her head was turned away from them toward me, her eyes shining with tears. Later she came to my door and wrote her name and address, the first ten numbers, the usual proof of literacy, and then, her message: "Mashi come again."

How long will the men's enthusiasm and the woman's anguish last? I could not know then, but do now. Until a young boy wanted a better education and the (ex) zamindar closed the schools. Enter "Maoism." Another story.[14] What I am describing is rather different from the self-conscious rectitude of so-called adult education classes. Let me translate for you the lines written for me, in the middle of our lesson and on his own, by the first man who came for his lesson today, knowing nothing but the Bangla alphabet: *"yele koto anando holo choley jabey abar kobey abey boley na"* (Here and at the end of the next paragraph I have omitted periods to give a sense of the trailing incompleteness of the punctuationless sentences.)

This is Bangla tribal creole that Mahasweta attempts to reproduce in her fiction and I cannot translate into English. My friend Sahan Sabar thought he was writing standard Bengali. I give witness to the attempt to translate which the sentence bears. I made two changes for him, assuring him that the first was just a variation. I did not change the most powerful mark of the creole—the absence of the "you"—*tumi*—an absence only poetry or affect would produce in standard Bangla. This is how Sahan's sentence would translate into standard English: "[You] came how much joy there was [you] will leave us doesn't say when [she] will return"

This subaltern gave me the gift of speech, already on the way to translation, because I had attended to his idiom, not because I helped him in distress. These Sabars, women and men, constantly translate for me, consciously, between their speech, their creole, my Bangla. *They* do not immediately need an anthropological dictionary of the Kheria language. There are a couple of those in the Columbia University Library. And these Sabars have "lost their language" in every way. They speak versions of Gaudiya prakrit, some of the many Sanskrit creoles that coalesced into modern Bengali a thousand years ago, give or take—I am no scholar. Today as we speak to accept our awards for translating well from the twenty-one languages of India, I want to say, with particular emphasis, that what the largest part of the future electorate needs, in order to accede, in the longest run, to democracy rather than have their votes bought and sold, is practical, simple, same-language dictionaries that will help translate idiom into standard, in all these languages. I hope the Akademi will move toward the satisfaction of this need, as we work to rearrange desires—don't ask an elder or a Babu for meaning, consult a book. (This hope, too, has been subsequently dashed. The priorities are primitivism, traditionalism, bourgeois culturalism, global competitionism. No surprises.)

For myself, I cannot help but translate what I love, yet I resist translation into English, the title of the next chapter. I never teach anything whose original I cannot read, and constantly modify printed translations, including my own. I think it is a bad idea to translate Gramsci and Kafka and Baudelaire into Indian languages from English. As a translator, then, I perform the contradiction, the counter-resistance, that is at the heart of love. And I thank you for rewarding what need not be rewarded, the pleasure of the text, a prayer to be haunted.

Let me end with my "Translator's Note" after I finished translating Aimé Césaire's *Une saison au Congo* this year:

> There are two theories of translation: you add yourself to the original or, you efface yourself and let the text shine. I subscribe to the second. But I have said again and again that translation is also the most intimate act of reading. And to read is to pray to be haunted. Césaire haunted me, as he was in turn haunted by Lumumba. Effacing my generation's disappointments, translating him with care, I understood in my nerve-endings that that generation of post-colonials wanted to undo the flimsy European gift of nation-identification and create a real force in the world, where a new kind of regionalism would undo cultural essentialisms. It did not succeed. But, speaking again and again Lumumba's dying speech in Act three Scene six— not veridical but true—where death appears as a promise to be in the land, and death's bloody foam as the sense of some coming dawn, I sensed in my nerves that that failure was not final. As I expressed this in public, my friend Souleymane Bachir Diagne, speaking from the first row, countersigned that sense—speaking of a persistent effort, the result always around the corner. I ask him, therefore, to introduce the text that it was my honor to translate. Let my translation lead you to the French.

CHAPTER TWELVE

Translating into English

'D LIKE to begin with what should to be an obvious point. That the translator should make an attempt to grasp the writer's presuppositions, pray to be haunted by the project of the original. Translation is not just the stringing together of the most accurate synonyms by the most proximate syntax. Kant's "Religion within the Boundaries of Mere Reason" is written with the presupposition that mere (rather than pure) reason is a programmed structure, with in-built possibilities of misfiring, and nothing but calculation as a way of setting right.[1] Since the eighteenth century, English translators, not resonating with Kant's philosophical presuppositions, have psychologized every noun, making Kant sound like a rational choice bourgeois Christian gentleman.[2] Kant's insight could have taken on board today's major problem—can there be a secularism without an intuition of the transcendental, of something that is inscrutable because it cannot be accessed by mere reasoning? Kant's project, to protect the calculus of reason by way of the transcendental as one parergon among four, was counter-intuitive to his English translators.[3]

I will add three more examples here to show the generality of the problem. In these, the lack of translators' sympathy stalled a possible use for each text, a use that relates to the limits of rational choice. This brings the examples into my chief concern: the responsibility of the translator into English. I hope some readers will care to follow the trajectory suggested by each.

When Marx wrote about the commensurability of all things, that it was "contentless and simple" *(inhaltslos und einfach)*, he was speaking as a materialist speaks of form.[4] Not as *form,* but as a thing without content. Generations of empiricist English translators have missed the point, not resonating with Marx's philosophical presuppositions, translated *inhaltslos* as "slight in content," and thus made nonsense out of the entire discussion of value. Marx's insight could have taken on board today's transformation of all things into data—telecommunication rendering information indistinguishable from capital. Marx's presuppositions, to control the inevitability of intelligible formalism in a materialist interest, were counter-intuitive to his English translators.

In his seminar on the gaze or glance, the eminent French psychoanalyst Jacques Lacan presents the scopic or apparently objectivizing sweeping glance as something like a symptom. To show his students this, Lacan cannot use proof. It is the very production of proof in the patient that Lacan is opening up. He therefore uses the interesting coinage *apologue*— apology, excuse, but also something that is just a little off the side of the *logos.* "I will tell you a little apologue," he says. *Je vais vous raconter une petite apologue.*[5] The naturalizing translator, thinking Lacan is just talking about people looking, translates this important sentence as "I will tell you a little story."

When the French historian Michel Foucault described the ground-floor of power as set up with "irreducible over-againsts" *(irréductible vis à vis),* he was trying to avoid transcendentalizing the empirical.[6] Humanist English translators, unable to resonate with Foucault's philosophical presuppositions, have translated "vis-à-vis" as "opposite," given content to a non-formalist intuition of form, and turned the argument into the micropolitics of power, understood as ordinary language.

Grasping the writer's presuppositions, then, as they inform his or her use of language, as they develop into a kind of singular code, is what Jacques Derrida, the French philosopher who has taught me a great deal, calls entering the protocols of a text—not the general laws of the language, but the laws specific to *this* text. And this is why it is my sense that translation is the most intimate act of reading, a prayer to be haunted.

I begin this way because I am a translator *into* English, not just *from* specific languages. Because of the growing power of English as a global lingua franca, the responsibility of the translator into English is increasingly complicated. And, although I chose my four opening examples in order to avoid cultural nationalism, it is of course true that the responsibility becomes altogether more grave when the original is not written in one of the languages of Northwestern Europe.

For a variety of reasons, the market for quick translations from such languages is steadily on the rise. Since the mid-1970s, it has been enhanced by a spurious and hyperbolic admiration not unrelated to the growing strength of the so-called international civil society.[7] In the 1970s, extra-state collective action in Europe, Latin America, Asia, and Africa concerned itself with issues such as health, the environment, literacy, and the like. Although their relationship with the nation-state was conflictual, there was still a relationship. Gradually, with the advance of capitalist globalization, this emergent force was appropriated into the dominant. These earlier extra-state collectivities, which were basically non-governmental entities, often with international solidarity, were now used to undermine the constitutionality (however precarious or utopian) of the state. Powerful international NGOs (non-governmental organizations) now control these extra-state circuits globally. Indigenous NGOs typically have a large component of foreign aid. This self-styled international civil society (since it is extra-state) has a large cultural component, especially directed toward gender issues. It is here that the demand for translation—especially literary translation, a quick way to "know a culture"—has been on the rise. At this point, we translators into English should operate with great caution and humility.

Yet the opposite is often the case. Meenakshi Mukherjee, the well-known feminist Bengali scholar of English literature, spoke to me of a person—she did not mention the name—who has recently turned her or his hand to translating from the Bengali. Upon repeated questioning about her or his proficiency in Bengali, this would-be translator has given the same answer: *"bangla porte jani,"* "I can read Bengali." We all know of such cases.

It is time now to mention the other obvious point—the translator must not only make an attempt to grasp the presuppositions of an author but also, and of course, inhabit, even if on loan, the many mansions, and many levels of the host language. *Bangla porte jani* is only to have gained entry into the outer room, right by the front gate.

At the time of writing, I was engaged in translating Mahasweta Devi's novel *Chotti Munda ebong tar tir—Chotti Munda and His Arrow*—published in 1980.[8] In the last paragraph that I translated I made a choice of level when I came across the phrase *"mohajoner kachhe hat pa bandha."* "Arms and legs in hock to the moneylender," I wrote. "In hock" is more in the global lingua franca than in the English that is one of the Indian languages. I had a running conversation about such choices with Sujit Mukherjee, the brilliant Indian translator from Bengali into English. But "mortgaged" would have been, in my judgment, an error of level, and would have missed the pun, "being tied up or trussed," present in the original.

Not that "in hock" catches the pun. But "hock" is sufficiently confusing in its etymology to carry the promise of nuances. The translator must play such games.

I'm less satisfied with my treatment of the phrase lower down in the paragraph, *"hoker kotha bollo na Chotti?"* as "Didn't Chotti speak of 'rights'?" *Hok,* in Bengali, a *totshomo* or identical loan from the Arabic *al haq,* is not rights alone but a peculiar mix of rights and responsibilities that goes beyond the individual. Anyone who has read the opening of Mahasweta's novel knows that the text carries this presupposition. I have failed in this detail. Translation is as much a problem as a solution. I hope the book will be taught by someone who has enough sense of the language to mark this kind of unavoidable failure, and that the rare reader will be led to the Bengali.[9]

This for me is an important task of translation, especially from languages that are dying, some fast, some slow, for want of attention. In our particular circumstances, we translators from the languages of the global South should prepare our texts as metropolitan teaching texts because that, for better or for worse, is their destiny. Of course, this would make us unpopular, because the implicit assumption is that all that "third world" texts need is a glossary. I myself prepare my translations in the distant and unlikely hope that my texts will fall into the hands of a teacher who knows Bengali well enough to love it, so that the students will know that the best way to read this text is to push through to the original. Of course, not everyone will learn the language, but one might, or two! And the problem will be felt. I should add here that I have the same feeling for Aristotle and classical Greek, Hrotswitha von Gandersheim and Latin, Dante and Italian—and, of course, Kant and Marx and German, Lacan and Foucault and French. It is just that these latter texts have plenty of teaching editions and the languages are not ignored. I received a contemptuous notice, I think, if memory serves, from *Kirkus Review,* some years ago, for preparing a volume of fiction by Mahasweta Devi with a preface and an afterword. Literature and philosophy do, of course, belong to different slots on a publisher's list, but I do contrast this with the abundant praise I have received over the last twenty-seven years all over the world for providing just that apparatus for a volume of philosophical criticism by Jacques Derrida.[10]

In this spirit I will turn now to *Ashomoyer Noteboi—Untimely Notebook—*by Farhad Mazhar, activist-poet from Bangladesh.[11]

Ashomoy is an interesting word. *Dushhomoy* would be "bad times" of course. But Nietzsche's use of *Unzeitmäßig,* typically translated as "untimely," as in *Untimely Meditations,* gave me a way out.[12] And a notebook is a place where meditations are jotted down.

Mazhar thinks of himself as "untimely" quite as Nietzsche does, indeed quite as Nietzsche believes genuine cultural figures must be: "Virtue . . . always swims against the tide of history, whether by combating its passions as the most proximate stupid factuality of its existence or by dedicating itself to being honorable while the lie spins its glittering web around it."[13] He offers no alternatives: "The untimely thinker, which is how Nietzsche viewed himself, does not work directly towards the establishment of another culture, in which his arguments might become 'timely'; rather, he is working 'against my age, and thereby influencing my age, and hopefully for the benefit of a future age.'"[14]

As Foucault suggests in "Nietzsche, Genealogy, History":

> If genealogy in its turn poses the question of the land that saw our birth, of the language that we speak, or of the laws that govern us, it is to make visible the heterogeneous systems which, under the mask of our "we," forbids us all identity. . . . [Another] use of history . . . uncovers the violence of a position taken: taken against ignorant happiness, against the vigorous illusions by which humanity protects itself, taken in favor of all that is dangerous in research and disturbing in discoveries.[15]

In pursuit of heterogeneity, Mazhar goes clear out of culture into nature, undertaking impossible translations from the animal world in a recognizably Nietzschean mode. We recall that this is precisely where Derrida locates Nietzsche as philosopher of life.[16]

> Now then notebook, will you get the Philip's
>   Prize this time?
> Try hard, try hard, by Allah's grace.
>
> Caution
> I'm copying down how the grass crawls
> I'm copying down how the jaguar grabs
> I'm slipping, my foot's missed its hold
> I'm copying down the problems on the way
>   along with the foot's heel
> Caution caution
> Earlier you had to fight standing
>   on the other side of the barbed wire

Now on both sides: Right and left, top and
    bottom, in water and on land . . .
Go get your teeth fixed by the alligator
From the snake a rubber spine
Go suckle the breasts of the bat
Hey my untimely notebook, the times are bad
    chum
Must walk with eyes peeled on all sides my
    friend
    Be careful!!
    Caution!!!

In the previous stanza, he speaks of the woman Nurjahan who was
stoned to death because she was supposed to have slept with someone
other than her husband. I can commend Mazhar's feminism and work out
his spiritual link with the anything-but-feminist Nietzsche but I cannot
work out the words *murtad* and *dorra* in lines 2 and 3:

Untimely notebook, I'm giving a fatwa,
    you're murtad
I'll dorra you a hundred and one times
    you're shameless
I'll fix you in a hole and stone you to death
    In front of the whole village
    You to Chhatakchhara, to Kalikapur
Must go, this time to die
Seek out a torn sari or a pitcher
Shariat witness, Allah has bred girls
    For the village elders and the world's rich men
Shariat witness, the task of imam and mollah
    is to fulfill Allah's will
Go faith go money go reaction go progress go
Go Jamayate Islami go imperialism go Subal
    go Sudam[17]
Go hand in hand twin brothers let's watch and
    be delighted . . .

I am unable to access *murtad* and *dorra* because they are *tatshomo*
words from Arabic. I add an explanation of this word and the companion word *tadbhabo*, words that were known to every Bengali schoolchild
when I went to high school in the early 1950s. I am not a Bengalist,

merely a translator in love with the language. What I am about to give you is a generalist's sense of things.

Tat in these two words signifies "that" or "it," and refers to Sanskrit, one of the classical languages of India, claimed by the Hindu majority. They are descriptive of two different kinds of words. *Tadbhabo* means "born of it." *Tatshomo* means "just like it." I am using these two words by shifting the shifter *tat*—"that" or "it"—to refer to Arabic as an important loan-source.

Through the centuries of the Mughal empire in India (1526–1857) and the corresponding Nawabate in Bengal, Bengali was enriched by many Arabic and especially Persian loan-words. Of course Bengali is derived from Sanskrit, which was by then "dead," so the relationship is altogether different. But learned and worldly Bengali gentlemen were proficient in Arabic, and especially Persian—the languages of the court and the law. The important entry of the British into India was by way of Bengal. It is at least the generalist's assumption that the British played the Bengali Hindus with promises of liberation from the Muslim empire. William Jones's discovery that Sanskrit, Greek, and Latin were related languages even gave the Hindus and the English a common claim to Aryanism, a claim to inter-translatability, as it were.[18] And, from the end of the eighteenth century, the fashioners of the new Bengali prose purged the language of the Arabic-Persian content until, in Michael Madhusudan Dutt's (1824–1873) great blank verse poetry, and the *Bangadarshan* (1872–1876) magazine edited by the immensely influential novelist Bankim Chandra Chattopadhyaya (1838–1894), a grand and fully Sanskritized Bengali emerged. Its Arabic and Persian components became no more than local color. This was the language that became the vehicle of Bengali nationalism and subsequently of that brand of Indian nationalism that was expressed in Bengali. The medium was simplified, expanded, and diversified into the contemporary Bengali prose which is the refined edge of my mother tongue, which I learned in school, and which did not allow me to translate *murtad* and *dorra*.

A corresponding movement of purging the national language Hindi of its Arabic and Persian elements has been under way since Independence in 1947. Such political dismemberments of language have become part of Partition Studies—as Serbian separates from Croatian, Czech separates from Slovak, and Cantonese is dismissed as a mere dialect of Han. The political production of internal translation requires a different type of analysis, which I will touch upon in my conclusion.

If the Arabic and Persian elements were purged out of Bengali, how do I encounter them as a translator today? I encounter them as part of a general movement in Bangladesh to restore these components. This is not to be confused with an Islamicization of the language, since there can be no question of transforming the Sanskrit base of Bengali. Indeed, Mazhar uses the Sanskrit-based vocabulary of Bengali with considerable flair. One may call this an attempt persistently to mend the breach of a partition that started—as I have indicated in my generalist tale—long before the named Partition of India in 1947. It is to restore a word-hoard that went underground.

What was created as East Pakistan in 1947 became independent as Bangladesh in 1971. Although there was an important political and military conflict that brought this about, it would not be incorrect to say that one strong factor of the mobilization of what was to become Bangladesh was the issue of language.[19] And indeed the naming of the new nation as Bangladesh was to shrink an older cartography. Bangladesh (Banglaland) is the name of the entire land area whose people use Bangla, or Bengali; or Bangla is the name of the language of the entire people of the land or desh called Bangladesh. Before the Independence-Partition of 1947, this would have been the entire British province of Bengal, including today's Indian state of West Bengal and the modern nation-state of Bangladesh, whose geographical descriptive could be East Bengal—in Bengali Paschim and Purbo Banga. Banga is the ancient name of a tract of land somewhat larger than the British province of Bengal. Thus the proper name of a pre-modern area and kingdom, displaced into the name of a Nawabship, translated into the colonial proper name of a province, expanded beyond a language area into the governmental abstraction of a Presidency—is now modernized to designate, not a language-area, but a bounded nation-state metonymically claiming the whole.

This may be seen as the celebration of partition, however benign. Since 1947, the Indian state of West Bengal (or Paschim Bango) is the western part of a place that does not exist. Unlike those who propose solutions such as calling it merely Bango, so that it too can claim the whole, by a more ancient name, I propose no nominative solution. Such a solution would finalize partition by making official the historically asymmetrical name of the whole for each geographically asymmetrical half. Even that could be undone, of course; for each half could say we are each the whole, in different ways. In the long run, it would not matter a great deal, for named places do not, strictly speaking, exist as such, since there are re-namings. If there is history, there is the re-naming of place. In this case as elsewhere, I am interested in the political mode of production of the collectively accepted existence of named places, whose "other names" linger on as archaic or residual, emergent as local alternative or opposition, always ready to emerge.[20]

If the establishment of a place named Bangladesh in a certain sense endorses the Partition of 1947, then the language policy of the state, strangely enough, honors that other partition—the gradual banishment of the Arabic and Persian elements of the language that took place in the previous century—and thus paradoxically undoes the difference from West Bengal. The official language of the state of Bangladesh, 99 percent Muslim, is as ferociously Sanskritized as anything to be found in Indian Bengali.

It is over against and all entwined in this tangle that the movement to restore the Arabic and Persian element of Bengali, away from its century-old ethnic cleansing, does its work. And it is because I grew up inside the tangle that, in spite of my love of Bengali, I could not translate *murtad* and *dorra*—though I could crack *ashamoyer* with Nietzsche.

I am only a translator, not a Bengalist. I can cite only two names in this movement: Akhtaruzzaman Ilias (1943–1998), the author of *Chilekothar Sepai* and the fantastic *Khoabnama;* and Farhad Mazhar, whose poem I was about to translate when I launched into this lengthy digression.[21] It may be claimed that these writers do a double bluff on the Sanskritized linguistic nationalism of Bangladesh.

At a meeting of the Sahitya Akademi I was immediately side-tracked into a translation of the word *huda* (about which more later), as an Arabic-origin Urdu word foreign to Bengali; and instructed by a learned etymologico-philosophical disquisition (a pale imitation of which I would be able to provide for Sanskrit-origin Bengali words) from a distinguished professor of Urdu from Kashmir. None of the Indian Bengalis could offer a translation.

Murtad and *dorra* can be translated as "apostate" and "whiplash." *Huda* so overwhelmed the discussion that they remained un-Englished at the Akademi meeting. I have withheld this information for so long because, as I was moving through various European and Asian countries, revising, I kept wondering how I would get to find the English equivalents! A chance encounter—someone reading Bengali web in the Bangkok airport must be Bangladeshi!—provided them at last.

It is my belief that unless the paleonymy of the language is felt by her in some rough historical or etymological way, the translator is unequal to her task. Strangely enough, I got this lesson at St. John's Diocesan Girls' High School in Calcutta, from Miss Nilima Pyne, a young Christian woman (we thought her ancient, of course) who had learned Sanskrit with heart and soul. She had quoted at us, when I was no more than eleven or twelve, that famous pair of Sanskrit tags, both meaning "there's a dry branch in the way." See if you can sense the complete dissonance in the two sets of sounds; be sure to mark the greater length of the vowels in the second example. I have not followed accepted phonetic transliteration, but given the closest Englishing of the Sanskrit sounds:

a. *shushkum kashthum tishthattugrey*
b. *neerasa taruvara poorata bhaati*

Can you sense the completely different ring of the two sentences? If you don't have a sense of Sanskrit, which is rather different from "knowing" Sanskrit, you cannot, of course. Sound and sense play together to show that translation is not merely transfer of sense, for the two lines "mean the same thing." Sanskrit is not just a moment in Benveniste.[22]

This was not a lesson in translation. But it was such instruction that allowed us to understand, three or four years later, Shakespeare's line with "the same meaning," metaphorizing enormity in the enormousness of the encompassing ocean:

This my hand,
Will the multitudinous seas incarnadine,
Making the green one red.

We transfer content because we must, knowing it cannot be done, in translation as in all communication, yet differently. We transpose level and texture of language, because we must, knowing that neither idiom nor sound goes over. It is this double bind that the best and most scrupulous translation hints at, by chance, perhaps. *Mimesis* hits *poiesis* by *tuchè*.[23] Translators from the languages of the global South into English have lost this striving. The loss is incalculable. Responsible translators from the languages of the global South into English therefore often translate in the shadow of the imminent death of the host language as they know it, in which they are nurtured.

Translating these two words in Mazhar I was also suggesting that the burden of history and paleonymy are added to this double bind. Arrived here I often hear, Not everybody can be so well prepared! Is there ever such a refusal of craftspersonly expertise for European-language translation? I suggest we pay no attention to such excuses and proceed to the next poem, where another kind of history is invoked.

This poem refers us not to Bengali in the history of the nation-state but in the inter-nationality of Islam. As already mentioned, Bengali is not of Arabic/Persian origin. It is not taken seriously as a language of Islam.

During the war that established Bangladesh, soldiers of the then West Pakistan regularly taunted East Pakistani soldiers and civilians as not "real" Muslims, no more than the force-converted dregs of Hinduism. (It may be worth mentioning here that Assia Djebar is most unusual in acknowledging Bengali among the non-Arabic Islamic languages: "Arabic sounds—Iranian, Afghan, Berber, or Bengali").[24] In this frame, Mazhar addresses Allah, as follows:

> **Bangla Is Not Yours**
> You've built the Bangla language with the crown of
>   my head and the roof of my mouth
> My epiglottis plays with the "ah" and the long "ee"
> Breath by breath I test the "om" and my chest's
>   beat
> Heartstrings ring in the enchanted expanse of the
>   con-sonant
>
> Oh I like it so, lord, I like the Bangla language so
>   much
> I lick it clean, greedy, as if paradise fruit.
> Are you envious? For in this tongue you never
> Proclaimed yourself! Yet, all day I keep at it
> Hammer and tongs so Queen Bangla in her own
> Light and power stays ahead of each and all, my dearest lord.
> Some ask today, So, Bangla, are you divine as well?
> You too primordial? Allah's alphabet?
>
> I'm glad Bangla's not yours, for if she were—
> Her glory'd raise your price, for no reason at all.

Let us look at the lines. *Dānt* is one of those particularly untranslatable idiomatic words: airs and graces, swelled head, hype—you see the choice I've made: "raise your price." What is interesting is that this word has been coupled with *behuda,* another Arabic *tatshamo* word that I have translated "unreasonably." Let me first say that there is a common Sanskrit-origin word—*ajotha* (Sanskrit *ayathā*)—that would fit snugly here. *Behuda* points at itself, incomprehensible to "the common reader." I believe now that the word is in general use in Bangladesh. As I have already mentioned, I received a lecture on the Arabic word *huda* from my learned colleague from Kashmir. I could best grasp his meaning by turning it into the English familiar. "Reason" in "for no reason at all" is an ordinary language word. Yet "reason" is also a word of great philosophical weight. *Huda* has a comparable range. What reason is being invoked here to claim a language connected to Revelation by imagination rather than by letter? This is a different argument from the right to worship in the vernacular, where, incidentally, content transfer must be taken for granted. I go everywhere in search of the "secular." I will come back to this later. Here is a hint that expanding religion beyond mere reason may bring with it a question of translating rather than recording the transcendental: the difference between "reasonable" and "rational" beyond Latinity.

Attempting to make the reader walk with the translator translating the poet translating his language through the history of nation-states and of inter-nationality toward the transcendental, I will cite three poems here with brief introductions.

First, "Lady Shalikh."

The shalikh is a household bird, with no claim to beauty or musical skill. Mazhar is invoking the simplicity of the malnourished rural Bangladeshi woman, not the famed beauties of Bengal. Mazhar is a feminist poet. (I cannot unpack this difficult sentence here.) What does it mean to make the common woman cry out to Allah, in desperate humility, as the poet had, in pride of language?

> In the garden of paradise a body-brown Shalikh
> Calls. O my life, did you hear on paradise branch
> Our kindhearted Shalikh calls with life and soul
> Calling her own words at Allah's great hall.
>
> Can you hear, can you see, our Lord,
> Holding the knee of her yellow gam straight
>   On gandam branch
> Hacking her throat with her humble beak in weak
> Abject low tones our Begum Shalikh calls?
>
> What have we asked, dear Lord, our hopes are
>   small
> Let our life's bird reside in paradise
> Even if a darkskinned girl, snub-nosed,
>   bandy-legged
> Eyes sunk with body's work, yet in Bengal
> A well-loved daughter, without her paradise
>   lost—
>
> Bird call, call with life and soul, even Allah's
>   heart does melt.

The next poem refers to Rabindranath Tagore, who has already been mentioned as a master fashioner of modern ethnically cleansed Bengali, a language that slides easily into English. Mazhar cannot disclaim his pervasive influence, but . . .

The Tagore Kid
Our sir Rabi is a huge big poet, white folks
Gave him the Nobel prize to vet his literary might
Just right. His dad and gramps
Ran after the Brits and gathered in the loot
Became landowners by own claim
But family faults ne'er stopped
His verse—he's now the whole world's poet.

I salaam him welcome him heartfelt
Yet my soul, dear lord, is not inclined
Towards him. Rabindra had his faults. His pen
Remembered many a lucky sage, saint, renouncers, and great men
But never in wildest dream did the name of
Prophet Muhammad come in shape or hint
To his pen's point, so I can never forgive.

But dear lord of grace, you please forgive that boy from Tagore
    clan.

In the last poem that I will cite, the poet addresses a figure within the Hindu tradition who was open to all others. Sri Ramakrishna Paramahansa (1836–1886), as he was known (see Chapter 7), was also a poet of the transcendental, although his medium was not literary verbality. He was not an intellectual and therefore could not alter the course of public language. But if *poiesis* is a making of the other that goes past *mimesis,* Ramakrishna must be called a poet in the general sense. Islam took its place among his imaginings and his iterations of the self. Because these moves acknowledged the irreducibility of the imperative to translate rather than its denial for the sake of identity, here Mazhar responds as part of that which is translated, not an "original," but an other. Here translation surprises the poet as no displacement at all, perhaps; the mode is not declarative and introduces a picture of the poet dancing in the othered mode: "Have I moved, then?"

In Ramakrishna's name Mazhar undertakes yet another translation or transfer into the transcendental, a messenger from the human mystic to God himself—the most easily recognizable name of the transcendental as such. And yet it is a translation: the poet articulates a plea for henotheist worship (a hibiscus for Kali) to achieve felicity in Allah's acceptance. He daringly offers to transport the Hindu hibiscus to the austere Allah of Islam. In the present of the poem, the transfer is forever performed.

Sri Ram Paramahansa
Have you seen the red hibiscus? You told that flower
    to bloom, in Bengal
So it does hang and bloom
Blood red—*haemoglobin* of blood
In petals perhaps, it glows in wood and plot.

I a hibiscus flower in your honor my lord
Will give into the hands of th' blessed one,
Sri Ramakrishna Paramahansadeb.
He'll give his little chuckle, gap-tooth glowing in
    laugh
And say "O my Sheikh's Boy, here you are, you've come?"

Have I moved, then? Nope, I didn't move
If going, I go the same way everywhere.
Entranced the lord of love dances in state
The sheikh boy dances equal, loving this lord.

By way of Kali when Paramahansa sends
Hibiscus to you lord, accept with love.

Ground-level, counter-theological Islam has managed such exchanges, perhaps not so spectacularly, wherever Islam has flourished. Today, when the great tradition of Islamic secularism is tarnished, it seems particularly important to allow poetry such as this to launch us on an imaginative journey that can be risked if reader and translator venture beyond the sanctioned ignorance that guards translation from the languages of the global South into English. The literature of Bangladesh does not appear prominently on the roster. Rokeya Sakhawat Hossain's *Sultana's Dream and Selections from the Secluded Ones* are resuscitated from time to time in an indifferent translation from the Feminist Press.[25] Otherwise it is the fashioners of that other Bengali and their descendants who get Englished. It is of course different with development material, but that is another story.

As writers like Mazhar attempt to enter the detheologized "religious," they question the premises of a superficial secularism. They are, in turn, incorrectly perceived as providing fuel for fundamentalists.

I started this essay with a reference to "Religion within the Boundaries of Mere Reason." I mentioned that a problem of translation does not allow us to see that in that text Kant considers with scrupulous honesty if secularism is possible without the possibility of thinking the transcendental. This task is absolutely crucial today. Those sanitized secularists who are hysterical at the mention of religion are quite out of touch with the world's peoples, and have buried their heads in sand. Class-production has allowed them to rationalize and privatize the transcendental and they see this as the welcome telos of everybody everywhere. There is no time here to connect this with the enforcement of rights, and the policing of education by the self-selected moral entrepreneurs of the self-styled international civil society—with no social contract and no democratic accountability. I can only assert here that the connection can and must be made. I hope I have been able at least to suggest that this state of the world has something to do with a failure of responsible translation, in the general and the narrow sense.

I have walked you through the hybridity of a single language. I want now to make a comment on the notion of hybridity that is the migrant's wish-fulfillment: irreducible cultural translation in any claim to identity. I wish translation could be so irreducibly taken for granted. The impossibility of translation is what puts its necessity in a double bind. It is an active site of conflict, not an irreducible guarantee. If we are thinking definitions, I should suggest the thinking of trace rather than of achieved translation: trace of the other, trace of history, even cultural traces— although heaven knows, culture continues to be a screen for ignoring discussions of class. If translation is a necessary impossibility, the thought of a trace looks like the possibility of an anterior presence, without guarantees. It is not a sign but a mark and therefore cannot signify an "original," as a translation presumably can, especially when assumed as definitively irreducible. I contrast a comfortable notion of a permissive hybridity to the thought of the trace because the former is associated, sometimes precisely by the assurance of cultural translation, with the sanitized secularism of a global enforcement politics. This permissive hybridity can also foster an unexamined culturalism which can indeed give support to fundamentalisms here and there. That bit of the migrant population that faces a repressive state as well as dominant racism becomes a confused metonym for this other, separate, global face of hybridity as translation.

If the European context brought us to the sense of problems in the global public sphere, the context of Bangladesh brought us to the question of secularism. In my last section I come back to what has always been one of my chief concerns: translation as reading. I examine here the problems of entering the protocols of a text, when the text seems to give way. I move to a singular example where the aporia of exemplarity—that the singular example loses singularity by entering the category "example"—is cleanly resolved by the poet himself into no more than a reader's choice:

> This book of poems, focused on a girlfriend, and dealing only with a plea for love is indeed a diary. . . . If you think only of me, this poetry is only a plea for love. . . . Yet, because any one part is applicable to many situations connected to love, social theory, politics, science and many other topics, therefore one should be able to find a successful realization of any kind of situation in the lives of any sort of reader, male or female.[26]

This book of poetry was first published in 1961 and then republished in 1962 under the title *Phire Esho Chaka* or *Come Back Wheel*. The book was dedicated to Gayatri Chakravorty. (The Sanskrit *chakra* of the surname means wheel and is transformed into *chaka* in modern Bengali. A cunning translation.)[27] Chakravorty did not know the poet, although she had noticed the intensity of his gaze. She left Kolkata for the United States in 1961. She did not read the poems, although she knew the fame of the book, and that it was dedicated to her. Many of the poems lament her absence, his loneliness without a response. It is not clear that such lamentations, included in poetry, require "response" in the ordinary way. Must the lost object not remain lost for the poems to retain their exact verbal contour? If reading is a species of translation, here was a rather singular double bind of translation, for a singular reader, with a specific proper name. Gayatri Chakravorty, not having read the poems, did not have to live this double bind.

In 2002, some forty years after the publication of the book, a facsimile edition of the manuscript has been published. This book, in the poet's impeccable hand, is entitled *Gayatrike* or *To Gayatri*. I was shown a review of this text by a colleague, and a woman in the family bought me a copy. I have now read these brilliant poems. There is no question of response, other than what you read here.

A face and body, a figure, is a cipher, to be deciphered, read. The figure cannot read itself. The poet's uncanny eye has deciphered Gayatri Chakravorty, pre-figured predicaments that she would like to think she averted in ways that he had counseled in those unread poems. At a certain point, the poet advises a different way of living:

> Not success outside,
> But a selfsame flowering as unstiff as the body's sleep
> Is what lovers want. . . .

Go on, try opening by yourself, like a shell would,
Fail, yet that bit of sand, the little sand that finds its way just in,
Will little by little be pearl, the proper success,
    Of movement.
If you want a life as easy and all nature, like the sleeper's pose,
Try breathing in the heart's interior fragrance. (p. 8)

This reader would like to think that the prayer to be haunted by the ethical is kin to that advice.

Benoy Majumdar (1934–2006) was in and out of mental hospitals for the last forty-odd years of his life. What is it for such a man to write: "I will now be mad, at last by insane claws / Will prise out the angel's home address, the door" (p. 30)? There are poems that delicately hint how "madness" must be managed, and poems that ask: "O time, where, at whose door shall I appear / With my armored charms, my naked ways" (p. 85)?

There is no question of response. The occasion of these poems has been translated into the transcendental. The facsimile edition ends with poems marked "not to be included in the printed version." I do not know if they are to be found in the printed versions. The last one of them is the only straightforward narrative poem in the sequence. The others are written "according to the psychological process by which we dream (setting together scene after scene)" ("Foreword," n.p.). Indeed, Gayatri Chakravorty is called "Dream-Girl" a number of times.

It is not possible to write about these poems briefly. There is spare praise of auto-eroticism, praise of the austere comforts of poetry, despair at loss of skill, a tremendous effort to imagine the smallest creatures, and the uncaringness of star and sky, to frame human frailty and loss, and a brilliantly heterogeneous collection of addressees. Sometimes the imagery is a rarefied dream-lexicon: nail, cave, delta, rain. I hope they will not be translated soon. At last I would like to translate them.

There are repeated references to oneself as a letter lying on the wrong threshold, destined to err, a plea to be called if some "social need" should arise:

Come and pick me up like torn bits of a letter
Put 'em together for curiosity's sake, read once and leave
As if to disappear, leaving them like a slant look. (p. 16)

There are reprimands to the frivolous girl, references to the future laughing at her sudden death (p. 36), cryptic judgments such as the following, where nothing in the poems allows us to decide if Dream-Girl is among the exceptions or the rule: "In very few women is there a supplement placed" (p. 3). I have been unable to catch the specificity of *ramani*—one of a handful of common words for woman—which carries the charge of *ramana*—the joy of sex. I have also been unable to catch the pun in *krorepatra* (translated "supplement")—literally "lap-leaf." What does the pun mean? This poet is uncharitable to women who merely breed and copulate.

It is this particular ambivalence in the poems that seems exciting for this translator to access, as she makes the mistake of thinking the named subject is she. Thus the ambivalence seems to offer a codicil to that bit in Coetzee's *Waiting for the Barbarians* that she had so liked: how does the other see me? Identity's last secret. Coetzee describes the Magistrate describing his deciphering effort thus: "So I continue to swoop and circle around the irreducible figure of the girl, casting one net of meaning after another over her. . . . What does she see? The protecting wings of a guardian albatross or the black shape of a coward crow afraid to strike while its prey yet breathes?"[28]

I am the figure of the girl, the translator thinks, making that easy mistake, and this book offers what the poet sees as he casts his net. I come up both ways, albatross and crow. This is a lesson: to enter the protocols of a text one must other its characters.

In the last poem in the facsimile edition, in and out of the book, since it is not meant to be included in the printed version, Gayatri Chakravorty or "my divine mistress" is translated into a declarative narrative of transcendental alterity. Response stops here, in the representation of response without end:

> I've grasped it surely, life on earth is done;
> I'm straight in heaven's kingdom, earth's body's shed.
> These heavenly kingdoms are indeed our home, and we
> Are just two spirits—Dream-Girl and I—this pair
> Divinely live in heaven's kingdom now. I see,
> That she's still that familiar youthful form,
> And stands with a greeting smile upon her lips.
> My divine mistress. I too have by desire kept a body,
> Even in heaven—healthful, like Dream-Girl's,
> As tall as she, no *glasses*, eyesight good,
> I am to her taste, a goodlooking young man.
> Smiling she speaks up—You're done, you've come at last,
> Now for the bliss of peace, fulfillment, thrill
> In body and mind, in deep immeasurable kind,

> Everything just so, as we would like it. Come.
> Next, in a clasp so deep, and deeper still a kiss,
> She promises that she will spend with me,
> An eternity of shared conjugal life. (p. 85)

What is it to be an "original" of a translation? This is what teaches me again the lesson of the trace. For a name is not a signifier but a mark, on the way to a trace. Benoy Majumdar makes Gayatri Chakravorty a hybrid, but not by the assurance of some irreducible cultural translation. The name as mark is caught between the place under erasure—crossed out but visible—on the handwritten title page—and its generalization as "my divine mistress"—*amar ishwari*.[29]

On the flyleaf of this book I find notice of something that no critic has spoken of so far, a prose book, presumably, entitled *Ishwarir Swarachita Nibandha—An Essay or Essays Composed by the Divine Mistress Herself*. The book was out of print, I heard, but about to be printed again. How shall I be encountered by myself in that text, where I think the poet has attempted to access Gayatri Chakravorty's thinking? Here is an allegory of translation, turned inside out.

This task remains. And it remains to try that second way of reading, impersonal or diverse situations connected to social theory, politics, science. I am back where I began. I must get around the seduction of a text that seems to be addressed to myself, more than most texts, and enter the author's presuppositions, where my youthful proper name is obliterated in the concerns of general readers, equally welcome.[30] As I do so, I must of course remember that those presuppositions have a history and a geography, and that I am a translator into English: double binds still unravished by mere globality.

CHAPTER THIRTEEN

Nationalism and the Imagination

IT HAS BEEN MY PERSISTENT argument that nationalism has no place in the politics of translation (see especially page 471). At the end of the previous chapter, narrating the ethnic cleansing of Bengali, an implicit critique of Bengali → Indian nationalism was made. At the very end of the chapter, in connection with a private/public switch, the question of readership was raised. In this chapter, we will discuss nationalism as an illicit private/public switch. The talk that serves as the basis for the chapter was written for presentation at the biennial meeting of the Commonwealth Association for Language and Literature, meeting that year in Hyderabad, India.[1] It was an object lesson in the complexity of interpellations when one spoke of nationalism responsibly.[2] For most of the "Commonwealth" folks I was Indian. For the Indians, I lived abroad and so was not a local. For the Bengalis, I was a Bengali first, "Indian" more for foreign consumption. I subsequently presented the talk in Beijing and the lesson was further nuanced, especially since the Tsing-Hua University Literature department was and was not "China." I had enough experience in the mud schools near the Laos border to be aware of this. I was also aware, as is the "global" face of the world, that China and India are nationalistic competitors for the driver's seat in the Asian century. The final presentation of the paper was at the Centre for Advanced Studies in Sofia, Bulgaria. That is the version I have included here, because Bulgaria's access to what I call "nation-think" is unusual: five centuries as part of the Ottoman empire, sovietization in 1948, emergence, in 1989, into the simulacrum of Westphalia in a world with global imperatives.[3] I have included the question and answer session, so that you will notice that, in the brilliant summary at the end, the Director misses the connection between nationalism and reproductive heteronormativity (RHN). Once again, the Centre for Advanced Studies in Sofia is not "Bulgaria." I mention this because what was perfectly acceptable in Kiossev's mock-summary at the end is of course not acceptable in my general argument. If you are speaking to "nations," you are begging the question. Imaginative de-transcendentalization has to be taught, persistently, because of the private-public hold of nation-think. But I get ahead of myself. Let us start again.

I am tremendously honored to be a guest of the Centre for Advanced Study in Sofia. What I read refers to India, although I am acquainted, of course, with U.S. nationalism also. Neither example is unique, but they are different. Your history would not produce the kind of nationalism that the history of India produced immediately after Independence, or the exceptionalist nationalism that has sustained the United States for so long.

Alexander Kiossev, the Director of the Centre, gave me a paper called "Ensuring Compatibility, Respecting Differences." That's what I asked the Bulgarian audience to do. I had been invited partly because the group was interested in translation. They had to translate the circumstances as I spoke. By contrast, in Hyderabad, I had to step into the "original." I sang all the songs mentioned in the next paragraph in the original Bengali!

I remember Independence. I was very young, but I was precocious. It was an incredible event. But my earliest memories are of famine: skeletal bodies dying in the streets, crawling to the back door begging for starch. This was the great artificial famine created by the British to feed the military in the Pacific theater in World War II. A bit later I learned the extraordinary songs of the Indian People's Theatre Association—the famous IPTA. Why were they political? One of you was asking me if literary representations could be political. In this case what happened was that section 144 of the Penal Code, enforcing preventive detention, was put in place to control resistance. But the British authorities did not understand the Indian languages, so theater fell through the cracks and the IPTA survived as a political organization. Like most Bengali children, I learned their extraordinary songs, and I will quote the refrain that haunts our cultural memory: "We won't give any more rice, for this rice, sown in blood, is our life." I didn't connect it to the British, only to class struggle.

The British were mentioned only in that street rhyme about the Japanese: "Do re mi fa so la ti / dropped the bomb on the Japanese / In the bomb, a cobra snake / the British scream: 'Oh, Lord, help, help!' "

The Japanese, we thought in Bengal, were bringing the British to their knees. We admired these Asians standing up to the British. Kolkata was evacuated at the time of my birth for fear of Japanese bombings. The Bulgarians were first with the Axis powers and then with the Allies. For us, it was happening at the same time. The largest number of dead in World War II was Indian soldiers fighting for the British. On the other hand, at India's eastern edge, there was this alliance with the Japanese and the Axis powers. Subhas Chandra Bose, a family friend, was a friend of the Japanese and the leader of the Indian National Army. He went off to Japan and from there to Germany and married a German wife. Kolkata airport is named after him. So there was this synchronic commitment to the Allies and to the Axis powers. The lines were crossed. For the Europeans it was the Holocaust, but for us it was a World War; it was the end of colonialism perhaps.

As I said, Kolkata was evacuated at the time of my birth. My mother refused to leave. My grandmother stayed too, so I was born in Kolkata. In 1946, I entered kindergarten. In October school closed. We lived in Kolkata right on the border of a Muslim quarter, on the edge of Sayad Amir Ali Avenue. Those areas were among the cruelest sites of the Hindu-Muslim violence. It was a politically mobilized violence. The country was going to be divided, and so people with whom we had lived forever, for centuries, in conflictual coexistence, suddenly became enemies. I was four years old; these are my first memories. So the cries would go up, celebrating the divine in a Hindu or a Muslim way. Even we children knew that each cry meant a knife blow, a machete blow. Those riots were not fought with guns. There was blood on the streets. It was the working-class people, the underclass people who were mobilized because the British and the upper-class folks had made a pact to separate the land. There was blood on the streets and I don't mean that metaphorically. These are my earliest memories: blood on the streets. What I am considering in this book is how this relief map of recent history is apparently flattened in the superficial contemporaneity accepted by unprepared imaginations at the top.

My parents were ecumenical secularist anti-casteists. I am an atheist but was born in a Hindu family. At night the house was full of Muslim women and children. My father brought them in from the neighboring low-income housing estate, which in those days was called a slum—but that's politically incorrect now. The men and my father were on the terrace. By contrast, Independence was a polite affair. Elation in the conversation of the elders, interminable political discussions, and remember, we were 300 years under the Islamic empire and from that a straight 200 years under the British, so it was big. (Who were the "we" here? Thus were the noxious seeds of Hindu identitarianism sown at Independence in spite of the unity talk. The double bind of nationalized independence with even the historical practice of freedom denied.)[4] Marching along wearing white and blue, waving flags, singing the inevitable songs by Tagore. The important event was Partition, the division of the country. Mother was out at the minor railway station every morning as the trains came in from the East, at dawn busy with refugee relief and rehabilitation, coming home battered in the middle of the evening. Overnight Kolkata became a burdened city; speech patterns changed.[5] If these were the recollections of Independence, the nationalist message in the streets created schizophrenia.

If there is anyone my age reading this who grew up in Kolkata and did not lead a hopelessly sheltered life, she will remember that in addition to the Hindi film songs, the plays that were broadcast over the loud speaker at every Durga Puja—Durga Puja is like "our" Christmas, a commercialized high holiday, a major event of ideological production—were *Siraj-ud-daula,* the story of the unhappy betrayed smart teenager Nawab, the Muslim king, who fought with Robert Clive, the guy who brought territorial imperialism into India; and *Mebar Patan,* a play which was written in my family a hundred years ago, coding the Rajputs ambiguously, so the Muslims became an ambiguous analogue to the British. These things are manageable in various ways—the British are our enemy; so are the Muslims—ambiguous, for the British may suddenly become our savior!

This hardy residual of the Muslim as not only enemy but evil is still being worked by the Hindu right: to translate the sentiment of a famous song from *Mebar Patan:* voluptuous sex is bad, mothers and wives are good and must be protected, the Muslims are the enemy. Yet this play was by a famous liberationist poet, whose songs are sung every Independence Day. I will translate a few sentences: "Does it behoove you to lie down in despicable lust, when town and country are in fear of the enemy, upon that chest devastated by the blows of the Muslim, are the arms of the paramour an appropriate adornment? Who will care to preserve his life, when mother and wife are in danger? To arms! To arms!" What my adolescent mind, growing into adulthood in the Kolkata of the 1950s, began to grasp was that nationalism was tied to the circumstances of one's birth, its recoding in terms of migration, marriage, and history disappearing into claims to ancient birth.[6] Its ingredients are to be found in the assumptions of what I later learned to call reproductive heteronormativity (RHN). That is why I quoted the song: RHN is in its every beat. Later in the United States, the important question was: Are you natural or naturalized? George Bush or Madeleine Albright? Bulgarian or Turk?

A variation: are you Indian or Muslim? Get it? When I look at Zhivkov's arguments that Bulgarians had an organized state before the Russians, they were Christians before the Russians, I think of this: ancient claims to things becoming nationalism by virtue of a shared ancestry.[7]

As I was growing up, then, I realized that nationalism was related to RHN as a source of legitimacy. As I moved to the United States and became active around the world, I realized that the alibi for transnational agencies—backed explicitly by exceptionalist nationalism(s)—was nationalism in the developing world. Gender was an alibi here even for military intervention in the name of humanitarian intervention. I believe with Eric Hobsbawm that there is no nation before nationalism although I do not locate nationalism as he does in the late eighteenth century.[8] Anticipating my argument in rethinking comparativism, let me add that if this nationalized globality loses the anchor of the first language that activates the metapsychological, the ethical instrument is seriously deactivated.

When and how does the love of mother tongue, the love of my little corner of ground become the nation thing? I say nation thing rather than nationalism because something like nations, collectivities bound by birth, that allowed in strangers gingerly, have been in existence long before nationalism came around. State formations change, but the nation thing moves through historical displacements and I think Hannah Arendt was altogether perceptive in suggesting that the putting together of nationalism with the abstract structure of the state was an experiment or a happening that has a limited history and a limited future. We are living, as Habermas says, in post-national situations.[9] And yet.

Pared down, the love of mother tongue, the love of my little corner of ground, is more like comfort. It is not really the declared love of country as in full-blown nationalism. When and how does the comfort felt in one's mother tongue and the comfort felt in one's corner of the sidewalk, a patch of ground, or church door—when does this transform itself into the nation thing? And how? Let us try to pare it down a little further. This rock bottom comfort, with which the nation thing conjures, is not a positive affect. I learned this in the eighteen years of my friendship with the Indian aboriginals for and with whom I worked. Unlike Mahasweta Devi, whose fiction I translate, I do not romanticize these aboriginals. I worked for them as a teacher and a trainer of teachers and it is not my habit to romanticize my students or their parents. To return to my argument: this rock bottom comfort in one's language and one's home with which nationalism conjures is not a positive affect when there is nothing but this, as I saw with these folks I worked with. I would not have known this as a metropolitan Kolkata person at the time of Independence, at the inception of the new nation-state from an established nationalism. When there is nothing but this, its working is simply a thereness. Please remember I am not talking about resistance groups, but people who accept wretchedness as normality. That's the subaltern; those are the folks with whom I worked. I learned this from below. When this comfort is taken away, there is a feeling of helplessness, loss of orientation, dependency, but no nation thing. At the extreme, perhaps a banding together, making common cause through reinvention of something like religious discourse into an ethics that can condone violence. This is the work of the early subaltern studies group of historians: tracking religion being brought to crisis as militancy that can mobilize a certain kind of violence—but not nationalism.

We are so used to the cliché that there is nothing private outside of Europe that we are unable to recognize that in this sphere, if it can be called that, it is the guarantee of the profound bottom-line shared unease of the removal of comfort that solders the band together. We have to understand that in a country as large and as socially layered as mine, nationalism doesn't work right through. This is different in Bangladesh, for example, because it is small; and different in the United States because of the relentlessness of the exceptionalism and the ubiquity of telecommunication.

The nationalism I have been describing operates in the public sphere. But the subaltern pre-affect where it finds its mobilizing is private, though this possibility of the private is not derived from a sense of the public, an underived private, imbricated with a comfort where human-animal is indeterminate for all of us, which has been difficult for European philosophy to think. Women, men, and queers are not necessarily divided along the public-private line everywhere. I have already let slip that nationalism is a recoding of this underived private as the antonym of the public sphere. When you begin to think nationalism, this underived private has been recoded, reterritorialized as the antonym of the public. Then it is as if it is the opposite of the public. This shift is historical, of course, but it is also logical. The subaltern is in our present, but kept premodern, as if the underived and unacknowledged private is only situated in a teleology.

I will not rehearse here the mostly Hegelian historical story of the emergence of the public sphere. In whatever nationalist colors it is dressed, whether chronological or logical, the impulse to nationalism is "we must control the workings of our own public sphere." The reclaiming of the past is in that interest. Sometimes nationalism leads to the resolve to control others' public spheres, although this is not a necessary outcome. With this comes the necessary though often unacknowledged sense of being unique and, alas, better—it's a quick shift—because born this way. (A training in literary reading, in suspending the self in getting the text to talk, might temper this one, need I add? False hope.)

Every diasporic feels a pull of somewhere else while located here. If we consider the model of exogamous marriage with reference to that sentence, we might have to revise the entire city/country model implicit in "Metropolis," and think that the women in gendering have always shared this characteristic with what we, today, have learned to call "Diaspora," even when it doesn't have much of a resemblance with what happened so long ago in Alexandria. And yet, metonymized as nothing but the birth-canal, woman is the most primitive instrument of nationalism.

I have here offered a reading of nationalism that allows us to see why, although nationalism is the condition and effect of the public sphere, nationalisms are not able to work with the founding logic of the public sphere: that all reason is one. It is secured by the private conviction of special birth, hopping right from the underived private comfort which is no more than a thereness in one's corner.

If nationalism secures itself by an appeal to the most private, democracy in its most convenient and ascertainable form is secured by the most trivially public universal—each equals one. That flimsy arithmetic, unprotected by rational choice, can also be manipulated by nationalism. I am not convinced that the story of human movement to a greater control of the public sphere is necessarily a story of progress. The religion/science debate makes this assumption, forgetting that the imagination, forgetting that literature and the arts belong neither to reason nor to unreason. That literature and the arts can support an advanced nationalism is no secret. They join them in the task of a massive rememoration project, saying, "We all suffered this way, you remember, this is what happened, you remember," so that history is turned into so-called cultural memory. Literature can then join in the task of a massive counter-rememoration project suggesting that we have all passed through the same glorious past, the same grand national liberation battles, the same religious tolerance or whatever. I am going to suggest by the end of this—because sometimes I am misunderstood—that the literary imagination can impact on de-transcendentalized nationalism. That is not what I am discussing here. I am supporting the cliché that imagination feeds nationalism, and going forward toward the literary imagination and teaching the humanities, through the teaching of the humanities to prepare the readerly imagination to receive the literary and thus go beyond the self-identity of nationalism toward the complex textuality of the international. I will come to that later.

I want now to share with you a lesson learned from the oral-formulaic. If the main thing about narrative is sequence, the main thing about the oral-formulaic is equivalence. Equivalence here does not mean value in the sense of commensurate. That was the Marxist definition in the economic sphere. I am speaking of value in a more colloquial sense. The oral-formulaic works by the assumption of equivalence. We learn from narrative by working at the sequence. We learn in the oral by mastering equivalence. Roman Jakobson famously offered equivalence as the poetic function. In typical modernist fashion he thought equivalence lifted the burden of meaning. My experience with the oral-formulaic presentation of Sabar women, these groups that I used to train teachers for until the local landlord took the schools away from me and handed them to the corporate sector—even that is gone now—has convinced me that it is the inventiveness in equivalence that makes something happen beyond the tonal and verbal monotony that turns off many literate sympathizers. The Sabar women are members of a tiny and unrepresentative group among India's eighty-two million aboriginals. They still practice the oral-formulaic, although they will soon forget this centuries-old skill. The hold upon orality is gender-divided here. The men's access to the outside world is wretched, working day labor for the Hindu villages, and since they don't themselves know that there are twenty-four hours in the day, they are cheated constantly. That is why I used to have these schools, to give the subaltern a chance at hegemony.

The men's access to the outside world is nonetheless more "open." When the men sing, the archived yet inventive memory of the oral-formulaic approaches rote. The men, and this is a very important distinction, inhabit enforced illiteracy rather than an orality at home with itself and with the great genealogical memories. The women, because of the peculiar situation of gender, were still practicing the oral-formulaic.

The precolonial name for the area where I worked is Mānbhum. It is not the name now. In the adjoining state of Jharkhand there is Singbhum, not the name on the map now. Precolonial names. To the south there is Birbhum, etc. Imagine the frisson of delight that passed through me the first time I heard these women weave a verse that began: *Mānbhuñār Mān rājā*, King Mān of Mānbhūm, using the precolonial name of this place that nobody uses. Then they even brought up another precolonial name. . . . There were other folkloric details that sped through my mind. The next line was even more delightful: *Kolkatar rajar pathorer dalan be*—"the king of Kolkata has a stone mansion." Kolkata was in the place of what I am calling "inventive equivalence." They were going to Kolkata, a little group for a fair, so they were honoring the king of Kolkata. They were preparing these songs. Kolkata is my hometown and I was thinking as I sang with the women in that remote room with no furniture, no doors and windows, no plumbing, no electricity obviously. In that remote room with no furniture but a 6-foot-by-9-foot sheet of polyethylene in some way associated with chemical fertilizer I thought, who would the King of Kolkata be? Kolkata is a colonial city and unlike older Indian cities had never had a Nobab; and indeed, unlike Bardhaman, Krishnanagar, Srihatta (Sylhet), Jashor, or Mymensingh, it had never had a Hindu Raja either. But the women were singing "The king of Kolkata has a stone mansion," where Kolkata occupied the place of a shifter, and who was I to contradict it?

I translate the fiction of Mahasweta Devi, who, in her personal politics, is somewhat feudal. She used to organize these tribal fairs in Kolkata where people came to look at them and buy handicraft, etc. That is why they were preparing. The building where this tribal fair actually took place in Kolkata is called *tathhokendra*—Information Center. What is the name of that place, one of the women asked me. Tathhokendra, I said. They produced the line *Tathhokendrer rajar patharer dalan bé*—"the King of the Information Center has a stone mansion." It would be better to keep it "Kolkata," I said, inwardly noting with wonderment that although they knew that Kolkata was a city with zoos and parks and streets and the Information Center only a building, and although they knew no king had power over them, the concept of sovereignty, which would put a space in apposition to archaic Manbhum or Barabhum, applied to both equally.

Here, then, is a thinking without nation, space-names as shifters, in a mythic geography, because of the power of the formulaic. In internationality the nation-state has such equivalence, now rationally determined. In globalization, no, because there the medium of value is capital. This is the sort of intuition that Lyotard and before him McLuhan had claimed for postmodernity, jumping the printed book in between. Their politics ignored the texture of subalternity, and equated it with internationality with no gap. Lyotard tried, in "The Differend," to undo it, but most readers did not make the connection. Without the benefit of postmodern argumentation such geographical intuitions are defined as premodern, by Hobsbawm as prepolitical. This group is not tied to counter-globalization. They are too subaltern to attack the indigenous knowledge or population control people and their avoidance of chemical fertilizers or pesticides (now destroyed) was then too recent and not connected to large-scale agriculture, and came more from deprivation than choice.

If, however, they had been connected to counter-globalization then they would accede to a nationalist moment, because the activist workers would speak nation to them. This is a nationalist moment in affective collectivity with no historical base, ultimately productive of neither nationalism nor counter-globalization, but rather of obedience disguised as self-help. Indeed one year I had added a line to their singing of locaters—names of "their" village (the Hindus deny them entry there), their district, and so on—"West Bengal is my state, India is my nation."

The next day a group of women larger than the group that went to Kolkata, and I, walked to the central village of the area. One of the protocols of these two-and-a-half-hour walks was that we sing at the tops of our voices. I longed for a camera person. (I am joking; I have never wanted anybody there.) I longed for a camera person as these aboriginal women and I walked in the sparsely forested plains of Manbhum, the women and I screaming "India is my country"—*bharat henak desh be*—again and again and again—the moment of access to nationalism—Gayatri Spivak traveling with the subaltern would then be caught on camera. Except that it wasn't access to nationalism, of course. The oral-formulaic can appropriate material of all sorts into its machine, robbing the content of its epistemic charge if it does not fit the inventiveness of the occasion—and this is what Jakobson thought was the poetic that takes away the meaning and is only equivalence. Indeed West Bengal or Paschim Banga—the name of the state—has long been changed into Paschim Mangal, a meaningless phrase with a Sanskrit-like aura. And the lines are only sung when Shukhoda wants to show me that she loves me still. (I haven't seen her for five years now; moved my schools away from the landowner's grasp.) I am not asking us to imitate the oral-formulaic. I am suggesting that the principle of inventive equivalence should be at the core of the comparativist impulse. It is not all that a fully elaborated comparativism does. But the principle would destroy the hierarchical functioning of current Comparative Literature, which measures in terms of a standard at whose heart are Western European nationalisms. Standing in the airport of Paris I have been turned off by the accent of upstate New York and turned to my mother and said in Bengali, "You can't listen to this." But she chided me, also in Bengali, "Dear, it is a mother tongue." (I will tell this story again.) That sense, that the language learned first through the infantile mechanism is every language, not just one's own, is equivalence. You cannot be an enemy of English. People say easily "English is globalization. It is destroying cultural specificity." Here is equivalence. It is not equalization, it is not a removal of difference, it is not cutting the unfamiliar down to the familiar. It is perhaps learning to acknowledge that other things can occupy the unique place of the example of my first language. This is hard. It's not an easy intuition to develop, yet this need not take away the comfort in one's food, one's language, one's corner of the world. Although even this the nomad can give up. Remember Edward Said quoting Hugo of St. Victor: "The man who finds his homeland sweet is still a tender beginner; he to whom every soil is as his native one is already strong; but he is perfect to whom the entire world is as a foreign land." The human being can give up even the facticity of language, but comparativism need not. What a comparativism based on equivalence attempts to undermine is the possessiveness, the exclusiveness, the isolationist expansionism of mere nationalism.

Why is the first learned language so important? Because it activates the public-private in every human infant, allows the negotiation of the public and the private outside of the public-private divide as we have inherited it from the legacy of European history. (Indeed, the "private" here is not even underived animal comfort, but metapsychological—inaccessible, catachrestic.) Language has a history; it is public before our births and will continue so after our deaths. Yet every infant invents it and makes it the most private thing, touching the very interiority of the heart. On a more superficial level it is this underived private that nationalism appropriates. A multilingual republic like mine with a national language for communication—Hindi—can in the literary sphere work the admirable comparativist move—my mother's move—recognizing that there are many first languages—24 if you don't count the aboriginals, 850 if you do. If we think that postcolonial literature is simply another name for post-imperial literature in the British Commonwealth, the former British empire, I am afraid that move is not made. And, in the context of the globe, we are thinking "Empire as such," of course. Every mention of the British Commonwealth in the initial essay has to be "translated" thus. This is the translation from postcolonial studies to the era of globalization. No specificity at the metropolitan end, only uniformization—data and capital. Everything else is damage control.

The British Commonwealth has an association called the Commonwealth Association. It is supposedly for the study of languages as well, and the Commonwealth has many languages. Cyprus, Malta, Burkina Faso, all these places were in the Commonwealth—who cares? So were fifteen African nations. But the association mainly becomes a clearinghouse for the exuberance of Global English. It should of course welcome a consideration of textual analyses of cultural work in the various languages of Africa and India. The tendency should now go beyond the question of translation into the possibility for the members of the old British Commonwealth to reopen what was closed by colonialism: linguistic diversity. The medium of communication can remain English, that gift of colonialism we can accept as convenience. But the work must become comparativist. That would indeed be the empire writing back in tongues. Ngũgĩ wa Thiong'o acted on comparable convictions nearly twenty-five years ago.[10]

Here is Maryse Condé, a francophone novelist from Guadeloupe. In the passage below, she is picturing the Caribbean upper class confronting subaltern Africa. An undisclosed West African subaltern speaker, possibly feminine, says to the French-speaking upper-class Véronique from Martinique: "What strangeness that country [*quelle étrangeté ce pays*] which produced [*qui ne produisait*] neither Mandingo, nor Fulani, nor Toucouleur, nor Serer, nor Woloff, nor Toma, nor Guerze, nor Fang, nor Fon, nor Bété, nor Ewe, nor Dagbani, nor Yoruba, nor Mina, nor Ibo. And it was still Blacks who lived there [*Et c'étaient tout de même des Noirs qui vivaient là!*]." The young woman passes this by, noting only her pleasure at being complimented on her appearance: "'Are all the women of that country as pretty as Mademoiselle?' I got a silly pleasure out of hearing this."[11]

Of course Bulgaria has been incredibly conscious of its languages, an amazing phenomenon. So to an extent this did not apply to my immediate audience, but on the other hand, a reminder of equivalence was still apposite. You must translate, you must think, said I. There is Africa. The Bulgarian colleagues had remarked that there would not be interest among students if African languages were introduced there. I could not begin to emphasize how important it is to change this.

Condé's Veronica does not hear the subaltern African woman's question. If the academy does not pick up the challenge of Comparative Literature, literatures in the Indian languages, like many literatures in regional languages, will not flourish on their own. This sentence applied to my Indian presentation. In globality, we are thinking the world. Indeed, in private conversation with a Bulgarian colleague who is working on Indian literature in English, I had said, "Don't kill us." If you compare the advances paid to a writer like Vikram Seth with the kind of money that the Indian language literatures make, it's amazing that these latter are still so powerful. A terrible sociology of knowledge is taking the name "Indian" away from them. A Columbia student recently offered a field called Indian Literature for his doctoral examination. "Surely you mean Indian literature in English," asked I. And he said, "I am following Amit Chaudhuri's definition that only literature in English written on the sub-continent can qualify as Indian." Salman Rushdie's word for the literature of all the Indian languages that he could not read was "parochial." Can one not suggest that the repeated narration of the immigrant experience, however varied the style, taking the relay from the presentation of India the exotic, into India-Britain or India-America as fusion, always focused on the writer's own corner, is also a bit "parochial?"

This is sociology of knowledge at work, creolizing the Indian languages artificially to English, undoing the separated yet hierarchically shared histories of North and South Indian literatures. In globality, this argument broadens to focus on the dungeons of the world republic of letters. In a double bind with the uniformization of English, I have long proposed not just an Indian Comparative Literature in a nationalist ghetto, but Comparative Literature as such, productively undoing the mono-cultures of the British empire, all empires and all revolutions. Women from Central Asia come to Columbia, because of our Harriman Institute, which used to be Soviet studies, and is now post-Soviet studies. They often come to talk to me, because I do feminism and Tashkent is close to India. One of the things they say is that they can't talk to their grandmothers. They speak Russian by choice and their native languages are no longer nuanced with meaning for them. This is often true in certain classes in India as well. If one begins to establish the outlines of a global Comparative Literature, one can at least hope that the deep linguistic consequences of the largely female sovietization described in Gregory Massell's *Surrogate Proletariat* can come undone.[12] In this context, I recall Marx's very well-known words: "The beginner who has learned a new language always re-translates it into his mother tongue. He can only be said to have appropriated the spirit of the new language and to be able to produce in it freely when he can manipulate it without reference to the old and when he forgets the language planted in him while using the new one." I am not translating from the Bengali when I am speaking English. Although I cannot translate my own Bengali into English—what I publish in Bengali remains in Bengali—other people find it very difficult to translate also, although they sometimes try. "To be able to produce in it freely when he can manipulate it without reference to the old and when he forgets the language planted in him while using the new one." This is what a translator should be—someone who can forget translation. This is a literal description both of good Comparative Literature *and* the kind of energy the dominant unifying languages can command. We cannot learn all the languages of the world in this kind of depth. But we can learn two: n + 1. And in the process restore the relief map of the world, flattened under one imperial formation. And it doesn't matter what you call that empire.

(What Marx does not consider, because he is rightly concentrated on separating revolution from enthusiasm and on teaching the worker a counter-intuitive view of the agency of capital, is that the rootedness of the mother tongue must supplement the abstractions of revolution. In the event it was the lack of practice of the ethical that laid the revolution low, aesthetic education remained confined to the bourgeois liberals who lost it when they entered the speed of globalization.)

Nationalism is the product of a collective imagination constructed through rememoration. It is the comparativist imagination that undoes that possessive spell. The imagination must be trained to take pleasure in such strenuous play. Yet social priorities today are not such that higher education in the humanities can prosper, certainly not in India as it is rising to take its place as a competitor in a "developed" world, and certainly not in the United States. The humanities are progressively trivialized and/ or self-trivialized into belles-lettristic or quantitative work. If I have learned anything in my forty-five years of full-time teaching, it is the tragedy of the trivialization of the humanities, a kind of cultural death. Unless the polity values the teaching of literature in this way rather than just literary history and content and a fake scientism, the imagination will not be nourished.

I am going to talk now about a few metaphors and then come to an end.

The first is time and woman. A general temporizing narrative enables individual and collective life. Simon Gikandi has worked with narratives that support genocide in the African context (he is himself Kenyan) and how the African can intervene in these narratives. Israel supports legitimized state violence with the so-called biblical narrative, but this is much broader.

The role of women, through their placement in the reproductive heteronormativity that supports nationalisms, is of great significance in this narrative. When we are born, we are born into the possibility of timing, temporalization: we are in time. This possibility we can grasp only by temporizing, thinking and feeling a before, which through a now will fall due in an after. Our first languaging seems almost coeval with this, for we are also born into it. Since, as I said, it has a before before us, we take from its already-thereness. And since we can give meaning in it, we can think ourselves into the falling-due of the future by way of it. It is this thought, of giving and taking, that is the idiomatic story of time into which the imposition of identities must be accommodated. Since it is usually our mothers who seem to bring us into temporalization, by giving birth, our temporizing often marks that particular intuition of origin by coding and re-coding the mother, by computing possible futures through investing or manipulating womanspace. The daughtership of the nation is bound up with that very re-coding. Another example of temporizing toward a future that will fall due is of women as holding the future of the nation in their wombs. It comes from the obvious narrative of marriage.[13] Language, mother, daughter, nation, marriage. The task of the literary imagination in the contemporary is the persistent de-transcendentalization of such figures. In other words, if you study this graphic as text, you can keep it framed in the imaginary, rather than see it as the ineffable cultural "reality" that drives the public sphere, the civic structure that holds the state. "Culture" is a rusing signifier. If you are committed to "cultural" nationalism while your "civic" nationalism is committed to a Group of Eight state, it is possible, though not necessary, that you work against redistributive social justice in the "culturally" chosen nation. This is very important as one moves up into neoliberal globalization.

Let me repeat: If we are committed to "cultural" nationalism while our "civic" nationalism is committed to a Group of Eight state, it is possible, though not necessary, that we work against redistributing social justice in the "culturally" chosen nation. Possible, even probable, but not necessary. Nationalism will give us no evaluative category here, if nationalism is confused with location. In other words, and I am giving you an Indian example—the NRI—which is the Indian shorthand for the non-resident Indian—or the PIO—person of Indian origin, who is given certain visa privileges by India (both describing the metropolitan diasporic only in the United States and perhaps in Britain)—is not necessarily good or bad. The issue is confused by the fact that the nationalist-left, the social-movement nationalist, who is now of course committed into national civil society, and the globalist-nationalist will compute "good" and "bad" differently. This is also going to happen, this is round the corner, vis-à-vis the Bulgarian nation-state, if and when it enters the European Union. This is an interested remark of course, for I am an NRI. But not only an interested remark. It is also to indicate the power and danger of taking "nationalism" as an unambiguous value today, or indeed ever. Today, when one section in the nation-state works hand in glove with the self-selected moral entrepreneurs of "the international civil society," how will the touchstone of nationalism alone allow us to read the situation, let alone act on it? An analysis of the lasting social productivity of disease- and poverty-eradication movements would be beyond the scope of this essay. Here I will simply repeat that nationalism is a deceptive category. I will turn Shelley's much-quoted remark around, set it on its head. In 1818, when Britain was entering capitalism, Shelley wrote: "We want the creative faculty to imagine what we know." I will turn that much quoted lamentation on its head: "We lack the cognitive faculty to know nationalism, because we allow it to play only with our imagination, as if it is knowledge." At this point, as I will keep on insisting, we must train the imagination, to be tough enough to test its limits: an aesthetic education. In globalized postcoloniality, we can museumize national-liberation nationalism, good for exhibitions, great exhibitions; we can curricularize national-liberation nationalism, good for the discipline of history. Learn about the great nationalist leaders, who are not speaking subalterns.[14] The task for the imagination is not to let the museum and the curriculum provide alibis for the new civilizing missions, make us mis-choose our allies. This whole business of redefining Eurasia. . . . A member of my Bulgarian audience asked if we were jealous—Eurasia is becoming the place where NATO plays. It is not a question of jealousy; it is a question of fear, a Radio Free Europe saying, "Yes, of course, the United States is a Central Asian power." There is Turkey, entering Europe, but Bulgaria is European in a different way for the rest of the world, although it is not sufficiently European by its own count, because what the Bulgarians call Europe provincializes them.

I want to end by speaking of the reinvention of the state. The phrase "nation-state" rolls off our tongue. Therefore it is the re-invention of the civic state in the so-called Global South, free of the baggage of nationalist identitarianism, and inclining toward a critical regionalism, beyond the national boundaries, that seems today to be on our agenda. Bulgaria is extraordinary in terms of regionalist possibilities, inherent in the history of its changing frontiers. To our inability to write anything but national allegories, and our fate to be merely parochial, has been added a new problem: "the presuppositions of poststructuralism and its paradoxical latently identitarian anti-identitarianism, its minoritarian antistatism, and its lack of a utopian anticapitalist critical horizon."[15] How can these words be applied to a philosopher who has read Marx as a messianist, who has written endlessly of a democracy to come?

As for me, I am altogether utopian, cherishing false hopes in spite of myself. I look toward a re-imagined world that is a cluster in the Global South, a cluster of regions. Of course it can only happen gradually. But as we make small structural adjustments, we should keep this goal in mind. It may produce imaginative folk who are not only going on about cultural identity (read "nationalism"), but turning around the adverse effects of the adjustment of economic structures. The state, as Hannah Arendt says, is an abstract structure. And you may have noticed that everything I have written turns around learning and teaching. One of the many tasks of the teacher of the humanities is to keep the abstract and reasonable civic structures of the state free of the burden of cultural nationalism. To re-peat: an imagination trained in the play of language(s) may undo the truth-claims of national identity, thus unmooring the cultural nationalism that disguises the workings of the state—disguises the loss of civil liberties, for example, in the name of the American "nation" threatened by terror. Again, "may." I will never be foolish enough to claim that a humanities education alone (especially given the state of humanities education today) can save the world! Or that anything can, once and for all. Or, even, that such a phrase or idea as "save the world" can be meaningful.

I have let this paragraph stand, if only to show the altogether recent provenance of gloom in my work.

My main topic has been the de-transcendentalizing of nationalism, the task of training the singular imagination, always in the interest of taking the "nation" out of nation-state, if I may put it that way. It sounds bad right after liberation. When I spoke in South Africa in the first memorial lecture after the lifting of Apartheid I spoke in this way. My message was not exactly popular. And then about ten years later, when the piece was included in an anthology, the editor said that I had been prescient to have spoken at that time of "the ab-use of the enlightenment from below."[16] At the time it had sounded too negative. I am saying therefore again and again—translate from someone who has had sixty years of independence, a little more than that—1947 to 2011—and see if it will translate, rather than simply saying "we cannot afford to think of the nation in that way now." This is where comparativism comes in. Hence a few obvious words about re-inventing the state, words that take us outside of an education only in the humanities, are not out of place here.

Economic re-structuring, as we know, removes barriers between national and international capital so that the same system of exchange can be established globally. Put so simply, there need not be anything wrong with it. Indeed, this was the fond hope of that long-lost mirage, international socialism.

But the individual states are themselves in such a predicament that their situation should be transparent. Mere nationalism, ignoring that economic growth is not automatic redistributive justice, can lead us astray here. Theatrical or philanthropic wholesale counter- or alter-globalism, whatever that might be, the demonstrations at Seattle or Genoa, for example, are not guarantees of redistributive justice either.[17] It has long been my view, especially as a feminist, that even liberationist nationalisms should treat a seamless identity as something thrust upon them by the opposition. In this context, Edward W. Said's rejection of the two-state solution in Palestine is exemplary.

Even before the advent of economic re-structuring, anyone working in the areas I spoke of could have told you that constitutional sanctions do not mean much there. But now, with state priorities increasingly altered, redistributive justice through constitutionality is less and less easy if not impossible. Philanthropy is now coming top-down from the international civil society; the state is being de facto (and sometimes de jure) un-constitutional, because it is asked to be managerial and take free-market imperatives; Human Rights Watch notices it and then the philanthropic institutions intervene. We in the South cannot usually engage constitutionally to achieve much—although for Habermas it was possible in the 1990s to speak of constitutional patriotism, in a European context, in a post-national world.[18] Such an attitude would today be unmindful of the current status of globality. As for patriotism, even more than nationalism, it is an affect that the abstract structure of a functioning state harnesses largely for defense: *dulce et decorum est pro patria mori.* I am back humming that childhood song from *Mebar Patan,* composed in gallant yet ideologically tarnished national liberationism: take up arms!

It is this effortful task, of keeping the civic structure of the state clear of nationalism and patriotism, altering the redistributive priorities of the state, creating regional alliances, rather than going the extra-state or non-government route alone, that the new Comparative Literature, with its alliances with the social sciences, might have worked at ceaselessly. I think feminist teachers of the humanities might have had a special role here. For behind this rearrangement of desires—the desire to win in the name of a nation—is the work of de-transcendentalizing the ruse of analogizing from the most private sense of unquestioning comfort to the most ferocious loyalty to named land, a ruse that uses and utilizes the axioms of RHN. Emmanuel Lévinas, for example, offers us the ruse as the establishment of a norm—the feminine establishing home as home—leading to the masculine exchange of language—which inexorably led, for Lévinas, to a politics of a most aggressive nation-statism, anchored in a myth of identitarianism long predating the historical narrative of the rise of nations.[19]

In August 2003, at the public hearing of crimes against women in Bangladesh, the jury had suggested (I was part of the jury) that the South Asian Association for Regional Cooperation, or SAARC, be requested to put in place trans-state jurisdiction so that perpetrators could be apprehended with greater ease, and survivor-friendly laws could support trafficked women, often living with HIV/AIDS, across state lines. Such feminist work would not only supplement the rich cultural mulch of the testifying women themselves, re-coding their lives through sex-work collectives working to monitor and advise; it would also, by supporting the sex-work awareness of these women, provide an active criticism of the

RHN that is making the United States withdraw aid from the most successful HIV/AIDS programs—as in Brazil or Guatemala—because they will not simply criminalize prostitution.[20] There multilingual and regional comparative work might have been productive.

In conclusion—a bare-bones summary, once again. Nationalism negotiates with the most private in the interest of controlling the public sphere. I learn the lesson of equivalence rather than nationalist identitarianism from the oral-formulaic. I owe a conversation with Etienne Balibar when he suggests that equivalence masks difference whereas equality acknowledges it. I cannot quite agree with him, though I do see his point. This leads me to propose a multilingual Comparative Literature of the former empires which will arrest the tide of the creolization of native literatures, although the discipline is moribund now.[21] This will not compromise the strength of writing in English. Higher education in the humanities should be strengthened so that the literary imagination can continue to de-transcendentalize the nation and shore up the redistributive powers of the regionalist state in the face of global priorities. Imagine this, please, for a new world around the corner, less likely than ever today.

Discussion

From the Audience: My question concerns the imagination, the literary imagination. If I understood correctly, when you talked about the appropriation of the mother tongue, of the first language, you described it in terms of not just appropriation, but something like ex-appropriation, which forbids such a distance from your own . . . Am I right?

Gayatri Spivak: Something like that, yes.

Audience: This is what permits the play of the imagination if I can say so. What if there is no conscious distance between you and your own first language, which will not permit you an imaginative act? For example, what if the literary imagination is not the imagination of the people?

Gayatri Spivak: Yes, it is a wonderful question, excellent question. I was talking only to my own group—in other words, teachers of humanities. I have learned something from people who in fact have a less intimate relationship with the official language, perhaps. I am not learning nationalism from them. Given their situation, they are bilingual in what they think is their own language, which is a creole and a version of Bengali. They switch constantly and some try to teach me Bengali. But the imagination I was talking about, related to people of my own kind all over the world, people who teach Comparative Literature, people who teach the humanities, people who are in the Commonwealth Association, people who think about the fact that an empire of some kind has come to an end. I learned something about Comparative Literature practice by reading what they were doing. But the imagination can operate in other ways as well. It is not just through the training of the literary imagination, which is what we do. It is possible that in social formations that are defective for capitalism, for example, in Muslim communities that are not mobilized for violent action against state terrorism right now, the old responsibility-based structure is called *al-haq,* a difficult word to translate. It is often translated "truth," but it is also "right," "birthright." It is the birthright of being able to take care of other people. On the other hand, what happens in these situations, and not just with Muslim communities, is that they stagnate because they are withdrawn from the mainstream, from the social productivity of capital. In that theater, the effort is to build infrastructure, to build a different kind of education, small work, but important work. Otherwise, because reproductive heteronormativity is the oldest and broadest institution in the world, responsibility-based structures become increasingly gender-compromised. This is not the place where I go to teach literary imagination, no, I am talking about tertiary education at universities, teaching Comparative Literature. In fact I want to connect the language-learning initiative that I am trying to put in place, since I am affiliated with an Institute for Comparative Literature and Society, with these kinds of work. There you have to learn from below what philosophy of education will survive in order to give an intuition of the public sphere without being destroyed by the others around them who do not want them to rise. That's a very different kind of teaching, but in the end, it does exercise the imagination, so that thinking of others doesn't remain a burden fated by gender-identity.

Alexander Kiossev: I would like to risk addressing just one point of your presentation: when you spoke about your personal utopia to detach the state, the civic state from cultural nationalism and to form certain regional heterogenic structures. I thought to myself that maybe Bulgaria and post-socialist Bulgaria is a realization of your utopia, because in fact the Bulgarian state practically abdicated from any national cultural policy. And the most important Bulgarian state institutions are imitating nationalism, they are not really nationalistic.

They are repeating nationalistic rituals, but these rituals are empty of any content. What happened is not a kind of civic paradise, but nationalism was appropriated by under-state structures, corporations, soccer fans, historians, a lot of different groups with different images. And what happens is that on this, let us say, under-public level, we have a lot of nationalisms in the plural. These nationalisms are feeling strange mass feelings, which could be called populism. Recently a party emerged which addressed these populist nationalistic feelings. All of a sudden this party became very powerful. I believe this is not only a Bulgarian case. I can give you German examples, I can give you Austrian examples, and Hayder and his party and a lot of other examples—Belgium, France . . . So in case the state abdicates from this traditional nationalistic politics, these feelings, call them nationalistic, call them patriotic, they just don't disappear. And it is very interesting what happens with them when certain groups and certain leaders appropriate these feelings with different causes.

Gayatri Spivak: Yes, this is a very good warning. We think this way, to counter the international civil society, which has no democratic social contract at all. It calls itself "civil society" simply because it is not the states, before it used to call itself "non-governmental," but that is kind of negative, so it became a civil society overnight. But what you are saying is absolutely correct. We want the state to be mindful of its redistributive obligations. As for nationalisms coming up everywhere, we are thinking about that old formula, a persistent critique. There are already existing regionalist organizations. The World Bank and the International Monetary Fund, when they began, wanted to do something like a welfare world outside of the socialist camp. Very quickly their imperatives changed. When they began, they too were regionalists because of this kind of imperative—the importance of regions rather than state boundaries. The World Bank's Indus valley water imperative, for example, did not honor the borders of India and Pakistan, it was the whole Indus valley. Today there is no way that it would not honor a national boundary—there was a flood action program in Bangladesh, although India holds the sources of those rivers. It is no surprise that, in Asia, regionalist organizations are largely economic. What we are trying to do is to recode these regions outside of—again that's why I like Hannah Arendt—the state boundaries, undermining the call for nationalism as ancient birth because the regions are diversified. This call will come all the time, that's why I was trying to say how important this affect is, it is not even an affect, it's the most un-derived private—it's not going to go away, that's why the word "utopia" is back there. It's not as if you will bring the kingdom of heaven into the world by just keeping the state abstract. But what we are talking about is that there should be an effort. For that there has to be nationalist stuff elsewhere, in curricula, in museums. I agree with you, it's too dangerous, it will come back. But cleaning nationalism outside of an identification with the state is also part of something that we do through languages, de-transcendentalizing the nation, etc. I don't think utopia will come, because it doesn't come, it is always "to come," as it were. It is a dangerous project, only less dangerous than the nationalist state in hock to globalization, making it rise against redistribution. I am expanding your warning beyond the state. Nationalism doesn't disappear with globalization either. We must be mindful.

From the Audience: So would you say that de-transcendentalizing the nation, we will re-transcendentalize the future? Because my intuition will be that once you step back from this transcendental meaning of the nation, you give it back to some other type of rituals. The nation-state collapses and then something comes back. Do you imagine a world without transcendental idols?

Alexander Kiossev: To redistribute the transcendental.

Gayatri Spivak: This is why I do believe that something like a literary training, which used to be given through cultural instruction, is a very important thing today. When I say the literary imagination de-transcendentalizes, when you think of something as literature, you don't believe in it, and yet you're moved. Martin Luther King gave a great speech in 1967 at Riverside Church in New York: "Beyond Vietnam." In that speech he says: "I speak in the name of someone who so loved his enemies that he gave his life for them." For him it was a transcendental narrative. For me it's a narrative. But narrative is an important thing to a literary person—that's de-transcendentalizing. So that's why I'm saying that work must go on, that's why I am saying the work of the humanities is not just a little cherry on a cake, while people do speed work and the world financializes the globe. There is that, too. So the work of the de-transcendentalization is a kind of training that should become part of this radical movement.

Audience Member: But there is no positive element into your program.

Gayatri Spivak: I say *de*-transcendentalization, ok, I could find a positive word. But there is a positive element in so far as this impulse, which I also call comparativist equivalence (my mother when she said "it is also a mother tongue") brings people together, that's not a negative thing—in fact one of the things that feminists from India, Pakistan, and Bangladesh do is undo the Partition.[22] Regionalism is a bringing-together kind of enterprise. In these areas of the world regional enmity is quite long-standing; therefore regionalism would be the positive thing. When I describe what the imagination does, I have for a moment this negative word—de-transcendentalizing. I teach in New York in the most powerful university in what some call the most powerful city in the world. And I don't teach South Asia, I teach English, I teach the language of the dominant. The students, undergraduates in my class, either go to Silicon Valley, or they go to become powerful in politics, or yet, these days, they want to help the world, human rights. It is them that I am also thinking about, not just people who are going to want something positive. These people are so ready, these children of the superpower, thinking that they are the best, it doesn't matter what color they are, that they are the reason why history happened and they can help the whole world. Take my words contextually, please. I teach in the United States among the elite and I teach in India among the subalterns. So I can't speak to the whole world wanting a positive program, but what I am asking for through de-transcendentalization is a deeply positive thing—to rid the mind of the narrowness of believing in one thing and not in other things—that's what I am talking about. And the future is indeed somewhat transcendentalized in this account, if we take it on the model of Kant's transcendental deduction, as a move needed to think something unavailable to evidence but necessary for experience to be possible.

Zornitsa Hristova: I would like to ask you to say a little bit more about these multilingual comparative studies. What is the added benefit of such multilingual comparative studies with regard to the existing representation of foreign languages in the university curriculum? It is already on the program, the vernacular languages are being studied and their literatures are studied as well. What is the added benefit of including the comparative as well?

Gayatri Spivak: To do it comparatively is to get a sense of the global and to get a sense of the historical, topological, and formal affinities between the literary as it springs up among peoples. When the powerful languages are taken as the language of translation and people read only in those powerful language translations, the fact of being translated disappears. This is not a helpful thing. First of all this is not helpful because when we teach at universities, we want to be correct and this is incorrect. It is bad academic work. That people should read Plato's "Republic" and not know that Plato did not think of republics and that it was only the Romans, who thought of "res publica," but in Plato's work it was called something else. If you read Aristotle's "Poetics" in English, you see imitation and poetry and you don't have a sense that Aristotle is actually doing a kind of rhythmic thing with students who might write tragedies—mimesis, poesis, mimesis, poesis. You don't get that sense. I think it is bad academic practice, because it is incorrect. So that's it—I don't know if it is a benefit, it is in the interest of good academic work. But indeed, if you want a broader context, you can go to the anthropologist Alton Becker, who, in *Beyond Translation*, proposes "lingual memory," very important in war and peace-making.[23] In order to be able to enter another space, and globalization enters other spaces constantly, you have to learn a language well enough to enter its lingual memory. A fantastic idea. In the *New York Times* there is a little series of formulas—as to how you speak to an Iraqi to convince him or her that you are a friendly person rather than an attacking soldier. I am afraid that those kinds of formulas, unless these Iraqis are presumed to be totally stupid, do not go too far. Michael Ignatieff said that on the desk of American officials in Kabul there are little tags that tell you how to say "thank you," "not today," etc. These people do it badly, assuming that the other is a fool. On the other hand, entering the lingual memory of subordinate languages perhaps makes for the imagining of a just world. I heard Simon Weathergood, an NGO worker in Sri Lanka, say: "Over the last five-six years I have been learning both Tamil and Sinhala and I now no longer feel that I have the same goals that I came in with." "Just don't change. Don't change, so few people do this," I said to him. If you have a good functioning foreign language situation at your university, where the vernaculars are taught well, you should be very grateful and your university is fortunate and you are fortunate. To introduce a comparativist view-point will enhance the democratic spirit.

From the Audience: I was thinking, while I was listening to your wonderful presentation and while I was trying to grasp the ideas during the first half an hour, about another brilliant Indian writer Arundhati Roy and her very deep novel *The God of Small Things*. Actually this is a novel about everything important in life—about death, about love, and about nation as well and national culture. It is a novel in defense of local languages, local cultures, but of course written in English and due to this fact it became famous around the world. So how would you comment on this fact that actually this is pro-nationalistic, but at the same time written in a global language.

Gayatri Spivak: Assia Djebar, whom I admire greatly, writes in French, although she is Algerian. But in the first page of her book *Women of Algiers in Their Apartments* she writes about the obligation of the stars. She says that the starry women are always called but they should become aware of what they are doing. The distance between the stars and the people is so great that the movements work because they adore their leaders. I am more interested in what is being written and not noticed and not read in the many Indian literatures. I root for comparativism there as well.

Tatyana Stoycheva: When we were talking about the nation-state project and the fact that it should be restructured, you also referred to Comparative Literature and the fact that it will become multilingual and it will apparently address new areas, but thinking about Comparative Literature emerging in the context where national literatures emerged and there being such tight connection between the two, wouldn't you expect Comparative Literature to restructure as well in the future? What would you anticipate or suggest?

Gayatri Spivak: Probably. I am not imaginative enough to predict. Comparative Literature, as established by the folks who came to the U.S. after the Second World War, was already regionalist in impulse. But whereas for René Wellek it was only that which pertains to the rhetorical text itself which was up for study, now it involves the social text as well. Perhaps that's the way it will go, Tanya. But for sure Comparative Literature will change, if it does not altogether disappear. We are not thinking of restructuring the state, we are questioning the seemingly inevitable coupling of nation and state, and thinking of a continuing reinvention of the state as what it always is supposed to be—the mechanics of redistribution. Restructuring is happening with neoliberalism, so that the imperatives supposedly become free-market, which is as free as all the regulations imposed by the great companies themselves, and the protectionisms written into World Trade. In the global North it is the dismantling of the welfare state. And of course, we haven't touched upon globalization and the digital. How a literary discipline changes in step with such conjunctural changes will become abreactively evident.

Tatyana Stoycheva: A rebirth of a discipline after the crisis?

Gayatri Spivak: Death of a Discipline was written only about the United States. I tend always to speak very much in context. I always carry the trace of what I do, where I am. My books are not universal messages. A French reviewer wrote, "Gayatri Spivak should have written this book in Bengali." I write a lot in Bengali, but he can't read it!

The situation of Comparative Literature is not the same in West Bengal! Every declaration of death, every elegy, says at the end that the person is reborn. *Death of a Discipline* is an elegy to Comparative Literature rather than simply an obituary although that seems to be called for now, with Comparative Literature programs closing here and there.

So is that it? Thank you for your wonderful questions, wonderful questions!

Alexander Kiossev: Everybody is exhausted. Before expressing my deep thanks to Professor Spivak, I will risk something quite personal. She started with an appeal that we should translate for ourselves her presentation and I did so for myself. It was a less-than-sophisticated translation, because I was unable to follow everything. Some stuff I really understood, other things I am still thinking about, third things remain a little bit vague for me, but at the end I experimented with a kind of comic summary of your lecture. So I would summarize the lecture in this way and this is my personal risk, it has nothing to do with the lecture itself: "Dear nations—this is the general message—dear nations, please, you were invented as imaginary narratives. After that, unfortunately you were institutionalized and you forgot your origin, you forgot that you are imaginary. Be kind enough, go back to the imaginary. You are fictive narratives and furthermore, please, be kind enough to compare yourselves. Then you will understand that you are not equal, you are equivalent."

Gayatri Spivak: Well done! Well done! You know what you forgot? Reproductive heteronormativity. But otherwise—beautifully done! I needn't have given the lecture, it takes two minutes!

And you, my anonymous readers, please go back to the beginning and see how, brilliant as this mock-summary might be, my project is not simply a re-reading of Ben Anderson.[24]

CHAPTER FOURTEEN

Resident Alien

THIS CHAPTER reads a text that pre-dates postcoloniality and certainly pre-dates globalization. It stages an aesthetic education as the training of an imagination for epistemological performance. An unwitting member of the imperial race goes native. When he discovers his racial affinity, he becomes an enlightened secular citizen of the colonized space.

Large-scale movements of people—re-named "diaspora"—is what defines our time. As a result, the premodern principle of demographic frontiers is encroaching upon imperial territorial frontiers. The new African, Asian, and other "diasporas" connect globally in unprecedented ways, seemingly putting in place a relatively seamless global contemporaneity, often in the name of a good life. Is there a lesson for upscale diasporics in globality in Tagore's novel *Gora,* the text for reading in this chapter? Is there a lesson here, in other words, for the international civil society? Only indirectly. Literature is not a blueprint for action.

A former Prime Minister of India, Mr. Inder Pal Gujaral, addressed a large group of prosperous Indians in New York in the fall of 1997, speaking warmly of the connection between Indians at home and abroad. Himself born in what is now Pakistan, the Prime Minister must have known that, in the metropolis, a connection also exists among South Asians that is rather larger than the Realpolitik on the subcontinent. (This seemed particularly apposite in 1999, with India and Pakistan at war. Breathing room for contextualized nationalisms in the metropole.) Some philosophers suggest that it is an ethics of hospitality that we must ponder now. But the contemporary metropolitan philosopher cannot conceive this demographic re-drawing of frontiers between place of departure and place of arrival. When they think hospitality or recognition, philosophers as different as Etienne Balibar, Jacques Derrida, and Charles Taylor, begin and indeed end with the migrant, although Balibar does offer an astounding re-definition of mass movements as movements of people. Even the global concept of "multitude" in *Empire* takes on a migratory cast: "the kinds of movement of individuals, groups, and populations that we find today in Empire, however, cannot be completely subjugated to the laws of capitalist accumulation."[1] In *Of Hospitality*, Derrida has opened hospitality into teleopoiesis—a structure that interrupts the past in the name of the future rupture that is already inscribed in it—but his specific figurations remain named *arrivant* or *revenant*.

The figure of the Resident Alien—a tax-paying non-citizen with a semi-permanent visa—remains outside this dynamic.[2]

Reda Bensmaia has recently called the immigrant intellectual in the metropolis a "phantom mediator."[3] Being Algerian by birth, he generalizes from the Algerian case. The way back is barred him, let us hope not for long. As for the South Asian case, there is not much ghostliness in the coming-and-going of the New Immigrant subcontinental intellectual and her counterpart on the mainland. It is a shuttling, and as well as a mediation, more worldly than ghostly. There is, by contrast, a sheltered ghostliness in the figure of the long-term Resident Alien, a curious residual—in Raymond Williams's powerful phrase—that seems to run counter to the contemporary tendency toward the emergence of virtual frontiers that are demographically defined. The figure of the long-term Resident Alien belongs to a tenaciously held territoriality that is also, of course, abstract, as all territoriality must be; yet, being without significant civil rights, the figure lacks access to the more salient abstractions of an everyday civility. Today, as metropolitan migrants establish mostly capitalist-cultural solidarities with their fellow country-folks in the old second and third worlds, it is silly to call ontopology archaic. That virtuality is accretive rather than privative. It creates the kind of para-state collectivities that was part of the shifting multicultural empires that have hitherto written the spatialized temporizing of the planet. By contrast, the Resident Alien, a vestigial postcolonial figure, belongs to postcoloniality in the narrow sense. I wrote "Imperative to Re-imagine the Plant" (Chapter 16) from this perspective, one useful stereotype of myself.

Rabindranath Tagore's *Gora* is set at a conjunctural moment of consolidation of a peculiarly "Indian" territoriality: the end of the 1857 Mutiny. Narrating, with such a consolidating moment as the external focalization, Tagore imagines the unwilling imperialist as a sort of "Resident

Alien." It is a curious act of hospitality where the host-guest relationship is reversed. This textual-figural analogy cannot be a narrative parallel to the situation of the "real" metropolitan resident alien today. And yet, much of the mysterious fun of literary reading, half-constructing relationships between singular and unverifiable figures, rises from such differences. And, if I dare say so, much of the tedium of a sociological *use* of literary examples arises from ignoring them. Paradoxically, the literature of cultural difference, when it reads the text as proof, in the name of identity, however mixed or lost, is peculiarly susceptible to such tedium. *Gora* is a singular novel, an unusual novel, a peculiar riff on mere nationalism, and a major experiment in Bengali fictional prose. I want to see my own civil status replicated in it. Can anything be gained from such a reckless and sinister disregard of speculative sobriety?

The novel was first published in serial form between 1907 and 1909. The story is well known. An Irish foundling of the Sepoy Mutiny grows up believing he is a Brahman's son and observes strict doctrinal Hindu orthodoxy as an expression of nationalism. At the seeming approach of death, his adoptive father reveals his alien birth to him, for he has not the right to perform the funeral rites of a Brahman. The father recovers, but Gora, relinquishing orthodox Hindu doctrine, emerges a true nationalist Indian. Gora's last utterances in the novel, already cited, after he knows his biological birth and national origin, will give us a sense of the use of women in the staging of this Resident Alien:

> Gora said, "Ma, you are my only mother. The mother whom I'd sought wandering—had herself entered my room, attending. You have no caste, no caste-judgment, no contempt—you are nothing but the image of our good! You are my Bharatvarsha, indeed . . ." A few moments later, he said, "Ma, will you call Lachmiya and tell her to get me now a *glass* of water?"[4]

Two tiny clarifications. In a polytheist culture, "image" is a divine image, without the weight of the monotheist metaphor. Lachhmiya is the Christian outcaste, from whose hands the earlier Gora, orthodox Brahman, could not accept drinking water, although there was no lack of affection. This sort of internalized caste-judgment is of course infinitely more powerful and dangerous than overt oppression. Tagore attempts to spectralize or disembody affection, the hardest task of all ideology critique.

Meenakshi Mukherjee discouraged us from drawing parallels between Tagore's *Gora* and Kipling's *Kim*. I accept her admonition as part of that general warning about narrative parallels. Yet the central similarity has been so often pointed out that not to mention it seems odd. *Kim*'s hero is Irish; in spite of an effort at British-style schooling, throughout the book he is more "Indian" than any of the natives, who remain irretrievably local. This too is part of that consolidation of territory, and yet, as I hope to suggest shortly, the discursive situation of the place is different. What I am calling the resident alien figure appears here as well, though its lineaments are startlingly different. There are other differences. *Kim* is picaresque, *Gora* a *Bildungsroman*. Kim does not grow; neither his residency nor his alienness is existential. A cultural commonplace of access to wisdom is stated by the plot of apprenticeship, of course. But Gora's nationalism is altogether subjectivized in rather an Aristotelian way: peripety and anagnoresis, reversal followed by removal of non-knowledge. And, if the delicate affective efficiency of women is part of gentrifying nineteenth-century Bengal, the women in *Kim* are stock types of magico-erotic instrumentality in a predominantly male world.

So much said, I will honor Professor Mukherjee in the breach. Away with narrative parallels. Let us concatenate the figural dynamics—the making-into-figure—of the two figures. The first move is to notice that they are nicknames—not proper names—that entitle, that provide the title, of these two considerable books. Will you move with me if I say that entitling nicknames have something like a structural relationship with the permanent resident alien's relationship to two communities? The proper name is more unilateral; it can claim locationist identity with assurance.

If the times produced the two nicknames, Gora and Kim—the characters as well as the books—they produced the times as well. These are what Michel Foucault would call "watershed texts." I carry the history of that condition-and-effect relationship between literary text and social text. As a reader, I can say "yes" to these texts—without which there is no reading—in two different ways. As I point out in "The Burden of English," Chapter 1 in this book, I am tied in with the comic hybrid in *Kim,* an M.A. from Calcutta University. By contrast, I am something like the implied reader of *Gora,* the emancipated secularist Bengali middle-class woman in the future anterior—what will have been. In both cases, my mother, Sivani Chakravorty, is closer to the mark. I left India before my M.A. She received hers, from Calcutta University in 1937. She grew up in Cornwallis Street, the area where most of *Gora*'s action takes place. And, since her degree was in Bengali Literature—or, as it used to be called then, "Indian Vernaculars," a phrase embarrassingly replicated in a recent *New Yorker* by Salman Rushdie—her generation read *Gora* as its immediate appropriate readers. I am here as my mother's proxy, as perhaps in life. But she was a U.S. citizen, a New Immigrant, for the last thirty years of her life. That too is part of the residual textuality of the

long-term Resident Alien today, tenaciously retentive of lost territorialities. "Figures in the carpet" is the lovely phrase of Henry James, the
American novelist, long-term Resident Alien in Europe. "Assigned
subject-positions," to quote Foucault again.

I cannot resist the temptation here to recount a teaching tale to this
audience. As part of my History of Literary Criticism Part I, I was hesi-
tantly teaching some Bhartrhari to my undergraduates. Normally, of
course, in this course, English Literature students read *Greek* antiquity:
Aristotle, Longinus, Plotinus. But since there are many kinds of English-
speaking Americans today, it seemed appropriate that my class should
read pre-Columbian, Arbi-Farsi, ancient East Asian, African; hence Bhartrhari, the seventh-century philosopher of grammar.

In the famous Book 3, Verse 3.3 of the *Vakyapadiya*—meaning simply
"Of Sentences and Words"—Bhartrhari suggests that the connection
between word and meaning, signifier and signified, *vācaka* and *vācya*, is
simply dependent upon a genitive suffix—what in English would be the
apostrophe "s," but, more commonly, the auxiliary construction with
"of": as in citizen *of,* resident *of.* Thus, Bhartrhari goes on, the identity
of word and meaning is, in the felicitous translation of Bimal Krishna
Matilal, "de-signated."[5] Identity is in the domain of signs. To explain
this to my diverse national-origin students, I used Foucault's sentence in
The Archaeology of Knowledge: "The position of the subject can be
assigned."[6]

I am rather dubious about explaining modern "culturally different"
writers simply in terms of "traditional" models.[7] Please remember that I
am not drawing parallels here. I am speaking of Bhartrhari and Foucault.
They had not read each other as far as I know. They were merely inspired
by a similar intuition: of the semioticity—sign-character—of identity.
The word is resident in the meaning by virtue of a case: the genitive. In
that spirit I would say that Tagore's *Gora* and Kipling's *Kim* are both
attempting to animate that indeterminate space of identity as sign,
dependent upon a case—the locative as the genitive *Adharadhikarana* as
samvandha—space as copula, rather differently.

The difference is felt in their being in language. Both Kipling and
Tagore are writing experimental prose. Kipling places a variety of "Indian English" that gets its punch from its distance from the standard English that is the primary medium of narration; rather like an expanded
version of Mark Twain's black dialect. This tradition has been appropriated by writers such as Rushdie and Farouk Dhondy; though not I think
by Amitabh Ghosh, Hanif Kureishi, Arundhati Roy. Tagore bends the
bones of Bangla. Hard to catch in translation.

The difference is also in their being in space. "India" does not name the same space for them. Is Sujit Mukherjee right in keeping the Bengali word *Bharatvarsha,* spelled in the Sanskrit way? I think I see his reasons. The Hindu-nationalist Gora would certainly fill that word with aggressively confected and prior religio-philosophico-cultural meaning. He entertains all his scandalized class-equals with such soliloquies. But that meaning—underlying all talk of "Indian values" today—is abreactive to imperialism—quite as the signifier "indigenous knowledge" is abreactive to biopiracy.

Kipling cannot enter that space, marvelously flowering in the furrow of a violated episteme, with a peculiar species of class-consent that Tagore's hospitality would recode—like Jawaharlal Nehru's invitation to Le Corbusier to build Chandigarh half a century later.[8]

No. Kipling could not enter that space. He had a vague idea of its worlding, and he treated the idea with contempt, as a merely "imagined community" would deserve. Writing only six years earlier, he locates his Kim in the para-colonial space where the project *was* to control shifting demographic frontiers by strict territorial lines. "India,"—the Greek name,—"Hindostan"—the central Asian name—is the name of a prize in a game. And Kim's picaresque apprenticeship is as a player in that "Great Game." No doubt this is also an effort to exculpate colonialism as feudalism—the feud as game, rather like two football teams, winner take all. It is Kipling's genius to stage the imperialist as child, a child who is in symbolic apprenticeship at once to the Game (British with collaborating Muslims) and to the ethical system (or Way) of Buddhism, concentrated in the lama alone, never the vehicle of internal focalization, and treated with affectionate derision by the Muslim players. This entire problematic is laid out in the final reunion—no anagnoresis here—between Master and disciple, hosted by Mahbub.

> "I was dragged from no river," said the lama simply. . . . "I found it by Knowledge." "Oh, ay. True," stammered Mahbub, divided between high indignation and enormous mirth . . . "It seems that I stand by [he says a bit later] while a young Sahib is hoisted into Allah knows what of an idolater's Heaven [he is wrong about the Buddhist "Nibban" put in the lama's mouth by Kipling, but that may be part of the staging] by means of old Red Hat. And I am reckoned something of a player of the Game myself! But the madman is fond of the boy; and I must be very reasonably mad too." "What is the prayer?" said the lama, as the rough Pushtu rumbled into the red beard.[9]

The "Great Game" was apparently a phrase invented by "Lieutenant Arthur Conolly of the 6th Bengal Native Light Cavalry . . . [who], aged 16, . . . [had] joined his regiment as a cornet."[10] To follow the trajectory of the Great Game as played in the Northwestern frontier area called "India" by Kipling as by Alexander the Great in 324 BCE, we flash forward to the *New York Times* of October 6, 1996. There we will find an item called "Afghanistan Reels Back into View."[11] A picture of "the bodies of Najibullah, left, and his brother hang[ing] from a Kabul traffic post." A crowd of peering men from behind, looking as much at the cameramen as at the backs of the bloody bodies, as far as one can tell. What is the lesson of this public spectacle? I quote the *Times:*

> In the months before Afghanistan's new rulers marched him from a United Nations compound in Kabul and summarily beat, shot and hanged him, Afghanistan's last Communist President, Najibullah, spent much of his time preparing a translation into Pashto, his native language, of a 1990 book about Afghanistan, "The Great Game," by the English writer Peter Hopkirk. Mr. Najibullah told United Nations officials that he wanted Afghans to read the Hopkirk text because of what they would learn from it of the 19th-century struggle between imperial Britain and imperial Russia for influence in Afghanistan. "They can see how our history has represented itself," he said. "Only if we understand our history can we take steps to break the cycle."

What characterized the para-colonial theater loosely called Afghanistan was that upon that stage, the masters masqueraded as the native. As in *Kim,* the Great Game was almost invariably played in disguise. Hopkirk's pages are strewn with pictures of British and Russian soldiers in Afghan, Persian, Armenian dress. This planned indeterminacy, like the indeterminacy of the demographic rather than territorial frontiers in this theater, is much closer to the postcolonial hybridized world of today than the nationalist colonialisms, which were as much a historically contained phenomenon as Bolshevism. If in Foucault's story, as told in *Discipline and Punish,* the transformation of the soldier into a docile body "could become determinant only with a technical transformation: the invention of the rifle," the rifle clinched no great narrative in Najibullah's.[12] Plate 35 in *The Great Game* shows a British officer in native dress surrounded by Afghans. "Many minor players," the caption runs, "were involved in the Great Game. An anonymous political officer (rifleless), hardly distinguishable from his companions, is seen here with friendly Afghan tribesmen," who all carry rifles, but are not called "soldiers." This picture is outside of Foucault's beautifully organized system, so beloved by the disciplines, but also "inside," for this is the wild counter-narrative, rifle-toting tribesmen and rifleless white soldier, that keeps the story of efficiency and leniency going in the metropolis.

Although the Afghan subalterns, "the people" according to Najibullah, were perhaps not sufficiently aware of the "Great Game," the principal players were, of course. I offer a reflection of the Kim-Gora relationship in a cracked mirror.

In 1886 Muhammad Mahfuz Ali, an Indian Muslim, translated his own book *The Truth about Russia and England: From a Native's Point of View* from Urdu into English. A move that Najibullah was obliged to reverse, as it were. It is interesting that even Mahfuz Ali, inimical to Afghanistan, himself on the one hand a loyal subject of the Crown, and on the other a Muslim, spoke of "the national spirit of the Afghan people." The bibliographer at the India Office Library informs me that the Urdu text is unavailable. What interests me is that Mahfuz Ali, very much the colonial subject—at one point he writes of "the oriental mind"; what had that phrase been in Urdu?—had thought that the appropriate translation of the Urdu word was "nation." Yet it is also quite clear that he was aware that Afghanistan, technically uncolonized, was not a repository of colonial knowledge. For in the same passage he calls the Afghans "a savage and united race"—that last word too is interesting—and Afghanistan a "wretched country." What had he meant by the word "nation" applied to people who did not share his own epistemic enclave?[13]

With respect, the problem with the brilliant body of speculation undertaken by Benedict Anderson and Etienne Balibar is that it cannot acknowledge that such questions (inhabiting the cusp where the rupture of colonialism is repeated or iterated within precolonial semiotic fields), although finally unanswerable, are worth pondering. The word that is translated "nation" names a hardy "residual," not an "emergent" which would allow us to claim that "citizenship"—the model of which is much more directly linked to the development of civil societies in Northwestern Europe—"and nationality have a single, indissociable institutional base."[14]

By transcribing the colonial subject into resident alien, by splitting the colonizer (Gora's biological Irish mother and her son) and rendering him indeterminate, by re-naming him "Gora"—of course the diminutive of Gourmohan—but also "Whitey," metonymically the colloquial nomenclature of the British soldier, Tagore re-writes Mahfuz Ali, and in the process messes with hospitality, in an impossible, impracticable model. That is its strength.

(It is not possible to do justice to *Of Hospitality* in parentheses. Here, suffice it to say that the question in *Gora* the novel, of Gora for the other characters in the novel, and for Gora the character himself does indeed come from abroad [*de l'étranger*].[15] What would it be to be hospitable to the invader? Gora attempts to imagine the *xenos*—the foreigner politically acknowledged as such [H, p. 5]—from below. [Strictly speaking, the above of the below, the colonized elite, a category not thinkable when we conceive of Socratic Greece in an opacity that conceals an oligarchy supported by an upwardly mobile slave population, an agist caste-bound queer population, and an instrumentalized female population.[16] I am not sure why Derrida quotes the stranger in Plato's *Sophist* who, contradicting old Parmenides, does not by that token want to be considered a patricide [H, p. 5]. It is, however, true that, in the heritage of colonialism, the question of patricide is the first question of teleopoesis [imaginative interruptions in structures of the past]—turning enemy into friend. In *Gora,* for example, agency is displaced onto the subjected. The foreigner must be welcomed by [forgetting] the murder of the fathers: Gora's biological Irish/British father and his collectivity. To Derrida's list of the indeterminate newcomer [H, p. 73] Tagore adds the impossible category of a member of the imperial race as one to whom a singular hospitality is shown in the embrace of the Indian [foster] mother, who is, strictly speaking, foreign to the foreigner, her [foster] son. Such hospitality puts the father's murder under erasure, only for the space of the book. To generalize it is to forbid resistance. Yet surely such a welcome is upstream from the political—a depoliticization that deconstructs the genealogical. The violent death of the biological father is finally obliterated in the novel by the banal failed death of the querulous and unwilling adoptive father, the colonized host.

This impossible colonizing foreigner, being, in history, though not in consciousness, part of the colonizing group, is the Law-of-forced-entry-as-Law that he questions. The encounter between the Law and the "Law," which is also the encounter between the Law and the foreigner [H, pp. 33, 35, 69], is in the brave scene on the boat, the bold scene with the white Magistrate, and the furtive silence at the father's bedside, which I read below. They are rather different from the encounters imagined by Sophocles or the Platonic Socrates, Derrida's authors. My apologies for this hasty reading of an important text. I have never been afraid to revise.)

In the para-colonial space for which Kipling's "India" is no more than a screen-identifier, a noun for which there is neither genitive nor locative to support a copula, there were repeated efforts at producing a colonial subject without the validating agency of colonialism. Abd-ur Rahman, the last nineteenth-century Amir of Afghanistan (fl. 1880–1901), had struggled to establish something resembling a "constitutional government" in Afghanistan. This was the peculiar failed Resident Alien program to which I referred in the opening of my essay. He had imported English men and women to train up Afghans, rather than encourage the production of the pharmakontic (medicine as well as poison) enabling

violation of the full-fledged colonial subject. The Afghan "national identity" is a provisional moment, of course, in the alternative inter-nationality
of Islam. It is fascinating to read the Amir's awareness of the diversity of
Islam and yet its provision for thinking a collectivity. For "the struggle
between imperial Britain and imperial Russia for influence in Afghanistan" was not unknown to him. But the production of the colonial subject in order to administer a settled colonial possession could not appear
on the agenda of this region, perceived always as an in-between, a buffer.
Between 1919 and 1929, Abd-ur Rahman's grandson Amanullah, by up-
bringing separated from his grandfather's tribal base, attempted to introduce a fantasmic "constitutionality," and was obliged to retire to Italy,
where he died peacefully in 1960. I think of E. M. Forster's Fielding, in *A
Passage to India,* retiring to Italy in the end, thinking, again and again,
that he had been mistaken in locating beauty in India. Remember Forster
too was speaking not of British "India," but a slightly para-colonial
space, a native state. The generation that came of age in the 1960s, my
generation, produced Najibullah, a man radicalized at University. He attempted once again to establish a "constitutional" state, this time with
the validating agency of communism. Gorbachev sold him out in the end.

There is no hope that anyone will question the identity of the monster
painted by John F. Burns, the *New York Times* correspondent: "Mr. Najibullah, who in life served the K.G.B.'s efforts to eliminate opposition to
Marxism, died a death as miserable as any his secret police meted out."
Under pressure from both the USSR and the United States, possibly because he was a capable and convinced man, he had resigned on the
promise of a government of unanimity. When that was not forthcoming,
he had sensed his vulnerability and made arrangements to leave his country. He was stopped at the airport and turned himself in to the United
Nations. Commenting on his demeanor on the eve of his resignation,
Diego Cordovez, the former Undersecretary General of the United Nations who negotiated the Soviet withdrawal from Afghanistan, remarked
in 1995: "He was not a scared or a nervous man; quite the contrary, he
seemed serene, fully in control, and ready to face all the ominous eventu-
alities that could follow the Soviet withdrawal."[17] In less than a year, the
Times had written his epitaph: a flunky of Stalinism.

Najibullah's translation remained unfinished. As we move back into
"India" or "Bharatvarsha," we are obliged to leave him hanging, like the
dead of the Sepoy Mutiny in Farhad Mazhar's poem "Jimmedar Bidroher
Lash" (The Corpse-Keeper of Revolt):

Lord, Dhaka's mosque is world-renowned
Much varied work on pillar and cloister. In British days

the Whites, right or wrong, put in place
th'Asiatic Society and researched it all
Here. In the white eyes
of whites the new Bengalis dig now
and look for things we see.
I wish them good luck. But doctor's degrees,
make them twice
as wily as their White forebears.

Lord, I'm an unlettered fool,
can't grasp the art of architecture, paint,
yet my heart aches empty
as I stand by the old Ganga.
The Sepoys seem to hang still on hangman's ropes
waiting for last rites, the ropes uncut,
their bodies still aloft, none to mourn,
to perform *zannat*.
Don't you mock me with minaret and arcade,
me, the corpse-keeper of revolt.[18]

I said earlier that Tagore re-inscribed and revised, turned around, and displaced Mahfuz Ali, the loyal Indian subject of the Crown as Gora. That is not quite correct, of course. It is Benoy, the major actor of *Gora*, Engels to Gora's Marx, who is Mahfuz Ali transmogrified. In order to appreciate this, let us see how Kipling pre-wrote him. I refer to the offensive and familiar passage, speaking to my worst fears, the resident made alien quoted in "The Burden of English" (Chapter 1 in this book):

> He became thickly treasonous, and spoke in terms of sweeping indecency of a Government which had forced upon him a white man's education and neglected to supply him with a white man's salary. He babbled tales of oppression and wrong till the tears ran down his cheeks for the miseries of his land. Then he staggered off, singing love-songs of Lower Bengal, and collapsed upon a wet tree-trunk. Never was so unfortunate a product of English rule in India more unhappily thrust upon aliens. (K, p. 286)

It is possible to say that Tagore himself, poet and love-song-writer from Lower Bengal, appropriates this subject-position in his magnanimous novel. But not quite. Kipling's Hurree Babu sang something like his songs. In conceiving Benoy, Tagore gives something like narrative flesh to Hurree Babu. The novel takes place between Benoy's "white man's education" and his job, that would not "supply him with a white man's salary." Here is the initial description of Benoy's situation: "College studies done with long ago, yet no entry into the real world as yet, Benoy's situation is such" (G, p. 1). I have already made the point that these are upper-middle-class Indians, the above of the below, the space of Frantz Fanon, perhaps. Ranajit Guha has recently made the point that *Hutum Penchar Naksha,* a Bengali riff on Charles Dickens's *Sketches by Boz,* takes place in the borrowed interval of carnival time, denoted in the text by the period between two cannon-shots from Fort William.[19] In the introductory chapter, before we have encountered Gora, the extended space of Benoy's nationalism occupies such a vacant borrowed interval: "he'd devoted himself to running committee meetings and writing for the newspapers," the sentence continues, "but his spirit was not fulfilled by this." It is as if *Gora* the novel, via Benoy, the educated Bengali, undoes Hurree Babu (a "love-song from lower Bengal," sung in the next paragraph by a robed minstrel may be a meta-narrative sign), and illuminates a liminal space of narrative time pulled out of *Kim,* in the sense that Keats's "Ode to a Grecian Urn" pulls out a space on a Grecian Urn remembered only by way of Keats's poem.[20] It is what classical rhetoric might call an ekphrastic displacement. The phrase or articulation from within a text is taken outside of the original: one kind of iteration, repeating as making-other. Tagore's novel operates an ekphrastic displacement of a moment of the colonial subject—between education and job—in *Kim.*

I am of course not suggesting that Tagore writes *Gora* in this way. I am reading *Gora* in this way. You can take it or leave it. My dear friend Meenakshi Mukherjee would probably have left it.

Within this space Gora makes his mistakes. When I read his story I think of the famous repetitive, epithetic tabulation of Vishnu Maya or Vishnu's illusion in *Candi,* discussed in "Moving Devi." It is as if Gora celebrates the trajectory of the goddess who is resident in all existants (in the *Seiend,* à la Heidegger) as error: *"yā devi sarvabhutesu bhrāntirupena samsthitā."* Don't get me wrong; I am not explaining a modern Indian text of secularism like a cultural Hindu conservative. The line is in praise of error, errancy.[21] And I have earlier described Gora's anagnoresis by way of Aristotle. For me Candi and Aristotle are both instruments to theorize with, as are Foucault and Bhartrhari.

I am emboldened in this by Tagore's introduction of Gora in the third person, citing the Sanskrit Pandit of his College, by way of an extremely well-known epithet of Siva—*"rajatagirinibha"* or Silver Mountain(–like). Rajatgiri is an epithet of Siva uttered by some little Hindu girls before daybreak, hoping for a good husband: *"Dhyāyennityam mahésam rajatagirinibham cārucandrāvatamsam."* That this connection was not far from the narrative and indeed from the *mythos* or plot of the narrative is confirmed in the opening conversation between Mother and Son (with an added bonus of a Freudian coincidence: the phallic mother): "My love, your mother did indeed follow ritual once. . . . Daily I molded a Shiva lingam [the holy phallus] and sat down to worship, and your Dad threw it away. . . . When I took you in my lap I let ritual wash away, do you know that?"

These introductory motifs and exchanges, full of dramatic irony, give us a sense of the role of woman in this novel, radical yet willingly subordinate. More about that at the end. Now two words about Gora's errancy.

As substance of Gora's error there are some persuasive discussions of the appropriateness of an ennobled Hindu India. This can be compared to the superb risk of playing the *vivādi* in a performance, the note in a raga that can break the raga, but can be used by a master artist. There is no reasonable refutation of Gora's espousal of orthodox Hinduism in the novel, only a narrative one: he discovers he is not a Brahman. It is only if we read the novel as novel that we say "yes" with affective sympathy to the end: that this is the best India: "What I wanted to be day and night but couldn't be, I am today. I am Indian today. In me today there is no conflict among Hindu, Muslim, and Christian society." This is in the affective declarative. If you read the text as a tract for the times, without entering its textual protocol, you cannot garner its strengths to undermine religious violence today. Gora's earlier (errant) monologues shine with conviction, full of textual value.

Reading him as a figure in a textuality that includes the social and the verbal, I point also at another line of *anagronesis*. Gora listens with distaste to a Bengali Babu and a British functionary mocking underclass pilgrims on a steamer. He leaves the First Class deck with this impassioned statement: "My place is not with the two of you together—my place is with those travelers. But, let me ask you not to oblige me to come to this class again" (G, p. 48).

In Tagore's hospitable representation of this imaginary incident, the Englishman acknowledges a bond with this noble position: "He walks quickly to Gora before alighting, lifts his hat slightly and says, 'I am so ashamed of my behavior—I hope you will forgive me'" (G, p. 48).[22] In-between, when Gora confronts Magistrate Brownlow to say "Since you have decided not to redress these wrongs, and since your ideas about the villagers are inflexible, then I have no other choice, I will encourage the villagers to stand in resistance against the police by their own efforts" (G, p. 180), it is again a Bengali Babu who says "Such people have not earned the right to absorb the best parts of an English education." The colonizer and the colonized are both split and split again by the text. (The place of woman as social agent within this split is staged in "Didi" [see "The

Burden of English"]. *Gora* stages woman as social instrument. I believe it is possible to argue a country-city divide here, but that argument would take us too far afield.)

I draw this textual line of the recurring split between colonizer and colonized to a bit of interior monologue toward the very end of the book. The European doctor enters with the Bengali family physician. Gora is still dressed in ritual clothes, with the marks of ritual upon his face and body. The doctor looks at him and thinks: "'Who is this person?' Before this Gora would have felt a resentment," Tagore continues, "at the very sight of an English doctor. Today he kept looking at him with a special eagerness [*bishesh ekta outshukyer shohit*] as he examined the patient. He kept asking himself the same question again and again, 'Is this man my closest kin here?'" (G, p. 472). No direct resolution to this is offered by the text. In a few pages we get the final series of declarations from which I have already quoted.

It is the grandeur of the text that identity is thus left dependent on case. If we wish to use this as a socially useful document, we must admit that the new demographic virtual frontiers are not located in such territorialities—the possessive case of identity is not derived from the locative any longer. We must become, in the Gramscian sense, permanent persuaders. You must attempt to displace *Gora* ekphrastically; iterate and situate it in the new virtualized locales. Today's NRI [non-resident Indian] is no Resident Alien. He is on the Internet, conjuring up Hindu nationalism. He is a DIPSO—dollar-income-private-sector-operator—sitting in Bangalore, India's first Silicon City but part of what Robert Reich has called the secessionist community of electronic capitalism, as I describe him in "Megacity." He is in the metropolis, recoding upward class-mobility (mimicry and masquerade) as resistance, destabilization, intervention. Can *Gora* be damage control? Probably not.

I left Najibullah hanging, as he must hang suspended when we celebrate our postcoloniality. Let us look at a displacement of his translation project, upon this terrain where the reverse hospitality of the colonized misfired.

A Swiss anthropologist had apparently noticed "primary school students changing out of their traditional clothes into their Western-style school uniforms while on the way to [the] school[s established by Abd-ur Rahman's grandson]."[23] In my fancy, that quick-change is grotesquely reversed in the difference between the smiling and plump Najibullah, dressed in suit and tie, shaking Gorbachev's hand—as depicted in a famous photograph—and the emaciated man, dressed in Afghani costume, hanging from the traffic post in Kabul. If we are to credit the second volume of the *Life,* Abd-ur Rahman had attempted to substitute trim European clothing for the voluminous attire of the male Afghan.[24] No translation from English to Pashto must ignore the translations from Pashto to English in an earlier dispensation. And the woman is elsewhere, even on this terrain, as a U.S. oil company strikes a deal with Taliban.

In my fancy, Najibullah was trying to provide a means to educate the people of Afghanistan to want a civil society, and to mourn a violent past. We supplement it by reminding his ghost of subalterns, of women, *if* we deserve that haunting. It is hard; for the languages are Farsi (Abd-ur Rahman), Urdu (Mahfuz Ali), Pashto (Najib)! And people keep saying English is the only language that matters on the subcontinent.[25] British colonialism is an enabling violation. Our point has long been that, in the house of language, we must remember the violation as well as the enablement. It does indeed provide a connection, as does something called "communism," with Najib. This is why I translate, and in closing I turn to my translation of Mahasweta Devi, and ask you to look at Mary Oraon, the central character of "Shikar," discussed in Chapter 2.

Derrida ends *Of Hospitality* with the story of a gang rape, but builds nothing on it. *Gora* ends with a call to Lachhmiya, the Christianized outcaste domestic worker, but builds nothing on it. Mahasweta takes the hybrid and puts a machete in her hand. Daughter of the rape of a Christian tribal domestic worker by a white imperialist displaced at Independence, Mary—with a Christian name as Gora has a Hindu—corrects the failure of decolonization by the solitary exercise of a wild justice, a reinscription of aboriginality. An impossible model, as all conceptual art must be. In her impossibility, she remains my favorite resident alien, a quick-as-a-flash reinscription of the majestic Gora. A bit of the history of Bengali literature is caught in that move. If you don't push deep language learning in globality, thinking it impractical and wasteful, that reinscription is erased, with the historicity of all literatures. False hope.

CHAPTER FIFTEEN

Ethics and Politics in Tagore, Coetzee, and Certain Scenes of Teaching

THIS ESSAY and "Righting Wrongs"[1] represent my highest hopes for the humanities. It was two years later that I realized that my convictions had been fed by an artificially preserved "authentic" tribal group in the interest of feudalist benevolence. That shock has been matched by the joining of political correctness and corporate funding at the other end. I have kept the outlines of this piece undisturbed because of the internal consistency of that deluded conviction. Read it with bemusement, then, and a suspicion of golden-ageist culturalisms.

It is practically persuasive that the eruption of the ethical interrupts and postpones the epistemological—the undertaking to construct the other as object of knowledge, an undertaking never to be given up. Lévinas is the generic name associated with such a position. This beautiful passage from *Otherwise than Being* lays it out, although neither interruption nor postponement is mentioned. That connection is made by Derrida.[2]

Here, then, is Lévinas, for whom Kant's critical perspectivization of the subject and the rigorous limits of pure theoretical reason seem to have been displaced by the structuralist hermeneutics of suspicion. For Lévinas, structuralism did not attend to what in Kant was the mechanism that interrupted the constrained and rigorous workings of pure reason: "The interests that Kant discovered in theoretical reason itself, he subordinated to practical reason, become mere reason. It is just these interests that are contested by structuralism, which is perhaps to be defined by the primacy of theoretical reason."[3]

The relationship between the postponement of the epistemological in Lévinas and the subordination of pure reason in Kant is a rich theme,

beyond the scope of this essay. Let us return to what Lévinas will perceive as a general contemporary hermeneutics of suspicion, related to the
primacy of theoretical reason: "The suspicion engendered by psychoanalysis, sociology and politics weigh on human identity such that we
never know to whom we are speaking and what we are dealing with
when we build our ideas on the basis of the human fact."[4] The political
calculus thematizes this suspicion into an entire code of strategy defined
as varieties of game theory and rational choice, combined with the spe-
ciousness of heritage politics. This can be verified across cultural difference, backward through history, and in today's global academic discourse.
Over against this Lévinas posits the ethical with astonishing humility:
"but we do not need this knowledge in the relationship in which the other
is the one next to me [le prochain]."

Kant thought that the ethical commonality of being (gemeines Wesen—
repeatedly mistranslated as "the ethical state") cannot form the basis of
a state. Surprisingly, there is a clear line from the face-to-face of the ethical to the state in Lévinas.[5] It has long been my habit to scavenge and tin-
ker in (ab-use) the field of practical philosophy. I will conserve from Kant
the discontinuity between the ethical and the political, from Lévinas the
discontinuity between the ethical and the epistemological. I will suggest
that the discontinuities between the ethical and the epistemological and
political fields are tamed in the nestling of logic and rhetoric in fiction.[6]
Whether this can be put to use in teaching today has become doubtful.

Assuming at that earlier stage that fiction could be used to teach living
in these postponing double binds, I could move to another bit of prose
on that page in Lévinas: "For reasons not at all transcendental but purely
logical, the object-man must figure at the beginning of all knowing."

The figure of the "I" as object: this representation of the holy man in
Lévinas does not match our colloquial and literal expectations. My general suggestion, that the protocol of fiction gives us a practical simulacrum of the graver discontinuities inhabiting (and operating?) the ethico-
epistemic and the ethico-political, can, however, take such a figure on
board; to produce this in the social field is impossible today. Yet some of
us will of course continue to want to say that fiction offers us an experience of the discontinuities that remain in place "in real life." That would be
a description of fiction as an event—an indeterminate "sharing" between
writer and reader, where the effort of reading is to taste the impossible status of being figured as object in the web of the other. Reading, in this special
sense, is sacred and will remain sacred, wherever the profane takes us.

In this essay I consider, because I was in that earlier more confident
mode, not only fiction as event but also fiction as task. I locate in Rabindranath Tagore (1861–1941) and J. M. Coetzee (1940–) representations

of what may be read as versions of the "I" figured as object and weave the representations together as a warning text for postcolonial political ambitions. I am obviously using "text" as "web," coming from Latin *texere*—"to weave."

In the second part of the essay I move into the field of education as a nation-building calculus. I examine planning as its logic and teaching as its rhetoric—in the strong sense of figuration.

On the cover of the first *Pratichi Education Report,* there is an artwork by Rabindranath Tagore, containing a poem, in English and Bengali, nestled in a tinted sketch, written and painted in Baghdad in 1932.[7] Here is the poem, in Tagore's own translation:

> The night has ended.
> Put out the light of the lamp of thine own narrow corner smudged
>   with smoke.
> The great morning which is for all appears in the East.
> Let its light reveal us to each other
> Who walk on the same path of pilgrimage.

The Bengali is slightly more active: *"Nikhiler alo purba akashe jolilo punyodine / Ekshathe jara cholibe tahara shokolere nik chine"* (The universe's light burns in the eastern sky on this blessed day / Let those who'll walk together recognize each other). These lines resonate with what might be the mission statement of the moral entrepreneurship of the international civil society today, which, however laudable, is put together, not by democratic procedure, but largely by self-selection and networking. I am aware, of course, of the same forces at work in "democracies." But the presence of mechanisms of redress—electoral or constitutional—however remote, produces a faith in electoral education, which is useless if our faith is put entirely in self-selected international helpers.

"Apoman," the poem Tagore wrote more than twenty years before this, after reading Kshitimohan Sen's translations of Kabir, is much darker.[8] In this poem, Tagore uses the exact phrase "human rights"—*manusher adhikar*—already at the beginning of the last century. What is to me more striking is that, instead of urging that human rights be immediately restored to the descendants of India's historical unfortunates, he makes a mysterious prediction, looking toward the historical future: *"apamane hote habe tahader shobar shoman"* (my unfortunate country, you will have to be equal in disgrace to each and every one of those you have disgraced millennially), a disgrace to which Kabir had responded.

How can this enigmatic sentence be understood? The idea of intertextuality, loosely defined, can be used to confront this question.

I will offer an anecdotal account of intertextuality. It will help us coast through Tagore's India, Coetzee's South Africa, and the space of a tiny group of *adivasi*s.[9]

In November 2002, Roald Hoffman, a Nobel Laureate chemist, gave a popular mini-lecture with slides in the basement of the Cornelia Street Café in New York. The topic was "Movement in Constrained Spaces," by which Hoffman meant the incessant microscopic movement that goes on inside the human body to make it function. To prepare for his talk, he had asked a choreographer from neighboring Princeton to choreograph a dance for the space of the stage, which is very small.[10] This is already intertextuality, where one text, Hoffman's, would make its point by weaving itself with another, the dance. A shot silk, as it were. Again, that venerable sense of text as in text-ile, and *texere* as weave.

The choreographer managed a pattern of exquisite and minute movements for two dancers, male and female, in that tiny space. And, at the back of the long and narrow bar, two singers, female and male, sang *"La ci darem a mano"* in full-throated ease. That wonderful aria from Mozart's *Don Giovanni,* sung with such force and skill, bought our choreographer the deep space of the bar, but also historical space—the space of an opera that has been heard and loved by millions for a few centuries. Yet her dancers gave something to Mozart as well. Full of lyric grace as a love song if heard by itself—a man telling his beloved the exquisite beauty of the place to which they will escape—*La ci darem* is, in context, a brutal seduction song of the most vicious class-fixed gendering, a gentleman seducing a confused farmgirl only to fuck, and the audience sharing the joke. The two impish and acrobatic dancers on the diminutive stage, wittily partnering, gave the lie to the possibility of any such interpretation.

This is intertextuality, working both ways. Just as the chemist gave the dancer the lie, somewhat, for the movements *he* spoke of made the dance possible, so did the dancers give Mozart the lie by taking away his plot. Yet each gained something as well.

But in this case it did not work completely. Mozart is too elite, too conventional, too old-fashioned, for a radical New York audience. They did not catch the allusion. When the boring literary academic referred to it in a timid question, the choreographer melted in gratitude.

This *is* sometimes the task of the literary academic. To restore reference in order that intertextuality may function; and to create intertextuality as well. In order to do a good job with the Tagore poem, I have to read Kabir carefully. And that will be another session with the fictive simulacrum of the helpless strength of the ethical.

"Helpless strength." Get it? Not a cash cow. Not something ignorant cost-analysts can ask a corporate university to close down. Not teaching only legalized greed to bring the whole world to crisis. Not helping from above, taking no historical responsibility for those who were disabled cognitively from suddenly using high-end help now.

J. M. Coetzee's novel *Disgrace* may be put in an intertextual relationship with Tagore's poem.[11] In representing *jare tumi niche felo she tomare bandhibe je niche*—the one you fling down will bind you down there—in rural South Africa, Coetzee offers an illustration of what that enigmatic prediction might mean: *"apamane hote hobe tahader shobar shoman"*—you will have to be equal in disgrace to all of them. Here too, intertextuality works two ways. Where Tagore alters his refrain in the last line: *"mrityumajhe hobe tobe chitabhashshe shobar shoman"*—you will then be equal to all of them in the ashes of death—thus predicting the death of a nation, Coetzee, writing an unsentimentally gendered narrative, makes his protagonist choose life. (I should add that Tagore's last stanza is somewhat more programmatic and asks for a call to all.)

Here is a plot summary of Coetzee's novel: David Lurie, a middle-aged male professor, sentimental consumer of metropolitan sex-work, seduces a student, and is charged with sexual harassment by the appropriate committee. He refuses to utter the formulas that will get him off. He leaves the university and goes to his possibly lesbian daughter Lucy's flower farm. The daughter is raped and beaten and he is himself beaten and badly burned. The daughter is pregnant and decides to carry the child to term. One of the rapists turns up at the neighboring farm and is apparently a relative of the owner. This farmer Petrus, already married, proposes a concubinage-style marriage to Lucy. She accepts. The English professor starts working for an outfit that puts unwanted dogs to sleep. He has a short liaison with the unattractive married woman who runs the outfit. He writes an operetta in a desultory way. He learns to love dogs and finally learns to give up the dog that he loves to the stipulated death.

These are some of the daughter Lucy's last words in the novel. Her father is ready to send his violated daughter back to her Dutch mother. Holland is the remote metropole for the Afrikaner:

> It is as if she has not heard him. "Go back to Petrus," she says. "Propose the following. Say I accept his protection. Say he can put out whatever story he likes about our relationship and I won't contradict him. If he wants me to be known as his third wife, so be it. As his concubine, ditto. But then the

child becomes his too. The child becomes part of his family. As for the land, say I will sign the land over to him as long as the house remains mine. I will become a tenant on his land." . . . "How humiliating," *he* says finally. . . . "Yes, [she says,] I agree, it is humiliating. But perhaps that is a good point to start from again. . . . To start at ground level. With nothing. Not with nothing but. With nothing. No cards, no weapons, no property, no rights, no dignity." (pp. 204–205; emphasis added)

Apamane hote hobe tahader shobar shoman.

Insofar as *Disgrace* is a father-daughter story the intertextuality here is with *Lear.* If Lucy ends with nothing, Cordelia in the text of *King Lear* begins with the word "nothing." That word signifies the withholding of speech as an instrument for indicating socially inappropriate affective value. In Cordelia's understanding, to put love in the value-form—let me measure how much—is itself absurd.

Indeed, in the first impact of the word "nothing" in the play, this protest is mimed in the clustering of silences in the short lines among the regular iambic pentameter lines. "*Cor.* Nothing, my lord. [six syllables of silence] / *Lear.* Nothing? [eight syllables of silence] / *Cor.* Nothing. [eight again] / *Lear.* Nothing will come of nothing: speak again" (I.i.87–90). The meter picks up and Cordelia speaks.

Now Cordelia shows that she is also a realist and knows that love in the value-form is what makes the world go around. She is made to chide her sisters for not thinking of the love due to their husbands: "Why have my sisters husbands if they say / They love you all?" (I.i.97–98).

Just as *Disgrace* is also a father-daughter story, so is *King Lear* also a play about dynastic succession in the absence of a son, not an unimportant topic in Jacobean England. It has been abundantly pointed out that the play's turnaround can be measured by the fact that "the presence of Cordelia at the head of a French army . . . marks the final horrific stage in the process by which Lear's division of the kingdom goes on turning the world upside down."[12] Thus the love due to fathers bows to the love due to husbands and is then displaced, as it were. It is this story of fathers and husbands, and dynastic succession at the very inception of capitalist colonialism, that *Disgrace* de-stabilizes, re-asking the question of the Enlightenment ("let those who will walk together get to know each other by the dawning universal *light*" [emphasis added], says the cover of the *Pratichi Report*) with reference to the public sphere and the classed and gendered subject, when Lucy, "perhaps" a lesbian, decides to carry the child of rape to term and agrees to "marry" Petrus, who is not (one of) the biological father(s).

Lucy's "nothing" is the same word but carries a different meaning from Cordelia's. It is not the withholding of speech protesting the casting of love in the value-form *and* giving it the wrong value. It is rather the casting aside of the affective value-system attached to reproductive heteronormativity as it is accepted as the currency to measure human dignity. I do not think this is an acceptance of rape, but a refusal to be raped by instrumentalizing reproduction. Coetzee's Lucy is made to make clear that the "nothing" is not to be itself measured as the absence of "everything" by the old epistemico-affective value form—the system of knowing-loving. It is not "nothing but," Lucy insists. It is an originary "nothing," a scary beginning. Who imagines that centuries of malpractice—*shotek shatabdir ashommanbhar*—can be conveniently undone by diversified committees, such as the one that "tried" David Lurie for rape Enlightenment-style?[13] Literature is not a blueprint for action, but is there a lesson for the feudality of the international civil society here? Even if there were, it would be in the double bind of the literary being just that.

"Unaccommodated man is no more but such a poor, bare, forked animal as thou art," Lear had said to Edgar's faked madness, erasing the place of the phallus: "a poor, bare, *forked* animal" (emphasis added). What does it mean, in the detritus of colonialism, for one from the ruling race to call for interpellation as "unaccommodated woman, a poor, bare, forked animal," and hold negotiating power without sentimentality in that very forkèdness? What if Lévinas's catachrestic holy man is a catachrestic holy woman, quite unlike the maternity that Lévinas embarrassingly places in the stomach in the passage from which I quoted? Is it a gendered special case, or can it claim generality, as making visible the difficulty of the postcolonial formula: a new nation? Without the practice of freedom. I repeat, neither *Lear* nor *Disgrace* is a blueprint for unmediated social policy. These are figures, asking for dis-figuration, as figures must. And it is the representation of the "I" as figured object—as woman relinquishing the child as property, as always, and as former colonizer in the ex-colony. This is how critique is operated through fictions, a critique no longer available in the rational choices of globality, at best—and only at best—manipulated by the hopelessly pre-critical models of the human mind presupposed by behaviorist economics, Barack Obama's choice of Cass Sunstein as the Head of the Office of Information and Regulatory Affairs.

I emphasize that it is not an equality in death—*mrityumajhe*. It is not the sort of equality that suicide bombing may bring. Suicidal resistance is a message inscribed in the body when no other means will get through. It is both execution and mourning, for both self and other, where you die with me for the same cause, no matter which side you are on, with the implication that there is no dishonor in such shared and innocent death. That is an equality in disgrace brought about by the withholding of response, or a "response" so disingenuously requiring duress as to be no response at all, as from Israel to Palestine.[14]

If Lucy is intertextual with *Lear,* Lurie is intertextual with Kafka's *The Trial,* a novel not about beginning with nothing, but ending like a dog when civil society crumbles. Here is the end of *The Trial,* where Josef K.'s well-organized civil society gives way:

> Logic is no doubt unshakable, but it can't withstand a person who wants to live. Where was the judge he'd never seen? Where was the high court he'd never reached? He raised his hands and spread out all his fingers. But the hands of one man were right at K's throat, while the other thrust the knife into his heart and turned it there twice. With failing sight K. saw how the men drew near his face, leaning cheek-to-cheek to observe the verdict. "Like a dog!" he said; it seemed as though the shame was to outlive him.[15]

This is how Lurie understands Lucy's remarks about "nothing but." Not as a beginning in disgraceful equality but the end of civil society (with the withdrawal of the colonizer?) where only shame is guaranteed continuity. This is a profound misunderstanding. And this brings me to the second point about literature. The literary text gives rhetorical signals to the reader, which lead to activating the readerly imagination. Literature advocates in this special way. These are not the ways of expository prose. Literary reading has to be learned. Metaphor leans on concept and concept on metaphor, logic nestles in rhetoric, but they are not the same and one cannot be effaced in the other. If the social sciences describe the rules of the game, literary reading teaches how to play. One cannot be effaced in the other. This is too neat an opposition, of course. But for the moment, let it suffice as a rule of thumb.

What rhetorical signal does *Disgrace* give to the canny reader? It comes through the use of focalization, described by Mieke Bal as "the relation between the vision and that which is 'seen.' "[16] This term is deemed more useful than "point of view" or "perspective" because it emphasizes the fluidity of narrative—the impression of (con)sequence as well as the transactional nature of reading.

Disgrace is relentless in keeping the focalization confined to David Lurie. Indeed, this is the vehicle of the sympathetic portrayal of David Lurie. When Lucy is resolutely denied focalization, the reader is provoked, for he or she does not want to share in Lurie-the-chief-focalizer's inability to "read" Lucy as patient and agent. No reader is content with acting out the failure of reading. This is the rhetorical signal to the active reader, to counter-focalize. This shuttle between focalization and the making of an alternative narrative as the reader's running commentary, as it were, used to be designated by the prim phrase "dramatic irony" when I was an undergraduate. You will see immediately how much more effortful and active this counterfocalization is than what that term can indicate. This provocation into counterfocalization is the "political" in political fiction—the transformation of a tendency into a crisis.[17]

Thus when Lurie asks, after Lucy's impassioned speech, "Like a dog?" Lucy simply agrees, "Yes, like a dog." She does not provide the explanation that the reader who can work the intertextuality will provide. *Lear* and *The Trial* are not esoteric texts. (But then neither was *Don Giovanni*, and not teaching the humanities is now encouraged!) We can sense the deep contradiction of a split understanding of postcoloniality here: between the risk of beginning with nothing and the breakdown of civil societies. If not, we can at least see that Lurie literalizes his daughter's remark and learns to love dogs as the other of being-human, as a source, even, of ethical lessons of a special sort. He is staged as unable to touch either the racial or the gendered other. These may be Lucy's last words, but the novel continues, focalizing Lurie loving dogs, avoiding bathos only by his obvious race-gender illiteracy, as we counter-focalize the absent Lucy.

Literary reading teaches us to learn from the singular and the unverifiable. It is not that literary reading does not generalize. It is just that those generalizations are not on evidentiary ground. In this area, what is known is proved by *vyavahāra,* or setting-to-work. Martin Luther King, in his celebrated speech "Beyond Vietnam," which I have already cited in Chapter 13, had tried to imagine the other again and again. In his own words, "perhaps the more difficult but no less necessary task is to speak for those who have been designated as our enemies. . . . Surely we must understand their feelings even if we do not condone their actions."

Here is a setting to work of what in the secular imagination is the literary impulse: to imagine the other who does not resemble the self. King, being a priest, had put it in terms of liberation theology, in the name of "the one who loved his enemies so fully that he died for them." For the secular imagination, that transcendental narrative is, I repeat, a narrative, singular and unverifiable. When it is set to work, it enters the arena of the probable: King's imagination of the Viet Cong. I believe this is why Aristotle said *poiesis* or making-in-fiction was *philosophoteron*—a better instrument of knowledge—than *historia*—because it allowed us to produce the probable rather than account for that which has been possible.

In my words on suicide bombing, I was trying to follow Dr. King's lead halfway, use the secular imagination as emancipatory instrument. When

I was a graduate student, on the eve of the Vietnam War, I lived in the same house as Paul Wolfowitz, the ferocious Deputy Secretary of Defense who was the chief talking head for the war on Iraq. He was a Political Science undergraduate, disciple of Allan Bloom, the conservative political philosopher. As I have watched him on television lately, I have often thought that if he had had serious training in literary reading and/or the imagining of the enemy as human, his position on Iraq would not be so inflexible. This is not a verifiable conviction. But it is in view of such hopes that humanities teaching acts itself out. These hopes are dashed by inanities like the "Next Big Thing."[18]

To repeat: literature is not verifiable. The only way a reading establishes itself—without guarantees—is by sharing the steps of the reading. That is the experience of the impossible, ethical discontinuity shaken up in a simulacrum. Unless you take a step with me, there will be no interdisciplinarity, only the tedium of turf battles.

Insofar as Lucy is a figure that makes visible the rational kernel of the institution of marriage—rape, social security, property, human continuity—we can check her out with Herculine Barbin, the nineteenth-century hermaphrodite who committed suicide but left a memoir, which Foucault edited and made available.

Herculine Barbin was a scholar—a diligent student who became a school mistress. But when she was named a man by doctors she could not access the scholarly position—of writing and speaking to a general public—that Kant secures for the enlightened subject in "What Is Enlightenment?"[19]

Let us look at Herculine/Abel's cautious elation at the moment of entry into the world of men:

> So, it was done [*C'en était donc fait*]. Civil status called me to belong henceforth to that half of the human race that is called the strong sex [*L'état civil m'appelait à faire partie désormais de cette moitié du genre humain, appelé le sexe fort*]. I, who had been raised until the age of twenty-one in religious houses, among shy [*timides*] female companions, was going to leave behind me a past entirely delightful [*tout un passé délicieux*], like Achilles, and enter the lists, armed with my weakness alone and my profound inexperience of men and things![20]

It is this hope—of entering the public sphere as the felicitous subject—that is dashed as the possibility of agency is annulled in suicide (p. 98).

Barbin cannot articulate the relationship between the denial of agency and the incapability to reproduce. Yet, Tiresias-like, he offers a critical account of marriage:

It has been given to me, as a man, the most intimate and deep knowledge of all the aptitudes, all the secrets, of the female character. I read in that heart, as in an open book. I count every beat of it. In a word, I have the secret of its strength and the measure of its weakness; and just for that reason I would make a detestable husband; I also feel that all my joys would be poisoned in marriage and that I would cruelly abuse, perhaps, the immense advantage that would be mine, an advantage that would turn against me. (p. 107; translation modified)

I presented "Can the Subaltern Speak?" as a paper twenty years ago. In that paper I suggested that the subaltern could not "speak" because, in the absence of institutionally validated agency, there was no listening subject. My listening, separated by space and time, was perhaps an ethical impulse. But I am with Kant in thinking that such impulses do not lead to the political. There must be a presumed collectivity of listening and countersigning subjects and agents in the public sphere for the subaltern to "speak." Herculine Barbin wrote abundantly, presuming a reader repeatedly. And yet she could not speak. Her solution would be the normalization of the multi-sexed subject, a civil and agential rather than subjective solution. There would then be a listening public who could countersign her "speech act."

In the arrangement of counterfocalization within the validating institution of the novel in English, the second half of *Disgrace* makes the subaltern speak, but does not presume to give "voice," either to Petrus or to Lucy. This is not the novel's failure, but rather a politically fastidious awareness of the limits of its power. By the general dramatically ironic presentation of Lurie, he is shown to "understand" Petrus by the neat reversal of the master-slave dialectic without sublation: "Petrus needs him not for pipefitting or plumbing but to hold things, to pass him tools—to be his *handlanger*, in fact. The role is not one he objects to. Petrus is a good workman, it is an education to watch him. It is Petrus himself that he is beginning to dislike" (pp. 136–137). Once again, the novel and Lurie part company, precisely on the issue of reading, of control. This is a perfectly valid reading, as is the invocation of the end of Kafka's *The Trial* to describe the difficult birth of the new nation. It is precisely this limited perfect validity of the liberal white ex-colonizer's understanding that *Disgrace* questions through the invitation to focalize the enigma of Lucy. It is interesting that Petrus's one-liner on Lucy shows more kinship with the novel's verdict: "'She is a forward-looking lady, not backward-looking'" (p. 136). If we, like Lurie, ignore the enigma of Lucy, the novel, being fully focalized precisely by Lurie, can be made to say every racist thing.[21] Postcoloniality from below can then be reduced to the education of Pollux, the young rapist who is related to Petrus. Counterfocalized, it can be acknowledged as perhaps the first moment in Lucy's refusal of rape by generalizing it into all heteronormative sexual practice: "'When it comes to men and sex, David, nothing surprises me any more. . . . They spur each other on. . . .' 'And the third one, the boy?' 'He was there to learn'" (pp. 158–159). The incipient bathos of Lurie's literalism ("like a dog" means love dogs; forgiveness from Melanie's parents means prostrating himself on the floor before them [p. 173]; loving dogs means letting one of them into the operetta [p. 215]; even the possibility that the last Christian scene of man giving up dog may slide into a rictus,[22] given the overarching narrative context) can be seen, in a reading that ignores the function of Lucy in the narrative, as the novel's failure, rather than part of its rhetorical web.

I want now to come to the second way in which Tagore's refrain can be understood: the failure of democracy.

The Pratichi Trust in India, to whose *Report* I have referred above, is doing astute work because it realizes that, if the largest sector of the electorate misses out on early education, democracy cannot function, for it then allows the worst of the upper sectors to flourish. Democracy sinks to that level and we are all equal in disgrace. When we read statistics on who wins and who loses the elections, the non-specialist-located middle-class as well as the rest of the world, if it cares, thinks it shows how the country thinks. No. In the largest and lowest sector of the electorate, there is a considerable supply of affect, good and bad; there is native sharpness and there is acquired cunning. But there is no rational choice. Election does not even pretend to be based on rational platforms. (This applies to the United States as well, in another way. But it would take me too far to develop that here.) Gendering must be understood simply here: female teachers are preferred, though they have less authority; gendering presuppositions must be changed through education, and so on.

There is little I can add to the Trust's magisterial work. After a general caution, that work in this sphere runs the risk of structural atrophy, like diversified committees in *Disgrace,* and therefore must be interrupted by the ethical, I will add a few codicils here and there.

Professor Sen, the founder of the Trust, supports the state in opposing "the artificially generated need for private tuition," artificial because generated by careless non-teaching in the free primary schools.[23] While the state waits to implement this opposition legally, I have been trying to provide collective "private tuition" to supplement the defunct primary schools, to a tiny sector of the most disenfranchised. It is my hope that private tuition in this form can be nationalized and thus lose its definition.

I will ask some questions in conclusion, which will make the direction of my thoughts clear. The one-on-one of "private" tuition—at the moment in the service of rote learning that cannot relate to the nurturing of the ethical impulse—is the only way to undo the abdication of the politically planned "public" education. "Private tuition," therefore, is a relation to transform rather than prohibit. The tutorial system at the other end of the spectrum is proof of this.

I must repeat that I am enthralled by the report and whatever I am adding is in the nature of a supplement from a literary person. The work of the Trust is largely structural. The humanities—training in literary reading in particular—is good at textural change. Each discipline has its own species of "setting to work"—and the texture of the imagination belongs to the teacher of literary reading. All good work is imaginative, of course. But the humanities have little else.

There is a tiny exchange on page 69 of the book: "On the day of our visit [to a school in Medinipur], we interviewed four children of Class 4. . . . Well, can you tell us something about what was taught? All four children were silent."

Part of the silence rises from the very class apartheid that bad rural education perpetuates.[24] The relationship between the itinerant inspector and the child is, in addition, hardly ethical.

Training in literary reading can prepare one to work at these silences. I will submit an example which it would be useless to translate here. It is lesson 5 from *Amader Itihash,* a Class 4 history book, specifically devoted to national liberation, one item in which is the story of Nelson Mandela. Let us overlook the implicit misrepresentation of Gandhi's role in Mandela's political victory in the lifting of apartheid, or the suggestive detail that the section on national liberation starts with George Washington. One cannot, however, overlook, if one is a reader of Bengali, the hopeless ornamentation of the prose, incomprehensible to teacher and student alike at the subaltern level, in the outer reaches of rural West Bengal. The point is not only to ask for "a radically enhanced set of commitments" "from the primary teachers," as the *Report* stresses. The real disgrace of rural primary education is that even the *good* teacher, with the best will in the world, has been so indoctrinated into rote learning that, even if s/he could understand the lugubrious prose and even if s/he had retained or imbibed enough general knowledge of the world—both doubtful propositions—the technique of emphasizing meaning is not what s/he would understand by teaching. Elsewhere I have emphasized this as the systematic difference in teaching between *baralok* and *chhotolok*— translated by Pratichi as high-born and low-born, brave attempts—*gatar khatano* and *matha khatano*—manual labor and intellectual labor does not quite translate the active sense of *khatano*—setting to work, then, not of the body alone, and of the mind as well—that keeps class apartheid alive. The common sight of a child of the rural poor trying to make the head engage in answer to a textbook question and failing is as vivid a figure of withholding humanity as anything in Tagore or Coetzee. The "silence" is active with pain and resentment.

The solution is not to write new textbooks, the liberal intellectuals' favorite option. The teachers at this level do not know how to use a book, any book, however progressive. Many of the textbooks, for instance, have a list of pedagogic goals at the top of each lesson. The language of these lists is abstract, starting with the title: *shamortho*, capacity. Sometimes, for nine or ten lessons in a row, this abstract title is followed by the remark: "see previous lesson." No primary or non-formal teacher over the last twenty-five years has ever noticed this in my presence, and, when informed of the presence of this pedagogic machinery, been able to understand it, let alone implement it. Given the axiomatics of the so-called education within which the teacher has received what goes for training, it is foolish to expect implementation.

There are progressive textbooks that try to combine Bengali and Arithmetic—the famous *Kajer Pata*. This combination causes nothing but confusion in student and teacher alike on this level. And frankly, it serves no specific purpose here. There are also books where some metropolitan liberal or a committee of them tries to engage what they think is a rural audience. I wish I had the time to recount the failure of their imagination case by case. There is no possibility of the emergence of the ethical when the writing subject's sense of superiority is rock solid. The useless coyness of these failed attempts would be amusing if the problem were not so disgraceful. Both Hindu and Muslim poets are included—communalism must be avoided at all costs, of course. The point is lost on these children—though a sort of equality is achieved. All poetry is equally opaque, occasions for memorization without comprehension, learning two-way meanings—what does *a* mean? *b;* and what is *b? a,* of course. The meaning of meaning is itself compromised for these children, these teachers. A new textbook drowns in that compromise.

Two girls, between 11 and 15 years of age, show me what they are being taught in primary school. It is the piece about South Africa. I ask them some questions. They have absolutely no clue at all what the piece is about, as they don't about any piece in the book, about any piece in any book. To say "they haven't understood this piece" would be to grant too much. The girls are not unintelligent. Indeed, one of them is, I think, strikingly intelligent. They tell me their teachers would go over the material again the next day.

The next day after school, we meet again. Did the teachers explain? "Reading *poriyechhe*" is the answer—an untranslatable Bengali phrase for which there are equivalents in all the major Indian languages, no doubt. They made us read reading would perhaps convey the absurdity? Any piece is a collection of discrete spelling exercises to be read in a high drone with little regard to punctuation. The scandal is that everyone knows this. It is embarrassing to put it in an essay about Tagore and Coetzee. Better to present social scientific surveys in English. This too is a way of disgracing the disenfranchised.

To continue with the narrative. After the girls' answer begins the process of explaining. As I have already mentioned, the experience of a head attempting but failing to set itself to work is killingly painful. Most of us interrupt such silences with noise, speak up and create a version of explanation to break the experience. At that point we think we are teaching although no teaching is taking place. Sometimes we learn to resist this by excruciating self-control that often fails.

In *Foe*, another novel by J. M. Coetzee, there is a moment when a character called Friday (as in *Robinson Crusoe*), an abducted savage with his tongue cut out, resists the attempt of the white woman to teach him how to write.[25] Varieties of such resistance in the ground-level rural classroom can be read as the anger of the intelligent child not being able to work his or her head. Such readings are necessarily off the mark. But the literary critic is practiced in learning from the unverifiable.

If the older girl was just frustrated by not grasping at all what I was trying to explain, the younger one, the strikingly intelligent one, faced me with that inexorably closed look, jaws firmly set, that reminds one of Friday, withholding. No response to repeated careful questions going over the same ground over and over again, simplifying the story of Nelson Mandela further at every go. These are students who have no concept or percept of the neighboring districts, of their own state of West Bengal—because, as the *Pratichi Report* points out, they have arrived at Class 4 through neglect and no teaching. How will they catch the reference to Africa?

Into the second hour, sitting on the floor in that darkening room, I tried another tack. Forget Africa; try *shoman adhikar*—equal rights. It was impossible to explain rights in a place with no plumbing, pavement, electricity, stores, without doors and windows. Incidentally, do people really check—rather than interrupt the painful experience of having failed to teach—the long-term residue of so-called legal awareness seminars? What is learned through repeated brushes with the usual brutality of the rural judiciary is not significantly changed by the conviction that the benevolent among the masters will help them litigate. What is it to develop the subject—the capital I—of human rights, rather than a feudal dispensation of human rights breeding dependency and litigious blackmail and provoking a trail of vendetta in those punishers punished remotely? Let us return to the schoolroom in gathering dusk.

It is common sense that children have short attention spans. I was so helpless in my inability to explain that I was tyrannizing the girls. At the time it seemed as if we were locked together in an effort to let response emerge and blossom with its own energy. The ethical as task rather than event is effortful. And perhaps an hour and a half into the struggle, I put my hand next to the bright one's purple-black hand to explain apartheid. Next to that rich color this pasty brown hand seemed white. And to explain *shoman adhikar,* "equal rights," Mandela's demand, a desperate formula presented itself to me: *ami ja, tumi ta*—what I, that you. Remember this is a student, not an asylum seeker in the metropole, in whose name many millions of dollars are moved around even as we speak.[26] This is just two students, accepting oppression as normality, understanding their designated textbook.

Response did emerge. "Yeses" and "nos" were now given; even, if I remember right, a few words uttered as answers to questions. In a bit I let them go.

The next morning I asked them to set down what they remembered of the previous day's lesson. The older one could call up nothing. The younger one, the more intelligent one, produced this: *"ami ja, tumi ta, raja here gachhe"*—what I, that you, the king is defeated. A tremendous achievement in context but, if one thinks of all the children studying under the West Bengal Board, including the best students from the best schools in Kolkata, with whom these girls are competing, this is a negligible result. I have no doubt that even this pitiful residue of the content of the lesson is now long lost and forgotten by the older one. The younger one is dead of encephalitis.

The incident took place about ten years ago. When the two girls were young women in high school, I spoke to them and their teachers. I stressed repeatedly the importance of explaining the text, of explaining repeatedly, of checking to see if the student has understood. A futile exercise. You do not teach how to play a game by talking about it. No one can produce meanings of unknown words. There are no dictionaries, and, more important, there is no habit of consulting dictionaries.

As I continued with the useless harangue, I said, "As two of you might remember, I spent two hours explaining Nelson Mandela to you some years ago. It is important to explain." A fleeting smile, no eye contact, passed across the face of the bright one, sitting in the last row. It is unusual for such signals to pass from her class to mine.[27]

The number of calculative moves to be made and sustained in the political sphere, with the deflecting and overdetermined calculus of the vicissitudes of gendered class-mobility factored in at every step, in order for irony-shared-from-below communication to be sustained at this level, would require immense systemic change. Yet, in the supplementary relationship between the possibility of that fleeting smile—a sign of the interruptive emergence of the ethical—and the daunting labor of the political calculus, we must begin with the end, which must remain the possibility of the ethical. That inconvenient effort is the uncertain ground of every just society. If the political calculus becomes the means *and* the end, justice is ill served and no change sticks. The peculiar thing about gendering is that, in Lucy's vision of "starting with nothing," in the reproductive situation shorn of the fetishization of property, in the child given up as body's product, the ethical moment can perhaps emerge—at least so the fiction says.[28]

I have recounted this narrative to make clear that although on the literary register, the register of the singular and the unverifiable (this story, for example, is unverifiable because you have nothing but my testimony) the suggestive smile, directed by indirection and a shared experience, is a good event; it has no significance in terms of the public sphere, to which education should give access. The discontinuity between the ethical and the political is here instrumentalized—between the rhetoric of pedagogy and the logic of its fruition in the public sphere. For the smile of complicity to pass between the *adivasi* and the caste-Indian, unprovoked, marks an immense advance. But it is neither a beginning nor an end, only an irreducible grounding condition.

When I was attempting to teach in that darkening room, I had no thought but to get through. It so happened that the topic was *shomanadhikar,* equal rights. Writing this for you, on the other hand, I put myself grandiosely in Tagore's poem: *manusher odhikare bonchito korechho jaare, shommukhe danraye rekehe tobu kole dao nai sthan*—those whom you have deprived of human rights, whom you have kept standing face-to-face and yet not taken in your arms. So, spending considerable skill and labor, to teach precisely the meaning of *shomanadhikar,* was I perhaps undoing the poet's description of the behavior of the Hindu historical dominant, denying human rights over centuries to the outcastes (today's *dalit*s) and *adivasi*s? The point I am laboriously making is that it is not so. Although the literary mode of instruction activates the subject, the capital I, in order to be secured it must enter the political calculus of the public sphere. Private voluntarism such as mine remains a mongrel practice between the literary and the rational, rhetoric and logic.

And so the reader of literature asks the social scientists a question. Is it not possible for the globally beleaguered state to institute civil service positions that will call, on a regular and optional basis, upon interested humanities professionals from the highest ranks to train ground-level teachers, periodically, yet with some continuity, gradually integrating and transforming the existing training structure, thus to deconstruct or sublate private tuition and slowly make it less possible for "a teacher of [sic] Birbhum village" to say: "How can we carry over the training to our classrooms? *Baro baro katha bala soja*—Talking big is easy."[29]

Before I had started thinking about the heritage of "disgrace," I had tried to initiate the production of same-language dictionaries in the major Indian languages, specifically for ground-level teachers and students. It came to nothing, because the situation was not imaginable by those whom I had approached, and because the NRI (non-resident Indian, Indian designation for diasporics) has other kinds of uses. Should the NRI have no role but to help place the state in metropolitan economic bondage? Is it not possible to think of subaltern single-language dictionaries as an important step toward fostering the habit of freedom—the habit of finding a meaning for oneself? Is it not possible to think, not of writing new textbooks, but of revising what is now in existence—to make them more user-friendly for the least privileged, even as such teachers and students are texturally engaged? I do not believe the more privileged child would suffer from such a change, though I can foresee a major outcry. It must be repeated: to foster such freedom is simply to work at freedom in the sphere of necessity, otherwise ravaged by the ravages of political economy—no more than "the grounding condition [*Grundbedingung*] for the true realm of freedom," always around the corner (C 3, p. 959).

Shakespeare, Kafka, Tagore, Coetzee, Amartya Sen. Heavy hitters. My questions are banal. I am always energized by that paragraph in the third volume of *Capital* from which I quote above, and where Marx writes, in a high philosophical tone: "The true realm of freedom, the development of human powers as an end in itself begins beyond [the realm of necessity], though it can only flourish with this realm of necessity as its ground." That sentence is followed by this one: "The reduction of the working day is its grounding condition." In Marx's text philosophy must thus displace itself into the everyday struggle. In my argument, literature, insofar as it is in the service of the emergence of the critical, must also displace itself thus. Its task is to foster yet another displacement: into a work for the remote possibility of the precarious production of an infrastructure, that can in turn produce a Lucy or her focalizer, figuring forth an equality that takes disgrace in its stride.

No one will take this task seriously any longer. The point is funding.

CHAPTER SIXTEEN

Imperative to Re-imagine the Planet

THIS IS PERHAPS the first time that I was asked to speak from above rather than be part of the evidence at an organ of the international civil society. Just as, for the budget of my schools in rural India, I use NGOs that were founded long before the word came into being, so was the Stiftung Dialogik a member of the international civil society long before the phrase came into circulation. I cannot say what I said to them to the international civil society today. The idea of planetarity came to me as I pondered the occasion. Like the subaltern not speaking, planetarity has been altogether misunderstood; as something like community, thinking of the world's resources, or yet, at the extreme, sustainability. Let me ask the reader to work out the difference, to see planetarity as the source of a double bind that will not bind.

I was honored to have been asked to give the first lecture in Stiftung Dialogik's new series on refugees and immigrants. I was aware of the responsibility of being the remote vehicle of the honor and affection bestowed by a philosopher upon the memory of his activist wife. In Hermann Levin Goldschmidt's own words: "together we remember those who were not allowed, as survivors, to bear witness for those who did not, testifying anew, and in many different ways, to a Jewish and Swiss commitment to the world as a whole."[1]

I was fortunate enough to deliver this paper in Goldschmidt's presence. I remember our spirited exchange two days later. It was clear to both of us that my remarks were a supplement to his notion of dialogics—freedom of contradiction without synthesis—critical of the comforts of both dialectics and pluralism.[2] In this version, I have marked the moments when the supplementary character of my argument breaks upon the text.

I was born during World War II. In the estimation of my generation in India, the War was, to use an obsolete German adjective that Marx often uses, *zwieschlächtig*. The horror of the Holocaust was what made it *European*. It was a *world* war because for us, with our quarter of a million dead fighting for the Allies and the highest number of military honors won by any national group—and subsequently for a number of colonies—the War was a remote instrument for the end of specifically territorial imperialism. Goldschmidt begins our era with the discovery of the *entire* world in the sixteenth century. The end of World War II made it possible for that entire world to become "nothing but neighbors." Goldschmidt gave me his *Frage des Mitmenschen und des Mitvolkes: 1951–1992* two days after the lecture.[3] There the interpretation of "love thy neighbor" as dialogics is unfolded. I come from a generation for whom the obligation, de-theologized, could also be located on the other side. As I said to Goldschmidt on that occasion, and we both smiled: "I do not speak to you from within your community." I contradict, then, freely.

Any narrativization of the restless limning of a world after the World War goes through many phases, large and small. Negotiated Independences redefined themselves as neocolonialism from the West. Failure of decolonization at home and large-scale Eurocentric economic migration began to fix the new world's demographic outlines. With the Fall of the Berlin Wall and the subsequent events in Eastern and Central Europe, these outlines have become altogether unstable. This is the moment when I was asked to speak to the Stiftung. Today the world has moved on.

I spoke as a person from the very first waves of postcolonial migration, a *Mitmensch* who is not a *Mitvolk*.[4] If anything I said should seem unpalatable to the audience, I asked them to put it down to the seriousness of my intent. Freedom, again, to contradict.

I came to the United States in 1961, when the virtualized demographic frontiers of the modern world were not yet set (I have spoken of this phenomenon in Chapter 14, "Resident Alien"). A bit of anachronistic nationalism clings to me still. I retain an Indian passport and remain no more than a permanent resident in the United States. However common this may be among European nationals, Asians and Africans emigrate to gain metropolitan citizenship. My small group, however, is in both worlds, deeply, without being quite of them. I believe that slight anomaly gives us a certain distance, which may be valuable. I am still working at the immediately postcolonial mandate of neighborliness rather than subjection. In that belief, I could, then, speak in a somewhat utopian strain, although already aware of the dystopia around the corner which we inhabit now. You will judge.

"Migration Studies" was then just beginning as an academic subdiscipline. At its most theoretical edges we didn't often stop to think of the difference between the cultural requirements of migration and allocthonic demographic patterns in the United States and in Europe, respectively. Yet it is precisely those differences that should have occupied us.

When we theoreticians of migrant hybridity allow ourselves to be concerned about the differences between the United States and Europe, we are of course and immediately aware that Europe is a conglomerate of relatively small units, each determined by its own colonial past. Here Switzerland, especially Zurich, with its history of republicanism, economic anonymity, and commitment to social welfare, itself stands as an anomaly. Statistical patterns of national origin among recent migrants to Switzerland do not reflect a colonial past. In order of volume, a recent count would give us, in 1997: Afghanistan, Bosnia, Mozambique, Rwanda, Liberia, Iraq, Croatia, Tadzhikistan, Burundi; the relative volume of guest workers would give us Italy, Spain, Portugal, Turkey. Switzerland has had a liberal, multicultural policy, however confined to "Europe," and is engaged in seeking new ways to make the policy sustainable. But, as one Swiss Political Scientist points out,

> to integrate foreigners in the same way as the native minority groups of the past will be much more difficult for Swiss society. . . . On the other hand Switzerland already has the highest proportion of foreigners of all European countries except Luxembourg, and integration of new immigrant groups could turn out to be a continuation of the successful historical experiment.[5]

It is in this context that I am proposing the planet.

I want simply to refer now to the role of a European nation-state in governmental and non governmental international aid, a question not often asked in the offices and agencies concerned with migrancy or multiculturalism. Unofficially, however, certain connections seem obvious to both. Donor agencies that support aid to the South through a nationalist logic of self-interest regularly caution that, unless the South is built up, the waves of underclass immigration from the so-called least developed countries will overflow into Northern civic life. That the so-called green revolution—high-yield agricultural aid—prevented a "red revolution" is a commonplace of the development lobby. Any serious consideration of equitable immigration laws and multicultural legislation would have to elaborate these connections between the national and the international in new ways. Of course it is practical that every government document should begin with "Rules of Exclusion" and "return-oriented training." Yet it may be apposite to think how much we are involved in the constitution of the space to which the refugees return. I have neither the familiarity nor the experience to undertake this in the Swiss case. I would enter this often virtual yet altogether clear, electronic yet human, network through interpretative strategies toward the minutiae of such well-known institutions as the Berne Declaration and the Novartis Foundation. And no New Yorker can forget that Switzerland is the other home of the United Nations.

It is in this context too, then, of the global face of the European nation and the inter-national divide, that I hear the imperative to re-imagine the planet.

In that era, then, of a breakneck globalization catching up speed, I proposed the planet to overwrite the globe. Globalization is achieved by the imposition of the same system of exchange everywhere. It is not too fanciful to say that, in the gridwork of electronic capital, we achieve something that resembles that abstract ball covered in latitudes and longitudes, cut by virtual lines, once the equator and the tropics, now drawn increasingly by other requirements—imperatives?—of Geographical Information Systems. The globe is on our computers. It is the logo of the World Bank. No one lives there; and we think that we can aim to control globality. The planet is in the species of alterity, belonging to another system; and yet we inhabit it, indeed are it. It is not really amenable to a neat contrast with the globe. I cannot say "on the other hand." It will not engage in a double bind.

(I hasten to add that I am not writing to endorse any and every use of the word "planet." I am writing, rather, for a position that has this particular (non)relationship to the global, as I explain below: a position whose defining other is the outer as such, that cannot serve as other, dis-locating a position that only seeks to control by digital quantification. The place where the buck of the double bind stops as the bind on all double binds. Toward the end of his life, Derrida grappled with the *animot* this way.)

In order to think the migrant as well as the recipient of foreign aid, we must think the other. To think the other, as everyone knows, is one meaning of being human. To be human is to be intended toward the other. If to be human is also to be an occasional and discontinuous animator of what we call timing and spacing, like and unlike all living creatures, we provide for ourselves transcendental figurations of what we think is the origin of this animating gift of animation, if there is any: Mother, Nation, God, Nature. These are names of alterity, some more radical than others.

Planet-thought opens up to embrace an inexhaustible taxonomy of such names including but not identical with animism as well as the spectral white mythology of post-rational science. If we imagine ourselves as planetary accidents rather than global agents, planetary creatures rather than global entities, alterity remains underived from us, it is not our dialectical negation, it contains us as much as it flings us away—and thus to think of it is already to transgress, for, in spite of our forays into what we metaphorize, differently, as outer and inner space, what is above and beyond our own reach is not continuous with us as it is not, indeed, specifically discontinuous. My efforts for the last decade tell me that, if we ask the kinds of questions you are asking, seriously, we must persistently educate ourselves into this peculiar mind-set. This is where I join hands with Goldschmidt. It is only then that we will be able to think the migrant as well as the recipient of foreign aid in the species of alterity, not simply as the white person's burden:

> Take up the White Man's burden—
> The savage wars of peace—
> Fill full the mouth of Famine
> And bid the sickness cease;
> And when your goal is nearest
> The end for others sought,
> Watch sloth and heathen Folly
> Bring all your hope to nought[6]

This—foreign aid and metropolitan migration—is the specific contradiction that I offer to the dialogic sensibility. It is interesting that *Die Frage des Mitmenschen* closes with the other Kipling poem: "Oh, East is East, and West is West, / And never the twain shall meet." The problem now is that, in globalization, with the disappearance of "East" and "West," North and South do meet.

Let me then modify my title: I speak of an imperative to re-imagine the subject as planetary accident.

The problem with thinking the migrant separately from the issue of international aid has been a narrowly dialectical vision of the other. Indeed, the word "recognition" in the title of one of the most influential books in this area puts us in mind of the Master-Slave dialectic: *Multiculturalism and "The Politics of Recognition."* I am speaking of course of the work by the eminent Hegelian Charles Taylor.

Taylor's excellent book defines an impossible unitary multicultural subject in terms of the politico-intellectual history of Northwestern Europe:

> To see what is new here, we have to see the analogy to earlier moral views. . . . This fact is part of the massive subjective turn of modern culture, a new form of inwardness, in which *we* come to think of *ourselves* as beings with inner depths. . . . This is the powerful moral ideal that has come down to *us*. (pp. 28–30; emphasis added)

On a practical level, this is incorrect. The only way we can bestow a modicum of plausibility upon such conclusions is by assuming the heritage of the imperialist adventures of Northwestern Europe as having completely obliterated politico-intellectual culture in its former subjects. By this assumption, what is left as simple "culture" for these subjects, who now want to be metropolitan citizens, is the part of unreason. There is no doubt here at all as to who is nominally the Master, however beleaguered. And, true to form, the Slave countersigns the Master by speaking unreason from below.[7] The word "culture," with its claim to a pattern of behavior beyond reason alone, is opposed to the claim of the culture of the European Enlightenment to Reason as such. In its paleonymic—as a name with a history, in other words—and in its idiomatic strength—multiculturalism performs a critique, however inchoate, of the limits of the rational structures of civil society.

Why must both sides be sure that a position of power signifies delicacy of human material, or indeed vice versa? A position of power means a position of power and actions to ensure its stability. Relative procedural honesty is efficient but not necessarily a guarantee of intelligence or independent moral excellence. And, mutatis mutandis, the migrant sometimes leaves a known pattern of corruption for an unknown one. Thus, although I speak to you here and now, the planetary mode of intending without guarantees must be urged on both sides. Otherwise, multiculturalist policy reduces itself to allowing unreasonable cultural practices as a sign of freedom, to the institutionalization of the interval between "colonial" and "pre-colonial" time, the negotiation of which ensured survival under imperialism proper. This institutionalization of the spacing of different methods of temporizing is deep-structurally marked in the gap between philosophical and political liberalism in John Rawls's *Political Liberalism*, which pays no explicit attention to a multicultural society.[8]

Planetary imaginings locate the imperative in a galactic and para-galactic alterity—so to speak!—that cannot be reasoned into the self-interest that extends as far as recognizing the self-consolidating other as the self's mere negation. It is perhaps this outrageous possibility that makes otherwise reasonable thinkers like Amartya Sen or Nancy Fraser speak of considerations of "capability" in Development strategy or "universal caregiving" as a general model for "post-socialist" society.[9] How can we provide adequate justification for giving care, for considering the capacity to help others as a basic human right? How can we inscribe responsibility as a right rather than an obligation? This is a paradox that has troubled intellectuals and philosophers as well as cultural leaders through the ages and is, indeed, one of the problems that most engaged Goldschmidt. He worried the problem tenaciously, drawing upon the Judaeo-Christian heritage. A random sampling within my meager circle of knowledge would yield us Plotinus justifying the ethical as a beautiful resonating: "the Soul must be trained—to the habit of remarking . . . the works of beauty produced not by the labour of the arts but by the virtue of human beings known for their goodness."[10] It would yield Hinduism offering a right to work but not to its labors—*karmanyebādhikaraste mā phalesu kadācana*[11]—and Islam in my part of the world, combining right and responsibility in the tremendous concept or figure of *haq*. I have spoken of it in "Translating into English," Chapter 12 in this book.

Haq is the "para-individual structural responsibility" into which we are born—that is, our true being.[12] Indeed, the word "responsibility" is an approximation here. For this structural positioning can also be approximately translated as birth-right. Whether it is right or responsibility, it is the truth of my being, in a not quite English sense my *haq*.

It is my conviction, although I cannot demonstrate it now, that this robust notion of responsibility is the one practiced by most precapitalist high cultures of the planet. The transcendental figuration of the origin of the imperative—*du sollst*—differs, of course, because it had to accommodate a rationally justifiable teleology. Yet it still retains the remnants of a planetary discourse in its two-worldism. By contrast, Islam, although a religion of the Book and therefore notionally two-world, carries the residuals of a nomadic past that thinks the earth, human habitation in community, as what I am calling a "planet," planetary, by implication, in practice, if not always by scientific computation. You will indulge me if I say that the "planet" is, here, as perhaps always, a catachresis for inscribing collective responsibility as right. Its alterity, determining experience, is mysterious and discontinuous—an experience of the impossible.

The more ecological practice of living, where the opposition between the human and the natural is made indeterminate, is, of course, the Aboriginal. If we are focusing only on problems of immigration in Switzerland, it has no bearing on our concerns, except insofar as the *Umwelt* is thought by the European. But if we are thinking the planet, it may not be irrelevant to mention that, precisely in the interest of global financialization, the *Encyclopaedia of Life Support Systems,* aided by UNESCO, must now define the Aboriginal as having no concern for the ecobiome!

(I now know that the ecobiome as transformed by centuries of progress bears no resemblance to what the Aboriginal had learned to protect. At the time of my speaking, my experience was misled by the fuedalist preservationism of the landowning class and its cohorts.)

Let us return to the episteme or mind-set that persistently undoes the conflict between right and responsibility. Our right or truth *is* to be responsible, in structurally specific ways. (The structure leads to hierarchy, to caste, to bureaucracy, which must be persistently undone.) The imperative comes *in* being-human, not necessarily in conscience, *from* planetary discontinuity. This is historically a precapitalist mind-set. Almost all examples of this that we have today are compromised by the victory of capitalist imperialism and by the conflict between different transcendental figurations of the source of the imperative for responsibility. On the other hand, so-called remedies for the current situation, whose goal still remains sustaining profit maximization, will only exacerbate the predicament that calls forth meetings such as the one I was addressing that evening.

As I have pointed out in Chapter 9 of this book, "What's Left of Theory?," the heritage of the public use of reason—shorthand for Enlightenment-model social engineering on the Left as well as the liberal-capitalist center—cannot think responsibility and right together. This contradiction—seen as that between reason and faith—is put beautifully by Goldschmidt: "we must learn to know, it is an enrichment; faith makes humble, it is to be gripped."[13]

Also in "What's Left of Theory?," I have indicated Mahmood Mamdani's understandable difficulty in thinking "responsibility." Michel de Certeau speaks with rare understanding of "*collective fragments of memory* [which] constitute, whether consciously or unconsciously, the roots or the 'fixed points' by which a collective irreducibility is engraved in individual members" (p. 161). Yet he too, like Mamdani, cannot get beyond the language of "collective *rights*" as "capable of balancing the economy that, in the name of individual rights, exposes the entire social reality to the great universal light of the market and of the administration" (pp. 290–291; emphasis added). On the other side, Lévinas's *autrui*—a nonspecific, pluralized otherness—is a nonphenomenological abstraction. His *visage*—too quickly translated as visage or face—is mostly a nominal construction from *viser*, to be directed toward, the verb of intentionality. The singular/universal remains a perennial moral dilemma, an ethical conundrum. Granted that this may be the outline of an irreducible experience of the impossible. But how can we loosen the bracket, how contaminate this austere landscape with the unevenness of grouped persons without falling into the abstraction of collective *rights*?

Learning the Aboriginal way of living as custodian of the planet—not part of your problem with immigration—is daily being compromised by the Development lobby's drive to patent not only so-called indigenous knowledge but the very DNA or life-inscription of the autochthone most separated from the cultures of imperialism. Bio-prospecting leads to bio-piracy, leading further to monocultures, leading to the death of biodiversity. Insofar as these rational projects are in the interest of globalization, you are indeed implicated in it, actively as capital, and passively as state.[14] Thus your goal, in spite of all appearances, cannot reduce itself to merely integrating the underclass immigrant into this economic dynamic. Think, therefore, the planet, as the merely imagined proper receiver and transmitter of imperatives.

Some years ago I received the hospitality of an Algerian migrant family in Lyons, France. M. Benmelouka had retired as foreman at the Ciba-Geigy factory after forty years of service there. There was no way I could say that I was on my way to Bangladesh, where I was joined in struggle in a movement against Ciba-Geigy and such companies, for the harm done to women and land through pharmaceutical dumping. The planet became invisible in mere personal goodwill.

Madame Benmelouka died earlier that year. I used to live in her empty tenth-floor apartment in Oran when it was still possible for me to go to Algeria. I remember her in her altogether less roomy apartment in Lyon, initiating me into the mysteries of the home dialysis machine on long loan from a local hospital through the National Health Service, and exclaiming "Vive la France!," even as she had exchanged invectives with a racist white girl at the telephone booth on the street. I cannot think that mixture of gratitude-in-racism as the goal of an enlightened multicultural policy.

In a magnificent passage in the "Critique of the Teleological Power of Judgment," Kant speaks of God:

> We can thus assume a righteous man [*einen rechtschaffenen Mann anne-hmen*] . . . who takes himself to be firmly convinced that there is no God. . . . He would merely unselfishly establish, rather, disinterestedly to establish the good to which that holy law directs all his power. But his effort is limited. . . . Deceit, violence, and envy will always surround him, even though he is himself honest, peaceable, and benevolent; and the righteous ones besides himself that he will encounter will, in spite of all their worthiness to be happy, nevertheless be subject by nature . . . just like all the other animals on earth, and will always remain thus until one wide grave devours [*verschlingt*] them all together . . . into the abyss of the purposeless chaos of matter from which they were drawn. . . . If he would remain attached to the appeal of his moral inner vocation . . . he must assume the existence [*Dasein*] of a *moral* author of the world, i.e., of God.[15]

I quote this passage rather than other, better-known ones because here, in a supplementary section of the Third Critique, Kant is writing with his guard down. Here the source of the imperative is frankly and repeatedly conceptualized as a supplement to Reason. I have argued this at some length in *A Critique of Postcolonial Reason*.[16]

The European secularism that took its strength from such moves, resting upon a division not only of Church and State but also upon the separation of public and private, will not stand to support a world devastated by the capitalist adventure. As a corollary to increasing globalization, whatever your national economic convictions, industries and services will privatize. This meaning of "private" is not, of course, identical with what is meant when we speak of the secular separation of the public and the private. However, given that welfare services that do not come under the rubric of corporate philanthropy are increasingly dependent, in this restructured world, upon voluntarism—the imperative for social welfare becomes increasingly "private," as we privatize.

There can be no doubt that "democracy" in the general sense is an unquestioned good. But there can be no doubt, either, that in our current predicament, confidence in the formal democratic structures of civil society as sanctioning a cultural—public or private—superiority from which to dispense bounty to the migrant cannot find support. In the decolonized world, we have seen—repeatedly—the appropriation of democratic structures—the vote as body count—to move the polity toward theocracy. Elections in the United States would be bathetic in their histrionics if the results were not so consequential. In the global context, precisely because the limits and openings of a particular civil society are never transnational, the transnationalization of global capital requires a post-state class-system. The use of women in the establishment of this system is the universalization of feminism of which the United Nations is increasingly becoming the instrument. In this re-territorialization, the collaborative non-governmental organizations are increasingly being called an "international civil society," precisely to efface the role of the state. Winston Churchill's *boutade* about democracy will no longer serve today if the system stands alone. It is necessary today at least to attempt to fill it with an agency other than a private goodwill whose imperatives are at best received from a supplement to reason. This developed postcapitalist structure must once again be filled with the more robust imperative to responsibility which capitalist social productivity was obliged to destroy. And, to repeat, the imperative must be understood and valued (an aesthetic education!) as *defective for capitalism* rather than necessarily *pre*-capitalist on an interested sequential evolutionary model. Capital, being the abstract as such, has no other path but toward globalization. Human beings are not only abstract, as even rational expectations must admit. Hence an unequally developed world, and hence, as I have argued above, its consolidation through the World Trade Organization. I quote that touchstone passage yet again.

> If however wages are reduced to their general basis, i.e. that portion of the product of his labour which goes into the worker's own individual consumption; if this share is freed from its capitalist limit and expanded to the scale of consumption that is both permitted by the existing social productivity . . . and required for the full development of individuality; if surplus labour and surplus product are also reduced, to the degree needed under the given conditions of production, on the one hand to form an insurance and reserve fund, on the other hand for the constant expansion of reproduction in the degree determined by social need; if, finally both (1) the necessary labour and (2) the surplus labour are taken to include the amount of labour that those capable of work must always perform for those members of society not yet capable, or no longer capable of working—. . . then nothing of these forms remains, but simply those bases [*Grundlagen*] of the forms that are communal [*gemeinschaftlich*] to all social modes of production.[17]

Acknowledging the tremendous social productivity of capital (rather roughly equivalent to economic growth in Development parlance), Marx wrote this subjunctive formula for the transition from capitalism to socialism, but did not live to specify, if he could have, the magic for its continued exercise. In the event, the planning was as disingenuous internally as it was systematically thwarted externally. The development of the welfare state thrived on the edge of multiparty democracies that prided themselves on a "liberal revolution." Under globalization, pushed by postcoloniality and a reported "ethnic cleansing" that often denies colonial constitution of history and applies a double standard on the legitimacy of mass destruction, that pride too is crumbling. Western critics like Jean-François Lyotard, seeing pride go in both social justice and economic growth, had diagnosed postmodernism.[18] I say, looking back to the impractical philosopher who had tried to turn economic growth around to social justice, that the subjunctive can move to an imperative only in terms of that responsibility-as-right fixed by a truth-in-alterity collective structure that happened to have been conceptualized as *haq*. This is my supplement to dialogics, from the other side. Use the Enlightenment from below, from a gendered *haq*-laced space, shorthand, this, for the training of the imagination for epistemological performance of a different kind, called an aesthetic education when institutionalized.

I want it to be understood that I am not speaking for Islam. It so happens that I have linguistic access to how the youngest people of the Book institutionalized the practice and thus began its effacement. How ethics separated itself from the law in the history of Islam has been recorded by Fazlur Rahman.[19] And, like most cultural logics institutionalizing responsibility, Islam has historically allowed the woman to take the other's part within it.

I should also mention that I am not speaking for cultural identity either. I was not born a Muslim. Indeed, as a caste Hindu, my identity-claims rest on an obliteration of the Muslim heritage of my national space. I am resolutely against the reduction of the ethics of alterity to a politics of identity, pro or contra, yours, ours, or theirs. What I am offering for our consideration is not historically Muslim, as was not the *Muselmann* in the concentration camp.[20] It is rather the lineaments of a social practice of responsibility based on an imperative *grounded* on alterity. As we have already noticed, Abdelkébir Khatibi has claimed that, in Islam, this grounding was writing rather than sacrifice.[21] I am not competent to investigate such niceties.

I am simply suggesting that, without an education into an epistemic transformation whose most efficient description I happen to find in *haq,* capital—industrial and finance—cannot be persistently checked and turned around to the interest of the social as practically laid out in the Marxian passage, which has not grown old. I am further arguing that this social practice of responsibility based on an imperative imagined as intended from alterity cannot today be related to any named grounding—as in Kant or Islam. This is where educating into the planetary imperative—assuming and thus effacing an absolute and discontinuous alterity comfortable with an inexhaustible diversity of epistemes—takes its place.

I am further suggesting that, rather than honoring the historical happenstance, that the rational machine of capital logic required the destruction of this understanding of the individual, and thus dismiss it as "precapitalist," we might imagine it animating and in-spiriting the abstract structures of democratic guarantees, which are indeed a great good. Speaking in South Africa, I have argued that democratic freedoms—both freedom from and freedom to—can be free as guarantees but can be exercised only when bound. Here also I resonate with Goldschmidt's work, but I cannot locate it in the dialogics of reason with a named faith. I must take another step—the contradiction between planetary *poiesis* (imaginative making) and a named faith with an inherited record. To Switzerland, the European nation-state with the longest history of liberalism—and conscientious about multicultural policy, however restricted—I said in 1997: bind it to a re-constellated planetary imperative to responsibility, seen as a right precomprehending becoming-human, where the proper name of alterity is not God, in any language. In the United States at least, children's multicultural education divides into two broad areas: education into tradition and education into modernity. The following random example will give a sense of the divide. If I had bothered to update it, I would have been swamped with examples, every day, on every front.

On August 23, 1997, New York 1 News reported approvingly on two children's programs. One, called "Passing On," trained them in Caribbean dance steps. The other, where they got t-shirts, took them to the floor of the New York Stock Exchange. This too is children's education: relegating "tradition" to "culture" and a past museumized into a dynamic present being played out on the subject's involvement with the Stock Exchange.

If in the area of cultural practice, multicultural demands circle around religious observance and (usually female) dress code; in the arena of education, multicultural demands, since they are usually emergent from economic migration (even when ostensibly seeking asylum), remain content to accept this divide.

I am asking you to imagine something different, much harder, not a quick fix. Something that you will never hear in discussions of multicultural policy. I am daring to take dialogics to its logical consequence: as a stereotyped example of an earlier-phase postcolonial still "responsible" within a monstrous hybrid "faith" without a Book—though constantly competing for one in "globalatinization"—I suggest that we have something to learn from the underclass immigrants, in the interest of a more just modernity: the remnants of a responsible pragma.[22] I am asking if together we can re-invent this pragma to fit, however unevenly, the democratic structures of civil society. I am therefore suggesting that both the dominant and the subordinate must jointly rethink themselves as intended or interpellated by planetary alterity, albeit articulating the task of thinking and doing from different "cultural" angles.[23] What is new here is that the dominant is educated, persistently to attempt, at least, to suspend appropriation in its own interest in order to learn to learn from "below," to learn to *mean* to say—not just deliberately non-hierarchically, as the U.S. formula goes—I need to learn from you what you practice; I need it even if you didn't want to share a bit of my pie; but there's something I want to give you, which will make our shared practice flourish. You don't know, and I didn't know, that civility requires your practice of responsibility as pre-originary right.

(This is still pertinent, but seems completely undoable now, because there are so many pretend ways in action.)

To teach this saying is the support that cultural workers and educators can provide globally. It requires earning a right to win responses from both sides—responsibility once more.

I think the real winners in this transaction will have been women, on both sides. Let this remain a conjecture for the future anterior, to be opened up, again and again.

How is this to be done? Civil policy makers will have to learn some languages, clearly. Thus it involves changes in civil service training as well. The structure of general education will have to change some as well. (It requires a shift in emphasis in education, especially in children's education, where the mind is set in habits.) The real requirement is diversified social tact, persuasion rather than coercion. I am not speaking of an easy or cheap change. But if the exchange is a two-way road, a practical dialogic, as I have proposed above, there can be no question of interfering with the languages of national and international governance, for those control the abstract structures of civil society.

Under imperialism, the colonized often suggested that they had the better spiritual and the colonizer the better material culture. This view has always been dismissed as at best disingenuous, and at worst hypocritical. It has repeatedly been pointed out that this slogan was one way of keeping women backward, as holders of spiritual culture. If structurally planetarized and persistently freed from the accouterments of the cultural markers of migrant national origin on the part of the subordinate, and equally persistently freed from the nationalist prejudices of the dominant, the truth of this perception can be tested.

Otherwise, as it stands today, demands for "cultural" autonomy within a multicultural state is no more than a reaction to xenophobia and the lack of access to untrammeled upward class-mobility, combined with reaction-formation to cover over the guilt at having left the very "culture" that one wishes to conserve. Once upwardly mobile, a counter-modernity is claimed for the entire spectrum by the section that moves up far enough to set cultural definitions.

I have spent a good long time speaking of re-constellating the responsibility-thinking of precapitalist societies into the abstractions of the democratic structures of civil society, to use the planetary—if such a thing can be used!—to control globalization interruptively, to locate the imperative in the indefinite radical alterity of the other space of a planet to deflect the rational imperative of capitalist globalization: to displace dialogics into this set of contradictions. It cannot be denied that I have been speaking of what may result in persistently critical institutional practice: politico-economic and ideologico-pedagogic accountability. The kind of lesson that I have learned from a more European ethical philosophy would suggest that institutional practice forgets ethical cautions, as follows: Our life is lived as the call of the wholly other, which must necessarily be answered (in its forgetting, of course, assuming there had been a gift in the first place in the subject's unanticipatable insertion into temporality), by a responsibility bound by accountable reason. Ethics as experience of the impossible—therefore incalculable—is lived as the possible calculus that covers the range between self-interest and responsibility that includes the politico-legal. Justice and law, ethics and politics, gift and responsibility are structureless structures because the first item of each pair is neither available nor unavailable. It is in view of justice and ethics as undeconstructible, as experiences of the impossible, that legal and political decisions must be made, empirically scrupulous but philosophically errant. (Even this opposition is not tenable to the last degree.) The calculus of the second item in each pair such as the ones named above is imperative for responsible action, always in view of this peculiarity. These pairs are not interchangeable, but move on an unconcatenated chain of displacements. In each case, the "and" in the pair opens up the task of acknowledging that the copula "and" is a "supplement" covering an indefinite variety of relationships, since the supplement both supplies a lack and adds an excess. When the thinking of this structureless structure turns to multicultural imperatives within a new Europe, it seems not to be able to move outside of thinking Europe as the giver—of hospitality, or neighborly love. It circles and recircles cosmopolitheia. This is, indeed, part of my response to Jean-Luc Nancy. This supremacism won't do any more.[24] As we have seen in the "Critique of the Teleological Power of Judgment," alterity becomes a mere supplement as the ethics of alterity changes to a politics of European identity. We must give to it a proper name within a planetary graphic, not within a continental metonymy. If religion is the mobilizable instrument of the subaltern, this will accommodate many subaltern pasts, release it from the dated burden of mere messianicity. We cannot simply feel accountability in terms of border crossings and free frontiers, while the head of the superpower state justifies NATO intervention in the name of an accountability where messianicity becomes indistinguishable from manifest destiny. We must think our individual home as written on the planet as planet, what we learn in school astronomy. In this defracted view of ethics, Space may be the name of alterity, not time, not nation, not mother, not *visage* as intending.

In conclusion, then, I repeat my invitation, sheltered within, but also a codicil to, Goldschmidt's thought. Imagine yourself and them—as both receivers and givers—not in a Master-Slave dialectic, but in a dialogic of accountability. Zurich must remember Geneva—where on a worldwide scale the gifts of the battered poor responsibility-cultures are being chained in Trade-Related Intellectual Property Rights, and military peacekeeping is imposing hasty binary explanations upon the heritage of older empires: Bosnia, Rwanda. In the interest of globalization. It is within this framework, thinking the world, not just the nation-state, that I say to all of us: let us imagine anew imperatives that structure all of us, as giver and taker, female and male, planetary human beings.

CHAPTER SEVENTEEN

Reading with Stuart Hall in "Pure" Literary Terms

A LAS, the only double bind here is that anybody so carefully trained in reading may not want to engage in globe-correcting politics. Produce large numbers of such readers and you may not need the correction. Utopia.

This, then, is a reading of Jamaica Kincaid's *Lucy*, based on the conviction that rhetorically sensitive approaches to literature enhance rather than detract from the political. Indeed, in order "to give an account, within a materialist theory, of how social ideas arise," it is possible to call upon the resources of a rhetorically sensitive reading of literature.[1] If *Lucy* is read without that sensitivity, it is a story about a situation, not a subject. If read in its literariness, however, it erases the migrant-as-victim into the unmarked ethical agent. There is a homology between that erasure and the classic Marxist transcription of the worker from victim to "agent of production." I read *Lucy*, paying attention to it as a paratactic event, as resisting "the preferred reading,"[2] the reading in black and white, the reading of the story as race-class-gender predicament of the migrant situation. This is not a popular position, but I have long drawn comfort from Stuart Hall's fighting words, which describe

> fundamental agreements . . . bind[ing] . . . opposing positions into a complex unity, . . . effect[ing] its systematic *inclusions* (for example, those "definitions of the situation" which regularly . . . "have access" to the structuring of any controversial topic) and *exclusions* (for example, those groups, interpretations, positions, aspects of the reality of the system which are regularly "ruled out of court" as "extremist," "irrational," "meaningless," "utopian," "impractical," etc.). (CM, p. 346)

Playing in such a "structured ideological field," in the academic work-place in the United States, the "Cultural Studies" style of work in litera-ture is today encouraged to remain narcissistic, question-begging, ridden with plot summary and stereotypes, citing sensational detail without method, a quick-fix institutionalization of heroic beginnings in Birming-ham. ("I don't know what to say about American cultural studies. I am completely dumbfounded by it.") I find myself insisting on restoring rhe-torical reading practices because I believe, in an irrational, utopian, and impractical way, that such reading can be an ethical motor that undermines the ideological field. If to be born human is to be born angled toward an other and others, then to account for this the human being presupposes the quite-other. Such presuppositions can battle bodies-without-organs like "the nation." This is the bottom line of being-human as being-in-the-ethical-relation. By definition, we cannot—no self can—reach the quite-other. Thus the ethical situation can only be figured in the ethical experience of the impossible. And literature, as a play of figures, can give us imaginative access to the experience.[3]

In today's United States, the ethical is dominantly inscribed into the phrase "human rights." Class struggle has given way to the impatient triumphalism of human rights expressed as politico-economic blackmail leading to military intervention; or to "the suppression of the savage," as in NGO "gender training," which swiftly suppresses primitive gendering in order to create the individual.[4]

I agree with Hall's prescient formulation that

> the various discourses . . . of individual "rights and duties," of "free agents," of the "rights of man" and of "representative democracy"—in short, the whole enormously complex sphere of legal, political, economic and philo-sophical discourses which compose the dense ideological complex of a modern capitalist society, all stem from or are rooted in the same premises upon which the market and the ideas of a "market society" and of "market rationality" are founded. . . . It is also crucial that "ideology" is now under-stood not as what is hidden and concealed, but precisely as what is most open, apparent, manifest—what "takes place on the surface and in view of all men." What is hidden, repressed, or inflected out of sight, are its real foundations. This is the source or site of its *unconsciousness*. (CM, pp. 324, 325)

It is this site of *unconsciousness* that a literary reading may open up. This is not a recommendation for the psychoanalytic investigation of lit-erature or society. "Unconsciousness" is a textual figure, not the uncon-scious. "It is . . . in this general sense that Althusser speaks of ideology as 'that new form of specific unconsciousness called 'consciousness' '" (CM,

p. 326). We can use another formulation here, and say that the text makes available "the hinterland of migrancy," in a rhetorical rather than a polemical frame.[5]

It is not that *Lucy,* or any novel, is a text for imitation. It is just that if we constitute ourselves as the implied reader of the novel, we move from rights as problem solving (the opening page of the novel) to responsibility as the ability to love (the end). If the first step of socialism is to claim rights, the second step is to acknowledge responsibility: "A training in literary reading is not a sphere where a socialism [as rights/responsibility], a socialist culture—already fully formed—might be simply 'expressed.' But [the literary classroom] is one place where socialist ethics might be remotely constituted. That is why ['literature'] matters. Otherwise, to tell you the truth, I don't give a damn about it."[6]

Events described in narrative fiction never really happen(ed). If we want to read narrative fiction in a specifically "literary" way, we have to admit that what happens on its pages is language or prose. Roman Jakobson, one of the leading linguists of our century, made the point that the specifically "poetic" or "literary" function of language is in play or at work where what matters is the message itself, not what the message says. Common sense tells us that Jakobson must be correct. Although we often treat narrative literature as if it is gossip about nonexistent people, or something the author is trying to tell us directly, in doing so we go against the specific nature of literature. The things described in narrative fiction did not really happen. And if the author were addressing you directly, he or she would find out who you were and write the message clearly in expository prose, perhaps using some examples, but certainly not simply "tell a story!"

What happens in literature *as* literature is the peculiarity of its language. I don't know all the literatures of the world. But the phenomenon that what happens in literature *as* literature is the peculiarity of its language applies to the literatures I can move around in: English, Bengali, French, German, Sanskrit, Hindi, Greek, Latin, Spanish, Italian—all Indo-European. It is of literature written in English that I mostly write, even more often of literature produced in the United States—"American Literature," as it is called. There I am confident that my bit of common sense will apply: What happens in literature *as* literature is the peculiarity or singularity of its language. Paradoxically, it is through attentive practicing of the singular rhetoricity of language that the imagination is trained for flexible epistemological performance. This is rather different from "learning about Antigua" (by chance the birthplace of the author) by the quick fix of fiction, or confirming foregone conclusions—pro or contra—about the experience of black au pairs in white liberal families. If "the same story" is told again in other words, it ignores the fictive or literary quality of fiction.

With this simple conviction in hand, I will read Jamaica Kincaid's *Lucy*.[7] What mainly happens in this novel is, I believe, parataxis.

According to the *Oxford Companion to the English Language*, "parataxis" means "punctuating two or more sentences as if they were one. Placing together phrases, clauses, and sentences, often without conjunctions, often with *and, but, so* and with minimal or no use of subordination." Etymologically, it means "placing side by side." It is borrowed from the name of a military formation. "Parataxis" is a fine old Greek word which has described this particular characteristic of linguistic practice for a thousand years or more.

I would even like to propose that, with this literary characteristic of placing side by side without conjunctions, *Lucy* resists and alters any reading that would categorize it only by its subject-matter—a story about a migrant governess, and therefore an instantiation of received ideas about hybridity and diaspora. There is such massive immigration into the United States that many books of so-called literary criticism do produce such categorization. Yet I think it may be said that if we paid attention to the singularity of the language happening in examples of narrative fiction, we would often find that that piece of work resists categorization by general remarks that we could make by considering simply its story line.

By looking at the singularity of language happening on the page, we do not ignore the story line. Language cannot happen without content. It is just that focusing on the singularity of the language allows us to notice that the literariness of literature makes the language itself part of the content. (This happens in life too, but we take it for granted. I would give you examples, if I weren't eager to get to parataxis, get to *Lucy*.)

Parataxis is to place side by side without conjunctions. The poet and critic Bob Perelman makes large claims for parataxis. But he also quotes an impatient critic who sees only its negative value: " 'It is the product of a generation raised in front of a television: an endless succession of depthless images and empty sounds, each canceling the previous one.' "[8] Perelman knows, however, that the power of language can only operate on the reader reading. And readers are made, not born. You have to learn to read, by way of aesthetic educations of diversified provenance. If the critic and teacher is able to produce readers who can receive the power of language, the power of parataxis (the power in language to withhold its own power of making connections) need not perish. That is why reading is taught, today institutionally, in the past culturally, in the family, gender-compromised, class-compromised, race-compromised, perhaps, but still taught, before today.[9] Thus I want not just to describe the novel, but to move step by step into a reading of the singularity of its language. And this kind of skill can only be seen as useless when language is being uniformized. The university is corporate, and our upper administration will not understand this.

The title is simply the first name of the central character. As you take the first step into the story, therefore, you realize that the putting together of the "I" that inhabits the name may be what it is "about," as you may with any text that names itself in this way. In order to see if it is so, and then, after taking note that indeed it may be so—"It was my first day," the book begins—you try to see how it is that the book goes about it. And you notice that the sentences seem mostly to be simply placed side by side: "It was all wrong. The sun was shining but the air was cold" (p. 5) is a pretty typical example.

But you notice something more. That the absence of connection that is the mark of a paratactic style infects the storyline as well. The singularity of the language—an overwhelming sense of parataxis (and how the relatively more connected passages negotiate it)—becomes a formal description, a homology for what the language describes. Because the Jakobsonian "poetic" or literary function takes over, we recognize it as a novel. This is partly what Roland Barthes taught us thirty-four years ago, in his powerful essay "Introduction to the Structural Analysis of Narratives": "It is therefore legitimate to posit a 'secondary' relation between sentence and discourse—a relation which will be referred to as homological, in order to respect the purely formal nature of the correspondence." Bits of narrative relate to each other to make a chain of meaning that is like a sentence laid out as a relief map.[10] In this novel the sentences and, seemingly, the narrative are arranged paratactically.

Let us look at a few passages.

"When they were gone away, I studied my books, and at night I went to school. I was unhappy. I looked at a map. An ocean stood between me and the place I came from, but would it have made a difference if it had been a teacup of water? I could not go back" (pp. 9–10).

This is an example of paratactic writing from the opening section, "Poor Visitor," where Lucy arrives in the United States as an au pair. Here is her description of parataxis on a higher level of homology—a description of "a famous building, an important street, a park, a bridge when built was thought to be a spectacle" (p. 3). These are places that are ranged one after the other, just like sentences in parataxis: "These places were points of happiness to me. . . . I would imagine myself entering and leaving them, and . . . entering and leaving over and over again—would see me through a bad feeling I did not have a name for" (ibid.). Entering and leaving over and over again to see one through a bad feeling without a name is the paratactic affective structure, the minimum with which the text sets out to establish the subject. We could think of this as the rhetorical representation of a withdrawal from affective connectives, whether before or after the diasporic cut, but prior to questions of hybridity.

"Now that I saw these places, they looked ordinary, dirty, worn down by so many people entering and leaving them in real life, and it occurred to me that I could not be the only person in the world for whom they were a fixture of fantasy" (p. 4). It occurred to me that I could not be the only person in the world living in affective parataxis: this is the minimal resource with which the subject sets out. (By "subject" I always mean the capital "I" that is the figure of the speaker or focalizer in the novel, neither subject-matter nor character.)[11]

It is in the third section, "The Tongue," that homological parataxis becomes the theme of the text. "Tongue" is a metonym for language itself.

(A metonym is as ancient a name as parataxis. It means "change of name." According to the *Oxford English Dictionary:* "a figure of speech which constitutes in substituting for the name of a thing the name of something closely related.")

Language or a tongue is that with which we communicate. But in this section, the tongue is a metonym for (the failure of) sexual contact. "Sucking tongue" (p. 43), in a marvelous appropriation of adolescent language, is shown to be without affective content even when accompanied by all the appropriate physical signs of affect: "For a long time I had understood that a sigh and shudder was an appropriate response to a tongue passing along the side of your neck" (p. 49).

We could pass this off as an accurate description of the sexual instincts of adolescent libido, but it is the power of repeated parataxis, entering and leaving experiences with licking and shuddering that relates more to the fact that this is narrative *fiction* we are reading. Here, for example, is a description of Mariah, Lucy's mistress, and her husband, Lewis: "After Lewis licked Mariah's neck and she leaned against him and sighed and shuddered at the same time, they both stood there, as if stuck together. . . . But to look at them, they seemed as if they couldn't be more apart if they were on separate planets" (pp. 48–49). And Lewis's loss of love for Mariah is discovered by the subject in the following way: "I saw Lewis standing behind Dinah, his arms around her shoulders, and he was licking her neck over and over again, and how she liked it" (p. 79).

Yet the "I" of *Lucy* does not grow into "something real" as she enters and leaves transactions with the tongue.

There is Hugh, her holiday love affair, where the reader senses some advance in loving. Yet her leavetaking from him has the classic paratactic connective. It is the singularity of the language rather than some hint of plot line that establishes the narrative cue. First, there is a sentence about her girl-friend Peggy, with whom she has very little in common. They had been disappointed in a boy they meet on an evening out in the City. That is what the subject recalls, without a connective, as she says goodbye to Hugh: "We [Peggy and I] were so disappointed that we went back to my room . . . and kissed each other until we were exhausted and fell asleep. Her tongue was narrow and pointed and soft. And that was how I said goodbye to Hugh, my arms and legs wrapped tightly around him, my tongue in his mouth, thinking of all the people I had held in this way" (p. 83). "And that was how." Not a logical connective, at all.

No. This is not a matter of an adolescent sexual initiation where the subject connects without connecting. This, to repeat, is parataxis as dominant narrative figure running reading, where the absence of conjunction is felt as absence, if we read for singularity of language, respecting literature as fiction. Kissing Peggy can have no useful affective correspondence with kissing Hugh on the story line.

In the next section we move to other body parts. If we are tracking prose happening, it is as if the subject is unable to enter whole persons. It is as if the ethical semiosis parsed by Melanie Klein is coming undone. When Lucy meets Paul, the reader again feels that a progress has been made in the skill of loving. And yet, if we pick up the prose signals, we encounter a body part—Paul's hands—and an aggressively paratactic presentation of a memory: "Paul's hands, as they moved about the tank, looked strange also; the flesh looked like bone, and as if it had been placed in a solution that had leached all the life away. And I remembered this" (p. 102).

This is followed by a most peculiar and lengthy memory of her disappointment that she was not sexually abused as a child. The sequence ends with the admission that she did not know what the genial abuser's hands were like: "But his hands—what did they look like? I did not know, and I never would know. And so it was"—surely the reader is meant to notice that this is altogether hopeless as a connective—"and so it was that hands, moving about in the fish tank—reminded me of some other hands lost forever in a warm sea" (p. 109).

The last section of the book is called "Lucy," and here this structure—of spatio-temporal progress measured paratactically—is particularly pronounced. "It was my first day"—the first line of the entire novel and a personal statement without anchor that soon marks a false hope—has changed to the austere and unassailable correctness of "it was January again," but the parataxis is thicker. "The world was thin and pale and cold again"; the sentence continues, "I was making a new beginning again" (p. 133). Certainly this chapter-opening has an ironic relationship to the book-opening. But my point is that this is not achieved by a resolution of parataxis—but rather, with the insistence on "again," its thickening.

One may say that for "Lucy" the chapter, *Lucy* the book is a "past," the subject's brief metropolitan history. It is therefore interesting that the chapter is insistent, in its figuration, not upon the seamlessness of the past and the present, or upon their discontinuity, but upon their paratactic relationship. They are arranged side by side. Suddenly, the past happens as past. "I had begun to see the past like this: there is a line; you can draw it yourself, or sometimes it gets drawn for you; either way, there it is, your past, a collection of people you used to be and things you used to do" (p. 137). Even the passage about spatio-temporal parataxis is given in parataxis. It is an abyssal homology. A paragraph follows where "I used to be" is repeated like an incantation. And then an announcement of the final movement of the novel, still relentlessly paratactic, describing the departure from the country of origin: "My leaving began on the night I heard my father had died" (p. 138).

The only way that this thickening of parataxis is interrupted is by the use of the word "remind." It is time now to speak of Lucy's mother. *Lucy* cannot inhabit the proper name "Lucy" because the subject resists what it perceives as an indistinguishability from the mother: "My past was my mother," the book says in the next to the last section, entitled "Cold Heart."

> I could hear her voice, and she spoke to me not in English or the French patois that she sometimes spoke, or in any language that needed help from the tongue; she spoke to me in language anyone female could understand. And I was undeniably that—female. Oh, it was a laugh, for I had spent so much time saying I did not want to be like my mother that I missed the whole story: I was not like my mother—I was my mother. (p. 90)

It is when she speaks of her mother that she signals beyond language: "not a language that needed help from the tongue"; and, earlier, "I had come to feel that my mother's love for me was designed solely to make me into an echo of her; and I didn't know why, but I felt that I would rather be dead than become just an echo of someone. *That was not a figure of speech*" (p. 36; emphasis added). This emphatic assertion of an unwanted continuity is also prior to hybridity or diaspora.

It is Mariah, with her sincere but historically contaminated desire to establish a multiculturalist feminist bond, who helps her, however unwittingly, to come to a resolution of this problem that a figure of speech—like parataxis—cannot control. (Is there a lesson for the international civil society here?) If we are reading the book as literature, this is the only real problem that the text can declare. "The times that I loved Mariah it was because she reminded me of my mother. The times that I did not love Mariah it was because she reminded me of my mother" (p. 58). This is the failed invitation to assimilate—benevolent multiculturalism inviting to dominant hybridity through "gender training." The subject grasps this in terms of the only model of continuity available to it: the good and bad mother.

> Mariah left the room and came back with a large book and opened it to the first chapter. She gave it to me. I read the first sentence. "Woman? Very simple, say the fanciers of simple formulas: she is a womb, an ovary; she is a female—this word is sufficient to define her." I had to stop. Mariah had completely misinterpreted my situation. My life could not really be explained by this thick book that made my hands hurt as I tried to keep it open. (p. 132)

This is the very end of the next to the last section. It is after this that we will graduate to the last section, named "Lucy," where a canny reader will hope for a fulfillment of the project of a book whose title is a first name. What is it that Mariah's book teaches the subject? That simply rejecting the explanation of woman as mother will not explain Lucy's life as woman. The section has one more sentence, which simply refers to the sentence in Mariah's book as "that." "My life was at once something more simple and more complicated than that: for ten of my twenty years, half of my life, I had been mourning the end of a love affair, perhaps the only true love in my whole life I would ever know" (p. 132).

This mysterious passage, describing a past that is bigger than the book, can be explained by Lucy's story about her mother, also given in this section: "I was not an only child, but it was almost as if I were ashamed of this, because I had never told anyone, *not even Mariah*. I was an only child until I was nine years old." The love affair mentioned in the previous passage had ended when she was ten,

> and then in the space of five years my mother had three male children; each time a new child was born, my mother and father announced to each other with great seriousness that the new child would go to university in England and study to become a doctor or lawyer or someone who would occupy an important and influential position in society. . . . Whenever I saw her eyes

fill up with tears at the thought of how proud she would be at some deed her sons had accomplished, I felt a sword go through my heart, for there was no accompanying scenario in which she saw me, *her only identical off-spring,* in a remotely similar situation. . . . As I was telling Mariah all these things . . . I suddenly had to stop speaking; . . . my tongue [mark this important metonym] had collapsed in my throat. (p. 130; emphasis added)

This is no cliché of so-called diasporic experience, for what is envied is the brothers' brighter diasporic future; nor is it a simple rage of black against white. If one wants to reduce *this* to a formula, one might say: the solution to our Mothers' cultural gendering in the country of origin is not Eurocentric economic migration felt as diaspora. Further, the quick "gender training," now offered by big non-governmental organizations like Oxfam, training women to be women, the newest twist of global feminism, however good hearted, is no solution. "Mariah wanted to rescue me" (p. 130). The problem is not solved by rage against Mariah. The telling of this story to her contradicts the book's paratactic vision of "the past," fulfills the text's dramatic irony, making it bigger than the narrator. To see how the resolution of this problem exceeds the book, we must digress.

It is well known that the word "diaspora" means something like "scattered abroad" *dia + speirein* (to sow). Moses predicted that the Jews would be dispersed if they did not obey the Ten Commandments, although "it is particularly to be noted that deportation to a foreign land . . . is not the *sole* prospect which the author holds out before his people, it is but one beside many other afflictions, most of which are to fall upon Israel in its own land."[12] Diaspora is one of the punishments a people suffers if it disobeys the law. In Deuteronomy, the book of the Old Testament where the curses are uttered, they are balanced against the rewards (indistinguishable at this stage from blessings) that are earned if the people obey. Deuteronomy was among the first books of the Bible to be translated into Greek, which gives us the word "diaspora."

> The Pentateuch [the first five books of the Bible] was translated into Greek in Egypt before the middle of the third century B.C. . . . The evidence shows that it was prompted by the need of Jews in Egypt for a version of the Scripture in the Greek language (then more familiar to them than Hebrew or even Aramaic) either for public use in the synagogue or for private reading and study.[13]

Diaspora is thus full of affect. The word is given wide currency among migrant groups today for the sake of the affect. But the connection with responsibility and reparation—we are here because we are guilty, by some unspecified guilt against the law—is now gone or legitimized by reversal: we are here because you are guilty. *Lucy* questions this easy reversal. We cannot evaluate diaspora from this text.

The narrative (rather than merely linguistic) style of *Lucy* delivers a devastating judgment upon herself and brings back the ancient diasporic thematic of responsibility and reparation. For her, "diaspora" or "migration" is a way of using parataxis, a severing of connection as a solution—rather than the source—of a problem. We receive the shock of that displacement in the very beginning of the novel: "Oh, I had imagined that with my one swift act—leaving home and coming to this new place—I could leave behind me, as if it were an old garment never to be worn again, my sad thoughts, my sad feelings, and my discontent with life in general as it presented itself to me" (pp. 6–7).

This does not mean that the themes that we have come to expect in novels of underclass female migration ("diaspora" in the Euro-U.S. today) are absent in *Lucy*. Some of the analysis and descriptions of Mariah do indeed fit those expectations. Indeed, here again we encounter distinctions in hybridity, a comment on the desire to claim hybridity:

> "I was looking forward to telling you that I have Indian blood [Mariah tells her, for example]. . . . But now . . . I feel you will take it the wrong way." . . . Wrong way? Right way? What could she mean? . . . My grandmother is a Carib Indian. . . . My grandmother is alive; the Indians she came from are all dead. . . . In fact, one of the museums to which Mariah had taken me devoted a whole section to people, all dead, who were more or less related to my grandmother. (p. 40)

"[H]er novel *Lucy* runs a rich white urban family through the shredder of a young black au pair's rage," a critic writes.[14] Yet to reduce the novel to just that race-class subplot is not only to miss that the subject here dismisses all museumization of cultures of origin but also the displacing power of parataxis.

Lucy is not able to love Mariah, *as she is not able to love anyone, as she is not able to love her mother*. In *Lucy*, Lucy is not defined simply by the binary opposition of "rich white" and "black au pair," by, as it were, Hegel's famous Lordship and Bondage dialectic, where what "the bondsman does is really the action of the lord." In the beginning, love itself is disparaged because Mariah can love.

Before we consider how the paratactic rhetoric of the novel works to question the self-indulgences of contemporary diasporism, let us consider the subject's inability to establish a connection with her proper name through the history of its other holders: John Milton's Lucifer and William

Wordsworth's Lucy; her inability, in other words, to inhabit colonial hybridity in comfort.

Kincaid's early education had been "anglophile." Could she have known that, like most of the English Romantics, Wordsworth undertook to rewrite Milton? I cannot know, and in the end perhaps it does not matter, or matters differently, as I will suggest at the close of the chapter, in a feminist way, a woman's way. But first the names themselves.

Her naming as Lucifer comes after her love affair with her mother has ended. "Under her breath she [my mother] said, 'I named you after Satan himself. Lucy, short for Lucifer. What a botheration from the moment you were conceived.' I not only heard it quite clearly when she said it but I heard the words *before they came out of her mouth*" (p. 152; emphasis added). Again, beyond (or short of) language.

Lucy resents her mother but accepts this name. "I did not grow to like the name Lucy—I would have much preferred to be called Lucifer outright—but whenever I saw my name I always reached out to give it a strong embrace" (p. 153).

Percy Shelley had suggested that, unbeknownst to the author, Milton's Satan, the light-carrying unbending rebel, is the hero of *Paradise Lost*:

> Nothing can exceed the energy and magnificence of the character of Satan as expressed in *Paradise Lost*. . . . Milton's Devil as a moral being is so far superior to his God as one who perseveres in some purpose which he has conceived to be excellent in spite of adversity and torture, is to one who in the cold security of undoubted triumph inflicts the most horrible revenge upon his enemy.[15]

A plot summary reading of *Lucy* may take on such a reading. But this praise of individualism is not enough for a mother-daughter relationship severed by economic migration in search, precisely, of possessive individualism. Before the book ends, the subject will claim Lucifer in a less transparent way, as she tastes the moral dilemma of diasporic guilt, when metropolitan multiculturalist judgment is accepted and transformed: "Mariah said that I was feeling guilty. Guilty! I had always thought that was a judgment passed on you by others, and so it was new to me that it could be a judgment you pass on yourself. Guilty! But I did not feel like a murderer; I felt like Lucifer, doomed to build wrong upon wrong" (p. 139). Notice once again Mariah's crucial role. The subject is now able to state the text's end, in the broadest possible sense: "The Lucy was the only part of my name I cared to hold on to" (p. 149), although the logic of the story would give this the lie.

In terms of the story, her naming by her mother may have happened before her reading of Wordsworth's "The Daffodils," and certainly before the visit organized by Mariah to show her the flowers that she had only read about but never seen. In textual time, however, this realization of what had been the epistemic violation of an earlier form of colonialism—memorizing Wordsworth in school—comes before. This scene of violation or makeover is what produces colonial hybridity. The general style of the passage continues to be paratactic. If we are reading only for "what the plot called for" (p. 6), the exchange between characters as "real" people can be read as expected: determined by received ideas of race and class; and by gendering as understood by a cultural difference imagined by an author who knows the dominant pretty well: "It wasn't her fault. It wasn't my fault. But nothing could change the fact that where she saw beautiful flowers I saw sorrow and bitterness" (p. 30).

But we must remember that what is being undermined by Mariah is not some authentic cultural experience of origin or identity, but the memory inscribed by a colonial poetry lesson upon a Caribbean island. That memory can be fitted into a thoroughly historically organized narrative, the story of colonial occupation. Yet, if we have been following the homologies of a general parataxis along various levels, we can even read that historical narrative itself as two "sentences," describing the same space, once as "precolonial," and again as "colonial," one after the other, one over the other, the other under the one, with no connection but violation, the type case of colonial hybridity. Nothing to celebrate, but a kind of intimacy with the other nonetheless, an enabling violation, the imaginative sedimentation of the civilizing mission. On this level of homology, it may be said that Lucy wants to save that parataxis from the too-quick ministrations of the metropolitan multiculturalist.

Jamaica Kincaid glosses this in her own case:

> And I thought how I had crossed a line; but at whose expense? I cannot begin to look, because what if it is someone I know? I have joined the conquering class: who else could afford this garden—a garden in which I grow things that it would be much cheaper to buy at the store? My feet are (so to speak) in two worlds, I was thinking as I looked farther into the garden and saw, beyond the pumpkin patch, a fox. . . . In the place I am from, I would have been a picture of shame. . . . In the place where I am from, I would not have allowed a man with the same description as such a woman to kiss me.[16]

Kincaid is talking about entering the imperial class by having a garden in the United States. She is not crossing the color line but a class line. She is not talking specifically about race, but about empire. In the essay from which this passage is quoted, the talk is of Mexico and the Aztecs, of the British Empire, of the hybridization of plants, of the prejudice in an Oxford reference book on gardening. It is a gloss on entering "Mariah"'s class as

Kincaid's work becomes a textbook read by immigrant schoolgirls in the schoolrooms of the new metropolis, United States, the postcolonial superpower. In the case of the old colonialism, which, famously, had wanted to breed "a class English in everything but blood," Lucy had bridged the gap of parataxis with duplicity, the technique of the colonial subject in the "past" of the book. Postcolonial history, not global contemporaneity.

Perhaps such daytime duplicities are exploded by dreams. After the first day that begins the new life—the book we hold in our hands—Lucy attempts to use the marks of her failure to conceal the failure of connection. She tells her dream of the night before, precisely to these new colonizers. All subjects made over by old colonialisms negotiate these alliances in the new metropolis. It is hard to put neat plus and minus signs—like "black" and "white." This is the typical postcolonial double bind. This is what Kincaid's text plays out, *as literature*. The subject gives us a clue. At the end of the first section, she tells her dream to both husband and wife, her masters, and Lewis simply makes fun of her in the name of Freud. Uncomprehending, the subject ends the first section with these words: "I had meant by telling them my dream that I had taken them in, because only people who were very important to me had ever shown up in my dreams. I did not know if they understood that" (p. 15). After this begins a section, entitled simply "Mariah," where a real bond is established, to be half-rejected because the mother must be half-mourned. And before that half-rejection can be signaled at the end of the book, one realization is given in a curiously flat paragraph that seems to escape parataxis:

> I had realized that the origin of my presence on the island—my ancestral history—was the result of a foul deed; but that was not what made me, at fourteen or so, stand up in school choir practice and say that I did not wish to sing "Rule, Britannia!" . . . I disliked the descendants of the Britons for being unbeautiful, for not cooking well, for wearing ugly clothes, for not liking to really dance. . . . If only we had been ruled by the French. . . . I understand the situation better now; I understand that my pen pal [from a French island] and I were in the same boat. (pp. 135–136)

If this is postcolonial solidarity, hard enough to achieve, alas, in the autobiographical passage there is the unease of diaspora. Kincaid worries that she has entered the conquering class at the expense of someone she knows, that her own people would be profoundly ashamed of her access to class privilege. The novel will play this out differently at its end.

Will Wordsworth, if I read him as a metonym for the imaginative riches of the colonizing tradition, offer Lucy an answer?

(A metonym, let us recall, is as ancient a name as parataxis. It means "change of name." The *Oxford Companion to the English Language* says it is "a figure of speech which designates something by the name of something associated with it." A figure of speech does not obey the handbooks exactly. You learn how to recognize them by family resemblance, as it were. We substitute the name "Wordsworth" for the name "colonial imagination," then. One is something more than an example of the other, since Kincaid is not writing us directly. Because he figures in a novel, I read "Wordsworth" here as a figure. But a figure cannot be stripped of content. It says something by the very logic that allows us to recognize it as a figure—a logic that rests not only on the history of the language but upon "empirical" history. The British took part of the West Indies. Wordsworth was taught to West Indian schoolgirls. That figures in our story. Our cue is daffodils. But Wordsworth had a famous Lucy. Some say his Lucy poems are his best work. And our story wants to fill that proper name with being. What was Wordsworth's Lucy like? Perhaps this can be called "intertextuality.")[17]

Wordsworth's Lucy had little being of her own, existing on the page only to inspire the poet. By the end of the Lucy sequence, death in infancy has emptied her name of all human and individual significance. One may say that, in the world of literature, where singularity of language is all that happens and remains, Lucy had died in order that the "I" of the poem might know what Karl Marx called species-life, and Hegel the innocence of not-doing *(Nicht-thun)*: "Nature is the human being's *body without organs,* that is to say nature in so far as it is not the human body."[18] Wordsworth's Lucy is immortal because Nature is her great body without organs, neither hearing nor seeing:

> No motion has she now, no force;
> She neither hears nor sees.
> Rolled round in earth's diurnal course,
> With rocks, and stones, and trees.

The subject of *Lucy* wants to be able to act in her proper name. The paratactic relationship with nature marks an even more intimate break than the suture of the precolonial and colonial worlds. It is a relationship—a relationship without relationship, Nature my body without organs, is before and after I am proper to myself, although always there. It is pre- and post-propriation. "My" birth and death are events within it. That relationship is before and after the gift of time, if there is any, that allows us to be proper to ourselves. Just weather. Planetary. Antidote to stupid globality, mean, racist, and benevolent.

Thus the Wordsworthian line leads only to a redoubled parataxis for the subject of *Lucy*. It leads not only to the parataxis between the mind-sets of the colonizer and the colonized, but also between species-life and species-being—being-nature and being-human. This last one is also the parataxis between genders if you like, since Wordsworth, like most men of two hundred years ago and many men now, used women to develop a sense of self (which then works a vice versa, Gramsci's sister-in-law, Wordsworth's sister, Shelley's wife, selfless caregivers, literary angels) and *his* Lucy may be a splendid example of that. The name misfires there as well. We have already seen the paratactic failures of connection between the subject of *Lucy* and men in sexualized gender roles.

As "Jamaica Kincaid," the author of *Lucy*, without any noticeable "feminist" declaration, wants to claim responsibility for the human part in nature. At the end of the passage I have already quoted, we saw her looking at a fox. Let us pick up where we left off: "That night, lying in my bed, I heard from beyond the hedge where he had emerged sounds of incredible agony; he must have found his prey; but the fox is in nature. . . . *I am not in nature.* . . . To me, the world is cracked, unwhole, not pure, accidental; and the idea of moments of joy for no reason is *very strange*" (emphasis added). It is the distinction between being-in-nature and being-in-culture, based on the traditional definition of the animal as such, that allows her the diasporic responsibility of the Eurocentric economic migrant, a displaced line of the unreasonable ethical guilt of the Jew in diaspora as outlined in Deuteronomy. For the responsible diasporic, that is the strangeness of felt joy, when I feel I may have entered the conquering class at the expense of people whom I might know. It is that uncertainty of the "might"—"what if" in the Kincaid passage—that is the secret of this responsibility. It is noticeable that Kincaid, again with no flags raised, takes the gender-active part also when she invokes the place left behind: "I would not have allowed a man with the same description as such a woman to kiss me."

Following the singularity of its language, reading *Lucy* as a piece of literature, we may glimpse a critique of a politically correct and self-indulgent bit of contemporary diasporism—a real playing out of colonial and diasporic hybridity, where diaspora is a class line, even if not perceptible from the metropolis. *Lucy* is a book of arrested passage.

We can follow this singularity page by page, sentence by sentence, word by resonant word, and our enjoyment of *Lucy* as literature will be enhanced. Here let us move to the very last sentence of the novel, which will show us that the subject will accede to her name somewhere outside of this text, this story. And in that accession, "Wordsworth" and "Mariah" will be revised, as well as the too-quick readings that reduce all diasporic narrative to victimage and/or resistance.

Let me explain the idea of something taking place outside the text. This cannot be "true," of course. Yet, if what happens in the literary text is the singularity of its language and that singularity is in its figuration, that figuration can point to the depth of the content by signaling that the content cannot be contained by the text as receptacle. To note this is not to say that the text has failed. It is to say that the text has succeeded in signaling beyond itself. It is high praise for the book, not dispraise. It may also be, if repeated with many texts, training for an activism with an eye to the future anterior, exceeding one's grasp.

It is through the logic embedded in figuration that the text points. As we know, metaphor is the chief of figures. *Lucy* ends with a metaphoric sequence that signals beyond itself.[19]

The subject of *Lucy* wants to be the subject loving, not merely the object of love. This may be represented by the sequence that closes the text. The opening of the notebook—a beautiful notebook that Mariah has given her as an expression of real solidarity, in response to the subject's remark that "my life stretched ahead of me like a book of blank pages" (p. 163)—may be the beginning of a new text, a text that will do what *Lucy* has only tried: to speak the subject in its own name. We had nothing but the first name—parceled out between Milton and Wordsworth—in the first try. This new text will be specifically hers. The subject writes her full name: Lucy Josephine Potter. ("Jamaica Kincaid" happened to have a three-tiered name as well: Elaine Potter Richardson.)

As she focuses upon her name, her inability to love "'someone so much that I would die from it'" (p. 164) overwhelms her. The tears come as a surprise, not motivated by the subject who wants to be herself. Yet they are not an example of affective parataxis. Unlike her own descriptions of sex, feeling is here securely tied to gesture—the shame brings the tears. Her name is washed away until there is nothing but a blur. The text that will live in this new (note)book cannot be an access to the self, but rather an access to others, through a self-annihilating love. "Wordsworth" had not been able to name the other as a self. But that other text toward which *Lucy* travels beyond its own pages will correct that error by turning the name of the self not into a blank but a productive blur.

Perhaps. That book, not being in language, has no guarantee. Characterologically, if one thinks of Lucy as a "real" person, there is also no guarantee in that contrary temperament. She "is" more like Milton's Lucifer. The text tugs in the other direction. The virtue of Jamaica Kincaid's book is this push-and-pull between "Lucy" and *Lucy*. For any promise of a step beyond is also a reminder that the text is staged as not performing that step. Once again, this is not dispraise, but praise of the text's organization, which it would perhaps be better to call "formalization."

This may, in the end, be the singularity of this text, a singularity it shares with *A Question of Power,* a novel by the Southern African writer Bessie Head. The migrant woman of color is not allowed to be the unmarked subject of loving. It is the benevolent master who is allowed to love the victim. When a novel that seems an obvious example of black diasporic writing inhabits a theme of unmarked loving, we cannot read it. In that other book, the love for Mariah, which cannot emerge because of the criticism of her inherited and therefore chosen way of life, will take shape for a reader, as much as her love for her mother, which cannot emerge out of hatred. Perhaps. Perhaps. For that is not a book, but simply a part of the task of reading this one. The book swings between symptom and critique.[20] Remember that in globalization, in its simulacral contemporaneity, we must learn to think of all ways to modernity as just history.

In an interview with Jamaica Kincaid, Leslie Garis quotes Henry Louis Gates Jr: "She never feels the necessity of claiming the existence of a black world or a female sensibility. She assumes them both. . . . We can get beyond the large theme of racism and get to deeper themes of how black people love and cry and live and die."[21]

Gates is right, of course. I should like to add a rider. Not just black people, but people. This is not to write off black specificity by claiming history-transcending universality for great art. It is to question why white specificity is unmarked as "white," whereas black specificity cannot choose to be so. When a novel that seems an obvious example of black diasporic writing inhabits a theme of unmarked loving, we cannot read it: "It seemed almost incidental that he was African. So vast had his inner perceptions grown over the years that he preferred an identification with mankind to an identification with a particular environment. And yet, as an African, he seemed to have made one of the most perfect statements: 'I am just anyone.' "[22]

This passage is the opening of *A Question of Power.* If we work at the weave of desire in it, we will get to what I find in *Lucy:* a longing for unmarked humanity, without denying black specificity; an access to the subjectship of loving, "perhaps . . . the whole universe . . . that was another perfect statement, to him—love was freedom of heart," writes Bessie Head. Like Lucy, Head's unmarked man is flawed in loving, more so, characterologically, because he is a man, and because he is not the protagonist.

I should like to repeat here something I said in an interview:

> Cultural studies is a study of teleiopoiesis [imaginative interruptions in struc-
> tures of the past], which is the domain of the metropolitan minority claim-
> ing a history that makes the metropolis possible. It's not the domain of what
> is called post-colonial criticism, which is to reclaim a history that was al-
> lowed to stagnate—on the way to an unmarked modernity. Chinua Achebe is
> the noblest model of this, and the moment of that innocent reclaiming is
> now past.

"Unmarked modernity" is the synchronic statement entailed by an
"unmarked being-in-time," where "cultural" identity seems "natural" and
pre-comprehended. One can then be the subject of loving rather than, at
best, an object of benevolence. *Lucy*'s longing points to what *may* be an
impossible book, but also may not. Perhaps. The difference between a
blank—an absence—and a blur—something there to remake.

We who are from subordinated cultures must ab-use the new as agents
as we mourn the past with appropriate rites as subjects—a necessary but
impossible task of cultural translation, bigger than any individual narrator. It is the singularity of the language of the novel that led me into this
reading; yet even this can have no adequate justification, for it may be
that the textuality of my stereotype of myself led me to this reading. The
power of fiction is that it is unverifiable. To learn to read fiction is to
work with this power.

The moment for postcolonial longing may be past. And Perelman writes:
"In the seventies, . . . faith in the rebirth of modernist ambition and of the
cultural centrality of poetry was easier to maintain. Today parataxis can
seem symptomatic of late capitalism."[23] When was the postcolonial, indeed? Even late capitalism has now given way to the late late show—
global capital.

Toni Morrison's *Beloved* stages not parataxis, but hypotaxis—a style
some say is the exact opposite of parataxis, where many sinuous clauses
modify and intermodify each other as the long sentences move dream-
like. And yet, just as *Lucy* finally uses parataxis to point to a connected-
ness outside the covers, perhaps, so does *Beloved* use hypotaxis, a style of
passing on and into the next sentence, to pronounce, in the end, "This is
not a story to pass on." Sethe, as daughter and mother, caught between
slavery and citizenship, can only half-mourn, as I argue in "Acting Bits/
Identity Talk," Chapter 7 in this book. Is this because women, by historical definition, not essence, relate differently or obliquely to the history of
language, especially public language—published literature—which is also
singular and unverifiable? (The matrilineality of slavery is no exception to

this.) If you take another famous American pair—Hemingway, fiercely paratactic, perhaps most so in *The Old Man and the Sea;* and Faulkner, text sinking under the weight of hypotactic sentences signaling a history that has gone awry by its very weight—you will not find such rhetorical irony. I do not offer this as conclusions, but questions. The only way to consider them is to read these texts in the singularity of their languaging. Otherwise, to tell you the truth, I don't give a damn about it.

Lucy shows a resistance to multicultural hybridization by falling on colonial hybridization, the subjectivity of the colonial subject. "The notion that only the multi-cultural cities of the First World are 'diaspora-ised' is a fantasy which can only be sustained by those who have never lived in the hybridised spaces of a Third World, so-called 'colonial', city."[24] I would now like to take a step beyond the novel, and conclude by introducing a problematic that the discussion of diaspora and the third world can take on board.

After the gradual dismantling of the big colonies and the New Immigration (after 1947 and 1965), and the dubious end of the Cold War (1989), a certain ideologeme has been cooking itself in the Euro-U.S. socius: that the migrant has no history and not enough class to make a difference. Over the years, my greatest debt to Stuart Hall has been his discussion of ideology. Hall's tracking of ideology helps me to pursue this ideologeme.

In 1981, Stuart Hall wrote: "The more or less continuous struggle over the culture of working people, the labouring classes and the poor . . . must be the starting point for any study . . . of the transformations of . . . popular culture" (DP, p. 227).

The stability of the factory floor disappeared overseas with post-Fordism, international subcontracting, and the progressive feminization of labor. The predominance of finance capital and the "spectralization of the rural" in globalization today (as I describe it in "What's Left of Theory?," Chapter 9 in this book) occlude the question of organized labor.[25] Willy-nilly, the removal of the place of origin of the migrant from the history of the present (although sometimes secure in the consolidation of a glorious past)—Etienne Balibar and Martin Bernal, let us say—reflects this seeming disappearance of the internationally differentiated question of class, so that even the new transnationalist radical, focused on the migrant as an effectively historyless object of intellectual and political activism, works to conserve a strengthened metropolis, culturally destabilized, but economically not displaced from its exploitative position, as the migrant is inserted into the circuit of hegemony. Here is "a very severe fracture, a deep rupture—especially in popular culture in the post-war period. . . . Not only a matter of a change in cultural relations between the classes, but of the changed relationship between the people and the concentration and expansion of the new cultural apparatuses themselves" (DP, p. 230). I feel that a rhetorical reading of *Lucy* can be expanded into a literary representation of "the criticism to which such an ideological complex is subjected by the first representatives of the new historical phase" (Gramsci, cited in DP, p. 237).

The paradox of this emergent ideological formation is precisely that, within the metropolis, it produces the simulacrum of liberating the masses from "their subordinate place." But the world is larger than the metropolis. We might therefore complicate the privileging of hybridity in the diaspora with the question of colonial hybridization in the interest of a looser and more global definition of class. Otherwise, and by a quite different kind of generalization,

> in the sphere of the state and juridico-political ideology, the *political* classes and class relations are represented as individual subjects (citizens, the voter, the sovereign individual in the eyes of the law and the representative system, [the migrant, the minority], etc.): and these individual political legal subjects are then "bound together" as members of the *nation,* united by the "social contract," and by their common and mutual general interest. (CM, p. 337; emphasis added)

I have emphasized the word "political" because the argument here is not only economic. This gives us the possibility of expanding the class argument into a consideration of the migrant as Janus-faced in the history of the present, especially when a second-, third-, or many-generation hyphenated metropolitan hybrid is called upon to fulfill a demographic political or economic agenda in the interest of the metropolis; play Madeleine Albright to the bombing of the Balkans.

CHAPTER EIGHTEEN

Terror: A Speech after 9/11

AM REVISING this as a debate continues over the new Islamic Cultural Center (always referred to as a "mosque") near the site of the World Trade Center towers. The issue is being used to discredit Barack Hussein Obama and to bring down the Democratic Party. The debate is actually a double bind, but cannot be perceived as such: a rational abstraction—the right to build on private property, over against outrage in the family of the victims, whose lives were casually extinguished, apparently in the name of Islam. It will be decided, one way or the other, as the victory of one side over the other. You figure out how a generalized aesthetic education as social support might have helped here.

I

The ruminations that follow arose in response to America's war on terror.[1] In order to preserve its historical detail, I have preserved the Bush-era references. The general argument applies, mutatis mutandis, to the present situation.

I started from the conviction that there is no response to war. War is a cruel caricature of what in us can respond. You cannot be answerable to war.

Yet one cannot remain silent. Out of the imperative or compulsion to speak, then, two questions: What are some already existing responses? And, how respond in the face of the impossibility of response?

When I thus assigned myself the agency of response, my institutionally validated agency kicked in. I am a teacher of the humanities. In the humanities classroom, I still believed, begins a training for what may produce a criticism that can possibly engage a public sphere deeply hostile to the mission of the humanities when they are understood as a persistent attempt at an uncoercive rearrangement of desires, through teaching reading. Before I begin, I would like to distinguish this from the stockpiling of apparently political, tediously radical, and often narcissistic descriptions, according to whatever is perceived to be the latest Euro-U.S. theoretical trend, that we bequeath to our students in the name of public criticism. Uncoercive rearrangement of desires, then; the repeated effort in the classroom. Thus I found myself constructed as a respondent.

A response does not only suppose and produce a constructed subject of response; it also constructs its object. To what, then, do most of these responses respond?

The "war," on the Taliban, repeatedly declared on media by representatives of the U.S. government from the president on down, was only a war in the general sense. Not having been declared by act of Congress, it could not assume that proper name. And even as such it was not a response to war. Today there is talk of reconciliation. The detainees in Guantánamo Bay, as we were repeatedly reminded by Right and Left, were not prisoners of war and could not be treated according to the Geneva Convention (itself unenforceable) because, as Donald Rumsfeld said, among other things, "they did not fight in uniform."[2] The United States is fighting an abstract enemy: terror. Definitions in Government handbooks, or UN documents, explain little. The war is part of an alibi that every imperialism has given itself, a civilizing mission carried to the extreme, as it always must be. It is a war on terror reduced at home to due process, to a criminal case: United States vs. Zacarias Moussaoui, a/k/a "Shaqil," a/k/a "Abu Khalid al Sahrawi," with the nineteen dead hijackers named as unindicted co-conspirators in the indictment, now serving a life sentence without parole.

This is where I can begin: a war zoomed down to a lawsuit and zoomed up to face an abstraction. Even on the most general level, this binary opposition will no longer stand. For the sake of constructing a response, however, a binary is useful. To repeat, then, down to a case, up to an abstraction. I cannot speak intelligently about the law, about cases. I am not "responsible" in them. I turn to the abstraction: terror-ism.

Yet, being a citizen of the world who aspires to live and prosper under "the rule of law," I will risk a word. When we believe that to punish the perpetrators as criminals would be smarter than, or even more correct than, military intervention, we are not necessarily moving toward a lasting peace. Unless we are trained into imagining the other, a necessary, impossible, and interminable task, nothing we do through politico-legal calculation will last, even with the chanciness of the future anterior: something will have been when we plan a something will be. Before the requirement of the emergence of a specific sort of "public sphere," corollary to imperial systems and the movement of peoples—when different "kinds" of people came to live together, such training was part of general cultural instruction.[3] After, it has become the especial burden of an institutionalized faculty of the humanities. I squash an entire history here. Kant's enlightened subject is a scholar.[4] In "Critique of Violence [*die Gewalt* is also Power and Force]" Benjamin writes: "What stands outside of the law as the educative power in its perfected form, is one of the forms of appearance of divine power."[5] I happen to be a Europeanist, but I have no doubt at all that historically marked intuitions about the importance of the educative moment is to be found in every cultural system. What seems important today, in the face of this unprecedented attack on the temple of Empire, is not only an unmediated intervention by way of the calculations of the public sphere—war or law—but training (the exercise of the educative power) into a preparation for the eruption of the ethical. I understand the ethical, and this is a derivative position, to be an interruption of the epistemological, which is the attempt to construct the other as object of knowledge. Epistemological constructions cover the broad spectrum between the domain of the law and formal and informal education, which seeks to know the other, in his or her case, as completely as possible, in order to punish or acquit rationally, reason being defined by the limits set by the law itself. The ethical interrupts this imperfectly, to listen to the other as if it were a self, neither to punish nor to acquit.

Public criticism today must insist that no amount of punishment, legal upon individuals, or military and economic upon states and collectivities—indeed, military and economic *rewards* such as invitation into alliances or entry into the World Trade Organization—is going to bring lasting change, an epistemic shift, however minor. We must also attend upon a preparation for the ethical upon which we must attend. And that is where the public epistemological responsibility of the humanities may be situated, but will no longer be allowed to function.

By contrast, the "War on Terror" has generated an intense resurgence of nationalism and some resistance, consolidated by an act of Congress: the Patriot Act. There was an unexamined assumption by academic intellectuals that, because the world economic system acts multi- and trans-nationally, even globally at the top, a seamlessly ideological post-nationalism is the contemporary episteme. That bit of irresponsible thinking has been given an indecent burial; an unintended consequence, but a consequence nonetheless. As I have been insisting, this assumption of seamless post-national contemporary is what requires the damage-control of an aesthetic education, not a top priority for tertiary education anywhere.

Women are prominent in this war on terror, this monstrous civilizing mission. We cannot ignore the very vocal, fresh-faced women shown by CNN at the helm of a U.S. aircraft carrier. One of them, unnervingly young, said to the viewers: "If I can drive an aircraft carrier I can drive any truck." This was in response to the most bizarre example of single-issue feminist patter that it has been my good fortune to hear from the mouth of a male CNN correspondent: "No one will be able to make sexist jokes about women drivers any more." All women? The "women of Afghanistan" are coded somewhat differently.[6]

Given this gender-prominence, a feminist critical theory must repeat that expanding the war endlessly will not necessarily produce multiple-issue gender justice in the subaltern sphere. The most visible consequences—the exacerbation of state terror in Israel, Malaysia, India, and elsewhere—have nothing to do with gender justice at all. If ruined Kabul is an "international city" of a rather different kind from Abd-ur Rahman's dream at the end of the nineteenth century, with perhaps a UN peacekeeping force in place, and constant access to the globalized version of U.S. local culture, something consonant with U.S. and UN gender politics will again emerge as part of social consciousness.[7] But these gender-sensitive groups will represent the subaltern as little as, indeed possibly less than, RAWA (Revolutionary Association of the Women of Afghanistan). There are now female U.S. combatants "making connections" with Afghan women. Time will not allow an analysis of this effort. There is no possibility, in an American protectorate, of gender holding the repeated and effortful turning of capital into social, which is the best of the counter-globalizing struggle. That happened in the era of the seventies "new" social movements in what we now call the "global South."

The most difficult thing as the emancipation of women by the United States is celebrated over and over again is an assessment of the Soviet regime. Middle-class women are emerging from where they were before the Taliban sent them underground. Everybody knows the United States created the Taliban. Indeed, in these times of quick-fix political education to match the flavor of the week, this is often the acme of left-liberal knowledgeability. But why were these women flourishing as professionals under the Soviet regime? There is a singular ignoring of the history of the development of the Afghan intelligentsia and its genuine involvement with the Left.[8]

There is an internal line of cultural difference within "the same culture." The emancipation of women has forever followed this line and that story is bigger than wars, if anything can be. I comment on it in Chapter 5, "Culture: Situating Feminism."

Another response to Terror has been to put quotation marks around it—to commodify it, relexicalize it for History and Geography, museumize it. At the soft end of this is the marketing of a sentimentalized 9/11 that is altogether offensive and continues to this day. To this a superficial but scrupulous public criticism of the visual culture industry can surely apply. Contained within it there are arresting metonyms that negotiate the area between the hard and soft:

> Behind an adjacent tarpaulin-cloaked fence topped with barbed wire [at Ground Zero] . . . splinters from the soaring television antenna that marked the highest point in New York City—1,732 feet into the sky—sit on their sides, right next to the punctured, debris-choked remains of Fritz Koenig's great spherical bronze sculpture, the former centerpiece to the trade center's ground-level plaza, interpreted as a symbol of world peace through trade. And nestled against the Koenig globe is . . . a charred and pitted lump of fused concrete, melted steel, carbonized furniture and less recognizable elements, a meteorite-like mass that no human force could have forged, but which was in fact created by the fiery demise of the towers.[9]

An objet trouvé, because "world peace through world trade" is a lie. Shades of Kant! And the forces are human. The Koenig globe—marked as was Yeats's lapis lazuli—has now been installed as a memorial at Historic Battery Park on the Eisenhower Mall near Bowling Green, adjacent to the Hope Garden. The Sphere, as it is called, is lexicalized into the text of New York as the capital of capital, into a phrase in the imaginary that will contain the signifiers History (Eisenhower, Battery Park), Space (Battery Park, Bowling Green, Garden), and Hope. "9/11" is as powerful as ever; Ground Zero remains a bit of a real-estate squabble, now solved.

Close to the event, there were the conceptual banalities accompanying what is no doubt much more interesting architecturally, at a number of shows, from which I choose at random a show called "A New World Trade Center" at the Max Protetch Gallery in New York.[10] At one end the most lasting memorial—a response to the time of terror by spacing—the classic model of writing—Stonehenge-model slabs fixing the exact position of the sun during the two attacks, "Zero Zones," designed by Raymund Abraham. At the other end the typical pomo exhortation to active forgetfulness: "Let's not even consider remembering. . . . What for?" offered by Foreign Office architects for their plioform snakelike towers. In between there were other conceptualities including a vaguely leftish

criticism of the towers as buildings: "Jet(tison) the past, out-of-sync anyway (US = bigness, power). Out of the Tower ruins will emerge generative
matter" (Thomas Mayne, Architects). The wildest of them, twin towers
of light, representing the inscription of the towers as noumenal rather
than phenomenal, was the temporary memorial chosen by the City.

Of all the responses, I find this middle-of-the-road trend the most reas-
suring. The Euro-U.S. has always been good at museumization. The quotation marks neutralize, although here too political art can fuel martial art
and the task of responsibility is never closed. This response is now mired,
of course, in the conflict between competition sculpture, the Lower Manhattan Development Corporation, and the conventions of mourning. And,
many conflicts later, the mosque dispute.

I come now to the second part of my remarks: what response to offer
in the face of the impossibility of response.

The stereotype of the public intellectual, from Fareed Zakaria, then with
Newsweek International (now CNN) to Christopher Hitchens, the free-
lance British gadfly, would offer statements describing U.S. policy, coming
out promptly in response to every crisis. This is undoubtedly worthy, often
requiring personal courage, but it is not a response. It enhances the cha-
risma of the intellectual and produces in the reader a feeling of being in
the thick of things. This type of cognitive mapping, heavily dependent
upon the fieldwork of frontline investigative journalists and humble
gatherers of statistics, legitimizes by reversal the idea that knowledge is
an end in itself or that there is a straight line from knowing to doing politics as human rights or street theater. But to respond means to resonate
with the other, contemplate the possibility of complicity—wrenching
consciousness-raising, which is based on "knowing things," however superficially, from its complacency. Response pre-figures change. Reading
Aristotle and Shelley, students typically ask: What is the difference between prediction and pre-figuration? The difference is, negatively, in the
intending subject's apparent lack of precision, in the figure; positively, it
is the figure's immense range in time and space. The figure disrupts confidence in consciousness-raising. That is the risk of a response that hopes
to resonate through figuration. When we confine our idea of the political
to cognitive control alone, this does not just avoid the risk of response;
it closes off response altogether. We end up talking to ourselves, or to our
clones abroad. Predictably, on left and right, you lose support when you
stop us-and-them-ing, when you take away the unself-critical convenience of doing good or punishing.

It is for such situations that Mahasweta Devi wrote: "There are people
for passing laws, there are people to ride jeeps, but no one to light the

fire."[11] (An aesthetic education may make people aware of this.) The response is in the fire. You get burned if you are touched and called by the other. If anything in what follows outrages you or seems not political enough, please remember this.

The traditional Left here in the United States and in Europe has by and large understood the events of 9/11 as a battle between fundamentalism and the failure of democracy. Being Indian, I look more at the Indian press, and the tone on the left there is less exclusivist. "Nineteen Arab men . . . brought their various frustrations onto four commercial aircraft," writes Vijay Prashad; "the impoverishment of other languages of social protest leads many young people to adopt the garb of Islam to articulate their alienation." Prashad's tone is fairly representative.[12]

By contrast, Noam Chomsky can be read as representing the dominant line on the U.S. Left: "'globalization,' or 'economic imperialism,' or 'cultural values,' [are] matters that are utterly unfamiliar to bin Laden and his associates and of no concern to them."[13] If, on the other hand, we think of the actants involved, politicized graduate students, rather unlike Chomsky's stereotype, we do not have to withhold from them the bitterness of understanding that, as the stakes in the Great Game shift, and Russia and the United States maneuver to come together over the black gold of the Caspian, bypassing the Taliban, who were flourishing on September 11, 2001, there was no hope that their cities would participate, to quote one of the innumerable World Bank Policy and Research Bulletins— this one entitled "Creating Cities that Work in the New Global Economy"— "in the changes [attendant upon world trade reaching more than $13 trillion in 1998, that] carry the promise of large gains for developing countries, but [only] expos[ure] to greater risks" to some among them.[14] Why can Islam not be a liberation theology for radicals from the middle-class elite as a great culture—called "Islam"—continues to get separated from the mainstream toward modernity? I hold no brief for liberation theology. Indeed, in the heyday of the gender-compromised Latin American liberation theology, I would often ask: "Why can't we have the liberation without the theology?" But the possibility must be granted if one is trying to imagine something different from the sorry stereotype.

I would agree with Professor Chomsky that the hijackers cannot be fully explained by globalization. But I would also agree with Vijay Prashad that 9/11, as it is being called now, is not just about religion. There is neither mourning nor execution without imagining the transcendental, and the transcendental, when imagined, has cultural names. But that is another matter, and, as I will argue in the final section, this set should not be given the blanket name "religion" too quickly. It is also true that a millennial confrontation is on record, as soon as Islam emerged out of its tribality, of which I as a Europeanist know the European side rather more. George W. Bush, if he had been literate, could have tapped the *Chanson de Roland*. Was it ever thus? I cannot know. Culture is its own explanations. Sayyid Qutb and Sheikh Ahmed Yassin tap into this too.

If this intuition—that culture is its own explanations—is credited, then anthropological ideas of culture and Marxist ideas of ideology hang out together. That "Muslims" explain things in terms of "Islam" and "Americans" in terms of "freedom" begins then to make a different kind of sense. The fragility of both under stress can then move, perhaps, toward understanding. The impersonal narrative of globalization: capital-formation producing, as much as managing, its crisis, explained as the progression from absolute state → colony → imperialism → empire is then less persuasive as the rational explanation of 9/11.[15] The explanation is contained rather in the ideology of thinking oneself the proper shadow of the transcendental—hence "global," in a historical as well as a contemporary sense. Thomas Aquinas wrenching Aristotle away from Ibn Rushd at the University of Paris in the thirteenth century is an example of this. This shadowy self-concept, unencumbered by history, but alive to visible injustice—military, political, and economic—is provided a semblance of access, speed, momentaneity by the Internet, producing a collectivity soldered by the intense male bonding of students living together, a political phenomenon well-known by all tertiary educators. It happens to soldiers too, of course, and guerillas—but I have easier access to the foreign student phenomenon. Through this access I am trying to go toward these uncanny young men. If MSNBC is to be believed, the one who actually flew the plane into the tower was eighteen years old! When Terry Castle writes with embarrassment about her fixation on the young soldiers in World War I, I perceive the risk-taking of a real response such as I too am attempting.[16]

No doubt the millennially imagined confrontation was present and communicated among the young men who executed the attack and who lie, unremembered, among the aggressively remembered 2,800. Although common sense would tell us that, once embarked upon the plan, it was the dream itself that enchanted them, and the millennial confrontational imaginary became the deepest of deep background.

Unremembered, yes. But when, in May 2002, New York presented a memorial, European and military in the spectacularity or visuality of its culture of mourning, they could not not welcome the seven hijackers who lie in that ground into the economy of Nature. There is no

apartheid in the transcendental, the abject relationship without relation to planetarity.

I will now quote at some length from the article "Temple Desecration
in Pre-Modern India" by Richard Eaton, published in *Frontline*.[17] But
first I want to mention a tiny but important detail that Syed Mujtaba Ali
recorded in his unpublished writings, that for centuries the Balkhi Afghans came to India to learn Farsi rather than go to Iran, and the major
premise of *Asia Before Europe*, that the Indian Ocean rim was a much
more important motor of cultural change than today's "national or religious identity"-based thinking.[18] It is also true that the connections between South Asian Islam, Iran, and Central Asia are historically strong.
Thus, even if we want to accept Chomsky's dismissal—they knew nothing of globalization—we can cite a cultural imaginary. Eaton writes of
"the sweeping away of . . . prior political authority," and continues:

> When such authority was vested in a ruler whose own legitimacy was asso-
> ciated with a royal temple . . . that temple was normally looted, redefined,
> or destroyed, any of which would have had the effect of detaching a defeated
> [king] from the most prominent manifestation of his former legitimacy.
> Temples that were not so identified but abandoned by their royal patrons
> and thereby rendered politically irrelevant, were normally left unharmed.

"It would be wrong," Eaton continues,

> to explain this phenomenon by appealing to an essentialized "theology of
> iconoclasm" felt to be intrinsic to the Islamic religion. . . . Attacks on images
> patronized by enemy kings had been, from about the sixth century A.D. on,
> thoroughly integrated into . . . political behavior [in the area]. . . . In short,
> from about the sixth century on, images and temples associated with dynas-
> tic authority were considered politically vulnerable.[19]

I am not speaking of intended rational choice. I am speaking of a cultural imaginary producing "reason," somewhat like the repeated marching band arrangement of the "Battle Hymn of the Republic" and the lav-
ish use of African-Americans in the preamble to the declaration of this
altogether catachrestic "war." It is possible to add to this by doing a riff
on the notion of dynasty displaced into lineages of class-mobility in the
U.S. context. I will do no more now than represent the confrontation
in September as the destruction of a temple—world trade and military
power—with which a state is associated. It may not be a referential message about the inequity of an ideology of trade and arms at all; not an
intended rational choice. And it helped that the buildings were tall, a fact
not unconnected with the representation of power. It is certainly reflected
on the other side in the Stonehenge-type projects, in the project that re-

flects twin beams of light as tall and thin as the erstwhile towers, "beacons of light as symbols of strength," or builds a World Art Tower behind an exact replica of Tower One, a hollow square arch flanking the filled one.

If the other side needs a temple, this side needs at least a word: "terror." Something called "terror" is needed in order to declare a war on it—a war that extends from the curtailment of civil liberties to indefinite augmentation of military self-permission.

Without the word "terror," this range of things, alibied in the name of women, cannot be legitimized.

I have been trying to open up that abstraction—"terror"—to figure out some possibilities. During these efforts, it has seemed increasingly clear to me that "terror" is the name loosely assigned to the flip side of social movements—extra-state collective action—when such movements use physical violence. (When a state is named a "terrorist state," the intent implicit in the naming is to withhold state status from it, so that, technically, it enters the category of "*extra*-state collective action.")[20] "Terror" is, of course, also the name of an affect. In the policy-making arena, "terror" as social movement and "terror" as affect come together to provide a plausible field for group psychological speculation. The social movement is declared to have psychological identity. In other words, making terror both civil and natural provides a rationale for exercising psychological diagnostics, the most malign ingredient of racism. I have neither the training nor the taste for such exercises. But I must still say that in the case of "terrorism"—sliding imperceptibly into "terror"—as social movement, the word is perhaps no more than an antonym—for "war," which names legitimate violence; but also an antonym, paradoxically, for peace. And here we could wander in the labyrinth where war and peace become interchangeable terms, although the status of war as agent and peace as object never wavers. Shades of Kant, again! We have come to accept the oxymoron: "peacekeeping forces." The United Nations High Commission for Refugees and Save the Children–UK, in a February 2002 report, asked peacekeeping missions to stop trafficking in women and girl children. Feminists agitate against the sexually rapacious behavior of "peacekeeping personnel."[21] The scandal of rape within the U.S. army is now well known. At the same time Barbara Crossette offers the conventional wisdom, in an article entitled "How to Put a Nation Back Together Again," that "faster-moving armies are necessary."[22] Here is the usual division between the various spheres of discourse, but they work within the same cultural imaginary, this time almost global: Conquering armies violate women.

Where "terror" is an affect the line between agent and object wavers. On the one hand, the terrorists terrorize a community, fill their everyday with terror. But there is also a sense in which the terrorist is taken to be numbed to terror, does not feel the terror of terror, and has become un-like the rest of us by virtue of this transformation. When the soldier is not afraid to die, s/he is brave. When the terrorist is not afraid to die, s/he is a coward. The soldier kills, or is supposed to kill, designated persons. The terrorist kills, or may kill, just persons. In the space between "terror" as a social movement and terror as affect, we can declare victory. Although civil liberties, including intellectual freedom, are curtailed, and military permissiveness exacerbated, although racial profiling deforms the polity and the entire culture re-designs itself for prevention, and although, start-ing on September 28, 2001, the UN Security Council adopts wide-ranging anti-terror measures; we can still transfer the register to affect and say: "We are not terrorized, we have won." And the old topos of intervening for the sake of women continues to be deployed. It is to save Afghan women from terror that we must keep the peace by force of arms. I want to distinguish the suicide bomber, the kamikaze pilot, from these received binaries.

Single, coerced yet willed, suicidal "terror" is in excess of the destruc-tion of dynastic temples and the violation of women, tenacious and pow-erful residual.

These comments on suicide bombing have provoked so much hostility that I include here some words of explanation that I offered to Dr. Mi-chael Bernet, in response to a specific query:

> I believe responsible humanities teaching strives at uncoercive rearrange-ment of desires in the student.
>
> An extreme violation of this responsibility is seen in groups such as Hamas or Islamic Jihad that coercively rearrange desires until coercion seems identi-cal with the will of the coerced. I, like many others, think that the conduct of these groups is tied to the extremist politics of the state of Israel. It must, however, be admitted that these groups are now out of control, not a little because it is not possible to credit any offer of "peace" as reliable.
>
> Those whose desires are re-arranged so as to undertake suicide bombing are typically the young, whose attitude to life is peculiarly vulnerable to such coercion.
>
> I am a pacifist, I cannot and do not condone violence, practiced by the state or otherwise. I therefore also believe that violence cannot be brought to an end by ruthless extermination. I believe that we must be able to imag-ine our opponent as a human being, and to understand the significance of his or her action. It is in this belief—not to endorse suicide bombing but to

be on the way to its end, however remote—that I have tried to imagine what message it might contain. Of course this does not mean each suicide bomber has these specific thoughts in mind! Here, too, I think things are out of control and whole generations have been affected. Mine may therefore be seen as the counsel of despair, but certainly not as an endorsement of violence.

It is convenient for the laws of war to distinguish between civilians and soldiers. It is just that there be law, but law is not justice. In view of justice and the discourse of the ethical, human life cannot be marked for death by positive law.

Single, coerced yet willed, suicidal "terror" is in excess of the destruction of dynastic temples and the violation of women, tenacious and powerful residual. It has not the banality of evil. It is informed by the stupidity of belief taken to extreme. It is we, who can no longer die young, who are banal, albeit with the banality of the merely quotidian. The Kantian sublime is, strictly speaking, and from the point of view of the spectator, for whom alone the sublime "is" sublime, stupid. The sublime is mindless. We bring it under something like control because "the rational vocation of our cognitive faculty" kicks in.[23] If in what I now say you feel distaste, even rejection, you will be tasting the *risk* in response. But do not mistake this for Stockhausen's aesthetic gush.[24] To legitimize the largest number killed by diagnosing "evil empire" is no good either way. That too is to close off response.

I am not suggesting that violence or the exercise of power, legitimized or delegitimized, is sublime in the colloquial sense. For me the word "sublime" (more than the German *Erhabene;* such is the force of English) has been forever marked by Kant. It names a structure: the thing is too big for me to grasp; I am scared; my moral will kicks in by the mind's immune system and shows me, by implication, that the big thing is mindless, "stupid" in the sense in which a stone is stupid, or the body is (*Oxford English Dictionary,* sense 2). I call the big mindless thing "sublime."

I am also not suggesting that political analyses and resistances and, on another level, aid and human rights are unnecessary. I am suggesting that if in the imagination we do not make the attempt to figure the other as imaginative actant, political (and military) solutions will not remove the binary which led to the problem in the first place. Hence aesthetic education in the exercise of the imagination.

Even within this suggestion, I am not describing all the acts of September 11, 2001 as "sublime" in the Kantian sense. It is an imaginative exercise in experiencing the impossible—stepping into the space of the other—without which political solutions come drearily undone into the continuation of violence. To paraphrase Devi: "there are many to offer political analyses and solutions, but no one to light the fire." Cultural instructions through the imagination in time of war are seen, at best, as aestheticization and, at worst, as treason. But that too is situational.

Suicide bombing—and in this case the planes were living bombs—is a purposive self-annihilation, a confrontation between oneself and oneself—the extreme end of auto-eroticism, killing oneself as other, in the process killing others. It is when one sees oneself as an object, capable of destruction, in a world of objects, so that the destruction of others is indistinguishable from the destruction of the self. The scary thing is that the destruction of the royal temple can be referenced as so transcendental a task that mere human lives become as nothing, theirs as mine. This is the moment one cannot, in principle, imagine—but no use covering that inability with that word again. We have no idea if these men had killed before—they don't seem different from foreign students anywhere. We hear from those phone calls from the planes that one of them cut a passenger's throat. It is a horrible detail. Was it to bring the aura of death into this "licensed lunacy," not merely to think it and have it happen, but pretend to have control over that *peu profond ruisseau calomnié la mort?*

Whatever it was, this act of global confrontation was neither resistance nor multitudinous. There is no such thing as collective death. It cannot be punished, despite the efforts at due process. It cannot be condoned as a legitimate result of bad U.S. policy abroad, as in the usual U.S.-centered political analyses. Such a gesture matches the media overkill to "mourn" the dead with every possible sentimentality, and thus attempt to contain the sublimity of Ground Zero. Many of us saw the second plane hit the second tower live (if that is the word) on that morning of September 11. That enclosed object, moving across a sunny sky quickly, with no special effects, hitting the tower and bursting into thick fire is "beyond Ate"—beyond "the limit that human life can only briefly cross."[25] Its unremarkable progress contained a collection of heterogeneous personal terror, connecting so desperately to transcendentality, that cannot be grasped. I cannot support violence rationally. But we must acknowledge the sublimity of terror, as in the inadequate name of a human affect beyond affect, rather than the catch-all name for any act of violence not authorized by the state.

The second plane, hitting, as seen live, can be imagined within the structure of the Kantian sublime conceived as a limit to imagining. On May 21, 2002, on *The David Letterman Show,* Diane Sawyer kept saying, "Charlie [Charles Gibson, the other anchorperson] and I were in denial as we were commenting"—and that denial is the moment in the structure described in the Analytic of the Sublime when the subject feels "displeasure from the inadequacy of the imagination."[26] I was watching that channel on September 11, 2001. I have no memory of their "denial," and that too computes. Commenting on the May 30, 2002 memorial for the removal of the last standing column of the World Trade Center, Richard Meyer said, "The moment I saw the second plane, I knew we were at war." That too can be a moment in the structure of coping with the sublime. It is the moral will at its most restricted: I can destroy the thing that scares me by force of response: war is a caricature of what in us can respond. I have suggested that suicide bombing undoes the difference between the bomber and his or her enemy. And I have suggested that, behind the smoke screens, the definitive predication of terror was "violent extra-state collective action," that a "terrorist state" disqualifies itself for stateship.

Insofar as the United States makes its own rules as it expands its war on terror, it allows "terrorist states" to concentrate and legitimize their policies. I am thinking, of course, of Israel and India, but so-called preventive anti-terror now spans a good part of the globe. It would be out of place here to offer accounts and analyses of such state terror. I hope you remember that I was lukewarm about the potted analyses that accompany each crisis. I will comment in closing on one isolated point for each case, points that relate to the question of public criticism—the training for ethics in the humanities.

First, then, Palestine. If 9/11 was a boy thing, in the struggle against Israel in Palestine we encounter female suicide bombers. I do not think this is a gendered phenomenon. Suicidal resistance is a message inscribed in the body when no other means will get through. It is both execution and mourning, for both self and other, where you die with me for the same cause, no matter which side you are on, with the implication that there is no dishonor in such shared death. It is only the young whose desires can be so drastically rearranged. I have no sympathy for those who train the young in this way. It is the extreme case of cultural instruction—coercion at the full, simulating choice, imagination represented as revealed truth. And this is where the dialogue must start—between a humanities training trivialized here and in extremis there. It is the *history* of this failure of cultural instruction re-coded as triumph that we must question, not the instruction itself. For that history, leading now to apartheid and unspeakable violence in *their* homeland, can be so narrativized as to persuade the young to die. (How many of us know about the Rohengyas, as 9/11 takes a world-historical place? Their gender has not been recoded.)

The female suicide bomber, thus persuaded, does not make a gendered point. Put them over against those female warriors on CNN and you will see that in suicide bombing there is no recoding of the gender struggle. When the dust settles, and at the moment it does not seem likely that it will settle over anything but the ruins of Palestine, the gender divisions will perhaps settle into the same or similar lines. Bhubaneswari Bhaduri, the subaltern in "Can the Subaltern Speak?," was a woman who used her gendered body to inscribe an unheard message; the bomber who died with Rajiv Gandhi, also a woman, did not. (It is interesting that in the male imaginary, the female suicide bomber is gender-marked by the reproductive norm. I am thinking of *The Terrorist,* a film made by an Indian Tamil about Sri Lanka, and of *The Cyclist,* the brilliant novel by Viken Berberian, a brave attempt to imagine the inner world of the suicide bomber.[27])

Even though I am trying to imagine suicide bombing without closing it off with the catch-all word "terror," the real lesson for the young potential suicide bombers may be that their message will never be heard. Even if a terrifying number of children become suicide bombers, they will remain exceptional, even as suicide is always an exceptional death—an impossible phrase. The most pathetic and most powerful thing about suicide bombing is that, like the ghost dance, its success is that it cannot succeed. In the face of this, public criticism can only repeat, taking the risk of responding with the utmost banality: it is not worth the risk.

I come, finally, to India. The conflict that emerged in the visuality of our everyday, in the context of the War on Terror, in the summer of 2002, was Kashmir. But if, in the Palestinian case, no one ever mentions that the West Bank is occupied territory, in the Indian case, the state of Gujarat, where genocidal violence against Muslim citizens is condoned by state and police, never makes it into the visualization of international public culture. Indeed, *The Economist* calls the Hindu attacks on Muslims in Gujarat "true but irrelevant."[28] In closing I want to cite these few words from a poignant piece by Harsh Mander—a former government official who resigned after writing this piece, which is available on the Internet.[29]

"I have never known a riot which has used the sexual subjugation of women so widely as an instrument of violence as in the recent mass barbarity in Gujarat," Mander writes, and then goes on to comment on the rule of law:

> As one who has served in the Indian Administrative Service for over two decades, I feel great shame at the abdication of duty of my peers in the civil and police administration. . . . The law . . . required them to act independently, . . . impartially, decisively. . . . If even one official had so acted in

Ahmedabad, she or he could have deployed the police forces and called in the army to halt the violence and protect the people in a matter of hours. No riot can continue beyond a few hours without the active connivance of the local police and magistracy.

My piece describes the long-term effort that subtends such necessary and immediate decisions. At the end of his piece, Mander invokes the ethical by way of a story,

> a story of the Calcutta riots, when Gandhi was fasting for peace. A Hindu man came to him, to speak of his young boy who had been killed by the Muslim mobs, and of the depth of his anger and longing for revenge. And Gandhi is said to have replied: If you really wish to overcome your pain, find a young [Muslim] boy, just as young as your son, . . . whose parents have been killed by Hindu mobs. Bring up that boy like you would your own son, but bring him up in the Muslim faith to which he was born. Only then will you find that you can heal your pain, your anger, and your longing for retribution.

If all through these pages I have urged the humanities to train the imagination so that the ethical interruption can postpone the attempt merely to know the other—even in Cultural Studies occupied with one's "own culture"—here the tables are turned. What is offered as the identity of the subject must be accessed in the imagination when every impulse is to repudiate it. It is no use saying, with the reverse fundamentalists, true Hinduism is not like this; or to exclaim, with the secularists, I am a secularist, I do not vote with these people. The toughest task is to imagine myself a Hindu, when everything in me resists, to understand what in us can respond so bestially, rather than merely to show cause, or to impose rules that will break, in every polity but a police state, unless prepared for by a sustained and uncoercive rearrangement of desires with moves learned from the offending culture.

As the humanities instruct us to instruct, critical theory distinguishes the discriminations of a global culture dominating our pitifully local mind-sets.

II

I taught at the University of Hawai'i–Manoa in the spring of 2003. Part of the job was to deliver public lectures. I had proposed "Terror" in advance of arrival. By the time I spoke, Iraq had broken. The University was profoundly politicized. The small enclave of native Hawai'ian students and faculty, the presence of Pearl Harbor and the military base—what one of them described as "weapons of mass destruction under the

Turtle[-shaped island]," the protest carried a peculiar poignancy—since the military base was one of the largest employers of the Hawai'ian underclass, in this place that had been forcibly annexed by "the bayonet constitution" of 1887.[30] I could not recycle the initial script. I have attempted to indicate its embedding in this short second section.

In the midst of what seemed to be a disastrous engagement with Iraq, I went back to reading Martin Luther King's "Beyond Vietnam," the 1967 speech he delivered at Riverside Church in New York, walking distance from where I live now. Again and again in the text of the speech, I found Dr. King exhorting us to "speak for those who have been designated as our enemies," because "the human spirit [does not] move without great difficulty against all the apathy of conformist thought within one's own bosom and in the surrounding world." "How do they judge us?," King asked. "When we ask why they do not leap to negotiate, these things must be remembered," he said. It was first in Hawai'i that I was able to connect my efforts to imagine the suicide bomber with these exhortations. I spoke there of the fact that this resonance with Dr. King's effort had received hostile responses from various persons and journals and this in itself was cause for alarm. I referred to the speech given in Ebenezer Baptist Church on April 30, 1967, which contained these powerful words:

> Don't let anybody make you think that God chose America as His divine messianic force to be—a sort of policeman of the whole world. God has a way of standing before the nations with judgment, and it seems that I can hear God saying to America: "You are too arrogant! If you don't change your ways, I will rise up and break the backbone of your power."

I wondered—even as I repeated the apologia offered to Dr. Michael Bernet—if these words applied to the curtailment of civil liberties, including intellectual freedom, the exacerbation of military permissiveness, the deformation of the polity through racial profiling and the re-designing of the entire culture for the prevention of auto-immunity, of which I spoke in section I. And now, of course, the world financial crisis brought about by greed.

I pointed out that we are now so used to the idea that it is the United States' responsibility as the new Empire to police the world that we quibble over containment or war, war over oil as opposed to a just war, assassination as opposed to regime change. I shared with that audience my comments, made to the then Provost of Columbia University, after listening to a crazy debate on Iraq between Alan Dershowitz and George P. Fletcher:

I felt that I could not actually ask only a question—to an extent the response could not come from what the debaters had presented. It was pretty unsettling to hear "It is sometimes better to do the right thing rather than the legal thing." This is of course the grounds for civil disobedience, but precisely because it is civil. We cannot speak of states operating in this way. When it comes to state practice, it turns to vigilantism, precisely because there is no authority to "disobey." I was also a bit unnerved that there were hands up in the room for condoning the right "to kill." Even one hand up for this is unnerving—since we were not speaking of capital punishment, which I do oppose, but which at least can be discussed within an idea of law. It is not correct to think that, because "inalienable" rights have been again and again violated, they do not exist. Surely, the difference between having torture warrants and having an individual policeman decide that torture was okay is that the latter can be punished if discovered! The problem with deciding in favor of legalized targeted assassination is surely that if a covert targeted assassination is discovered, then, at least, in perhaps a utopian vision of the rule of law, such a thing can be retroactively punished? It was troublesome to see how a debate presumably on our right to invade Iraq turned into such a rhetorical tirade against Palestine. (Here I would want to use stronger words.) The repetitive condemnation of Palestinians showed no ability to imagine them in a material context where Israel figured as anything other than "a good figure." This is where George Fletcher's idea in *Romantics at War*, that romanticism was simply a variety of irrationalism, may be questionable.[31] We must call the glass half-full rather than half-empty. Romanticism was a strike for a robust imagination—for me, it is summarized in Shelley's remark, precisely in the context of the beginnings of capitalism, that "we want the creative faculty to imagine that which we know." It is the ability to imagine the other side as another human being, rather than simply an enemy to be psyched out, which is the greatest gift of romanticism. What I was saying the other day about the humanities comes in here, because this is the terrain where a solid grounding in the humanities allows one to think the spirit rather than the letter of the law, and not think of the imagination as mere unreason. Although I do think that Mike Davis, in his new book *Dead Cities,* is somewhat over the top, he certainly does have a good deal of documented material that would not allow us to think that we are above the law because we will never be irresponsible with weapons of mass destruction.[32] Not to mention Agent Orange! I grant that I am somewhat outside the grounds of the debate because historical experience makes me very uncomfortable with the pre-comprehended assumption on both sides that America should think of itself as having an imperial mandate. I admit that George Fletcher's repeated assertion that there are no good or bad states, but equal states, can be read as a questioning of this pre-comprehension. It troubled me then that there were student hands up in that Law School auditorium condoning murder, albeit to be carried out by the state. This too is a coercive rearrangement of desire.[33]

And such a possibility makes it necessary to call upon the robust imagination, once again, to undo the binary opposition between bad cop and good cop—and remember that they are both cops. The impulse to help by *enforcing* human rights, by giving things, giving money, commodifying literacy, ignoring gender-consciousness, has a relationship with the impulse to kill. I quote Kant: "Although . . . there can still be legally good actions, [if] . . . the mind's attitude is . . . corrupted at its root . . . the human being is designated as evil."[34] Today, with the endorsement of the assassination of Sheikh Yassin, the backbone of the rule of law is broken.

Martin Luther King was a Christian, "the field of his moral vision" was religious, and he was by profession a man of God. It was his reliance upon the transcendental that gave him his strength. In "Religion within the Boundaries of Mere Reason," Kant investigates if a secularism is possible without some intuition of the transcendental that cannot be reasonably enforced. His answer is "no," because mere reason is by nature unwilling to a moral working through *(Bearbeitung).*[35] It merely likes to patch a minus with a plus, push legally good actions with no attention to the mind's corrupt attitudes. Kant has the courage, in this text, to compare the bloody violence of the aboriginal to the bloodless malice of the academic scene. In the house of mere reason, he cannot allow himself to move from determinant to reflexive judgment, to philosophize without the Aboriginal as human example, as he had done in the *Critique of the Power of Judgment,* two years before.[36]

In the same way, we would say that the heavenly rewards, sounding so mediaeval in English translation (as a translator I have something to say about this), that we associate with Islamic "terror," may be compared with the calculative or carrot-and-stick push-and-pull with which the management of peace and war is undertaken by the new imperial interests: here a human rights violation, there an economic sanction, as it were. Kant calls this tit-for-tat approach to salvation *Nebengeschäfte,* generally translated "secondary tasks," relegating the work of the ethical state to the moral will alone. I believe Jacques Derrida is right in suggesting that a persistent critique of these *Nebengeschäfte,* calculative reason standing in for moral labor, must be taken as a primary task in a multicultural and multi-faith world.[37] This task is absolutely crucial today. Those sanitized secularists who are hysterical at the mention of religion are quite out of touch with the world's peoples, and have buried their heads in the sand. Class-production has allowed them to rationalize and privatize the transcendental and they see this as the welcome telos of everybody everywhere, without historical preparation for this particular class-episteme.

Radical alterity, an otherness that reason needs but which reason cannot grasp, can be given many names. God in many languages is its most recognizable name. Some have given it the name of "man," some nation, nature, culture. Kant's good faith was reflected in his acknowledgment that mere reason "needs" the transcendental. It is this good faith that allows our more stringent position, recognition of a repeatedly de-transcendentalized radical alterity, to co-exist, however discontinuously, with faith itself, always watchful for the calculative.

These are untimely words in a world of urgency. But times are always urgent and cultural preparation—now reflected in the teaching of the humanities—is always for the long haul.

III

I had begun making the connection to Kant and that led me to secularism. The disclaimer in the paragraph below is a continuation of the unwillingness to recycle that had set in in Hawai'i, I think. Our session at the Modern Language Association (MLA) had been set at the same time as a memorial panel for Edward W. Said, who had died three months earlier. I was unhappy to be absent from that session, and realized how much my comments were a supplement to Said's magisterial work on the secular critic, who resembles the scholar, the *Gelehrte,* the hero of the Kantian Enlightenment, in being "oppositional" to every system, the individual who resists systems.[38] I wanted to look at "ordinary people." Here, then, is that third text—ordinary people following Kant and Said— with its recalcitrant opening:

> This is not a polemic against the current state of war. There are others more capable of offering informed polemic. It is also the case that, given the indifference and arrogance of the war-makers, the recitation of polemic in non-policy-oriented conferences has limited usefulness. Further, I do not believe stockpiling of details about what is obviously true—that politics is misrepresented as religion by war-makers when the occasion suits—will do anything for secularism. Secularism is not a mind-set—it is an abstraction that must be protected. It is no use thickening it with affect, like narrative "new math." No. Located as we are at the university, it is both the university and the secular that we need to rethink.

The university is in the world. And the world's universities are, no doubt, of the "European model [which], after a rich and complex medieval history, has become prevalent . . . over the last two centuries in states of a democratic type."[39] Yet that structure does not operate everywhere with the same degree of efficiency, the same degree of informed consent or critique, with the same quality or connection with the state. As the best in the United States think more and more of world governance, in the name of sustainable development and ethical globalization, and human rights—to oppose the murderous collusion of the military and the economic—in the context of *world* governance, then, we must think of all of these different *kinds* of universities, rather than just generalize from the universities we know, as if the world were one. If we move through the spectrum, the ideas we will see circulating among students and teachers will be "cultural identity," "cultural difference," "national sovereignty," "minority politics." More often than not, these issues shade off into varieties of religious freedom. I hasten to add that this is not invariably the case.

The historical place and nature of state religions are of course important. But since an active culture is the least tangible part of human behavior, the signs that spell "culture" for a mobilized collectivity are often indistinguishable from signs that can easily spell "religion." Religion in this sense is the ritual markers of how we worship and how we inscribe ourselves in sexual difference. These are performative gestures of being-human, needing no referential "evidence," being between nature and super-nature, a precarious place that needs such semiosis constantly. It is a place that captures and controls the possibility of the transcendental by writing it as that which is worshiped. We have seen that Kant dismisses this ground-level institutionality of religion, synonymous, as it were, with the automatic negotiations of culture, as *Nebengeschäfte*. This eighteenth-century point of view is still around in those who preach "the true religion has been hijacked into something terrible" or "a few bad examples are corrupting the whole." There is nothing necessarily wrong with those sentiments. But if we are thinking secularism, we must come to terms with this perennial level of something that we might as well call religion, but just as well call culture, which is always ready to bite because it *is* a species of proto-public sphere, in Said's word an "affiliation-in-filiation," for brothers and sisters of brothers, honorary brothers. It is neither possible nor desirable to be precise here. And Samuel Huntington is so wrong because he performs a precise identification between religion and culture.[40] In this imprecise and imbricated normality, it is not a question, strictly speaking, of belief, but of something *like* linguistic competence. And the competence is called on, demanding different levels of semantic negotiations, in different psychopolitical situations. Gendering plays a strong role here, with different levels of acquiescence, even consensuality. Indeed, it can be said that this is the groundrock of the semantics of gender, the weave of permissible narratives. The preparation for secularism is political: to work for a world where religion can shrink to this mundane normality.

In order to sustain such a world, assuming its establishment, it is the skills we teach in the humanities that we need. I am speaking, of course, of the skills of reading, of catching the generic difference between registers of language, with the hope of a "setting to work" to meet the world in which we live, in order to read Martin Luther King's example of one who so loved his enemies that he died for them as a narrative, singular and unverifiable. It should be clear from my description of the situation of religion that secularism—which I will define in a moment—is a persistent critique; a persistent setting to work to recognize language as system rather than ground for belief. If we are to keep working for such a world we must partially (only partially) undo the lesson of the last few European centuries and massively redo the program of disenfranchised histories. It sounds pretty scary put this way. But if we think of it as a collective enterprise that we undertake in the classroom it need not work that way. (How hard I worked at that stage to keep doubt away!)

If the signs that spell "culture" for a collectivity are often indistinguishable from signs that can easily spell "religion," this can also be true of a "culture" that fetishizes mere reasonableness. In its most sublime mode, Kant shows this in "Religion within the Boundaries of Mere Reason." I have spoken of this text in passing. Let me spend a few moments on it now.

Although he made an attempt to show that all religions tended toward dramatizing the role reason must play in order to ensure an ethical collectivity, there was no doubt in Kant's mind that Christianity is "the first true *church*."[41]

This conviction, that the Judaeo-Christian is *the* secular religion, is the prejudice that still rides us and is only legitimized by reversal as in Sayyid Qutb's work on Islam. If the Judaeo-Christian is seen as the religion of reason, de-transcendentalized into secularism, that is *also* a description of capturing and controlling the possibility of the transcendental as that which is worshiped, the characteristic of religion-as-culture that I advanced above.

My point is that, whatever your politics or your religion, the place of reason in whatever secularism might mean remains implacable. If reason is to be our ally, and there is no compromise on that one, it cannot be fetishized, as in the most common version of secularism, laundered Judaeo-Christianity. Today's soft option, "teaching tolerance," is of course a good thing. But as Kant's real effort at tolerance two centuries ago, at the end of "Mere Reason," shows us, tolerance allows you to de-transcendentalize all other religions but the religion-culture language that governs your own idiom. Basically, it's the same problem as with cultural relativism.

Tolerance, such an easy virtue in theory, is difficult to practice. It is, at best, a private virtue. A "tolerant" state is a secular state. We are talking the juridico-legal, not the psychological. It flourishes best when religion is de-transcendentalized into something like linguistic competence, which is most easily done in the absence of the need to mobilize, not when it is privatized by a particular class.

It is clear, in other words, that the two pieces of machinery bequeathed to us by the European eighteenth century—the separation of Church and State and the separation of the public and the private—are too race- and class-specific and indeed gender-specific to hold up a just world. Privatization of the transcendental works for a handful. Our world shows us that secularism is not an episteme. It is a faith in reason in itself and for itself protected by abstract external structures—the flimsiest possible arrangement to reflect the human condition: under the circumstances, I invite you to think of secularism as an active and persistent practice, an accountability, of keeping the structures of agency clear of belief as faith. Secularism is too rarefied, too existentially impoverished to take on the thickness of a language. It is a mechanism to avoid violence that must be learned as mere reasonableness. It is as thin as an ID card, not as thick as "identity."

What role can we play in promoting the practice of secularism rather than simply "being secular?" Think of the role religious belief has in fact come to play in the contemporary multicultural university, and you will see that "being secular" is often a matter of preserving the letter of secularism. What I am going to suggest is not going to insist that there is some enlightened spirit of secularism for which we ought to initiate new conversion rites, but that we ought to acknowledge that secularism is only ever in the letter, and that we ought to train fiercely to protect it as such. No religion has a special privilege to it.

(At the 2003 Annual Convention of the MLA, I was fortunate enough to receive many proofs of resonance. One of the most important came from my old friend Phil Lewis, who commented that this was my most important contribution to the thinking of a broad-based secularist practice: that it was only ever "in the letter." "But," said Phil, "it will be difficult for people to understand, Gayatri." I think the training that is now required is for the sake of this understanding, that secularism is a set of abstract reasonable laws that must be observed to avoid religious violence.)

At this point it should also be clear that any assertion of the "universalism" of reason-based secularism is suspect for me because it finesses the fact that such assertions are based on the assumption that the University—the place designated for the training in deep subjective change—is not only an institution of class-mobility, but of a specifically

European-style class-mobility. However European the model of the modern University may be, our commitment to multiculturalism resists that scenario. Indeed, even the description of the forum at the MLA reflected that in its goal of presenting "visions of the contemporary university that go beyond the Europe–North American axis." It is precisely the figure of "the universal secular intellectual" that will no longer suffice for what the university must produce today.

It is in order to think the alternative that I turn to Kant, for he was the philosopher who gave the best articulation to the universal secular intellectual as produced by the university: it is when a scholar writes for all times and all places that he is enlightened. For singular individuals of our generation, that is still a noble ideal, and that is where I have placed Said's thinking of secular criticism.

Yet accompanying Kant's wonderful statement about publishing come exhortations to be obedient on the job where we would expect a statement of public freedoms. If we look at Kant's philosophical writings, especially "Religion within the Boundaries of Mere Reason," written at the end of his life, we will see that Kant's idea of a common ethical life—a *gemeines Wesen* for which the translation "public sphere" would be altogether inadequate—is not based on the separation of the public and the private but on the fact that all human beings have the *same* reason and therefore the goal of humanity is collective. (The Church, which is a public institution, also messes with the private.) As I have tried to argue, it is upon the universality of reason that the promise of secularism is also based. Because Kant was deeply aware of the limits of reason, he asked himself if it was possible to forge a species of what we might as well call secularism that would incorporate intuitions of the transcendental. Let us see how he solved his problem and what we, who must be fair to our debt to Kant and yet must undo—ab-use—him, can learn from him.

To begin with, although reason is one, and indeed that is the ground of ethical commonality, Kant fractures that unity, rather more than we do when we put our blind faith in secularism as we understand it. (Kant himself always asserted that the various reasons were different forms of appearance of the same reason. What I am describing here can take that on board.) Between the fractured functions of reason, Kant establishes a skewed relationship. Pure reason, of which Kant is most suspicious, is the highest function of reason. And mere reason, which is what we work with every day and which can only be accountable—*zurechnungfähig* rather than responsible—is inimical to moral labor. Therefore, in describing how we would philosophize the moral in pure reason, Kant asks us, literally, to make room for—*einräumen*—the *effects* of grace.

If this is too Eurocentric, it is because I need to question the reading of Kant that is used to justify world governance.[42] There is a certain degree of self-confidence in such justifications, whereas Kant's relentless honesty makes him shackle reason.

In the spatial institution of pure reason, then, we must make room for "the effects of grace." And, in the last section of this last "critique," where he is speaking of world governance, with repeated theological references (since he is fighting the theological faculty), he insists that a global institution based on ethical commonness of being is impossible. The ethical cannot be immediately institutionalized.

I learn many of my ways of reading the past from Marx and this is where I want to read Kant as Marx read Aristotle, with admiration but with the historical acknowledgment that he could not imagine the value-form. Even within his brilliantly fractured model of the oneness of reason Kant spoke of "effect of *grace*" (emphasis added) because he could not imagine a European-style university where the theology faculty was not dominant. We have to run with the revolutionary force of the word "effect," clear out of the theological into the aesthetic. "Effect" comes as close as Kant can get to de-transcendentalizing Grace. Grace is caught in the figure of something like a metalepsis—the effect of an effect. Since pure reason—or indeed any kind of reason—cannot know the cause, all that is inscribed is an effect.

Hannah Arendt commented on the political potential of Kant's thinking of the aesthetic.[43] What I am proposing links up with that thought. Most of us are familiar with the slightly off-key English translation of the aesthetic: purposiveness without purpose. We know that Kant tells us that the aesthetic gives practice to the faculty that can represent without objective concepts. Then, ever the thinker of checks and balances, in the Third Critique, Kant straps in the tendency of the imagination to shoot too far by emphasizing the task, not of reason, but of understanding.

In "Religion within the Boundaries of Mere Reason," Kant implicitly, and to a large extent without acknowledgment, shifts the task of representation-without-concept—figuration—to the figuring of Grace as near-metalepsis—unverifiable effect of an effect—to a parergon or outside-work of pure reason. It is not understanding that is now a check on the Imagination, as it was in the Third Critique. It is figuration that supplements mere reason's calculative moral laziness.

I apologize for the abstruseness of this last paragraph. Universalist multiculturalism would go down much better. But bear with me for just a few more pages.

In support of my reading, I offer the fact that "Religion within the Boundaries of Mere Reason" is an extended allegorical or dis-figuring reading of the New Testament—a species of liberation theology. And I am now going to make a suggestion that I hope won't rattle you. We will go back to suicide bombing.

Liberation theology works because it literalizes the metaphorology of a religious culture. Suicide bombing works the same way. I am not equating the two, nor am I endorsing either. The only thing they share is bad gender politics. Over the past few years, I have been trying to imagine suicide bombing because I am convinced that to dismiss it as pathological, murderous, or aberrant is to speak from the positions I have already discussed. Have you ever heard Palestinian mothers lament the transformation of their sons and daughters to suicide bombers by the current situation? This is what I was speaking of at the outset when I said that the ever-accessible bilinguality between religion and culture as idiom becomes mobilized in situations. If liberation theology mobilizes by literalizing the metaphor, in the case of suicide bombing we see the recoding of religious narrative as referential in the narrowest sense.

But training in the humanities does neither of these two moves—it teaches us to learn from the singular and the unverifiable. If the university is to be secular, it requires a sustained epistemic effort that can only come from the humanities. The idea that secularism can be supported by training in political science and law alone belongs to privative disciplinary formations, where the subject's control is customarily left unquestioned. It is the humanities that can provide continuing practical instruction in de-transcendentalizing the radically other—re-inventing grace as necessary metalepsis—a lesson learned by undoing the prophet of that earlier style.[44] The humanities must learn to detrivialize themselves and to stake their suitable place at the University of this troubled century. I am utterly appalled by conservative young colleagues who insist with amazing insularity on teaching "only literary skills"—what are they?—because the students arrive untrained; as the world breaks around them.

If we want to take up the challenges of the twenty-first century, we must also learn languages. The simplified reading I have offered of Kant would be impossible from even the best translations into English. And we must not look for the vicissitudes of the translation for the word "secular" as applied to states and societies in "the rest of the world."

No. The task is to find something like the "secular/transcendental" binary in the many languages of the world rather than offer abstruse translations of the English or the metropolitan words. *Din aur dunya* and *jāgatik o paromārthik* are the two I work with as candidates for undoing: the two major religions of India. Indeed, I came up with the definition of religion as ritual markers of how we worship—*ki korey thakur pujo kara hoy*—as I was speaking to a rural woman in West Bengal on December

16, 2005, a barefoot teacher who was completely incapable of explaining the lesson on religion written in the elementary school textbook.

I close as I began, exercising my institutional validation as a teacher of narrative. I open *Baby No-Eyes,* a novel by the Maori writer Patricia Grace.[45] My friend and colleague Carolyn Sinavaiana helped me teach this book and gave an impressive account of the Maori world-view that did not acknowledge the distinction between public and private but rather a circulatory commonness among all its members. I mention above Kant's notion of the ethical common being and the oneness of reason. As I argued about Buchi Emecheta's rewriting of the Enlightenment some years ago, these characteristics of Kant's thought allow it to be pliable outside its European provenance.[46] But what it remained for me to point out was that the last chapter of the novel ended at a university where the newest Maori learns to "Try Opposite," the most succinct lesson in the imagination moving away from identity as reference. If Toni Morrison's *Beloved* is a novel about the shift from Africa to African-America, this novel is on the cusp from the move from Aotearoa to New Zealand. It is upon such historical changes that the persistent effort at keeping the university secular—by persistently de-transcendentalizing the radically other into a space of effect, persistent acknowledgment of religio/culture as idiom rather than ground of belief—is placed into the hands of the pedagogy and scholarship of the humanities.

That I felt so strongly for an aesthetic education as the remedy after 9/11 shows what a strong conviction in a soldiering teacher is now broken, more by the full corporatization of the university, I realize re-reading this essay for revision, than by any other characteristic of globalization.

CHAPTER NINETEEN

Harlem

ERE IS THE SITE of a major double bind. How deny "development" to the disenfranchised? This is where the Du Bois/Gramsci lesson—aesthetic education for the subaltern, so that hegemony is grasped responsibly—becomes crucial. Mere nostalgia, that would celebrate those "tribals in aspic," for example, indulged in by Mahasweta Devi and Gopiballabh Singh Deo, is useless here. If anything, this piece showcases the precariousness of the way from "freedom from" to "freedom to," as well as paying attention to the fact that capitalist "development" must, persistently, subalternize. Today, when U.S. racism has suborned conservative Christian African America for a future subalternization that will help this, it is even more important to remember this. I will be forgiven if I no longer have the conviction that this memory will survive.

Alice Attie showed me her photographs of Harlem.[1] The images haunted me and interpellated me as a New Yorker. A month before this, twenty-one photographs of the base of the eleventh-century Brihadiswara temple in Thanjavur, taken in 1858 by a captain in the British army, had beckoned. What was that interpellation? I have not come to grips with that one yet, but it launched me for a while on the question of photographs and evidence of identity. Harlem moved onto a big map.

In Dublin I could juxtapose the Harlem images with allochthonic Europe. What is it to be a Dubliner? Romanian, Somali, Algerian, Bosnian Dubliners? What is it to be a high-tech Asian Dubliner, recipient of 40 percent of official work permits? Diversity is class differentiated. How does the anti-immigration platform "Return Ireland to the Irish" relate to the ferocious dominant-sector culturalism that is reconstituting Harlem today? A class argument subsumed under this culturalism, pronouncing received antiglobalization or pro-working-class pieties, will nicely displace the question. This became part of my argument.

In Brazil's Bahia, I learned what the movimento negro owed to African America in the United States. In Hong Kong in 2001, I saw that the word "identity" attached to the name of a place such as Hong Kong indicated yet another species of collectivity: postcolonial. Between Great Britain and China, the Hong Kong cultural worker staged a loss of identity. If the quick sketch of Dublin foregrounds the class division in diversity, the staging of Hong Kong makes visible the fault lines within what is called "decolonization."[2]

In 1996 the Taiwanese artist Tsong Pu thought of his work *Map* (Figures 2a and 2b) as marking a contradiction between "lucid Chinese names and maps, and [the] ambiguous concept[s] of China and [its] names," questioning precise identities, as set down by names and maps.[3] He was perhaps inserting Hong Kong, via repatriation, into the confusion of the question of two Chinas; of one country, two systems. The year 1997 was the official repatriation, the promise of a release. The artist could be conceptualizing this as a frozen series of bilateralities—no more than two chairs, a small rectangular table, rather emphatically not round. Hong Kong and the PRC, Hong Kong and Britain, UK and PRC: bilateralities. The rough concrete block, commemorating the promised release, in fact imprisons the two unequal partners. (Only one chair back has something like headphones attached.) Rough concrete blocks weigh down bodies that must drown without trace. The chairs are empty, no bodies warm them, they cannot be used. The figure "1997" is engraved on one side of the block and embossed on the other. To what concept might this refer? To the strength of the piercing of that date into the history of the city-state as it displaces itself? To the fact of piercing out, but not through? The power of conceptual art is that, as the visual pushes toward the verbal, questions like these cannot be definitively answered.

Culture as the site of explanations is always shifting. The cultural worker's conceptualization of identity becomes part of the historical record that restrains the speed of that shift or drift. It feeds the souls of those in charge of cultural explanations, who visit museums and exhibitions. The British critic Raymond Williams would call this restraining effect the "residual" pulling back the cultural process.

I spent five months in Hong Kong. I never saw anyone looking at *Map*. Culture had run away elsewhere.

The photograph of Ethernet delegates (Figure 3) is a dynamic mark of identity, sharing in the instantaneous timing of virtual reality. The

"Ethernet" band can be put away tomorrow but is always available around the corner. Conceptuality moves on a clear path here—from the slow cultural confines of postcoloniality as repatriation into the quick fix of the culture of global finance. What is the relationship between the innocence and charm of these young people and the occlusion of class interests?

Who sends the collective messages of identity? Who receives them? It is surely clear that Tsong Pu may not have been the real sender of the many messages that his piece can project. And of course I, a female Indian

莊普在展覽廳內的作品 "地圖" 共有兩部分，第一部分是用中國地圖切割再拼貼成一條長紙條，在展覽開始時圍出一個類似台灣島的地形，之後形狀由觀眾自由調整。

第二部分是一座1997的紀念碑。作者將一桌兩椅凝固在水泥內，以白色的座台為基。碑的前後都顯示 "1997" 字樣。

Tsong Pu's work in the Exposition Hall, Map, comprised two parts. For the first part Tsong cut up a Chinese map and reassembled it into a strip. At the beginning of the exhibition, it was arranged in the shape of the island of Taiwan. The shape was then to be altered freely by visitors.

The second part is a 1997 monument. A table and two chairs were stuck together with cement. The object was supported by a white base. On both sides of the monument read "1997".

Figure 2a: Map (mixed media), Tsong Pu (1996). Exhibition catalog, Hong Kong University of Science and Technology. Reproduced with the permission of the HKUST Center for the Arts.

academic teaching English in the United States for over two-thirds of her life, may not be its felicitous receiver. I want to keep the question of the sender and the receiver in mind as I move myself from Port Shelter, China, to Harlem, United States. Who sends, and who receives, when messages assuming collectivities are inscribed? What are identities in megacities like Hong Kong and New York where floating populations rise and fall? Harlem is a famous place, "a famous neighborhood rich in

Figure 2b: Map (detail), Tsong Pu (1996). Exhibition catalog, Hong Kong University of Science and Technology. Reproduced with the permission of the HKUST Center for the Arts.

culture," says PBS. If the intellectual and the artist stage Hong Kong as emptied of cultural identity, the general dominant in New York is now interested in pronouncing Harlem as metonymic of African America in general. If the texture is so multiple, how may we imagine globality? It is best to sharpen the imagination rather than collect and classify an impossible embarrassment of content.

In 1658 Peter Stuyvesant, the Dutch governor of New Netherland, established the settlement of Nieuw Haarlem, named after Haarlem in the Netherlands. Throughout the eighteenth century, Harlem was "an isolated, poor, rural village."[4] In the nineteenth century it became a fashionable residential district. Following the panic of 1893, property owners rented to blacks, and by World War I much of Harlem was firmly established as a black residential and commercial area, although race and class cross-hatching was considerable.[5] From then until the 1990s, Harlem was the scene of fierce deprivation and fierce energy. The chief artery of black Harlem is 125th Street. Columbia University, a major property owner in the area, spreads unevenly up to the edge of 125th. Since the 1990s, Harlem has been the focus of major economic "development," and the property ownership graph is changing. Part of the "development" package seems to be an invocation of a seamless community and culture marking the neighborhood, on left and right, finally working in the same interest, the American dream. The United States thinks of itself as "global" or "local"

Figure 3:   Ethernet delegates.

interchangeably. At this point, nothing in the United States, including Harlem, is merely counterglobal.

This article is not part of the voluminous social history of Harlem, now coming forth to code development as freedom in the name of culture. I have not the skill. Robin Kelley's introduction to Attie's *Harlem on the Verge* integrates the photographs into that particular stream.[6] I only raise questions. (Now, revising, I locate the question that was always there: can an aesthetic education nuance the American Dream? At best, it's a chance. Today, we are in the worst-case scenario for the duration.) That is my connection to Aaron Levy's *Cities without Citizens*.[7] Like Levy, I question archivization, which attempts not only to restrain but also to arrest the speed of the vanishing present, alive and dying. I question the evidentiary power of photography. The question changes, of course. Here on the Upper West Side of New York, the question becomes: in the face of class-divided racial diversity, who fetishizes culture and community? The only negative gesture that I have ever received from a black person in New York has been from a near-comatose drunken brother in the 96th Street subway station who told me to "take my green card and go home." That is not culture-turned-racism but a recognition of the class division in so-called diversity. At the end of the day, my critical position (though, as he noticed, not my class position or my class interest) is the same as his.

W. E. B. Du Bois describes the African-American at the end of the nineteenth century as "two souls . . . in one dark body, whose dogged strength alone keeps it from being torn asunder."[8] In the development and gentrified "integration" of Harlem today, the hyphen between these two souls (African and American, African-American) is being negotiated. Therefore Alice and I attempt teleiopoiesis, a reaching toward the distant other by the patient power of the imagination, a curious kind of identity politics, where one crosses identity, as a result of migration or exile.[9] Keats tries it with the Grecian urn, Joyce with the Odyssey, with the Wandering Jew. We beg the question of collectivity, on behalf of our discontinuous pasts, her mother in Damascus, I in India, as New Yorkers. If the Ghost Dance accesses something like a "past" and grafts it to the "perhaps" of the future anterior, teleiopoiesis wishes to touch a past that is historically not "one's own" (assuming that such a curious fiction has anything more than a calculative verifiability, for patricians of various kinds). We must ask, again and again, How many are we? Who are they? as Harlem disappears into a present that demands a cultural essence. These are the questions of collectivity, asked as culture runs on. We work in the hope of a resonance with unknown philosophers of the future, friends in advance.

The Encyclopedia Britannica says "Harlem as a neighborhood has no fixed boundaries." Of course the *Encyclopedia* means this in the narrow sense. For Attie, a photographer with a Euro-U.S. father and a mother from Damascus, and for me, resident alien of Indian origin, these words have come to have a broader meaning. It has prompted us to ask: what is it to be a New Yorker? We are New Yorkers, Alice and I. Our collaboration is somewhat peculiar in that I emphasize our differences rather than our similarities. In the summer of 2000, I said, "Alice, you're not to mind the things I say about you. One thing is for sure. The photos are brilliant." She came up to me from behind, gave me a hug and kissed me on my neck. You decide if these words are a record of betrayal.

"For the past thirty years," Alice wrote in her field notes, "I have lived on 105th Street and West End Avenue, a fifteen-minute walk from the heart of Harlem in New York City. Only recently, in April of 2000, did I venture into this forbidden territory and experience a community of warmth, generosity, openness, and beauty. The dispelling of some deeply embedded stereotypes has been a small part of the extraordinary experience I have had walking the streets and conversing with the residents of Harlem."[10]

I have lived in the United States for forty-nine years and in Manhattan for nineteen. I went to Harlem the first week of arrival, because my post office is there. Someone in my office warned me that it might be dangerous. In the middle of the day! I have been comfortable in Harlem since that first day, perhaps because Harlem gives me the feel of, although it does not resemble, certain sections of Kolkata. But write about Harlem? Identitarianism scares me. That is my identity investment in this. It is in the interest of the catharsis of that fear that I have tried this experiment and asked: How do we memorialize the event? I have tried to avoid the banalities of globalized contemporaneity and asked: As "culture" runs on, how do we catch its vanishing track, its trace? How does it affect me as a New Yorker? Has the dominant made it impossible to touch the fragility of that edge?

Eine differente Beziehung.[11] This is a Hegelian phrase, which describes the cutting edge of the vanishing present. The present as event is a differancing relationship. I could add a modest rider to that. By choosing the word *Beziehung* rather than *Verhältnis* for relationship, Hegel was unmooring the present from definitive structural truth claims, for he invariably uses the latter word to indicate the structurally correct placement of an item of history or subject. I must repeat my question: how does one figure the edge of the differancing as past, as something we call the present unrolls? For it is important in figuring the preservation of culture as "heritage" as the future "develops," usually without an imagination trained in epistemological performance, constructing past and future as objects of knowing?

I myself have been making the argument for some time now that on the ethical register, precapitalist cultural formations should not be regarded in an evolutionist way, with capital as the telos. Indeed, this is the main argument of "Imperative to Re-imagine the Planet," Chapter 16 in this book. I have suggested that culturally inscribed dominant mind-sets that are defective for capitalism should be nurtured for grafting onto our dominant. (I now believe this has become institutionally impossible.) This is a task for which all preparation can only be remote and indirect. It does, however, operate a baseline critique of the social Darwinism implicit in all our ideas of "development" in the economic sense and "hospitality" in the narrow sense. I am a New Yorker. As Harlem is being "developed" into mainstream Manhattan, how do we catch the cultural inscription of delexicalized cultural collectivities?

(To lexicalize is to separate a linguistic item from its appropriate grammatical system into the conventions of another grammar. Thus a new economic and cultural lexicalization, as in the development of Harlem, demands a delexicalization as well.) Identitarianism is a denial of the imagination. The imagination is our inbuilt instrument of othering, of thinking things that are not in the here and now, of wanting to become others. I was delighted to see, in a recent issue of the Sunday *New York Times* devoted to the problem of race, that Erroll McDonald, a Caribbean American editor at Pantheon Books, thinks that "at the heart of reading is an open engagement with another, often across centuries and cultural moments."[12] In the academy, the myth of identity goes something like this: the dominant self has an identity, and the subordinate other has an identity. Mirror images, the self othering the other, indefinitely. I call this, in academic vocabulary, an abyssal specular alterity.[13] To look for the outlines of a subject that is not a mirror image of the dominant, we have to acknowledge, as does Erroll McDonald, that any object of investigation— even the basis of a collective identity that we want to appropriate—is other than the investigator. We must investigate and imaginatively constitute our "own" unclaimed history with the same teleiopoietic delicacy that we strive for in the case of the apparently distant. The most proximate is the most distant, as you will see if you try to grab it exactly, in words, or, better yet, to make someone else grab it. If we ignore this, we take as demonstrated the grounds of an alternative identity—that which we set out to establish. This may be useful for combative politics but not so for the reinvention of our discipline.[14] Yet the combat cannot be forgotten. That is indeed the point of the entire book.

I asked Alice to give me pictures that had inscriptions, no live figures. The humanism of human faces, especially in a time of mandatory culturalism, guarantees evidentiary memories, allows us to identify the everyday with the voice of recorded and organized public protest. "Of a necessity the vast majority of [the Negroes in Harlem] are ordinary, hard-working people, who spend their time in just about the same way that other ordinary, hard-working people do."[15] These inscriptions, each assuming a collectivity, are a bit exorbitant to both public protest and the mundane round. The inscriptions are now mostly gone. New building has replaced them. Already when they were photographed, there was no longer sender or receiver for these collectivities, in a sense that is different from the way this may be true of all messages, although the messages could still be read. This is the eerie moment of delexicalization, congealing into a "past," even as I speak. Inscriptions are lexicalized into the textuality of the viewer, and it is the unexpected that instructs us. Therefore I asked for shots that inscribe collectivities and mark the moment of change. We are both parts of the text—New Yorker is a collective term. How many are we? We are residents of Morningside Heights. How much of us is Harlem? How is synoikismos possible?[16]

Wake Up, Black Man (see Figure 5a) is on the wall of a landmark warehouse on 123rd Street. Today, with the knowledge that the building is standing skeletal and gutted, after passing through consideration by Columbia University, Robert De Niro, and a community group that would have turned it into a cultural center, it seems more interesting that the message was on a warehouse. My fellow critic is still the brother in the subway station. No amount of pious diversity talk will bridge the constant subalternization that manages the crisis of upward class mobility masquerading as the politics of classlessness. Who is this Black Man and to what would he have awakened? Who wrote on the warehouse wall? Was it a felicitous writing surface? Questions that have now disappeared.

I come from an inscribed city, Kolkata, whose inscriptions are in the mode of disappearance as the state of West Bengal moves into economic restructuring. The inscriptions of Kolkata, in Bengali, are never read by international commentary, Left and Right. As I write, I have a vision of writing a companion piece for my hometown. How will it relate to the early imperial photographs, imprints taken by egg white smoothed on waxed paper, of the temple inscriptions that set me to read photographs? (see Figure 4a). Questions that must be asked before the Kolkata street inscriptions disappear.

The entire argument of this chapter—the fragility of the differantiating moment—is captured in the difference between the photograph in Figure 4a and a contemporary digital representation.*

In the era of globalization, a simulation of the original would be a fake or art. And that's not our point. To grab that—an aesthetic education.

Figure 4a: Photograph by Linnaeus Tripe (1858), Canadian Photographic Society.

* *Figure 4b:*   Photograph by the author.

"To grab" → "to grip" = *greifen* → *Begriff* = concept. I've played this out in and through Yeats in "Culture: Situating Feminism," Chapter 5 in this book. For the general argument about feminism, it is not without interest that the metaphor in "concept" is shared with the motor of reproductive heteronormativity.

I am not suggesting that there is any kind of located meaning to an inscribed collectivity as the movement of differantiation is taking place. That, too, is a hard lesson to learn. On the other side is the convenience of facts. Alice and I have resolutely kept to rumors, with the same boring "authenticity" as all poorly edited oral history. Selected facts confound the ordinary with the resistant, thus fashioning identitarianism, culturalism. Our sources do not comment on the inscriptions, but rather on the built space. The gutted warehouse is an architectural moment in the spectrum between spatial practice (here inscription) and ruin (not allowed by developers), as the disappearing movement is taking place, the differantiating moment as the present becomes past, indefinitely.

Let us create a pattern. Here is "Wake up people," on an old Harlem storefront, which grandly and inadvertently provides an allegory of reading "MOVING" (Figure 6). Discontinuous inscriptions, the old economy a space for inscribing, both under erasure, both gone, united in Harlem's current seamless culturalism. You can tell the lost word is "Black" simply by that "k," "up" is assumed, "male female, young old," once tied to my allegory of reading, is, at the time of photography, anchorless. Indeed, what Harlem has and others use is now covered over. The object is not just lost by the covering over. It is the lost object in the future of the new Harlem.

Let us read Figure 7, *Keep Out,* as an effective allegory of the anonymity. No one is sure as to who has asked whom to keep out of this lot. Here there is no built space yet to distract the inhabitants' attention. The inscription commands reading, yet is meaningless. It is now gone. The small, rubble-strewn, empty lot surrounded by barbed wire has been flattened. No one knows what will come up there. We could know if we made it a new political science (I am on the editorial board of a journal of that name) research project, with predictable results. I am keeping the convenient conclusions at bay; they can have the predictable pluses and minuses depending on the investigators'; but the inhabitants are not there. (I had thought to check at time of revising, but Attie had the right idea. She had not noted the location, just made this note: "This was the only *Keep Out* sign that I came across in my year of photography throughout Harlem.")[17]

Records (Figure 8) is a storefront on 116th Street that has been filled with concrete. The current inhabitants of the tenement above are relative

Figure 5a: *Wake Up, Black Man,* Alice Attie (2000).*

* *Figures 5b and 5c:*   In these two photographs by Aniruddha Das, we see the new building on the site and what the black man has awakened to, with a rupture we can analogize with that between the work of the dream and waking life.

Figure 6: *Male/Female*, Alice Attie (2000).

Figure 7: *Keep Out*, Alice Attie (2000).

newcomers, Haitians, who are suspended between the history of the store and the imminent future. The small notice is in French because it acknowledges this floating present. For the English speaking, a more austere notice: "NO/sitting/standing/loitering. Thank you. Owner." The amiable Haitians, in suit and tie of a Wednesday evening, may have put this up. I didn't ask. One thing is sure. The only name scribbled on the soft concrete—"Allen"—is not the signatory of the message, and not only because of the absent patronymic. The archaeologist would undo the implausible text: Owner Allen.

An allegory again? I am a reader of words, not a drawer of foregone conclusions from images read as if evidentiary. Therefore inscriptions.

I placed *Buster Moved* (Figure 9) next. This is a memorial on which Robin Kelley comments movingly.[18] Here a felicitous public space of mourning/inscription is moving into that anonymous public space that memorializes the differantiating present as it disappears. Neither Robin nor I will know "Buster." This is in excess of the general structure without structure where all mourning, seeking to establish traffic with a transcendental intuition, is definitively unmoored. There is no guarantee that Buster is still at 1972 7th Avenue. We have not looked for him.

Figure 8: Records, Alice Attie (2000).

An article such as this one can have no ending. We are commenting on culture on the run, the vanishing present. But there is a closure for the historical record, the "residual" restraint that I mentioned in my opening. The Lenox Lounge (Figure 10) will remain—a different urban text will sediment meaning as it lexicalizes the lounge into the historical record. The insistent culturalism of *Harlem Song* at the Apollo Theater and the various television programs is the ideological face of that lexicalization. It will appropriate the Harlem Renaissance and the New Negro.[19] Indeed, it can appropriate the theme of loss in a golden nostalgia. In a show at the Museum of the City of New York, there are some images devoted to Harlem—and they belong to that genre.[20] That, too, is how architecture inhabits the spectrum between spatial practice and ruins. By scholarly hindsight a collectivity will be assumed or assigned to have intended this bit of built space. That will be a structural truth claim. The anonymous, provisional, ghostly collectivities inscribed in and by these photographs, the edge of changeful culture caught on camera, will be delexicalized. This is an aporia of history, forever monumentalizing the stutter in the classic identity claim "I am (not) one of us." Memory has a "posterior anteriority"—an "I was there" before the fact—to which the historically established so-called cultural memory can only aspire.[21] "Living" memory sustains us because it privatizes verifiability, effectively canceling the question. The incessant production of cultural memory aspires to the public sphere by a species of subreption, the word Kant uses to designate the attribution to nature of a sublimity that actually belongs to

Figure 9:   Buster Moved, Alice Attie (2000).

our "respect for our own determination."[22] It is a word that, in ecclesiastical law, means the "suppression of truth to obtain indulgence." By using this word for the built-in or constitutive character of the production of cultural memory, I draw a structural parallel with Kant's use of the word and have no intention to tie it to Kant's argument about nature and the moral will. The problem, at any rate, is not so much truth and falsity as public verifiability of culture by history.

To situate the lexicalization of the Lenox Lounge, I recall once again that moment in W. E. B. Du Bois's *The Souls of Black Folk*—the outsider's hospitable entrance into Afro-Am.

The Souls of Black Folk is the prototype of the best vision of metropolitan cultural studies. At the head of each chapter, Du Bois takes a line of an African spiritual and writes it in European musical notation. There we note the move to convert the performative into performance—an active cultural idiom lexicalized into the encyclopedia or the museum—that is at the core of it. This is how the Lenox Lounge will enter the historical record—in a New World notation.

The Du Bois of the last phase moved to a different place. Disaffected with the United States, the Pan-African Du Bois became a citizen of Ghana in Africa. We situate the traces of the other, ghostlier demarcations of col-

Figure 10:   Lenox Lounge, Alice Attie (2000).

lectivity caught in Attie's photos with the obstinate remnants of Du Bois's cherished *Encyclopedia Africana,* emerging from anonymity in contemporary Ghana, as the official encyclopedia of Africa thrives. What we offer here is related to that refusal to disappear. Du Bois's call for a state where "the crankiest, humblest and poorest . . . people are the . . . key to consent of the governed," seeking to redress Marx's regret at the end of "The Eighteenth Brumaire of Louis Bonaparte," that the lumpen proletariat could not "represent themselves," is now being claimed by the moral entrepreneurs of the international civil society who would represent the world's minorities without a democratic mandate.[23] I will go on to comment on Marx's statement (see page 432).

What is it for Du Bois, the African-American who made that hyphenation possible, to become American-African? Hong Kong, British until the day before yesterday, asks this question in terms of Asia and the United States, as Asian-American intellectuals come back after repatriation. For Dublin, Irish America is the next parish, whereas Little Bosnia is elsewhere.[24] These are movements in different directions. We must place Harlem in this world if we want to claim a supplement to globalism.

What are the remains of the event as *différance?* What is the responsibility of the memorializing collectivity? What mark will the old, imprecise, ghostly "singularity"—the scattered "Harlem" of these inscriptions— leave on film as the historical archives define it for scholarly use in a present that will cut itself off from it? A handful of photographs, deducing a collectivity from the ghost's track. These questions lead to different conclusions if you remember that politics is gendered.

The inscribed collectivities in the photographs are hardly ever women, and of course, never queer. This can be read in many ways. I have made the argument in another context that specific women's access to activism, not necessarily feminist activism, is socially produced in ways rather different from the male mainstream. I will not reproduce that argument here. I will repeat that, especially in the case of developmental activism, collectivity is constantly subsumed under the prevailing religion of individualism and competition, and this is true even of women. The activist may speak of collectivities, even work for groups of people, but it is the individuals who enter history. Thus the *New York Times* and the well-known liberal Left journal *The Nation* have picked up the cases of Dorothy Vaughan, whose old Harlem reconstruction project is going to be taken over by the gourmet supermarket Citarella, and Una Mulzac, who founded Liberation Bookstore in 1967 (Figure 11) and was threatened with eviction in 2000.[25]

They may not be immediately lexicalizable, like the Lenox Lounge, for which we go to Toni Morrison, Hortense Spillers, bell hooks, Queen

Latifah, Maya Angelou. But they are, as it were, convertible to the format of the lexicon. We do not have their photographs, because they do not belong to the anonymous unclaimable delexicalized collectivities. We are not privileging delexicalization or anonymity; we are memorializing the moment before obliteration. It is in that caution that I now turn to a couple of images of "representative" Harlem women, unconnected to the inscriptions of collectivities (Figures 12 and 13).

The lesson that I have learned over the last decades is that, unless there is infinite patience, not just in one of us but in all of us to learn from below, we cannot stand for their collectivity, if anyone ever can, when freedom from oppression, from not having rights, turns around, one hopes, to the freedom to be responsible. It is always Mandela on the Springboks that one quotes: "We have to surprise them with restraint and generosity."[26]

Thus, to that impossible "if only . . . ," I add the statement from Assia Djebar that I have already cited (see page 109): "If only I could cathect [*investir*] that single spectator body that remains, encircle it more and more tightly in order to forget the defeat!" This is where developing the possibility of "being silent together," perhaps, becomes our task. This task is unverifiable, and the desire to claim it on the part of the one above who wants to be downwardly mobile is strong. Because "woman" remains a special case, there are human figures here—as if in a rebus. Their distance from the inscription of collectivities is part of a "thing-presentation"

Figure 11:   Liberation Bookstore, Alice Attie (2000).

rather than a "word-presentation," to analogize somewhat irresponsibly from Freud to signify a position behind access to collective verbality.[27]

Here now are prosthetic inscriptions of female collectivity: buttocks, shoes, hats, heads (Figures 14–17). There was a gap in the window of

Figure 12: Fish & Chips, Alice Attie (2000).

Figure 13:   Real Estate, Alice Attie (2000).

Coco Shoes and in Virgo Beauty Salon Restaurant through which one could glimpse the inside. Today this kind of combination and merger has been institutionalized on another level of capital abstraction. But here there is no attempt at coherence. To the outsider today the storefronts mark a doubling that seems humorous, naïve, perhaps witty. Was it always thus?

Now Corvette, one of the original large businesses in Harlem (Figure 18). Driving down 125th Street toward the Triboro Bridge, Alice saw this blazing storefront as she was growing up. At the time of picture taking, there were rumors: what would come in its place? HMV, Old Navy, Modell's, Starbucks, Sony? Corvette is gone now and in its place is Duane Reade.

Here is one of Attie's shots of the future, this one a palimpsest of old Harlem revamped ("THE UNITED CHURCH OF PRAYER FOR ALL PEOPLE") and held reversed in the new globo-America (Figure 19). The power to displace the new lexicalization, perhaps? But I am not speaking of individuals. I am talking about the disappearance of disenfranchised or disabled collectivities as we develop. I am talking about everyday social Darwinism, not only the survival of the fittest but also, if one thinks of the patter of the developers, "the burden of the fittest." Remember the

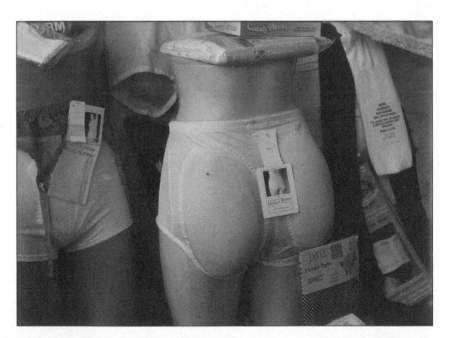

Figure 14:   Perfect Comfort, Alice Attie (2000).

Figure 15:   Coco Shoes, Alice Attie (2000).

Figure 16:   Hats—Exercise Faith, Alice Attie (2000).

Figure 17: *Virgo Beauty Salon*, Alice Attie (2000).

Figure 18: Corvette, Alice Attie (2000).

innocence of the bearers of "Ethernet"? Through an indoctrination into a relentless culturalism in the dominant, these kids will get the charge of the New Empire, not the bereft instrumentality of the high-tech Hong Kongers.

As it was, this picture took its domestic place with the international critique of my interlocutor in the subway station (Figure 20). "I had a dream, it is for you to fulfill it," Martin Luther King weeping. Now, the tears painted over, the mural shines with fresh color between a new Lane Bryant and the old "Kiss." A bit of a Lenox Lounge here, although not quite so royal. (I revise on the 2010 anniversary of King's speech, and the conservative tele-journalist Glenn Beck has reclaimed King for racism.)[28]

In 1939–1941, "a few dozen [anonymous male] photographers fanned out to every corner of every borough [of metropolitan New York] to shoot virtually every building then standing."[29] The purpose here is not to memorialize but to construct a database for tax purposes. I have seen fourteen of these. "If only I could cathect that single spectator body that remains, encircle it more and more tightly in order to forget the defeat!" (Figure 21).

Could those anonymous male photographers have imagined a situation in New York City when, more than sixty years later, this wish would be expressed, by way of an Algerian and a half-Syrian sister, by a female East Indian New Yorker? That is the force of the "perhaps," the undecidability of the future on which we stake our political planning. Nothing

Figure 19:   United House—Disney,
Alice Attie (2000).

may come of it. But nothing will survive without this effort. Love feeds research. It is a love that can claim nothing.[30]

Was there a failure of love in that silent independent short film *Orchard Street* in the Lower East Side of New York City, made by Ken Jacobs in 1956, nine years before Lyndon Johnson relaxed the quota system in U.S. immigration law? Because I am somewhat critical of the film, I felt hesitant about asking Mr. Jacobs to let me include clips, although I believe that he is no more caught in his time than we are in ours. White male independent filmmakers like him were attempting to distinguish themselves from Hollywood. Before the age of political correctness, the film betrays certain stereotypes, which give legitimacy to identity politics. The beautiful young East Asian woman, dressed in what could be sexwork clothes, sashays across the screen. The white child on a tricycle moves out of the screen at speed. A pair of African-American legs in baggy trousers sweeps refuse up and down the screen, the only repeated shot in this short film. You wouldn't have guessed that Malcolm X was active in the city at this time. To be a New Yorker is also to keep the neighborhoods separate.

I close with the permissible narrative of what disappears as development happens. "What is an endangered species?" asked the wall text of Cynthia Mailman's exhibition in the Staten Island Institute of Arts and Sciences (Figures 22–24). "Simply put," the text continued,

> it is any organism whose population has declined to the point of possible extinction. During the past 400 years the human species has played an impor-

Figure 20:   I Had a Dream, Alice Attie (2000).

tant role in the extinction of certain species. The most celebrated extinctions in recent times involve birds. The passenger pigeon, which once occurred in flocks numbering in the millions, the Carolina parakeet, great auk and Labrador duck all succumbed to the pressures of either overhunting or habitat destruction, all within a relatively short period of time. . . . We have to rely on the artist's renderings of the fringed gentian [warns the text], chokecherry and blue marsh violet since all have disappeared from the Staten Island landscape.[31]

The intent to memorialize can be signified by way of the frames, in the style of medieval illuminated manuscripts. And, because nature is presumed to be without history in this time frame, a species here can presumably come back as the same from the verge of extinction.

Figure 21:   A Lost City, Frozen in Time (1940). Tax Photographic Collection, Municipal Archives of the City of New York.

"This magnificent raptor," runs the wall text for this one, "was once on the verge of extinction due to thinning of its eggshells caused by pesticidal spraying. A ban on the use of DDT in the 1970s, coupled with Federal protection, paved the way for a successful comeback. In the 1990s it was removed from the endangered species list" (Figure 24).

Figure 22: Turn of the Century Wetlands, Staten Island, Cynthia Mailman (1999). Eco-Illuminations exhibition, Staten Island Institute of Arts and Sciences, 2000.

Figure 23: Turn of the Century Wetlands, Disappeared Flora, Staten Island, Cynthia Mailman (1998). Eco-Illuminations exhibition, Staten Island Institute of Arts and Sciences, 2000.

This romantic conviction ("no hungry generations tread thee down") is dubious at best. "Biologically, the gene pool is badly impoverished; ecologically, its relation to the environment is radically altered. Are the herds of bison raised in national parks 'the same' as the herds the Indians hunted?"[32] But it is certain that there can be no hope of a successful comeback as a repetition of the same for inscribed collectivities, forever vanishing. A seamless culturalism cannot be as effective as federal protection and a ban on DDT.

At the Staten Island institute, this head is part of the permanent collection (Figure 25). The curator, Ed Johnson, writes as follows:

> The story of its finding is perhaps best told by George F. Kunz, who presented the head at a meeting of the Natural Science Association of Staten Island on 10 May 1884. . . . "The features are too well cut for a common off-hand piece of work by a stonemaker: the style is not Egyptian or Eastern; rendering it unlikely that it is a part of an antiquity thrown away by some sailor; it is rather Mexican, and still more resembles Aztec work. This leads to the inference that it is possibly of Indian origin."

Johnson also comments on the name "Lenape" given to the Indian head: "A term derived from the Unami language, meaning 'common,' 'ordinary,'

Figure 24:   United States of America, Turn of the Century, Cynthia Mailman (1999). Eco-Illuminations exhibition, Staten Island Institute of Arts and Sciences, 2000.

or 'real' people." For convenience, used to describe the Indians who lived on Staten Island and New Jersey in late prehistoric and early historic times.[33] It is indeed convenient to have one serviceable name; as in the case of Yoruba, collectively naming, for convenience, the delexicalized collectivities of Òyó, Ègbá, Ègbádò, Ijèsà, Ijèbú, Ekítí, Nàgò into a single colonial name.[34]

Where does originary hybridity begin? What, indeed, is it to be a New Yorker? We must push back on the trace of race in identity rather than insist on exclusive culture in order to ask that question. This is not to forget that the other side oppresses in the name of race, but its opposite: not to legitimize it by reversal.

The naming of the Lenape loosens us from location, as does the convenience of Yoruba. Music mixes it up; jazz is hybrid at the origin.

The "originary" is a move—like the clutch disengaging to get a stick-shift car moving. The originary is precisely not an origin. Thus the most recent arrival engages that originary move as well. Alice and I are caught in it. In the fierceness of divisive identitarianism and/or benign diversitarianism, how many such New Yorkers are we? What are the implications of corporate promotion of culture as tax shelter as in today's Harlem? New York is also the foremost financial center in the United States, perhaps in the world. Was there ever a felicitous sender and receiver of those inscriptions that Alice photographed?

Figure 25: *"Lenape" Stone Head,* Bill Higgins (2000). Staten Island Institute of Arts and Sciences.

Let it be marked here that I live now where the Lenape walked, to go down to the river to fish and catch clams and oyster: 158th Street and Riverside Drive:

In April 1609, Henry Hudson sailed his ship the Half Moon up a river that would eventually bear his name, looking for passage to the Pacific. On the

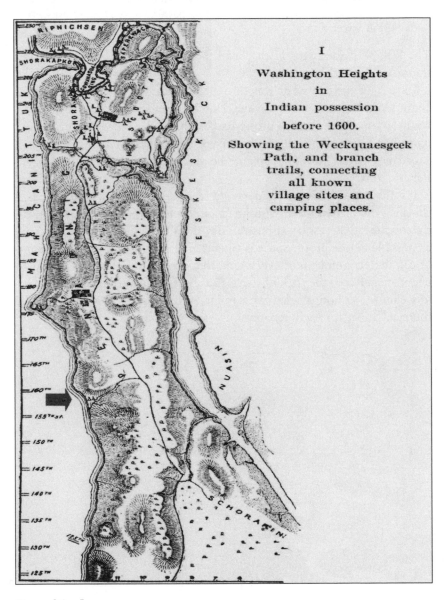

Figure 26:   Lenape map.

river's right bank stretched a verdant island some 13 miles long. The Native American Lenape people called it Manna-hatta, roughly translated as "island of many hills." Approximately two-thirds of the way up the island, in line with present-day 158th Street, Hudson and his crew passed a fishing camp, though in April, the Lenape people had probably not made their yearly migration to that spot yet. . . . Archeological evidence exposed during the construction boom of the early 1900s revealed that the Native American Lenape had once maintained a seasonal fishing camp at the foot of present-day 158th Street.[35]

The Lenape made maps in the head. Figure 26 shows a paper map of their land. I live there now.

I live right next to what was once "New Harlem": "Within a quarter century of Hudson's 1609 voyage, Dutch colonists had settled in lower Manhattan and by 1637, a group had established a village in the flat expanse just south of the hills the Lenape people called *Penadnic*. The Dutch called their village New Harlem and the rocky heights to the north, Jochem Pieter's Hills."

It is the negotiability of senders and receivers that allows teleiopoiesis, touching the distant other with imaginative effort. The question of negotiability, like all necessary impossibilities, must be forever begged, assumed as possible before proof. Space is caught in it, as is the calculus of the political, the economic, and everything that writes our time. I ask you to negotiate between the rock of social history and the hard place of a seamless culture, to honor what we cannot ever grasp. Is there anyone out there any more for such negotiations, except in name?

CHAPTER TWENTY

Scattered Speculations
on the Subaltern and the Popular

ERE I AM in the belly of the beast, arguing subalternity with a
second academic generation of U.S. subalternists in the presence
of the first generation of brothers always claimed as authorities—
with the father, Ranajit Guha (affectionately nicknamed "Pope" by the
brothers) absent in Australia.[1]

(It may be added that the first claim to subaltern studies, after metropolitan publication, came from Latin America via the University of
Pittsburgh.[2] Currently the claim has developed in France, Germany, Belgium, and Spain, on the part of the first generation of immigrant European students and academics, especially women. This is comparable to the
rise of Cultural Studies in the United States. In Italy, scholars hold on to
Indian Subaltern Studies, with a bit of Marx, a bit of Gramsci.[3] The U.S.
subalternists are led by South Asianists.

The "subaltern" as a concept has dissipated itself in the work of the
brothers in interesting ways. Foucault's unilinear criticism of "governmentality" [with bio-politics now added, as in Hardt and Negri] has inspired some of their most interesting writings.[4] It is therefore appropriate,
for example, that Michele Spano should be energized by Dipesh Chakrabarty's definition of the subaltern: "the figure of the difference that governmentality all over the world has to subjugate and civilize."[5] The earlier
Antonio Negri inherited this unilinear opposition to the state from Louis
Althusser.)

I have insisted throughout this book that Gramsci's attitude toward
the state sees it as both medicine and poison and leads to a permanent
educative activism. This has been corroborated, for me, by the conviction

that, in a global situation where the undoing of the possibility of a welfare state or dismantling already existing welfare states is required for the march of capitalism, "governmentality" has been made minor; and, when rampant, it was indifferent to the subaltern (as opposed to the working class or the deserving poor), incidentally obliged to keep difference in place. In such a situation, in response to metropolitan romanticization of something called the "subaltern," it is problematic to reproduce the voice of French or "French" ex-bourgeois critics of the twentieth century, impatient with the fruits of Second International Communism while distracted by a seemingly intractable Communist Party.[6] When I do so, I learn that governmentality subsumes the subaltern imperfectly, so that the subject remains unable to sabotage the Enlightenment. Why do we teach if we feel teaching is unnecessary? What I wrote must be read with these additions in mind.

Subaltern is to popular as gender is to sex, class to poverty, state to nation. One word inclines to reasonableness, the other to cathexis—occupation through desire. "Popular" divides between descriptive (as in presidential or TV ratings) and evaluative (not "high," both a positive and a negative value, dependent on your "politics") and contains "people," a word with immense range, from "just anyone" to the "masses" (both a positive and a negative political value, depending on your politics). The reasonable and rarefied definition of the word "subaltern" that interests me is: to be removed from all lines of social mobility.

The disciplinary interest of literary criticism is in the singular and the unverifiable. In "Can the Subaltern Speak?" it was the peculiar and singular subalternity of the young Bhubaneshwari Bhaduri that seemed of interest. Her story was my mother Sivani Chakravorty's testimony. The question of veridicality—of the evidentiary status of testimony, sometimes taken for granted in unexamined oral history—has to be thought of here.

Gilles Deleuze's notion of singularity is both complex and simple. In its simplest form, the singular is not the particular because it is an unrepeatable difference that is, on the other hand, repeated—not as an example of a universal but as an instance of a collection of repetitions. (Derrida will come to call this the "universalizable.") Singularity is life as pure immanence. As the name Bhubaneshwari Bhaduri became a teaching text, it took on this imperative—repeat as singular—as does literature.[7]

If the thinking of subalternity is taken in the general sense, its lack of access to mobility may be a version of singularity. Subalternity cannot be generalized according to hegemonic logic. That is what makes it subaltern. Yet it is a category and therefore repeatable. Since the general

sense is always mired in narrow senses, any differentiation between subalternity and the popular must thus concern itself with singular cases and
thus contravene the philosophical purity of Deleuze's thought.[8]

The starting point of a singular itinerary of the word "subaltern" can
be Antonio Gramsci's "Southern Question"—a discussion specifically of
underdeveloped Southern Italy—rather than his more general discussions
of the subaltern. I believe that was the basic starting point of the South
Asian Subaltern Studies collective—Gramsci, a communist, thinking beyond capital logic in terms of unequal development. Subsequently, Partha
Chatterjee developed a nuanced reading of both Gramsci and Foucault.[9]

It is from "Some Aspects of the Southern Question," then, that we can
move into Ranajit Guha's "On Some Aspects of the Historiography of
Colonial India."[10] "Subaltern" in the early Guha was the name of a space
of difference. And the word was indistinguishable from "people."

Although Guha seems to be saying that the words "people" and "subaltern" are interchangeable, I think this is not a substantive point for
him. At least in their early work, the members of the Subaltern Studies
collective would not quarrel with the notion that the word "subaltern"
and the idea of the "popular" do not inhabit a continuous space.

Subalternity is a position without identity. It is somewhat like the strict
understanding of class. Class is not a cultural origin, although there is
working class culture. It is a sense of economic collectivity, of social relations of formation as the basis of action. Gender is not lived sexual difference. It is a sense of the collective social negotiation of sexual differences
as the basis of action. Race assumes racism. Subalternity is where social
lines of mobility, being elsewhere, do not permit the formation of a recognizable basis of action. The early subalternists looked at examples where
subalternity was brought to crisis, and a basis for militancy was formed.
Even then colonial and nationalist historiography did not recognize it as
such. Could the subaltern speak, then? Could it have its insurgency recognized by the official historians? Even when, strictly speaking, they had
burst the outlines of subalternity? This last is important. Neither the
groups celebrated by the early subalternists nor Bhubaneshwari Bhaduri,
insofar as they had burst their bonds into resistance, were in the position
of subalternity. No one can say "I am a subaltern" in whatever language.
And subaltern studies will not reduce itself to the historical recounting of
the details of the practice of disenfranchised groups and remain a study
of the subaltern, in the sense in which the term is now useful.

Subalternity is where social lines of mobility, being elsewhere, do not
permit the formation of a recognizable basis of action. Both Gramsci and
Guha imply this, of course. But I came to it through Marx.

I came to it through the very well-known and misunderstood passage in the *Eighteenth Brumaire,* which I have repeatedly invoked in this book, where Marx is talking about class formation in two ways, about how the same group of people are and are not a class, depending upon whether they have a consciousness of class. Marx comes to the conclusion that small peasant proprietors in France are a class, to use contemporary language, as a constative, but not as a performative. It is in that connection that he writes: "They cannot represent themselves; they must be represented." That passage, about the difference between the two ways of being a class, was what gave me a sense of what I later learned to call the difference between subalternity and agency. Agency was the name I gave to institutionally validated action, assuming collectivity, distinguished from the formation of the subject, which exceeds the outlines of individual intention. The idea of subalternity became imbricated with the idea of non-recognition of agency. Did Marx intend this? I believe so. When I came across Bhubaneshwari's story, the resource that was to hand produced the account that this woman's resistance in extremis was not recognized. It was unfortunate that I used the metaphor of not-speaking for this. It caused a lot of confusion. Indeed, many readers think that metaphor applies to the widows burned on husbands' pyres. This leads to further confusion.

The line from the Marx passage to Bhubaneshwari Bhaduri can be discerned if we look at Marx's German. The best English translation goes: "They are therefore incapable of asserting their class interest in their own name." In the German it is *Sie sind daher unfähig, ihr Klasseninteresse im eigenen Namen . . . geltend zu machen.*[11] Because of the absence of infrastructural institutions, which are the condition and effect of class-consciousness, "they could not make their class-interest count," to have what they are saying and doing be recognized as such.

The early subalternists accepted this as the challenge of their new historiography. Their sources were the texts of an elite that was constituted by this non-recognition. They could not therefore deduce subalternity from the textual or archival evidence. They solved the problem by putting forward a "negative consciousness."[12] And I, instead of noticing that they were finessing the problem, said they were using essentialism strategically. But essentialism is always used strategically, to bypass or acknowledge difference. Today, realizing that subalternity is a position without identity—that like the value-form it is contentless—I cannot think that the project is to fill it with a "negative" essence. Subaltern content takes on identity, names itself "people." "People" becomes a slogan too quickly. To appreciate Gramsci's vision, we must know that, outside of such politics, subalternization does not stop. I have not been able to get my hands on Peter Hallward's book. But I understand he thinks this is just too non-specific and therefore not political.[13] Some people think an interest in the subaltern takes us away from secularism. I have tried to answer that charge in "Terror: A Speech after 9/11," Chapter 18 in this book.

> To want to hegemonize the subaltern, of which the subalternist revision of historiography is an important but relatively autonomous part, transforms the academic intellectual into a "permanent persuader."[14] The subalternists, having chosen to persuade a change in the historiography of the nineteenth, and the first half of the twentieth centuries in India, exhausted that vein when the project became a part of curricula. They seem now engaged in excellent postcolonial exercises away from the subaltern classes. Alternatively, there is some recounting of the details of the practice of disenfranchised groups. This is useful work, but only constative, there is no effort here to touch the subaltern or, with the energy with which historiographic practice is questioned, to question the political strategy that appropriates the disenfranchised in the interest not of governmentality, but democracy as body count, hardly bio-politics either. This is, of course, perfectly compatible with established ideas of the role of the academic intellectual. Contemporary political conduct, as it is now studied by the subalternists, does not rise to the status of the texts of the elite in earlier work. It is not decoded and contrasted to that which it subverts: the conformity of the subaltern to its own social norms. I am suggesting, of course, that this, the decoding and subverting of the elite text, was the "performative" part of early subalternist work, in the interest of changing historiography. Today, there is no residue of that earlier clandestine attempt to graft this performative and the constative of correct historical description.[15]

The oral version of what became "Can the Subaltern Speak?," titled "Power and Desire," was presented before I had read the first volume of *Subaltern Studies*. Perusal of that book and the subsequent meeting with the collective represented such a change in intellectual direction that it led to the placement of the initial theoretical coding upon a collective (rather than singular) phenomenon: Sati-reform: white men are saving brown women from brown men. That incendiary sentence, come back to haunt our time, does not apply to the abstract virtue of the reform itself, of course. In the essay the reform is called "in itself admirable!"[16] In order for the presuppositions of the reform to reach the affective field of the popular, however, a kind of involvement with subaltern female subjectivity had to be undertaken that was inconsonant with colonialism. Although the essay did not fully theorize the connection between this absence of affective/epistemic change with the non-recognition of Bhubaneshwari's "resistance," that is its burden. Thus the focus of subalternity in the essay remained the singular woman who attempted to send the reader a message, as if her body were a "literary" text. The message of the woman who hanged herself was one of unrecognizable resistance, an unrecognizable refusal of victimage by reproductive heteronormativity. As already mentioned, I had learned the importance of making unrecognizable resistance recognizable from "The Eighteenth Brumaire," a rather different recognition from the one touted by today's liberal multiculturalism.[17]

The only criticism of the subaltern studies group in "Deconstructing Historiography" was that they were gender-blind. In the next volume, Ranajit Guha produced "Chandra's Death," where the dead woman also remained singular.[18] There too the theme is reproduction. But the woman is a victim, without even the minimal activity of suicide.

What I am now suggesting is that constative subaltern studies, radical in its place and time, was questioning colonial and nationalist as well as Marxist historiography. Its connection to the performative was to attempt to expand the horizons of historiography. I am suggesting that their focus on the bringing into crisis of subalternity *by* the subaltern, and its non-recognition because they could not make it *count* for such historians as Eric Hobsbawm, who called such activity "pre-political," inevitably called for another kind of "setting-to-work," to which most of them did not rise. I am suggesting that Gramsci also called for such a setting-to-work in his conception of the organic intellectual. The call is for another performativity, a contamination of the outlines of historiography by its own place in history, so that the subaltern is not merely protected by "negative consciousness," as the new historiography continues endlessly to read the archives against the grain. Such work is useful, but only, at best, for correcting the constative.

In *Primitive Rebels,* Eric Hobsbawm enters into the intimacy of the ethnographer with the communities he describes as "pre-political."[19] He believes in accessing the mind-set of the other, "getting a 'feel' for them" (p. v), yet he finds comfort in knowing that some of his subjects will never read his books (p. vi). This is disciplinary protection of another kind. In my interdisciplinary intervention, I began to see (this is, of course, an abreactive stereotyping of myself) that, however ethnographic his practice, Hobsbawm did at least call them pre-political, not pre- or para-historical, nor merely anthropological, so perhaps he was not quite as culpable as the nationalist historiography that could not make these people count as history. Yet Hobsbawm too was stopping the problem of the unrepresentability of the subaltern (position) with no more than ethnographic regret.

Gramsci, the thinker of subalternity as an amendment of mere capital logic, had, in his figuration of the organic intellectual, given us an idea of expanding the horizon of historiography as an activity. In an extended consideration, I would question the concept-metaphor of the "organic," but that would not lead to a disagreement with Gramsci's general point.

This entire book is driven by the notion of subalternity, which in turn drove a classically aesthetically educated, class-displaced Southern European named Antonio Gramsci. I will therefore not linger on a specific analysis here. Suffice it to say that, when I first delivered this lecture, the subaltern I proposed was somewhat more impervious than Gramsci's. There are at least two reasons for this. First, Gramsci's thought-world had seemed to be more mono-gendered than it was. And, subalternity as position without identity computed differently in a world where the role of the Communist Party as envisaged by Gramsci in his jail cell was significantly different from anything that either we or the early subalternists could imagine.[20] This too has changed with the sweeping mandates of the international civil society. And one particular insight of Gramsci's has remained pertinent throughout: "The intellectuals are the dominant group's 'deputies' exercising the subaltern functions of social hegemony and political government."[21] I add here Raymond Williams's dynamic sense of the "dominant" as defined by its ceaseless appropriation of the emergent, as it is forced into mere alternative from the actively oppositional, the lines shifting, another one of my touchstones. Hobsbawm's and the early subalternists' limiting of the subaltern within the historiographical may be seen as such an appropriation. By contrast, it was the intention of saving the singular oppositional that the example of Bhubaneshwari Bhaduri taught me so long ago. That message in her body led outside disciplinary limits.

Gramsci's description of the organic intellectual fits the vast network of U.S. tertiary education well: "the 'organic' intellectuals which every new class creates alongside itself and elaborates"—Gramsci uses this word in the strong sense of "working through"—"in the course of its development, are for the most part 'specialisations' of partial aspects of the . . . activity of the new social type which the new class has brought into prominence."[22]

I think it can be argued that there is such a connection between the gradual emergence of a global secessionist managerial class, and a self-styled international civil society of self-selected moral entrepreneurs with no social contract—with the transference of power from Britain to the United States in the middle of the last century—and the transmogrification of the subaltern into the humanist figure of the "people," a noun that cannot enter into singularity. Our conjuncture needs "people," a pluralized general category that has no necessary class-description.[23] In a broad understanding, the subaltern historian as the historian of the popular is the organic intellectual of the class-shuffle between the old and new imperial worlds. Gramsci had expanded class-logic to think of bringing the subaltern into hegemony. This new development recodes both class-logic and the Gramscian task for corporate fundraising to purchase virtue for capitalist globalization.

Insofar as one can examine one's own production, I situate my concern with subalternity within this narrative. One must think that this can help produce an effort not to be helplessly confined within one's class-culture of origin, an effort not to be fully determined by history. One recalls with embarrassment Gramsci's further description: "The mode of being of the new intellectual can no longer consist in eloquence, which is an exterior and momentary mover of feelings and passions, but in active participation in practical life, as constructor, organizer, 'permanent persuader' . . ." This may seem too radical if your goal is the constative, but there is no gainsaying that Gramsci is looking to "generat[e] by a joint and simultaneous grafting . . . of the performative and the constative."[24] I defend this effort by quoting Gramsci further, and questioning both "the position assumed by the social complex of intellectuals [whose philosophy] can be defined as the expression of that social utopia by which the intellectuals think of themselves as 'independent,' autonomous, endowed with a character of their own, etc.," and, on the other hand, those old-style new historiographers who have forgotten that "school is the instrument through which intellectuals of various levels are elaborated."[25]

What we are speaking of, then, is the bringing of the subaltern from the deduced *subject* of crisis to the logic of *agency*. Can this be equated with the activation of singularity into multiplicity? I think not.

Singularity was a questioning of the universal-particular dyad. The singular is repeated, with a difference. That is how the "human" is repeated-in-difference in single humans, prior to the construction of personhood or individuality. It is a powerful concept, anchored in good sense, questioning both universalism and identitarianism. Such differently repeated singularities collectively are a multiplicity. This is not an empirical collective, not, in other words, a multitude. As long as we remember these are ways of thinking, always inclined to the empirical, we can continue to work. If we reduce them to the empirical alone, turn subaltern into popular, we are merely disputatious chroniclers.

If the repetition of singularity that gives multiplicity is the repetition of difference, agency calls for the putting aside of difference. Agency presumes collectivity, which is where a group acts by synecdoche: the part that seems to agree is taken to stand for the whole. I put aside the surplus of my subjectivity and synecdochize myself, count myself as the part by which I am metonymically connected to the particular predicament, so that I can claim collectively, engage in action validated by that very collective. A performative contradiction connects the metonymy and the synecdoche into agential identity.[26] All calls to collectivity are metonymic because attached to a situation. And they work by synecdoche. Now in order to be able to restrict singularity by agential intuition, an immense labor of infrastructural change, to make resistance count *(geltend),* to make it recognizable, must be undertaken. This is where aesthetic education kicks in, sees the way reasonable agency is nestled in the permission to be figurative—the right to the metonym/synecdoche political performance of collectivity. I will give an example in a moment. But let me say here that this is where the humanities can reclaim a part of history for the "human" as it plays with qualitative social science. To mistake this for classical humanism is to ignore history and politics. The outlines of historiography must be contaminated if it wishes to continue as subalternist. Making something count is not counting things, on the way to quantification. (Quantification has won. The imaginative social sciences bite the dust more discreetly than the humanities, beggars at the global feast.)

I have said that the "singular," as it combats the universal-particular binary opposition, is not an individual, a person, an agent; multiplicity is not multitude. If, however, we are thinking of potential agents, when s/he is not publicly empowered to put aside difference and self-synecdochize to form collectivity, the group will take difference itself as its synecdochic element. Difference slides into "culture," often indistinguishable from "religion." And then the institution that provides agency is reproductive heteronormativity (RHN). It is the broadest and oldest global institution. You see now why just writing about women does not solve the problem of the gendered subaltern, just as chronicling the popular is not subaltern studies. In search of the subaltern I first turned to my own class: the Bengali middle class: Bhubaneshwari Bhaduri and Mahasweta Devi. From French theory that is all I could do. But I did not remain there. In the middle class, according to Partha Chatterjee, Bhubaneshwari Bhaduri was metaleptically substituting effect for cause and producing an idea of national liberation by her suicide. Chatterjee's argument is that an idea of national liberation was produced by so-called terrorist movements.[27] A daring and "Clytemnestra-like" project for a woman.

In the subsequent years the gendered subaltern, for me, kept moving down the social strata. Class is not the exact word here because we are speaking of an area beside capital logic. Relative autonomy does not apply here, first, because autonomy is a marked concept. Secondly, because, in the commonplace agential sense, there is minimal agential autonomy in engendered subalternity. My discussion of Mahasweta Devi's "Doulati the Bountiful," in *Outside in the Teaching Machine*, describes a literary representation of the female subaltern as holding up the rural economy.[28] This downward trajectory came to relate to home working, permanent casuals, more orthodox doubts of the Marxist analysis of the female laboring body as the agent of production.

As you can see, however, in what I am writing today, the problems that emerged out of "Can the Subaltern Speak?"—the problem of subjectship and agency, and the call to build "infrastructure" in the colloquial, not the Marxist sense, so that agency would emerge—have not left me. At that stage already, I saw agency as institutional validation, whereas subject formation exceeded the borders of the intending subject, to put it brutally briefly once again. And I saw reproductive heteronormativity (RHN) as the broadest global institution. Now, in addition, I see agency as the play of self-synecdochizing in a metonym. To "restore rights to the people" without laying the groundwork for this (political) will can be well-intentioned, but only that, and at best.

In general, the leaders of collectivities—"good" or "bad"—have the right to the metonym/synecdoche complex. That the rank and file do not sometimes gets overlooked. That I believe is the difference between "good" and "bad" movements. My foray into teacher-training for the subaltern is because they also are citizens, *the* name for hegemony. In order to work for them, I set aside my differences—Columbia Professor, dollar income, classed caste-birth, and all that comes with them. I synecdochize myself as nothing but a citizen of India, which is where my tribal students, their parents and relatives, and I can form a collectivity, in search of agency. On the other hand, they are not free to put aside their differences. The effort is to build infrastructure so that they can, when necessary, when the public sphere calls for it, synecdochize themselves. The solution, as I see it, is not to celebrate or deny difference, but find out what inequality brings about its use and who can deny it on occasion. The solution is also not to create "a politics of recognition" where this problematic is altogether ignored. The solution cannot come to us from the international civil society, distributing philanthropy without democracy.[29] I believe the existing debates about contingency and universality have not taken this into account.[30]

Here is another example, from the other end of the spectrum. Donald Pease the Americanist was recently suggesting that in the wake of 9/11, with civil liberties constrained by the Patriot Act and the general atmosphere of suspicion and fear, the will of the citizen of the United States has become separated from the state.[31] This too is a kind of subalternity because the part is no longer part of the whole, and therefore the power to self-synecdochize has been taken away. Bruce Ackerman had suggested some years ago that "We the people" in the U.S. polity are not engaged on an ordinary day. It's only when there are transformative Supreme Court decisions and popular mandates that they act.[32] And now Donald Pease was suggesting that even that has been changed. He, however, was not able to see that RHN kicks in here as well. Although the citizen is subalternized inside the nation-state—the United States—outside in the world agency is reclaimed, generally in the name of gender. Gender is the alibi for much U.S. violence abroad. That has as little persuasiveness for the thinking of subalternity as a position without identity as does gender-oppression in the name of cultural difference. "People" will play into both these extremes. If we grasp subalternity as a position without identity we will think of building infrastructure for agency. Ethical sameness cannot be compromised. The point is to have access to the situation, the metonym, through a self-synecdoche that can be withdrawn when necessary rather than confused with identity.

I always hesitate to talk about my teacher-training efforts. But, if I am going to suggest that the task is to take Hobsbawm a step further, to make the anthropologist construct her object as a teacher for a different end, learn to learn from below, *from* the subaltern, rather than only study him (her), I have to make an attempt. In a social science audience, I can call it "fieldwork." Then you can take a small example and people will not dismiss you. In a social science audience I can call it "case studies." It is a small undertaking going on for twenty-five years and it has its place in the movement of the subaltern as I am describing it. (The reader will remember the brutal eye-opener in the middle of it.) My project has become more and more not only to study the subaltern (always in the sense of "cut-off from lines of social mobility") but to learn (as from figuration—because I am a literary person) from them in order to be able to devise a philosophy of education that will develop, for want of a better expression (since I don't write about this fieldwork, generalizable phrases don't come immediately), the "habits of democratic behavior," or "rituals of democratic behavior," or "intuition of the public sphere." (To what end, I now ask, though I will not give up. In the Introduction I expressed a hope that from a subaltern intellectual may come ideas that will bear fruit. False hope?)

By now it should be clear that "insertion into the public sphere" means for me the effort to create the possibility of metonymizing oneself for making oneself a synecdoche, a part of a whole, so that one can claim the idea of the state belonging to one. That is a citizen: the state is in the citizen's service. This is hopelessly idealistic, especially in the context of a repressive state, in the current era of globalization where the state is more and more reconfigured as not the agent of redistribution, but the agent of repression. The idea of relating to the state in a country as multilingual and multicultural, as many-leveled as India—and to a degree such differences exist everywhere—unless you want to go through nationalism/fascism, you must be able to metonymize/synecdochize yourself, understand the part by which you are connected to that abstract whole so that you can claim it. It's not even the right to metonymize oneself, but it's the possibility. This kind of work can only be a supplement to much more quick-fix, problem-solving work. But if it isn't there then subalternization remains in place and accounts of popular practice as political society remain constative.

This is where the responsibilities of borrowing Gramsci's word have brought me. It is the next stage of the work with a trajectory of the subaltern. Not to study the subaltern, but to learn. I'm a humanities teacher. I'm not a historian or an anthropologist. My disciplinary formation is to expand the capacity to learn and teach reading in the most robust sense— not only to classify, record, and describe. It is not a neat divide, but "scholarship" is more instrumental here. Therefore, the disciplinary doors of history and anthropology are closed to me. I have chosen a reading task: to learn from these collectivities enough to suture rights thinking into the torn cultural fabric of responsibility; or, to vary the concept-metaphor, activate a dormant ethical imperative. (I have quoted Gramsci's uncanny intuition of this on page 8.) The text is text-ile. To suture here is to weave, as in invisible mending.[33] The work takes me to the breakup of rural welfare in China, and the transformation of indigenous knowledge in South Africa. And this brings me to the new subaltern, about whom I have written elsewhere.[34]

So far I have spoken of the old subaltern, withdrawn from lines of social mobility, in terms of an educational enterprise that in a supplementary way tries to release the possibility of self-abstraction, self-synecdoche. Merely trying to release the possibility—it won't happen in the classroom tomorrow. By infrastructure, I had earlier meant the effort to establish, implement, and monitor structures that allow subaltern resistance to be located and heard. In the interim years, through the electronic circuits of globalization, the subaltern has become greatly permeable. Much of a pastiche of "global" culture is lexicalized in a fragmentary fashion in the underclass public world. (To lexicalize is to separate a linguistic item from its appropriate grammatical system into the conventions of another grammar, as I have explained in Chapter 19, "Harlem," in this book.) But the permeability I speak of is the exploitation of the global subaltern as source of intellectual property without the benefit of benefit sharing,[35] pharmaceutical patenting, and social dumping. This is the bottom edge of bio-politics. A little ownership of governmentality, persistently supplemented by aesthetic education, would be useful here! I take my lesson from the failure of the ownership of the means of production. Call it the Gramscian shift to civil society as poison/medicine if you like.

There is no permeability in the opposite direction. That is where the permanent effort of infrastructural involvement is called for. I am not speaking of organizing international conferences with exceptionalist "examples" of subalternity to represent collective subaltern will. The subaltern has no "examples." The exemplary subaltern is hegemonized, even if (and not necessarily) in bad faith. This must be distinguished from the desperate and hardly perceptible effort at faking subaltern collecting initiative by the leaders of counter-globalist resistances. I have called it "feudality" without "feudalism." I don't think it's a good idea at this point to take a real position against it, because I know where the desperation comes from.

Here too I will speak of tapping subjectship for the sake of agency, as in teacher training among the subaltern. For what we need is not only legitimate benefit sharing. We need also to prepare the field for sharing, however incomplete. Professor Hayden, whom I cite in note 35, speaks of Mexico. I have some experience of South Africa in terms of the transformation of indigenous knowledge into intellectual property. My limited experience would tell me that even as organizations such as the *Indigenous Knowledge Systems of South Africa Trust* are trying to make benefit-sharing equitable, they remain complicit with the idea that the transformation of indigenous knowledge systems into data is an unquestioned good. And that there need be no attention paid, beyond the descriptive attention of anthropology and archeology. The only alternative seems to be to say, "This is as good as what the heritage of the European world calls science." I do talk about the problem with the Hindu nationalist claim, in India, that the ancient texts of the Vedas offer us "Vedic science."[36] The problem of the Hindu Right is not that it cares for Vedic science, but that it uses it to prove that it is best, that it can oppress others in its name, that India belongs to it. The Hindu Right is not subaltern![37] The traditional healers in South Africa cannot be immediately compared to the Bharatiya Janata Party, although the fear of religious violence should be always around the corner. From within the humanities, I want to claim the traditional healer's sense of all history as a big now; I want to claim the sense of myth as being able to contain history, and keep de-transcendentalizing belief into the imagination. I remain a "lonely gun-runner," as I have heard myself described, turned into "permanent persuader," now trapped in the machine. Turn the traditional healers' performative into performance, not just transform it into data, was my hope, imitating Du Bois, but that too helps "development"—without an aesthetic education. The unintended consequence of it can also become an appropriation for religious fundamentalism, just as the intended consequence of the data transformation is exploitation. This is the cleft stick—the double bind—for the new subalternist.

To historicize the subaltern, then, is not to write the history of the singular. It is the active, scrupulous, and vigilant contamination of historiography from the constative through the disciplinary performative into the field of the historical possibility of what we can only call the present. Here the difference between the old and the new subaltern is only conjunctural. The category of the "popular" seems altogether tame when compared to this dynamic.

CHAPTER TWENTY-ONE

World Systems and the Creole

BEGAN THIS PIECE with a reference to Didier Coste's idea that Comparative Literature should go back to Romantic aesthetics by way of classical comparativist universalism. I pointed out that my efforts were identical with his, with the difference of perspective generated by the inadequacies of the former. I believe it was Coste who had suggested that I should have written *Death of a Discipline* in Bengali. I also believe that we should attend to the "good" Euro-U.S. comparativists who are proposing solutions confronting the discipline. We are with them; they should not find us dangerous. In that spirit, I was delighted, in 2005, to have been asked to respond to a paper by Wai Chee Dimock, like me a Westernized Asian comparativist. Again in the spirit of establishing alliances, I sketched out first the broad points of solidarity between Dimock and myself and then pointed to some suggestions for the kind of future work that can arise out of this undertaking, different from Coste's more traditional one.

First I found common ground in our reaction to the encyclopedist and cartographic work of Franco Moretti: "I would like," Dimock wrote, "to caution against what strikes me as [Moretti's] overcommitment to general laws, to global postulates operating at some remove from the phenomenal world of particular texts." This resonated with what I had written in *Death of a Discipline,* although I was, admittedly, a little stronger: "The world systems theorists upon whom Moretti relies . . . are . . . useless for literary study that must depend on texture."[1] Thanks to initiatives such as Dimock's, we can begin to emphasize the altogether obvious point: in order to do distant reading one must be an excellent close reader. Close reading for distant reading is a harnessing of aesthetic education for its own counter-example. We can call this a double bind, in keeping with the theme of this book. In the intervening years, what I have noticed is that the followers of Moretti often categorize by subject matter, but that was not part of that evening's discussion.

I also attempted to find common ground in Dimock's idea that "the epic is a cross-over phenomenon." I wanted to take this past simply noting the kind of intertextuality where a modern text clearly alludes to an ancient one, "encoding the temporal within the lexical," to quote Dimock. I suggested, as an example of this, that Maryse Condé's slim novel *Heremakhonon* deploys epic time in the management of narrative time. Clearly, with the disappearance of robust orality, the epic tendency could not just shrivel. Rather than call deliberately large-scale narrative undertakings "epic" by a species of descriptive metaphor of size and complexity, we could call Condé's attempt to train the memory of the reader by the impersonal heterogeneity of "historical" times a displacement of epic play. . . . Although I did not mention this at the time, you can see that this training is an aesthetic education in the "contemporaneity" of globalization. *Heremakhonon,* with its rich epic dimension—loosely named "Africa," "Islam," "decolonization," and the like (unitary names suppressing the plural epic as monoculture does biodiversity)—then opens the door closed by Aristotle when he compared the slim tragedy to the massive performative epic.[2] It is a large and generic door, closed when history, tied to the self-determination of the individual, began to be written on a gradual incomprehension of the miraculous *mnemic* scripting of orality. . . . To say that the timing of the text is hybrid is to learn to read its epic dimension and witness this acknowledgment.

In these three essays the tone is lighter. I am, after all, also a Comp Lit professor. Let's forget saving the world, how best do we do our job? We've had it with being dismissed as non-serious, poco presentist folks. So build bridges, agree where you can, but also make concrete suggestions. Here now is such a suggestion.

Dimock does not suggest, as do I, that in such use of narrative time, literature touches orature; but her argument can clearly take it on board. What in the more expanded argument confronts the scandal of Africa in globalization can here take a more teacherly stance. Comparative Literature has never treated the techniques of orature except formulaically. Is there another way?

For her distant reading, Dimock turns to anthropology as a model. I do of course most heartily endorse this move. Here I would like to elaborate a little and again, I feel confident that Dimock's approach can take this on.[3] I should mention that it is not really "literary anthropology" that Dimock uses as her model.

(My response was composed with reference to an earlier version of Dimock's essay. The phrase "literary anthropology" was used in its initial paragraphs:

> "I was in Beijing a few weeks ago," she had then started, and was struck by a phrase that seemed to come up again and again even in the handful of articles that I happened to be reading: "literary anthropology." This is not a phrase we use very much in this country; in fact, with the exception of Wolfgang Iser, I don't recall seeing it anywhere else. I (would?) like to borrow it as a preface to this talk, as a summary and apology for the very immodest claim that I seem to be making: namely, that in order to think about the epic and the novel in conjunction, we need an analytic frame that has to be measured in terms of continents, an analytic frame that reflects, not the life of a single nation, and not the life of a single language, but something like the life of the species as a whole, in all its environments, all its habitats across the planet.

SET AND SUBSET

"Anthropology" is probably the right word for this kind of undertaking. Of course, as we know, the discipline has its own internal problems, not least of all being its long history of entanglement with colonialism and indeed racism of various sorts. But, as a discipline adjacent to and yet not reducible to literary history, it does serve as an interesting heuristic partner. One of the most important differences, it seems to me, is that anthropology is, by and large, an empirical discipline, and brings with it a self-consciousness about what we might call the conditions of its empiricism: the size of the sampling population, the scope of the claim that flows from it, and the extent to which it can be said to constitute a unit of analysis. It is this self-consciousness that allows anthropology to operate on two alternating and complementary registers, bouncing one off against the other: one macro and the other micro, one, much larger than the scale of literary history, and the other, much smaller. The smaller scale is obvious enough: anthropology is a study of local knowledge, it is dedicated to a self-contained population, a subset of human beings. But this subset matters, I think it is fair to say, because it is a subset, because there is a larger set to which it belongs. This larger set answering to the name of the "human" is the implicit but also indispensable ground of anthropology. It becomes a discipline at all because this larger set is a meaningful set, a meaningful unit of analysis. And the database that goes with it is coextensive with the life of the species as a whole; it extends to every part of the planet where human beings happen to be. It is this relation between set and subset and the coextension of the former with the bounds of the human that I'd like to map onto our own discipline. There is no reason why literary history should not be construed as being parallel to anthropology in this particular sense: committed both to a local population and to an unlocal idea of species membership. There is no reason, in fact, why it should not work as a switch mechanism between these two, between a subset of human expression, and a species-wide definition of the set. The term that I'd like to propose for this switch mechanism is the term "genre."

I have kept my earlier comments because, although Dimock has now jettisoned literary anthropology and taken on fractal geometry to explicate Lévi-Strauss on kinship, her presuppositions about the relationship of literature to culture remain unchanged.

My point, which I keep repeating, is that I am one of them—five big names thinking to respond to a "crisis in Comparative Literature" rather different from the one that René Wellek was responding to: Pascale Casanova, Didier Coste, David Damrosch, Wai Chee Dimock, Franco Moretti.[4] I also repeat my interested difference, to which it is not necessary to give a violent name, as does Coste. There is much greater violence in the "value-added" testing of teachers, where teaching is commoditized in terms of customer data, in terms of which teachers in the United States are judged and sacked.[5] My difference is that these critics all want to classify in a cruder and less informed way than the old literary historical and generic classificatory attempts. My comments on the universalizability and generalizing characteristic of the literary have been sketched out all through the book.[6] Here Dimock, opposing Moretti's encyclopedism, goes into a balance rather cruder than Schiller's and altogether less nuanced than Marx's differentiation between human and species.

I stumbled on the idea that imperialism was an "enabling violation" at least thirty years ago. Subsequent work willy nilly located our class, now global, as the beneficiary, not only by birth, but by other circumstances as well. I have never been able to think of descriptive arguments for counter- or alternative modernities as anything but specific to this amorphous "class." Globality can save us if we assert that everything now is what "modern"—not counter-, not alternative—*is*, and live up to the task of disciplinary revision. Not every "European" invented the steam engine, not every "American" the telephone. Capital is the mysterious motor; we fight its implacable choices epistemologically.)

"Literary anthropology" is the genre of anthropology that deploys autobiography powerfully—Lévi-Strauss on the Nambikwara, Mick Taussig in his various writings, James Clifford, Kiran Narayan.[7] They are rather far from claiming the species as set. That gesture would belong more to what is today called physical anthropology, whose borders mingle with genetics. This too is not Dimock's terrain. It seems to us that Dimock is using masterfully what Kant, in the opening of his *Anthropology from a Pragmatic Point of View,* writes about fiction as a source of anthropological knowledge.[8] Here, too, I declare alliance. When I began my postcolonial journey with "Three Women's Texts and a Critique of Imperialism," written in the early 1980s, I struck out for literature as "cultural self-representation."[9] Dimock's insistence on close reading is faithful to Kant. In an appendix to *The Critique of Pure Reason* on the regulative use of the ideas of pure reason, Kant speaks of the making sense-perceptible of three basic ideas of conceptualizing logic. When doing so, Kant says, the investigating subject, the philosopher, takes the concept as a perspective, as on a hill, and sees a horizon, as a circle. The subject continues to develop the concept and finds more and more circles appear, newer horizons. When the case won't fit a circle, the seeker pushes the figure until it becomes an ellipse; and a parabola, and perhaps all the figures of geometry as a circle bent out of shape (Kant doesn't list them), until he (always a he in Kant, of course) comes upon the asymptote, two parallel lines running side by side, meeting only at infinity. You never get to empirical particularity when you are making logic palpable, says Kant, for the entire exercise is still only analogical.[10]

A merely reasonable system, such as the kind of analogical classification envisaged by distant reading, in other words, will not yield the singular.

Yet another point of entry for me is Virgil in the novels of J. M. Coetzee. Indeed, Virgil is in *Disgrace* as well, along with *King Lear* and Kafka's *The Trial.*

I will now make a tiny suggestion that will, at first, seem contrary to Dimock's conclusions. But in fact, it will lead to further work that can only secure her general argument, her claims to the world.

I would suggest that Latin is not a "foreign" language to Dante. The conversation between Virgil and Dante is in Latin, not in a foreign language. When Dante wrote *De vulgari eloquentia* in Latin, he referred to it as the language with a grammar.[11] All the various speeches that together make up "Italian" are simply vulgar (popular) speech—Latin creole, as it were—mutatis mutandis in the spirit of Proust's Marcel:

(The French words we are so proud of pronouncing accurately are themselves only "howlers" made by Gallic mouths in mispronouncing Latin or Saxon ... the longstanding mutilations that our ancestors, by speech defects, the intonation of some ethnic vulgarity, or mispronunciation inflicted on Latin and Saxon words, in a way that later elevated them into the grammarians' noble statutes).[12]

In the Latin Middle Ages, even Provençal is not a foreign language, but another Latin creole. Out of all the "Italian" creoles, Dante chooses curial Florentine, the most elegant version of his beloved Tuscan, as the one most worthy. It is not too far-fetched to say that, for Dante, Latin is *sanskrt* (refined), and vulgar speech—all those "Italians"—is *prakrt* (natural). If we look at playwrights such as Bhasa (fl. third century CE) or Kalidasa (fl. fifth century CE), we find them using Sanskrt and at least three Prakrts (the vulgar eloquence out of which the languages of North India consolidated themselves, my mother tongue Bengali in the late eleventh century). I would therefore like to place this within a more general phenomenon of creolity rather than take Aristotle's casual mention of foreign words as my model as it was Dimock's. (Indeed, the passage on the capacity of the epic to extend its own bulk has nothing to do with foreign words and large kinship structures at all.) Aristotle was not keen on the epic, as the close of the *Poetics* will show. And in translations other than Else's, in the Loeb bilingual edition, for example, γλοττου is translated "rare words," rather than "foreign."[13] My own inclination would be to follow the "wordy" authorized by the Greek-English Lexicon. The *Poetics* is as much a creative writing lesson as it is literary theory. Aristotle is cautioning future writers of tragedy against ponderous language.[14] The epic can get away with heavy language. It is a vulgar narrative form. Be sure not to use such stuff in tragedy, drama with a socially therapeutic mission. I think it is not a good idea to draw a foreign language rule for works that are "epic" in a sense rather far from Aristotle's day. On the other hand, creolity, as I have sketched it above, is about the delexicalization of the foreign. (To lexicalize is to separate a linguistic item from its appropriate grammatical system into the conventions of another grammar, as I have repeatedly reminded the reader of this book [see pages 406 and 583n.37].) It will yield us a history and a world.

(Dimock was conscientious enough to look up two specialist books on Dante, Latin, and Italian, in response to my gentle nudge. I am grateful to her for this. My point, however, was not to check up on scholarship, especially from the late 1950s, when some of the allocthonic metropolitan concepts I carry around had not yet reared their teratological heads. The point is to imagine a time when the name "Italian" is shaky—to imagine a different mind-set—dare I say episteme? I cite my postscript and remind the reader that, in my initial response, this is why I had quoted Proust, to be helped along in the task of imagining, an epistemological performance repeatedly called for in global "contemporaneity." I quote myself quoting Rilke, in a piece where I wrote of the Indic episteme (structure of feeling?) that gives us avatar, as not grasped by experts or filmmakers.[15]

> It is within this general uneven unanticipatable possibility of avatarana or descent—this cathexis by the ulterior, as it were, that the "lesser" god or goddess, when fixed in devotion, is as "great" as the greatest: *ein jeder Engel ist schrecklich.* How did Rilke know? Perhaps "culture" is semi-permeable by the imagination? Am I not cynical enough about Comparative Literature? *Mea maxima culpa.* I still go by Shelley's warning, always apposite [but now historicized and politicized, as you now have seen in the Introduction and Chapter 4, "The Double Bind Starts to Kick In"]: "We want the creative faculty to imagine that which we know.")

Dimock's work invites us to look beyond Latin into the word "genre." The Indo-European cognates in Sanskrit yield us both "gnosis" and "genesis," and in Sanskrit we find *jnana,* "gnosis," but also *jati* and *jnati,* "nation" and "kin." All these words are related to the word for knee, *janu, genoux,* use of gender (another genre word) as rape, kneeing into forcible entry, to engender.

This is what makes me a bit leery of the model of family: father, mother, competitive patricidal brothers, sisters emerging as support. No kinship system, alas, is composed only of cousins, as Dimock would have it. Yesterday I listened to my dear old friend Lord William Wallace of Saltire deliver to us his response to the question posed by the Catholic Conference of Bishops and the Archbishop's Conference of the Church of England: Is there a "European" war? What we heard was a model of trusteeship, of protecting non-European peoples as they make the transition into modernity, not the white man's burden, Wallace insisted. This fraternocracy takes us on to the family tree, which Nietzsche and Foucault had revised. I feel such a strong bond with Dimock's work that I would ask her to rethink family as creolity.

(Dimock has loosened the concept of family a good deal in the second version. I am grateful for this, but I would ask her to give it up altogether. "Rhizome" is a good choice and, to see how one can leave family behind via the rhizome's dismantling of the root, I invoke creolity again. There is a short checklist in my postscript. The French postcolonials mentioned there go a long way with the rhizome, away from "the family of man."[16]

In order to get away from the family romance, Dimock goes to fractal geometry. I am as suspicious of humanists metaphorizing the latest developments in science through their pseudo-popularizing descriptions as I am of nonspecialists offering Mesopotamia as evidence. I will not call the repeatable universalizable difference in singularity a "strange attractor" from chaos theory as does the self-help book that I use to keep my blood pressure under control.[17] This sort of irresponsible analogizing leads to pretentiousness in our students. Do we really need fractal geometry to tell us "the loss of detail is almost always unwarranted?" I keep insisting on learning languages, the old access to literary detail, rather than analogizing from descriptions of fractal geometry or chaos theory. What warms the cockles of my old-fashioned heart is that Dimock will not give up close reading, however far she fetches to justify it within the current rage for filing systems.)

I mentioned Kafka and Shakespeare, not just Virgil, in Coetzee. If we take creolity and intertextuality (rather than kinship connections and genre) as models that coexist with Dimock's rethinking of the epic and the novel, we can welcome *Ulysses* and *Finnegans Wake* into the enclosure. In "Ethics and Politics in Tagore, Coetzee, and Certain Scenes of Teaching" (Chapter 15 in this book), I have suggested that you can even welcome Rabindranath Tagore.

Perhaps this expansion of Dimock's point of view, as expressed by me, already happens in her next book. For now, I will say that "The Law of Genre," the Derrida text from which Dimock quotes, will allow this. The figure that Derrida offers, over against the border policing that he and Dimock repudiate, is "invagination," where a part insistently becomes bigger than the whole. In creolity one can find a persistent invagination that will make room for our alliance.

In conclusion, I offer a bit of an abject postscript for my word "planet." I made Jonathan Arac change his over-enthusiastic blurb for me as the proponent of "planetary comparative literature" to a description of me as trying to be a "planetary reader." Here I give my reasons, which will repeat what Chapter 16, "Imperative to Re-imagine the Planet," lays out in full. I spoke of planetarity in an address to a Swiss organization— Stiftung-Dialogik—in 1997. They had been formed to give shelter to refugees from the Third Reich. In the mid-1990s they were changing to accommodate refugees from various countries of Asia and Africa, torn asunder by violence and poverty. To mark this change, they asked me to offer a keynote. I was asking them to change their mind-set, not just their policy. And I recommended planetarity because "planet thought opens up to embrace an inexhaustible taxonomy of such names including but not identical with animism as well as the spectral white mythology of post-rational science." By "planet-thought" I meant a mind-set that thought that we lived on, specifically, a planet. I continue to think that to be human is to be intended toward exteriority. I have repeated this in many ways in this book. And, if we can get to planet-feeling, the outside or other is indefinite. Therefore I wrote (see page 339), more or less:

> If we imagine ourselves as planetary accidents rather than global agents, planetary creatures rather than global entities, alterity remains underived from us, it is not our dialectical negation, it contains us as much as it flings us away—and thus to think of it is already to transgress, for, in spite of our forays into what we metaphorize, differently, as outer and inner space, what is above and beyond our own reach is not continuous with us as it is not, indeed, specifically discontinuous. My efforts for the last two decades tell me that, if we ask the kinds of questions you are asking, seriously, we must persistently educate ourselves into this peculiar mind-set.

To explain: If we planet-think, planet-feel, our "other"—everything in the unbounded universe—cannot be a self-consolidating other, an other that is a neat and commensurate opposite of the self. I emphasize "education" in the passage above, and I mean specifically training the imagination, "aesthetic education," here reduced to Comp Lit in the classroom. Gifted folks with well-developed imaginations can get to it on their own. The experimental musician Laurie Anderson, when asked why she chose to be artist-in-residence at the National Aeronautics and Space Administration, put it this way: "I like the scale of space. I like thinking about human beings and what worms we are. We are really worms and specks. I find a certain comfort in that."

She has put it rather aggressively. That is not my intellectual style, but my point is close to hers. You see how very different it is from a sense of being the custodians of our very own planet, for god or for nature, although I have no objection to such a sense of accountability, where our own home is our other, as in self and world. But that is not the planetarity I was talking about.

Planetarity, then, is not quite a dimension, because it cannot authorize itself over against a self-consolidating other. In that mind-set, there is no choosing between cultures. It is the place of "unaccommodated man," to use Shakespeare's words, which I thought Coetzee's Lucy gendered: "a poor, bare forked animal."

If I seem hesitant about claiming the planet, I also have a cautionary word about harnessing Mesopotamia. I insist that I share these precautions with Dimock because I feel a strong alliance with her. As a modernist, I too feel the need to approach the medieval and ancient worlds. If I remind ourselves that a string quartet and a spider must not be conceptually related because they both have eight legs, it is because I too have indulged in making preposterous connections. As I have tried to point out in the cases of Aristotle and the epic, and Dante and Latin, people in different historical periods think differently, they inhabit different epistemes. We cannot take the English word "foreign" as a felicitous synonym for the word γλοττου spoken by Aristotle to his students and use it to construct a world system. (There is evidence that Aristotle thought he was himself a "stranger" because he was from Stagira, whereas Plato was a citizen of Athens. How does "foreign" figure here?) We cannot read if we do not make a serious linguistic effort to enter the epistemic structures presupposed by a text. Aristotle and Dante are far enough from us, but Mesopotamia is quite another story. The responsibility of the comparativist entails a greater familiarity with the language(s) and patterns of thought of that remote theater than our elation at finding "foreign" elements everywhere—that allows us to repeat what may be a bit of a literary-critical cliché—the epic as world system.

Some years ago, the Metropolitan Museum of Art in New York had an extraordinary exhibition on the "Art of the First Cities." The exquisite objects gave us a glimpse of a comparativism before the letter, a world system before our world. I remember reading of an extraordinary linguistic phenomenon in that distant world:

> [At the Old Babylonian Schools] the students were not simply learning the technique of calligraphy but were also studying Sumerian, a language that had long ceased to be spoken and that bore no resemblance to the Akkadian they spoke at home.... The language was long dead and was a typical "nonmother tongue," taught by old men to young boys who would hardly ever get to use it outside the school environment.[18]

How would a simple idea of "foreign" be negotiated in this space?

Postscript

When I proposed creolity rather than kinship as a model for comparativist practice to Dimock, I was thinking of Dante and Latin. It was clear to me that, for a very long time, the idea of one normative language and many "natural" ones was a much more powerful idea than the accident of there being many languages. When Ibn Rushd was translating Aristotle, he was not translating from a foreign language because to earn the right to translate was for him to make the language of the original his own. Marx was catching the tail end of this idea in his injunction about how to learn a foreign language in "The Eighteenth Brumaire of Louis Bonaparte."[19] I felt that it would be good if we thought of the great order of the literary as a kind of virtual and inaccessible normativity, and of our own methodological attempts as varieties of creole, testifying to their practical usefulness. Revising, I consulted the basic texts of the contemporary debate on creolity.[20] The entire debate is worth contemplating. Here I will content myself with citing Édouard Glissant, the initiator of the movement. Glissant's word for what I am seeking to describe is "relation." To generalize this notion he writes, among a thousand provocative things, for example:

> Let us try to recapitulate the things we don't yet know, the things we have no current means of knowing, concerning all the singularities, all the trajectories, all the histories, all the denaturations, and all the syntheses that are at work or that have resulted from our confluences. How have cultures— Chinese or Basque, Indian or Inuit, Polynesian or Alpine—made their way to us, and how have we reached them. . . . No matter how many studies and references we accumulate (though it is our profession to carry out such things properly), we will never reach the end of such a volume; knowing this in advance makes it possible for us to dwell there. Not knowing this totality does not constitute a weakness. . . . Relation is open totality; totality would be relation at rest. Totality is virtual.[21]

My affinity with Glissant's thinking should be immediately clear. Glissant's work is particularly useful as an antidote to the understandable but unfortunate comparativism that wants to begin with the "fact" that "literatures the whole world over were formed on the national model created and promoted by Germany at the end of the 18th century."[22] Here too I concur with Édouard Glissant's wisdom, warning non-Europeans from joining in this contrived collectivity: "if one is in too much of a hurry to join the concert, there is a risk of mistaking as autonomous participation something that is only some disguised leftover of old alienations"; he gives an astute account of the kind of comparativism the enthusiasts of world literature would require: "In order to 'comprehend' and thus to accept you, I have to bring your solidity to the ideal scale which provides me with themes for comparisons and, perhaps, judgments. I have to reduce."[23] An unintended consequence of work such as Dimock's can be to give support to such "interaction, out of which ghouls of totalitarian thinking might suddenly reemerge." I hasten to add that I have a great deal of sympathy with Professor Casanova, from whom I cited that symptomatic sentiment about the originality of the German eighteenth century. I caution her simply because I have learned the hard way how dangerous it is to confuse the limits of one's knowledge with the limits of what can be known, a common problem in the academy.

We cannot not want to tie up all the loose threads in any world. Yet today more than ever that desire must be curbed, for everything seems possible in the United States now. If we want to preserve the dignity of that strange adjective "comparative" in comparative literature, we will embrace creolity. Creolity assumes imperfection, even as it assures the survival of a rough future. In the creolization of the world's past, comparativists of all stripes can hang out together. Join us.

CHAPTER TWENTY-TWO

The Stakes of a World Literature

For Ralph Cohen

I F FRANCO MORETTI is hard control, Didier Coste and Wai Chee Dimock are soft control and so is David Damrosch. I wanted to work with these colleagues rather than be defined as an outsider, and this was a paper I presented, initially in Istanbul, in David's presence, in an effort at a dialogue, just as I had done so with Dimock in 2005. Charles Bernheimer, in his response to the 1997 ACLA report, had suggested "that multiculturalist comparatism begins at home with a comparison of oneself to oneself," figuring out the hybrid elements in any investigating self and comparing the histories in a literary way.[1] Didier Coste had, as we have seen, asked us to go back to the "cautious multiculturalism" of "classical comparative literature" in search of acceptable universalisms. Dimock recommended a swing between worldwide close reading and literary anthropology. Casanova gave us a reality check and told us that literature began in the European eighteenth century. Franco Moretti gave us encyclopaedist distant reading in the face of a global knowledge explosion. These colleagues were trying, yet all were bound in the double bind of Europe as guide to disciplinary objectivity and "Europe" as these investigators' national origin. (In the case of Dimock and Spivak, the "colonial subjectship" comes into play at "European origin.") I have done no more than make the double bind fully visible and signaled a loss of hope. To students I suggest Wellek, from the outskirts of Europe, writing something that can be expanded, though class-bound, as Asia and Africa attempted to expand Marx. (But look at what happened there without the Gramscian supplementary role of aesthetic education for the subaltern. Mao's monstrous cultural revolution was a simulacrum of Gramsci's insight into epistemological labor.) Here is Wellek:

The only right conception seems to me a resolutely "holistic" one which sees the work of art as a diversified totality, as a structure of signs which, however, imply and require meanings and values. Both a relativistic antiquarianism [World Literature?] and an external formalism [distant reading?] are mistaken attempts to dehumanize literary study. Criticism [epistemological performance?] cannot and must not be expelled from literary scholarship.[2]

Embroiled in academic politics, Wellek opposed what gives us the instrument of ab-use: the critique of "humanism" that saw it as phallogocentrism, fratrocentrism. That tradition continues in Bernheimer, who takes nothing else from Wellek. We must rescue him from the teaching machine, and remember that he is combating the nationalism and patriotism coming in after the two great wars of the twentieth century:

> A cultural power politics is recommended [by Ernst Robert Curtius]: everything serves only the strength of one's nation. I am not suggesting that the patriotism of these scholars was not good or right or even high-minded. I recognize civic duties, the necessity of making decisions, of taking sides in the struggles of our time. I am acquainted with Mannheim's sociology of knowledge, his *Ideology and Utopia,* and understand that proof of motivation does not invalidate the work of a man.

Wellek also sees this as an opposition and goes for "internal formalism" as does Schiller for balance. I'm not a man, I'm not afraid of invalidation any more. I'm not only a woman—de Man's Schiller was already there—but an old woman.[3] I try to recognize that "making decisions" and "internal formalism" are in a double bind that can never be solved, but protects decision making if the world is right; but our world is out of joint with globalization. Some of the projects above will be appropriated by the dominant for the politically correct ghetto. Let us consider this a frame for my olive branch to my colleague and friend: David Damrosch.

This is a practical text as it inhabits my work and life. I dedicate the text to Nimai Lohar, the only illiterate member of the rural poor vanguard with whom I work in India. In the spoken forum, I sing a line from a folk song that this man sang for me during my December 2008 visit to the schools. Because he is illiterate, Nimai still sings, but is embarrassed to do so in front of the others. We cannot read this as "subaltern literature." It is a song that Nimai has learned as part of his cultural conformity. He interprets it well, but not in a surprising way. The line that I sing goes: *Mon kore uribar torey, bidhi dey na pakha.* A careless translation would go: I wish to fly but fate gives me no wings. Carefully and literally, it would go: my mind makes for flying, but—and then the word *bidhi,* which can mean "law," "justice," as well as "fate/God"—*bidhi* does not give wings. I sing and read it because it can also describe our own stakes in world literature.

Kant said that the concept of the world in general is a regulative idea of merely speculative reason. We are able to think that every experiencing being, perhaps even animals, assumes a world. On the model of Walter Benjamin's effort to understand language, I could make up a corresponding title: "World as Such and the Worlds of Experiencing Beings."[4] Such efforts are not much more than a method of inquiry that makes us feel we are avoiding assuming a world *and* self as self-evident ground for empirical inquiry. This needs to be made more precise, but for lack of preparation I will take the next step. Let us remember that in this method of inquiry, we take a step backward.

Upon this uncertain ground hardly secured by our method of inquiry, the English word "literature" is not yet useful. Nor are all its romance homonyms, securely placed in German *Literatur,* for historical reasons that we cannot consider here. All the translations of this word into other languages are part of the object of investigation, not yet instruments for it. Please mark my repeated use of "not yet." The dispute between Steven Owens and Rey Chow, cited in David Damrosch's book, does not attend to this "not yet."[5] They transform it into an "either-or" and lose the thread of thought before it can be secure in its insecurity.

Not only are the European words for "literature" not yet useful when we take the backward steps necessary for this type of inquiry, even the claims made by the "great non-western" civilizations, of historically having had words that could have, or did, serve the same, similar, or better functions than "literature" in the European context, become less than useful, here and now. And indeed here the Rey Chows and the Steven Owenses of the current dispute show their sharing of a similar set of values. For the counter-claims of the diasporas to the status of "literature" in the current situation are also not yet useful.

Let us rather try to think of a space filled by what is neither reason nor unreason yet seems irreducible. This is of course the space, literally, of dreams, that most literal of texts that help experiencing beings fill up the gaps in presupposing a world. Can one even think of this space as that between what experiencing beings can make and what they need? The irreducible filling up of this space has been a site of struggle that we call history and culture simply because there seems to be change constituted here and grounded in the shape of a struggle. There is no subsistence hunting, no subsistence gathering, no subsistence farming, no subsistence economy. A repeatable difference inhabits each: the irreducible difference between needing and making. As I sought to strike a keynote, a low tone that will sound behind and while and ahead, for a conference in Istanbul, I asked the Turkey- or U.S.-centered audience to think this shape as not only ever-different but also ever-repeatable. Thus it is not only history but also singularity, in the strictest sense given us by post-Spinozan thought. Here the human differentiates itself from the animal by proposing belief. That space of difference, between how much the experiencing being can make and how much need, is filled with belief, in a simulacrum of reason. It is here that the line between human and animal is made to waver. (That is the space where the "creative," the excess—from capital to art— lodges. Belief closes this off, and yet cannot close it fully—always open to (de-)transcendentalization by the imagination, trained or untrained.) This is religion. I would like to believe, from what little I know of the world I assume, that the economy of belief and wonder (for want of a better word) is a characteristic of the definitive predication of a chunk of the experiencing being; it can and has become a tug-of-war, a battle, battles, wars. The economy itself is the mark of what we here today can call literature and hope to be understood, whatever that might mean. This economy marks the arrogance of the French eighteenth century, even greater than the German Orientalism of the same period. Of that more later.

If the literary is grasped by way of this intuition, Sheldon Pollack's comment shows its dangerous pathos.[6] For him, as for me, the intuition of literature comes from what I would like to believe, from what little I know of the world I assume. This is because the assumption of a world in order to distinguish the agent of assumption from other experiencing beings becomes deeply personal, even when and as always it must embrace all persons and beings. The first step out of worldliness and the make-need difference, then, is also the first instrument of humanism, of all sorts. Discourses of worldliness are autobiographical in genre and confessional in institution, even when their interest is exactly not so.[7]

Some years ago I spoke in Istanbul about Edward Said's luminous book *Orientalism* and pointed at that important sentence: "Much of the personal investment in this study derives from my awareness of being an 'Oriental' as a child growing up in two British colonies."[8] Out of that autobiographical confession, Said spends a lifetime constructing and criticizing the making and breaking of world literatures, though he never points at the narrative of de-Ottomanization.

Let us now look at David Damrosch. He begins his book with a splendid scholarly intention: "What follows is an essay in definition, a celebration of new opportunities, and a gallery of cautionary tales" (WWL, p. 36).

But in the end he comes around to our way of acknowledging the instrumentality of world literature, its role in assuring us a special place in the space of experiencing beings: "I have given you my world literature, or at least a representative cross-section of it. . . . Different readers will be obsessed by very different constellations of texts" (WWL, p. 281). I want to keep emphasizing that even this pattern, many steps down from Kant's stark world, is upstream from the story of colonialism's (Goethe) and capitalism's (Marx) insistence on world literature.

What I have been describing is that to define world literature is to be part of a description, the description of stakes emerging. Pascale Casanova's work, and I mention her because she is a model here, is consonant with the spirit of the French eighteenth century, which gains its greatest strength from a resolute unconcern for the neutralizing of the insecure grounds of security, although not invariably. Thus world literature, in my loosening of those words, is an event that continues to escape the experiencing being as it shapes itself as a "task" within this frame, which is also itself a task. When I presented a keynote entitled "Subduing Byzantium," at a conference in Pécs, Hungary, a self-styled "borderless" city which, with Istanbul and a city in the Ruhr, whose name escaped me as I was writing, not really like Auerbach in Turkey, in Ranigram village in Birbhum where my only mechanical aid was that hurricane lantern that I mention so often in my work, was going to be the European cultural capital. Erfurt, I think. Derrida had been a frequent visitor to Pécs, so they described the necessity to neutralize the event as "pushing back *différance*." Here at least, neutralizing the event is seen as an ongoing task, the task of seeing secured origins as secure. To speak a language that is not yet obscure everywhere, this means to ignore the transcendental deduction rather than persistently de-transcendentalize it. You cannot enter a certain Europe any other way. Locke already knew this (PR, p. 231). In my response to the audience in Hungary, I said, as indeed I said to the audience in Istanbul, cultural capitals of the United States of Europe, if only for a day or year: "Is our obligation to challenge '*différance*' to be taken as task or event? Are the Balkans and Europe an adequate allegory of East-West? Or are these three cultural capitals yet another undoing of Byzantium?" Seen as task, this is the securing of security that comes from the empiricization of certain philosophical contingencies that turned figure/logic into history and gave us "Europe," the "United States," "the globe." I have called this an enabling violation for a very long time. I heard Orhan Pamuk in his conversation with Andreas Huyssen in New York say that entering Europe will make Turkey more tolerant. At the World Philosophy Day organized by UNESCO, I heard Professor Aminata Diaw Cissé of

Senegal say, after an elaborate paper on Rousseau, that to ignore the French eighteenth century was to deny the gender freedom that came to Muslim women through such a European alliance. I understood these positions; I even agree. I was born before Indian independence, and my last visit to India was in the wake of the November 2008 terrorist attacks in Mumbai. Nearly three decades ago, in "Can the Subaltern Speak?," I excoriated the Hindus and praised the British for good juridico-legal reforms in the interest of gender. But the question of world literature—what is neither reason nor unreason yet seems irreducible—is exactly to supplement persistently this necessary security for agential practice of a certain model. Supplement: to fill a lack and to add. "Literature" (what is neither reason nor unreason yet seems irreducible)—persistent task for the experiencing being. Step back.

Luca Scarantino, the Italian philosopher in the School of Preti, has tried to understand cultural difference in terms of how different cultural traditions have historicized the transcendental.[9] This is an ambitious and good effort in tracking the securing of the unsecurable, although still within the enclosure that secures the human in the name of history alone. This must rely on the distinctions, themselves remote from the speculations with which we began, between cultures, with Europe as the "tolerant" mediator. Comparable is the reliance upon the distinction between *national* literatures and "world" or "comparative" literatures, itself remote from the speculations with which we began, which the question "What is World Literature?" must presuppose. In effect, both David Damrosch and Djelal Kadir's work asks "What is the world of World Literature," in their different ways, and can take on a questioning of the assumption that there are nations, nations based on languages, and therefore based on literatures. At one end, of course, we have Hannah Arendt's careful critique of these assumptions on the basis of the European experience after World War II.[10] But above and beyond, we have Africa. The question of Africa, unfortunately, gives the lie to our thinking if we want to define it as definition, even description; although not if we think of it as contemplating stakes, *l'enjeu*. An empirical consideration of the history of colonialism in Africa shows the contingency of our assumption about nations. As a non-specialist, I have found A. Adu Boahen's *African Perspectives on Colonialism,* with its rich maps and tenacious text, immensely useful.[11]

Both Franco Moretti and David Damrosch, different as they are in their ways of thinking, cite Goethe and Marx together in the matter of world literature. I would like to point at a difference. In spite of his determination by colonialism and capitalism, upon which Damrosch comments with panache, Goethe is able, I think, to imagine the aporetic nature of world literature. Marx is not. For Goethe, the category of "world literature" is in the mode of "to come." Not for Marx. "National litera-ture is now rather an unmeaning term; the epoch of World literature is at hand, and every one *must strive* to hasten its approach" *(Nationallitera-tur will jetzt nicht viel sagen, die Epoche der Weltliteratur ist an der Zeit, und jeder muss jetzt dazu wirken, diese Epoche zu beschleunigen)*, says Goethe, open ended. "From the numerous national and local literatures, there arises a world literature" *(aus den vielen nationalen und lokalen Literaturen bildet sich eine Weltliteratur)*, says Marx, secure.[12] What imagination can surmise, scientific socialism cannot.

Let me now spend some minutes on Marx's problem.

Gramsci's hope (see pages 9–10):

> The mode of being of the new intellectual can no longer consist in eloquence, . . . but in active participation in practical life, . . . superior to the abstract mathematical spirit; from technique-as-work one proceeds to technique-as-science and to the humanistic conception of history, without which one remains [a] "specialist" and does not become [a] "leader" (specialist + politico).[13]

Marx's mistake was to think that the workers' self-interest would de-cline if the secret of social productivity were revealed. Some had thought that the solution lay in ethical instruction. It was Gramsci's genius to understand that the point was to deconstruct Marx by inserting the lever in Thesis Three and epistemologizing the project: instrumentalizing the new intellectual to produce a "revolutionary" subject as proletario-subaltern intellectual, so far invariably lost in the vanguardism of the immediate aftermath of revolutions. A disinterested episteme can allow and with-stand the interruption of the ethical. Study humanism, said Gramsci, in somewhat the same spirit as some of us say deep language learning and literary textuality train the ethical reflex. Because he was educated into a humanism, Foucault could write, supporting Nietzsche, that liberty is a by-product of oppression, thus emphasizing our conviction (not taken into account by Marx) that freedom from does not lead directly to free-dom to, or to gloss it, leads to freedom to claim rights; to think of respon-sibility as a freedom, you need that very humanist education which teaches rebellion against it.[14] Indeed, there is no freedom but freedom from, deter-mined by oppression. Rights are bound to occasions.[15] Freedom to re-sponsibility is in a double bind with aesthetic education. It is in a struc-tureless structure with the ethical.[16]

You notice that Gramsci's injunction will travel far in today's context, when Marx's abstract average (or quantification) has stepped fully into the arena of the political. The data-form is now the preferred form of value, I have argued elsewhere.[17] Hardt and Negri have filled this form with the possibility of a worldly conversation and action that fills the space of the thought where reason cohabits with something that is not-quite not-unreason. I have argued the difficulty of this in the Introduction. Gramsci's words—that just the mathematical intuition is not enough—sound the warning about confidence in the secured unsecure as secure that underlies scientific world-literaturism. Yet the phrase "humanist history" is not fully acceptable, even if it is the site of the double bind inhabited in a generally unacknowledged way by all the critics that I have just indicated. (An aesthetic education might displace you into a Captain Ahab or a Senanayak.) Gramsci was not a philosopher, at least not in the time allowed him, and in the circumstances that were his lot, capable of stepping altogether backward. But he certainly knew that grounds apparently secured by the heritage of the great European revolution needed to be loosened. (Here comparing *Latinitas* with Sanskrit education is a forgetfulness that we are looking at notes, and an inability or refusal to place a prevailing sentiment within the precarious unfinished scaffolding of the entire life.)[18] We must read Gramsci's *Prison Notebooks* knowing that he was writing a kind of shorthand. With this appreciation of the protocols of Gramsci's writing after 1926, I have been trying to open up the phrase "humanist history" beyond its own confines, so that it can be the light that goes a little way into the place where, to quote my Hungarian friends, differance is pushed back and back and "World Literature" ceases to have its homely specificity.

In the Introduction I have considered at length Gramsci's "techno-scientific" knowledge, "superior to mathematical abstraction." I have pointed there at Gramsci's implicit realization that Marx's humanist education provided him with an understanding of free sociality that created a double bind with the uniquely Marxian meaning of the social. It arises from the "double character" of labor, that as abstraction it can be exchanged, consumed, and produce more (surplus) value, whereas as personal use-value it produces an object that is consumed and extinguished, is the "jumping-off point" *(Springpunkt)* around which an understanding of political economy turns, and resides in the subsequent homeopathy or medicine/poison double-character *(pharmakon)* of labor quantification ("abstract average" in Marx), based on this understanding. I have pointed out that Marx did not theorize the subject of this homeopathy. Why should the agent of the "social" as quantification used for agential freedom of intention from capitalism devote their freed intention to the building of a welfare society, where the "social" is understood, by Marx and

Marxists, in a general humanistic sense? The impulse to build a just society in a humanistic as well as aesthetically trained way is lodged in the play of the word "social"—on the one hand the ferociously original adjective *gesellschaftlich* or *vergesellschaftet* in the sense of an association based on labor quantified as *pharmakon* and, on the other hand the fuzzy noun, openly inhabits that "literary" space—the space between need and capacity to make. Indeed, the only common thing in the double bind, what makes it a double bind, in fact, is this space. It was Marx's genius to have seen that capital arises here as well. This is where Gramsci steps in. He wants to connect the proletarian and subaltern intellectual as inhabitants of this shared space.

Gramsci, I suggest in the Introduction, was right in thinking the project epistemological. One must attend upon the interruption of the ethical. It cannot be part of a plan directly. This conclusion I have amplified a bit above.

When I was among the respondents to a brilliant presentation by Professor Casanova, I had used two other bits of Gramsci. One was the thought of the "organic intellectual," intellectuals continuous with a certain mode of production of value. If globalization is understood as re-structuring in order to establish the same system of exchange, the argument embraces all of us. I had also used Gramsci's insistence that historical and comparative grammars are always a site of struggle—an account of what wins—suggesting that Gramsci's "language" can easily be read as "literature," to develop the analogy. The passage is worth reading again.[19]

It is always exciting to choose the winning side. For students of literature in Turkey, I had reminded my audience in Istanbul, there is a particular poignancy in this as Osmanli nostalgia is reterritorialized as European triumphalism, recoded in turn as the sobriety and responsibility of participating in the establishment of a world standard by way of the French and German eighteenth and nineteenth centuries and the U.S. twenty-first.

Damrosch's book is full of moments that acknowledge the double bind of such projects not only with such projects but what that space of difference between making and reading can perhaps offer us as experiencing being—the possibility of a humanism, always to come—as Goethe rewrites Marx before the letter. Since it is no secret that capital rises in that space as well, the relationship between the apparent nationalism of capital and the wealth of languages in the world can be one of supplementarity rather than quantification—Greenwich Mean Time, give up close reading, and so on. Damrosch describes the United States this way:

"formerly provincial and now metropolitan" (WWL, pp. 27–28). Between "provincial" and "metropolitan" is Gramsci's space of struggle, which Damrosch hardly erases. I walk with him to pull him back into it.

He is ready to be pulled for, if I understand *What Is World Literature?*, it proposes that some texts qualify as "world literature" for a variety of reasons, among them a sort of archetypal unity in humankind. We tell the same stories. But in order to learn to recognize this, says Damrosch, you must learn history and languages. Not just "technique-as-science," but a "humanistic conception of history." A good creed that points at a level playing field in a selective past when the present builds itself on false promises. Of course, my point (and Gramsci's) is that what is selected out is the space of subalternization that must be disavowed for a polity to function.

For me, the best reason for walking with David Damrosch is his plea for collectivity. For me, the "philosophico-literary"—the aesthetic in aesthetic education—is the means for persistently attempting collectivities to come. Our stakes are not identical, but I keep hoping that they can walk together. Here is Damrosch: "It is far from clear how to proceed if we want to broaden our focus beyond one or two periods or national traditions: who can really know enough to do it well?" (WWL, p. 284).

Rabindranath Tagore seems to have made it into world literature. Asked a hundred years ago to speak, precisely, on Comparative Literature, he changed the phrase to "world literature"—*bishsho shahitto*—because "Comparative Literature" translated literally as a phrase is ridiculous in Bengali.[20] I wish there were time to relate this to the Owens-Chow dispute. I will simply say that in that essay, Tagore, usually uninterested in left politics, offers two metaphors, striking workers and *bajey khoroch*— literally bad spending—in everyday conversation wasting money, in Tagore's hands undoubtedly wasting resources. I have a full-length essay in Bengali on this subject, but that will not travel. I throw this metaphor into your hands and suggest that perhaps Tagore is hinting exactly at a way of turning around the use of that space of difference from "social" as useful quantification to "social" as human welfare where Marx failed, putting "world literature" in an unachieved present. Except this is a different kind of turnover, for we are not speaking of the proper use of the social productivity of capital. Tagore is proposing, dare I say it, a species of potlatch to fill that space. To recode the potlatch is one way of describing the stakes of world literature. Another is to rediscover tragedy as an important genre. Not to say fate has given us wings, so we are flying. Monty Python had given us a version of *Waiting for Godot* where Godot

THE STAKES OF A WORLD LITERATURE   465

arrives on a bus. Let us discover how the exuberance of global literature can learn to say *bidhi dayna pakha*.

Thinking gender at the end is often my custom because reproductive heteronormativity is the world thing with which we have always secured the space between making and need. The child as excess has assured the father an immortality of which the mother has been the custodian. Here, too, it can help us to think the recoding we are imagining, women's work, even now, even here.[21] Indeed, one of the problems with the field of world literature studies is that it is not often attendant to gendering.

Gender is our first instrument of abstraction.

Let us look back upon the working definition of culture offered in "Culture: Situating Feminism" (Chapter 5): Culture is a package of largely unacknowledged assumptions, loosely held by a loosely outlined group of people, mapping negotiations between the sacred and the profane, and the relationship between the sexes. There and in the Introduction, I have tried to explain how gender-abstraction institutes and sustains "culture." With the help of that explanation, I have read an uncharacteristic locating of the feminine by Paul de Man in Schiller's speculation about the aesthetic. I have attempted to turn this into an allegory of our work of reading and training the imagination for epistemological performance. I have suggested that this can perhaps be achieved in the mode of "to come," if we try, again and again, to reverse and displace the ancient binary until "woman" is a position without identity. I cannot replay the entire scenario here. I hope you will recall those moves and, in a gesture of activist reading, compute that this is also how Gramsci's shorthand phrase "humanist history" can be expanded in today's context, and this is how we must instrumentalize ourselves as the new intellectuals in the hope of a good world in the aporetic mode of "to come." In a previous book I announced a death, and here I announce a hopelessness—we cannot achieve a world literature that we must hope for, because life and hope are too easily claimed by the camp of mere reason. To repeat, then, sabotaging Schiller takes a historically "gendered" shape. You will be surprised how often I have to remember this as the savage turf-battles within the humanities buffet my everyday.

It would have been appropriate to end my walk with David Damrosch with the passage from Derrida's *Rogues* that I had quoted in the Introduction. But now that Verso wants a book called "Against World Literature: On Untranslatability in Comp Lit," that too is claimed, by the book business, the machine that claims these words as well, of course. I quote Derrida's words nonetheless: "It remains to be known, so as to save the honor of reason, how to *translate*. For example, the word *reasonable*.

And how to pay one's respects to, how to . . . greet . . . beyond its latinity, and in more than one language, the fragile difference between the *rational* and the *reasonable*."[22] Let us transpose this task to the synonyms for *world*, the fragile difference between *world* and *universe* beyond Indo-European and repeat, from within that infinite effort, not otherwise: *mon korey uribar torey bidhi deyna pakha*. False hope.

CHAPTER TWENTY-THREE

Rethinking Comparativism

I N THE TWO PREVIOUS ESSAYS I have given you a sample, by no means exhaustive, of my negotiations with my discipline in the matter of an aesthetic education in the era of globalization. It seemed that there was always an issue of controlling the other through knowledge production on our own terms, and an ignoring, therefore, of the double bind between Europe as objective and subjective ground, judge and defendant. In this essay I offer my rule of thumb for the times. Think of all languages as having the mechanism to prepare an infant for the world, therefore equivalent; learn comparativism not only from texts of disciplinary method but reach-out techniques in material studied. The essay is in the disciplinary mode, having been commissioned by the Comparative Literature issue of *New Literary History*.

What is it that one "compares" in Comparative Literature?

Goethe's *Weltliteratur* is usually invoked when talking about the beginnings of a comparative literature. The other story is Spitzer and Auerbach in Turkey. There is also the story of the rise of the discipline of Comparative Literature to intellectual prominence in the United States in the period following World War II, largely as a result of the migration to the United States of a group of noted European comparativists seeking asylum from totalitarianism. This group had a great influence in fostering the theoretical transformation of literary studies and in bringing about fundamental changes in national literature studies. But to think of comparative literature as comparative had something to do with the notion of *la literature comparée* in France—where comparison implicitly referred to the standards of the French eighteenth century. As I have pointed out, this attitude is reflected in the fundamental premises of Pascale Casanova's work today and in general disciplinary practice.[1] René Etiemble's *Comparaison n'est pas raison* attempted, in 1968, to combat that impulse in a manner that is still favorably comparable to much that goes on in the Euro-U.S. today.[2] But in terms of the questions we are asking, it is still too much within the internationalist side of Cold War logic—going no further than the front-line languages of India and East Asia, with a somewhat paternalistic approach. Whatever the outcome of that debate, and whatever the status of the classical traditions of Asia, Comparative Literature within the United States remained confined to European literary regionalism. After the Cold War, the division between a Eurocentric Comparative Literature and geopolitically oriented "Area Studies" seemed to have become less tenable than before. But comparison in favor of the European tradition has remained in place.

Seen another way, comparison assumes a level playing field and the field is never level, if only in terms of the interest implicit in the perspective. It is, in other words, never a question of compare and contrast, but rather a matter of judging and choosing. When the playing fields are not even continuous, the problem becomes immense. Most metropolitan countries acknowledge the problem simply because of the volume of migration in recent decades. There a certain degree of levelness (entry into the circuit of citizenship, desired when denied) is already established. I, on the other hand, write as I have always written, as soon as I began to publish in the 1970s, with a sense of the world rather than the demands of immigrants, in themselves also and of course a powerful disciplinary initiative. I would, however, like to distinguish my position, simply because it does not arise from "the forcing of cultures into greater proximity." Charles Bernheimer wanted Comparative Literature to include "subaltern perspectives."[3] As I have regularly noted, I am just as regularly asked to help curate shows that will, give or take the culture, "bring the barrio to the museum." This is to misunderstand even the way in which denial/desire/demand work in the establishment of the class cross-hatched space of migrant generations in metropolitan space. The degree of systemic change necessary for such transference to take place is precisely the issue.

It is absurd to expect a humanities discipline to bring about these changes. We are speaking of the establishment of citizenship structures within states where welfare is being eroded because national capital is supposed to be continuous with international capital in globalization. What a humanities discipline within the teaching machine can do here is altogether indirect—non-absolutist quality control in admissions, sane curricular change, etc. The result of the steady influx of people from elsewhere into the metropolis and the attendant demands, as one section of this group becomes relatively class-mobile, are reflected in Comparative Literature in the last few decades in the following way: Each literary tradition, tied to a dominant language group, confronts the narratives produced by this Eurocentric history, more or less. Thus we have a confrontation of Comparative Literature and East Asian languages; Comparative Literature and South Asian languages; Comparative Literature and Central/North Asian languages are just stirring. Comparative Literature and Arabic/Persian/Turkish shades off into Orientalism as such ("a manner of regularized [or Orientalized] writing, vision, and study, dominated by imperatives, perspectives, and ideological biases *ostensibly* suited to the Orient [sometimes indistinguishable from immigrant nostalgia today]") and, through Bulgarian, into Ottoman Studies and Balkan Studies.[4] The modern period in each of these language groups relates in a different way to that main tradition, which remains "Europe" as affected by Eastern European theory filtered through France.[5]

We are not speaking of Cultural Studies here. Very generally speaking, I think it is safe to say that Cultural/Ethnic Studies, generally considered to be the political corrective to Eurocentric Comparative Literature, legitimizes the implicit comparison by reversal. This is of course too sweeping a generalization, and would have to be modified in any extended discussion.

Mainstream Comparative Literature divided over French theory. It has been touched also by the transformation of German theory through the fall of mere socialism. One consequence of these circumstances was the flight of intellectuals and the rise of comparativism. The much more resplendent social philosophical consequence of that was Hannah Arendt and the Frankfurt School.

This is the set we consider when we think of rethinking comparativism. When we, the first generation of U.S. Ph.D.'s in Comparative Literature were graduate students in the 1960s, we took a certain pride in asserting that the word "comparative" in our discipline was a misnomer, that the point about Comparative Literature was that it did not exactly "compare." For the last few years, some of us have been trying to rethink comparativism, within the discipline, by pondering how exactly Comparative Literature does not compare, and how that not-comparing can shelter something affirmative.

I think the solution we found in the 1960s is not quite for these times. Those of us who belonged to the U.S. mainstream of comparative literature found affinity among national literatures in place of what the verb "compare" offers: not only the etymological "pairing with" but also some hint of ranking. We found a strong ally in the theory of archetypes, psychoanalytic with C. G. Jung and R. D. Laing, literary-historical with Thomas O. Brown and Northrop Frye. Notions of the collective unconscious allowed us to bypass the problem of comparison and ranking. That line of work has found a strong champion today in my colleague and friend David Damrosch, whom I discussed in "The Stakes of a World Literature," Chapter 22 in this book. I admire his work so greatly and so enjoy working with him that I should make clear that in this context, now, my thinking is different from his.

What was especially useful for us in those early days was the study of *topoi,* sets of imageme-narrateme-philosophemes that seemed to travel without either historical or psychic ballast across the history of literatures and cultures that make us: code geography, write our world. The Greek god Apollo and the Hindu goddess of learning, Saraswati, share the swan as a familiar. Ernst Robert Curtius was our guide here.[6] Wellek has situated him in European patriotism; that great scholar was also an "Orientalist" in an expanded Saidian sense. In the 1990s, I wrote on "Echo" in this manner, finding in the non-agential voicing of the Greek mythological figure a way to think about woman's fate, particularly in postcoloniality. That essay still seems to me persuasive enough to be included in this book. As graduate students we had been helped by the topological phenomenologies of Gaston Bachelard, Maurice Merleau-Ponty, and Georges Poulet.[7] I still recognize those trajectories in Lévinas (though not as a place-holder for comparison) and, of course, in the work of Jacques Derrida, whose brilliant topological slides do indeed teach us to think about relations without relations between diverse European texts.

Encompassing structures and archetypo-topical texture, not strictly polarized, helped us think affinity in place of mere comparison. We know today that those great networks of affiliations work by way of exclusions. Apollo and Saraswati quietly ignore those who have no right to learning. It is perhaps not too contentious to point out also that, in today's divided world, to discover varieties of sameness is to give in too easily to the false promises of a level playing field. The United States is still the world's policeman.[8] I do not need to remind you of this.

I am standing with my mother in Charles de Gaulle airport in Paris. For a week we have fed our ears on academic French. Suddenly I hear an exchange in the harsh accents of upstate New York. I turn to my mother and say, in Bengali, roughly this: "Hard to listen to this stuff." And my mother: "Dear, a mother tongue." My mother, caught up as she was in the heyday of resistance against the Raj, still extended imaginative charity to English.

I have told this story before and will say it again. Today I hold on to the fact that there is a language we learn first, mixed with the pre-phenomenal, which stamps the metapsychological circuits of "lingual memory."[9] The child invents a language, beginning by bestowing signification upon part-objects (Melanie Klein). The parents "learn" this language. Because they speak a named language, the child's language gets inserted into the named language with a history before the child's birth, which will continue after its death. As the child begins to navigate this language it is beginning to access the entire interior network of the language, all its possibility of articulations, for which the best metaphor that can be found is—especially in the age of computers—"memory." By comparison, "cultural memory" is a crude concept of narrative re-memorization that attempts to privatize the historical record.

Comparative Literature imagines that each language may be activated in this special way and makes an effort to produce a simulacrum through the reflexivity of language as habit. Here we translate, not the content, but the very moves of languaging. We can provisionally call this peculiar form of translation before translation the "comparison" in Comparative Literature.

This is not to make an opposition between the natural spontaneity of the emergence of "my languaged place" and the artificial effortfulness of learning foreign languages. Rather, it is to emphasize the metapsychological and telecommunicative nature of the subject's being-encountered by the languaging of place.[10] If we entertain the spontaneous/artificial opposition, we will possibly value our own place over all and thus defeat the ethical comparativist impulse. Embracing another place as my creolized space may be a legitimation by reversal. We know now that the hybrid is not an issue here. If, on the other hand, we recall the helplessness before history—our own and of the languaged place—in our acquisition of our first dwelling in language, we just may sense the challenge of producing a simulacrum, always recalling that this language too, depending on the subject's history, can inscribe lingual memory. In other words, a sense of equivalence among languages, rather than a comparison of historico-civilizational content. Etienne Balibar has suggested that equivalence blurs difference, whereas equality requires them. Precisely because civil war may be the allegoric name for an extreme form of untranslatability, it is that "blurring" that Comparative Literature needs.

I am not making claims of cultural equivalence, the unexamined dull anthropologism of cultural relativism. If you do not assume language to be isomorphic with cultural formation, you cannot move to such convictions. The apparent discrepancies in cultural power, measured on the grid of place to space, are meaningful in terms of the language's relative elaboration and importance. They become a matter of constative historical inquiry and performative resistance in the present, always waiting for what will have happened.[11] This is why we must remain mindful that the assumption of equivalence is upstream from all the historical language battles of postcoloniality and neocolonial power that are still being fought and must continue to be fought. I repeat that this is not nativism; any language or languages can perform this function. If in situations of migration the first language is lost, it is still a loss—not because of any kind of nationalist nostalgia, but because that originary, metapsychological constitution of ethical semiosis is de-activated. I think there is some kind of historical process that shifts those mechanisms into the newly chosen "naturalized" "first" language—which operates most successfully in the second generation.

Our rethinking of comparativism starts, then, with the admission that as language, languages are equivalent, and that deep language learning must implode into a simulacrum of lingual memory. We must wait for this implosion, which we sense after the fact, or, perhaps, others sense in us, and we thus enter into a relationship with the language that is rather different from the position of a comparer, a charter of influence, who supposedly occupies a place above the linguistic traditions to be compared. In other words, I have had enough of being told that imperialism gave us the novel.

Comparative Literature, then, begins to insist on the irreducibility of idiom, even as it insists on translation as commonly understood. When we rethink comparativism, we think of translation as an active rather than a prosthetic practice. I have often said that translation is the most intimate act of reading. Thus translation comes to inhabit the new politics of comparativism as reading itself, in the broadest possible sense.

In the name of comparativism as equivalence, we are prepared to undertake a serious and continuous undoing of nationalist or national language–based reading. We have not moved too far from the regionalist impulse of the initial vision of European Comparative Literature. We have simply announced a worldly future. It is our hope that, in this process, the performativity of comparativism will face the task of undoing historical injustice toward languages associated with peoples who were not successfully competitive within capitalism. With the added proviso that these languages attempt to establish an interconnection among themselves through our disciplinary and institutional help. This will take us a step outside the necessarily nation-centered and culture-centered frontiers of the United Nations.

The idea of a subaltern collectivity of languages and literatures outside of national-language restrictions is a difficult one. In order to take the diversified subaltern or less-taught languages out of enclavist or collectivist pedagogy and politics, to save Comparative Literature from unacknowledged and exclusivist comparison, structural and epistemological changes are required. I will quote some prose here that reflects a long, ongoing effort at institutional change. The implicit terms of resistance—this is against globalization—entrenches comparison beyond the discipline, indeed situates the discipline upon contemporary cognitive topography, in a negligible niche. I leave this caution here, proceed to the institutional passages, and close with two readings that can only look forward to the necessary yet impossible institutional guarantee of access to equivalence.

> Even as we want to include Europe and necessarily the United States in any version of a globalized world, we also recognize that our efforts cannot succeed without a thorough-going program of the less-taught languages of that world. . . . This latter group could only be taught for a few semesters, with insufficient quality control, by insufficiently trained instructors, and with no possibility of students moving on to a major or a doctoral track. This lack of parity between established and less-taught languages goes against the very spirit of an enlightened globalization of the curriculum. This is matched by the lack of parity between teachers of language and teachers of literature in all US universities. . . . The labor is, of course, immense. It will involve faculty development seminars, postdoctoral fellows, extensive and new recruitment procedures, and the involvement of national professional associations. There must be a consortium, since the less commonly taught languages are many, the need is acute, no single university could hope to cover all bases and, given distant learning resources, the first stages of language learning could easily be shared.[12]

It is in view of the resistance to institutional change that I often speak of the humanities supplementing globalization by providing a world. The worldliness of our new Comparative Literature could be a key element in this continuing and persistent effort. For, given the differential between the "first" language and others, the equivalence that would formalize our new Comparative Literature will never be fully established. We must always work in the element of simulacra, putting in place a bond between the world's neglected languages. The literature of Okinawa will then take its place with the wisdom songs of Ghana, and the historical fables of the Popol Vuh.

I want to make a methodological point before I conclude. We start from an assumption of linguistic equivalence which rests on language's capacity to inscribe. Always with one language as accidental standard, we escape national restrictions and create the simulacrum of equivalence through deep language learning across the spectrum of the subaltern languages of the world. The diversity and singularity of idiom remain a constant reminder of the singularity of languages. The absence of material equivalence provokes historical study. Within this procedural frame, how do we read now as comparativists?

Over the last few years, teaching the introductory course in Comparative Literature and Society to graduate and undergraduate alike, I have drawn a conclusion: in disciplinary method we remain astute. Attention to idiom, demonstration through textual analysis, acquisition of expertise in plotting the play of logic in rhetoric and vice versa. Insofar as our object of investigation is concerned, however, we acknowledge as comparativist any attempt that the text makes to go outside of its space-time enclosure, the history and geography by which the text is determined. Thus disciplinary convention expands toward what would otherwise escape it, and the field expands greatly, in many ways.

I now test my notion of textual comparativism with a look at Medoruma Shun's short story, translated "Hope."[13]

"Hope" has been called "the first post-colonial work of Okinawan literature."[14] Like all *post*coloniality, it looks forward to an undecidable future. Its very title, "Hope," out of joint with the narrative content, gives us a sense of this. How can it help us in the task of rethinking Comparative Literature in view of such an undecidable future?

By my disciplinary responsibility I would have to undertake the difficult journey of entering Japanese idiom and its relationship to the idiom of Okinawa. I would have to plot the relationships as I would, with appropriate differences, in Ireland, or Hong Kong. I am ill-prepared for this. What I can attempt now is the lesson of reading—locating an impulse toward comparativism in this new sense in the story itself.

The story is about a sacrifice and a suicide. Upon a scene of political conflict, such a double gesture often reflects a comparativism of last resort: a plea to the political other to recognize equivalence, to respond, and, finally, to end oppression. I have been long attracted to this species of comparativism, attempting to go outside of the space-time enclosure, when that enclosure means oppression, colonial or gendered or both, undoing history and geography by inscribing the body with death.

I place the story of "Hope" in that genre, with "Can the Subaltern Speak?," with suicide bombing in Palestine, with Viken Berberian's *The Bicyclist,* with Santosh Sivan's *The Terrorist,* a film dealing with anti-colonial resistance and gender in Sri Lanka (see "Terror," Chapter 18).

One of the characteristics of this species of comparativism in extremis is the double bind between ethics and politics. This too is a theme that attracts me greatly.

(Comparativism in extremis is not a disciplinary choice of method. It can be located in our objects of investigation if it is represented. Comparativism in extremis is a political gesture when response [perhaps based on that lesson of equivalence in a context broader than our discipline] is denied. I have given above a few examples of such representation, including "Hope." *Bamako,* a film I will discuss at the end of this essay, is a teaching text, not a representation of comparativisim in extremis. The film hopes that its lesson—the difference between resistance and the people—will be learned. Other examples of the representation of comparison in extremis—merely indexed—is a line in Rabindranath Tagore that I have discussed in Chapter 15. Speaking of the people to whom human rights were denied millennially in India, he writes: *"mrityumajhe hobe tobe chitabhashshe shobar shoman"*—"you [addressing his "unfortunate country"] will then be equal to all of them in the ashes of death," thus predicting the death of a nation. The only thing that will make me equal to you, because you deny response, is a shared death. This is also the theme of Ernesto Cardenal's poem "Prayer for Marilyn Monroe" [1965], made into a film by the Instituto Cubano de Arte e Industria Cinematográfico, where the items of comparison are Marilyn Monroe, with her desperate life on the one hand and the millions of dead children in Latin America on the other, standing in as victims of the U.S. system, a place of no response. Cardenal is a priest, a liberation theologian—for him in death the two sides were equal in God's eyes, comparison as equivalence in extremis. Perhaps it may be said that our lesson of learning equivalence, practicing equivalence, indexing a small epistemic change or shift, may come to facilitate a world where comparison in extremis will no longer be required.)

A double bind, then. Between ethics (I must not kill) and politics (I can have a "response" from my non-respondent[s] only in a shared death).

To some the double bind, laboriously repeated throughout this book, may seem a dangerous idea. And yet, to deny its pervasiveness leads to failed revolutions. Paradoxically, to acknowledge its pervasiveness does not lead to unqualified success. This is its danger. I put you in mind of the detailed discussion of the double bind in the Introduction, and remind you that this paradox by no means exhausts the power and danger of the double bind. The one thing that we can propose is that the fiction and reality of comparativism in extremis often makes visible the double bind between ethics and politics.[15]

The fiction suggests formulaically that the political situation requires the violence of sacrifice: "*What Okinawa needs now is not demonstrations by thousands of people or rallies by tens of thousands, but the death of one American child.*"[16] Yet the ethical unacceptability of violence requires the destruction of the political subject or actor. The pull of the ethical is so strong that the political act cannot be described as willed: "Just as fluids in the bodies of a small creature that is frightened suddenly changes into poison, [so] this deed of mine is natural and what had to happen [*hitsuzen*] for this island, I thought." And the pull of the political is so strong that the act representing the ethical is also a sacrifice and a destruction. The impossibility of containing the ethical subject in its worldly envelope is indicated in the text by the management of time:

> At the moment that I *reclosed* the trunk, the sun *broke* through the cloud veil that *covered* the sky. I *am* sweating, and I *break out* in goose bumps. I *crossed* the forest on foot . . . and *returned* home. . . . The air conditioning *doesn't* work . . . I *lower* the windows but I *pour* with sweat. I *went* up to Naha city. . . . I *pour* a bottle of gasoline on my jacket and pants. . . . A group of junior high schoolchildren *came* running.[17]

The sweating and sacrificing body breaks through into the present tense as the narrative progresses in the past tense. The body reenters the narrated past as an object before language in the last sentence.

On the side of the dominant, there is the longing for a release from the double bind between nationalism (the political) and responsibility (the ethical). Thus Oe Kenzaburo repeats a phrase in 1969: "Is it possible to change to a Japanese who is not a Japanese?"[18]

The dominant can also refuse this longing and simply deny the double bind. Here is a comment from the staff of the Japan Policy Research Institute: "Americans are likely to be shocked by Medoruma's subject matter and tone." It is a well-meaning comment, for the staff then proceed to list U.S. marine criminal activity against Ryukyuans, especially females. Yet to separate nationalism and responsibility is precisely a denial of the double bind that can reduce resistance to the politically correct.

One of the incidental but altogether astute moments in "Hope" is where the narrator recognizes that every inhabitant of the island is not infected by what I am calling comparativism in extremis—the necessity to call for a response from the colonizer. The first gesture from an islander is the innocent one of joy at seeing a known person on TV! And the last gesture is the equally innocent frivolity of the children kicking the agent reduced to object. Between these two gestures of innocence lies the story, apparently useless. Commemorated in fiction, it becomes useful if we learn how to read as we mark time toward a comparativism of equivalence.

Without this, we cannot pick up the message if an artist points at the distance between protest and the people. Abderrahmane Sissako's film *Bamako* (2006), for example, is regularly read like a documentary of protest by most policy-oriented folks.

The film stages a trial, in the compound of a traditional African compound, by African judges and lawyers, with the participation of two white lawyers on either side, of the World Bank, for its crimes in Africa. The trial is contained within fragments of local action and a slim subplot about the death of a charismatic singer's husband.

The new comparativism can read this film as a filmic discourse on epistemic discontinuity in the welding of place. We notice how much of the staging is in terms of a relief map of languages, colonial but also local. The trial is framed by a community where only the ones who have graduated into the discursive practice of the good whites are able to "speak the truth." The director took care to point this out by making the subplot with a singer very attractive, by closing the film with her, focusing on her husband's death and making clear that it has little to do with the main argument. The high point of eloquence in the film, and deliberately, if you notice the framing, is the good white guy (apparently the director just gave them the parts and said, "Now speak")—and makes us think precisely about the problem. There are also the moments of grassroots choice when access to the "trial" of the World Bank is turned off by the young men of the village, the real agents of collaboration with the destruction of the country. The bridge agents are a woman who is accused of not fitting the evidentiary structure and, on another level altogether, the traditional healer who utters (apparently in a language not necessarily understood by the "native speakers"). The complexity of the framing is evident also in the presence of the film within the film, an exaggerated eye-catching African Western.

The entire film can be a figuration of why resistance against the transnational agencies misfires. But it is inconvenient and counter-intuitive to understand this.

A few images now merely to suggest how the film might figure the separation, indeed the discontinuity, between resistance and the people. It is not without significance, surely, that the World Social Forum had had a meeting in Bamako just before the film's release. I will repeat my earlier points to relate them to the images.

We are looking at a symbolic trial of the World Bank, staged in an African compound in Bamako. Sissako places two persons outside the frame: the charismatic female singer who would travel easily into the musical circle of global protest, and the traditional healer (see Figures 27 and 28). The name of the film appears on the screen after those two placings outside of the work.

Figure 29 shows the woman singing simply to show her forceful presence in the film. Indeed this bit is used to promote the film—although it is not part of the trial, where the participating Africans have achieved sufficient continuity with the European Enlightenment to be able to criticize its travesty:

Now to images where, in the film, Sissako distinguishes carefully between the difference in the response.

First, the good white guy testifying against the World Bank (Figure 30). He speaks in metaphors and the audience is shown responding collectively.

Figure 27:   Singer interrupts film to have bustier laced.

Next, the black woman testifying (Figure 31). She is less eloquent and speaks more statistics. The response is more singular, less public.

Then the traditional healer, who finally intervenes, out of place (Figure 32). This is an undecidable moment, the moment of a double bind. For, if Mamadou Diouf is right, the Africans here do not necessarily understand what he sings. It may indeed be a procedural complaint on his own behalf. The response is mysterious, a pattern of close-ups of individual faces. We contemplate the distinction between singularity—repeatable difference—and the individual subject.

Figure 28: Healer leaves trial.

Figure 29: Singer's dynamism.

Contrast the much more innocent and open response to the African Western film within a film (Figure 33). This too is discontinuity from the trial. The African Western, with Danny Glover starring, is a generic opposite from *Bamako,* the film in which it is embedded. That is already a representational discontinuity. Further, the kind of innocent joy in such bloody mayhem that is portrayed in the mother and daughter is remote indeed from a critique of Western benevolence, from position in society within that enclosure, as represented by the "educated" Africans participating in the trial.

Figure 30:   Good white guy.

Figure 31:   Black woman testifying.

Without over-parsing, it remains noticeable that there are no white women in the film, no global feminist solidarity as is evident at the World Social Forum. Gender is the alibi for the entire spectrum of good and bad globalizing intervention. Has a criticism been represented here on the workings of the screen? For, as I have mentioned, Sissako takes care to present a taxonomy of black women, roughly in terms of distance from the European Enlightenment, if you like. And the implicit possibility of a male solidarity is shown across the color-class line, across the line where the black African has achieved rational epistemic continuity with the

Figure 32:   Healer singing.

Figure 33:   Innocent response to African Western.

white European. When Maître Rapaport—incidentally an actual person—interrupts on the side of the prosecution, his white colleague says to him, not waiting for procedure: "Shut up," with a gesture behind his rump (Figure 34).

When M. Rapaport addresses the court, the men active in the village world of unofficial micro-governance (please contrast this to world-governance) disconnect the loudspeaker, also without waiting for procedure (Figure 35).

Figure 34: "Shut up."

Figure 35: Africans disconnect loudspeaker.

Sissako and I have slipped in the question of gender, bigger than capital, since both sides are caught in reproductive heteronormativity and use gender as an instrument, an alibi—"the surrogate proletariat"; a question that the organized left intellectual, out of touch, expects only women and queers to ask, which is why a feisty philosopher like Agnes Heller, deeply sympathetic to women, says she is "against 'feminism.' "

Thus we track comparativism in our objects of investigation, even as we reproduce epistemological conditions of first-language learning in foreign-language learning: an aesthetic education. History and politics come in here, details imagined robustly rather than shored up for the will to power and control through knowledge. Utopia in the classroom.

Working a century ago, Frantz Boas clearly indicated the need for deciding if the cultures of "primitive" places had independent origins or were influenced by transmission. To compare seemed to be the only solution. The time for that initial anthropologistic comparativism is long over for us. Undoubtedly we should not rule out the contrast between historically independent origin and a comparativist study of dissemination from our discipline. In order to be able to do this as part of the discipline, however, we have to take a step back and perform the epistemological difference, looking forward to an epistemic difference "to come": the lesson of thinking the equivalence of language, potentially, in a diversified metapsychological theater.

CHAPTER TWENTY-FOUR

Sign and Trace

A S WE HAVE SEEN in "Imperative to Re-imagine the Planet" (Chapter 16 in this book), speaking to a European philanthropic organization in 1997, I thought of globalization in this way:

Globalization is achieved by the imposition of the same system of exchange everywhere. It is not too fanciful to say that, in the gridwork of electronic capital, we achieve something that resembles that abstract ball covered in latitudes and longitudes, cut by virtual lines—once the equator and the tropics, now drawn increasingly by other requirements—imperatives?—of Geographical Information Systems. The globe is on our computers. No one lives there; and we think that we can aim to control globality. The planet is in the species of alterity, belonging to another system; and yet we inhabit it, on loan. It is not really amenable to a neat contrast with the globe. I cannot say "on the other hand."

Anish Kapoor has taught me to add to this thinking of globalization. This is also a reason why I end this book with these two essays, stepping out, but not completely, from the academic enclosure. In the previous chapter I pointed out that "truth in painting" has no guarantees; here I point out that that situation has similarities to our attempt to parse the global.

I can think of *Memory* (Figure 36) as one of those flattened, one-dimensional representations of the globe, given flesh.

Perhaps it resembles more a dirigible—early instrument of global war—tamed now into a blimp, vehicle of minor commercial enterprise. Because globalization rears its ugly head wherever we look today, let me continue to think of the object as something like a globe. When I saw this in the first representations, it was the color of dried blood, only slightly less vibrant than the violent beckoning reds of "My Red Homeland," resembling an inner organ of beast or fowl that a gigantic Mr. Leopold Bloom would eat with relish. I know nothing about color symbolism. It is, however, noticeable that the current coloring is a more sober rust-orange, not the vibrant shit-colored yellow of *Homeland,* or the cold whites and deep blues of *Whiteout* or *My Body Your Body;* and not, of course, the shining of the mirror-work, as *Memory* submits itself to oxidation for the next couple of years. To borrow Kapoor's phraseology, this object does not carry mirroring. If I understand the viewing openings in the body of the work—one in Berlin, two in New York, looking into a tiny seamless interior—no indication of the grills, or perhaps just a glimpse—latitude and longitude perhaps? suggestions of fabrication, at any rate—they promise the depth, with all the allure and menace of a void leading us to individual deaths, that we inevitably secure as a world inside the globe. A rusting exterior, and each tile, unique, fashioned separately—a critique of the universalizing desire of globalization in the allegory of making.[1]

This is the "looks like" school of "truth in painting" with a vengeance. But at least for the general viewer in the museum, among whom I count

Figure 36: Memory, Anish Kapoor, 2008, Cor-Ten steel, 14.5×9×4.5 meters. Courtesy of Solomon R. Guggenheim Museum, New York. Photograph: David Heald.

Figures 37a and 37b: *Marsyas,* Anish Kapoor, 2002, PVC and steel. Installation view at Tate Modern. Photo: John Riddy. Courtesy of Tate, London.

myself, the non-representational is an active forgetfulness of the representational. I permit myself therefore to say that this "globe/blimp" has all the clumsy immensity of a mere world, and that this may be the point. I didn't know this in my 1997 thinking of globalization.

The size of *Marsyas* (Figures 37a and 37b) taught Kapoor that no one sees the whole thing at once.

And in *Memory,* he has made that part of the plan. I will speak of what the imagined viewer might also see in the seamless interior when I get on to the trace, but now let us think only of the ambiguous "my world" viewed through designated openings and stop there: the being makes its own history but does not choose the part.

Many have noticed that *Marsyas* wants to escape its enclosure. Marsyas the satyr had the ambition to go outside of the human enclosure and beat Apollo at his own game. More of this, too, later. If it is true that Kapoor has made the lesson of Marsyas part of the plan of *Memory,* then the lesson has been staged as also a reminder of the body as measure. And the idea of something inside that is bigger than the outside, earlier than *Marsyas,* is also there. Already in 2000, Laurent Busine writes of *Melancholia* (Figure 38):

> This sculpture does not allow us to say that the circle is included in the square or, conversely, that the square is inscribed in the circle because, even if, by measuring them, the circle is seen to be of equal diameter as the sides of the square, that is no more for us than information which does not influence the vision. . . . Have we not already stated that there is a difference between these forms, which in a certain way, rearrange the world into black and white; shadow and light; *masculine and feminine;* North and South . . . ?[2]

My thinking holds the globe!

Derrida has described this beautifully as "invagination":

> This upper or initial boundary, which is commonly called the first line of a book, is forming a pocket inside the corpus. It is taking the form of an *invagination* through which the trait of the first line, the borderline, splits while remaining the same and traverses yet also bounds the corpus. . . . There is only content without edge—without boundary of frame—and there is only edge without content.[3]

The concept-metaphor is of the womb.

Reproductive heteronormativity (affectionately RHN) has us in a double bind—it enables even as it disables, medicine as well as poison. It is in that spirit that I recall here my two best teachers, who taught me that a work wants. And that we should not read the work as a fulfillment of that want—but rather as a staging of the wanting. I cobble together the invagination of *Marsyas* with the "unhomeliness"—Anthony Vidler's word—of "the female genital organs.[4] This *unheimlich* place, however, is the entrance to the former *Heim* [home] of all human beings, to the place where each one of us lived once upon a time and in the beginning."[5]

I connect it with the innocent bump—the navel of the dream—on the wall of *When I Am Pregnant,* with all the holes, with the red loincloth-like *Cloak,* the *Mother as a Mountain,* and those installations, matching the *Double Corner* that hung in the corners of the room at the recent show at the Gladstone Gallery, where the actively forgotten representation can be only that of castration.[6]

Figure 38:   Melancholia, Anish Kapoor, 2004, PVC and steel, 680 × 1120 × 3600 cm. Photo: Phillippe De Gobert. Courtesy of MAC, Grand Hornu: Lisson Gallery, London.

Homi Bhabha has written some stunning stuff on Kapoor, among which is his idea that Kapoor represents emptiness. I'd gloss it some and say that Kapoor puts together "textual blanks" in the tradition of Stéphane Mallarmé. The emptinesses, the blanknesses that analogize with white spaces on the page are framed by the trace of a texting—an edge, a rim, a lip, a shore that lends depth to the emptiness, even direction. I am reminded of Derrida's remarks, made forty years ago: "*thought* is here for me a perfectly neutral name, the textual blank, the necessarily indeterminate index of a future epoch of differance."[7]

The here and now carries the trace of the directedness of a thought in the future. A lot of directions in that blank space.

Shall I call the depthed blank space a hole? Again, in that recent conversation, Kapoor reiterated his interest in holes. If the body as trace is unavoidably a measure for the heroism of sculpture, the body-with-holes is the most archaic source of human signage, RHN, the seeming cause and effect of the finite animate. Here all is analogy, all is "looks like," all is even literal resemblance. The tremendous blue hole under the blue cover in the false wall *(My Body Your Body)* "looks like" a vulva at one angle, and is crooked "like a penis" at another—overheard in the museum. An elegantly dressed, early middle-aged woman hunkers down to peer into the "Inwendig volle Figur." The doubled labias *(Double Corner)* watch from the top left corner of a room to remind us of the uncanny (see Figures 39a and 39b).

Yet, as we have all known for some time, women differently from men—and this is not just 1970s feminism—the cutting edge produces the letter.[8] Here too a resonance. Being cut off from a homeland allows us a "homeland." Jeremy Waldron has written of it perceptively: "To congratulate oneself on following 'the norms of my community,' is already to take a point of view somewhat external to those norms, rather than to subscribe wholeheartedly to the substantive commitments that they embody."[9] Jacques Derrida has warned about it as "ontopology": "an axiomatics linking indissociably the ontological value of present-being [*on*] to its *situation,* to the stable and presentable determination of a locality, the *topos* of a territory, native soil, city, body in general."[10] Kapoor has heeded and issued such warnings. His homeland is also the name of a pigment. It is clear that he plays with the double bind of the demands of the museums in the Euro-U.S. metropole—between globalization and homeland. He is described variously by the mayors and dignitaries of the cities where he shows: "acclaimed British artist" (Unilever); "sculptor of Indian origin now resident in London" (Malaga); "l'artiste anglais" (Nantes). Svayambhu (sui generis) for him is a

Figure 39a: *My Body Your Body,* Anish Kapoor, 1993, fiberglass and pigment. Photograph: David Regen. Courtesy of the artist and Gladstone Gallery.

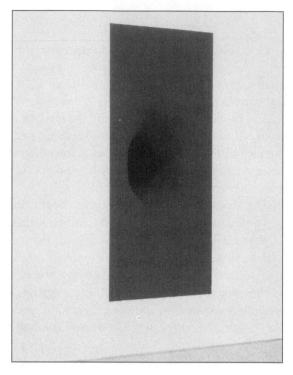

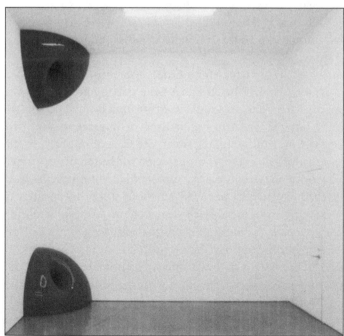

Figure 39b: *Double Corner,* Anish Kapoor, 2008, fiberglass and paint. Photograph: David Regen. Courtesy of the artist and Gladstone Gallery.

modern common noun in Northern Indian languages, without the authority of the Primum Mobile which would be roughly its meaning in sanskritic high Hinduism. He commemorates rather the animist objet trouvé whereby the subaltern undoes the grand Sanskrit elite meaning, and he imitates that impudence by turning the great Svayam (Self with a capital *S*) into rearranged museum space if not wind and water, his Svayambh having its meaning altered by the red object passing through doorways and other openings. The irony would be unavailable to the solemnity of the foreign India-fancier or the radical renouncer of myth and identity politics. It is time to turn to the lesson of the studio.

Many have noted that Kapoor's work seems allusive as well as significant or referential: "his proto-forms are allusive rather than representational. . . . There's no overt symbolism."[11] I want to agree with this and rewrite allusion as trace. There are signs and there may be traces (hinting at something that left *this* mark). It is not a break between words and picture/objects—the verbal and the visual—although it may seem so. In *Finnegans Wake*, his last work, maybe James Joyce tried to take the master sign-system—language—into traciness: "Maltomeetim, alltomatotetam, when a tale tarries shome shunter shove on. Fore auld they wauld to pree."[12] Non-expressive, non-compositional art shuttles the sign≠trace route, both ways.

Anish Kapoor said in Boston, recently: "It can't be helped that the body is the measure." It was an interesting exchange. The interlocutor's word had been "man." Kapoor quietly substituted "body." Sign to trace. But "man"—the holder of signs—still interferes. The subject remains "a stain in the field of vision."[13] *Finnegans Wake* is infinitely rationalized, as if all those traces were signs after all. Proving that Joyce himself, ceaselessly manufacturing traces out of more and more riddling signs, is fighting a losing battle, or—playing to lose? We can't know. Only that "man" interferes with "body"—for the adjective "human" had been implicit in the artist's rejoinder to his questioner, namely, "The [human] body is the measure." "It can't be helped."

Thus it is that, faced with Kapoor's *Memory* I have said "looks like . . . ," "feels like . . ." A trace is worked out by means of analogies by the human tracker. Who knows how the non-humans do it? The tracking of the trace continues through the animal into the animate and yes, the inanimate "world." "Man" must think this tracing as genetic "script," "cells reading," molecules "re-acting," until the atom just "splits." No use rewriting that split as trendy French *partage*. For even that "split" is old news in our post-particularity. "Our?" Who, we?

Thus, if Kapoor tries to get below, above, upstream from, the human, and build a huge hollow red installation with a slow steel knife, motor-driven,

cutting into the massy redness at a pace so slow as to be nearly impercep-
tible, and call it *Past, Present, Future,* a lover would still be heard to
murmur, "but the paint here is not getting really pushed around by that
cutting edge." Ah, but representation, even when only of an analogical
abstraction, tracing—is a losing battle. Or is the artist playing to lose?
Unknowable. The most striking thing when Kapoor speaks is his humility. "I am interested in the old questions that I cannot answer." Catch the
trace is the oldest problem in the book. Again, a resonance: at Derrida's
death, I wrote of his take on sexual difference: "I, the son, am the mother's
trace, and the father's sign."[14] I wish I knew how to do a Jewish riff on
Kapoor, whom I've heard referred to as "the Indian Jew."

Just after I had my first walk through Kapoor's studio, I spoke to a
group in Austria: "We will have to be able to think that for each one of
us and groups of us, globalization is an island of languaging in a field
of traces. Just descriptively, upstream from politics, globalization is an
island of languaging in a field of traces."

Here now is the passage that I have previously cited. There I had not
made the connection to globalization. Now you see what the visual can
teach us. It gives us an appropriate and corrective model of an understanding of the globe in any other way than through data and capital. And yet
meaning always tends toward the sign, so the lesson is never learned. That,
too, is damage control, and something to remember when too much is
claimed for music:

Globalization is an island of languaging in a field of traces.

What, then, is a trace? always remembering that it is not an "isness."
A sign system promises meaning. A trace does not promise anything. It is
something that seems to suggest that there was something before. Think
of the world's richness of languages. And then think of what happens
with the visual. I myself began to think of this much more carefully, when
I was with Anish Kapoor three or four weeks ago. He is making a co-
lossal sculpture for the Guggenheim and I was asked to write an essay, so
I spent three days with Anish. As I'm trying to figure out what it is that
this very smart guy wants, I am beginning to realize that he is trying to
represent traces—*Zwischenräume der Zeit.*[15] That's not a sign system;
it's like a *Spur* (German word for "trace"). It's like elephant shit on the
forest floor. It can be either, that there were elephants here. Or it could
be, that you are hallucinating. Or yet it could be, that someone put it
there in order to be a decoy for you. Or it could be that you are mistaken,
elephant shit does not look like that at all, or— . . . indefinite "inventory
without traces." A trace is not . . . a sign. In this connection one inevitably thinks of the established patriarchal convention, still honored by most

legal systems, that I, especially if I am recognizable as a man, am my father's sign and my mother's trace. What is important for us within my argument is that, rather than theorize globalization as a general field of translation which, in spite of all the empiricization of apparently impersonal mechanical translation, in fact privileges host or target, ceaselessly and indefinitely, we should learn to think that the human subject in globalization is an island of languaging—unevenly understanding some languages and idioms with the "first" language as monitor—within an entire field of traces, where "understanding" follows no guarantee. A new call for a different "non-expressional" art, a different "simultaneous translation."

If, then, for me, looking at Kapoor, globalization became supplemented as an island of language in an ocean of traces, I have to go back to the polarization denied by this intuition: namely, that art is visual, not verbal; that "language" can be used here only metaphorically—by a rule of language, certainly—but not literally, that too a rule of language, of course. Then the question of truth in the visual, implicated in all non-expressive art, perhaps in all art, looms. And what might a trace be, in this understanding of globalization opened up for me by a walk through Kapoor's studio? Let us spend a few moments on these questions.

To repeat: globalization makes us live on an island of language in an ocean of traces, with uncertain shores ever on the move. This "we" extends all the way from those who can view Anish Kapoor at Guggenheims to the unending circulation of labor export from the global South. Each member or collectivity belonging to this tremendously large group understands one or a few languages and is sure that the other organizations of noises are meaning-full but not for him or her. Language and trace are here in a gender-differentiated taxonomy rather than merely opposed.

Why did I get this sense of globalization in Kapoor's studio? Let us approach this question stealthily and indirectly.

To repeat, on a more ponderous register, let us say that language is a system that promises verifiable conceptual meaning. Everybody knows that the performance of a language is full of mystery, but that clear promise is always there. A trace, by contrast, seems to suggest an anteriority of some sort, altogether unverifiable. The thin figure of the trace lurks in the crannies of nuanced human endeavor—from the risk-taking decisiveness of politics to the grandeur of philosophy in its fullness. I have suggested in the Introduction to this book that Immanuel Kant's philosophy of pure reason may be a "management of the undermining risk of the trace" (see page 23). I have also suggested that Derrida submitted to his disciplinary elders in 1968 that the thought of the trace can curb the universalizing arrogance of language: "I have attempted to indicate a way out of the closure of this framework via the 'trace,' which is no more an effect than it has a cause, but which in and of itself, without extra-textual gloss [*hors texte*], is not sufficient to operate the necessary transgression."

The universalizing ambition of globalization would here qualify as a species of transgression, and Derrida feels that the thought of the trace might curb it in the epistemic sphere. And the curb is a solution in the field of the vanity of human wishes held up by capital.

In a certain sense the nonverbal visual traffics always in traces. In another sense it is ever tempted, in its allegorical reaches and tendencies, to usurp linguisticity. Kapoor is a major player in this double adventure: keep the freedom of the trace—and at the same time see if you cannot hit the precision of the verbal—the impossible dream of a globalization attempting "worldliness" in the museum: the orange blimp with a door or two.

For Kapoor, the shit-object *(Blood Stick)* is not only the representation of the trace of an unlikely body, perhaps—as indeed shit as Spur (trace) or spoor, as I literalized in Austria. It is also "writing of the body"—where, if you literalize, you will go toward the medical. But Kapoor is no organicist—"of the body" is contingent here, shit as writing is impersonal, we are into artificial intelligence and telecommunication, witness the computerized machine in the corner of the studio that "prints" cement-shit, and will one day build a house. Non-expressive signing of what is seen as the very production of the subject. Here is how Lévinas describes it:

> The possibility of a representation that is constitutive, but already rests on the enjoyment of a real completely constituted indicates the radical character of the uprootedness of him who is recollected in a home, where the I, while steeped in the elements, takes up its position before a Nature. The elements in and from which I live are also that to which I am opposed. The feat of having limited a part of this world and having closed it off, having access to the elements I enjoy by way of the door and the window, realizes extraterritoriality and the sovereignty of thought, anterior to the world to which it is posterior. *Anterior posteriorly:* separation is not thus "known"; it is thus produced. Memory is precisely the accomplishment of this ontological structure.[16]

Here is the range, then: at one end the saving vulnerability of the trace, which will not allow the transgression of globalization; at the other end, the control of the philosophical edge of the verbal, producing the "human" impersonally. This is Kapoor's space: rational and physiological, a common sense that is uncommon; nothing in-between. If we are speaking of globalization, it is not the usual anecdotal kind that asks us to include something called "India" in a supposedly neutral art space; that at least is clear.

Watching this stuff can give play to the reflexes of the viewer away from signage and away from the temptations of universalization. Am I dreaming that thus shuttling we may practice toward the ethical? Only if the transgressive desire to go toward signage, and thus toward the universal, is re-arranged. It can happen in the performance of the *viewing*: I live on loan upon the planet. I am a glitch/blip on the cycle that pushes up the daisies. Space-talk by way of traces. *Finnegans Wake* might message to Berlin and New York: "Soft morning, cities! I am spacy tracing."[17]

I want to talk now a bit about two of the networks in the performance of the *making*. The two are of course in a close embrace: the maker views as much as the viewer makes. Yet differently: ethics (performance of viewing), politics of viewing (first network of making), politics (second network of making).

All this to apologize for launching an analogy here. As follows:

The wall of the museum had to be opened and monumental cranes utilized, to bring *Past, Present, Future* and *S-curve* into the gallery. For *Memory*, the floor had to be reinforced, but since each tile was brought in separately, the walls did not have to be breached. *Marsyas*, representing a breaking through the museum walls, had to be installed inside by massive mechanical assistance.

We have spoken of the lesson of *Marsyas*, soft membrane stretched so tight that it is and seems hard, broken into bits by the (human) body's gaze. We have also spoken of the intertextuality with Greek polytheism which echoes the trace-sign battle: Marsyas, human musician, mere trace competing, with Apollo, master of the sign—losing struggle confused productively in myth with playing to lose—body flayed inside out, stretched red membrane, gigantic flute, held as if it wishes to escape, the silvering on the back of the mirror trying to trump the looking *Glass*, "the clapper of a truth that tilts, that cl—."[18] But *Memory* turns outside in. "Judd did the body, and now I must turn it inside out," Kapoor said in Boston. Kapoor must play (Marsyas playing) Apollo, know/show the whole object in little, so that it may become wholly inaccessible in the museum. "To measure up to the heroic propositions of sculpture—making scale an instrument" in more senses than one, his remarks, again, in Boston.

Insofar as a proposition—A is B—is the measure of reason, it is the heroic, the measure of man as the creator-hero. Man rising up to the proposition is Freud's fable of the emergence of the ego into the reality-principle.

In order for this to happen, a minutely detailed metapsychological psychic apparatus must dovetail through the stricture (a constraint that structures) of repression. (So far in this book, we have connected this with first language learning.) The constraints structure. As the mindspace (whatever it is) crosses the structuring fence, force-lines change into recognizable feelings. The ego moves into proposition-land. Subject gets predicated. A is B. As Freud famously said, it is only when repression fails that the subject goes askew, and the analyst tracks the trace to a healing narrative of signs. We get a trace-signing of the psychic apparatus balancing itself so that it can retain its hold upon the proposition in public exchange—even when the "public" is just the rational ego in conversation with itself—in the inbuilt healing work of the dream. That there can be no answer to the question "Who dreams?" is proof of the power of the fable.

I can find an analogy to this fable in "Kapoor's" measuring up to the heroic propositions of sculpture. "Kapoor" imagines the work. It is a truism for the least serious student of art that the imagination has no fixable subject. The star-system strives to deny this, as does the copyright, but the fact remains. "Who imagines?" is a public representation of the impossible question "who dreams?" I must keep the analogy loose: let me call the Director of Aerotrope, the engineering company involved in developing the geometry of the form, Christopher Hornzee-Jones; Allard Bokma, the man at Centraalstaal, the steel company in The Netherlands that is fabricating the work; and Lammert Osinga, the ship builder who is working on the stiffeners that will join all the 140 Cor-Ten steel tiles to one another—so that the globe/blimp can, in some only partially perceived bit of "objective truth" we learn in school, float in water if freed from the enclosures that produce the subject of the proposition—the constraining structurers of the real. Let us call the army of technicians in white jumpsuits the enforcers of the metapsychological, attentive to every detail. The ego tinkers, but only just. It remembers the dream. *Memory* was a "working title," now memorialized. As the sculpture-space (whatever it is) crosses the structuring boundary, technicity becomes art. The question "Who made this?" is the absurd auteurism that plagues photography as well. The unconscious may not have a vote in a working democracy but it can confabulate the museum. "Anish Kapoor" is as vulnerable as any proper name, only more so.

Yet that huge misshapen "globe/blimp" that only the dreamer and the dream-workers should "see" is now hypertextually available online, thus defeating sculpture's heroic proposition and re-opening Derrida's question: how would Freud have fabulated the psyche had he known the Internet? . . .

"I am I am I. All creation shivers with that sweet cry." Yeats's blissful ("bliss" is *jouissance* for those of you who care) heterotautological proposition is what keeps us going. In the name of "elongating time" the dreamworker unmoors us from this saving proposition. We are lost in the fun house. There are mirrors everywhere, creating virtual space by technical imaginings as they destroy the human image—though not completely. Just as a stopped analogue clock gives the correct time twice a day, so in the fable of measuring up to the proposition truth-as-exactitude is just a particular case of fiction, and so are we more jolted because, in some of the more complex mirrorings, we are mirrored "exactly" now and again, only to be startled by "loss of reality" in our outlines, our positions. I am reading this, but can the vulgar bejeweled investors (rather different from the old "civilized" elite—same difference) by whom I, an old unconnected woman (Baubo) was resolutely ignored at the opening reception at the museum? By this time, I ask you to figure out why an aesthetic education might have helped art step forth toward justice.

In *C-Curve,* I suddenly seem to step forth, a third of the way out of the mirror, niftily standing with whoever happens to flank me on grounding conditions expanded and extended. In *S-Curve,* Narcissus loses her outline, not in conclusion, as in Rilke's mirror elegy, but right in the middle, as her eyes are made to cross by the dip in the mirror. Bernard Tschumi taught me how to activate space but these things activate space on their own.

Who makes that happen? Oops, wrong question. Go rather on the other side of the "S," to the matched curve where Echo appears, and gives your voice back to you, and by chance you perform the gratuitous act of speaking up in the museum.

You begin to see it's not about the body as measure. It's about those mirrors. *"Spiegel, noch nie hat man wissend geschrieben, Was ihr in eurem Wesen seid."* Was Rilke waiting for Anish, who says that to "elongate time" is the sculptor's task, just as he says elsewhere that "intimacy implies the shortening of the distance between the viewer and the viewed?"

E-long-ate, shorten. "Long" and "short" are time/space words. Long time/long distance, short time/short distance. Time lengthened or shortened is time timed by space. Is it this spacing that Rilke described as *"Zwischenräume der Zeit"*—time's interstices? Laurie Anderson as "Long time no see?" Time and space—sign and trace, not a neat cut, of course. Not only by the body's measure, but by objects. The mirror stage. We look at a pesky item in *1000 Names,* by itself recognized as a cross between a marketplace cork hat and a solid mound of color powder, by a person with sufficient cultural information. And then, at a certain angle,

there it hangs from the upper edge of *S-Curve,* like a ripe red Indian cap-
sicum or chili pepper. This is Hindu polytheism, not Greek. Most foreign
commentators emphasize, again, the high Hindu explanation. That explanation can take on board a hundred and eight, just as easily. There is
nothing sacred about a thousand. What is generally missed is the subaltern model of these objects in the tin-box corner-shop, matching E. M.
Forster's description of the framed sampler in the kitsch of an Indian
temple "God si love," in the place of "God is love."

I saw the dream-object of *Memory* in miniature in Kapoor's studio in
London. Globalization was on my mind, and you know what I learned: a
fluctuating island of signs in a sea of trace.

This lesson applies even, in the most brutal sense, to this very object,
this *Memory,* as it does to all art as investment in a capital market, enhanced by globalization. This is the second network, the second performance of making. The circuits of capital, circuits of the abstract average,
move through various transformations by way of the data-form. This is
a circuit of traces of various kinds, if one bothers to track them. Nothing
will "signify" in this maelstrom of traces, always suggesting that someone,
somewhere, made a move, or perhaps not. This is exactly not the "inventory without traces" that Gramsci imagined as a description of the material for the historian-subject of the rural poor, cut off from the state, that
I quoted earlier. There the historian must be in search of signs. Here, at
the global end, not confined to the state, the trace suffices; it is not universalizable and today there is an entire virtual economy that is never realized into money or goods; there is the non-signifying barter-swap of de-
rivatives and futures, and finance capital capitalizing on exchange. Upon
this terrain—a useless metaphor—the data-form doesn't "signify" anything. It is de-substantialized, as in Marx's original argument about the
substance of money. What is given is a trace without a text.

Within this immense field of traces, the works themselves are islands
of meaning, engaged in the old game of trace and sign, (not exactly) the
visual and the verbal, that viewer and critic endlessly decode. The context is provided by general expedients: "looks like, feels like . . ."; the
unmarked Euro-U.S. as the general: Donald Judd, Sol LeWitt, Richard
Serra; and the region-marked ontopology: my red homeland, the Indian
Jew. And the island of proper names—Afinsa, B&O Hightex, Fondazione
Prada, Gaz de France, Interlaken, Tumi, Unilever, Union Fenosa—offers a
simulacrum of the being making history.

Derrida was unusual as a philosopher in claiming the trace as a solution:
to the old problem of universalizing the trace into a sign, thinking lan-

guage as prime mover. In mid-career, Derrida walked with painters and photographers, and prayed to be haunted by Tlingit coffin makers, perhaps to learn how trace folks traffic in signs. In the end, nothing was enough to step into the human-animot *différance*.[19]

Walking with Anish Kapoor in his studio, listening to him talk to his friend in public, I learned to think what I have written in these pages. As you walk with him in the museum, think yourself on the trace sign shuttle to check out the exhilaration of not going through to the meaning. Until nothing is enough, nothing suffices. We (no longer we are in) the planet.

CHAPTER TWENTY-FIVE

Tracing the Skin of Day

HOPELESS, I step out of the corporatized university, in the world and in the discipline. I move into visual material in conclusion, for this has been in the patronage and investment circuit for rather a longer time than electronic globalization. Into the gallery, the museum, an elite space, offering a lesson that will go unheeded, even as the artist moves forward. Classic aesthetic education, even in Schiller's day. Yet here, the learning of reading is put to the strictest test, for there are no guarantees. A demanding cooldown at the end, if you like.

Looking at Chittrovanu Mazumdar's *Nightskin* I start in the middle room, in the middle. Everything here started, said the artist to me, with a vision of something like lips, like tiny doors, like petals, opening and closing, a space, a hole, a slit. A middle. Think hymen, if you like, but I wouldn't, immediately. I will think position, without phenomenal identity and, since all cleansed things carry at least a trace of the phenomenon, the trace thing here can be the female sexual thing—but as a trace, not a symbol.

At the simplest mechanical level, the lips opening and closing are "originary," not at the origin. They must be staged as opening and closing for the show to start, in the middle. I saw this ritual a number of times and felt the "lips," windows with louvers and latches, some of which we can manipulate ourselves, shutters slowly opening and closing by themselves, sometimes housing raging fires that seemingly continue to rage in secret, mostly placed in aggressive and menacing early-industrial machines, "stern, rivet-studded, metallic military fastnesses," movable on equally aggressive squat wheels, animal-machines on parade, running interference for the vaunted invisibility of the digital.[1] I can think that this leads into the virtuality of the "natural," emerging from those open lips, bearing the mark of uterine trauma, life as death. Melanie Klein. The First Room. But only as trace. This is neither conceptual art nor digital idealism. Let me call this "wise" art for the moment.

All visual art, a field of traces, may well tend toward sign-status, especially when the viewer is obliged to speak about it. Let me then quote the previous chapter on the subject of the trace:

> There are signs and there may be traces (hinting at something that left *this* mark). It is not a break between words and picture/objects—the verbal and the visual—although it may seem so. . . . Catch the trace is the oldest problem in the book. . . . What, then, is a trace? always remembering that it is not an "isness." A sign system promises meaning. A trace does not promise anything. It is something that seems to suggest that there was something before. . . . It's like elephant shit on the forest floor. It can be either, that there were elephants here. Or it could be, that you are hallucinating. Or yet it could be, that someone put it there in order to be a decoy for you. Or it could be that you are mistaken, elephant shit does not look like that at all, or— . . . indefinite "inventory without traces." A trace is not . . . a sign.

What is important here is that, for Chittrovanu, unlike Kapoor, the human body is not the measure. He is attempting to go the other way from the merely human program to catch the trace. What organizes human semiosis, reproductive heteronormativity (RHN), is here shorn of the articulatory elements that produce social significance, thus gendering, and thus "culture" itself. In verbal cultural critique, some of us speak often of "position without identity." That is the other end of talk, thinking abstraction, with bits of the empirical clinging to it, constantly on the way to coding. The trace generates talk that cannot move up to systemic coding Marx thought of the trace as "insufficient," "incomplete," "because the representation-series never concludes." The general equivalent, shedding its thingliness, becomes something like a sign-system. Yet he must take us back into understanding traces, for only that will transform the quality of the detail of our lives, make the spirit uneasy, train for change without waiting for vanguardism to transgress the collective spirit.[2] Gramsci will build on this to lead to an incandescent political passion.[3] Nietzsche complicates matters by commenting on the actual move from trace to sign as a concealment of the spirit's moral determination:

> The entire history of a . . . custom can in this way be a continuous sign-chain of ever new interpretations and revisions [*Zurechtmachungen*] whose causes do not even have to be related to one another but, on the contrary, in some cases succeed and alternate with one another in a purely chance fashion.[4]

Kant re-wrote something like a field of traces as the cold abstractions of philosophizing: the transcendental deduction.[5]

Chittrovanu is thus in an altogether radical tradition and more radical with it, working with things, paint, pictures. He protects the trace away from the promise of the sign. This is exactly not conceptual art. Even the references to its own visuality, the bits of color in the First Room, the plangent, brilliant, glowing colors of the Middle Room, are witty denials of the conceptual. I can think the mystery of the metapsychological as the allegory of reading here. But as beckoning trace, not as the fulfilled promise of the psychoanalytic system.

Trace travels, with no guarantees. Trace teaches, lessons that the subject soaks up. Traveling on the dingy near-empty train on the New York City subway toward the vanished World Trade Center as I write these words, I am remembering the old number 9 train (I ride the number 1), the line destroyed by 9/11—coming into the City on that terrible day. Suddenly there is a gap in the slimy wall too close to the train, and Chittrovanu's plangent blue shines in. I begin then to sense glowing reds sometimes, my eyes focused outside the train, at the pressing in rough wall. I feel the doors as lips opening and closing, the subway is traced onto *Nightskin*. This is not evidentiary; I must get back from this tracing to the rooms.

"What does 'experimentation'/'alternative'/'radical' mean to you?" asks Paula Sengupta. Disingenuously, Chittrovanu says: "It's normal, isn't it?"[6]

Most of what is written on Chittrovanu mentions his French connection. His mother was French, French theory, and so on. I myself find these nation-state-specific concerns somewhat peculiar and I certainly cannot presume to produce the requisite Bhartrhari to prove the superiority of his Indianness. (His own description of his Frenchness is altogether moving: "the strange magic of a completely different world.") Derrida seems apposite in the story of the trace, as will *Kali* in the First Room.

Early on, Derrida thought of himself as a philosopher of the trace. I have quoted these lines often:

> Since language, which Saussure says is a classification, has not fallen from the sky, differences have been produced, they are produced effects, but effects which do not have as cause a subject or a substance, a thing in general, an existent somewhere present, and itself escaping the play of *différance*. If such a presence were implied in the most classical fashion, in the concept of cause in general, we would have to speak of an effect without a cause, which very quickly would lead to speaking of no effect at all. I have attempted to indicate a way out of the closure of this framework via the "trace," which is no more an effect than it has a cause, but which cannot suffice by itself, outside the text, to operate the necessary transgression.[7]

This passage assumes that the philosopher's predication is to move on out from the seduction of showing cause. As artist, Chittrovanu keeps a tight leash. Traced, the opening-and-closing puts us in mind of the hymen, but no linking—no *enchainement*—happens, no cause shown. There is indeed a stand-up, coffin-sized closed room, with flowered red satin walls, redolent with the nuances of an enclosing female erotic space and a felicitous male occupant, a helpful locus for the viewer to solidify the concept. All seems well. We hear the celebrated *thumri* of the lover's return and music resonant with it to secure the theme of sex for pleasure, the easiest riff, accommodating many permutations of aesthetics and sexual politics. Yet the looped soundtrack contains philosophical ruminations that have little or no connection with that consolation prize. What are these lines from the German poet Rilke doing there: "links of light, corridors, stairs, thrones, spaces of being, shields of rapture, torrents of unchecked feeling"?[8] I can "read" this mysterious room as a site where the failure of the articulation of the trace of the hymen into sexual semiotics is staged. For the Rilke lines will end: "and then suddenly, singly, *mirrors*." The music resonates with the greatest promise possible—the promise of meaning within a sign-system, only, deliberately to disappoint—so that the tough project of the work can succeed in failing. Oedipus, the staging of the opposite failure—not to mind the sign-system into which RHN is articulated—so humankind may be warned, laments that articulation: "O marriages, marriages, you put us in nature, and putting us back again, reversed the seed, and indexed fathers, brothers, children, kin-blood mingled, brides, women, mothers, a shameful thing to know among the works of man."[9] It is marriage that gives us the symbolic, and gives meaning to the aesthetics of copulation from whore to courtesan, catamite to paramour—separates the human from the animal through kinship inscription, making incest possible in performative contradiction. Chittrovanu hangs short of this slide. Now we begin to get a sense of the First Room. We will not go there yet, but it is all about human and animal. It is first, but we go there from the middle. Here in the Middle Room the lips open and close, tracing the hymen, but not consolidating it into the articulated chain of sexual difference as reference.

Let us now walk around the room. There are a couple of these antique-looking machines, close to the ground, looping over a lit screen. A few things to say here: the opening and closing of the hymen—coded as inside/outside in Derrida—is here, in a visual matrix, also coded as, speaking loosely now, nature/culture. Chain of displacements, level of abstraction, trace it as you walk through. (The First Room has prepared us for this, but I am not ready to go there yet.) Let us say culture is city-scapes, people—and nature is flower, leaf, water. I, a word-smith, can only mime the non-access to a sign-system and, in spite of myself, make it seem a failure. That is the power of Chittrovanu's sight-smithing, as it were, his para-conceptuality, his counter-intuitive intuition: that, in this work, who wins the way into the apparent coherence of the rhetorico-conceptual sign-system clearly loses.

I walked around in this room as *Nightskin* was being set up. I saw these flow machines when they were turned off—the black of switch-off—and when the loop wasn't working yet—a clear pellucid blue, the subway station blue as a waiting stillness—the bosom of the steady lake; just as I saw "Sony" in the margins of yet another one of the big lugubrious machines. These accidental viewings seemed consonant with the work. Techno-miraculous digitality simulates an empirical version of so-called virtuality, and so its slip can't show. Over against this is the post-Beaubourg public architecture, showing scaffolding—inside out. *Nightskin* is neither here nor there; its place is not within the current history of the artist's consciousness, aka style. "I suffer the questions," Chittrovanu quietly says.[10] This is an allegory of no-arrival at meaning and so can accommodate "every discoloration of the stone," as Yeats wrote in "Lapis Lazuli," here every clumsiness of the lugubrious machines, including accidents. There is no failure. Who loses wins. But to get here is difficult, as I have been repeating.

Now we begin to see the para-conceptual conceptuality of the many little windows for opening, half-opening, half-closing, and closing on the standing machines (Figure 40). Haunting pictures, one with two moons. Nature not nature.

While I was at the show, I heard a suggestion that these photographs be made available as a separate series. It'll be an admirable acquisition, a series without seriality. And we begin to "make sense" out of the walls of unnatural roses, water trickling down the immense face of a flat machine: the "nature" end of an opening and closing—species-life. "Make sense of." No one wins here, either. It's not so easy to "decide" not to be human, to swim against that rush. Perhaps that's what the show stages. Remember, no failure either . . . Like skipping ropes. The Third Room.

We'll get there later. Now we step back into the First Room and look at the dead cow disintegrating (Figure 41) until it's nothing but the configurations of ground—an important word, surely.

Chittrovanu traces the ground as end/origin, sticking with an animal, not graduating into the human. We now know that there is some connection here with that remark of Oedipus bitterly addressing marriage. It took away his mere animality, made him break the Law, and be bound by the double bind of incest. Hegel goes the other way with Antigone: the rendering of the corpse into the economy of nature is for him a celebration of *satkar*. It is a story of the general (universal) human ethical equivalent, fighting the animal:

> These powers are other communities, whose altars the dogs or birds defiled with their corpses, who were not raised into unconscious universality through

Figure 40:   Open Window with Moon Picture, from Chittrovanu Mazumdar, "Undated: Nightskin" (2009), 1 × 1 Art Gallery, Dubai.

Figure 41:   Dead Cow, from Chittrovanu Mazumdar, "Undated: Nightskin" (2009), 1 × 1 Art Gallery, Dubai.

the return to elementary individuality owed them, but have remained above ground, in the sphere of reality, and as the power of divine law, now receives a self-conscious effective universality.[11]

Tryamvaka is celebrated in the *Mahamrtyunjaya* as sweet-smelling, for the *asatkrta* body would stink. Wordsworth celebrates Lucy—a human child—as passively "alive," "roll'd round in earth's diurnal course, with rocks and stones and trees." When Wallace Stevens writes "beauty is immortal in the flesh," he isn't thinking of dead animals, but Chittrovanu is. "Documentary fictionalized" (AK). Sign traced. Fiction can be a place of traces, less so in the verbal than the visual.[12]

And on one of these tremendous digital prints, with bits of color announcing their visuality, there is a demure and elegant classic Kali, poised sideways, queered, as it were, not the straight orthodox authentic tribal goddess but an objet trouvé, as the artist assured me (Figure 42).

No sweet-smelling porter of divine law she. She carries rather the burden of the trace, a goddess in suspension on the print, hanging in mid-air, a goddess through sacrifice to whom the mere animal might have been sacralized, a mythologically non-reproductive goddess of course elaborately endowed with motherhood. Again, nothing jells. The goddess remains ex-orbitant to the celebration of the grounding of the animal. This is not a loop; the story has an ending. The end is the biggest loop of all, the ecological cycle, bigger even than RHN, with which we make meaning.

Figure 42: Kali, from Chittrovanu Mazumdar, "Undated: Nightskin" (2009), 1 × 1 Art Gallery, Dubai.

Contained within the ecobiome, we can do good or ill. This responsibility is ours. But you cannot access that great loop. Its cousin is planetarity. And the disintegrating animal integrates into it—otherwise than being.[13]

This is the First Room.

We transit now to the Third.

Here with quiet fanfare is the human theater where non-consolidation of meaning out of RHN is most counter-intuitive. Let us say that here the viewer is taught to look and feel the staging of the comfort of learning. I have often said that art for me is visual opportunities for the didactic, and so I feel particularly comforted by the protocols of this room.

First the obvious impossibility to see all the screens at once, often used by conceptual artists to make a point about what Barthes used to call "the writable."[14] In Chittrovanu's hands, it is a conceptual handle that reminds us of bigger non-conceptual entities. There are fragments that bring together all the short and truncated thematic chains. Women veiling and unveiling, unedited letters, now texted, that remind us of the philosophical soliloquy in the little room in the Middle Room, and waves, waves, waves—again repeating all the lost traciness. "Flowing water, cries, the lights of a city at night, the wail of an infant, a woman alone, sirens and traffic sounds, stained walls and doors and windows, a female voice pleading, a placid pig wallowing in the filth and murk of its natural habitat, fragments of a diary" (AK). This is also my least loved room, because I had the chance to go through it many times, in comfort. Perhaps it's good for the first-time visitor to have an ekphrasis of the tracing lesson, like Achilles' shield in Homer, which tells the entire tale of the *Iliad,* or, better yet, the *Viswarupadarsana* in the *Gita,* where Kṛṣṇa eats the synchronic action. Yet, can tracing ever be caught in ekphrasis? When you go back in, figure out the answer yourself, and forget it. For here, in the visual, the lesson of reading is the toughest. There are no guarantees at all.

Envoi

Grounding error, safety from the horror of planetarity, double bind within mere humanism . . . upon this precarious terrain, read the title as an aesthetic education in the era of globalizability.

Notes

Preface

1. Jacques Derrida, *Psyché* (Paris: Galilée, 1987), p. 9.
2. Most recently in Paris, in two unpublished lectures: "Femmes, langage, culture et politique à l'heure de la mondialisation postcoloniale," with Etienne Balibar, Le Merle Moqueur; and "Paroles subalternes: Politique culturelle du féminisme et du postcolonialisme," with Eric Fassin, Ecole Normale Supérieure; Paris, January 25, 2010. I have recently discovered what may be a secret origin, but would I know? See the chapter on the rehabilitation program in Nayanika Mookherjee, *The Spectral Wound: Sexual Violence, Public Memories and the Bangladesh War of 1971* (Durham, NC: Duke University Press, 2011). "French Feminism in an International Frame" and "Draupadi" are included in Gayatri Chakravorty Spivak, *In Other Worlds: Essays in Cultural Politics* (New York: Routledge, 2006), pp. 184–211, 245–269. "Three Women's Texts" and "Can the Subaltern Speak?," both much revised, are included in Spivak, *A Critique of Postcolonial Reason: Toward a History of the Vanishing Present* (Cambridge, MA: Harvard University Press, 1999), pp. 113–148, 246–311.
3. Emmanuel Lévinas, *Otherwise than Being, or, Beyond Essence*, trans. Alphonso Lingis (Pittsburgh: Duquesne University Press, 1998).
4. "Touched by Deconstruction," *Grey Room* 20 (Summer 2005): 95–104; "Notes toward a Tribute to Jacques Derrida," *differences* 16.3 (Fall 2005): 102–113, reprinted with additions in Costas Douzinas, ed., *Adieu Derrida* (London: Palgrave Macmillan, 2007), pp. 47–60.
5. Percy Bysshe Shelley, "A Defence of Poetry," in Bruce K. McElderry Jr., ed., *Shelley's Critical Prose* (Lincoln: University of Nebraska Press, 1967), p. 28.
6. Christopher Lasch, *The Culture of Narcissism: American Life in an Age of Diminishing Expectations* (New York: Norton, 1979).

Introduction

1. Support from the popular media: Peggy Orenstein, "Forcing ourselves offline may be the path to true knowledge" ("The Way We Live Now: Stop Your Search Engines," *New York Times Magazine,* October 25, 2009, p. 11).

2. Claus Offe is aware of this contemporaneity. Thinking of Eastern Europe as a "unique example," he calls it a simultaneity and a dilemma. In globalization every site is contemporary and yet also unique. We therefore call it a double bind. Offe is also aware of a need of what we are calling an "aesthetic education," but cannot of course say so. These are the ways it comes out: "As macroevents have assumed an incredible speed, the painful task of patient waiting falls upon individuals" and "is it possible to *generate* this kind of patience and civilized behavior where they are lacking, by the judicious use of political resources and institutional reforms?" ("Capitalism by Democratic Design? Democratic Theory Facing the Triple Transition in East Central Europe," *Social Research* 58.4 [Winter 1991]: 869, 872, 887, 888).

3. Derrida rightly writes that the modern university everywhere is a variation on the medieval European model. Jacques Derrida, "The University without Condition," in *Without Alibi,* trans. Peggy Kamuf (Stanford, CA: Stanford University Press, 2002), pp. 202–237. And here is a bit from an e-mail I wrote to the charming vice-chancellor of Mahatma Gandhi University in Kerala: "I have only recently been invited to participate in the elite tertiary and post-tertiary institutions in India, where English (which I believe is also an Indian language) can be understood. Although I feel most at home there, because of the presence of critical intelligence such as Sanal Mohan's and Thomas Joseph's (and many others, I feel sure), I cannot linger there precisely for that reason." Schiller is at home there as well. Affirmative sabotage.

4. Obama's minimalist acknowledgment of this is in his appointment of behavioral economists to change the desires of consumers (Benjamin Wallace-Wells, "Cass Susstein Wants to Nudge Us," *New York Times Magazine,* May 16, 2010, pp. 38–44).

5. In a broader compass, our sympathies would lie with someone like Lúcio Flávio Pinto, who is "suspicious of contemporary bromides about 'sustainable development,' which he regards as 'no more than an ideology until now, used to sugar the pill, smooth the international public opinion' and soothe the consciences of what he calls the 'colonial' consumers, both in and outside Brazil. Enabling humans to learn 'how to use' the Amazon 'without destroying it' is the region's greatest challenge, he says" (Reed Johnson, "On the Beat in the Amazon: Brazilian Journalist Lúcio Flávio Pinto Has Spent More than Four Decades Trying to Right Wrong While Staying Alive and Out of Jail," *Los Angeles Times,* May 18, 2008, p. F8). Pinto's remarks imply a hands-on epistemological project, a great challenge.

6. I think of Gramsci as a democratic communist rather than a liberal democrat. I hope that is clear from my references to him here. For a critique of the liberal appropriation of Gramsci, see Georgio Barratta, "Gramsci among Us: Hall, Said, Balibar," *Anglistika* 9.1 (2005): 9–43.

7. Hannah Arendt, *On Violence* (New York: Harcourt, Brace, Jovanovich, 1970), p. 27.

8. Tillie Olsen, *Tell Me a Riddle* (New York: Dell, 1961); Christine Brooke-Rose, *Subscript* (Manchester, UK: Carcanet, 1999) and *Life, End of* (Manchester, UK: Carcanet, 2006). A reading of Olsen is included in *Du Bois Rewrites History* (Cambridge, MA: Harvard University Press, forthcoming).

9. Friedrich Nietzsche, *The Gay Science,* trans. Walter Kaufmann (New York: Vintage, 1974), cited and discussed in Jacques Derrida, *Spurs,* trans. Barbara Harlow (Chicago: University of Chicago Press, 1979). Old women, in this view, are scary because their withered genitals, beyond the seductions of sexuality, are free of masculine thrall, and therefore they are wise about humanity. It seems likely that Nietzsche received his information from Clement of Alexandria, whose own source for this particular rite of Demeter is far from definitive (Clement of Alexandria, *Exhortation to the Greeks,* trans. G. W. Butterworth [Cambridge, MA: Harvard University Press, 1968], pp. 41–43); for the doubtful provenance for the rite, see G. E. Mylonas, *Eleusis and the Eleusinian Mysteries* (Princeton, NJ: Princeton University Press, 1961); and J. M. Coetzee, *The Age of Iron* (New York: Random House, 1990); Coetzee, *The Lives of Animals* (Princeton, NJ: Princeton University Press, 1999); Coetzee, *Elizabeth Costello* (New York: Viking, 2003); Coetzee, *Slow Man* (New York: Viking, 2005).

10. "Thinking Academic Freedom in Gendered Postcoloniality," in Gayatri Chakravorty Spivak, *Space and Place* (Kolkata: Seagull Books, forthcoming).

11. Consider Haiti, where black people established Liberty, Equality, Fraternity; or Uzbekistan, our partner in the War on Terror. For a thumbnail summary of the Haitian case, see "Haiti's Lesson," *Economic and Political Weekly* 45.5 (January 30, 2010), pp. 5–6; for Uzbekistan, see Craig Murray, *Murder in Samarkand: A British Ambassador's Controversial Defiance of Tyranny in the War on Terror* (London: Mainstream, 2006).

12. For a brilliant discussion, see Diana K. Reese, *Reproducing Enlightenment: Paradoxes in the Life of the Body Politic: Literature and Philosophy around 1800* (New York: de Gruyter, 2009).

13. The ab-use of the Enlightenment has to be thought through in terms of the irregular but tenacious residual/dominant presence of clan politics in different parts of the world. Kathleen Collins offers a provocative summary in *Clan Politics and Regime Transition in Central Asia* (New York: Cambridge University Press, 2006). Raymond Williams's model of "culture" as the dance of archaic/residual/dominant/emergent/oppositional/alternative/pre-emergent needs to be expanded to understand the heterogeneity of the ab-user (Raymond Williams, *Marxism and Literature* [New York: Oxford University Press, 1977], pp. 121–127). We also have to think of the irregularity of the enabling violations of varieties of imperialisms, and the influence of Americanization-as-globalization placed upon this uneven terrain with historically specific groups as receivers of a sort. Where is the intellectual in this phantasmagoria? What is it for Chengiz Aitmatov, the "liberal" novelist, to have supported

Akaev, the physicist gradually transformed into clan-managing autocrat, torture-approver?

14. Gregory Bateson, *Steps to an Ecology of Mind* (Chicago: University of Chicago Press, 2000), p. 272 (hereafter cited in the text as EM, with page numbers following).

15. As was clear, for example, from "Toward a Common Morality," neuroscience cannot help us here, even as it firmly undermines the plausibility of free will (September 11, 2009, United Nations). We are stuck with the training of the individual subject. On the occasion cited, most eloquent on this theme was Maxwell R. Bennett, Professor of Neuroscience at the University of Sydney.

16. Sigmund Freud, "Fetishism," in *The Standard Edition*, vol. 21, trans. James Strachey (New York: Norton, 1961–), p. 152 (hereafter cited in the text and notes as SE, with volume and page numbers following).

17. William Wordsworth, *The Prose Works of William Wordsworth,* ed. Warwick Jack Burgoyne Owen and Jane Worthington Smyser (Oxford: Clarendon Press, 1974) (hereafter cited in the text as LB, with page numbers following).

18. Marx, "Theses on Feuerbach," in *The German Ideology* (New York: International Publishers, 1988), p. 121. I now understand this is Engels's *felix culpa* (see W. F. Haug, "Gramsci's 'Philosophy of Praxis,'" *Socialism and Democracy* 14.1 [Spring–Summer 2000]: 1–19). Dermot Ryan has indicated Wordsworth's interest in innovative education systems (Dermot Ryan, "Writing, Imagination, and the Production of Empire from Adam Smith to William Wordsworth," Ph.D. dissertation, Columbia University, 2007).

19. Coleridge might be altogether more democratic here, since his humanist theory of the imagination is a description of being-human for the human being in general.

20. Antonio Gramsci, *Selections from the Prison Notebooks,* ed. and trans. Quintin Hoare and Geoffrey Nowell Smith (New York: International Publishers, 1971), p. 298 (hereafter cited in the notes as SPN, with page numbers following).

21. Derrida, *The Animal That Therefore I Am,* trans. David Wills (New York: Fordham University Press, 2008).

22. Derrida, *Without Alibi,* trans. Peggy Kamuf (Stanford, CA: Stanford University Press, 2002), p. 202. Derrida calls it a "profession of faith," thus inviting us to follow the labyrinthine framing of the original "Profession of Faith" in Rousseau's *Émile.* He cannot escape a version of humanism in speaking of the humanities, but must ask us to route that predicament by an intertextual invitation.

23. "Western Marxism and the Legacy of the New Social Movements," paper presented at Actuel Marx conference on Altermodialisme/Anticapitalisme, University of Paris–Sorbonne, October 5, 2007; given as "Revisiting Postcolonialism," Centre for Cultural Studies, Goldsmiths College, University of London, November 7, 2007. The embedding reference for the passage from Gramsci is to Antonio Gramsci, "The Problem of the School," in David Forgacs, ed., *The Antonio Gramsci Reader: Selected Writings 1916–1935* (New

York: NYU Press, 2000), p. 40. Cf. Joseph Stiglitz, *Globalization and Its Discontents* (New York: Norton, 2003): "We recognize today that there is a 'social contract' that binds citizens together, and with their government" (p. 78). Citizens are made, through a class apartheid broken by what I am calling "an aesthetic education."

24. I am grateful to Stathis Gourgouris, *Dream-Nation: Enlightenment, Colonization, and the Institution of Modern Greece* (Stanford, CA: Stanford University Press, 1996), p. 45, for this felicitous formulation.

25. SPN, p. 366.

26. "I therefore call the explanation of the way in which concepts can relate to objects a priori their transcendental deduction, and distinguish this from the empirical [evidentiary] deduction" (Kant, *Critique of Pure Reason,* trans. Paul Guyer and Allen W. Wood [Cambridge: Cambridge University Press, 2000], p. 220) (hereafter cited in the text and notes as PR, with page numbers following). This will always be the sense in which I will use this phrase in this book.

27. SPN, pp. 365–366.

28. Ibid., p. 10.

29. A conservative writer like Hervé de Carmoy, wanting white Europe and white United States to unite in fraternity, still relates as in a cracked mirror with what we are proposing. He wants an eighteenth-century-style, rational, epistemic transformation of these favored subjects so that the world can be saved (Hervé de Carmoy, *L'Euramerique* [Paris: PUF, 2007], pp. 9, 57, 65, 76). Our effort would destabilize and relocate this project, sublated into an unrestricted dialectic, always at a loss, losing in view of a future anterior. Srinivas Aravamudan's forthcoming *Enlightenment Orientalism* gives us a sense of the Enlightenment's desire for the Orient, through romance and novel and the institutionalization of literature. The relationship between our desire for the Enlightenment displaced into ab-use into a carefully modulated worldly practice and the place of an aesthetic education in that set and Aravamudan's argument is also "cracked" of course.

30. Voltaire, *Candide,* trans. Theo Cuffe (London: Penguin, 2009) offers a cartography of the discursive field ready for these changes.

31. Denis Cosgrove, *Apollo's Eye: A Cartographic Genealogy of the Earth in the Western Imagination* (Baltimore, MD: Johns Hopkins University Press, 2001), p. 19.

32. I mention this again in "The Stakes of a World Literature" (Chapter 22 in this book).

33. In *Clan Politics,* Kathleen Collins undoes the opposition between the Euro–U.S. and "the rest of the world" along these lines. In the process, she makes clear the historical frame within which Gramsci may have had a special grasp of the relationship between democratic communism and clans, which makes him appear so timely today.

34. Immanuel Kant, "Toward a Perpetual Peace," in *Political Writings,* trans. H. B. Nisbet (Cambridge: Cambridge University Press, 1991), pp. 93–130 (hereafter cited in the text as PP, with page numbers following).

35. Kant, PR, p. 602.

36. Derrida and Anne Dufourmentelle, *Of Hospitality,* trans. Rachel Bowlby (Stanford, CA: Stanford University Press, 2000). Invited to keynote 2010's European Cultural Capital, "the borderless city" Pecs in Hungary, I had the greatest possible visa difficulties because my passport was lost for a day! A variation, surely, of policing truth-telling.

37. Kant, PR, pp. 219–221. "Democracy" combines with "religion" in clan politics. The next quoted passage is from p. 384.

38. I have in fact inserted material from the translation by Werner S. Pluhar (Indianapolis, IN: Hackett Publishing, 1996), p. 372, because the Guyer and Wood translation seems to divert from Kant's text. (I thank Patricia Kitcher for leading me to it.) The general idea is that "in freedom" pure reason, precisely by bringing forth a causality, limits the practical idea.

39. I have given the two German words translated "absolute" to show that in the first usage, where the German uses the philosophical word *absolut,* we are looking at the limiting condition imposed by pure reason in its practical function, in other words, how pure reason behaves, as it were. In the second case, the colloquial German word *schlechthin* relates to how we philosophizing humans should behave. An aesthetic moment. I force the text to say: pure reason provides no object for practical reason's programmed "as ifs."

40. Jon Elster, *Ulysses and the Sirens: Studies in Rationality and Irrationality* (Cambridge: Cambridge University Press, 1984). I must also of course mention the gender politics (women tempting men) and class politics (sailors must bind him and stuff their own ears with wax), if I take Ulysses' pre-commitment as the characteristic European ideal.

41. George Caffentzis, "The Peak Oil Complex, Commodity Fetishism, and Class Struggle," *Rethinking Marxism* 20.2 (2008): 313, 317. "Another World Is Possible" is most prominently the slogan of the World Social Forum.

42. Friedrich Schiller, *On the Aestheic Education of Man: In a Series of Letters,* trans. Elizabeth M. Wilkinson and L. A. Willoughby (Oxford: Clarendon Press, 1982) (hereafter cited in the text and notes as AE, with page numbers following). It is not unimportant to remember that the letters were written to Friedrich Christian, Duke of Schleswig Holstein-Augustenburg.

43. Discussed at length in "Translating into English" (Chapter 12 in this book).

44. Spivak, *A Critique of Postcolonial Reason: Toward a History of the Vanishing Present* (Cambridge, MA: Harvard University Press, 1999), p. 22.

45. Prabhat Patnaik, "Challenges before Higher Education in Developing Societies," *Social Scientist* 37.434–435 (2009): 21–32.

46. Derrida, *Rogues: Two Essays on Reason,* trans. Pascale-Anne Brault and Michael Naas (Stanford, CA: Stanford University Press, 2005).

47. The following five paragraphs are taken from Spivak, "Notes toward a Tribute to Jacques Derrida," *differences* 16.3 (Fall 2005): 104–106; reprinted with additions in Costas Douzinas, ed., *Adieu Derrida* (London: Palgrave Macmillan, 2007), pp. 49–51.

48. The translators have a difficult time with this particular aspect of Kant, of course. But in the course of these paragraphs, even the most astute translators make curious decisions. For *"so stellet sich etwas vor"* (something thus

sets itself out), we read "I represent something"; *"was da geschieht"* becomes "an occurrence" rather than "what takes place there" (PR, p. 310). *"Anschauung"* is translated "experience" rather than "intuition" in the crucial sentence "By means of the understanding the very same order and constant connection in the series of possible perceptions is produced and made necessary as would be encountered a priori in the form of inner intuition (time)" (PR, p. 311).

49. Derrida, "Différance," in *Margins of Philosophy*, trans. Alan Bass (Chicago: University of Chicago Press, 1982), p. 12.

50. Derrida, *Rogues*, p. 121.

51. Derrida, *The Animal*, p. 48.

52. David Golumbia, *The Cultural Logic of Computation* (Cambridge, MA: Harvard University Press, 2009), p. 16 captures the spirit of my understanding well.

53. Paul de Man, *Aesthetic Ideology* (Minneapolis: University of Minnesota Press, 1996), p. 147.

54. "Ideology represents the imaginary relationship of individuals to their real conditions of existence." Louis Althusser, "Ideology and Ideological State Apparatuses (Notes towards an Investigation)," in *Lenin and Philosophy, and Other Essays,* trans. Ben Brewster (New York: Monthly Review Press, 1971), p. 162. Althusser seems to expand the general principle of neurosis to ideological survival. See Freud, "Formulation on the Two Principles of Mental Functioning," SE 12, pp. 213–225. The word translated as "functioning" is *Geschehens,* something more like occurrences or happenings. We are of course suggesting that philosophizing in Kant can be seen as one of these "occurrences," reasonably textualized by Kant as critique.

55. Spivak, *Death of a Discipline* (New York: Columbia University Press, 2003).

56. I take my sense of figure from a specific Derridian use. Discussing Hegel in *Glas,* Derrida moves to the literary at a certain point: the figurative. Derrida is identifying the family as working figuratively in order to suppress a double bind in Hegel: "For now, this determinate moment of the family, this finiteness, figures," and Derrida's parenthesis "(for now I leave a very large opening for this word) figures the system's totality." For Derrida, the name of the double bind in Hegel is the Jew, as for me the double bind of the (universal Euro-U.S.) subject is the schizophrenic, especially in globalization. It is interesting that Derrida computes the figure in terms of reproductive heteronormativity (RHN; see Chapter 5, "Culture: Situating Feminism," in this book): "When one rashly says that the finite family furnishes a metaphoric model or a convenient figuration about the language of philosophical exposition, a pedagogical ease, a good way to speak of abstract things to the student while playing with the familiarity of family signification. . . . Even then what the absolute familiarity of the signification is must be known." There's RHN; why is it that everybody knows it? What is the absolute familiarity of something? "If that can be thought and named without the family then one needs to ascertain that the finite family in question is not infinite already in which case what the alleged metaphor would come to figure would be already in

the metaphor." What the alleged metaphor (of the family) would come to figure would be already *in* the metaphor. In the strictest analogy, yet keeping in mind that all analogies are also and necessarily, ultimately false, I say, then, that what the alleged metaphor (of the universal Euro-U.S. subject—unacknowledged as metaphor, taken as truth) would come to figure (schizophrenia as the radical loss of subject) is already *in* the metaphor.

57. Among contemporary thinkers who recommend empire in one form or another—and there are many—at the extreme edge are those who simply recommend empire for empire's sake, as it were, saying that because they are powerful, by winning wars they bring peace; the United States should behave more like an empire. Historical analyses such as Niall Ferguson's or Mark von Hagen's can take on board the argument from "enabling violation" (Niall Ferguson, *Colossus: The Rise and Fall of the American Empire* [New York: Penguin Books, 2005]); Jane Burbank and Mark von Hagen, "Coming into the Territory: Uncertainty and Empire" [unpublished manuscript]). Deepak Lal understands the "enablement" but not the "violation": "Despite nationalist and Marxist cant, this first liberal order [the British empire] was hugely beneficial for the world, particularly its poorest" (Deepak Lal, *In Praise of Empires: Globalization and Order* [New York: Palgrave, 2004], p. 207). For him, Woodrow Wilson overthrew Westphalia (p. 192). He dismisses "human rights, democracy and freedom" as the rallying cry of "this Western jihad" (p. 209). I have myself often criticized the international civil society and its human rights sector. Extremes meet. The epistemological matter is taken care of by a simple formula: "Modernize without Westernizing" (p. 203). His solution? "The multinational bureaucracies of some of the technical multilateral agencies could be absorbed into the new imperial [U.S.] bureaucracy" (p. 75). Since these are wish-fulfillment dreams, any thought of the tremendous double binds implicit in any such effort cannot be thought of by him. In Ferguson's case, the cynicism about ignoring the bi-polarity of capital/capitalism is altogether striking. Acknowledging that "the difficulty with the achievements of empire is that they are much more likely to be taken for granted than the sins of empire" (p. xxi), he asks the question, "Can you have globalization without gunboats?" (p. xix) and comes to a conclusion, at the end of his 351-page book, in favor of "the United States shifting from informal to formal empire," although it might mean "a great many small wars like the one in Afghanistan" (p. 314). It is within the context of this faith in empire that he notes the occasional project of training into citizenship, in Australia or Africa, and of course, India. You cannot ignore this enablement in the violation; this is the mochlos, the lever to turn the collaboration between the abstractions of capital and the class-ignoring of culturalist identitarianism into productive ab-use. Again, if thought of as real epistemological effort, some thought of the effort involved in its implementation, in bringing the will into desiring the possibility of law must be imaginable! Joseph Stiglitz's three popular books are representative of a welfare-state liberal position. He takes for granted that integration into an equitable globalization is the only solution for "developing" countries and it is the responsibility

("burden"?) of the "developed" countries to transform themselves accord-
ingly. He is certainly critical of the "colonialism" of the IMF and the inequi-
ties of the WTO (Stiglitz, *Globalization and Its Discontents* [New York:
Norton, 2003], pp. 39–42, 71; Stiglitz and Andrew Charlton, *Fair Trade for
All: How Trade Can Promote Development* [New York: Oxford University
Press, 2005]), but this general attitude of the developed folks' burden leads
to a "good" imperialism, certainly the best we can hope for. *Discontents* does
indeed look for a mind-set change across degrees of "development," but
what I am calling a "good imperialism" comes clear if you look at the representative passage on page 216 of *Discontents* beginning "The greatest challenge is . . . in mind-sets." "An imperialistic desire attempts the global imposition of its values and fundamental structures of government and modes of
thought worldwide" (Ugo Mattei, "A Theory of Imperial Law: A Study on
U.S. Hegemony and the Latin Resistance," *Indiana Journal of Global Legal
Studies* 10.38 [2003]: 401–402). Our way to lay down the possibility of
epistemic change is contained in *Aesthetic Education*. Stiglitz's notion of
"asymmetries of information" (p. xi) can lead to our way, if attention is paid
to the difference between information control and learning to read, information or anything. His notion of education is of course as access to jobs
(p. 59). He can take on Gorz (*Critique of Economic Reason* [London: Verso,
1989]), but the Bloomsbury side of Keynes, which is what we are looking to
ab-use, necessarily escapes him. By *Making Globalization Work*, however,
the emphasis seems to have swung toward enforcement for the many excellent policy suggestions that he has assembled, to create a balance between
the economic sphere and "basic values" (Stiglitz, *Making Globalization
Work* [New York: Norton, 2006], pp. 129–132, 155, and passim). But what
are these values? How are they manufactured? Such questions drive us but
Stiglitz has no time for us. His idea is to enforce "good behavior" (p. 159).
This change begins to resemble the justified impatience of the human rights
lobby locally and globally, which is also beginning to swing toward enforcement. Solid formal classroom discussion and extensive informal questioning
make it clear that it is the general assumption that the financial sector cannot
police itself unless "forced" to do so. I have no patience with upper-middle-
class theorists who implicitly justify a "political society" based on this species
of conviction—generalized—coming from the postcolonial urban underclass.
On the other side, Charles Tilly's conviction that "bearing burdens for the
common good," and making it possible that a government will provide equitable treatment to the subaltern, does indeed lead to a "transformation and
an enhancement," but our quick summary should illustrate that such transformations and enhancements irreducibly require epistemological production
of the internal conditions of citizenship which may be potentially capable of
wrenching its external conditions without interminable global benevolence and
an unquestioning insistence on enforcement alone (Charles Tilly, *Democracy*
[Cambridge: Cambridge University Press, 2008], pp. 96, 185). With Gramsci
and Du Bois one might want to see things in a different light: that without a
rearrangement of desires toward the impossible willing of the law, persistently

and epistemologically inscribed, there is no looking forward to a just society. Today the law is seen as little more than an instrument of enforcement. Keynes questioned this from within the Bloomsbury group. It is well known that the United States imposes its domestic laws internationally to regulate world trade. I first learned this in Bangladesh in the mid-1980s. In her article "Empire's Law," Susan Marks gives a sober account of how to integrate this into Hardt and Negri's declaration of a rupture between imperialism and Empire (*Indiana Journal of Global Legal Studies* 10 [2003]: 449–446). It is of course abundantly clear to those who work for epistemological rearrangement that enforcement is not a practical unitary goal. This is where Hardt and Negri also remain conservative (Michael Hardt and Antonio Negri, *Multitude: War and Democracy in the Age of Empire* [New York: Penguin, 2004], p. 247 and passim). Their idea of democracy in this book ignores the double bind between ipseity and alterity that rides democracy from Plato to Gandhi. The absence of war cannot be defined as democracy. I remain bemused by these two fellow travelers. I cannot fully endorse their notion of the contemporary scene, as Empire sublating the Dream of America, to be sublated by a multitude that must come into itself. But insofar as they say that "the multitude is not a spontaneous political subject but a project of political organization, thus shifting the discussion from being the multitude to making the multitude," I can go along with them, although for me epistemological shifting is a preparation rather than a political organization. I can never accept, however, that the multitude "authors" itself in "an un-interrupted process of collective self-transformation" (Hardt and Negri, *Commonwealth* [Cambridge, MA: Harvard University Press, 2009], pp. 169, 173), producing a desire for a real, rather than the actually existing, commonwealth in a robust extra-moral sense. This needs a reality-check. The universities are not yet ready for burning. The humanities have not yet become useless in principle. Godot has not arrived, does not arrive. Posthumanism has not been achieved; we can only ever be on the way. "A universe of productive linguistic networks"—their phrase (Hardt and Negri, *Empire* [Cambridge, MA: Harvard University Press, 2000], p. 385)—must take into account that because of the immense linguistic richness of the world, we cannot always understand each other (this beyond the irreducible mis-understanding in successful human communication even monolingually) and some might want to preserve that mystery in the face of the data-based clarity of globalized capital in the service of a world. And the service sector, forever celebrated by the right, cannot just be given the new sexy name "immaterial production"! If they are interested in a future just world, they might wish to ask Judith Butler's question: "What is a life?" (Judith Butler, *Frames of War: When Is Life Grievable?* [New York: Verso, 2009], p. ix). It is not enough to imply, as they do, that in biopolitics (ill defined, if at all, in their three challenging books) the body is the mind (Hardt and Negri, *Multitude*, p. 337 and passim). In an age of exponential genomic and neurological techno-research, it is no longer particularly radical to hold this position. Without the habits of democratic reflexes (I am with them in their celebration of habit in *Multitude,* pp. 197ff.), there is no democracy. Different kinds of (con)text-specific aesthetic education will remain the long-term moving base of this, in this variegated world of ours, forever not yet a globe. Samuel Eisenstadt's "Multiple Modernities" (*Daedalus* 129.1 [Winter 2000]: 1–29)— already implicit in Saussure (for Saussure, "the holistically systemic character of each synchronic position makes it irrelevant by what succession of prior moves it has been reached; interesting as the question may be for its own sake, it has nothing to do with the given synchronic state of the game"; Boris Gasparov, "Freedom and Mystery" [unpublished manuscript])—seems much more coherent with the contemporaneity of globalization. Jon Solomon has cogently written of an "imperial Nationalism circulating among US leftists," and counseled "look[ing] beyond the categories of sovereignty and civiliza- tional difference in our approach to the violence of financial capitalism" (unpublished e-mail). If the Internet and the network are taken as their alle- gory of reading the multitude, much is excluded. As for the World Social Forum (WSF), many of its members already know that. Their problem is that by taking (capitalist) globalization for granted, they share the dangers of ig- noring the necessary bi-polarity. The WSF, as analyzed in Jose Corrêa Leite's excellent book *The World Social Forum: Strategies of Resistance,* trans. Traci Romine (Chicago: Haymarket, 2005) remains in the line of Kant's "good imperialism." How do we know that, given the chance, the workers will not go the way of Enron (pp. 189–191)? As I have repeatedly argued elsewhere, "consciousness-raising" is no substitute for patient epistemological care. Other- wise there's no training when the oppressed emerges from "freedom from" to "freedom to." My argument in this book is that the top needs an aesthetic education. Otherwise the imagination is not strongly enough trained to real- ize that "social movements" are co-opted by state and elite, with different agendas, ceaselessly. Leite correctly regrets that the WSF as such cannot ac- cess the national/local. Yet the metonymization of Mumbai as "far removed from Western political culture" has the aura of Foucault finding his other in ancient Greece! It is excellent that the book includes Naomi Klein's incisive critique. Yet Klein's critique can hardly be distinguished from the old social- ist one (p. 174). There again we turn to Gramsci, learning from the fall of international socialism. You cannot build "another world" with today's WSF. Marx's nineteenth-century vision, turning the Enlightenment goal of the public use of reason on its head, must be seen as epistemological in its bur- den. The reader must have guessed by now that I stay in touch with dumbed- down ideological wisdom from the pages of the Sunday *New York Times.* I continue to quote from it to combat academic complaints about impractical- ity and high theory. A comment on how enforcement alone is insufficient, then: "Drawing on dozens of historical conflicts, the manual's [the *Counter- insurgency Field Manual* adopted in 2006 by the U.S. Army and Marines] prime conclusion is the assertion that insurgencies cannot be defeated with- out protecting and winning over the general population, regardless of how effective direct strikes on enemy fighters may be" (James Glanz, "Historians Reassess Battle of Agincourt," *New York Times,* October 25, 2009). And my handwritten marginal note: "If war succeeds thus, surely also peace." You get the picture. Our position is, of course, that only capital and data can globalize. Everything else is re-coding, knavish to foolish damage control. In the face of "the dilemma of simultaneity" Claus Offe counsels: "Macroevents have assumed an incredible speed, . . . individual actors . . . need . . . patience in order not to interfere with the 'creative destruction' which will follow the price and property reform in a perfectly intended manner, although by making use of their newly won civil rights they would be quite capable of doing so" (Claus Offe, "Capitalism by Democratic Design? Democratic Theory Facing the Triple Transition in East Central Europe," *Social Research* 58.4 [Winter 1991]: 887). Charles Tilly says his reading tells him that "a certain level of trust [is] a necessary condition of democracy" (*Democracy,* p. 93). Patience, trust—where are these virtues coming from? Who trains for these any more? Yet the universities curb the humanities. In a mode that is as fictive as a professional sociologist can use, in "a series of half-proven conjectures," Tilly gives the go-ahead: "If these conjectures are even roughly correct, we have been tracing not just an interesting set of political transformations, but a path to the enhancement of human capability and welfare" (pp. 184, 185). An aesthetic education.

58. Charles Isherwood, "A Healthy Dose of Misery for Company," *New York Times,* October 26, 2008, p. 6.

59. Marx, *Capital,* vol. 1, trans. Ben Fowkes (London: Penguin, 1990), pp. 131–132.

60. Derrida, *Rogues,* p. 54; Wilhelm Reich, *The Mass Psychology of Fascism* (New York: Farrar, Straus & Giroux, 1970); the actual passage is probably a loving rejoinder to Jean-Luc Nancy's idea of a community of singularities.

61. Jean-François Lyotard, *Libidinal Economy: Theories of Contemporary Culture,* trans. Iain Hamilton Grant (Bloomington: Indiana University Press, 1993); Jean-Joseph Goux, "French Freud: Structural Studies in Psychoanalysis," *Yale French Studies* 48 (1972): 38–72.

62. Perry Anderson, *In the Tracks of Historical Materialism* (Chicago: University of Chicago Press, 1984).

63. Harry Braverman, *Labor and Monopoly Capital: The Degradation of Work in the Twentieth Century* (New York: Monthly Review Press, 1974), and Georg Lukacs, *History and Class Consciousness: Studies in Marxist Dialectics,* trans. Rodney Livingstone (London: Merlin Press, 1967) will have to stand in for a much longer list here.

64. Gilles Deleuze and Felix Guattari, *Anti-Oedipus: Capitalism and Schizophrenia,* trans. Robert Hurley, Mark Seem, and Helen R. Lane (Minneapolis: University of Minnesota Press, 1992).

65. Lewis H. Morgan, *Ancient Society* (Cambridge, MA: Harvard University Press, 1965).

66. I have referred to Derrida's dilemma regarding the "human" in the humanities in note 22.

67. V. I. Lenin, "Draft Theses on National and Colonial Questions for the Second Congress of the Communist International," in *Collected Works,* trans.

Julius Katzer (Moscow: Progress Publishers, 1965), vol. 31, pp. 144–151; Lenin, *Imperialism, the Highest Stage of Capitalism* (New York: International Publishers, 1937); and Christine Buci-Glucksmann, *Gramsci and the State*, trans. David Fernbach (London: Lawrence and Wishart, 1980).

68. Sophocles, *Oedipus the King*, 1403–1407; translation mine, as literal as possible, to show that Oedipus reproaches marriage for the inscription of human kinship, which then makes incest possible. Sophocles stages Oedipus as not learning the Law of the Father. It is the chorus, on hire from play to play, that is given the task of making an example out of him. Oedipus the King opens the play with a reference to a mythic collective birth outside of heterosexual copulation. It is almost as if there is a challenge here to the general applicability of the law that can only be a grounding error.

69. David Halperin, *Saint Foucault: Towards a Gay Hagiography* (New York: Oxford University Press, 1995), p. 62.

70. De Man, *Aesthetic Ideology*, p. 154. A good example of Schiller's usual remarks on women is to be found in AE, p. 213 and passim.

71. Derrida, *Rogues*, pp. 156, 159.

72. De Man, *Allegories of Reading: Figural Language in Rousseau, Nietzsche, Rilke, and Proust* (New Haven, CT: Yale University Press, 1979), p. lx.

73. An almost identical statement is made in the introduction to *Rhetoric of Romanticism* (New York: Columbia University Press, 1984), pp. vii–ix, without the generational reference, but with the poignant metaphor of "taking refuge" in "more theoretical inquiries into the problems of figural language."

1. The Burden of English

1. Ngũgĩ wa Thiong'o, *Decolonizing the Mind: The Politics of Language in African Literature* (Portsmouth, NH: Heinemann, 1986), p. xi.

2. R. K. Narayan, "English in India," in *A Story-Teller's World* (New Delhi: Penguin India, 1989), pp. 20–23.

3. Rabindranath Tagore, "Didi," in *Galpaguchchha*, vol. 2 (Calcutta: Visva-Bharati, 1975). Translations are my own.

4. I have given a historical account of this alienation outside of the classroom in "Once Again a Leap into the Post-Colonial Banal," paper delivered at the Davis Center for Historical Studies, Princeton University, March 1, 1991. This needs to be modified by the altogether brilliant account of alienation in Marilena Chaui, *Between Conformity and Resistance*, trans. Maite Conde (New York: Palgrave, 2011).

5. I have kept these pathetic attempts to write for a fantasmatic "Indian" audience, completely unnecessary except to solve the so-called cultural double bind, too easily. The Rashtriya Sevika Samiti is a women's Hindu Nationalist organization, established in 1936, with ideals of motherhood, social work, and leadership.

6. David Hardiman comments on the peasants' misplaced belief that the British would give them direct access to vengeance as justice (discussion after "The Peasant Experience of Usury: Western India in the Nineteenth Century," paper

delivered at the Davis Center for Historical Studies, Princeton University, April 12, 1991).

7. I have kept to the Indian custom of referring to a famous person by the first name to preserve the aura of my Indian audience.

8. For the importance of the assignment of reported, direct, and indirect speech and style, see V. N. Vološinov, *Marxism and the Philosophy of Language,* trans. Ladislav Matejka and I. R. Titunik (Cambridge, MA: Harvard University Press, 1986), part III.

9. Madhu Kishwar, "Why I Do Not Call Myself a Feminist," *Manushi* 61 (November–December 1990): 2–8.

10. Rudyard Kipling, *Kim* (New York: Viking Penguin, 1987), pp. 210–211.

11. For an example of such a misunderstanding, with reference to the relationship between philosophy and literature, and based on minimal documentation, see the chapter on Derrida in Jürgen Habermas, *The Philosophical Discourse of Modernism: Twelve Lectures* (Cambridge, MA: MIT Press, 1987).

12. Binodini Dasi, *My Story and My Life as an Actress,* trans. Rimli Bhattacharya (New Delhi: Kali, 1998). For a reading of this text in the context of women's autobiographies, see Partha Chatterjee, "Their Own Words: An Essay for Edward Said," in Michael Sprinker, ed., *Edward Said: A Critical Reader* (Oxford: Blackwell, 1992).

13. Tagore, *Gora,* trans. Sujit Mukherjee (India: Sahitya Akademi, 1997). The passage quoted is from p. 477; translation modified.

14. I am grateful to Ranes Chakravorty for reading out this paragraph to me, when my own *Gora* was inaccessible and the library did not have one.

15. Mahasweta Devi, "The Hunt," in *Imaginary Maps: Three Stories,* trans. Gayatri Chakravorty Spivak (New York: Routledge, 1993), pp. 1–18 (hereafter cited in the text as IM, with page numbers following). See also Chapter 2.

16. The elegantly staged representation of Sarada Devi as the rural woman denoting cultural choice and victory in the general text of imperialist seduction is a complex variation on the thematics we are discussing (Swami Gambhirananda, *Srima Sarada Devi* [Calcutta: Udbodhan, 1954], pp. 1–6). I have discussed this at greater length in "Imagination, not Culture: A Singular Example," William James Lecture, Harvard Divinity School, April 10, 2008.

17. There are a handful of prominent whites of this genre who receive a great deal of publicity (on a less exalted register, like middle-class husbands who cook). They offer an eagerly grasped standby for cultural representation as alibi. One thinks of their role in Richard Attenborough's *Gandhi* (1982), in the conception of the hero of *Dances with Wolves* (1990), and in countless other subsequent films that the reader can fill in.

18. The artificial separation between colonial (roughly British) and neocolonial (roughly U.S.), migrant and postcolonial, covers a wide field. Howard Winant, for example, makes the claim that *"in the postmodern political framework of the contemporary United States, hegemony is determined by the articulation of race and class"* (Howard Winant, "Postmodern Racial Politics in the United States: Difference and Inequality," *Socialist Review* 20.1

(January–March 1990): 137; emphasis in original. "Postmodern" is used here in the (to me) unsatisfactory sense of neocolonialism as being not only after the phase of modernization but also entering a phase after orthodox socialist radicalism. A curricular re-constellation as is being proposed here might have broader implications than one imagines.

19. The *Nātya Sāstra* is a compendious text on dramaturgy, theater, music, dance, and the like, written by various hands between 200 BCE and 200 CE. My dismissive tone is directed toward those critics who deny Indian performance modernity by referring everything back to "tradition." More about this text is included in "How to Read a 'Culturally Different' Book," Chapter 3 in this book.

20. For a sober accounting of the debates, see J. P. Naik and Syed Nurullah, *A History of Education in India*, 2nd rev. ed. (London: Macmillan, 1951). The recent reference is to Sanjukta Panigrahi, discussion after lecture demonstration with Eugenio Barba, at the Conference on Inter-Cultural Performance, Bellagio, February 20, 1991. The denigration of "rote" learning as opposed to "analytic" knowing is no longer as clearly on the agenda and shows evidence of an unquestioning ideological (and therefore often unwitting) acceptance of nineteenth-century imperialist universalism. The project would be to re-inscribe the presuppositions—of knowledge before understanding—proposed in some Indian Speech Act linguistics which challenge British Speech Act theory (Bimal Krishna Matilal, "Knowledge from Linguistic Utterances," in *The Word and the World* [Delhi: Oxford University Press, 1990]).

21. For the contrast between Binodini's testimonial and Tagore's literary representation of the insulted wife playing, precisely, Manorama, see "Manbhanjan," in *Rabindra Racanabali*, vol. 7 (Kolkata: Paschim Banga Sarkar, 1961), pp. 282–289.

22. It is not to denigrate feminism to point out that feminist ambition in the colonial nineteenth century must involve competition and class-ambition. For a discussion of this in the Western context, see Elizabeth Fox-Genovese, *Feminism without Illusions: A Critique of Individualism* (Chapel Hill: University of North Carolina Press, 1991). Here too the relationship between colony and the West is complex, not merely oppositional. The fact that powerful men suppressed Binodini's ambition points at another complex relationship between feminism and the critique of capitalism.

23. The connection between the dramatic representation of lust and drama proper is available in reverse in Damodargupta's *Kuttinimatam* (see Mandakranta Basu, "*Lasya*: A Dramatic Art?," in Bimal Krishna Matilal and Purushottam Bilimoriya, eds., *Sanskrit and Related Studies: Contemporary Researches and Reflections* [Delhi: Sri Satguru, 1990]).

24. Hanif Kureishi, *The Buddha of Suburbia* (New York: Viking Penguin, 1991).

25. Sensitively argued in "Location, Intervention, Incommensurability: A Conversation with Homi Bhabha," *Emergences* 1.1 (1989): 63–88.

26. J. D. Salinger, *The Catcher in the Rye* (Boston: Little, Brown, 1951); Iris Murdoch, *Under the Net, a Novel* (New York: Viking Press, 1954).

27. Rudyard Kipling, *The Jungle Book* (New York: Penguin, 1987).

28. The criticism comes from Tracey, a politically mature African-British woman. In our classroom, we would have to develop the point of this criticism, significantly different from the desire of the white.

29. Martin Amis, *London Fields* (New York: Harmony Books, 1989). I quote this from a trendy English novelist somewhat bloody-mindedly, because Amis too is in a world transformed by migrants. His villain is "multiracial" in his choice of women. But the staging of identity in migrancy is not Amis's burden. Hence this sentence about life and acting does not attach to a multiracial character. They remain victims. Our best students will have to come to grips with the fact that the epistemic fracturing of the colonial reader is no longer a marginal event.

30. Nadine Gordimer, *July's People* (New York: Viking Penguin, 1981).

31. Jan Nederveen Pieterse, *Israel's State Terrorism and Counterinsurgency in the Third World* (Kingston: NECEF Publications, 1986), p. 4. My extrapolations refer to the specific case of Israel and Palestine. Again, the student can link the international press with autobiography, Brit Lit, and vernacular literature if the teacher fills in Pieterse's passage. The pedagogic interest is, always, to globalize and politicize the burden by pointing at linked differences rather than divisive turf battles.

32. I have discussed this cluster in Spivak, "War and Cultures," lecture at the Power Plant Gallery, Toronto, February 24, 1991. Lars Engle makes a persuasive case for this passage as the characteristic irruption of the Freudian "uncanny" (Lars Engle, "The Political Uncanny: The Novels of Nadine Gordimer," *Yale Journal of Criticism* 2.2 [1989]: 120f). I think, however, it is more fruitful to consider the "uncanny" as inhabiting the past and the present and the future—always under the skin of the familiar everyday—rather than only a "post-revolutionary" future conceived as a future present in sequential narrative time. I also think that we should take note of "July"'s real name. The uncanny lurks under the skin of the everyday as Mwawate always lives in the skin that is always called July by his masters.

33. See Spivak, "'Draupadi' by Mahasweta Devi," in *In Other Worlds: Essays in Cultural Politics* (New York: Routledge, 2006), pp. 253, 266.

34. Figures received from the University Grants Commission, May 9, 1991.

2. Who Claims Alterity?

1. I have told the outlines of one such negotiation in "Marginality in the Teaching Machine," in Spivak, *Outside in the Teaching Machine* (New York: Routledge, 2009), pp. 58–85 (hereafter cited in the notes as OTM, with page numbers following).

2. I am drawing here as usual upon the difficult but most perceptive passage in Gilles Deleuze and Felix Guattari, *Anti-Oedipus: Capitalism and Schizophrenia,* trans. Robert Hurley, Mark Seem, and Helen R. Lane (Minneapolis: University of Minnesota Press, 1992), p. 10.

3. Michel Foucault, *The History of Sexuality,* vol. 1: *An Introduction,* trans. Robert Hurley (New York: Pantheon, 1978), p. 93; translation modified.

4. Marx, *Capital*, vol. 1, trans. Ben Fowkes (London: Penguin, 1990), p. 143 (hereafter cited in the text and notes as C 1, with page numbers following).

5. I am increasingly inclined to relate the Marxian and Foucauldian enterprises in terms of a theory of value. Marx needed the money-form, finding other forms defective. Foucault needed what Marx would call the total or expanded form, where semiotic chains came into being and were dissolved, finding Marx defective. In 1987, this is how it summarized: Foucault's use of "utterance" (*énoncé*) in the following passage is clearly not the linguistic one. It is a "name" (not identical with what it names, thus "catachrestic" as a common noun) that is the best loan-word that can be found under the circumstances. As such, it is possible to show that it is not incoherent with Marx's analysis of capital and capitalism, although the relationship between levels and strategies are complex. Foucault's own sense of his relationship with Marx is most interesting and has to be examined according to the methods of an older intellectual history. With this in mind, let me add that I use "archives" in the sense of the following passage: "The archive defines a particular level: that of a practice that causes a multiplicity of utterances to emerge as so many regular events. . . . Between tradition and oblivion, it reveals the rules of a practice that enables utterances both to survive and to undergo regular modification. It is the general system of the formation and transformation of utterances" (Foucault, *The Archaeology of Knowledge and the Discourse on Language,* trans. A. M. Sheridan Smith [New York: Harper Torchbooks, 1972], p. 130; translation modified). For another view of the relationship, see Barry Smart, *Foucault, Marxism and Critique* (London: Routledge, 1983). See Michael Ryan, "The Limits of Capital," in his *Marxism and Deconstruction: A Critical Articulation* (Baltimore, MD: Johns Hopkins University Press, 1982), pp. 82–102, for the argument that the economic and political are necessarily implicated in Marx.

6. "The value-form, whose fully developed shape is the money-form [today "virtual money" must still go through the possibility of "money as such," which is why an infinitely expanding stock market loses "value," in another sense], is content-less and simple" (C 1, pp. 89–90).

7. Gayle Rubin, "The Traffic in Women: Notes on the 'Political Economy' of Sex," in Rayna B. Reiter, ed., *Toward an Anthropology of Women* (New York: Monthly Review Press, 1975), pp. 157–210. It is curious that neither Deleuze and Guattari nor Rubin investigates value.

8. For a definition of the "subaltern," see Ranajit Guha, "On Some Aspects of the Historiography of Colonial India," in *Selected Subaltern Studies,* ed. Ranajit Guha and Gayatri Chakravorty Spivak (New York: Oxford University Press, 1988), pp. 37–44.

9. She stands unnoticed and implicit in the cracks of much carefully written documentation in the social sciences. Think, for example, of the "young wives" in Kalpana Bardhan's densely woven essay "Women, Work, Welfare and Status: Forces of Tradition and Change in India," *South Asia Bulletin* 6 (1986): 9. I had written in the earlier version: "Fiction makes her visible." For a multiculturalist example halfway between social science and fiction—assuming the opposition is tenable—see Spivak, *A Critique of Postcolonial Reason: Toward a History of the Vanishing Present* (Cambridge, MA: Harvard University

Press, 1999), pp. 406–409 (hereafter cited in the text as CPR, with page numbers following).

10. Carl E. Pletsch, "The Three Worlds, or the Division of Social Scientific Labor, circa 1950 to 1975," *Comparative Studies in Society and History* 23.4 (October 1981): 565–590. For an alternative self-conception of a "third force" of nonaligned nations emerging from the Bandung Conference of 1955, see Nigel Harris, *The End of the Third World: Newly Industrializing Countries and the Decline of an Ideology* (London: I. B. Tauris, 1986). The idea of the North-South division of the globe as the only viable one did not get going until 1989 and the fall of the Wall for most nonspecialists.

11. See Gauri Viswanathan, *Masks of Conquest: Literary Study and the British Rule in India* (New York: Columbia University Press, 1989).

12. At that stage, I was still thinking of internal colonization only in terms of Samir Amin, *Unequal Development: An Essay on the Social Formations of Peripheral Capitalism,* trans. Brian Pearce (New York: Monthly Review Press, 1976), p. 369. By the time of "Bonding in Difference," in Donna Landry and Gerald Maclean, eds., *The Spivak Reader* (New York: Routledge, 1996), pp. 23–25, I had begun to realize the scope of that story. The discontinuities, torsions, and disymmetries of this phenomenon now form a rather large part of my work.

13. Most elaborately in "Scattered Speculations on the Question of Value," in Spivak, *In Other Worlds: Essays in Cultural Politics* (New York: Routledge, 2006), pp. 212–242. It is interesting to see that the National Governors' Report, issued in Washington on February 24, 1989, calls for more language learning and culture learning, because otherwise the United States will be "outcompeted." In the context of the shortfall from the subsequent culture wars and the endless milking of the global subject, that last remark seems a bit quaint today.

14. Since this writing, such retrospective hallucinations in the field of fiction are drawing large advances. See Spivak, "Bajarer Opor . . . ," *Ananda Bazar Patrika,* August 1, 1999. The phrase is from Jean Baudrillard, "The Precession of Simulacra," in *Simulations,* trans. Paul Foss, Paul Patton, and Philip Beitchman (New York: Semiotext[e], 1983), p. 22. The following paragraph draws on Baudrillard's general argument about the divided globe.

15. This argument is also completely dated now. For transnational and trendy multiculturalist postcoloniality that disavows history by invoking nothing but space, see the discussion of "demographic frontiers" in "What's Left of Theory?" (Chapter 9 in this book).

16. This is the section that, in slightly different form, appeared in *The Statesman,* August 15, 1987.

17. Literally, in Sanskrit, "the Sorrow of Jawaharlal." Jawaharlal Nehru was independent India's first Prime Minister. In the *Bhagavadgītā,* an authoritative text of Hindu practice, "the Sorrow of Arjuna" *(Arjunaviṣādayoga)* opens the action. Krishna, a divine incarnation, is Arjuna's charioteer and steers him onto the path of just war, a metaphor for life in the world. This metaphor has gained new life since 1992, when Finance Minister Manmohan

Singh "liberalized" the Nehruvian protected economy, and opened India to the depredations of international capital, creating a tiny consumerist and a smaller managerial class as ideological representatives of the "nation" as the outlines of the state were loosened.

18. At first publication, I had revised the speech by saying that the extraordinary social power of the upwardly class-mobile British Muslim community displayed in the Salman Rushdie case had shown that the distinction between the U.S. and British subcontinental diaspora is no longer clear-cut. I think today I would make the argument in terms of the general American turn in Britain, displayed as well by Tony Blair's love affair with Bill Clinton, whose future in this U.S. election year (1999) provides an interesting bit of grist for the mill of political speculation. I would also make the connection in terms of the rise of Hindu nationalism or *Hindutva,* in India, supported by a large part of the international diasporic community. A bit of investigative work that a group of us did about that phenomenon was unaccountably—I was referred to another member of our collective when I asked for an explanation—turned down by a leading U.S. multicultural journal. (My hunch is that unalloyed criticism of diasporas did not sit well with the editorial policy of the journal.) I hope this piece, "Vasudhaiva Kutumbakam: The Internet Hindu," will see publication in a Subaltern Studies volume sooner or later. (This hope is now gone. I have spoken of this species of unease in the Introduction; see page 19.)

19. John Hutnyk points at the resistant potential of diasporic South Asia–based music, for which my descriptive tags are inept. See Sanjay Sharma, John Hutnyk, and Ashwani Sharma, eds., *Dis-orienting Rhythms: The Politics of the New Asian Dance Music* (Atlantic Highlands, NJ: Zed Books, 1997).

20. See "Scattered Speculations on the Question of Cultural Studies," in OTM, pp. 287–320.

21. For a bit of a discussion, see the conclusion of "Reading Satanic Verses," in OTM, pp. 244–272.

22. In the post-Soviet world this list has exploded as the United States uses the cultural politics of asylum as part of its manifest destiny.

23. All events—including culture and war—remake the material of history. There is no such thing as remaking history as such. The discipline consolidates hegemonic remakings as history as such. The discipline of history in India—conservative in its choice of canonical method even when radical in its sentiments—resists efforts, especially from outside the discipline, to remake the disciplinary method. A random example: "There is a fear that any rendering of objective history into a morphological exercise like any other art might turn an entire school of decent historians into an array of cognoscenti who are just involved with style, form, and techniques of representation. Both history and art have their separate domains, one based on reality, the other fictional" (K. M. Panikkar, "History from Below," *Hindustan Times,* February 26, 1989). This is again a reminder that there are other battles to fight than just metropolitan centrism. This too is a difference between internal colonization and decolonization.

24. This awkward and heavy sentence is written for interpretive instantiation in the classroom. By contrast, as I have argued elsewhere, clear and rousing pieces like Nancy Fraser, "Solidarity or Singularity? Richard Rorty between Romanticism and Technocracy," *Praxis International* 8.3 (October 1988): 268–270, remain lists of ingredients making like recipes.

25. "Editor's Comments," *Public Culture* 1.1 (Fall 1988): 3.

26. I use "paralogical" in the sense given to it by Jean-Francois Lyotard, *The Postmodern Condition,* trans. Geoff Bennington and Brian Massumi (Minneapolis: University of Minnesota Press, 1984), p. 61.

27. Mahasweta Devi, "The Hunt," in *Imaginary Maps: Three Stories,* trans. Gayatri Chakravorty Spivak (New York: Routledge, 1993), pp. 1–18 (hereafter cited in the text as IM, with page numbers following).

28. I have explained the Derridian use of "figure" in note 56 of the Introduction. That sense resonates here as well.

29. I have discussed this point at greater length in "Poststructuralism, Marginality, Postcoloniality and Value," in Peter Collier and Helga Geyer-Ryan, eds., *Literary Theory Today* (Cambridge: Polity Press, 1990), pp. 219–244; reprinted in *Sociocriticism* 10 (1989): 43–81; reprinted in Padmini Mongia, ed., *Contemporary Postcolonial Theory: A Reader* (New York: Arnold Press, 1996), pp. 198–364; reprinted in Diana Brydon, ed., *Postcolonialism: Critical Concepts* (New York: Routledge, 2000), pp. 57–84.

30. There is a description of one of these—"Bobby" by Raj Kapur—in Clark Blaise and Bharati Mukherjee, *Days and Nights in Calcutta* (Garden City, NY: Doubleday, 1977), pp. 143–146. See also "How to Read a 'Culturally Different' Book," Chapter 3 in this book.

31. For a description of this connection in Marx and Engels, see V. G. Kiernan, *Marxism and Imperialism* (Edinburgh: Edward Arnold, 1974), p. 188. Many artists, including E. M. Forster and Satyajit Ray, make this connection.

32. See Amin, *Unequal Development,* p. 380.

33. Marx, *Capital,* vol. 3, trans. David Fernbach (New York: Viking Books, 1981), p. 732. Within the narrative, Marx is describing usurer's capital.

34. It is only if "internal colonization," and its corollary, "united ethnic voice," are the presuppositions that such a judgment can become "authoritative." Thus Ngũgĩ wa Thiong'o: "It is important that we understand that cultural imperialism in its era of neocolonialism is a more dangerous cancer because it takes new subtle forms and can hide even under the cloak of militant African nationalism, the cry for dead authentic cultural symbolism and other native racist self assertive banners." See "Literature and Society," in his *Writers in Politics* (London: Heinemann, 1981), p. 25.

3. How to Read a "Culturally Different" Book

1. R. K. Narayan, *The Guide* (New York: Penguin, 1980) (hereafter cited in the text by page numbers alone).

2. Richard Hoggart, *The Uses of Literacy: Aspects of Working-Class Life* (New York: Oxford University Press, 1970); Stuart Hall, *Culture, Media, Language:*

Working Papers in Cultural Studies (London: Hutchinson, 1980). Work produced from a black British subject-position, such as the early and influential *The Empire Strikes Back: Race and Racism in 70s Britain* (London: Hutchinson, 1982), has a singularly different aura from its effect on post-colonial self-representation in Indo-Anglian writing.

3. Shashi Tharoor, *The Great Indian Novel* (New York: Arcade, 1989). This information is provided in the biographical blurb in the inside back cover.

4. Dipesh Chakrabarty notes the divide, but does not account for it in his "Open Space/Public Place: Garbage, Modernity and India," *Economic and Political Weekly* 27.10–11 (March 7–14, 1992), pp. 541–547: "Until the Salman Rushdies arrived on the scene and made the intellectual ferment of modern India more visible to the outsider."

5. G. V. Desani, *All About H. Hatterr* (New Paltz, NY: McPherson, 1986).

6. For "hyperreal," see Jean Baudrillard, "The Precession of Simulacra," in *Simulations,* trans. Paul Foss, Paul Patton, and Philip Beitchman (New York: Semiotext[e], 1983), p. 2.

7. Vološinov proposed a classification of literary form in terms of the reporting of speech (V. N. Vološinov, *Marxism and the Philosophy of Language,* trans. Ladislaw Matejka [Ann Arbor: University of Michigan Press, 1973], pp. 115–123). I have commented on the problems of bilingual representation of subjectivity with reference to Nadine Gordimer's *July's People* in "The Burden of English," Chapter 1 in this book.

8. R. K. Narayan, *My Days: A Memoir* (London: Penguin, 1989), p. 167.

9. In this respect the visible "difficulty" of *Glas,* trans. John P. Leavey Jr. and Richard Rand (Lincoln: University of Nebraska Press, 1986) is less "bewildering" than the philosophical prose of *Of Spirit: Heidegger and the Question,* trans. Geoffrey Bennington and Rachel Bowlby (Chicago: University of Chicago Press, 1989), where Derrida "follows" every principle of style developed in his thought so implicitly that an uninstructed or too-quick reading can and often does interpret his grave denunciation of Heidegger's betrayal of himself in his later politics as an apology!

10. The best-known elaboration of this argument is to be found in M. H. Abrams, *The Mirror and the Lamp: Romantic Theory and the Critical Tradition* (New York: Oxford University Press, 1971).

11. This is one of the supporting arguments in that part of Foucault's work that is interested in a chronological narrative of discursive formations. The argument is most persuasively made in Michel de Certeau, "The Formality of Practices: From Religious Systems to the Ethics of Enlightenment (the Seventeenth and Eighteenth Centuries)," in *The Writing of History* (New York: Columbia University Press, 1988), pp. 147–205.

12. Narayan, *Memoir,* p. 48.

13. Narayan is thus able to make this sweeping generalization, worthy of a Macaulay: "All imaginative writing in India has had its origin in the *Rāmāyana* and the *Mahābhārata*" (Narayan, "The Problem of the Indian Writer," in *A Story-Teller's World* [New Delhi: Penguin India, 1989], p. 14). The problem of "English in India" becomes a jolly safari arranged by some better-bred

version of the India Tourist Board. Is Narayan naive or ironic in the following passage? "In the final analysis America and India differ basically though
it would be wonderful if they could complement each other's values. . . . One
may hope that the next generation of Indians (American grown) will do better by accepting the American climate spontaneously or, in the alternative, by
returning to India to live a different life" (ibid., p. 30). It is significant that
only on the Raj is he uncompromisingly dismissive: "The Raj concept seems
to be just childish nonsense, indicating a glamorized, romanticized period
piece, somewhat phoney" (ibid., p. 31). His word on decolonization is back on
the track of general niceness (perhaps we should allow for the fact that this
piece was first published in the U.S. *TV Guide*): "With all the irritants removed [at Independence], a period of mutual goodwill began between the
two countries" (ibid., p. 33). It is possible that, as a result of this general
avoidance of conflict, Narayan is a preferred author in the underclass multicultural classroom in Britain (information received from Badar Nissar Kaler,
Oxford).

14. Narayan, *Memoir,* pp. 168–169.
15. For découpage see Derrida, "Mes Chances," in Joseph Smith and William
    Kerrigan, eds., *Taking Chances* (Baltimore, MD: Johns Hopkins University
    Press, 1984), p. 28.
16. E. M. Forster, *A Passage to India* (New York: Harper Torchbooks, 1952),
    pp. 283–322.
17. Frédérique Apffel Marglin, *Wives of the God-King: The Rituals of the Devada-
    sis of Puri* (Delhi: Oxford University Press, 1985). This book has been criti-
    cized by Indian scholars, but the politics of that criticism is itself a text for
    interpretation.
18. Narayan would like this not to be so ("After the Raj," in *A Story-Teller's
    World* [New Delhi: Penguin India, 1989], p. 32), and the Malgudi novels
    might have some unspecified regional specificity. *The Guide* does not carry
    specific regional signals.
19. Making dancing acceptable as a full-fledged career, inserting *Odissi* into the
    classical repertoire, has its own "feminist" histories, in quite a different space
    from subalternity. My conversations with Sanjukta Panigrahi, an *Odissi* dancer
    of my own generation and class, whom I have already mentioned, brought
    this home to me yet once again. This history must not be allowed to take first
    place. And the role of the quiet proto-feminist mothers of this generation
    who, working with immense innovativeness behind the scenes, made their
    daughters' career-freedom possible must not be obliterated in the accounts
    of the daughters' struggles.
20. Baudrillard, "Precession," p. 16.
21. Marglin, *Wives,* pp. 67, 73.
22. Ibid., p. 11.
23. Amrita Srinivasan, "Reform or Conformity? Temple 'Prostitution' and the
    Community in the Madras Presidency," in Bina Agarwal, ed., *Structures of
    Patriarchy: State, Community and Household in Modernizing Asia* (Delhi:
    Kali for Women, 1988) (hereafter cited in the text as AS, with page numbers

following). One wonders how seriously one should examine Marglin's claim of solidarity with Mrs. Besant. Annie Besant (1847–1933) was a brilliant woman of unremitting activism and extraordinary enthusiasms: for Christianity, atheist secularism, Socialism, and Theosophy/India, respectively. It is well-known that her aim for India was "Self-Government within the Empire" ("Manifesto," included in Raj Kumar, *Annie Besant's Rise to Power in Indian Politics 1914–1917* [New Delhi: Concept, 1981], p. 139). Indeed, her Theosophist millenarianism "was to bring about a universal, theocratic state under whose firm, wise rule men could not but behave as brothers" (Anne Taylor, *Annie Besant: A Biography* [New York: Oxford University Press, 1992], p. 277). As Taylor comments further, her "historical account of India's spiritual past [was] heavily biased towards Hinduism. . . . Indians as well as Europeans blamed her for inciting race hatred and caste hatred. . . . 'A democratic socialism controlled by majority votes, guided by numbers, can never succeed,' she wrote as early as 1908; 'a truly aristocratic socialism, controlled by duty, guided by wisdom is the next step upward in civilisation'" (pp. 311, 327, 313). Her attitude toward Indian women was consonant with her conviction that "knowledge of British ways and political methods [would lead] to India's strengthening" (Kumar, *Besant's Rise*, p. 102), and with her "approval [of] a proletariat in the condition of a child, ready to be governed, ready to admit the superiority of its elders" (Taylor, *Besant*, p. 313). I recommend a browse through a document like Besant's *Wake Up, India* (Adyar: Theosophical Publishing House, 1913) for a sense of her attitude to Indian women's education. It is no underestimation of her commitment, but a recognition of her historical inscription, to acknowledge that "Victorian and Edwardian feminists collaborated in the ideological work of empire, reproducing the moral discourse of imperialism and embedding feminist ideology within it" (Antoinette M. Burton, "The White Woman's Burden: British Feminists and the Indian Woman, 1865–1915," *Women's Studies International Forum* 13.4 [1990]: 295). If Marglin's throwaway claim had been serious, her own invocation of a century's difference between herself and Besant would have led to considerations of the relationship between imperialism and neo-colonialism, liberal humanism and cultural relativism. Who decolonizes? And how?

24. Manavalli Ramakrishna Kavi, ed., *Natyasastra: With the Commentary of Abhinavagupta* (Baroda: Central Library, 1926), vol. 1, V. 103–125.

25. Hari Narayan Apte, ed., *Sangitaratnākara,* vol. 7 (Gwalior: Anandasrama, 1897), pp. 3–16.

26. Aparna Chattopadhyay, "The Institution of 'Devadasis' According to the Kathasaritsagara," *Journal of the Oriental Institute* 16.3 (March 1967): 216–222. The famous reference in Kalidasa's *Meghaduta* is not necessarily a reference to the institution.

27. Mandakranta Bose, "*Lāsya:* Dance or Drama?," in Bimal Krishna Matilal and Purushottama Bilimoria, eds., *Sanskrit and Related Studies* (Delhi: Indian Books Centre, 1990), pp. 125–134. I am grateful to Dr. Bose for allowing me to summarize unpublished material.

28. "Sublate" is a newish translation of *Aufhebung,* usually translated as over-coming or superseding, words that do not keep the colloquial German aura of preserving in a higher way while destroying the lower way.

29. The technique of analogizing from individual pathology through the history of the language to the history of culture can perhaps do no more than figure forth the impossibility of ever performing this task successfully. For a bold excursion into this area, one might consult Freud's essay on the word "un-canny," which still stops short of the cultural history of gendering (Freud, "The Uncanny," in *The Standard Edition,* vol. 17, trans. James Strachey [New York: Norton, 1961–], pp. 218–256).

30. Gyan Prakash has theorized this resistance in terms of precapitalist/precolonial and capitalist/colonial/postcolonial discursive productions (without reference to gender) in Prakash, *Bonded Histories: Genealogies of Labor Servitude in Colonial India* (New York: Cambridge University Press, 1990). Activists in the field interpret this resistance in various ways. From a distance it gives rise to theories about the "natural" inferioriy of ethnic/racial groups, classes, and genders. A certain variety of armchair resistance refuses to recognize its real-ity as well as its critical potential.

31. *Shramshakti* (New Delhi: National Commission on Self Employed Women & Women in the Informal Sector, 1988), p. liii.

32. For more on SEWA (Self-Employed Women's Association), see Sheila Allen and Carol Wolkowitz, *Homeworking: Myths and Realities* (London: Mac-millan, 1987), p. 149.

33. "I am using 'feminism' here in a loose sense. a) Work for the removal of so-cial practices based on and perpetuating exploitation of women; b) follow-up support so that implementation of a) does not in fact become impossible through masculist and class reprisal; and c) education so that men and women want to be free of gender-bias and not consider the consequences of gender-freedom demeaning to themselves as men and women, and necessarily destruc-tive of the social fabric." Spivak, "Marxist Feminism," *Frontier* 23.24 (January 26, 1991), pp. 68–69.

34. Gail Omvedt, "Devdasi Custom and the Fight against It," *Manushi* 19 (1983): 17.

35. Discussion of Panigrahi's performance, Conference on Inter-cultural Perfor-mance, Bellagio, Italy, February 18, 1991. Ms. Ajayi's questioning was most perceptive, and revealed the difference in approach between performer and academic theorist. The bit about the film is the only part that relates to my argument.

36. Srinivas Aravamudan, "Being God's Postman Is No Fun, Yaar: Salman Rushdie's *The Satanic Verses,*" *Diacritics* 9.2 (Summer 1989): 3–20.

37. C. N. Srinath, *The Literary Landscape: Essays on Indian Fiction and Poetry in English* (Delhi: Mittal, 1986), pp. 7–8.

38. The author of the novel would endorse this sentiment. See Narayan, "After the Raj," in *A Story-Teller's World,* p. 32.

4. The Double Bind Starts to Kick In

1. Gayatri Chakravorty Spivak, "Righting Wrongs," in *Other Asias* (Oxford: Blackwell, 2008), pp. 14–57.
2. Susan Bazilli, *Putting Women on the Agenda* (Johannesburg: Ravan Press, 1991), p. 15. Some reading-work has to be deployed in order to discover the practical agreement between Bazilli and myself.
3. Conversation between Robert Reich and David Bennahum on "Into the Matrix" (http://www.reach.com/matrix/meme2-02.html). The next quotation from Reich is also from this source.
4. *The United Nations and the Advancement of Women: 1945–1995* (New York: United Nations, 1995), p. 180.
5. Karl Marx, *Capital,* vol. 3, trans. David Fernbach (New York: Viking Books, 1981), p. 1015.
6. Saskia Sassen, *Globalization and Its Discontents* (New York: New Press, 1998).
7. I am trying to condense the thinking in my second paragraph (it was the opening one in the original version) in the typography of (im)possible. This contorted enablement is a valid option, of course, but now I feel it has no effect in the world at large.
8. "Forum," *National Geographic* 195.2 (February 1999), n.p.
9. Joan C. Tronto, *Moral Boundaries: A Political Argument for an Ethic of Care* (New York: Routledge, 1993), p. x. The next passage is from pp. 2–3. If you look at the debates in Rebecca Whisnant and Peggy DesAutels, eds., *Global Feminist Ethics* (Lanham, MD: Rowman & Littlefield, 2008), you'll see that the mainstream woman as such is still defined as basic Euro-U.S., anglo-clone.
10. I have explicated my understanding of the Kleinian position in "Translation as Culture," Chapter 11 in this book.
11. For an example of bad haunting, see Owen Heatherley, "Lash Out and Cover Up: Austerity Nostalgia and Ironic Authoritarianism in Recession Britain," *Radical Philosophy* 157 (September–October 2009): 4, with the proviso that we do not confuse the effortful exercise of hauntology with either mere nostalgia or ideological production.
12. Elinor Solomon Harris, *Virtual Money* (New York: Oxford University Press, 1997).
13. Erla Zwingle, "Women and Population," *National Geographic* 4 (October 1998): 44–45. The general sentiment of the piece is altogether admirable: "'Don't look at people like an ant heap,' one expert urged. 'These are individuals'"(p. 38). My remarks can only signal at the responsibility attendant upon such statements.
14. *Ecologist* 27.2 (March–April 1997): 42. Resistance to this was certainly already afoot in the 1990s, but I think the aura of a Nobel Prize for Bangladesh has calmed this down. In order to keep abreast of resistance, I read local newspapers at the time, quite in the same way as old-fashioned Area Studies researchers do. *The Daily Star* and *Inkilab,* both Dhaka-based, carried news

items reporting people's retaliation upon a microlending, World Bank–
supported NGO (Proshika) after the death of three women and an infant, arrested for microloan default (July 6, 1997). My convictions remain the same,
but my work now is hands-on. It was amusing to see the *Economic and Political Weekly* commenting in 2010 on the problems with microlending (M. S.
Sriram, "Microfinance Turns into a Nightmare," *Economic and Political Weekly*
55.43 [October 23, 2010], pp. 10–13). I don't believe radical reporting achieves
much any more, although it should, of course, continue; it has greater evidentiary value than an aesthetic education.

15. Women's World Bank publicity flier, 1998.

16. Assia Djebar, "Forbidden Gaze, Severed Sound," in Djebar, *Women of Al-
    giers in Their Apartment,* trans. Marjolijn de Jager (Charlottesville: Univer-
    sity Press of Virginia, 1992), p. 141. I have remembered this passage in the
    title of my memoirs, forthcoming from Verso: "If Only."

17. Bazilli, *Putting Women on the Agenda,* pp. 217–247.

18. See Mahmood Mamdani, *Citizen and Subject: Contemporary Africa and the
    Legacy of Late Colonialism* (Princeton, NJ: Princeton University Press, 1996).

19. Bazilli, *Putting Women on the Agenda,* p. 220. Gordon Brotherston com-
    ments on such innovative hybrid existence in Guatemala in "Debate Regard-
    ing the Evidence in *Me llamo Rigoberta Menchú,*" *Journal of Latin American
    Cultural Studies* 6.1 (1997): 93–103; Peggy Rockman Napaljarri and Lee
    Cataldi speak of this among the Warlpiri in Central Australia in their intro-
    duction to *Yimikirli: Warlpiri Dreamings and Histories* (San Francisco: Harp-
    erCollins, 1994), pp. xvii–xxiv.

20. Samuel Taylor Coleridge, *Biographia Literaria,* ed. John Shawcross (Oxford:
    Oxford University Press, 1907, reprint 1967), chapter 13: "On the Imagina-
    tion, or Esemplastic Power," vol. 1, pp. 195–202; chapter 14: "Occasion of
    the Lyrical Ballads," vol. 2, pp. 5–12.

21. It helps that I had written of this long ago in "The Letter as Cutting Edge,"
    in Spivak, *In Other Worlds: Essays in Cultural Politics* (New York: Rout-
    ledge, 2006), pp. 3–19. The Shelley passage is in Percy Bysshe Shelley, "A
    Defence of Poetry," in Bruce R. McElderry Jr., ed., *Shelley's Critical Prose*
    (Lincoln: University of Nebraska Press, 1967), p. 28.

22. Colin McGinn, "Hello HAL," *New York Times Book Review* (January 3,
    1999), retrieved from the New York Times Internet archives. The article re-
    views Ray Kurzweil, *The Age of Spiritual Machines: When Computers Ex-
    ceed Human Intelligence* (New York: Viking, 1999); Hans Moravec, *Robot:
    Mere Machine to Transcendent Mind* (New York: Oxford University Press,
    1999); and Neil Gershenfeld, *When Things Start to Think* (New York: Henry
    Holt, 1999). This brand of popular material has increased exponentially in the
    last decade. See David Golumbia, *The Cultural Logic of Computation* (Cam-
    bridge, MA: Harvard University Press, 2009). I do not necessarily accept the
    binarity between human and robot as the last instance that is being offered
    here. But that is another story.

23. Meaghan Morris, "On English as a Chinese Language: Implementing Glo-
    balization," in Brett de Bary, ed., *Universities in Translation: The Mental*

Labour of Globalization (Hong Kong: Hong Kong University Press, 2010), p. 188.

24. Matthew Arnold, *Culture and Anarchy* (New York: Bobbs-Merrill, 1971), p. 37.

25. Walter Pater, *The Renaissance* (London: Collins, 1961), p. 222.

26. Virginia Woolf, *A Room of One's Own* (New York: Harcourt, 1929), pp. 4–5; emphasis added (hereafter cited in the text as RO, with page numbers following). The bit on Woolf is poached from Spivak, "Arguments for a Deconstructive Cultural Studies," in Nicholas Royle, ed., *Deconstructions: A User's Guide* (Oxford: Blackwell, 2000), pp. 14–43.

27. W. E. B. Du Bois, *The Selected Writings of W. E. B. Du Bois*, ed. Walter Wilson (New York: Mentor, 1970), p. 51; and "The Negro Mind Reaches Out" in Alain Locke, ed., *The New Negro: An Interpretation* (New York: Arno Press, 1968), pp. 392–397.

28. Chinua Achebe, "An Image of Africa: Racism in Conrad's *Heart of Darkness*," in *Hopes and Impediments* (New York: Doubleday, 1988), pp. 1–20.

29. See also Gayatri Chakravorty Spivak, *Du Bois Rewrites History* (Cambridge, MA: Harvard University Press, forthcoming).

5. Culture

1. Simone de Beauvoir, *The Second Sex*, trans. H. M. Parshley (New York: Knopf, 1953).

2. Frederick Engels, *The Origin of the Family, Private Property, and the State* (New York: International Publishers, 1972).

3. Betty Friedan, *The Feminine Mystique* (New York: W. W. Norton, 1963).

4. Hélène Cixous, "Laugh of the Medusa," in Isabelle de Courtivron and Elaine Marks, eds., *New French Feminisms* (Amherst: University of Massachusetts Press, 1980), pp. 245–264.

5. Gayle Rubin, "The Traffic in Women: Notes on the 'Political Economy' of Sex," in Rayna Reiter, ed., *Toward an Anthropology of Women* (New York: Monthly Review Press, 1975), pp. 157–210.

6. If, on the other hand, we proudly distinguish ourselves from these corrupt Ottomans, all we have to do is to look at myriad articles like James Glanz, "Fraud Inquiries Point to Lapses in Iraq Projects," and the scandals surrounding federal, state, and local governments (*New York Times*, March 14, 2010, p. 1). The difference is that we have enforcement. One of my chief arguments in favor of an aesthetic education is that enforcement alone cannot become the mark of a so-called free society. I therefore suggest an ab-use rather than a regressive and self-centered, genre-blind imitation, such as the femivores' (see page 129).

7. Walter Benjamin gets around this by calling education "divine violence" (Benjamin, "Critique of Violence," in M. Bullock and M. W. Jennings, eds., *Selected Writings of Walter Benjamin*, vol. 1: *1913–1926* [Cambridge, MA: Harvard University Press, 1996], pp. 236–252). Melanie Klein's repeated juxtaposition of the desire for knowledge and the destructive, sadistic, controlling

impulses is a case in point. The metapsychologicality of the subject's programming—both topography and space, and history and time—is the locus of the transcendental (Melanie Klein, *The Psycho-Analysis of Children,* trans. Alix Strachey [New York: Free Press, 1975], pp. 174, 245, and passim).

8. For a brilliant metaphoric description of the distinction between the evidentiary *(savoir)* and the intuitive *(instinct),* see Lacan, *Écrits,* trans. Bruce Fink (New York: W. W. Norton, 2006), p. 680.

9. See my discussion of this in "More on Power/Knowledge," in Spivak, *Outside in the Teaching Machine* (New York: Routledge, 2009), pp. 27–57.

10. David Livingstone, *Missionary Travels and Researches in South Africa* (London: John Murray, 1857), p. 10.

11. This is a well-known but often misunderstood, deeply ironic remark to be found in Marx, "The Eighteenth Brumaire of Louis Bonaparte," in *Surveys from Exile,* trans. Ben Fowkes (New York: Vintage, 1974), p. 239. I have discussed this in Spivak, "Looking Back Looking Forward," in Rosalind Morris, ed., *Can the Subaltern Speak? Reflections on the History of an Idea* (New York: Columbia University Press, 2010), pp. 227–236.

12. See, for example, Madhu Bhushan, ed., *Casting Curious Shadows in the Dark: The South Asia Court of Women on the Violence of Trafficking and HIV/AIDS* (Bangalore: W. Q. Judge Press, 2003).

13. Spivak, *A Critique of Postcolonial Reason: Toward a History of the Vanishing Present* (Cambridge, MA: Harvard University Press, 1999), p. 223.

14. For the acronym PLATO, see Spivak, "Feminism and Critical Theory," in *In Other Worlds: Essays in Cultural Politics* (New York: Routledge, 2006), pp. 89–92.

15. Peggy Orenstein, "The Femivore's Dilemma," *New York Times Magazine* (March 14, 2010), pp. 11–12; Voltaire, *Candide* (1759), trans. Theo Cuffe (New York: Penguin, 2005), p. 95.

16. Karl Marx, *Capital,* vol. 3, trans. David Fernbach (New York: Viking Books, 1981), pp. 1015–1016.

17. Although the guarantee was not firm. Exactly the same items are being audited again.

18. For two examples among many, see Fareed Zakaria, "Illiberal Democracy," in *The Future of Democracy: Illiberal Democracy at Home and Abroad* (New York: Norton, 2003), pp. 89–118, and Jack Snyder, *From Voting to Violence* (New York: Norton, 2000).

19. Paulo Freire, *Pedagogy of the Oppressed* (London: Continuum, 2000), p. 35 and passim. Freire's word *"conscientização,"* famously translated as "conscientization" in an earlier translation, is given as "critical consciousness" in the new 30th Anniversary Edition. The discussion of the concept takes place in chapter 3.

20. Medha Chandra, "Grassroots Environmental Claim Making and the State: The 74th Constitutional Amendment Act in Kolkata, India," Ph.D. thesis, University College London, 2006.

21. "Commencement Address to Smith College Class of 1979," *Smith Alumnae Quarterly* 70 (August 1979), pp. 8–10.

22. The ontico-ontological difference in Heidegger is predicated upon the intuition that one cannot include in the philosophy of being the unmediated details of daily being. A corresponding epistemo-epistemological difference would be predicated on the intuition that the method of constructing an object of knowledge is determined by a mind-set that cannot be "known." The idea of a habit of mind (as, for example, we encounter it in Wordsworth or Gramsci; see page 6) is close to the concept of the mind-set or episteme. Rearranging desire attempts to engage the mind at this level, where the student is constructing a "world" for knowing and, of course, for acting upon.

23. Whereas in my book *Other Asias* (Oxford: Blackwell, 2008), neither for nor by subalterns, I can take a principled non-identitarian position. For another contrast, read Kristin Bumiller ably writing, in the U.S. context, a book with the title *In an Abusive State: How Neoliberalism Appropriated the Feminist Movement against Sexual Violence* (Durham, NC: Duke University Press, 2008), and put it over against Syed Mujtaba Ali's thoughts as the Afghan tribesmen were deposing Amanullah because women were going to get medical training. Since Mujtaba Ali's book on Afghanistan has never been translated, the entire passage is worth quoting: "But the question is: is Amanullah [King of Afghanistan, 1919–1929] truly an infidel? The tremendous argument that the mullahs now advanced could not be withstood by a single word from a Shinwari or a Khugiani. The mullahs said, 'Didn't you see with your own eyes that Amanullah sent one score Kabuli girls to Mustafa Kamal [President of Turkey]; when they spent a night in Jalalabad, didn't you see that they got in and out of the motor car with marching steps right in the middle of the market like shameless unveiled creatures?' It is true that many Shinwaris and Khugianis had come to Jalalabad on that market day and did see unveiled Kabuli women. It is also further true that Gazi Mustafa Kamal Pasha never received a *good conduct prize* [emphasis in original] from the Afghan Mullahs. An 'idiot' still said, apparently, that the girls were going to Turkey to learn medicine. Apparently, hearing this, the Shinwaris had roared with laughter and said, 'Lady doctors! Who has ever heard that women can be doctors! Why not say the girls are going to Turkey to grow mustaches!' Who will then open their eyes and remind them, that Shinwari women work in the fields and barns unveiled, who will explain that if old Granny is more expert at attaching a turmeric poultice and putting a leech on a forehead than men, then why shouldn't Kabuli women be able to learn medicine? But these are silly debates, fruitless discussions. Some of them mentioned the real reason. But as to how true it was, research could not reveal. Apparently Amanullah had imposed a tax of five coins of the realm upon each Afghan to increase the revenue of the kingdom" (Ali, "Deshe Bideshe," in *Racanabali* [Kolkata: Mitra o Ghosh, 1974], p. 29; translation mine).

24. This is self-criticism, not self-congratulation, but who knows? A labyrinth . . . See Derrida, *The Animal That Therefore I Am,* trans. David Wills (New York: Fordham University Press, 2008), p. 82.

6. Teaching for the Times

1. For further discussion of this point, see Spivak, "Constitutions and Cultural Studies," *Yale Journal of Law and the Humanities* 2.1 (Winter 1990): 133–147.

2. Robin Blackburn, *The Overthrow of Colonial Slavery, 1776–1848* (London: Verso, 1988), pp. 123, 124.

3. For the specifically East Asian origin "model minority," see Colleen Lye, *America's Asia: Racial Form and American Literature, 1893–1945* (Princeton, NJ: Princeton University Press, 2005). The main argument of *A Critique of Postcolonial Reason* was the appropriation of the native informant's position by the upwardly mobile postcolonial in the metropolis (see Spivak, *A Critique of Postcolonial Reason: Toward a History of the Vanishing Present* [Cambridge, MA: Harvard University Press, 1999] [hereafter cited in the text as CPR, with page numbers following]). I am not unsympathetic with this group, but I ask for auto-critique in terms of the self-marginalizing appropriation. This should be understood as the premise of the chapter.

4. Joan Wallach Scott, "The Campaign against Political Correctness: What's Really at Stake?" *Change* (November/December 1991): 39, 43.

5. Ibid.

6. Pierre Bourdieu, "The Philosophical Institution," in Alan Montefiore, ed., *Philosophy in France Today* (Cambridge: Cambridge University Press, 1983), p. 2.

7. For performative and constative, see, of course, J. L. Austin, *How to Do Things with Words* (Cambridge, MA: Harvard University Press, 1962).

8. Jacques Derrida, "Force of Law: The 'Mystical Foundation of Authority,' " in "Deconstruction and the Possibility of Justice," *Cardozo Law Review* 6.5–6 (July–August 1990): 971.

9. Some of these philosophical moves are to be found in the discussion of the aporia between the experience of the impossible and the possibility of the political in Derrida, *The Other Heading: Reflections on Today's Europe,* trans. Pascale-Anne Brault and Michael B. Naas (Bloomington: Indiana University Press, 1992), pp. 45–46. I am critical of the author's self-staging in the piece.

10. Herbert Marcuse, "Repressive Tolerance," in Robert Paul Wolff and Barrington Moore Jr., eds., *A Critique of Pure Tolerance* (Boston: Beacon Press, 1965), p. 116.

11. Aihwa Ong, "Colonialism and Modernity: Feminist Re-Presentations of Women in Non-Western Societies," *Inscriptions* 3–4 (1988): 90. Although I have some problems with the details of Professor Ong's argument, I am fully in accord with her general point.

12. Derrida, "Force of Law," p. 947.

13. Karl Marx, *Capital,* vol. 3, trans. David Fernbach (New York: Viking Books, 1981), pp. 1015–1016.

14. Amy Tan, *The Joy Luck Club* (New York: Ivy Books, 1989) (hereafter cited in the text as T, with page numbers following).

15. I will speak in greater depth about the Black Reconstruction in my forthcoming book, the substance of my Du Bois lectures at Harvard in November 2009.

16. The fact that this struggle did not mean the same thing for the Jewish and the black sectors of the district brings forth both the element of competition and the pedagogically negotiable epistemic space of the old immigrants that I have touched on above. These examples make clear that abstract talk of the politics of difference and different histories do not go too far unless we consider only the "white" as dominant. For details of the event, see Maurice R. Berube and Marilyn Gittell, eds., *Confrontation at Ocean Hill-Brownsville: The New York School Strikes of 1968* (New York: Praeger, 1969).

17. José David Saldívar, *Border Matters: Remapping American Cultural Studies* (Berkeley: University of California Press, 1997); and Ramón Saldívar, *The Borderlands of Culture: Américo Paredes and the Transnational Imaginary* (Durham, NC: Duke University Press, 2006). For border-culture work, Guillermo Gomez-Peña is best-known to the general audience.

18. Jack D. Forbes, *Black Africans and Native Americans: Color, Race and Caste in the Evolution of Red Black Peoples* (New York: Blackwell, 1988) (hereafter cited in the text and notes as F, with page numbers following).

19. It would, for example, be interesting to play this narrative in counterpoint with Hortense Spillers, "The Tragic Mulatta," in Elizabeth A. Meese and Alice Parker, eds., *The Difference Within: Feminism and Critical Theory* (Amsterdam: John Benjamin, 1989), or with the more extensive Deborah E. McDowell and Arnold Rampersad, eds., *Slavery and the Literary Imagination: Selected Papers from the English Institute, 1987* (Baltimore, MD: Johns Hopkins University Press, 1989). For a more extended discussion of the Foucault material, see Spivak, "More on Power/Knowledge," in *Outside in the Teaching Machine* (New York: Routledge, 2009), pp. 27–57.

20. This argument is generally present in extant scholarship. For a random and superior example, I offer Russell R. Menard, "The Africanization of the Lowcountry Labor Force, 1670–1730," in Winthrop D. Jordan and Sheila L. Skemp, eds., *Race and Family in the Colonial South* (Jackson: University Press of Mississippi, 1987), pp. 81–108.

21. Contrary to some established opinion, Forbes makes a convincing case that the crucial descriptive mulat(t)o is a displacement of the Arabic muwallad-maula (F, pp. 141f). The importance of Islam in discussions of imperial formations is illustrated here from below as elsewhere from above. For the general reader, the sources are Samir Amin, *Unequal Development: An Essay on the Social Formations of Peripheral Capitalism,* trans. Brian Pearce (Boston: Monthly Review Press, 1976), and the last chapter of Perry Anderson, *Lineages of the Absolutist State* (London: New Left Books, 1974).

22. Sigmund Freud, *The Standard Edition,* vol. 14, trans. James Strachey (New York: Norton, 1961–), pp. 93, 101.

23. Giovanni Arrighi, Terence K. Hopkins, and Immanuel Wallerstein, *Antisystemic Movements* (London: Verso, 1989), p. 21. The following phrase is on p. 20.

24. Marcuse, "Repressive Tolerance," p. 91.
25. Begum Rokeya Sakhawat Hossain, "Lady-Prisoner," in *Rokeya-Rachanabali* (Dhaka: Bangla Akademi, 1984), p. 473; translation mine.
26. Paul de Man, *Allegories of Reading: Figural Language in Rousseau, Nietzsche, Rilke, and Proust* (New Haven, CT: Yale University Press, 1979), p. 205. The following phrase is from pp. 208–209.
27. Naila Kabeer, "The Quest for National Identity: Women, Islam and the State in Bangladesh," in Deniz Kandiyoti, ed., *Women, Islam and the State* (Philadelphia: Temple University Press, 1991), pp. 115–143. The quoted phrase is on p. 138.
28. A striking exception is the poetry of Farhad Mazhar.
29. Discussion with National Press Club, broadcast on CSPAN, September 28, 1991.
30. "Process of Writing," in *Declaration of Comilla* (Dhaka: UBINIG, 1991), p. xiii.
31. Assia Djebar, *Fantasia: An Algerian Cavalcade,* trans. Dorothy S. Blair (New York: Quartet Books, 1985) (hereafter cited in the text as D, with page numbers following); translation modified.
32. Frantz Fanon, *A Dying Colonialism,* trans. Haakan Chevalier (New York: Grove Weidenfeld, 1965), pp. 65–66, 67.
33. It would be interesting to work out the itinerary of Rolland's exile from the energetic analysis of 1848 in Marx's "The Eighteenth Brumaire."

7. Acting Bits/Identity Talk

1. Assia Djebar, *Fantasia: An Algerian Cavalcade,* trans. Dorothy S. Blair (New York: Quartet Books, 1985) (hereafter cited in the text as D, with page numbers following). For detail on Ibn Khaldûn, see Albert Hourani, *A History of the Arab Peoples* (Cambridge, MA: Harvard University Press, 1991), p. 1.
2. See David Prochaska, *Making Algeria French: Colonialism in Bône, 1870–1920* (Cambridge: Cambridge University Press, 1990), and David Kopf, *British Orientalism and the Bengal Renaissance* (Berkeley: University of California Press, 1969).
3. For a discussion of the work of these two philosopher-linguists, see Bimal Krishna Matilal, *Words and the World* (Delhi: Oxford University Press, 1990). All the "Indian" words that follow this sentence are spelled according to the transcription of Sanskrit orthography, although in the Bengali pronunciation they sound quite different, and the Bengali alphabet is quite different from the Sanskrit *devangari* alphabet, although descended from it. Another rift of history that English obliterates.
4. I will, later in the chapter, disassociate myself from the view that U.S. multiculturalism is, according to Arthur M. Schlesinger, "The disuniting of America." In the Indian context, however, I felt that I must speak out against separatism. I am not a situational relativist. One must take account of situations because one acts according to imperatives.

5. "Pro-pose" takes me back to an earlier discussion in my paper of the famous line of Nagarjuna: *Nāsti ca mama kācana pratijñā* (roughly, My proposition is not there at all). Incidentally, my description of deconstruction-work here found a nice bit of vindication. In the last chapter of *Specters of Marx: The State of the Debt, the Work of Mourning and the New International*, trans. Peggy Kamuf (New York: Routledge, 1994), Derrida shook the stakes of *ahamvāda* in Marx to release the multitudinous iterations of an *idamvāda*. Mechanical Marxists will not want to know it.

6. The only air-conditioned interior I entered in the area was the spacious room of the old British Circuit House, now the offices of the Sub-Zonal Relief Co-ordinator. I thank the Co-ordinator, Muhammad Omar Farooq, for permission to quote his letter to the Commander of the Joint Task Force:

Excellency,

For long years your people waited with patience and struggled with determination and shed tears and blood till your tryst with destiny came true, and on the fourth of July 1776 came the fruition of years of ceaseless and relentless struggle with the establishment of independence and liberty, equality and fraternity. Your elders and the fathers of your constitution endeavored to establish "a government of the people, by the people and for the people" so that liberty, equality and fraternity could flourish and grow in strength from day to day, and democracy could reign supreme.

Your elders had a dream and therefore they struggled to establish democracy, because they knew perhaps better than any one else that human qualities could not blossom without democracy, liberty, equality and fraternity. It is not a mere coincidence and chance that, these very qualities have so deeply mingled with your blood through the generations that, like the statue of liberty standing guard on the gateway to America, you, your colleagues and offsprings have chosen to be the sentinels of liberty, equality and fraternity the world over.

Excellency, as you passed from bondage to freedom and independence, we passed from independence to slavery and bondage, and we were a nation lost. It was through and after long years of struggle and sacrifice that, we were finally able to throw off our chains and fetters. Today, democracy in our country is reborn. It is young, hardly a few months old. But within these few months it has had its baptism of fire, with the fateful and devastating Cyclone and Tidal surge of 29 April, 1991, which rocked our people to their roots and caused devastation on a scale hitherto unknown, and left them in a state of complete shock and bewilderment.

But our people are resilient, they are born in cyclones and tidal bores, and they grow and live with them. For them, cyclones and tidal bores are almost so to say a natural habitat. With fortitude, and indomitable courage our people withstood the scourge of the cyclone, which was like a holocaust. Inspiration and unshakable assistance from friends like you helped to get us back on our feet sooner than later, and move boldly ahead. You and your sea angels, helped, facilitated and expedited the process of our recovery. For this, we will remain indebted. We have no words adequate to express our gratitude.

But above all, it was your conduct your Excellency, which perhaps was the well-spring of inspiration and hope. Your memorable words still echo and ring in our ears. These have left an indelible imprint on hearts and minds. You likened democracy in our country to a young plant which needed extreme care and attention to flower and blossom. You had as you said, come to nurture and water the roots of this young plant, for according to you there could be no humanity without democracy. Your words and action have once again, convinced us that our road to progress and development was only one—the road of democracy.

We are encouraged, re-assured and emboldened that, we have such committed friends and well wishers to help us establish democracy on a firm footing. We are sure and confident that in the achievement of this goal we have to succeed, because we simply cannot afford to fail—for that would be our very doom.

Excellency, long after the departure of yourself and your sea-angels, the memories of your short but memorable stay on our shores, will fondly come back again and again to our minds—because these are memories which one simply cannot forget, or wish away.

As for yourself Excellency, to many of us you were perhaps the Philosopher King of Plato. I am sure this is but only a partial description of your qualities of head and heart. These are the qualities which have endeared you to all of us, and again these are the qualities which have made you a wonderful and fine American, and an even more wonderful and finer human being, and a leader of men.

Excellency, with the co-operation and unity that was so happily evident during your stay, between our two friendly countries, it makes one feel that with sincerity, honesty and human love as the basis of all human relations "peace and good will amongst men" would indeed prevail and the "Kingdom of Heaven" would come true here on this very planet of ours—dear mother earth.

Excellency, kindly permit me to beg forgiveness for having taken up so much of your valuable time. I would like to convey to you and through you to all your colleagues—the sea-angels, our sincerest thanks and gratitude. You have permanently made us indebted.

No comment is surely needed here about the fracture between claimed "national identity" and being-in-the-land.

7. I have commented on this and the following paragraph in the text in *Other Asias* (Oxford: Blackwell, 2008), pp. 78–96.

8. Karl Marx, *Early Writings,* trans. Rodney Livingstone and Gregor Benton (Harmondsworth: Penguin Books, 1975), p. 328.

9. Smadar Lavie, *The Poetics of Military Occupation: Mzeina Allegories of Bedouin Identity under Israeli and Egyptian Rule* (Berkeley: University of California Press, 1990).

10. Luce Irigaray, "The Fecundity of the Caress: A Reading of Levinas, *Totality and Infinity*, Section IV.B: 'The Phenomenology of Eros,'" in *Face to Face with Levinas*, ed. Richard A. Cohen (Albany: SUNY Press, 1986), p. 232.

11. AM, "Calcutta Diary," *Economic and Political Weekly* 26.8 (February 23, 1991), p. 403.

12. See Spivak, "Inscription: Of Truth to Size," in *Outside in the Teaching Machine* (New York: Routledge, 2009), pp. 206, 202–204 (hereafter cited in the notes as OTM, with page numbers following). A few stray sentences are inserted here.

13. For an alternative view of the use of the word "culture," see Spivak, "Narratives of Multiculturalism," in Thomas W. Keenan, ed., *Cultural Diversities* (New York: Verso, 1995). It is salutary but perhaps too simple to call the "conceptual phantasm of community, the nation-state, sovereignty, borders, native soil and blood" "archaic" and "primitive" because "made more outdated than ever . . . by tele-technic dislocation" (Derrida, *Specters*, p. 82). It is in displacement, within the stagings of origin and willed exodus, that these tenacious affects create new terrains of struggle. You cannot shame them away by calling them outdated, even as you cannot secure the fantasmatic origin by bloodshed.

14. Arthur M. Schlesinger Jr., *The Disuniting of America: Reflections on a Multicultural Society* (New York: Norton, 1998).

15. Guillermo Gomez Peña, performance tape. The state of "illegal" immigration has worsened in the intervening years. The paperless (undocumented) are subalterns in the strict Gramscian sense; they cannot achieve the state (Gramsci, *Selections from the Prison Notebooks*, ed. and trans. Quintin Hoare and Geoffrey Nowell Smith [New York: International Publishers, 1971], p. 52).

16. Toni Morrison, *Beloved* (New York: Plume Books Edition, 1987) (hereafter cited in the text as B, with page numbers following).

17. For a longer discussion of this, see Spivak, "Theory in the Margin: Coetzee's *Foe* reading Defoe's *Crusoe/Roxana*," in *The Consequences of Theory*, ed. Jonathan Arac and Barbara Johnson (Baltimore, MD: Johns Hopkins University Press, 1990), pp. 171, 173.

18. Spivak, "Signs and Trace," catalog essay for Anish Kapoor, *Memory* (Berlin: Deutsche Guggenheim, 2008), pp. 56–75; Spivak, "Tracing the Skin of Day," in Chittrovanu Mazumdar, *Undated: Nightskin* (Dubai: 1×1 Art Gallery, 2009), pp. 17–25.

19. Jacques Derrida, *Glas*, trans. John P. Leavey Jr. and Richard Rand (Lincoln: University of Nebraska Press, 1986), pp. 207b, 208b (hereafter cited in the text as G, with page numbers following).

20. Rather than provide an English translation, I refer the reader to the entire complex problematic in Derrida, *Of Spirit: Heidegger and the Question*, trans. Geoffrey Bennington and Rachel Bowlby (Chicago: University of Chicago Press, 1989), pp. 129–136.

21. Jacques Derrida, "Economimesis," *Diacritics* 11.2 (Summer 1981): 3–25.

22. See Clarice Lispector, "The Smallest Woman in the World," in *Family Ties*, trans. Giovanni Pontiero (Austin: University of Texas Press), pp. 88–95.

23. Kamalkumar Majumdar, *Antarjaliyatra* (Calcutta: Subarnarekha, 1981), p. ix.
24. I have expressed my view of Ramprasad Sen in greater detail in "The Politics of Translation," in OTM, pp. 200–225.
25. Marie-Aimée Hélie-Lucas, "Women Living under Muslim Laws," *South Asia Bulletin* 10.1 (1990): 73.
26. Ted Swedenburg ("Palestinian Women Now: Tradition and Difference in the 1936–39 Revolt: Implications for the Intifada," paper presented at Marxism Now: Tradition and Difference Conference, December 2, 1989, University of Massachusetts) makes this point for one of the most important global sites of contestation.
27. Claudine Hermann, *The Tongue Snatchers,* trans. Nancy Kline (Lincoln: University of Nebraska Press, 1989), p. 7.
28. For the patriarchality of signatures in identity, see Derrida on Nietzsche, in "Logic of the Living Feminine," in *The Ear of the Other,* trans. Peggy Kamuf (New York: Schocken Books, 1985), pp. 3–19. It is this logic that we must ab-use as we act bits, talk identity.

8. Supplementing Marxism

1. The early Lacan is canny when he suggests that there is a yawning gap between Hegel and Freud in that the former, locating the connection between subject and knowledge in "desire," assumes that "from the outset and right to the end, the subject knows what it wants," while "Freud reopens the joint between truth and knowledge to the mobility out of which revolutions arise" (Lacan, "The Subversion of the Subject and the Dialectic of Desire," in *Écrits,* trans. Bruce Fink [New York: Norton, 2005]; translation modified). In other words, even if in Myanmar (2009–), in Tunisia (2011), and for Wikileaks (2009–) the digital is instrumental for dissemination of information and maintaining transparency, the epistemological task, persistently mobilizing the joint between truth and knowledge to produce imaginative suppleness for the possible practice of freedom, remains in place. An aesthetic education.
2. This assumes purity of motives in leaders, of course. I have developed the difference between the two "socials" in "Limits and Openings of Marx in Derrida," in Spivak, *Outside in the Teaching Machine* (New York: Routledge, 2009), pp. 107–110 (hereafter cited in the notes as OTM, with page numbers following). Even if an entire society were composed of what Marx called "the agents of production," the positive use of class-consciousness by every member of that society would need something other than reason, something that would have rendered into "habit" (as Gramsci would say) the conviction that the other (or society as a big Other) was more important than the self, relearning class-consciousness as the lesson of responsibility. Even apart from the fact that no society is composed thus, the human mental theater cannot learn responsibility fully. "Ethical teaching" whittles away at the impossibility. (The reader will add the epistemological reterritorialization

indicated in the Introduction.) As for the risks mentioned in my text, let me offer two examples from the Armenian post-Soviet case: "[Harnush] HACO-PIAN [one of eight women in the 260-member Armenian parliament]: Only if there is a strong economy, a good standard of living. Only after these are secured can people pay attention to the humanitarian and benevolent goals. . . . [Rouben] SHOUGARIAN [Assistant to the President for Foreign Affairs]: . . . I guess first we look to the West for technical assistance, to the civilized world and then to Oriental countries" (Michael M. J. Fischer and Stella Grigorian, "Six to Eight Characters in Search of Armenian Civil Society amidst the Carnivalization of History," in *Perilous States,* ed. George Marcus [Chicago: University of Chicago Press, 1994], pp. 95, 116). And Armenia is not representative of capitalism and socialism (wedded in a "mixed economy" in the post-Soviet context), repeating the mistake of ignoring the prior importance of the lesson of responsibility. We will no doubt hear differently from the Tatars, the Bashkirs, the Kazakhs, and the other members of the Commonwealth of Independent States and the Russian Federation. For the disconnect between clan politics and the "modern" state, see Kathleen Collins, *Clan Politics and Regime Transition in Central Asia* (New York: Cambridge University Press, 2006). Stalin is an example of a rational analysis run to the extreme consequences of the ignoring of responsibility, the body politic hacked to pieces to fit the "rational" diagram as an alibi. We must remember that a Western European rememoration of Marx, however important, is a comparatively minor episode. For more on Armenia from a continentalist outside, see Spivak, *Other Asias* (Oxford: Blackwell, 2008).

3. For "pure" formulations of this, see Harry Braverman, *Labor and Monopoly Capitalism: The Degradation of Work in the Twentieth Century* (New York: Monthly Review Press, 1975), and Harry Cleaver, *Reading Capital Politically* (Austin: University of Texas Press, 1979).

4. Karl Marx, *Capital,* vol. 1, trans. Ben Fowkes (London: Penguin, 1990), p. 132.

5. Sorry, Terry Eagleton and others of the same mind (see Eagleton, "In the Gaudy Supermarket," *London Review of Books* 21.10 [May 13, 1999], pp. 3–6). I write this odd typography in the hope that some patient reader will know why plain prose has to be tortured in order to grasp a deep problem in the heart of Marx's writings that has destroyed rational postrevolutionary state-building.

6. Derrida, "Différance," in *Margins of Philosophy,* trans. Alan Bass (Chicago: University of Chicago Press, 1982), p. 17.

7. Derrida, "Passions," in *Derrida: A Critical Reader,* ed. David Wood (Oxford: Blackwell, 1992), p. 15.

8. Derrida, "Force of Law: The 'Mystical Foundation of Authority,' " in "Deconstruction and the Possibility of Justice," *Cardozo Law Review* 6.5–6 (July–August 1990): 947.

9. For Bloomsbury Fraction, see Raymond Williams, *Problems in Materialism and Culture* (London: Verso, 1982), pp. 148–169. For the secularism debate,

see Gil Anidjar, "Secularism," *Critical Inquiry* 33 (Autumn 2006): 52–77. For the colonial subject and Human Rights argument, see Spivak, *Other Asias*, p. 15.

10. Karl Marx, *Capital*, vol. 3, trans. David Fernbach (New York: Viking Books, 1981), pp. 1015–1016. All thought of capitalism and/or socialism is inaugurated in difference, the most obvious being lodged in the notion of life as the pursuit of the happiness of me and mine as opposed to others, on the one hand; and as responsibility toward others, on the other. It is dependent, in other words, on the general law of *différance* (which is not a law, being itself grounded in splitting). But, and perhaps more important, the relationship between capitalism and socialism is also susceptible to the passage on *différance* quoted in my text, roughly as follows: As the passage referred to in *Capital*, vol. 3 would show, socialism is not in opposition to the form of the capitalist mode of production. It is rather a constant pushing away—a differing and a deferral—of the capital-ist harnessing of the social productivity of capital. Because of the impossibility of the fully ethical, the calculations toward this *différance* get constantly jerked around the other way, the movement as much like a hardly arrested vibration in everyday decisions as like the broad-stroke swings between the public and the private sectors charted in Stephen Resnick and Richard Wolff, "Lessons from the USSR: Taking Marxian Theory the Next Step," in Bernd Magnus and Stephen Cullenberg, eds., *Whither Marxism? Global Crises in International Perspective* (New York: Routledge, 1995), pp. 207–234. It scares me to think of the risks of attempting in more than merely an academic way the double-sided program laid out in the early Derridian project in the passage quoted in the text, in terms of capitalism and socialism; yet it is the substance of organized and unorganized economic resistance. If this resistance is conceived as end rather than figured as *différance*, it gives us the Marxian description referred to in the text.

11. The European suppression of this voice in colonized Africa in the 1920s is signaled in W. E. B. Du Bois, "The Negro Mind Reaches Out," in Alain Locke, ed., *The New Negro: An Interpretation* (New York: Arno Press, 1968). This tendency is still prevalent in full force.

12. Djebar computes it in terms of women in Algeria (Djebar, "Forbidden Gaze, Severed Sound," in Marjolijn de Jager, trans., *Women of Algiers in Their Apartment* [Charlottesville: University Press of Virginia, 1992], pp. 133–151). Leila Ahmed tracks it historically in the world at large, with the metropolitan migrant group as a crucial part, in her book *The Quiet Revolution* (New Haven, CT: Yale University Press, 2011). Joachim Bergman gives a splendid description: "Desire, agency, the contextually created and varying 'sign', identity, subjugation in so many layers (man, woman, the west), political agency as identity, the Other's effect on the group, the white woman saving the brown woman—not only from the brown man but from herself, the will to replace one rigid system with another—more rigid, globalisation, national identity and the Other—it is all there. And that is just starters!" (unpublished communication).

13. See *The Nara Document* (1994), http://whc.unesco.org/archive/nara94.htm, asking the custodians of world sociality (not in either of the Marxian senses, but in the sense of the UNESCO) to "preserve" intangibles. And now culturalism has expanded beyond the located-migrant boundary. See, for example, Debarshi Dasgupta, "My Book Is Red," http://www.outlookindia.com/article.aspx?265325. In this article I see the first example (there may also have been others, of course) of a repressive postcolonial government trying to undermine the real problem and manage its own crisis, by taking a culturalist way out, and convincing metropolitan readers who readily confuse this with the metropolitan problem with bilingualism. The problem is class apartheid; the way that the rural Indian subaltern "Maoists," now collected and desperate, are dealing with the problem is by killing individual corrupt government and police functionaries in the area. Intellectual leftists have taken sides by rationally re-coding this as revolutionary struggle without any epistemological effort. To undermine even this by substituting tribal language textbooks may be useful for the actual armed struggle, but will have only negative consequences, if the battle is won by this means alone. If they really wanted to get these people moving to access to citizenship, the way is not investing in tribal language textbooks with no other change. It is similar to putting women on the quota system. When the state preserves its structure of power in every other way, the ambitious and the exceptional go to the Bengali language schools. What happens in Jharkhand, the new(ish) tribal state, for example, is that there is a Santali section (tribal language state vernacular), and sections in Bengali and Hindi, and most ambitious people even choose Bengali over Hindi, the local dominant and general national language. If one is going to make reforms of this sort, there has to be a systemic base. I write at such length here because it is proof of my telegraphic sentence about *pouvoir savoir* on another register. Otherwise the Huntingtons of the world cite the statistics of how the underclass chooses and thus defeat the argument about bilingualism, which belongs with the middle-class need to transform the performative into performance, the culture wars, the canon debates, all good things when undertaken by the middle class (Samuel Huntington, *Who Are We? The Challenges to America's National Identity* [New York: Simon & Schuster, 2004]). Ganesh Devy, a former Professor of English, who is cited in the article as the spokespeson for neutralizing the struggle via tribal-language textbooks, is a "collector," not an activist.

14. Derrida, "Mochlos; or, the Conflict of the Faculties," in *Logomachia: The Conflict of the Faculties,* ed. Richard Rand and Amy Wygant (Lincoln: University of Nebraska Press, 1992), p. 11.

15. *The World Bank and the Environment* (Washington, DC: World Bank, 1992), pp. 106, 107. This passage was included in the original version. As we move through the years, the annual reports give us a coded account of the use of indigenous knowledge, now always with the word "sustainable" in there, the indigenous peoples helping sustain the bank. The latest publication is *Environment Matters* (2009), http://go.worldbank.org/DHIO2J5UV0.

16. I use "caress" here in the philosophical sense given to it by Luce Irigaray in "The Fecundity of the Caress: A Reading of Levinas, *Totality and Infinity,* 'Phenomenology of Eros,'" in *An Ethics of Sexual Difference,* trans. Carolyn Burke and Gillian C. Gill (Ithaca, NY: Cornell University Press, 1984), pp. 185–217. I have discussed this essay at greater length in OTM, pp. 163–171.

17. For invagination, the part also larger than the whole containing and contained by the part, see Derrida, "Law of Genre," in *Glyph* 7 (1980): 202–229.

18. Derrida, *Of Grammatology,* trans. Gayatri Chakravorty Spivak (Baltimore, MD: Johns Hopkins University Press, 1976), pp. 141–164.

9. What's Left of Theory?

1. Karl Marx, *Capital,* vol. 1, trans. Ben Fowkes (London: Penguin, 1990), p. 277 (hereafter cited in the text and notes as C 1, with page numbers following).

2. Aristotle, *The Nicomachean Ethics,* trans. H. Rackham (Cambridge, MA: Harvard University Press, 1994), pp. 332–333; translation modified.

3. The attempt to philosophize it leads to theology. It is "nothing else than the historical process of divorcing the producer from the means of production" (C 1, p. 875).

4. Is it too fanciful to say Marx is a strange sort of Kantian here, turning from the reflexive to the determinant judgment, from autonomy to heteronomy, in order not to participate in the poverty of a philosophy that goes too fast to solve problems? At any rate, Marx downshifts.

5. Perry Anderson, *Considerations on Western Marxism* (London: New Left Books, 1976).

6. This insight undergirds a large part of the political argument of Deleuze and Guattari's *Anti-Oedipus.* It would be hard to isolate a specific passage. See Gilles Deleuze and Felix Guattari, *Anti-Oedipus: Capitalism and Schizophrenia,* trans. Robert Hurley, Mark Seem, and Helen R. Lane (Minneapolis: University of Minnesota Press, 1992).

7. Foreign Policy in Focus, a joint project of the Institute for Policy Studies and the Interhemispheric Resource Center, produces briefs that give the nonspecialist an idea of these dynamics.

8. Some years ago, Kali for Women (New Delhi) made an excellent documentary on Hindu widows leading a peculiar communal life in the holy town of Vrindavana. The English subtitles (middle-class sentiment emoting on their victimage) did not reveal that there was a strong cynical critique of the institution of marriage and a woman's lot in much that these widows said. A failure of translation, a difference in class culture. And then, a few weeks ago, John Burns at the *New York Times,* simply commenting on the widows' lot, again quoting, again pitying, again deploring their victimage. The subaltern is made to unspeak herself.

9. I use the words of the final Foucault because he was trying to understand ethics in its institutional coding, rather than in the deconstructive unmoor-

ing of the thematics of conscience (Michel Foucault, *The History of Sexuality*, vol. 3: *The Care of the Self,* trans. Robert Hurley [New York: Vintage, 1990]).

10. This is of course a modification of Kant's famous line: "If only freedom is granted, enlightenment is almost sure to follow" ("What Is Enlightenment?," 1784).

11. Karl Marx, *Capital: A Critique of Political Economy,* vol. 2, trans. David Fernbach (New York: Vintage, 1978), p. 131 (hereafter cited in the text as C 2, with page numbers following).

12. Karl Marx, *Capital,* vol. 3, trans. David Fernbach (New York: Viking Books, 1981), pp. 1015–1016 (hereafter cited in the text as C 3, with page numbers following).

13. Here is an example of a simple power semiotic, outside the context of my managerial specimens, of course. At my university, one of the signs of "power," not necessarily connected with sheer intellectual or pedagogic excellence, is the square footage of your living quarters. The desire to give others space—as an ethical desire—gets quenched here, as of course, if you care more for your living than your being-othered, does any (irrational?) desire to live in a snug space.

14. As always, I use "miraculating" in the sense given to the word by Deleuze and Guattari, *Anti-Oedipus,* p. 10.

15. Mahmood Mamdani, *Citizen and Subject: Contemporary Africa and the Legacy of Late Colonialism* (Princeton, NJ: Princeton University Press, 1996), pp. 203, 201.

16. See Susan Bazilli, ed., *Putting Women on the Agenda* (Johannesburg: Ravan Press, 1991), and Neville Hoad, "Between the White Man's Burden and the White Man's Disease: Tracking Lesbian and Gay Human Rights in Southern Africa," *GLQ: A Journal of Lesbian and Gay Studies* 5.4 (1999): 559–584.

17. Michel de Certeau, *The Capture of Speech and Other Political Writings,* trans. Tom Conley (Minneapolis: University of Minnesota Press, 1998), p. 161.

18. Jacques Derrida, *Glas,* trans. John P. Leavey Jr. and Richard Rand (Lincoln: University of Nebraska Press, 1986), p. 1b.

19. Raymond Williams, *Marxism and Literature* (New York: Oxford University Press, 1977), p. 123.

20. Virginia Woolf, *A Room of One's Own* (New York: Harcourt, 1929), pp. 4–5 (hereafter cited in the text as RO, with page numbers following). In this mode, Woolf cannily inscribes the connection between Western feminism and imperialism. As I insist, her fictive fiction-writing woman can do so because her "aunt, Mary Beton . . . died by a fall from her horse when she was riding out to take the air in Bombay" (p. 37).

21. Here is John Perry Barlow on the cybernetic instant enlightenment of Hmmma, a 14-year-old African boy. "See? The kid gets it. He is introduced to the computers and the Net, and 30 seconds later he knows the thing to do in this new economy is gain some attention. Advertise!" (Barlow, "Africa Rising,"

Wired magazine, January 1998, p. 8, http://www.wired.com/wired/archive/6 .01/Barlow.html). We are of course not discussing collective problem solving by faxes and such, although what long-term effect the short-run successes have is another story.

22. Karl Marx, *Early Writings,* trans. Rodney Livingstone and Gregor Benton (Harmondsworth: Penguin Books, 1975), p. 282.

23. Derrida, *Aporias,* trans. Thomas Dutoit (Stanford, CA: Stanford University Press, 1993) (hereafter cited in the text as A, with page numbers following). The passage quoted below is from pp. 12–13; translation modified.

24. It cannot be repeated often enough that both *The Communist Manifesto* and *The German Ideology* were written before Marx saw the revolution of 1848. That for me is the epistemic cut, not some attitude to humanism or Hegel.

25. Marx, *Grundrisse: Foundations of the Critique of Political Economy,* trans. Martin Nicolaus (New York: Vintage, 1973), pp. 471–493. It is as if there is a seamless continuity between Marx's nineteenth-century remarks and the United Nations publication *An Urbanizing World: Global Report on Human Settlements* (Oxford: Oxford University Press, 1996).

26. Aristotle, *Poetics,* trans. W. Hamilton Fyfe and W. Rhys Roberts (Cambridge, MA: Harvard University Press, 1991), pp. 84–85.

27. Similar implications of the Asiatic mode of production have been discussed at greater length in Spivak, *A Critique of Postcolonial Reason: Toward a History of the Vanishing Present* (Cambridge, MA: Harvard University Press, 1999), chapter 2.

28. James O'Connor, *Natural Causes: Essays in Ecological Marxism* (New York: Guilford Press, 1998) shares many of the presuppositions of this essay, explains them with much greater scholarship and authority, but finally creates an articulation of ecologism and Marxism. I see a productive rupture where he sees a potential continuity. But we are allies.

29. Etienne Balibar, *Masses, Classes, Ideas: Studies on Politics and Philosophy before and after Marx* (New York: Routledge, 1994), p. 146.

30. The earliest example I know comes from Derrida, *Of Grammatology,* trans. Gayatri Chakravorty Spivak (Baltimore, MD: Johns Hopkins University Press, 1976), p. 140. This move in Derrida is related to the impulse that makes Nietzsche investigate truth and falsity in "an extra-moral sense." The banality, the complicity with its opposite of the general sense of a concept-metaphor, often escapes Derridians. This is why he kept rejecting "good conscience deconstruction," I believe.

31. The infinite delicacy with which he "corrects" Nancy on comparable grounds in Derrida, *Politics of Friendship,* trans. George Collins (New York: Verso, 1997), p. 48n.16 is exemplary.

32. Ranajit Guha, "On Some Aspects of the Historiography of Colonial India," in *Subaltern Studies,* vol. 1 (Delhi: Oxford University Press, 1982), p. 8. Checking the passage for reference, I see that he says something slightly different, but the difference may prove interesting to the reader.

33. Mahasweta Devi, "Pterodactyl, Puran Sahay, and Pirtha," in *Imaginary Maps: Three Stories,* trans. Gayatri Chakravorty Spivak (New York: Rout-

ledge, 1993), pp. 95–196 (hereafter cited in the text as PT, with page numbers following).

34. For a nuanced scholarly account of how this should be responsibly stated, see Colin Renfrew, *Archaeology and Language: the Puzzle of Indo-European Origins* (Cambridge: Cambridge University Press, 1988).

35. Sigmund Freud, "The Uncanny," in *The Standard Edition*, vol. 17, trans. James Strachey (New York: Norton, 1961–), p. 245. Luce Irigaray's "Plato's Hystera," in *Speculum of the Other Woman,* trans. Gillian C. Gill (Ithaca, NY: Cornell University Press, 1985), pp. 243–365, is also a reinscription of this text of Freud. The irony that Irigaray, victim of masculism, writes from below and Mahasweta, descendant of colonizers, writes from above would of course be missed by the sanctioned ignorance of liberal multiculturalism.

36. V. I. Lenin, *Imperialism: The Highest Stage of Capitalism* (New York: International Publishers, 1993), p. 22.

37. UNESCO, *Encyclopedia of Life Support Systems,* www.eolss.net/.

38. For rare and relevant documentation in this context, see Najma Sadèque, *How "They" Run the World* (Lahore: Shirkat Gah, 1996), pp. 28–30. My only objection to this brilliant pamphlet is that it does not emphasize the production of the colonial subject in imperialism and thus cannot emphasize our complicity, which we must acknowledge in order to act. I keep quoting this text rather than some more "scholarly" work because of its directness and its simplicity, more appropriate to the general state of ignorance of the basic principles of these issues for the left academic in the human sciences. See also Spivak, "Bajarer Opor . . . ," *Ananda Bazar Patrika* (August 1, 1999).

39. I am referring, of course, to Salman Rushdie's remarks in the *New Yorker* (June 23 and 30, 1997), pp. 50–61, and the publication of Salman Rushdie and Elizabeth West, eds., *The Vintage Book of Indian Writing, 1947–1997* (London: Vintage, 1997), containing writing only in English. Aamir Mufti, "Orientalism and the Institution of World Literature," *Critical Inquiry* 36.3 (March 1, 2010): 458–493, has an excellent discussion of this phenomenon.

40. De Man, *Allegories of Reading: Figural Language in Rousseau, Nietzsche, Rilke, and Proust* (New Haven, CT: Yale University Press, 1979), p. 301. I have altered two words. I invite the reader to ponder the changes. There are, of course, plenty of references to these movements in mainstream journals such as *The Ecologist* and in the New Social Movement support groups in the United States such as the International Waters group. In academic left literature not specifically connected to the third world, the best we can do is something like O'Connor's "thousands of groups (formal and informal) and dozens of political parties in Africa, Asia, and Latin America are evolving programs that include elements drawn from both the old political Left and ecology. Clearly, radical ecology is becoming a force to reckon with, and to work with, and to defend and advance" (O'Connor, *Natural Causes,* p. 15). Although this statement overlooks the crucial difference between party politics and these alliances, it acknowledges their long-term existence and makes no claim to leadership. His chapter on "International Red Green Movements"

(pp. 299–305) is the shortest in the book, and has the obligatory references to Mexico and the Narmada. Rosalyn Deutsche's *Evictions: Art and Spatial Politics* (Cambridge, MA: MIT Press, 1996), certainly a breakthrough for New York–based Cultural Studies, faults "new social movements" for generally "positivist" understanding of social practice, without ever defining them. I have no doubt she is thinking of Euro/U.S.-based identity politics of one sort or another, including environmentalism; but cannot of course be sure. That she is not aware of the powerful global parabasis to which I am referring seems certain. Yet she faults "traditional left intellectuals" (undoubtedly confined to the phantom U.S. Left and her own take on the gender-debates forever commemorated by the 1960s so-called New Left): "Masculinism as a position of social authority is also about the authority of traditional left intellectuals to account for the political condition of the entire world. What measures does it take to reestablish this authority in the name of the public?" (p. 312). Deutsche celebrates "an essential limitlessness" (p. 275)—a species of anti-essentialist essentialism—where "public space" is finally seen to be "structured like a language." This is the problem with Derridians that I refer to above. The lesson about the problem with making language your explanatory model of last resort might have been learned even from "Structure, Sign and Play in the Discourse of the Human Sciences," in Derrida, *Writing and Difference,* trans. Alan Bass (Chicago: University of Chicago Press, 1978), pp. 278–295. Deutsche's basic good sense in the New York context is fortunately at odds with these theoretical pronouncements. She clearly knows that limitlessness requires the drawing of limits that must remain open, and thus is bound; that the structure of language is forever compromised with reference. (One interesting conclusion to be drawn from her work is that, even as the subaltern in the Southern Hemisphere is the focus of spectral networking, the category of the "homeless," everywhere, fills the place of the earlier definition of the subaltern: beings cut off from all lines of mobility. On the homeless as subject of freedom, see Jeremy Waldron, "Homelessness and the Issue of Freedom," *UCLA Law Review* 39.2 (1992): 295–324. On the other side of the spectrum, it is interesting that, as of March 21, 1998 (Conference on "Does America Have a Democratic Mission?", University of Virginia), Lawrence Eagleburger, George Bush's Secretary of State, had not heard the words "New Social Movement"!

41. Paul Virilio/Sylvère Lotringer, *Pure War,* trans. Mark Polizzotti (New York: Semiotext[e], 1997), pp. 13–14.

42. Virilio, *Open Sky,* trans. Julie Rose (New York: Verso, 1997), p. 71; translation modified. Virilio's book *Popular Defense and Ecological Struggles,* trans. Mark Polizzotti (New York: Semiotext[e], 1990) is all about European theories of war.

10. Echo

1. Christopher Lasch, *The Culture of Narcissism* (New York: Norton, 1983). For a socialist-feminist reading of Lasch's book, see Michèle Barrett and

Mary McIntosh, "Narcissism and the Family: A Critique of Lasch," *New Left Review* 135 (September–October 1982): 35–48.

2. See Catharine A. MacKinnon, *Are Women Human? And Other International Dialogues* (Cambridge, MA: Harvard University Press, 2006), and Kelly Oliver, *Women as Weapons of War: Iraq, Sex and the Media* (New York: Columbia University Press, 2007).

3. Frédrique Delacoste and Priscilla Alexander, eds., *Sex Work: Writings by Women in the Sex Industry* (Pittsburgh: Cleis Press, 1987).

4. Sigmund Freud, "On Narcissism: An Introduction," in *The Standard Edition*, vol. 14, trans. James Strachey (New York: Norton, 1961–), pp. 93–94, 101 (hereafter cited in the text as SE, with volume and page numbers following). See also Anahid Kassabian and David Kazanjian, "From Somewhere Else: Egoyan's Calendar, Freud's Rat Man, and Armenian Diasporic Nationalism," *Third Text* 19.2 (2005): 125–144.

5. My point lately has been that Oedipus had trouble with Oedipus (see Chapter 25, "Tracing the Skin of Day," in this book), that Sophocles' Oedipus questions the Law of the Father. The play begins with an alternative possibility of human birth. The implications are coiled in the labyrinth of Derrida, *The Animal*. See Jacques Derrida, *The Animal That Therefore I Am*, trans. David Wills (New York: Fordham University Press, 2008).

6. See Spivak, "Time and Timing: Law and History," in John Bender and David Wellbery, eds., *Chronotypes: The Construction of Time* (Stanford, CA: Stanford University Press, 1991), pp. 99–117.

7. See Spivak, "The Politics of Translation," in *Outside in the Teaching Machine* (New York: Routledge, 2009), pp. 200–225 (hereafter cited in the text and notes as OTM, with page numbers following).

8. V. S. Naipaul, *India: A Wounded Civilization* (New York: Knopf, 1977), pp. 107–23; see also Naipaul, *India: A Million Mutinies Now* (New York: Knopf, 1977), passim. In the case of the United States, here is a peculiar rag-bag, all denominated "narcissism": "After all the machinations of leftist sects, homosexual activists, self-indulgent businessmen, therapeutic functionaries, would-be and actual politicos and others, the killer continues to punctuate the real tragedy: the total domination and helplessness that define clientage in organized capitalism" (Adolph Reed Jr., "Narcissistic Politics in Atlanta," *Telos* 14.48 [Summer 1981]: 105).

9. Lévinas, *Otherwise than Being or Beyond Essence*, trans. Alphonso Lingis (The Hague: Martinus Nijhoff, 1981).

10. Derrida, "Geopsychanalyse—'and the rest of the world,'" in Christopher Lane, ed., *Psychoanalysis of Race* (New York: Columbia University Press, 1998), pp. 65–90.

11. Spivak, *A Critique of Postcolonial Reason: Toward a History of the Vanishing Present* (Cambridge, MA: Harvard University Press, 1999), p. 116 (hereafter cited in the text as CPR, with page numbers following).

12. "Kant's categorical imperative is thus the direct heir of the Oedipus complex" (Freud, "The Economic Problem of Masochism," in *The Standard Edition*, vol. 19, trans. James Strachey [New York: Norton, 1961–], p. 16)

(hereafter cited in the notes as SE, with volume and page numbers following) might be the most self-assured declaration of this affiliation. For more extensive documentation, see, of course, the Kant entry in the index to SE 24, p. 212.

13. Jon Elster, *Ulysses and the Sirens* (Cambridge: Cambridge University Press, 1979). Elster, who is writing directly about Odysseus as the felicitous subject of the European Enlightenment, misses out on the usefulness of the sailors, with enforced wax in their ears, who are essential for his enlightened behavior. Class rather than gender or race. I hope the reader will work this out.

14. Sigmund Freud, "Analysis Terminable and Interminable," in SE 23, pp. 211–253; see also Derrida, "The Force of Law: The 'Mystical Foundation of Authority,'" trans. Mary Quaintance, in Gil Anidjar, ed., *Acts of Religion* (London: Routledge, 2002), pp. 228–298.

15. Bimal Krishna Matilal, *The Word and the World: India's Contribution to the Study of Language* (Delhi: Oxford University Press, 1990), pp. 70–71.

16. Investigations of Echo in Indic discourse would lead us into the rational linguistic tradition of *dhvani* and *pratidhvani,* quite apart from mythic and epic narrative.

17. Georg Wilhelm Friedrich Hegel, *Aesthetics: Lectures on Fine Art,* trans. Thomas M. Knox, vol. 1 (Oxford: Clarendon Press, 1975), p. 361.

18. Ovid, *Metamorphoses,* 2nd ed., trans. Frank Justus Miller (Loeb Classical Library) (Cambridge, MA: Harvard University Press, 1966), book I, line 3 (hereafter cited in the text and notes as M, with page and line numbers following); translations modified.

19. Freud, "Group Psychology and the Analysis of the Ego," in SE 18, p. 130.

20. Luce Irigaray, "Sexual Difference," in Toril Moi, ed., *French Feminist Thought: A Reader* (Oxford: Oxford University Press, 1987), p. 122.

21. Ellie Ragland-Sullivan, "Jacques Lacan: Feminism and the Problem of Gender Identity," *Sub-Stance* 11.3 (1982): 6–19.

22. Jacques Lacan, "The Mirror Stage as Formative of the Function of the I as Revealed in Psychoanalytic Experience," in *Écrits: A Selection,* trans. Alan Sheridan (New York: Norton, 1977), pp. 6, 7.

23. Ibid., p. 2.

24. The notion of an underived fiction is borrowed from Derrida, *Limited Inc,* trans. Samuel Weber (Evanston, IL: Northwestern University Press, 1988), p. 96. Jacqueline Rose indicates the difference between Freud and Lacan without commenting on the relative philosophical banality of Lacan's position. She shows that in the later Lacan the subject's move from primary to secondary narcissism is the move from the Imaginary to the Symbolic. What interests me, as my final extended comments on Claire Nouvet will show, is that although the insertion into the Symbolic seems to invite a consideration of the Echo-response situation, Rose does not mention her: "the two moments of [the mirror] phase, that of the corporeal image [which Lacan describes as primary narcissism], prior and resistant to symbolisation, and that of the relation to the other [the place of secondary narcissism], ultimately

dependent on such symbolisation" (Jacqueline Rose, *Sexuality in the Field of Vision* [London: Verso, 1986], pp. 178–179).

25. For an extensive treatment of the Narcissus tradition and narcissism, see Louise Vinge, *The Narcissus Theme in Western European Literature Up to the Early 19th Century*, trans. Robert Dewsnap (Lund: Gleerups, 1967). (Professor Georgia Nugent has pointed out to me that there is a mythic tradition of Echo as coupled with Pan which is rather different from the Ovidian narrative. An ethical-instantiation reading focuses on a narrativization rather than a myth. I look forward to a historical meditation upon the vicissitudes of Echo in the history of myth, but that is not my concern here.) Any consideration of Narcissus and narcissism would fall into the literary and the psychoanalytic. I have not considered them in detail in my text because they do not, strictly speaking, have much bearing on a performative ethical reading in the context of feminism in decolonization. Among the Christian allegorical readings in the Ovid *moralisé*, we find Echo interpreted as "good reputation" and in Christine de Pisan's *Epistre d'Orthea* as "anyone who asks for help in great need" (see Vinge, *The Narcissus Theme*, pp. 94, 101). I have no doubt that an extended look at these texts with a gender-sensitive theoretical perspective would yield exciting results. Although not particularly gender sensitive, Joseph Lowenstein's *Responsive Readings: Versions of Echo in Pastoral, Epic, and the Jonsonian Masque* (New Haven, CT: Yale University Press, 1984) is a more theoretical and sympathetic analysis of the trajectory of Echo than Vinge's older study. He is, however, interested in the "myth of Echo," that which remains across rhetorical narrativizations, "as the myth of cultural memory" (p. 5). His Echo is caught between "the genius of myth, of sorts" and the "phenomenology of acoustical reflection itself" (pp. 10, 9). When he speaks of ethics, he is analyzing the structuring of stories rather than the conduct of the rhetorical texture of storying as instantiations of ethical responsibility (p. 132). To be sure, the predicament of the self-conscious feminist allied by class with imperialism has something in common with the romantic notion of the self-conscious artist as Narcissus (Rousseau's *Narcisse*, Friedrich Schlegel's *Lucinde*), for those texts emerge at the height of Western European colonialism and imperialism. The trajectory of romanticism is so well traveled that I will wait for future criticism to lay bare that common ground from this political perspective. Since Echo's role is not significantly an independent position in psychoanalytic treatments, I have paid little or no attention to the growing literature on identification from this perspective. In conclusion, I have addressed "psychoanalysis" in a general way.

26. For the definitive discussion of this passage, see John Brenkman, "Narcissus in the Text," *Georgia Review* 30 (1976): 293–327.

27. Strictly speaking, there is another bit of reported speech in the narrative. When Narcissus cries *veni!* (Come!) Ovid does not give the perfectly possible echo—*veni!* (Come!)—or even, with a little trick of vowel length, again perfectly acceptable within echo as a phenomenon, "I have come!" (I am grateful for this latter suggestion to Professor Georgia Nugent.) In this particular

case, it seems as if there is an embarrassment of successful response here, as opposed to the ethically more useful bit that I discuss. And indeed the style of Ovid's reportage is also noticeably different. If in the *fugis/fugi* reporting, Ovid reports Narcissus as receiving back the words he said, in the *veni/veni* reporting, Ovid gives Echo a plenitude of voicing: *vocat illa vocantem* (M, p. 150, line 382, she calls him calling, calls the calling one, voices the voicer). The ethical-instantiation reader must choose between a gendered agency that can speak its desire within gendering, where the narrator reports her (internalized constraint as a version of) fulfilled choice, or a gendered aporia that goes beyond mere (historically contaminated) intention. For our part, a greater responsibility beckons in the instantiation of the possibility that history is in all respects larger than personal goodwill.

28. The reader will notice that I too have played a translator's trick here, substituted the Greek Lethe for the Latin Styx. Latin does not have an exact equivalent of *aletheia* for truth (thereby hangs Heidegger).

29. Jacques Derrida, "Signature Event Context," in *Margins of Philosophy*, trans. Alan Bass (Chicago: University of Chicago Press, 1982), p. 318.

30. For the importance of reported speech in the Law of Genre, as I have insisted, we must elaborate a position from V. N. Vološinov, *Marxism and the Philosophy of Language*, trans. Ladislav Matejka and I. R. Titunik (Cambridge, MA: Harvard University Press, 1973), pp. 115f. I have attempted to do this in the context of multiracial representation as well (unpublished colloquium, Congress of South African Writers, Cape Town, August 15, 1992).

31. Derrida, *The Post Card: From Socrates to Freud and Beyond*, trans. Alan Bass (Chicago: University of Chicago Press, 1987), p. 123; translation slightly modified. Cited in Derrida, "Pour l'amour de Lacan," in Natalia S. Avtonomova, *Lacan avec les philosophes* (Paris: Albin Michel, 1991), pp. 416–417.

32. Derrida, "Le Facteur de la vérité," in *Post Card*, pp. 413–496; also Derrida, "The Force of Law: The 'Mystical Foundation of Authority,'" in "Deconstruction and the Possibility of Justice," *Cardozo Law Review* 6.5–6 (July–August 1990): 264 and passim.

33. Assia Djebar, *Fantasia: An Algerian Cavalcade*, trans. Dorothy S. Blair (New York: Quartet Books, 1985) (hereafter cited in the text as F, with page numbers following).

34. Derrida, *Of Grammatology*, trans. Gayatri Chakravorty Spivak (Baltimore, MD: Johns Hopkins University Press, 1976), p. 175.

35. Here and elsewhere, I am struck by the affinities and differences between Djebar and Derrida, two compatriots separated by ethnocultural and sexual difference. If in *Glas* Derrida kept the name of the mother a blank by the positioning of the "L" (French *elle*=mother) on the page, and the female thing unnamed by contrasting *Savoir absolu* to *Sa* (the third person singular genitive with an unspecified female object), Djebar keeps the autobiographical culture-divided female subject's name a blank by the ruse of proper naming. (*Sa* is everywhere in *Glas*. For the placing of the "L," see Jacques Derrida, *Glas*, trans. John P. Leavey Jr. and Richard Rand [Lincoln: University of Nebraska

Press, 1986], p. 261b. For a general commentary, see Gayatri Chakravorty Spivak, "*Glas*-Piece: A *Compte rendu*," *Diacritics* 7.3 [Autumn 1977]: 22–43.)

36. See the listing under *tzarl-rit,* in *Dictionnaire pratique arabe-français,* ed. Marcelin Beaussier (1871; reprint, Algiers: La maison des livres, 1958); quoted in F, p. 221.

37. See the listing under *tzarl-rit,* in *Dictionnaire arabe-français,* ed. Albert de Biberstein-Kazimirski (Paris: Maison-neuve et cie, 1860); quoted in F, p. 221.

38. In the context of a traditional culture that is fully oral in its beginnings, I would like to refer here to the African National Congress Women's Charter of 1954 (see Raymond Suttner and Jeremy Cronin, *30 Years of the Freedom Charter* [Johannesburg: Raven Press, 1986], pp. 162–164).

39. Assia Djebar, "Forbidden Gaze, Severed Sound," in Marjolijn de Jager, trans., *Women of Algiers in Their Apartment* (Charlottesville: University Press of Virginia, 1992), pp. 133–152.

40. Claire Nouvet, "An Impossible Response: The Disaster of Narcissus," *Yale French Studies* 79 (1991): 103–134 (hereafter cited in the text and notes as IR, with page numbers following). I am grateful to Dorothea von Mücke for bringing this essay to my attention.

41. Ibid., p. 111. Yet on the next page, Nouvet makes a peculiarly characterological move by assigning to Narcissus one, rather than another, phenomenal affect—fear rather than pride—and constructs a new reading on it. As the next sentence of my text will suggest, such a slippage is good "polytheist" practice, and problematic only if one sees character and figure in opposition.

42. I have commented on the "monotheist" habit of the imagining of the subject of the ethical decision in a number of texts, most accessibly in "Not Virgin Enough . . . ," in OTM, pp. 193–199, and in "Moving Devi," in Gayatri Chakravorty Spivak, *Other Asias* (Oxford: Blackwell, 2008), pp. 175–208.

43. Max Müller, *Lectures on the Origin and Growth of Religion: As Illustrated by the Religions of India* (London: Longmans, 1878), pp. 260–316. He, like all German Orientalists, did of course unquestioningly accept the existence of an "Aryan" race.

44. The first quoted phrase is from Derrida, "The Force of Law," p. 255, and the second, a passage already cited here, from Derrida, "Mochlos; or, the Conflict of the Faculties," in *Logomachia: The Conflict of the Faculties,* ed. Richard Rand and Amy Wygant (Lincoln: University of Nebraska Press, 1992), p. 11; the French original of this quotation is to be found in Derrida, *Du droit a la philosophie* (Paris: Galilée, 1990), pp. 408, 424.

45. Incidentally, this shift is reflected in Derrida's move from "reticen[ce]" because the ethical "presupposes . . . the self" (Derrida and Pierre-Jean Labarriere, *Alterités* [Paris: Osiris, 1986], p. 76; cited in IR, p. 103) to ethics as "the *experience* of the impossible" ("The Force of Law," p. 264, that this move is particularly significant for Derrida is indicated by the fact that in the latter Derrida is citing an earlier piece by himself. In the general methodology of *The Animal,* "an experience of the impossible"—the way to an inclusive epistemology—is itself shown to involve a mad contortion that never quite grasps or *begreift.*

46. Is this because of Lacan's unseen presence? "Two factors emerge from this preliminary delineation of the Imaginary—the factor of aggression, rivalry, the image as alienating on the one hand, and the more structurally oriented notion of a fundamental mis-recognition as the foundation of subjectivity, with the image as salutary fiction, on the other" (Rose, *Sexuality in the Field of Vision*, p. 175). The difference between the subject's history and mythic story being that in myth it is a "knowledge" rather than a misrecognition, and the fiction is not "salutary" in a curative sense. Oedipus does sleep with his mother; he does not just want to.

47. Maurice Blanchot, *The Writing of the Disaster*, trans. Ann Smock (Lincoln: University of Nebraska Press, 1986), pp. 125ff.; cited in IR, pp. 128ff.

48. See André Green, *Narcissisme de vie, narcissisme de mort* (Paris: Minuit, 1983) (hereafter cited in the text as NVM, with page numbers following) (my translations).

49. Luce Irigaray will undo this in her brilliant *je, tu, nous: Toward a Culture of Difference*, trans. Alison Martin (New York: Routledge, 1993).

50. The best reading within this epistemo-teleology is Juliet Mitchell's (although I am not sure why she writes that "Narcissus never believed that what he saw in the pond's mirror was himself"): "The mirror did not give him himself, because the only one in the world he had to tell him where he was, was Echo, the absolute other, to whom none could get attached because she would not listen [why?] and who did no more than repeat the words of Narcissus's own self-fascination. But no one could have done any more; for Narcissus is confined in intra-subjectivity" (Juliet Mitchell, *Psychoanalysis and Feminism* [Harmondsworth: Penguin, 1975], pp. 38, 39).

51. Samuel Weber, *The Legend of Freud* (Minneapolis: University of Minnesota Press, 1982) (hereafter cited in the text as LF, with page numbers following).

52. As Jacqueline Rose has pointed out, in the mature Lacan the Imaginary slides into the Symbolic, primary into secondary narcissism. A single sentence will have to suffice here: "Hence, the symbolic equation that we rediscover between these objects arises from an alternating mechanism of expulsion and introjection, of projection and absorption, that is to say from an imaginary interplay" (Lacan, "The Topic of the Imaginary," in *The Seminar of Jacques Lacan: Book 1, Freud's Papers on Technique* 1953–54, trans. John Forrester [New York: Norton, 1988], p. 82). This is still, of course, a continuist simplification of Freud's discontinuous dynamics, what Weber calls "the play of speculation." I refer my reader to Freud's reverse definitions of speculation and science, quoted on page 222.

53. Wallace Stevens, "Peter Quince at the Clavier," in *The Collected Poems of Wallace Stevens* (New York: Vintage Books, 1990, c1954), pp. 89–91. The lines of the poem read, "Beauty is momentary in the mind— / . . . But in the flesh it is immortal."

54. James Joyce, *Finnegans Wake* (New York: Faber and Faber, 1939), p. 13.

11. Translation as Culture

1. What follows is my own interpretative digest of Melanie Klein, *Works,* vols. 1–4 (New York: Free Press, 1984). Giving specific notes is therefore impossible. The details may also not resemble orthodox Kleinian psychoanalysis.

2. Jacques Derrida, *Given Time I: Counterfeit Money,* trans. Peggy Kamuf (Chicago: University of Chicago Press, 1992).

3. This more colloquial sense is where we locate Charles Taylor, *Multiculturalism and the Politics of Recognition* (Princeton, NJ: Princeton University Press, 1994).

4. I have referred to this example in Spivak, *A Critique of Postcolonial Reason: Toward a History of the Vanishing Present* (Cambridge, MA: Harvard University Press, 1999), p. 404.

5. Peggy Rockman Napaljarri and Lee Cataldi, trans., *Yimikirli: Warlpiri Dreamings and Histories* (San Francisco: HarperCollins, 1994), pp. xvii, 20. The immense labor of thinking the relationship of this "mnemonic mapping" with "satellite positioning technology offer[ing] a definitive solution to this question, which some claim has troubled us from our origin: where am I?" must be undertaken without foregone conclusions. (Laura Kurgan and Xavier Costa, eds., *You Are Here: Architecture and Information Flows* [Barcelona: Museum of Contemporary Art, 1995], p. 121. The entire text, especially the visuals, should be studied with an "active" perusal of *Yimikirli,* which may now be impossible. The necessary yet impossible task of cultural translation is made possible and ruined by the march of history.)

6. Napaljarri and Cataldi, *Yimikirli,* p. xxii.

7. A. B. Lord, *The Singer of Tales* (New York: Atheneum, 1965).

8. The film is based on Rabindranath Tagore's novel *Gharé Bairé.* In an essay on translation it should be noticed that the English title is a mistranslation. It does not catch the delicacy of the threshold effect of the original, which is in the locative case, and might translate as "inside outside," or the more literal "at home/abroad."

9. I have discussed the hospitality of the subordinated toward the dominant in Spivak, "Arguments for a Deconstructive Cultural Studies," in Nicholas Royle, ed., *Deconstructions: A User's Guide* (Oxford: Blackwell, 2000), pp. 14–43.

10. One of the most important concept-metaphors in Sanskrit aesthetics. Literally, "resonance."

11. Gayatri Chakravorty Spivak, *Outside in the Teaching Machine* (New York: Routledge, 2009), pp. 197–200.

12. The Jnanpith Award, instituted on May 22, 1961, is given for the best overall contribution to literature by any Indian citizen in any of the languages included in the VIII Schedule of the Indian Constitution. Mahasweta Devi won it in 1996.

13. I understand that the West Bengal State Academy of Letters has since then issued a student dictionary. My own efforts are now halted in red tape.

14. A zamindar is a landowner who became a tax collector for the British at the time of the Permanent Settlement of Bengal in 1793. (See Ranajit Guha, *A*

Rule of Property for Bengal [Paris: Mouton, 1963].) To see how tribals are "used" as cannon fodder in the name of "Maoism," see Nirmalangshu Mukherjee, "The State of the War," http://www.outlookindia.com/article .aspx?277662, and Prasenjit Bose, ed., *Maoism: A Critique from the Left* (Delhi: LeftWord, 2010).

12. Translating into English

This chapter was first presented as a keynote address on January 17, 2001, at the Sahitya Akademi (the National Academy of Letters), at a conference of translators. Since India has at least twenty-two languages, the internal translators were not all knowledgeable about Derrida, Foucault, and Lacan, though Kant was known to some, and Marx, of course, to all.

1. Immanuel Kant, "Religion within the Boundaries of Mere Reason," in Allen W. Wood and George di Giovanni, eds., *Religion and Rational Theology* (Cambridge: Cambridge University Press, 1996), pp. 39–215.

2. It is not that translators since the eighteenth century have not been aware that problems exist. The best-known is the *Willkür-Wille* distinction, which the great translator T. K. Abbott translated as "elective will" and "will," respectively, thus coming close to the sense of the mere mechanical ability to select one thing rather than the other, preserved in the ordinary language associations of "whim" or "willfulness" attached to Willkür. This is why, as John R. Silber notes, Kant associates Willkür with heteronomy rather than autonomy. Silber seems to me to be correct in suggesting that "the discovery and formulation of meanings for these terms was . . . one of Kant's foremost achievements in the *Religion* and in the *Metaphysic of Morals*. . . . The evolving complexity of Kant's theory of the will is missed by the English reader unless they can know when Kant is using '*Wille*' and when he is using '*Willkür*'" ("Introduction," in Kant, *Religion within the Limits of Reason Alone*, trans. Theodore M. Greene and Hoyt H. Hudson (New York: Harper, 1960), p. lxxxiv.

3. "Parergon" is Kant's word, describing a task that is outside the limits of the work undertaken ("Mere Reason," p. 96 and passim). It is to be noticed that these parerga belong not only to the work of mere reason but to that of pure reason as well. To discuss this detail is beyond the scope of this chapter.

4. Karl Marx, *Capital,* vol. 1, trans. Ben Fowkes (London: Penguin, 1990), p. 90.

5. Jacques Lacan, "The Line and Light," in *The Four Fundamental Concepts of Psychoanalysis,* trans. Alan Sheridan (New York: W. W. Norton, 1978), p. 95.

6. Michel Foucault, *The History of Sexuality,* vol. 1: *An Introduction,* trans. Robert Hurley (New York: Pantheon, 1978), p. 96.

7. For an assessment of the limits of the international civil society, see Satendra Prasad, "Limits and Possibilities for Civil Society Led Redemocratization," *Prime* (2000), pp. 3–28; for a somewhat unexamined encomium, see Homi

K. Bhabha, "Democracy De-realized," in Okwui Enwezor, ed., *Documenta 11, Platform 1: Democracy Unrealized* (Ostfildern-Ruit: Hatje Cantz, 2002), pp. 346–364.

8. The translation appeared in 2002 (Kolkata: Seagull Books).

9. I have discussed the ambivalence of *al haq* in "Imperative to Re-imagine the Planet," Chapter 16 in this book. Patrick Wolfe has an interesting comment about "hock" and *haq*, an unwitting coupling on my part: "I have nothing to base this on, but I can't help feeling that your text isn't the first place that these words have met up. In English, 'hock' has to do with ransoming— opposing groups (men and women, tenants and landlords, etc) mock-kidnapped each other (tying up and trussing were involved) at Easter time and dues had to be paid for their return. A fair amount of ransoming went on during the Crusades. A practice associated with Saracens, hence the Arabic loan-word? Wild and woolly, I may well be suffering from a William Jones complex, but no doubt there's a philologist somewhere who'd know" (private communication).

10. *Of Grammatology,* of course.

11. Farhad Mazhar, *Ashomoyer Noteboi* (Dhaka: Protipokkho, 1994), p. 42; translation mine. I have discussed this poem in another context in Spivak, *A Critique of Postcolonial Reason: Toward a History of the Vanishing Present* (Cambridge, MA: Harvard University Press, 1999), pp. 362–363n (hereafter cited in the notes as CPR).

12. Friedrich Nietzsche, *Untimely Meditations,* trans. R. J. Hollingdale (Cambridge: Cambridge University Press, 1983).

13. Ibid., p. 106; translation modified. See also pp. 22, 55, 60, 95, 146, 206, and 251.

14. Gianni Vattimo, *Nietzsche: An Introduction,* trans. Nicholas Martin (London: Athlone, 2002), pp. 31–32.

15. Michel Foucault, "Nietzsche, Genealogy, History," in *Language, Counter-Memory, Practice: Selected Essays and Interviews,* trans. Donald F. Bouchard and Sherry Simon (Ithaca, NY: Cornell University Press, 1977), pp. 162–163; translation modified.

16. Derrida, *Of Spirit: Heidegger and the Question,* trans. Geoffrey Bennington and Rachel Bowlby (Chicago: University of Chicago Press, 1989), pp. 54 and 57n.3.

17. Friends of the Hindu god Krishna. Mazhar typically mingles the Hindu and Muslim elements of Bengali culture. More about this in the text.

18. I have discussed this at greater length in CPR. Homi Bhabha misses this important and substantive religion/caste point when he quotes Alexander Duff as relating English and the Brahmins as proof of the merely formal irreducibility of hybridity (Bhabha, "Commitment to Theory," *Location of Culture* [New York: Routledge, 1994], p. 33).

19. For discussions of the Bangladeshi language movement, see *Chinta* 22–23 (March 15, 2000): 20–25.

20. I have discussed this in terms of the name "Asia" in "Our Asias," in *Other Asias* (Oxford: Blackwell, 2008), pp. 209–238.

21. Akhtaruzzaman Ilias, *Chilekothar Sepai* (Dhaka: University Press, 1995); Ilias, *Khoabnama* (Dhaka: Maola Brothers, 1996).

22. Emile Benveniste, *Indo-European Language and Society,* trans. Elizabeth Palmer (London: Faber, 1973).

23. Aristotle, *Poetics,* trans. W. Hamilton Fyfe and W. Rhys Roberts (Cambridge, MA: Harvard University Press, 1991), p. 29.

24. Assia Djebar, "Overture," in *Women of Algiers in Their Apartment,* trans. Marjolijn de Jager (Charlottesville: University Press of Virginia, 1992).

25. Rokeya Sakhawat Hossain, *Sultana's Dream and Selections from the Secluded Ones,* trans. Roushan Jahan (New York: Feminist Press, 1988).

26. Benoy Majumdar, *Gayatrike* (Kolkata: Protibhash, 2002), "Foreword," n.p. (hereafter cited in the text by page numbers alone).

27. I have just read Derrida's *Rogues* (*Rogues: Two Essays on Reason,* trans. Pascale-Anne Brault and Michael Naas [Stanford, CA: Stanford University Press, 2005]) (before *Voyous* [Jacques Derrida, *Voyous: Deux essais sur la raison* (Paris: Galilée, 2003)] was translated as such, in fact). His luminous and anguished words on the wheel ("The Roue," in *Voyous,* pp. 19–41; in *Rogues,* pp. 1–2) add greater poignancy to this singular narrative.

28. Cited in Spivak, *Death of a Discipline* (New York: Columbia University Press, 2003), p. 22.

29. I am using Derridian language here. The editor of the facsimile edition thinks there is some connection between Benoy's perceptive glance and my "spreading Derrida," as she puts it (Kankabati Dutta, "À Propos," n.p.). Perhaps there's something there, but she has got her dates wrong. I started teaching Derrida (and Lacan, and Foucault) in the 1960s, not the 1980s.

30. I was in Kolkata for two nights recently, after this essay was submitted to the editors. It was the time of the justly celebrated Calcutta Book Fair. There seemed to be a Benoy Majumdar revival. I acquired the slim *Complete Works.* I read this, written in 1992, thirty-one years after book publication, in a letter: "Gayatri Chakravorty was a student at Presidency College, and came First Class First in English in her B.A., in 1960 or 1961 A.D. [actually 1959], thinking that she alone would understand my poems the book *To Gayatri* was addressed to her, and therefore I called the book *To Gayatri,* and I wrote in the book what I had to say to her" ("Patraboli," *Ishwareer Swarachito Nibandha o Anyanya* [Kolkata: Pratibhash, 1995], p. 3).

But also this, in 1986, in an interview, twenty-five years later: I wanted to ask [says the interviewer]—Were you in love with Gayatri?

Hey, no—I only knew her for two or three days—she was a famously beautiful student of English literature at Presidency College—then she went off somewhere—to America or some place, I'm not sure.

Then why write poems about her?

One must write about someone, after all. Can one write forever about mango trees, jackfruit trees, and tuberoses? ("Phire Esho Chakar Nam Paribartan Shommondhe," *Kabyoshamogro,* vol. 1 [Kolkata: Pratibhash, 1993], p. 162.)

Benoy had in fact never exchanged a word with Gayatri. Translator's note: the three items in the last sentence seem exotic in English. They are the Bengali equivalent of: "apples and pears and red, red roses," let us say. I include these passages here in the interest of bibliographical detail. To think through their implications will take time.

13. Nationalism and the Imagination

1. The Indian version of this chapter was published as "Nationalism and the Imagination," in C. Vijayasree, Meenakshi Mukherjee, and Harish Trivedi, eds., *Nation in Imagination: Essays on Nationalism, Sub-Nationalisms and Narration* (Hyderabad: Orient Longman, 2007), pp. 1–20; reprinted in Italian translation in *aut aut* 329 (January–March 2006): 65–90.

2. In Althusser's formulation, interpellation refers to the mechanism by which ideology creates the subject by "hailing" the individual. For Althusser, ideology "represents the imaginary relationship of individuals to their real conditions of existence." See Louis Althusser, "Ideology and Ideological State Apparatuses (Notes Towards an Investigation)," in *"Lenin and Philosophy" and Other Essays*, trans. Ben Brewster (New York: Monthly Review Press, 1971), pp. 127–186.

3. Bulgaria was under Ottoman control for almost five centuries. It became an Ottoman vassal state in 1372 and was incorporated into the Ottoman Empire in 1396; the Russo-Turkish War (1877–1878) resulted in the formation of an autonomous principality of Bulgaria in 1878, but it was not until 1908 that full independence was recognized. See, for example, R. J. Crampton, *Bulgaria* (Oxford: Oxford University Press, 2007), pp. 18–23, 150–189. The identity of the nation and the state is generally associated with the Peace of Westphalia (1648), often thought of as one of the inaugurations of the Enlightenment. See, for example, R. Paul Churchill, "Hobbes and the Assumption of Power," in Peter Caws, ed., *The Causes of Quarrel: Essays on Peace, War, and Thomas Hobbes* (Boston: Beacon Press, 1988), p. 17.

4. Khaled Ziadeh, *Neighborhoods and Boulevard,* trans. Samah Samad (New York: Palgrave, forthcoming), gives a superb picture of this sort of change.

5. Moinak Biswas's film *Sthaniya Sambaad* (directed by Arjun Gourisaria and Moinak Biswas, Black Magic Motion Pictures, 2009) attempts to capture this moment and these changes.

6. I have discussed these circumstances, and the imperative to invert them to give truth a chance, in "Constructing a Personal Past," 5th Dilip Kumar Roy Memorial Oration, Kolkata, 2010.

7. A member of the People's Liberation Insurgent Army during World War II, Todor Khristov Zhivkov (1911–1998) was Bulgaria's authoritarian ruler for thirty-five years, first as secretary of the Bulgarian Communist Party's Central Committee (1954–1989) and then as president (1971–1989). The Zhivkov regime's assimilation campaign, begun in 1984 and continuing until the regime's fall in 1989, sought to force all ethnic Turks to renounce Muslim cultural practices. See, for example, Crampton, *Bulgaria,* pp. 352–381.

8. Eric J. Hobsbawm, *Nations and Nationalism since 1780: Programme, Myth, Reality* (Cambridge: Cambridge University Press, 1990).

9. Jürgen Habermas, *The Postnational Constellation: Political Essays* (Cambridge: Polity Press, 2001).

10. Ngũgĩ wa Thiong'o, *Decolonising the Mind: The Politics of Language in African Literature* (London: J. Currey, 1986). See Chapter 1.

11. Maryse Condé, *Heremakhonon,* trans. Richard Philcox (Washington, DC: Three Continents, 1982), p. 24.

12. Gregory Massell, *The Surrogate Proletariat: Moslem Women and Revolutionary Strategies in Soviet Central Asia 1919–1929* (Princeton, NJ: Princeton University Press, 1974).

13. This paragraph is quoted from Spivak, *Other Asias* (Oxford: Blackwell, 2008), p. 123.

14. Edward W. Said makes this curious claim in the revised edition of *Orientalism* (New York: Pantheon, 1994), p. 335.

15. James Penney, "(Queer) Theory and the Universal Alternative," *Diacritics* 32.2 (2002): 3–19.

16. Joan Vincent, ed., *The Anthropology of Politics: A Reader in Ethnography, Theory, and Critique* (Oxford: Blackwell, 2002), pp. 452–459.

17. There were powerful street demonstrations that stopped international meetings of the World Trade Organization (WTO) in Seattle (1999) and Genoa (2001). It is, however, U.S. domestic protectionism that has caused much more harm to the WTO.

18. Jürgen Habermas, "Citizenship and National Identity: Some Reflections on the Future of Europe," *Praxis International* 12.1 (1992): 1–19.

19. Emmanuel Lévinas, *Totality and Infinity: An Essay on Exteriority,* trans. Alphonso Lingis (Pittsburgh: Duquesne University Press, 1969), pp. 154–156.

20. The role of the Oscar-winning documentary *Born into Brothels: Calcutta's Red Light Kids* (directed by Zana Briski and Ross Kauffman, THINKFilm, 2004) in misrepresenting the situation—and a good deal of it through lack of access to verbal idiom—is something that could be discussed here.

21. I am not speaking of the wonderful idea of creolity that emerges from the work of Édouard Glissant (Jean Bernabé, Patrick Chamoiseau, and Raphaël Confiant, *Éloge de la créolité,* trans. M. B. Taleb-Khyar [Paris: Gallimard, 1993]; Maryse Condé and Madeleine Cottenet-Hage, eds., *Penser la créolité* [Paris: Karthala, 1995]; Édouard Glissant, *Caribbean Discourse: Selected Essays,* trans. Michael Dash [Charlottesville: University of Virginia Press, 1989]; Glissant, *Poetics of Relation,* trans. Betsy Wing [Ann Arbor: University of Michigan Press, 2003]). I have asked the entire discipline of Comparative Literature to take creolity as its model in "World Systems and the Creole," Chapter 21 in this book. Here I speak of creolization, in the narrow sense, from above, a compromising of our many mother tongues.

22. Urvashi Butalia, *The Other Side of Silence: Voices from the Partition of India* (New Delhi: Penguin, 1998); the entire Bangladesh experiment is a site of this uneasy regionalism.

23. Alton L. Becker, *Beyond Translation: Essays toward a Modern Philology* (Ann Arbor: University of Michigan Press, 1995). See Chapter 21.
24. Benedict Anderson, *Imagined Communities: Reflections on the Origin and Spread of Nationalism* (New York: Verso, 1983).

14. Resident Alien

1. Michael Hardt and Antonio Negri, *Empire* (Cambridge, MA: Harvard University Press, 2000), p. 397; Etienne Balibar, *Masses, Classes, Ideas: Studies on Politics and Philosophy Before and After Marx*, trans. James Swenson (New York: Routledge, 1994); Charles Taylor, *Multiculturalism and the Politics of Recognition: An Essay* (Princeton, NJ: Princeton University Press, 1992).
2. Alien residency in the United States is, at least technically, open to all foreign nationals upon fulfillment of certain conditions. The government of India has started, as of August 15, 1999, the issuance of "a person of Indian origin" (PIO) passport, with all appurtenances of citizenship but voting rights. An interesting illustration of identitarianism within metropolitan multiculturalism.
3. Reda Bensmaia, "The Phantom Mediators: Reflections on the Nature of the Violence in Algeria," *Diacritics* 27.2 (1997): 85–97.
4. Rabindranath Tagore, *Gora*, trans. Sujit Mukherjee (New Delhi: Sahitya Akademi, 1997), p. 477 (hereafter cited in the text as G, with page numbers following) (translation modified whenever necessary).
5. Bimal Krishna Matilal, *The Word and the World: India's Contribution to the Study of Language* (New York: Oxford University Press, 1990), p. 96 and passim.
6. Michel Foucault, *The Archaeology of Knowledge*, trans. A. M. Sheridan Smith (London: Routledge, 1972), p. 95; emphasis added.
7. Once again, Harish Trivedi, "India and Post-colonial Discourse," in Harish Trivedi and Meenakshi Mukherjee, eds., *Interrogating Post-colonialism: Theory, Texts and Contexts* (Shimla: Indian Institute, 1996), pp. 231–247, is astute on this point.
8. Freud wrote that the uncanny could appear in fiction as it could not in the psyche. Tagore's fiction creates a full-fledged program—an affective apprenticeship using women—of alien residency. Neither Abd-ur Rahman—the Afghan Amir (about whom more below)—nor Nehru could swing that outside of colonialism, para (about which more later) or post.
9. Rudyard Kipling, *Kim* (New York: Viking, 1987), pp. 333–334 (hereafter cited in the text as K, with page numbers following).
10. Peter Hopkirk, *The Great Game: The Struggle for Empire in Central Asia* (New York: Kodansha, 1994), pp. 123–124.
11. This part of the piece is elaborated at much greater length in Spivak, "Foucault and Najibullah," in *Other Asias* (Oxford: Blackwell, 2008), pp. 132–160. Afghans are the largest group of migrants to Switzerland. The reader might find it interesting to recall my suggestions in "Imperative to Re-imagine the Planet," Chapter 16 in this book, for planetary conduct toward them and

other refugees as a more just asylum ethics. Transnational literacy attempts to make the global writable of capital-as-impossible-abstraction readable, again and again, as permanent parabasis, locating paratactically in fragmented narratives. This agenda despairs over metropolitan identity politics, which has, of course, its own situational justifications.

12. Michel Foucault, *Discipline and Punish: The Birth of the Prison,* trans. Alan Sheridan (New York: Pantheon, 1977), p. 163.

13. Muhammad Mahfuz Ali, *The Truth about Russia and England: From a Native's Point of View* (Lucknow: London Press, 1886), p. 51. "Besides, the oriental mind"—we read in the next paragraph—"does not much appreciate a friendship which is based on high principles and noble intentions—a friendship which is always insisting on dealing in a straightforward and honest way with all questions, political or otherwise. For instance, the Ameer [of Afghanistan] could never perhaps understand how it would be consistent with real friendship on the part of the British Government to help him only on condition that he never entertained any aggressive aims towards his neighbours" (p. 51). I should like to detect irony in this passage but cannot in the absence of the Urdu text.

14. Etienne Balibar, "Globalization/Civilization 2," in Jean-François Chevrier, ed., *Politics-Poetics* (Ostfildern-Ruit: Cantz, 1997), p. 786.

15. Jacques Derrida and Anne Dufourmentelle, *Of Hospitality,* trans. Rachel Bowlby (Stanford, CA: Stanford University Press, 2000), p. 5 (hereafter cited in the text and notes as H, with page numbers following).

16. Assia Djebar's impulse toward placing Delacroix, or the French Captain who occupied Algiers, into teleiopoiesis, shares something of this impulse from the above of the below, but she foregrounds that subject-position as a woman (see Assia Djebar, "Forbidden Gaze, Severed Sound," in *Women of Algiers in their Apartment,* trans. Marjolijn de Jager [Charlottesville: University of Virginia Press, 1992], pp. 134–136, and Djebar, *Fantasia: An Algerian Cavalcade,* trans. Dorothy Blair [London: Quartet, 1989], p. 7).

17. Diego Cordovez, *Out of Afghanistan: The Inside Story of the Soviet Withdrawal* (New York: Oxford University Press, 1995), p. 374.

18. Farhad Mazhar, "The Corpse-Keeper of Revolt," in *Ebadatnama 1* (Dhaka: Prabartana, 1989), p. 36; translation mine.

19. Ranajit Guha, "A Colonial City and Its Times(s)," in Partha Chatterjee, ed., *The Small Voice of History* (Ranikhet: Permanent Black, 2009), pp. 409–434; Charles Dickens, *Sketches by Boz and Other Early Papers, 1833–39,* ed. Michael Slater (Columbus: Ohio State University Press, 1994).

20. The song itself is a meta-narrative sign insofar as it reterritorializes what Kipling could only understand with contempt. It is by Lalan Shah (1774–1890), a major Bengali mystic poet of the cusp of the eighteenth into the nineteenth century. Tagore's relationship with the poetry and music of Lalan is still to be researched. Edward C. Dimock's good-hearted essay "Rabindranath Tagore—'The Greatest of The Bauls of Bengal' " (University of Chicago, Committee on Southern Asian Studies, no. 1, 1959, pp. 33–51) makes the same critical/historical error as Jeffrey J. Kripal, in designating Ram Prashad

a tantric (see Spivak, "Moving Devi," in *Other Asias* [Oxford: Blackwell, 2008], p. 343); Santosh Chakrabarti, *Studies in Tagore: Critical Essays* (New Delhi: Atlantic), pp. 106–112 gives the received academic account in West Bengal. It is certainly true that Lalan Shah was in the last year of his long life in his residence in Seuria the year Tagore moved to nearby Silaidaha as a young landowner. The song is famous. Benoy wants to write it down. He doesn't and the action of the story begins, in its place, as it were. Gerard Genette would place it within his range of "substitutions," the definitive predication of the figure as such (Gerard Genette, *Figures of Literary Discourse*, trans. Alan Sheridan [New York: Columbia University Press, 1982], p. 94 and passim). It is as if the entire novel is a figure for what is staged as the undone at the beginning of the text, as a precolonial locatedness that is out of reach of the thinker or sponsor of the imperial resident alien, a located catachresis.

21. Revising I notice that Derrida frames Kant's famous injunction to tell the truth even if it endangers a guest—thus breaking the law of hospitality—in Kant's thinking of the right to lie (H, pp. 63f). The general teleopoietic hospitality of *Gora* allows the stranger to err before he can acquire permanent residence.

22. I have commented elsewhere on the conjunctural connections between Tagore and W. E. B. Du Bois (Spivak, "Deconstruction and Cultural Studies: Arguments for a Deconstructive Cultural Studies," in Nicholas Royle, ed. *Deconstructions* [Oxford: Blackwell, 2000], pp. 14–43). This nod to the good British spirit reminds me of Du Bois's "the South is not 'solid' " (Du Bois, *The Souls of Black Folk*, in *The Oxford W. E. B. Du Bois*, vol. 3, ed. Henry Louis Gates Jr. [New York: Oxford University Press, 2007], p. 92).

23. Barnett R. Rubin, *The Fragmentation of Afghanistan: State Formation and Collapse in the International System* (New Haven, CT: Yale University Press, 1995), p. 76.

24. Abd-ur Rahman Khan, *The Life of Abdur Rahman, Amir of Afghanistan*, vol. 2, ed. Sultan Mahomed Khan (Karachi: Oxford University Press, 1980), pp. 43–45.

25. Spivak, "Bajarer Opor," *Ananda Bazar Patrika*, August 1, 1999.

15. Ethics and Politics in Tagore, Coetzee, and Certain Scenes of Teaching

This chapter was first presented at the Centre for Social Sciences in Kolkata, India. I have not changed the second part significantly in order to give the U.S. reader the sense of how alien ethical discourse might seem on a remote terrain.

1. Gayatri Chakravorty Spivak, "Righting Wrongs," in *Other Asias* (Oxford: Blackwell, 2008), pp. 14–57.

2. Derrida, *Adieu to Emmanuel Levinas*, trans. Pascale-Anne Brault and Michael Naas (Stanford, CA: Stanford University Press, 1999), pp. 51–53.

3. Emmanuel Lévinas, *Otherwise than Being, or, Beyond Essence*, trans. Alphonso Lingis (Pittsburgh: Duquesne University Press, 1998), p. 58; translation modified.

4. Ibid., p. 59; translation modified. There is a footnote in the text to Paul Ricoeur's *Conflict of Interpretations*, trans. Don Ihde (Evanston, IL: Northwestern University Press, 1974), p. 99. The next quoted passage is from the same page.

5. See Derrida, *Adieu to Emmanuel Levinas*, pp. 29–33 for a discussion of this.

6. I first learned to notice this from Derrida's article "White Mythology," whose subtitle is "Metaphor in the Text of Philosophy" (Derrida, *Margins of Philosophy*, trans. Alan Bass [Chicago: University of Chicago Press, 1982], pp. 209–271).

7. Pratichi (India) Trust, the *Pratichi Education Report*, intro. by Amartya Sen (Delhi: TLM Books, 2002).

8. Rabindranath Tagore, Poem No. 108, *Gitanjali*, 20 Ashadh 1317 BE (i.e., approximately 1910). The title "Apoman" would have been acquired at a later stage, as the poems in *Gitanjali* had no titles. Kshitimohan Sen's Bengali translations of *Kabir* were read and discussed by Rabindranath long before he published his own English translations of them. See Rabindranath Tagore, trans., *Kabir, Songs of Kabir*, trans. from Kshitimohan Sen (New York: Macmillan, 1915).

9. "Adivasi" is the name used commonly for so-called Indian tribals, by general account the inhabitants of India at the time of the arrival of Indo-European speakers in the second millennium BCE.

10. Diann Sichel, "Mass, Momentum and Energy Transport (Living Space)"; Dancers: Josiah Pearsall, Melanie Velo-Simpson; Singers: Wendy Baker, Erik Kroncke.

11. J. M. Coetzee, *Disgrace* (New York: Viking, 2000).

12. William Shakespeare, *King Lear* (Cambridge, MA: Harvard University Press, 1959), Arden Edition, p. 141.

13. For an analysis of this rhetorical question, see Rosalind C. Morris, "The Mute and the Unspeakable: Political Subjectivity, Violent Crime, and 'the Sexual Thing' in a South African Mining Community," in *Law and Disorder in the Postcolony*, ed. Jean and John Comaroff (Chicago: University of Chicago Press, 2006), pp. 57–101.

14. Since 1983, when I delivered "Can the Subaltern Speak?" as a lecture at the Summer Institute at the University of Illinois in Champaign–Urbana, I have been interested in suicide as envoi. Partha Chatterjee reminded me in conversation (October 31, 2003) that the "cause" is metaleptically constructed by the suicide, as the effect of an "effect." My point is that Lucy is not represented as the "subject" of a "cause." Her representation may be read as Lévinas's object-human as the figure that subtends all knowing, including the cognition of a cause. About suicide bombing I speculate at greater length in "Terror: A Speech after 9/11," Chapter 18 in this book.

15. Franz Kafka, *The Trial*, trans. Breon Mitchell (New York: Schocken Books, 1998), p. 231.

16. Mieke Bal, *Narratology: Introduction to the Theory of Narrative* (Toronto: University of Toronto Press, 1985), p. 100.

17. Karl Marx uses this to describe why the tendency of the rate of profit to fall
does not result in increasingly lower profits (Marx, *Capital,* vol. 3, trans.
David Fernbach [New York: Viking Books, 1981], pp. 365–366 and passim)
(hereafter cited in the text as C 3, with page numbers following).
18. See Patricia Cohen, "The Next Big Thing in English: Knowing They Know
That You Know" (*New York Times,* April 1, 2010); and the accompanying
series of blogs on "Neuro Lit Crit" (http://roomfordebate.blogs.nytimes.com
/2010/04/05/can-neuro-lit-crit-save-the-humanities/). None of the commentators had been present at a meeting arranged by the United Nations on September 11, 2008 with eminent neuroscientists to see if they could provide an
ethics for the world. All the participants (except the man working for the Air
Force) vehemently insisted that this was not possible. To understand literature or philosophy as such by way of neuroscience is like testing out the
roundness of the world by walking across it, or telling the time by the theory
of relativity. To respect the experiencing being that lives and dies in spite of
impersonal scientific descriptions is becoming less and less possible. The
imagination cannot sustain the double bind.
19. Immanuel Kant, "An Answer to the Question: What Is Enlightenment," in
Practical Philosophy, trans. and ed. Mary J. Gregor (Cambridge: Cambridge
University Press, 1996).
20. *Herculine Barbin: Being the Recently Discovered Memoirs of a Nineteenth-
Century French Hermaphrodite* (no trans. given) (New York: Pantheon,
1980), p. 89; translation modified.
21. For a debate over such readings, see Peter D. McDonald, "Disgrace Effects,"
Interventions 4.3 (2002): 321–330, and David Attwell, "Race in Disgrace,"
Interventions 4.3 (2002): 331–341.
22. This possibility of an uneasy snigger (as well as the "giving up") may mark
something irreducible, the seeming "abyss"—we think also of the incessant
back-and-forth of the abyssal—between the "I" of the "I think" and the presumed self-identity of the animal: "This automotricity as auto-affection and
self-relation, even before the discursive thematic of an utterance or of an *ego
cogito,* indeed of a *cogito ergo sum,* is the character that one recognizes in
the living and in animality in general. But between that self-relationship (that
Self, that ipseity) and the *"I"* of the *"I think"* there is, it seems, an abyss"
(Derrida, *The Animal That Therefore I Am,* trans. David Wills [New York:
Fordham University Press, 2008], pp. 49–50; translation modified). The dull
effort of a cogitative Lurie has an abyssality that must not be forgotten as we
attempt to acknowledge the enigmatic historiality of the mixed-race postcolonial child of rape deliberately given up as property for the adopted father,
Black Christian, a Petrus upon which rock the future, guaranteeing tenancy
for the colonial-turned-native, is founded. It is not the object-human as a
figure with nothing that comes before all else, but the look of the naked animot (a word that the reader must learn from the book by Derrida I am citing; a word [mot] that marks the irreducible heterogeneity of animality).
This is Derrida's critique of the philosophical tradition of the West. I have
often felt that the formal logic of Coetzee's fiction mimes ethical moves in an

uncanny way. The (non)relationship between the cogitation of animality and the setting-to-work of gendered postcolonialism in *Disgrace* may be such an uncanny miming. The "dull decrepitude" of the former is where equality in disgrace is impossible; we cannot disgrace the animot. It is the limit of *apamane hote habe tahader shobar shoman;* and to call it a limit is to speak from one side. Since my ethical texts are Kant, Lévinas, and Derrida, and my fictions are "Apaman," *Disgrace,* and the uncoercive rearrangement of desire, I have not considered J. M. Coetzee's staged speculations about animality and the human in "Lives of Animals" (in Amy Gutmann, ed., *The Lives of Animals* [Princeton, NJ: Princeton University Press, 1999]).

23. Pratichi (India) Trust, *Pratichi Education Report,* p. 10.
24. I have developed the idea of the role of rural education in maintaining class apartheid in "Righting Wrongs."
25. J. M. Coetzee, *Foe* (New York: Penguin, 1986).
26. Clyde Prestowitz, *Rogue Nation: American Unilateralism and the Failure of Good Intentions* (New York: Basic Books, 2003) argues that the United States wants to make everyone American and there left and right meet. The same, I think, can now be said of Europe. This is too big a topic to develop here. What I urge in the text is the need to imagine a world that is not necessarily looking for help.
27. Her name was Shamoli Sabar. She is memorialized in figure 1.2 of my "Righting Wrongs," p. 49. She was one of the signatories of the petition. I offer this essay to her memory.
28. We have to have an idea of how fiction can be made to speak through the transactional heading beyond the limits of the author's authority, which would expose the frivolousness of a position such as Rajat Ray's in *Exploring Emotional History: Gender, Mentality, and Literature in the Indian Awakening* (New Delhi: Oxford University Press, 2001), pp. 79, 115n.28.
29. Pratichi (India) Trust, *Pratichi Education Report,* p. 68.

16. Imperative to Re-imagine the Planet

1. Hermann Levin Goldschmidt, *Freiheit für den Widerspruch* (Schaffhausen: Novalis, 1976), p. 198.
2. Ibid. and passim.
3. Hermann Levin Goldschmidt, *Die Frage des Mitmenschen und des Mitvolkes: 1951–1992* (Zurich: Nyffeler, 1992).
4. Goldschmidt's perception, that the refugee breaks this continuity, may be compared to Giorgio Agamben's extension of Hannah Arendt's perception of this: "by breaking the continuity between man and citizen, nativity and nationality, they [refugees] put the originary fiction of modern sovereignty in crisis" (Giorgio Agamben, *Homo Sacer: Sovereign Power and Bare Life,* trans. Daniel Heller-Roazen [Stanford, CA: Stanford University Press, 1998], p. 131).
5. Wolf Linder, *Swiss Democracy: Possible Solutions to Conflict in Multicultural Societies,* 2nd ed. (New York: St. Martin's Press, 1997), pp. 35–36.

6. Rudyard Kipling, "The White Man's Burden," *McClure's* 12 (February 1899).

7. Georg Wilhelm Friedrich Hegel, *The Phenomenology of Spirit*, trans. A. V. Miller (Oxford: Clarendon, 1977), p. 116. In Hegel the slave or, more correctly, the bondsman sublates "its own being-for-self"—Miller unaccountably translates this as "sets aside," not even the more conservative "supersedes," "overcomes," or yet "transcends"—"and in so doing itself does what the other does to it." Interesting parallels to various forms of migrant mimicry can be drawn from here.

8. In his Dewey lectures (Columbia University, October 19–23, 1998), Ronald Dworkin proposed a theory of democracy "upstream from cultural difference rather than downstream," as in Rawls.

9. Best developed, perhaps, in *Inequality Reexamined* (Cambridge, MA: Harvard University Press, 1992). See also Amartya Sen, "Capability and Well-Being," in Amartya Sen and Martha Nussbaum, eds., *The Quality of Life* (Oxford: Clarendon, 1993), pp. 30–53. For Nancy Fraser, see Fraser, *Justice Interruptus: Critical Reflections on the "Postsocialist" Condition* (New York: Routlege, 1997).

10. Plotinus, *The Enneads*, trans. Stephen MacKenna, 4th ed. (New York: Pantheon, 1969), p. 63.

11. "Your right is only to work, never to its fruits" (*Srimadbhagavadgita* 2.47; translation mine).

12. This Arabic word is much disputed in Islamic theology. I am commenting on perceived usage. *Haq* is also an Arabic-origin word in my mother tongue (Bengali) and in my national language (Hindi).

13. Goldschmidt, *Freiheit für den Widerspruch*, p. 13.

14. See Mae-Wan Ho, *Genetic Engineering: Dream or Nightmare: The Brave New World of Bad Science and Big Business* (Bath, UK: Gateway, 1998).

15. Kant, *Critique of the Power of Judgment*, trans. Paul Guyer (Cambridge: Cambridge University Press, 2000), pp. 317–318; translation modified.

16. Spivak, *A Critique of Postcolonial Reason: Toward a History of the Vanishing Present* (Cambridge, MA: Harvard University Press, 1999).

17. Karl Marx, *Capital*, vol. 3, trans. David Fernbach (New York: Viking Books, 1981), pp. 1015–1016.

18. Jean-François Lyotard, *The Postmodern Condition: A Report on Knowledge*, trans. Geoff Bennington and Brian Massumi (Minneapolis: University of Minnesota Press, 1984).

19. Fazlur Rahman, "Law and Ethics in Islam," in Richard G. Hovannisian, ed., *Ethics in Islam* (Malibu, CA: Undena, 1985), p. 15.

20. That name marked the absolute failure of dialogics. "Primo Levi has described the person who in camp jargon was called 'the Muslim,' der Muselmann—a being from whom humiliation, horror and fear had so taken away all consciousness and all personality as to make him absolutely apathetic" (Agamben, *Homo Sacer*, pp. 184–185). I am inviting you to desacralize that person into a productive contradiction.

21. Abdelkébir Khatibi, "Frontières," in "Entre psychanalyse et Islam," *Cahiers Intersignes* 1 (Spring 1990): 13–22.

22. Derrida's nice phrase in "Faith and Knowledge: The Two Sources of Religion at the Limits of Reason Alone," trans. Samuel Weber, in Jacques Derrida and Gianni Vattimo, eds., *Religion* (Stanford, CA: Stanford University Press, 1998).

23. Gramsci was once again prescient enough to think through a version of this from his one nation-state-based, Europeanist point of view which, like all his insights, could not find development (Antonio Gramsci, *Selections from the Prison Notebooks*, ed. and trans. Quintin Hoare and Geoffrey Nowell Smith [New York: International Publishers, 1971], pp. 330–331).

24. It seems to me that Derrida recognizes this in his repeated references to Islam in "Faith and Knowledge." Note 28 (p. 73) recognizes "Islamism" as "also develop[ing] a radical critique of what ties democracy today . . . to the market and to the technoscientific reason that dominates it." And on pp. 55–56, where he asks: "Does not the globalization of demographic reality and calculation render the probability of such a 'context' ['I understand Judaism as the possibility of giving the Bible a context' (Lévinas)] weaker than ever and as threatening for survival as the worst, the radical evil of the 'final solution'?" and suggests that "this question is perhaps the most grave and most urgent for the state and the nations of Israel . . . also all the Jews, and . . . all the Christians in the world," he perhaps acknowledges this again in the next, incomplete sentence: "Not at all Muslims today" (see Derrida, "Faith and Knowledge"). As I have made clear in my text, I am not speaking of the "religion" named "Islam."

17. Reading with Stuart Hall in "Pure" Literary Terms

"Pure literary terms" is a citation from Stuart Hall in "The Formation of a Diasporic Intellectual," in David Morley and Kuan-Hsing Chen, *Stuart Hall: Critical Dialogue in Cultural Studies* (London: Routledge, 1996), p. 498. My thanks to Jean Franco and Deborah White for critical readings, and Bill Michael for research assistance.

1. Stuart Hall, "The Problem of Ideology—Marxism without Guarantees," *Journal of Communication Inquiry* 10.2 (1986): 29.

2. Hall, "Culture, the Media and 'the Ideological Effect,'" in James Curran, Michael Gurevitch, and Janet Woollacott, eds., *Mass Communication and Society* (London: Edward Arnold 1977), p. 344 (hereafter cited in the text as CM, with page numbers following).

3. This passage, on ethics and literature, is quoted from "The Double Bind Starts to Kick In," Chapter 4 in this book.

4. I have discussed this in "Feminism without Frontiers," unpublished lecture, Institute for Research on Women and Gender, Columbia University, February 1, 1999, with reference to Sarah Cummings, Henk van Dam, and Minke Valk, eds., *Gender Training: The Source Book* (Amsterdam: Royal Tropical Institute, 1998).

5. Hall, "The Hinterland of Science: Ideology and the 'Sociology of Knowledge,'" in *On Ideology* (London: Hutchinson, 1977), pp. 9–32, discusses the

same kind of relationship that I am suggesting between the literary and the geopolitical "scientific" implications of metropolitan multiculturalism.

6. Hall, "Notes on Deconstructing 'The Popular,'" in Raphael Samuel, ed., *People's History and Socialist Theory* (London: Routledge, 1981), p. 239; wording altered (hereafter cited in the text as DP, with page numbers following).

7. Jamaica Kincaid, *Lucy* (New York: Farrar, Strauss, Giroux, 1990) (hereafter cited in the text by page numbers alone).

8. Bob Perelman, "Marginalization," in *Language Writing and Literary History* (Princeton, NJ: Princeton University Press, 1996), p. 62.

9. The political implications of extreme parataxis—schizophrenia—are elaborated in Gilles Deleuze and Felix Guattari, *Anti-Oedipus: Capitalism and Schizophrenia,* trans. Robert Hurley, Mark Seem, and Helen R. Lane (Minneapolis: University of Minnesota Press, 1992).

10. Roland Barthes, "Introduction to the Structural Analysis of Narratives," in Stephen Heath, trans., *Image-Music-Text* (New York: Hill and Wang, 1977), p. 84. The passage quoted is from the first part of the essay and mired in binary oppositions. The word "legitimate" gives a hint of this. By the end of the essay, Barthes is much wilder, moving from homology to definitions that want not "to strain the phylogenetic hypothesis!" (p. 124). Thus my invocation of paratactic contamination of the story line is not altogether out of the Barthesian line.

11. For "focalization," and the distinction between "story" and "text" that I will invoke below, see Shlomith Rimmon-Keenan, *Narrative Fiction: Contemporary Poetics* (New York: Methuen, 1983), chapters 2–6.

12. S. R. Driver, *A Critical and Exegetical Commentary on Deuteronomy,* 3rd ed. (Edinburgh: T. and T. Clark, 1978), p. 304.

13. F. G. Kenyon, *The Text of the Greek Bible,* 3rd ed. (London: Duckworth, 1975), p. 14.

14. Diane Simmons, *Jamaica Kincaid* (New York: Twayne, 1994), p. 1.

15. Percy Bysshe Shelley, "A Defence of Poetry," in Bruce K. McElderry Jr., ed., *Shelley's Critical Prose* (Lincoln: University of Nebraska Press, 1967), p. 24.

16. Kincaid, "Flowers of Evil," *The New Yorker,* October 5, 1992, pp. 159, 158.

17. Michael Riffaterre, *Text Production,* trans. Terese Lyons (New York: Columbia University Press), 1983. For another description of intertexuality, see "Ethics and Politics in Tagore, Coetzee, and Certain Scenes of Teaching," Chapter 15 in this book.

18. Karl Marx, "Economic and Philosophical Manuscripts," in *Early Writings,* trans. Rodney Livingstone and Gregor Benton (Harmondsworth: Penguin Books, 1975), p. 328; translation modified. The Hegelian passage is to be found in Hegel, *The Phenomenology of Spirit,* trans. A. V. Miller (Oxford: Clarendon, 1977), p. 488.

19. It may be worth recalling that Barthes assigns the metaphoric to "sapiential discourse" (Barthes, "Introduction to the Structural Analysis," p. 84).

20. Perelman, "Marginalization," pp. 61, 69.

21. Leslie Garis, "Through West Indian Eyes," *New York Times Magazine,* October 7, 1990, p. 80.
22. Bessie Head, *A Question of Power* (New York: Pantheon, 1973), p. 11.
23. Perelman, "Marginalization," p. 62.
24. Stuart Hall, "When Was 'The Post-colonial?' Thinking at the Limit," in Iain Chambers and Lidia Curti, eds., *The Post-Colonial Question: Common Skies, Divided Horizons* (London: Routledge, 1996), p. 250.
25. By "spectralization of the rural" I mean that biodiversity, genetic engineering, chemical fertilizers, and other globalizing phenomena engage the rural directly in the circuit of a disembodied, hi-tech, electronified capitalism, bypassing industry. It is interesting to note that the IMF concentrated only on energy and agriculture, not on industry at all, in order to restructure the Russian economy to integrate it into the global system. The entire question of IMF-sponsored reform is brilliantly discussed in Boris Kagarlitsky, *The Mirage of Modernization,* trans. Renfrey Clarke (New York: Monthly Review Press, 1995), and Roger Burbach, Orlando Núñez, and Boris Kagarlitsky, *Globalization and Its Discontents: The Rise of Postmodern Socialisms* (London: Pluto Press, 1997). See also Chapter 9.

18. Terror

1. The first version of this chapter was delivered at a conference, "Responses to War," in the Feminist Interventions series run by the Institute for Research in Women and Gender at Columbia University. I thank Rosalind Carmel Morris for inviting me to participate in it.
2. This is not as silly as it may sound. In an interesting article in *The American Prospect,* Anne-Marie Slaughter also mentions this as an important reason: "the convention governing prisoners of war defines unlawful combatants as participants in an armed conflict who abuse their civilian status to gain military advantage: those who do not carry arms openly and do not carry a 'fixed distinctive sign' such as a uniform or other insignia that would identify them as soldiers" (Slaughter, "Tougher than Terror," *American Prospect,* January 28, 2002, p. 2).
3. Livy, *History of Rome,* Book I, 58–60, recalling the founding of the Roman Republic, places it in Lucretia's fear that she should be represented as having slept with a "man of base condition."
4. Kant, "What Is Enlightenment?," in James Schmidt, ed., *What Is Enlightenment? Eighteenth-Century Answers and Twentieth-Century Questions* (Berkeley: University of California Press, 1996), pp. 58–64.
5. Walter Benjamin, "Critique of Violence," in *Reflections: Essays, Aphorisms, Autobiographical Writing,* trans. Edmund Jephcott (New York: Schocken, 1978), p. 297; translation modified.
6. See Kelly Oliver, *Women as Weapons of War: Iraq, Sex, and the Media* (New York: Columbia University Press, 2007).
7. Abd ur-Rahman Khan, *The Life of Abdur Rahman, Amir of Afghanistan,* 2 vols. (New York: Oxford University Press, 1980). The issue of "gender," the

abstraction of sexual difference, itself discursive since always posited as a difference, for both dominant and subordinate, is never absent from a society. I say "again" because, as I say in my text, the issue of civil justice for women can be charted along the story of the often-thwarted development of the Afghan intelligentsia. As far as I know, that story has not been put together between covers. One can start from the loss of the Silk Road monopoly, or from Abd-ur Rahman.

8. Gregory J. Massell, *The Surrogate Proletariat: Moslem Women and Revolutionary Strategies in Soviet Central Asia, 1919–1929* (Princeton, NJ: Princeton University Press, 1974); Fazal-ur-Rahim Marwat, *The Evolution and Growth of Communism in Afghanistan (1917–1979): An Appraisal* (Karachi: Royal Book Co., 1997).

9. Eric Lipton and James Glanz, "A Nation Challenged: Relics; From the Rubble, Artifacts of Anguish," *New York Times,* January 27, 2002, section 1, p. 1.

10. "A New World Trade Center: Design Proposals," Max Protetch Gallery, New York, January 17–February 16, 2002.

11. Mahasweta Devi, "Douloti the Bountiful," in Devi, *Imaginary Maps: Three Stories,* trans. Gayatri Chakravorty Spivak (New York: Routledge, 1993), p. 88.

12. Vijay Prashad, *War against the Planet: The Fifth Afghan War, Imperialism, and Other Assorted Fundamentalisms* (New Delhi: LeftWord, 2002), pp. 7, 27.

13. Noam Chomsky, "The Theatre of Good and Evil," http://www.zmag.org/chomskygsf.htm.

14. "Creating Cities that Work in the New Global Economy," *World Bank Policy and Research Bulletin* 10.4 (October–December 1999): 1.

15. This is the general argument of Michael Hardt and Antonio Negri in their *Empire* (Cambridge, MA: Harvard University Press, 2000). As I have made abundantly clear, I no longer share their confidence.

16. Terry Castle, "Courage, mon amie," *London Review of Books* 24.7 (April 4, 2002): 3–11.

17. Richard M. Eaton, "Temple Desecration in Pre-Modern India," *Frontline* 17.25 (December 9–22, 2000): 62–70.

18. Syed Mujtaba Ali, *Works,* vol. 7 (Kolkata: Mitra & Ghosh Publishers, 1974–). The tradition continues. President Hamid Karzai's graduate degree is from an Indian university.

19. Eaton, "Temple Desecration," pp. 64–65. To understand why the distinction between "India" and "Afghanistan" is in this context spurious, see Martin W. Lewis, *Myth of Continents: A Critique of Metageography* (Berkeley: University of California Press, 1997), pp. 13, 14, 213.

20. As already mentioned, former U.S. Secretary of State Lawrence Eagleburger did not know what New Social Movements were at the Conference on Does America Have a Democratic Mission, University of Virginia, March 19–21, 1998. Indeed, the useless definition of terror is quoted in Chomsky, *9-11* (New York: Seven Stories Press, 2001), p. 54. *Rogues* by Derrida is an entire book on the possibility of rogue states.

21. United Nations High Commission for Refugees and Save the Children–UK, "Note for Implementing and Operational Partners on Sexual Violence and Exploitation: The Experience of Refugee Children in Guinea, Liberia and Sierra Leone," February 2002.

22. Barbara Crossette, "How to Put a Nation Back Together Again," *New York Times,* Week in Review section, November 25, 2001, p. 3.

23. Kant, *Critique of the Power of Judgment,* trans. Paul Guyer (Cambridge: Cambridge University Press, 2000), p. 141. "The Analytic of the Sublime" appears on pp. 128–212.

24. It was widely reported that the composer Karlheinz Stockhausen had, days after September 11, made remarks to journalists in Hamburg to the effect that the attack on the World Trade Center was a work of art. "Attacks Called Great Art," *New York Times,* September 19, 2001, section E, p. 3.

25. Jacques Lacan, "The Splendor of Antigone," in *The Ethics of Psychoanalysis 1959–1960: Seminar Book VII,* trans. Dennis Porter (New York: Routledge, 1992), pp. 262–263.

26. Kant, *Critique of the Power of Judgment,* p. 141.

27. *The Terrorist,* Santosh Sivan, 1998; Viken Berberian, *The Cyclist* (New York: Simon & Schuster, 2002).

28. "The Weakest Link: Pakistan," *The Economist,* June 1, 2002, p. 11.

29. Harsh Mander, "Cry, the Beloved Country: Reflections on the Gujarat Massacre," http://www.sabrang.com/gujarat/statement/nv2.htm.

30. For bayonet constitution, see Jon Kamakawo'ole Osorio, *Dismembering Lahui: The History of the Hawai'ian Nation until 1887* (Honolulu: University of Hawai'i Press, 2002).

31. George P. Fletcher, *Romantics at War: Glory and Guilt in the Age of Terror* (Princeton, NJ: Princeton University Press, 2002).

32. Mike Davis, *Dead Cities, and Other Tales* (New York: New Press, 2002).

33. Informal response to "The War in Iraq: Is It Legal? (Does It Matter?)," debate between George Fletcher, Ruth Wedgwood, and Alan Dershowitz, Columbia Law School, November 15, 2004.

34. Kant, "Religion within the Boundaries of Mere Reason," in Allen W. Wood and George di Giovanni, eds., *Religion and Rational Theology* (Cambridge: Cambridge University Press, 1996), p. 78.

35. Ibid., p. 95.

36. Gayatri Chakravorty Spivak, *A Critique of Postcolonial Reason: Toward a History of the Vanishing Present* (Cambridge, MA: Harvard University Press, 1999), pp. 26–29n.32.

37. Derrida, "Faith and Knowledge," in Gil Anidjar, *Acts of Religion* (New York: Routledge, 2002), pp. 40–101.

38. Edward W. Said, "Secular Criticism," in *The World, the Text, and the Critic* (Cambridge, MA: Harvard University Press, 1983), pp. 1–30; Said, "Gods That Always Fail," in *Representations of the Intellectual* (New York: Columbia University Press, 1994), p. 120.

39. Derrida, "The University without Condition," in *Without Alibi,* trans. Peggy Kamuf (Stanford, CA: Stanford University Press, 2002), p. 202.

40. Samuel Huntington, *Clash of Civilizations and the Remaking of World Order* (New York: Touchstone, 1997).

41. Kant, "Religion within the Boundaries of Mere Reason," p. 181.

42. It would require a great deal of space and time to support this statement adequately. Suffice it to refer to the close of the document signed by Jacques Derrida and Jürgen Habermas in the *Frankfurter Allgemeine* on May 31, 2002. Derrida's position on Kant is altogether more nuanced, as evidenced by his many writings on Kant throughout his career.

43. Hannah Arendt, *Lectures on Kant's Political Philosophy* (Chicago: University of Chicago Press, 1990).

44. Derrida had warned in "Différance" that an effect without a cause would lead to a first cause. Kant's near-metalepsis of grace still has God in the offing, although Kant is careful to bind this possibility in every way, one of the most important being the discussion of the hypothetical use of reason (Kant, *Critique of Pure Reason*, trans. Paul Guyer and Allen W. Wood [Cambridge: Cambridge University Press, 2000], pp. 590–604). Derrida's argument would be that to locate the effect of grace in texts would not necessarily invoke a causeless cause (Derrida, "Différance," in *Margins of Philosophy*, trans. Alan Bass [Chicago: University of Chicago Press, 1982], p. 17). This, put another way, is the de-transcendentalization of the radically other, the causeless cause, the persistent effort of a training in the humanities.

45. Patricia Grace, *Baby No-Eyes* (Honolulu: University of Hawai'i Press, 1998). The passage referred to is from p. 293.

46. Spivak, "Interview with Jane Gallop," in Jane Gallop, ed., *Polemic: Critical or Uncritical* (New York: Routledge, 2004), pp. 179–200.

19. Harlem

1. See Alice Attie, *Harlem on the Verge* (New York: Quantuck Lane Press, 2003). For this chapter in full color, see Spivak, *Harlem* (Kolkata: Seagull Books, forthcoming).

2. Kar Wai Wong's film *Chungking Express* (1994) stages this by robbing well-established cinematic idiom—French New Wave, American noir, and gangster movies—of all the expected semantic charge. On the cultural studies front, Ackbar Abbas's work comments most extensively on this cultural denuding: "Hyphenation: The Spatial Dimensions of Hong Kong Culture," in Michael P. Steinberg, ed., *Walter Benjamin and the Demands of History* (Ithaca, NY: Cornell University Press, 1996), pp. 214–231; Abbas, "Hong Kong: Other Histories, Other Politics," *Public Culture* 9 (1997): 293–313. Meaghan Morris, a relative newcomer to Hong Kong, bypasses this history as she plunges into global Hong Kong in "On English as a Chinese Language: Implementing Globalization," in Brett De Bary, ed., *Universities in Translation: The Mental Labour of Globalization* (Hong Kong: Hong Kong University Press, 2010), pp. 177–196.

3. Tsong Pu, *Journey to the East 1997* (Hong Kong: HKUST Center for the Arts, 1997), p. 92.

4. Gilbert Osofsky, *Harlem: The Making of a Ghetto* (1966; reprint, Chicago: Ivan R. Dee, 1996), p. 71. I am grateful to Brent Edwards for sharing some references. Some of the prose is a paraphrase of the *Encyclopedia Britannica* entry.

5. For an unsentimental account of this, see Jervis Anderson, *This Was Harlem: 1900–1950* (New York: Noonday, 1981).

6. Robin Kelley, "Disappearing Acts: Capturing Harlem in Transition," in Attie, *Harlem on the Verge,* pp. 9–17.

7. Aaron Levy, *Cities without Citizens: Statelessness and Settlements in Early America,* Rosenbach Museum and Library (Philadelphia), July 8–September 28, 2003.

8. Du Bois, *The Souls of Black Folk,* in *The Oxford W. E. B. Du Bois,* ed. Henry Louis Gates Jr. (New York: Oxford University Press, 2007), vol. 3, p. 3 (hereafter cited in the notes as ODB, with volume and page numbers following).

9. Derrida speaks of teleiopoiesis in George Collins, trans., *Politics of Friendship* (New York: Verso, 1997). I have connected it to cultural work in "Deconstruction and Cultural Studies: Arguments for a Deconstructive Cultural Studies," in Nicholas Royle, ed., *Deconstructions: A User's Guide* (Oxford: Blackwell, 2000), pp. 14–43.

10. These words are somewhat modified in the headnote to the acknowledgment to Attie, *Harlem on the Verge,* p. 119.

11. Cited in Derrida, "Différance," in *Margins of Philosophy,* trans. Alan Bass (Chicago: University of Chicago Press, 1982), p. 14.

12. Amy Finnerty, "Outnumbered: Standing Out at Work," *New York Times,* July 16, 2000. Mr. McDonald, you may have "decided Derridean deconstruction wasn't for me," but this liberating statement, standing alone in an issue full of clichés, shows that you can't take the Yale out of Erroll.

13. If one credited the Lacanian narrative, this would be a kind of group mirror stage, to be superseded by the symbolic (Jacques Lacan, "The Mirror Stage," in *Écrits,* trans. Bruce Fink [New York: Norton, 2006], pp. 75–81). I can hang in with this kind of generalized psychoanalytic talk only as long as it remains general.

14. To see how this ruse works for constitutions, see Derrida, "Declarations of Independence," *New Political Science* 15 (1986): 7–15; and Derrida and Mustapha Tlili, eds., *For Nelson Mandela* (New York: Seaver, 1987).

15. James Weldon Johnson, *Black Manhattan* (New York: Da Capo Press, 1991), p. 161.

16. This is Edward Soja's term for that sort of living together that is the motor of history (Soja, *Postmetropolis: Critical Studies of Cities and Regions* [Malden, MA: Blackwell, 2000], pp. 12–18).

17. Unpublished communication.

18. Attie, *Harlem on the Verge,* p. 14.

19. *Harlem Song* by George C. Wolf, dir. George C. Wolf, Apollo Theatre, New York, July 8–December 29, 2002; Alain Locke, *The New Negro* (New York: Atheneum, 1970). Of the many television programs, PBS's *Walk through Harlem* is the most exemplary. Its slim accompanying volume, Andrew S. Dolkart

and Gretchen S. Sorin, eds., *Touring Historic Harlem: Four Walks in Northern Manhattan* (New York: Landmarks Conservancy, 1997), is a superb example of the scholarly lexicalization into a seamless history, a continuous geography.

20. Michael Henry Adams, "Harlem Lost and Found," Museum of the City of New York, May 3, 2003–January 4, 2004.

21. Lévinas, *Totality and Infinity: An Essay on Exteriority,* trans. Alphonso Lingis (Pittsburgh: Duquesne University Press, 1969), pp. 169–170.

22. Kant, *Critique of the Power of Judgment,* trans. Paul Guyer (Cambridge: Cambridge University Press, 2000), p. 141. See also Spivak, *A Critique of Postcolonial Reason: Toward a History of the Vanishing Present* (Cambridge, MA: Harvard University Press, 1999), p. 11n.18.

23. Du Bois, *Darkwater: Voices from within the Veil,* in ODB 19, p. 73. On the role of the international civil society in today's world, I have a serious difference with my long-term ally and dear friend Homi Bhabha. I hope to discuss this with him in the near future. The passage from Du Bois is cited in Homi K. Bhabha, "Democracy De-realized," in Okwui Enwezor, ed., *Democracy Unrealized: Documenta 11-Platform 1* (Ostfildern-Ruit: Hatje Cantz, 2002), p. 360. The full passage is "In future democracies the toleration and encouragement of minorities and the willingness to consider as 'men' the crankiest, humblest and poorest and blackest peoples, must be the real key to the consent of the governed" (ODB 19, p. 73). The ellipses should be noticed. Du Bois's piece is indeed about "the old cry of privilege, the old assumption that there are those in the world who know better what is best for others than those others know themselves, and who can be trusted to do their best. . . . They say of persons and classes: 'They do not need the ballot'" (ODB 19, p. 68). I am making the point that self-selected moral entrepreneurs fit this description. I will not comment here on the folly of drawing in the Lévinas of *Otherwise than Being* to endorse that role. Du Bois's use of the feminine metaphor in the subtitle of his book also bears further inquiry.

24. See, for instance, Kieran Allen, "Immigration and the Celtic Tiger," in Gareth Dale and Mike Cole, eds., *The European Union and Migrant Labour* (New York: Berg, 1999), pp. 91–111; and Khalid Koser and Melisa Salazar, "Ireland," in Steffen Angenendt, ed., *Asylum and Migration Policies in the European Union* (Berlin: Deutsche Gesellschaft für Auswärtige Politik, 1999), pp. 217–227. I thank Benjamin Conisbee Baer for inspired research assistance.

25. Nina Siegal, "A Legendary Bookstore Gets a Last-Minute Lease on Life," *New York Times,* July 30, 2000. See also Kathleen McGowan, "Fish Store Buys Bakery, Harlemites Say Deal Stinks," *City Limits Weekly,* May 22, 2000, www.citylimits.org/content/articles/weeklycontents.cfm?issuenumber =96. The bookstore has since closed because of Una Mulzac's advancing age and consequent frailty.

26. Thomas L. Friedman, "Surprise, Surprise, Surprise," *New York Times,* August 21, 2010, http://www.nytimes.com/2010/08/22/opinion/22friedman.html? _r=1&scp=1&sq=Thomas+Friedman+Mandela&st=nyt.

27. Jean Laplanche and J.-B. Pontalis, *The Language of Psycho-analysis,* trans. Donald Nicholson-Smith (New York: Norton, 1973), pp. 447–449, provides a list of the documentation to consult.

28. http://www.c-spanvideo.org/program/HonorRall.

29. Jim Rasenberger, "City Lore: A Lost City, Frozen in Time," *New York Times,* July 30, 2000, query.nytimes.com/gst/abstract.html?res=F10C11F83D590C 738FDDAE0894D8404482. The following two quotations are from the same source.

30. I have recently been reminded, by way of a publication request, that I had read the sentence "This thought weighs nothing [*pèse rien*]" in the 1960s, translating Derrida (see Spivak, "Reading *De la grammatologie*," in Sean Gaston and Ian Maclachlan, eds., *Reading Derrida's* Of Grammatology [London: Continuum, 2011]). Conservative radicals will dismiss this as silly nihilism, and my use of the catachresis "love" as aestheticizing politics. Loss of allies is also a loss of hope. I will not seemingly change the conviction to get allies. Glenn Beck cannot be our role model.

31. *Eco-Illuminations: The Art of Cynthia Mailman,* Staten Island Institute of Arts and Sciences, September 23–December 31, 2000.

32. Henry Staten, unpublished communication.

33. Printout given at the museum.

34. Henry John Drewal and John Mason, eds., *Beads, Body, and Soul: Art and Light in the Yorùbá Universe* (Los Angeles: UCLA Fowler Museum of Cultural History, 1998), p. 278.

35. Matthew Spady, *The Ground beneath Our Feet,* exhibition mounted on the occasion of the centenary of "The Grinnell," 800 Riverside Drive. The next quotation and the map are taken from the same source.

20. Scattered Speculations on the Subaltern and the Popular

1. For a more personal account for some of the same material, see Gayatri Chakravorty Spivak, "In Response: Looking Back, Looking Forward," in Rosalind Morris, ed., *Can the Subaltern Speak? Reflections on the History of an Idea* (New York: Columbia University Press, 2010), pp. 227–236.

2. John Beverley, *Subalternity and Representation: Arguments in Cultural Representation* (Durham, NC: Duke University Press, 1999).

3. The work of Sandro Mezzadra is particularly fruitful here.

4. Shahid Amin and Shail Mayaram seem more committed to researching subaltern groups in the old way at home and abroad.

5. Dipesh Chakrabarty, *Provincializing Europe: Postcolonial Thought and Historical Difference* (Princeton, NJ: Princeton University Press, 2000), p. 94.

6. Wendy Brown's insights on the shrunken role of the neoliberal state are apposite here. See Wendy Brown, "Neo-Liberalism and the End of Liberal Democracy," *Theory and Event* 7.1 (2003): 1–26.

7. Gilles Deleuze, *Logic of Sense,* ed. Constantin V. Boundas (New York: Columbia University Press, 1990). See also Antonio Negri, "Spinoza's Anti-

Modernity," *Graduate Faculty Philosophy Journal* 18.2 (1995): 1–15, where singularity is related to Spinoza's notion of ethical singularity. All reading carries this imperative, but literature admits to this most readily.

8. Here Derrida is once again useful. Derrida, "Shibboleth: For Paul Celan," in Geoffrey H. Hartmann and Sanford Bunick, eds., *Midrash and Literature* (New Haven, CT: Yale University Press, 1986), p. 325.

9. Partha Chatterjee, *Nationalist Thought and the Colonial World: A Derivative Discourse* (Minneapolis: University of Minnesota Press, 1993), pp. 24, 29–30, 43–50. The Gramsci reference is to Antonio Gramsci, "Some Aspects of the Southern Question," in *Selections from Political Writings (1921–1926)*, trans. and ed. Quintin Hoare (New York: International Publishers, 1978), pp. 441–462.

10. Ranajit Guha, "On Some Aspects of the Historiography of Colonial India," in *Subaltern Studies: Writings on South Asian History and Society*, no. 1 (New Delhi: Oxford University Press, 1982).

11. Marx, *Surveys from Exile*, trans. David Fernbach (New York: Vintage, 1992), p. 239; Marx, *Marx-Engels Werke*, vol. 8 (Berlin: Dietz, 1982), p. 198.

12. Spivak, "Subaltern Studies: Deconsructing Historiography," in *Subaltern Studies: Writings on South Asian History and Society*, no. 4 (New Delhi: Oxford University Press, 1985).

13. Peter Hallward, *Absolutely Postcolonial: Writing between the Singular and the Specific* (New York: Manchester University Press, 2001). I now have read the book. It carries the mark of a dissertation, and is contained within a specific academic debate, unrelated to the concerns of this book.

14. Gramsci, "The Intellectuals," in *Prison Notebooks*, vol. 2, trans. Joseph A. Buttigieg (New York: Columbia University Press, 1996), p. 243.

15. The idea of such grafting comes from Derrida, *Politics of Friendship*, trans. George Collins (New York: Verso, 1997), p. 32; translation modified. Derrida is speaking of teleiopoiesis, creatively miming the distant other, which can be stretched to describe the early subalternist reach toward the subaltern. It should be mentioned that Derrida concept-metaphorizes J. L. Austin's restricted distinction between the performative and the constative (J. L. Austin, *How to Do Things with Words* [Cambridge, MA: Harvard University Press, 1962]). The relationship between Derrida's performative/constative grafting philosopher and Gramsci's organic intellectual is worth study. Derrida taught Gramsci's work in the late 1970s at the Ecole Normale Supérieure in Paris.

16. In a much-revised form (that phrase was never revised), it is now to be found in Spivak, *A Critique of Postcolonial Reason: Toward a History of the Vanishing Present* (Cambridge, MA: Harvard University Press, 1999), p. 290 (hereafter cited in the notes as CPR).

17. Charles C. Taylor, *Multiculturalism and the "Politics of Recognition"* (Princeton, NJ: Princeton University Press, 1992).

18. Guha, "Chandra's Death," in *Subaltern Studies: Writings on South Asian History and Society*, no. 5 (New Delhi: Oxford University Press, 1987), pp. 135–165.

19. Eric Hobsbawm, *Primitive Rebels: Studies in Archaic Forms of Social Movement in the 19th and 20th Centuries* (Manchester: Manchester University Press, 1959), pp. v, vi (hereafter cited in the text by page number only).

20. This is what John Beverley has called Gramsci's "vanguardism" (Beverley, *Subalternity*, p. 139).

21. Gramsci, "The Intellectuals," p. 12.

22. Ibid., p. 6.

23. Here the current subalternists and their critics, Hardt and Negri, the authors of *Empire*, meet. "Multitude" is as dangerous a hypostatization of singularity (in Spinoza it remains singular) as "people" is of subalternity.

24. Derrida, *Politics of Friendship*, passage referenced above. I have suppressed "without a proper body" because that may not have been part of Gramsci's plan. That such efforts have no identity is a problem for historian and political activist alike. This is where the imagination of the humanities, the aesthetic that judges without an objective concept (I paraphrase Kant), is useful for work.

25. Gramsci, "The Intellectuals," pp. 8, 10.

26. The classic analysis is in Derrida, "Declarations of Independence," trans. Thomas W. Keenan and Thomas Pepper, *New Political Science* 15 (Summer 1986): 3–19.

27. Unpublished conversation, already cited.

28. Gayatri Chakravorty Spivak, *Outside in the Teaching Machine* (New York: Routledge, 2009), pp. 78–95.

29. Alas the United Nations' noble Millennium Project suffers from this. I do not intend, of course, to denigrate its awesome scope and the good intention of its framers.

30. There is a good discussion of the debates in James Penney, "(Queer) Theory and the Universal Alternative," *Diacritics* 32.2 (Summer 2002): 3–41. I cannot lay claim to Penney's theoretical sophistication. But I offer my approach as an open-ended response to Penney's important question: "If we acknowledge that Left-leaning cultural criticism has in the last decade or so reached a virtual consensus that the Foucault-style postmodern emphasis on difference, specificity, and particularity necessarily features either (a) a socioeconomic short circuit misrecognizing the fact that, by virtue of the lack of closure of the general social field (the barred Other for Lacanians, the structural necessity of suture/articulation for the 'radical democrats'), any expression of a 'particular' political interest always manifests either an implicit 'call' to the universal or a formally necessary 'gesture' of universalization, how is the very concept of the universal to be elaborated?" (p. 9).

31. Donald E. Pease, "The Global Homeland State: Bush's Biopolitical Settlement," *boundary 2* 30.3 (Fall 2003): 1–18.

32. Bruce A. Ackerman, *We the People*, vol. 1: *Foundations*, and *We the People*, vol. 2: *Transformations* (Cambridge, MA: Harvard University Press, 1991, 1998).

33. I am told that a Pakistani poet has also used the metaphor of invisible mending or *rafu*. There is no copyright on metaphors. The task is to set them to work.

34. See Gayatri Chakravorty Spivak, "The New Subaltern: A Silent Interview," in Vinayak Chaturvedi, ed., *Mapping Subaltern Studies and the Postcolonial* (London: Verso, 2000), pp. 324–340.
35. For one example of this among many, see Cori Hayden, *When Nature Goes Public: The Making and Unmaking of Bioprospecting in Mexico* (Princeton, NJ: Princeton University Press, 2003), and "Benefit-Sharing: The Public at Stake," paper presented at "Contested Commons/Trespassing Publics: A Conference on Inequalities, Conflicts and Intellectual Property," January 6–8, 2005, New Delhi, India.
36. This seems to be the main argument against the subalternists offered by Sumit Sarkar, *Beyond Nationalist Frames: Relocating Postmodernism, Hindutva, History* (New Delhi: Permanent Black, 2002), and Meera Nanda, *Prophets Facing Backwards: Postmodern Critiques of Science and Hindu Nationalism in India* (New Brunswick, NJ: Rutgers University Press, 2003), and against Spivak by Hallward, *Absolutely Postcolonial*. Who can deny that the phrase "position without identity" has a "postmodernist" smell? I hope by distinguishing it from the abstract-posing-as-concrete menace of the "people," I have been able to make a case for our position.
37. Professor Romila Thapar drew my attention to Shrinivas Tilak, "Taking Back Hindu Studies," http://sulekha.com/expressions/articledesc.asp?cid =307085. This piece is an excellent example of how the so-called diasporic re-lexicalizes material into the grammar of "the West and the rest," as understood by the upwardly class-mobile hyphenated immigrant in the metropole. I wrote CPR analyzing this phenomenon. Tilak has not read it. He seems not to have read "Can the Subaltern Speak?" either, since he does not cite it. If he had read it, he could hardly have missed the fact that it was a harsh critique of the Dharma-Shastra staging of Sati. It is amusing that, although he takes me as his authority, he also participates in the general anti-intellectual putdown of Spivak: "One cautionary note! Spivak can be unnecessarily dense and obtuse when approached for the first time. A good stepping stone and guide to her thought is *Gayatri Chakravorty Spivak* by Stephen Morton ([London: Routledge,] 2003). He also provides a comprehensive bibliography of her works updated to 2003 (including her famous 1985 essay 'Can the Subaltern Speak? Speculations on Widow-Sacrifice')." In other words, Mr. Tilak can credit a "Western" interpretation of an "authentic Indian" scholar when it suits him! The only thing I can say about this dangerous nonsense is that when I was offered Stephen Morton's book by a colleague, I was chagrined by his representation of me, especially where he attempts to explain my attitude to war in the last pages of his book! One is not responsible for one's readers, although I am ever grateful for attention.

21. World Systems and the Creole

1. Wai Chee Dimock, "Genre as World System: Epic and Novel on Four Continents," *Narrative* 14.1 (2006): 90.
2. See Aristotle, *Poetics,* trans. W. Hamilton Fyfe and W. Rhys Roberts (Cambridge, MA: Harvard University Press, 1991), pp. 115–117.

3. I have discussed this part of my response with Professor Rosalind Morris.

4. René Wellek, "Crisis in Comparative Literature," in Stephen Nichols, ed., *Concepts of Criticism* (New Haven, CT: Yale University Press, 1963), pp. 282–295.

5. Sam Dillon, "Formula to Grade Teachers' Skill Gains Acceptance, and Critics," *New York Times,* September 1, 2010.

6. See Danny Butt's discussion of this in "Whose Knowledge? Reflexivity and 'Knowledge Transfer' in Postcolonial Practice-Based Research," preprint of keynote paper delivered at "On Making" symposium, University of Johannesburg, October 15, 2009, http://dannybutt.net/2009/10/whose-knowledge -reflexivity-and-knowledge, p. 9. My argument takes Butt's general argument from polarity to double bind, and shifts postcolonial to global—two not unrelated moves.

7. For most of these writers, a look at their general bibliography will suffice. For a discussion of the travelogue element in Lévi-Strauss's treatment of the Nambikwara, see Derrida, *Of Grammatology,* trans. Gayatri Chakravorty Spivak (Baltimore, MD: Johns Hopkins University Press, 1976), pp. 107–140.

8. Immanuel Kant, *Anthropology from a Pragmatic Point of View,* trans. Robert B. Louden (Cambridge: Cambridge University Press, 2006), p. 5.

9. Gayatri Chakravorty Spivak, *A Critique of Postcolonial Reason: Toward a History of the Vanishing Present* (Cambridge, MA: Harvard University Press, 1999), p. 243 and passim.

10. Immanuel Kant, *Critique of Pure Reason,* trans. Paul Guyer and Allen W. Wood (Cambridge: Cambridge University Press, 2000), pp. 600–601.

11. Dante, *De vulgari eloquentia* (New York: Cambridge University Press, 1996).

12. Marcel Proust, *Sodom and Gomorrah* (*In Search of Lost Time,* vol. 4), trans. John Sturrock, ed. Christopher Prendergast (London: Penguin, 2003), p. 139; and Proust, *In the Shadow of Young Girls in Flower,* trans. James Grieve (New York: Viking Penguin, 2004), p. 330.

13. Aristotle, *Poetics,* pp. 94–95, 84–85.

14. "Among the constraints on plot that Aristotle lists are the following. Note that they are all phrased negatively—i.e., as constraints. . . . All of these constraints are rooted in the fact that intersentence coherence in Indo-European languages is achieved primarily by tense" (A. L. Becker, *Beyond Translation: Essays toward a Modern Philology* [Ann Arbor: University of Michigan Press, 1995], pp. 32–33). Here is an "anthropologist" who has spent his intellectual life upon the relationship between languages. Worth listening to as we comparativists move out onto what are, for us, and wrongly, uncharted seas.

15. And indeed, to be fair to the experts, they take the mind-set for granted. Max Müller had figured out what Rilke imagined in his notion of henotheism (Friedrich Max Müller, *Lectures on the Origin and Growth of Religion as Illustrated by the Religions of India* [London: Longmans, 1882], p. 277 and passim). When Pulgram (one of Professor Dimock's sources) writes "[Dante's] prescription for the creation of a volgare illustre (so called of course not in the sense of 'vulgar' but only in opposition to learned Latin) . . . runs counter

to what one would consider the normal formation of a literary standard language" (Ernst Pulgram, *The Tongues of Italy: Prehistory and History* [Cambridge, MA: Harvard University Press, 1958], p. 55), he is commenting on Dante's poetics of creolity, although he would be scandalized to be told so, which went counter to scientific linguistics. When he writes of "a new written language in Italy [around 800 CE], which one can no longer call Latin, but at best Neo-Latin, or Italian" (p. 411), or says that the stiff written Italian of the early nineteenth century was "another Classical Latin" (p. 64), he is using that epistemic presupposition without theorizing it. What is over against the mother tongue is not a foreign language but a learned language. As for Cecil Grayson, Dimock's other source, his work on Leon Battista Alberti (1404–1472) conveys his sense of the culture/nature/culture relationship, as historically conceived, between Latin, "Italian," and Italian (Leon Battista Alberti, *La prima grammatical della lingua volgare* [Bologna: The Vatican, 1964]).

16. *The Family of Man* (MoMA Exh. #569, January 24–May 8, 1955) was composed of "503 photographs grouped thematically around subjects pertinent to all cultures, such as love, children, and death. . . . The photographs included in the exhibition focused on the commonalties that bind people and cultures around the world and the exhibition served as an expression of humanism in the decade following World War II" (www.MoMA.org). "The professed aim of the exhibition was to mark the 'essential oneness of mankind throughout the world.' During the time it was open, The Family of Man became the most popular exhibition in the history of photography" (www .learningcurve.gov.uk). We cannot go back to that cold war sentimentality in the name of rethinking the discipline!

17. Jon Kabat-Zinn, *Wherever You Go, There You Are* (New York: Hyperion, 1994), p. 240.

18. Joan Aruz and Ronald Wallenfels, eds., *Art of the First Cities: The Third Millennium B.C. from the Mediterranean to the Indus* (New Haven, CT: Yale University Press, 2003), p. 455.

19. Marx, *Surveys from Exile*, trans. David Fernbach (New York: Vintage Books, 1992), p. 147.

20. Jean Berubé, Patrick Chamoiseau, and Raphaël Confiant, *Eloge de la créolité*, trans. M. B. Taleb-Kyar (Paris: Gallimard, 1993); Maryse Condé, ed., *Penser la créolité* (Paris: Karthala, 1995); Édouard Glissant, *Caribbean Discourse: Selected Essays,* trans. Michael Dash (Charlottesville: University of Virginia Press, 1989); Glissant, *Poetics of Relation*, trans. Betsy Wing (Ann Arbor: University of Michigan Press, 2003). I am grateful to Brent Hayes Edwards for his help.

21. Glissant, *Poetics of Relation*, trans. Michael Dash (Ann Arbor: University of Michigan Press, 1997), pp. 153, 154, 171.

22. Pascale Casanova, "Literature as a World," *New Left Review* 31 (January–February 2005): 78.

23. Glissant, *Poetics of Relation,* pp. 120, 190; the next quoted passage is from p. 131.

22. The Stakes of a World Literature

1. Charles Bernheimer, "Introduction," in Bernheimer, ed., *Comparative Literature in the Age of Multiculturalism* (Baltimore, MD: Johns Hopkins University Press, 1994), p. 11.
2. René Wellek, "Crisis in Comparative Literature," in Stephen Nichols, ed., *Concepts of Criticism* (New Haven, CT: Yale University Press, 1963), p. 294. The next quoted passage is from p. 288.
3. Unpublished lecture, Goldsmiths College, London University, May 11, 2009.
4. Immanuel Kant, *Critique of Pure Reason,* trans. Paul Guyer and Allen W. Wood (Cambridge: Cambridge University Press, 2000), p. 613 (hereafter cited in the text as PR, with page numbers following); Walter Benjamin, "On Language as Such and on the Languages of Man," in *Reflections: Essays, Aphorisms, Autobiographical Writings,* ed. Peter Demetz (New York: Schocken Books, 1986), pp. 314–332.
5. David Damrosch, *What Is World Literature?* (Princeton, NJ: Princeton University Press, 2003), pp. 19–20 (hereafter cited in the text as WWL, with page numbers following).
6. Sheldon Pollock, "Cosmopolitan and Vernacular in History," *Public Culture* 12 (2000): 594–595.
7. Derrida, *The Animal That Therefore I Am,* trans. David Wills (New York: Fordham University Press, 2008), p. 22.
8. Edward Said, *Orientalism: Western Conceptions of the Orient* (New York: Pantheon, 1978), p. 25.
9. Luca Scarantino, "Violence and Cultural Dialogue: Generosity as an Epistemic Feature," in *Dünya Felsefe Günü Bildirileri: Papers of the 2007 World Philosophy Day* (Ankara: Türkiye Felsefe Kurumu, 2009), pp. 299–307.
10. Hannah Arendt, *The Origins of Totalitarianism* (New York: Harcourt, 1976), pp. 267–302.
11. A. Adu Boahen, *African Perspectives on Colonialism* (Baltimore, MD: Johns Hopkins University Press, 1987).
12. Johann Wolfgang von Goethe, *Conversations with Eckermann, 1823–1832,* trans. John Oxenford (San Francisco: North Point Press, 1984), p. 132 (emphasis added); Karl Marx and Frederick Engels, *The Communist Manifesto,* ed. John E. Toews (Boston: Bedford/St.Martin's, 1999), pp. 66–69.
13. Antonio Gramsci, *Selections from the Prison Notebooks,* ed. and trans. Quintin Hoare and Geoffrey Nowell Smith (New York: International Publishers, 1971), p. 10.
14. Michel Foucault, "Nietzsche, Genealogy, History," in *Language Counter-Memory, Practice,* trans. Donald Bouchard and Sherry Simon (Ithaca, NY: Cornell University Press, 1977), pp. 139–164.
15. Discussed in *Thinking Academic Freedom in Gendered Postcoloniality* (Cape Town: University of Cape Town Press, 1992); forthcoming in a revised edition from Seagull Books, Kolkata.

16. This is discussed at length in chapter 2 of Spivak, *Other Asias* (Oxford: Blackwell, 2008).
17. Spivak, *Other Asias*, pp. 253–254.
18. Sheldon Pollock, *The Language of the Gods in the World of Men: Sanskrit, Culture, and Power in Premodern India* (Berkeley: University of California Press, 2006), pp. 571–572.
19. Antonio Gramsci, *The Gramsci Reader: Selected Writings, 1916–1935,* ed. David Forgasc (New York: New York University Press, 2000), p. 355.
20. *Rabindra Racanabali,* vol. 6 (Kolkata: Paschim Banga Sarkar, 1961), pp. 762–781.
21. A representative article here would be Wendy Sigle-Rushton and Jane Waldfogel, "Motherhood and Women's Earnings in Anglo-American, Continental European, and Nordic Countries," *Feminist Economics* 13.2 (2007): 55–91.
22. Derrida, *Rogues: Two Essays on Reason,* trans. Pascale-Anne Brault and Michael Naas (Stanford, CA: Stanford University Press, 2005), p. 159.

23. Rethinking Comparativism

1. Pascale Casanova, *The World Republic of Letters,* trans. M. B. DeBevoise (Cambridge, MA: Harvard University Press, 2004). This was the ground of J. Hillis Miller's criticism of Chinua Achebe's essay on *Heart of Darkness,* for example (J. Hillis Miller, *The Ethics of Reading* [New York: Columbia University Press, 1987]).
2. René Etiemble, *Crisis in Comparative Literature,* trans. Herbert Weisinger and Georges Joyaux (East Lansing: University of Michigan Press, 1966).
3. Charles Bernheimer, ed., *Comparative Literature in the Age of Multiculturalism* (Baltimore, MD: Johns Hopkins University Press, 1994), p. 44.
4. Edward W. Said, *Orientalism* (New York: Pantheon, 1994), p. 202.
5. The best example of this filtering for general reading remains Roland Barthes, "Introduction to the Structural Analysis of Narratives," in Stephen Heath, trans., *Image/Music/Text* (New York: Hill and Wang, 1977), pp. 79–124.
6. Ernst Robert Curtius, *European Literature and the Latin Middle Ages,* trans. Willard R. Trask (1953; reprint, New York: Harper & Row, 1963).
7. For a checklist, one might think of Gaston Bachelard, *The Psychoanalysis of Fire,* trans. Alan C. M. Ross (Boston: Beacon Press, 1964); Bachelard, *Water and Dreams: An Essay on the Imagination of Matter,* trans. Edith R. Farrell (Dallas: Dallas Institute Publications, 1983); Bachelard, *Poetics of Space,* trans. Maria Joles (Boston: Beacon Press, 1958); Maurice Merleau-Ponty, *Phenomenology of Perception,* trans. Colin Smith (London: Routledge & Kegan Paul, 1962); Merleau-Ponty, *The Visible and the Invisible,* trans. Alphonso Lingis (Evanston, IL: Northwestern University Press, 1968); Georges Poulet, *Studies in Human Time,* trans. Elliott Coleman (Baltimore, MD: Johns Hopkins University Press, 1956); Poulet, *The Interior Distance,* trans. Elliott Coleman (Baltimore, MD: Johns Hopkins University Press, 1959); Poulet,

Metamorphoses of the Circle, trans. Carley Dawson (Baltimore, MD: Johns Hopkins University Press, 1966).

8. U.S. policing of Latin America is particularly well documented in Lars Schulz, *Beneath the United States: A History of U.S. Policy in Latin America* (Cambridge, MA: Harvard University Press, 1998).

9. Alton L. Becker, *Beyond Translation: Essays toward a Modern Philology* (Ann Arbor: University of Michigan Press, 1995), p. 12.

10. "It would be bad natural history to expect the mental processes and communicative habits of mammals to conform to the logician's ideal" (Gregory Bateson, *Steps to an Ecology of Mind* [Chicago: University of Chicago Press, 2000], p. 180).

11. For the structure of constative-performative-attendance, see Derrida, *Rogues: Two Essays on Reason,* trans. Pascale-Anne Brault and Michael Naas (Stanford, CA: Stanford University Press, 2005), pp. 151–152.

12. In the hope of increasing institutional attention, I have included these words also in "Translation in the Undergraduate Curriculum" (ADFL *Bulletin* 41.2 [2009]: 26–30) and will probably continue to re-cite them indefinitely.

13. For an expert account of the story, see Ikuo Shinjo, "Homoerotikusu no seijiteki haichi to 'reisen': Okinawaeno/ kara no manazashi no koso," *Frontiers of Gender Studies* (F-GENS) Annual Report Number 5 (2005), Ochanomizu University. Presented as "The Political Formation of the Homoerotics and the Cold War: Battle of the Gazes at and from Okinawa," at the American Comparative Literature Association Annual Conference at Princeton University, March 23–26, 2006.

14. Quoted in *Japan Policy Research Institute (JPRI) Critique* 6.12 (1999), www.jpri.org/public/crit6.12.html.

15. This may be the moment to suggest that the pervasive presence of the acknowledgment of the double bind in Derrida's work can allow us to think of deconstruction as a philosophy of (praxis as) the double bind. In Deleuze and Guattari's *Anti-Oedipus* (trans. Robert Hurley, Mark Seem, and Helen R. Lane [Minneapolis: University of Minnesota Press, 1992]), the attempt to think schizophrenia in a more general sense leads to the French title (subtitle in the English): "Capitalism and Schizophrenia."

16. Shun Medoruma, "An Okinawan Short Story," trans. Steve Rabson, *JPRI Critique* 6.12 (1999), www.jpri.org/public/crit6.12.html; emphasis in original. All quotes are from this translation. Translation often modified.

17. I have emphasized the tensed words to show the play of present and past tenses.

18. Oe Kenzaburo, *Okinawa Notes* (Tokyo: Iwanami Shoten, 1970), p. 16. I am grateful to Shinjou Ikuo for making this text available to me. I thank Norie Oka for producing a digest at short notice.

24. Sign and Trace

1. To see the visuals that go with this sentence, please consult Germaine Celant, *Anish Kapoor* (Milan: Charta, 1998); Anish Kapoor, *Marsyas* (London: Tate

Publishing, 2002) and *My Red Homeland* (Malaga: Arte Contemporaneo, 2006).

2. Laurent Busine, "Plus belle q'une peau tendue entre un carré et un cercle," in *Anish Kapoor: Melancholia* (Hornu: Arts contemporains, 2004), pp. 5, 13; translation mine; emphasis added.

3. Derrida, "Law of Genre," *Critical Inquiry* 7.1 (Autumn 1980): 70.

4. Anthony Vidler, *The Architectural Uncanny: Essays in the Modern Unhomely* (Cambridge, MA: MIT Press, 1992).

5. Sigmund Freud, "The Uncanny," in *The Standard Edition,* vol. 17, trans. James Strachey (New York: Norton, 1961–), p. 245.

6. For one among many examples, see Kapoor, *My Red Homeland,* p. 57.

7. I have commented on this passage in Spivak, "Reading *De la grammatologie,*" in Sean Gaston and Ian Maclachlan, eds., *Reading Derrida's* Of Grammatology (London: Continuum, 2011), p. xxxiii.

8. This is once again a reference to Spivak, "The Letter as Cutting Edge," in *In Other Worlds* (New York: Routledge Classics edition, 2006), pp. 3–19.

9. Jeremy Waldron, "What Is Cosmopolitan?," *Journal of Political Philosophy* 8.2 (June 2000): 227–243.

10. Derrida, *Specters of Marx: The State of the Debt, the Work of Mourning and the New International,* trans. Peggy Kamuf (New York: Routledge, 1994), p. 82.

11. Nicholas Baume, ed., *Anish Kapoor: Past, Present, Future* (Cambridge, MA: MIT Press, 2008), p. 22.

12. James Joyce, *Finnegans Wake* (New York: Viking, 1961), p. 336.

13. Lacan, "Of the Gaze as Objet Petit a," in *The Four Fundamental Concepts of Psychoanalysis,* trans. Alan Sheridan (New York: Norton, 1978), p. 53.

14. Spivak, "Notes toward a Tribute to Jacques Derrida," *differences* 16.3 (Fall 2005): 102.

15. Rainer Maria Rilke, *Duineser Elegien* (Leipzig: Insel, 1931).

16. Emmanuel Lévinas, *Totality and Infinity: An Essay on Exteriority,* trans. Alphonso Lingis (Pittsburgh: Duquesne University Press, 1969), pp. 169–170.

17. The line in Joyce is "Soft morning, city! Lsp! I am leafy speafing" (Joyce, *Finnegans Wake,* p. 619).

18. Derrida, *Glas,* trans. John P. Leavey Jr. and Richard Rand (Lincoln: University of Nebraska Press, 1986), p. 229.

19. Most poignantly staged in the cusp between the discussion of Lévinas at the end of the first essay and the discussion of Lacan at the beginning of the second in *Animal,* that the English loses by translating the repeated *cela ne suffit pas* in various different phrasings (Derrida, *The Animal That Therefore I Am,* trans. David Wills [New York: Fordham University Press, 2008], pp. 118–119; Derrida, *L'animal que donc je suis* [Paris: Galilée, 2006], pp. 162–163).

25. Tracing the Skin of Day

1. I occasionally cite Anjum Katyal's notes because she walked the walk with me around these rooms (hereafter cited in the text as AK).

2. Marx, *Capital,* vol. 1, trans. Ben Fowkes (London: Penguin, 1990), pp. 154, 156; translation modified. This is not the place for a theoretical expansion of this unorthodox digest of Marx's discussion of the value-form.

3. Gramsci, *Selections from the Prison Notebooks,* pp. 139–140.

4. Nietzsche, *On the Genealogy of Morals and Ecce Homo,* trans. Walter J. Kaufmann (New York: Vintage Books, 1969), p. 77; translation modified.

5. Immanuel Kant, *Critique of Pure Reason,* trans. Paul Guyer and Allen W. Wood (Cambridge: Cambridge University Press, 2000), p. 221.

6. Unpublished interview provided by Anjum Katyal. The next quoted passage is also from this interview.

7. Derrida, *Margins of Philosophy,* trans. Alan Bass (Chicago: University of Chicago Press, 1982), pp. 11–12; translation modified.

8. Rainer Maria Rilke, *Duino Elegies,* trans. Edward Snow (New York: North Point Press, 2000), p. 13.

9. *Oedipus the King,* 1403–1407; translation mine, as literal as possible, to show that Oedipus reproaches marriage for the inscription of human kinship, which then makes incest possible. Sophocles against myth as destiny.

10. Unpublished interview provided by Anjum Katyal.

11. Georg Friedrich Hegel, *The Phenomenology of the Mind,* trans. J. B. Baillie (New York: Harper, 1967), p. 495; translation modified.

12. A confession: I read Derrida slowly, checking the translation (because I am obliged to teach in English), following up every reference, checking texts in languages unavailable to me with learned friends, accounting for their possible position vis-à-vis deconstruction; often with Benjamin Baer, Eduardo Cadava, Brooke Holmes, Rosalind Morris—so that sometimes these readings are collective. When I wrote this essay I had not yet come to pages 50 and following of *The Animal That Therefore I Am,* which, as I now find, corroborate my vulgar ruminations about Derrida's thinking of the trace. I have just come, alone, to pages 54 to the top of page 56 this morning, and I must say I cannot not stop press to quote this passage: "The animal in whose tracks [*à la trace*] therefore I am (following), and who picks up [*relève*—also translates the Hegelian *Aufhebung*] traces, who is it? Does it speak? Does it speak French? Imagine it signing a declaration, one trace among others, in the first person, *je, je suis.*" This also is the temptation that Chittrovanu shares, suffers, and follows with greater freedom—visually, pushing inevitably toward the verbal, and pushing back, as artist and viewer share being-human.

13. Emmanuel Lévinas, *Otherwise than Being, or, Beyond Essence,* trans. Alphonso Lingis (Pittsburgh: Duquesne University Press, 1998).

14. Roland Barthes, *S/Z,* trans. Richard Miller (New York: Hill and Wang, 1974), p. 4 and passim.

Acknowledgments

A previous version of "The Burden of English" appeared in Rajeswari Sunder Rajan, ed., *The Lie of the Land: English Literary Studies in India* (Delhi: Oxford University Press, 1992), pp. 275–299.

A previous version of "Who Claims Alterity?" appeared in Barbara Kruger and Phil Mariani, eds., *Remaking History* (Seattle: Bay Press, 1989), pp. 269–292.

A previous version of "How to Read a 'Culturally Different' Book" appeared as "Feminism in Decolonization: *Once Again a Leap* into the Postcolonial Banal," *differences* 3.3 (1991): 139–170. Copyright 1991 by Brown University and *differences: A Journal of Feminist Cultural Studies*. All rights reserved. Reprinted by permission of the publisher, Duke University Press. A revised version was reprinted as "How to Teach a 'Culturally Different' Book," in Francis Barker, Peter Hulme, and Margaret Iversen, eds., *Colonial Discourse, Postcolonial Theory* (Manchester: Manchester University Press, 1994), pp. 126–150. Reprinted by permission of Manchester University Press and the volume editors.

A previous version of "The Double Bind Starts to Kick In" appeared as "A Moral Dilemma," in *What Happens to History: The Renewal of Ethics in Contemporary Thought,* edited by Howard Marchitello, pp. 215–236, copyright © 2001, reproduced by permission of Taylor and Francis Group, LLC, a division of Informa plc.

A section of "Culture: Situating Feminism" previously appeared as "Why Does Zamyn Place 'Culture' at the Centre of Its Analysis?" for Zamyn, an independent analytical agency.

A previous version of "Teaching for the Times" appeared in *The Journal of the Midwest Modern Language Association* 25.1, "Oppositional Discourse" (Spring 1992): 3–22. A revised version appeared in Jan Nederveen Pieterse and Bhikhu Parekh, eds., *The Decolonization of Imagination: Culture, Knowledge, and Power* (London: Zed Books, 1995), pp. 177–202.

A previous version of "Acting Bits/Identity Talk" appeared in *Critical Inquiry* 18.4 (Summer 1992): 770–803. A revised version appeared in Dennis Crow, ed.,

Geography and Identity: Exploring and Living Geopolitics of Identity (College Park, MD: Maisonneuve Press, 1996), pp. 40–72.

A previous version of "Supplementing Marxism" appeared in *Whither Marxism? Global Crises in International Perspective,* edited by Bernd Magnus and Stephen Cullenberg, pp. 109–119, copyright © 1995, reproduced by permission of Taylor and Francis Group, LLC, a division of Informa plc.

A previous version of "What's Left of Theory?" appeared as "From Haverstock Hill Flat to U.S. Classroom, What's Left of Theory?" in *What's Left of Theory? New Work on the Politics of Literary Theory,* edited by Judith Butler, John Guillory, and Kendall Thomas, pp. 1–39, copyright © 2000, reproduced by permission of Taylor and Francis Group, LLC, a division of Informa plc.

A previous version of "Echo" appeared in *New Literary History* 24.1, "Culture and Everyday Life" (Winter 1993): 17–43.

A previous version of "Translation as Culture" appeared in Isabel Carrera Suárez, ed., *Translating Cultures* (Oviedo: Dangaroo Press, 1999), pp. 17–30; a revised version appeared in *parallax* 6.1 (January–March 2000): 13–24.

A previous version of "Translating into English" appeared in Sandra Bermann and Michael Wood, eds., *Nation, Language and the Ethics of Translation* (Princeton, NJ: Princeton University Press, 2005), pp. 93–110.

A previous version of "Nationalism and the Imagination" appeared in C. Vijayasree, Meenakshi Mukherjee, and Harish Trivedi, eds., *Nation in Imagination: Essays on Nationalism, Sub-Nationalisms and Narration* (Hyderabad: Orient Longman, 2007), pp. 1–20.

A previous version of "Resident Alien" appeared in David Theo Goldberg and Ato Quayson, eds., *Relocating Postcolonialism* (Oxford: Blackwell, 2002), pp. 46–65.

A previous version of "Ethics and Politics in Tagore, Coetzee, and Certain Scenes of Teaching" appeared in *Diacritics* 32.3–4 (Fall–Winter 2004): 17–31. A later version appeared in Elleke Boehmer and Rosinka Chaudhuri, eds., *The Indian Postcolonial: A Critical Reader* (London: Routledge, 2011), pp. 195–213.

A bilingual version of "Imperative to Re-imagine the Planet" appeared in Willi Goetschel, ed., *Imperatives to Re-imagine the Planet/Imperative zur Neuerfindung des Planeten* (Vienna: Passagen, 1999).

A previous version of "Reading with Stuart Hall in 'Pure' Literary Terms" appeared as "Thinking Cultural Questions in 'Pure' Literary Terms," in Paul Gilroy, Lawrence Grossberg, and Angela McRobbie, eds., *Without Guarantees: In Honor of Stuart Hall* (London: Verso, 2000), pp. 335–357.

"Terror: A Speech after 9/11" was first delivered at a conference, "Responses to War," in the Feminist Interventions series run by the Institute for Research in Women and Gender at Columbia University. I thank Rosalind Carmel Morris for inviting me to participate in it. A later version of the essay appeared in *boundary 2: An international journal of literature and culture* 31.2 (2004): 81–111. Copyright 2004 by Duke University Press. All rights reserved. Reprinted by permission of the publisher, Duke University Press.

A previous version of "Harlem" appeared in Eduardo Cadava and Aaron Levy, eds., *Cities without Citizens* (Philadelphia: Slought Books, 2004), pp. 58–85. A later version appeared in *Social Text* 81, 22.4 (Winter 2004): 113–139. Copyright 2004 by Gayatri Chakravorty Spivak. All rights reserved. Reprinted by permission of the publisher, Duke University Press. A full-color version is forthcoming from Seagull Books.

A previous version of "Scattered Speculations on the Subaltern and the Popular" appeared in *Postcolonial Studies* 8.4 (2005): 475–486. Copyright 2005 by Gayatri Chakravorty Spivak.

A previous version of "World Systems and the Creole" appeared in *Narrative* 14.1 (January 2006): 102–112.

A previous version of "The Stakes of a World Literature" appeared, in Turkish translation, in E. Efe Cakmak, ed., *Dunya Edebiyati Deyince* (Istanbul: Varlik, 2009), pp. 35–39.

"Rethinking Comparativism" was originally commissioned by the Comparative Literature issue of *New Literary History*. It appeared in *NLH* 40.3 (Summer 2009): 609–626.

A previous version of "Sign and Trace" appeared in the catalog for *Memory* (2008), a sculpture by Anish Kapoor commissioned by the Deutsche Guggenheim (Berlin: Deutsche Guggenheim, 2008), pp. 56–75.

A previous version of "Tracing the Skin of Day" appeared in the catalog for Chittrovanu Mazumdar's *Undated: Nightskin* (Dubai: 1×1 Art Gallery, 2009), pp. 17–25.

Index

Note: Page numbers followed by *f* indicate figures.

Etiemble, René, *Comparaison n'est pas raison,* 468
Evidentiary and intuitive, distinction between, 125, 536n8

Family and creolity, 449–450
Family law and "custom," 109–110
Family of Man, The (exhibit), 585n16
Fanon, Frantz, *A Dying Colonialism,* 155
Fantasia: An Algerian Cavalcade (Djebar), 155–157, 158–160, 230–231, 556n35
Faulkner, William, 370
"Fecundity of the Caress" (Irigaray), 165
Female suicide bombers, 385–386
Feminism and culture, 122, 124–129; culture, engagement with capital, and problem solving, 129–136; ethnicity, transnational literacy, and teaching, 149–155; Marx and, 187; Native American practices and utopian socialism, 149
Feminist readers, *The Guide* and, 80–90
"Femivores," 129
Ferguson, Niall, 516n57
Feuerbach, Marx's theses on, 7, 183
Finnegans Wake (Joyce), 491, 495
First Nations. *See* Native Americans
Fish & Chips (Attie), 417f
Flatulence, xi, 174
Fletcher, George, *Romantics at War,* 389
Foe (Coetzee), 170, 330
Forbes, Jack D., 147–149
Forster, E. M., 45, 80, 498; *A Passage to India,* 310
Foucault, Michel, 58, 78, 197, 199, 257, 260, 304, 305, 429, 461, 525n5, 529n11, 548n9
Frage des Mitmenschen und des Mitvolkes: 1951–1992 (Goldschmidt), 336, 339
"Freedom of choice," 130
Freud, Sigmund, xii, 5, 10, 123, 150–151, 496, 565n8; "On Narcissism, An Introduction," 218–219, 221; psychoanalysis and Narcissus, 218–227, 239–240, 555n25, 555n27
Friedan, Betty, 123
Friere, Paulo, 133, 536n19
Fynsk, Christopher, 139

Gandhi, Mahatma, 248
Gandhi, Rajiv, 386
Gangesa, 221
Garis, Leslie, 368

Gates, Henry Louis, Jr., 368
Gayatri Chakravorty Spivak (Morton), 583n37
Gender: aesthetic education and, 30–33; as alibi for U.S. violence abroad, 439; capital/culture aporia and, 105–110; class and study of English literature, 37; ethics, electronic capitalism, and the founding gap, 98–105; war on terror and gender justice, 375, 574n7. *See also* Reproductive heteronormativity (RHN)
Genetic engineering, 188, 190
Gerber, Ava, 240
German Ideology, The (Marx and Engels), 550n24
Gerusalemme Liberata (Tasso), 239
Gharé Bairé (Tagore), 559n8
Ghosh, Gautum, *The Voyage Beyond,* 176–180
Gikandi, Simon, 288
Glas (Derrida), xi, 172–175, 201, 515n56, 556n35
Glissant, Édouard, 453
Globalization: other women and learning in the field, 98–110; trace and Kapoor's work, 484, 492–499
God of Small Things, The (Roy), 298
Goethe, Johann Wolfgang von, 13, 460–461, 467
Goldschmidt, Hermann Levin, xiv, 335–336, 342, 570n4; *Frage des Mitmenschen und des Mitvolkes: 1951–1992,* 336, 339
Gomez Peña, Guillermo, 54; "Border Notebook," 169, 171, 172, 543n15
Gora (Tagore), xiii, xiv, 44–45, 52; Resident Alien and, 301, 302–315
Gorbachev, Mikhail, 310, 314
Gordimer, Nadine, *July's People,* 53–55, 524n32
Governmentality, subaltern and, 429–430
Grace, Patricia, *Baby No-Eyes,* 398
Grameen Bank, 106–107
Gramsci, Antonio, 2, 3, 464, 498, 501, 510n6, 513n33, 572n23; instrumentalization of the intellectual, 7–8; Marx and, 26–27, 200–201, 203; *Selections from the Prison Notebooks,* 461–463; "Some Aspects of the Southern Question," 431; subalternity and, 429, 434–435, 436, 581n15; "technoscientific knowledge," 10, 28–30
Great Game, The (Hopkirk), 307